MW00476201

CULTURAL MATURITY

Also by Charles Johnston:

The Creative Imperative: Human Growth and Planetary Evolution

Necessary Wisdom: Meeting the Challenge of a New Cultural Maturity

Pattern and Reality: A Brief Introduction to Creative Systems Theory

The Power of Diversity: An Introduction to the Creative Systems Personality Typology

An Evolutionary History of Music: Introducing Creative Systems Theory Through the Language of Sound (DVD)

Hope and the Future: An Introduction to the Concept of Cultural Maturity

Quick and Dirty Answers to the Biggest of Questions: Creative Systems Theory Explains What It Is All About (Really)

Online:

The Institute for Creative Development: www.CreativeSystems.org

Cultural Maturity-A Blog for the Future: www.CulturalMaturityBlog.net

Creative Systems Theory: www.CSTHome.org

Cultural Maturity: www.CulturalMaturity.org

The Creative Systems Personality Typology: www.CSPTHome.org

An Evolutionary History of Music: www. Evolmusic.org

CULTURAL MATURITY

MATURITY

a guidebook for the future

*with an introduction to the ideas
of Creative Systems Theory*

Charles M. Johnston, MD

The Institute for Creative Development (ICD) Press
Seattle, Washington

Cover design by Les Campbell

Author photo by Brad Kevelin

Library of Congress Control Number: 2011911382

First printing 2015

CULTURAL MATURITY

Further Evidence

Going Forward

Appendices

Where We Stand:
A Time of Great Risk
—and Great Possibility

The future is ever a misted landscape
No man foreknows it, but at cyclical turns
there is a change felt in the rhythm of events.

ROBINSON JEFFERS

I'M A PSYCHIATRIST BY TRAINING, but the larger part of my life's work concerns how we can best make sense of the times in which we live and what lies ahead for us as a species. People often refer to me as a futurist. A better term, given where I put my attention, might be "cultural psychiatrist."[1] Most futurists focus primarily on technological advances. My greater interest lies with the psychological, social, and leadership capacities that humanity will need to effectively address the questions that most define our time and that will most determine our future.

One conclusion stands out in my efforts. The future will require from us not just fresh ideas, but a fundamentally greater sophistication in how we think and act. To put it simply—but I think quite precisely—the critical questions ahead demand of our species an essential "growing up," what I call a new *Cultural Maturity*.

---

1   The term "cultural psychiatrist" is sometime used to refer to the cross-cultural study of mental illness. The way I use the term is more encompassing.

The concept of Cultural Maturity is a formal notion within Creative Systems Theory, a comprehensive framework for understanding how human systems work that was developed by myself and colleagues over the last forty years.[2] *Cultural Maturity: A Guidebook for the Future* closely examines the concept of Cultural Maturity and its implications for addressing the critical challenges before us. It also introduces the thinking of Creative Systems Theory.

This book's goal is to help readers think differently, and *deeply*, about today's critical challenges, both to appreciate the greater human maturity required by the tasks before us and to understand how to make that maturity manifest in our personal and collective choices. It is written for people wanting a deep understanding of the changing times we live in, and in particular, for people who wish to develop the capacities needed to provide effective and wise leadership as we look ahead.

The Basic Notion

The concept of Cultural Maturity starts with the essential question of how best to understand current times. But it quickly confronts a more specifically provocative question. It asks if it is correct to assume, as is our tendency, that the profound advances that have given us modern age institutions and ways of thinking mark some final achievement, whether further new chapters in our human story may lie ahead. The concept of Cultural Maturity argues that further chapters are not just possible; they are necessary, if our human future is to be bright.

Most of us recognize—whether consciously or not—that a kind of cultural "growing up" is needed today. We grasp that dealing with nuclear proliferation in an ever more technologically complex and globally interconnected world will require us to relate in more mature ways. Similarly, people recognize that addressing the overwhelming array of environmental concerns before us will demand a newly mature acceptance

---

2   See www.CreativeSystems.org for links to Creative Systems Theory–related sites. Where I use formal Creative Systems language, I will capitalize terms and on first usage also put terms in italics—as here with the phrase *Cultural Maturity*.

of responsibility for the planet's well-being. People's more immediate frustrations also show a beginning appreciation of this need for greater maturity. With growing frequency, people today respond with disgust—appropriately—at the common childishness of political debate, and at how rarely the media presents information that appeals to more than adolescent impulses.

At the very least, we appreciate that a sane and healthy future will require us to be more intelligent in our choices. Most of us also recognize something further. We get that it is essential, given the magnitude of the challenges we face and the potential consequences of our decisions, that our choices be not just intelligent, but wise. Cultural Maturity is about realizing the greater nuance and depth of understanding—one could say "wisdom"—that human concerns of every sort today demand of us.[3]

The concept of Cultural Maturity helps us in three important ways: First, it provides an overarching, guiding story for our time, a way of understanding the kinds of choices that will most serve us going forward. Second, it delineates new human capacities that will be needed if we are to effectively address the essential challenges before us as a species. And third, it describes how the future will require that we understand in some fundamentally new, more complete[4] and sophisticated ways, and at least points toward the characteristics of such new thinking. Shortly, I will expand on each of these ways in which the concept benefits us and make clear how each of them is essential.

In one sense the concept of Cultural Maturity is simple. Indeed we need not even think of it as a concept, rather just an observation. In using words like "childhood," "adolescence," or "adulthoodÆ to describe stages in individual personal development, people may quibble about details as far as just what specific stages involve, but the fact of general development stages is not something we question. In a similar way, Cultural Maturity is a developmental notion. I will argue that when

---

3   Here I mean wisdom in a very specific sense. See "Personal Maturity, Cultural Maturity, and the Mechanisms of Wisdom" in Chapter Seven.

4   When I use the word "complete," I do not at all mean finished. I mean simply that an idea better takes into account all that needs to be considered.

we examine it closely, it similarly becomes obvious. That it is not now obvious is a product only of the fact that we are just now making entry into the new realities that it describes.

At the same time, and for related reasons, the concept of Cultural Maturity does not let us off lightly. New developmental chapters necessarily stretch us, and as you shall see, Cultural Maturity's changes do so in some particularly fundamental ways. I will describe how culturally mature perspective challenges familiar assumptions of every sort—political, religious, philosophical, aesthetic, and scientific. It requires a willingness to expand how we understand—and how we engage the world—in every part of our lives, and in ways we can only begin to grasp.

How I Got Here

A bit about how I arrived at the decision to write this book helps put what I hope to achieve in these pages in context. When I was in my twenties, I stumbled upon an intriguing way of thinking about how human systems grow and evolve—human systems of all sorts: individuals, relationships, organizations, and societies.[5] I wrote about these ideas in my 1984 book, *The Creative Imperative*. They later filled out to become Creative Systems Theory.

In developing Creative Systems Theory, I found particular fascination with the perspective its ideas provided for understanding cultural change—for making sense of how cultural systems grow and evolve. At first it was the way these cultural change concepts helped me better appreciate the past that I found most striking—how they provided insight into why our human story has progressed in the ways that it has.

But I soon recognized that these ideas also had more immediate and practical implications. They could help us understand the often-confusing times in which we live. Creative Systems Theory's big-picture vantage predicts that challenges we face today should be requiring us to turn first pages in an important next chapter in the human endeavor. I saw that understanding what those challenges ask of us clarifies much

---

5   See "Creative Systems Theory Patterning Concepts" in Chapter Six.

about current human circumstances. I also saw that the next chapter in culture's developmental story is not just predicted, but happening. I coined the term "Cultural Maturity" to have a readily graspable way to talk about it.

The recognition that the concept of Cultural Maturity provides perspective for understanding today's essential tasks dramatically altered my life's direction. I realized that a major portion of my life's work needed to focus directly on today's challenges. And I saw that it needed to focus specifically on Cultural Maturity and the necessary changes it entails.

I found myself struck increasingly by how, if there is a single, core "mental health" crisis in our time, it is a crisis of story—ultimately, a crisis of human purpose. Familiar cultural narratives have today stopped serving us as they once did—be this the American Dream, opposing political ideologies, the beliefs of our various religious traditions, or progress's promise of ever onward-and-upward scientific discovery and technological advancement. Because people lack compelling pictures of what our times are about, and also what may be possible, all too frequently they wander aimlessly, or confuse the superficial excitement of the next big thing with real meaning and direction. Individually and collectively, we also often make dangerously shortsighted decisions.

The concept of Cultural Maturity offers an antidote to this crisis of purpose. I saw that it not only provides a new guiding narrative, it helps us make sense of the more sophisticated ways of understanding and acting that will be necessary if we are to effectively address the challenges ahead.

Acknowledging this significance, I joined together with colleagues to start a nonprofit think tank and center for leadership training— the Institute for Creative Development—to explore Cultural Maturity's implications and to further develop the ideas of Creative Systems Theory. I knew that the Institute's work would not be easy, given that our interest lay with human abilities that, at best, we were only beginning to understand. But it was obvious that what we endeavored to do together could not be more important. The Institute brought together exceptional people from around the world to confront many of the most important questions of our time. It also trained people in the new, more sophisticated leadership capacities that the future's new questions will increasingly demand. It was a time of rich inquiry and deeply fulfilling collaboration.

But after leading the Institute for eighteen rewarding years,[6] I saw that a further phase in my own life and work would be required. Given the great practical significance of the ideas and approaches we had drawn on, it was important that they be made available to a wider audience. And if these notions had a significant place in the history and evolution of understanding—as they must have if they effectively reflect this needed new chapter in our human story—they warranted further research to substantiate that significance. I stepped down from my formal leadership role to do additional research and to write.

This book is one of three related works I wrote during the twelve years that followed. Each has similar intent—to help people understand the times we live in and to make sense of what the future will require of us—but each is written for a different audience. *Hope and the Future: An Introduction to the Concept of Cultural Maturity* is a short work intended for a general audience wanting to better understand the tasks humanity now faces. *Quick and Dirty Answers to the Biggest of Questions: Creative Systems Theory Explains What It Is All About (Really)* is intended for people who find particular fascination in overarching inquiry. It describes how the new kind of understanding we need today, besides helping us address modern-day challenges, also brings a new maturity and creativity to more ultimate sorts of concerns. Of the three books, it most explicitly establishes culturally mature perspective's significance in the larger history of ideas.

Cultural Maturity: A Guidebook for the Future is the most detailed, comprehensive, and leadership-focused of the three books. It also most directly applies the ideas of Creative Systems Theory to the tasks ahead. It is intended for those who have serious interest in developing the new kinds of skills and capacities that future leadership will require in all parts of our lives.

The first half of the book fleshes out the concept of Cultural Maturity by reflecting on today's new challenges and the new ways of thinking,

---

6   The Institute existed as a "bricks and mortar" institution from 1984 through 2002. Today, the Institute's work continues online (see www. CreativeSystems.org) and internationally.

acting, and relating that they increasingly require of us. It expands on ideas presented in *Hope and the Future*, examining both the major demands and the potentially great rewards that come with Cultural Maturity's changes. The second half of the book turns more specifically to the ideas of Creative Systems Theory. It looks at how the theory offers conceptual evidence for the concept of Cultural Maturity that makes the concept hard to dispute. It also examines how Creative Systems Theory provides an example of the new kind of conceptual tool that we will more and more need if we are to effectively make our way in times ahead.

Today's New Challenges

A basic observation links the book's reflections: We as a species confront a broad array of new challenges—from terrorism, to climate change, to the task of effectively addressing the increasingly complex moral/ethical concerns that more and more permeate our choices— that will be very difficult, if not impossible, to address if we remain limited to the ways we have understood and related in times past.

Below I've put a few new challenges from the many that we will address in the book in the form of questions. Clearly, if we can't get our minds around such essential concerns, we will pay a high price. None of these questions can be escaped, and with each the potential consequences if we fail to address it are considerable:

- How, given the growing availability of weapons of mass destruction, do we best support a safe human future?

- How do we successfully address the very real possibility of environmental catastrophe?

- How, in times ahead, will we deal with the numerous new concerns that require global decision-making— such as terrorism and the need for stable and trustable global economic structures?

- How will love work in the future, with gender roles and expectations today in such flux?

- How do we effectively address our modern health care delivery crisis?

- How do we make good moral decisions without the clear cultural guideposts of times past?

- Is modern representative democracy a final and ideal form of government or do further chapters in how we think of governance and government lie ahead?

- How do we best define progress if our contributions are to result in real human advancement?

These questions share essential characteristics. Certainly each is inescapably important. But as you shall see, they also share a requirment to leave behind familiar assumptions and think in new ways. We will examine how each of these questions challenges us to bring a complexity and dynamism to how we understand and act that before now we have not been capable of. Indeed, many of these questions are God-like in their implications—if we had encountered them before, we would have considered them the province of deities, not mere mortals.[7] With each of these concerns, not only finding the answers, but even just usefully framing the questions requires us to venture into new territories of understanding and experience.

These questions also share a more ultimately provocative commonality. What each of these very different new questions ask of us is, in the end, the same. We will examine how Cultural Maturity's needed next chapter in how we understand makes each of these questions newly addressable. Fully grasping any of them requires us to stretch how we think. And putting new conclusions into practice stretches us considerably further. But from the perspective of Cultural Maturity, questions

---

7   We find a simple example in the need, today, to make complex moral decisions without clear, culturally defined moral codes. Later we will look at how each of the other questions I have listed is also, in this sense, God-like in its implications.

such as these become not just answerable, they become fascinating and compelling, invitations to venture forth in essential new ways.

The pace at which culturally mature perspective has become inescapably important has been surprising even to me. Cultural Maturity's changes in the end address humanity's long-term well-being, but they are becoming increasingly pertinent to immediate concerns. Fifteen years ago, my colleagues and I at the Institute for Creative Development were deeply engaged with all these questions. But when we spoke to the public, we found that we couldn't expect people to immediately be on the same page with us. At that time—a very short time ago—people tended to see most of these issues as blue-sky concerns: if not unimportant, at least not immediately critical. In my public appearances, I found that I spent the larger portion of my time arguing for the simple fact that these questions were worthy of people's attention.

How quickly things change. The 9/11 attacks on the New York World Trade Center made the global nature of potential conflict inescapable, and highlighted how outmoded our past ways of thinking about safety and defense have become. Growing evidence for global climate change and its potentially cataclysmic effects has become increasingly impossible to ignore. Major upheavals in financial markets have turned conjecture about needed changes in global economic structures from the most rarified of academic inquiry to common street-corner conversation. Increasing acceptance of gay marriage along with broader changes in cultural mores today require people to rethink their most basic ideas about love and the family. The health care delivery crisis, along with a wide array of amazing, yet two-edged scientific advances (such as the manipulation of the human genome) are bringing new, more collective moral/ethical controversies ever more to the fore in our attention. Partisan pettiness has come more and more to undermine effective governmental decision-making. And the increasingly obvious fact that what we can do is not always what we should do has made it ever more clear that we need to revisit not just how we are to succeed at progressing, but just what progress should mean.

Today only outright denial could allow us to avoid the critical significance of these and other big-picture concerns, issues that only a very short time ago seemed of distant importance. And the need for new ways thinking and acting if such questions are to be effectively addressed is, for a growing number of people, coming to seem obvious. Once people are familiar with the new capacities that the concept of Cultural Maturity makes possible, those capacities and the new kinds of answers that result from them too can seem remarkably straightforward—in the end, like common sense. What is different is that this is a kind and degree of common sense that before now we could not have fully understood, or tolerated.

A friend recently asked me, only partly tongue in cheek, whether I thought we were facing an end to civilization. The world is changing so rapidly and disruptively that a person could certainly think so. My response to his query changed the subject, but in a way that has generated a rich and continuing conversation. I think it accurate that we face an end, but in a much more interesting sense than his question implied. We face an end to one important chapter in our human story and, with the beginnings of Cultural Maturity's needed "growing up," the start of another we are just beginning to fully understand.

Putting Who We Are in Motion

This inquiry differs from most writing about the future in several key ways. First is its scope: This is big-picture, long-term inquiry. The larger portion of writing that addresses what may lie ahead is more concerned with the next "must have" gadget, the next election, or the next business cycle. While all the questions I listed in the previous section have immediate pertinence, they are also relevant to our ultimate human well-being. Certainly the concept of Cultural Maturity is.

A second key way in which this inquiry is different is in where it most often directs its attention. The thinking of most futurists who are at all concerned with the long term focuses on the technological, on future invention and its implications. This inquiry's interest includes the technological—advances in technology are radically changing our world and will play a key role in making Cultural Maturity possible. But it gives primary attention to more explicitly human concerns: the future of war and peace, of intimacy and the family, of governance, of morality, of scientific perspective, of our relationship with nature and with the sacred.

There are multiple reasons for this emphasis. As a start, the human dimension is the part of the future's puzzle to which each of us—whatever our age, skills, beliefs, or profession—can most contribute. It is also the case that very few of the important problems we will face in times ahead can be solved by technical means alone. At the very least, successfully addressing them will depend on the values we bring to applying technological solutions. It will also depend on the greater sophistication of thought and relationship that Cultural Maturity makes possible.

Also, perhaps surprisingly, the more human dimension includes the parts of the puzzle that we can know most about. It has never been possible to predict technological invention with any confidence. Certainly today's world is far different from that of climate-controlled covered cities and personal flying transporters envisioned in the 1950s and '60s for the turn of the century. But while we can't always predict what will happen in the broader cultural sphere, there is much we can say about the challenges it will present. It turns out that there is also a great deal we can know about the values, social structures, and ways of making sense of the world that will be required to address those challenges successfully.

A further key way in which this inquiry differs from most writing about the future is central to this book's conclusions: The concept of Cultural Maturity puts how we think about culture in motion. It describes how cultural assumptions evolve over time. And of particular importance, it sees the times in which we live as continuing that evolution. More commonly, if we have thought of culture as evolving at all, we have made our current period in culture an ideal and end point. The concept of Cultural Maturity makes it clear that our time is as much defined by change as any other. Indeed, it proposes that what most defines our time is change of a particularly pivotal sort.

Thinking of culture as an evolutionary process for some people can at first feel foreign, but with familiarity doing so becomes obviously important. When I work as a psychiatrist with individuals and couples, I pay special attention to whether the issues and concerns brought up are specific to the lives of the people I'm seeing or whether, instead, they reflect questions that we all face at certain times in our lives. In my efforts as a cultural psychiatrist, I have found it increasingly inescapable that beyond the many specific challenges we face as a species, the most important tasks of our time are of the latter, more "developmental" sort.

Events we've witnessed around the globe in recent decades—in the Middle East, in Central and South America, in Eastern Europe, Southeast Asia, and Africa—illustrate this developmental sort of cultural change. We've seen dramatic shifts, often with the overthrow of long-entrenched authoritarian regimes. While the results have often been of a two-steps-forward, one-step-back sort, we see in these changes a general impetus toward more democratic sensibilities.

Cultural Maturity's changes are fundamentally different in their implications. The kind of change that produces the emergence of democratic principles happened for the modern West well back in our history—in the U.S. with our original emancipation from colonial rule and the first forging of constitutional documents. But Cultural Maturity's changes are in a similar sense evolutionary. In a related way, they are products of their time—in this case, our time. Our current stage in culture's evolution—that which gave us our modern concept of the individual, institutional democracy, free-market economics, contemporary religion, and the scientific age—could not be more significant. The concept of Cultural Maturity confirms that Modern Age values and Modern Age institutions have served us well. But it also makes clear that values of a more sophisticated sort, along with more maturely conceived institutions, will be needed for times ahead. The concept of Cultural Maturity describes that next essential chapter in our human story.[8]

It is interesting that even people who recognize that fledgling democracy movements around the globe involve changes of a developmental, "next-chapter" sort still commonly assume that the modern West's current beliefs and institutions reflect some last word. The concept of Cultural Maturity argues that developmental changes yet

---

8   One might appropriately ask if "species maturity" might be a more appropriate term. Yes and no. Cultural Maturity is not just about individual cultures. It is a global phenomenon. But it is also the case that different cultures reside at different stages in cultural development—something that is increasingly important to appreciate if relationships between the world's peoples are to be well understood and healthy. (Note that making such distinctions with the needed subtlety is tricky. Culturally mature perspective is needed if our thinking about cultural stage differences is not to reflect bigotry more than considered insight.)

ahead will make possible the human capabilities essential to going forward. It also argues that without these further changes, a future rife with significant disorientation and anguish becomes a very real possibility.

The idea that we stand at the threshold of changes that are fundamentally significant has been voiced in different ways by important thinkers throughout the last century. Former Czech president Václav Havel expressed it in a 1994 speech when he observed that, "Today, many things indicate that we are going through a transitional period, when it seems that something is on the way out, and something new is painfully being born." And anticipating the need for change of such depth decades earlier, Albert Einstein famously stated that "We shall require a substantially new manner of thinking if mankind is to survive." Numerous others—philosophers, politicians, scientists, theologians, and more—have reached similar conclusions. But just what those changes entail and how they might be possible is unclear even in the best of formulations. And the more simplistic of proposals are naïve at best. The concept of Cultural Maturity offers a frame for understanding such necessary changes that makes gut-level sense and that is also backed by solid evidence.

The Concept of Cultural Maturity

The kind of "growing up" that the concept of Cultural Maturity refers to is of a specific sort. It is not uncommon today to hear the assertion that we must somehow grow up in our thinking, but most often if we listen closely to what is implied, we hear little that is helpful. The person speaking is arguing, simply, that others should think more like he or she does. The claim can come from widely different positions of advocacy—from the political left or the political right, from a spiritual interpretation of truth or an interpretation that makes scientific observation what it is all about. Cultural Maturity's growing up is wholly different.

It will take the book as a whole to fully develop the concept of Cultural Maturity and flesh out its implications. But to get started, you can think of Cultural Maturity in terms a sequence of related change processes. Each kind of change is today fundamentally reordering what it means to be human.

The first concerns how culture's guiding rules on all fronts—unswerv-ing national alliegiances, clear moral codes, tight bonds in community, and more—are becoming less and less reliable. Our times challenge us to step beyond the comforting surety of familiar cultural guideposts and assume a new responsibility in the choices we make both in our daily lives and as cultural beings. Globalization explains part of this new requirement. It is hard to hold fast to the absolutes of one's own culture when the unquestioned beliefs of different cultures can be so decidedly at odds. But the concept of Cultural Maturity proposes that the dimin-ishing power of past absolutes also has deeper origins.

The next kind of change pertains to those deeper origins. It con-cerns our relationship as individuals to our cultural contexts. In times past, culture has functioned like a symbolic parent in the lives of individuals. It has provided us with our rules to live by and, in the process, given us a sense of identity and connectedness with others. Culture's parental dictates have also protected us from truths that would before have been beyond us to tolerate—how complex things can be, limits to what may actually be possible, the depths of life's uncertainties.

The consequences of moving beyond what always before has been a mythologized relationship is Janus-faced, at once about loss and possibility. We feel loss because the diminishing effectiveness of familiar truths combined with the diminishing power of cultural authority more generally leaves us without familiar sureties. But in stepping beyond our past mythologized relationship with culture, we also at least gain the ability to choose outside the bounds of convention. Often we discover whole new kinds of options.

The final change process is embedded in this new picture and has particular significance for this inquiry. I've proposed that today's new questions require us to think and act in new, more mature and com-plete ways. The concept of Cultural Maturity describes how today's changing relationship between culture and the individual does more than provide greater freedom of choice. It brings with it fundamental changes in how we see the world and, more generally, in how we un-derstand—specific cognitive changes.

This additional kind of change is essential. If our future is to be bright, we can't stop with just a loss of guideposts. The general notion that traditional absolutes are not serving us as before is a common theme in what people speak of as "postmodern" perspective. But what comes next after our guideposts are gone? If we merely lose traditional guideposts without gaining some new source of understanding, the best that can result is the illusory freedom of an "anything goes" world. Later we will look at how postmodern thought, while historically significant, at best reflects recognitions of a transitional sort.[9] We need a further, deeper kind of change if today's loss of past guideposts is not just to set us adrift.

The concept of Cultural Maturity addresses each of these change processes and describes how, in the end, they reflect aspects of a single larger process. When fully grasped, the concept offers rewards very difficult to attain in other ways. Earlier I briefly noted three ways the concept of Cultural Maturity benefits us and promised to say more about each of them. Each contribution will be essential to a healthy human future.

First is how the concept of Cultural Maturity provides a practical and compelling new guiding story. I've described how the cultural narratives we have known and lived by now fall decidedly short. Just as important to recognize is how the new stories put forward today to replace them at best capture pieces of a larger picture. We have a wide array of such new options to choose from. Do we think of our time as a dramatic new Information Age offering endless potential for the human species? As a time of aimlessness, decay of traditional institutions, and loss of basic cultural civility? Or, with the end of the Cold War, as a period of new hope for a peaceful and democratic world? Do we think of this moment as a time of profound environmental crises that might be beyond our power to solve? As a spiritual New Age? As a time of moral downfall, of impending Armageddon?

While these various candidates for a new guiding story each address things that we feel—at the very least, they reflect real hopes or fears—none, by itself, fully explains what today we witness around

---

9   See "Cultural Maturity, Ideology, and Limits" in Chapter Three; "Truths, Responsibility, and the Postmodern Contribution" in Chapter Five; and "Postmodern/Constructivist Scenarios" in Chapter Nine.

us. And none succeeds at providing reliable and compelling guidance. Cultural Maturity's notion of an essential new step in our collective human development provides both perspective that takes us beyond the limited worldviews implied in these more familiar and often-warring candidates, and concrete guidance for moving forward.

Second, there is the way that the concept of Cultural Maturity helps us make sense of the human capacities we will need going forward. It is important to note that the implications of doing so go beyond just understanding. By clarifying what needed new capacities ask of us, the concept of Cultural Maturity offers us a chance to practice them, build the muscles we need for making good choices. And because deeply making sense of needed capacities—and certainly making the needed new capacities effectively manifest—necessarily engages us in Cultural Maturity's cognitive changes, doing so helps to bring the required greater human maturity more generally into being.

And third, there is how the concept of Cultural Maturity points toward the new ways of thinking that we will need if we are to effectively make our way—both what makes such new kinds of ideas possible and just what they must look like. This further contribution is essential if we are to effectively address today's increasingly complex, and often God-like, challenges. Cultural Maturity's cognitive changes support the development of whole new kinds of conceptual tools that can help us effectively engage a future that will certainly be both bewildering and deeply fascinating. The developmental ideas that underlie the concept of Cultural Maturity provide an important illustration. With the second half of the book, needed new ways of understanding—and in particular how Creative Systems Theory provides illustration—become our primary focus.

We don't have to look into the future to see any of these essential rewards. I will describe how we have witnessed first-step culturally mature contributions in multiple fields—science, psychology, art, religion, government, and more—over the last hundred years. The recognition that the needed changes are already in process is important for deeper reasons than just encouragement. Views that merely criticize the present and see solutions only in some far-off future rarely provide useful insight. We will examine how such views not only tend to produce deadening cynicism; they commonly involve distortions that make their conclusions ultimately dangerous—and simply wrong.[10]

We tend not to think of the word "maturity" as terribly sexy, but put in this context it could not be more so. Certainly guidance that works is provocative simply through its effectiveness. But maturity, too, is where we humans find greatest ultimate meaning and fulfillment—as those who know it in their personal lives will attest. In the long term, it is also where we as a species will find ultimate meaning and the full expression of human possibility. The idea of a needed cultural "growing up" offers a powerful picture of what can lie ahead and a practical road map for going forward. And Cultural Maturity's changes make that road map not just something we can consider, but something we can apply—in our daily lives and more broadly.

A "Threshold" Time

In getting started, it is essential that we appreciate just how deeply Cultural Maturity's changes ask new things of us, how they involve fundamental reexamination—fully a leap in understanding. We must be careful with this kind of assertion. Every generation in its own way sees itself as reinventing the world. That noted, we can recognize also that history has periodically required radical new things of us. While many of a time's tasks follow fairly logically from the tasks of realities that precede it, cultural breaks occur that are more dramatic. The most life-altering of these have delineated not just next paragraphs in the cultural story, but new chapters—thus we speak of new epochs and ages. Cultural Maturity's changes are of this next-chapter sort.

Certainly the new questions I just listed point toward this kind of conclusion. The idea that we face new kinds of human challenges is, by itself, not radical. But recognizing the depth of those challenges— for example, the degree that they require more than just technological solutions—is at least provocative. So, certainly, is how they touch on every part of our lives. More radical is the recognition that addressing these new challenges will require new kinds of human skills and capacities, how effectively taking them on they will demand ways of act-

---

10   See "Scenarios for the Future" in Chapter Nine.

ing and relating—and kinds of understanding—that before now have not been needed or possible. The recognition that the new skills and capacities required for addressing what may often seem to be wholly distinct challenges come together in the idea of a now essential cultural "growing up" is more specifically radical.

I often use a simple image to represent the experience of engaging the tasks of Cultural Maturity (see Figure I-1). At its most basic, it depicts what we experience with any developmental leap. Without some later additions,[11] it doesn't fully capture what is unique about Cultural Maturity's particular developmental changes, but even in this simplified form, it provides a good reference. Think of engaging the tasks of Cultural Maturity as similar to stepping through a doorway into a new world of experience.

Fig. 1-1. Cultural Maturity's Threshold [12]

---

11   See "Cultural Maturity's Cognitive Reordering" and "Cultural Maturity and Polarity" in Chapter Two.

12   The diagram on the book's cover is a stylized representation of Cultural

Before we step across that doorway's threshold, the new kinds of ideas and social structures that Cultural Maturity makes possible are not understandable to us. Indeed, we tend not to even recognize why we might need them. Critical new challenges may directly block our way, but still remain largely invisible. When we are able to step over that threshold and through the doorway, new challenges become increasingly obvious and important. And the changes that culturally mature perspective describes become clearly what right choice and action are about.

Later, drawing on Creative Systems Theory, I will describe how the new challenges we face today engage us not just in a new cultural chapter, but in one of particular importance—a defining hinge point in culture's evolving story.[13] Cultural Maturity is not as much about marching in the streets as previous major cultural change points were—certainly it is not in the same sense about toppling regimes. But, as you will see, ultimately its changes are more revolutionary than what we have encountered with previous transitional times.

The threshold image helps clarify two different ways I will talk about Cultural Maturity's changes. Each follows from the developmental nature of the maturity metaphor. First, I will apply the concept of Cultural Maturity as a minimum requirement for addressing, or even really just understanding, our time's new questions. We will look at the kinds of understanding that can best get us over that threshold and how certain kinds of ideas are going to leave us short no matter how well meant or how complexly and intelligently they are conceived. Here the book's tone will be uncompromising. Ideas that stop short—and often they are some of our favorites—become not just partial, but dangerous, when we face challenges of today's new sort.

I will also talk of Cultural Maturity as a "territory" of experience—what we find on the other side of that threshold. We will examine in depth what Cultural Maturity's new world of choice and understanding looks like and asks of us. Here, in making comparisons, my language will shift from qualitative—is a particular idea maturely conceived?—

Maturity's threshold.

13   See "History—and Life—as a Creative Narrative" in Chapter Seven.

to quantitative—how many steps into culturally mature reality does a particular way of thinking or acting take us? At our best today, we are able to take only a few solid steps. And these are but a few of many more that over the decades and centuries ahead will be necessary. But even baby steps, as these surely are, are of major consequence.

Culturally Mature Leadership's "Threshold Tasks"

I've noted that this book is the most leadership-focused of my three more recent efforts. The observation that Cultural Maturity is in the end about leadership gives us one of the clearest ways to talk about Cultural Maturity's changes. Needed new leadership capacities provide the book's starting point.

Here I use the word "leadership" in a way that expands the term's usual definition. Culturally mature leadership will be critical to leading nations and organizations, certainly, but it will be just as essential to making good choices as lovers, friends, or parents. The needed new kind of leadership involves everyone—none of us gets to escape its demands. The concept of Cultural Maturity also makes clear that the future will require not just good leadership, or even exceptional leadership, but a new, specifically more mature, sophisticated—and wise—kind of leadership.

The simplest way to put it is that culturally mature leadership challenges us in a critical new sense to "hold life large." It demands that we step beyond ways of thinking that before have protected us from experience's bigness and engage life with a fullness and subtlety— with a kind of head-on courage—that before now has not been needed or possible. Culturally mature leadership requires that we leave behind once helpful, but now limiting and dangerous, easy-answer solutions. It requires that we surrender ideological conclusions of all sorts and address life in ways that are more nuanced and complete.[14]

But we can also be more specific. The book's early chapters juxtapose examples of today's new questions and challenges with an examination of the new leadership capacities that we will need if we are to effectively address them. While the origins of today's major new concerns can be

---

14   Chapter One will look closely at how ideology works and at its relationship to culturally mature perspective.

very different,[15] at the same time, as I've described, we find important parallels in what effectively confronting them will require of us, parallels that can take us a long way toward understanding Cultural Maturity and its changes.

Using the needed new leadership capacities as a starting point provides a particularly direct—in-the-trenches—way to engage our quarry. If you, the reader, accept that successfully addressing today's new questions will require new, more mature human capacities, then agreeing with or even fully understanding the concept of Cultural Maturity's more theoretical foundations is not essential. You can get right to work learning about and developing the capabilities that leadership for the future will require. (In a bit, I will clarify how even this approach can't be as simple as we might like, but it gives us a solid place from which to begin.)

Making reference to the doorway image, I will use the term "threshold task" to describe the various parts of what is being asked of us. Each task relates to an aspect of life's bigness that today's new questions require us to engage with a whole new kind of maturity and directness. The book's first half is devoted to a close examination of three such threshold tasks.

The first threshold task turns our attention to the critical importance of getting our minds around today's complexities. We will look at how the world is becoming ever more complicated and how newly complex questions can leave us overwhelmed. We will also look at how, in times past, cultural absolutes—and ideological beliefs more generally—have protected us from how complicated life can be, and how, today, such protection increasingly puts us at risk. You will see how Cultural Maturity's changes make us both more comfortable with complexity and better able to maneuver in a multifaceted world.

The question of how nations are to relate peacefully in the future shines a particularly useful light on the way ideology has before protected us from complexity. It also makes the dangerous consequences of

---

15   Some are simple products of where our human successes have taken us. Others are direct consequences of now-outmoded assumptions. And others are themselves the results of Cultural Maturity's new realities. See "The Origins of Modern Complexity" in Chapter Two.

continuing to cling to ideological belief particularly difficult to ignore. We confront an age-old proclivity: Always before in human history, social identity and our sense of purpose and security have required that we regard our own kind as in some way "chosen." Simultaneously, as part of the same mechanism, we've projected the less savory parts of ourselves—our inner demons—onto some other group, making it our polar opposite "evil other."[16] Our future well-being hinges on our ability to get beyond such reactive, easy-answer assumptions. Combine "chosen people/evil other" thinking with today's readily available weapons of mass destruction, and the necessity of moving beyond us-versus-them ideology becomes inescapable. To safely and creatively make our way in times ahead, we must learn to think and relate in ways that better acknowledge the multifaceted complexities both of the other peoples we engage and of ourselves.[17]

Narrow, reactive thinking is not limited to global relations, and ideological assumptions today present dangers wherever we find them. The categories are endless—the conflicting beliefs of various religions and ethnic factions, warring political convictions, bigotries of every sort, conflicting philosophical allegiances. We will look at how such easy-answer conclusions not only obscure needed answers, they keep us from recognizing the real questions. Today's challenges require more encompassing, more mature and systemic kinds of understanding.

The maturity of perspective that is needed to more directly address this first aspect of life's bigness might seem beyond us to achieve. But in fact we have already begun to take solid steps. An example: Few people anticipated the fall of the Berlin Wall—certainly no one

---

16   We tend to focus on specific differences in belief when trying to make sense of conflict on the world stage—whether it be political or religious. Such specifics are in fact most often secondary to the role that polarization—a "chosen people" set against ignorance or worse—has played in solidifying social identity. Such polar identification manifests in different ways at different stages in cultural development but has otherwise been universal though history.

17   If globalization is the only factor reshaping relations, we are in real trouble. By itself, globalization, by pushing together cultures that reside in fundamentally different cultural stages, becomes a formula for calamity.

predicted the suddenness of its collapse. Particularly important as far as our first threshold task is just how it fell. The Berlin Wall fell ultimately not because of decisions made at the top, but because of a shift in the beliefs of common people on both sides of the wall, and in human society more broadly. And that shift in belief had less to do with a change in ideology than with people becoming, in effect, bored with ideology itself.[18]

Threshold task number two shifts our attention to the fact of limits. We confront the importance of better acknowledging real limits and learning to relate to such limits more maturely. We will look at how past beliefs have protected us, much like they protected us from complexity, by shielding us from the disturbing fact of real limits. Ideological beliefs, by their nature, hide myths of limitlessness. In a similar way, too, this further protection from life's bigness is no longer consistent with a safe and healthy world.

Historically, our response when we have come up against apparent limits has been heroic—we have fought to defeat them and move unswervingly forward. This has served us. Much that is greatest in past human achievement—the building of great cities, the elimination of devastating diseases, the exploration of the far reaches of outer space—has come from our successful conquering of limits. But today, increasingly, we confront limits that cannot be defeated in the old ways—such as limits to the planet's resources, fundamental economic limits, and critical limits to what we can ultimately know and predict. We must take these limits seriously if our amazing human inventive capacities are not to be our undoing.

We will examine how rethinking our relationship with limits requires not just greater wisdom and courage, but also more nuanced and mature ways of understanding. Traditional assumptions give us only two options: heroic victory or defeat. Not surprisingly, many people today feel defeated, and not just with regard to specific issues before us, but more generally. Humanity's future well-being hinges on our ability to understand limits of all sorts in more mature and sophisticated ways.

---

18 What we saw was more significant than just some liberal siding with peace. Throughout the book, we will observe how Cultural Maturity takes us beyond the traditional positions of both the Left and the Right.

We will look at how effective leadership in times ahead must stand willing to accept hard facts—unswervingly acknowledge real limits. We will also examine what may at first seem a surprise—how maturely acknowledging limits can reveal essential options that before we could not recognize. The best new leadership models advocate approaches that are more humble in their acceptance of real limits. As a result, they are also more powerful.

Our third threshold task is even more basic, both in what it asks and where it leads: We must rethink the yardsticks, the fundamental values and truths, that we use to make our choices. We can think of this developmental task as itself having three parts. Each has an essential role if we are not to wander aimlessly—and often dangerously. First, we need to take new responsibility for the truths we apply. I've described how before now, culture in its parental guise has provided us with ready rules and guideposts: clear moral codes along with generally agreed-upon assumptions about God, science, and truth more generally. We also need to reconceive the measures we use to guide us in all parts of our lives in ways that are more complete, more systemic. Finally, we need to bring a dynamism and detail to the distinctions we make that has not before been needed or possible. We will look at how the ability to engage each of these truth-related challenges follows directly from Cultural Maturity's cognitive reordering.

One example of this third task ties with particular directness to the question of narrative, to the imperative of finding a story that works for our time: We need to rethink traditional ideas about what constitutes human advancement—our ideas about wealth and progress. In an important new sense, we are becoming responsible not just for how we act and for our day-to-day beliefs, but for our larger understanding of who we are collectively. Such greater responsibility requires not just greater awareness, but that we revisit our cultural "bottom lines" and conceive of them more systemically. In the Modern Age, we've come to define advancement almost exclusively in terms of economic expansion, technological dominance, and individual benefit. In the future, our definitions of wealth and progress must be more embracing—at the very least more sustainable and more directly attentive to an ultimate good. Leadership in times ahead must advocate for a more full and complete—we could simply say "wise"—definition of progress and a rethinking of our human endeavor more generally.

Actually, the in-the-trenches strategy the book's first half applies can't be quite as simple and straightforward as these basic descriptions might suggest. A couple of factors will necessarily add to the challenge, even with this approach that draws so directly on specific examples and engages new skills and capacities in such a concrete fashion. In its own way, each factor offers additional insight into the nature of our task.

First, we confront a chicken-and-egg reality: Grasping the needed new capacities with real depth itself requires culturally mature perspective. This kind of situation is not unique to Cultural Maturity. It is a conundrum we face with any new understanding that is a product of change of a developmental sort. But we can't escape it, and it will often result in what might seem like simple assertions being ultimately more demanding of us than we had first imagined.

It is also the case that theory will necessarily have an important role even in these introductory reflections—often a more prominent role than many people, particularly those of a more practical bent, might choose. As much as possible I will make the argument for Cultural Maturity through examples, but theoretical perspective proves particularly valuable on multiple fronts. Certainly the fact that Cultural Maturity is not just about thinking new things, but also about thinking in some wholly new ways is critical and requires careful reflection. There is also how we face the essential task of separating the wheat from the chaff in our thinking. When we confuse the needed "growing up" with things it is not, the notion becomes trivial and a distraction from the tasks at hand. We need theory—and often particularly sophisticated theory— to make the needed distinctions. In addition, effectively going forward will require whole new sorts of theoretical formulations—specific new kinds of tools for our conceptual toolbox.[19]

But, complicating factors acknowledged, the in-the-trenches approach of looking at new challenges and needed new leadership capacities provides a particularly good point of departure. At the very least, it

---

19   I will conclude the book's more theoretical sections with brief references to some of the practical implications of what I have described. These short "threshold lessons" will help clarify what mature decision-making is and is not about, in direct, immediately applicable ways.

offers basic reassurance. The observation that new challenges will require similar new skills and abilities suggests that our situation may not
be as frightening and chaotic as our ever more demanding world can
sometimes feel. And we encounter a more specific kind of reassurance
in the recognition that these new skills and abilities needed to address
today's challenges follow naturally as products of Cultural Maturity's
changes. Cultural Maturity's cognitive reordering gives us the tools we
need to begin effectively engaging those challenges.

This approach also provides important beginning insights with
regard to strategy. We can think of the three threshold developmental
tasks I have described simultaneously as requirements for moving
forward and as leverage points for doing so. This is how things work
with any developmental process. But the fact that culturally mature
perspective involves a more conscious relationship to experience than
understanding in times past gives this fact a new level of significance.[20]
Every time we successfully engage one of these tasks, in some way, large
or small, our actions take us up to Cultural Maturity's threshold and
begin to reveal culturally mature possibility.

In the end, applying any of the new skills and abilities that result
opens the door not just to specific new solutions, but also to Cultural
Maturity's new world of experience more broadly. The resulting greater
maturity of perspective changes everything. We will examine how taking
on these three threshold tasks makes each aspect of our lives—our values,
relationships of every sort, how we understand, and the institutions we
craft—more dynamic and complete. Engaging them makes us direct
participants in today's needed next chapter in our human narrative.

The Evidence

These various capacity-related observations capture the first of four
kinds of evidence I will draw on to support the concept of Cultural
Maturity. Over the next six chapters, we will examine how culturally
mature perspective helps us address each of these aspects of life's

---

20   This more conscious relationship to change is implied in the way
     Cultural Maturity takes us beyond culture's past role as mythic parent.
     See "Cultural Maturity's Cognitive Reordering " in Chapter Two for a
     closer look at how it follows directly from Cultural Maturity's changes.

bigness—its multifaceted complexity, the fact of real limits, and the depths of the truths we need to engage if we are to make ultimately wise and effective choices. Each threshold task gets a couple of chapters, one that generally introduces its demands and a second that more deeply engages its implications.[21]

The second kind of evidence for Cultural Maturity, and the foundational insight for Chapter Seven, is more specifically developmental. We will examine closely how limited versions of these same threshold tasks can be found with the shift that defines maturity in our individual lifetimes. We will look, also, at how we encounter something related with the mature stages of human change processes wherever we find them. The recognition of developmental parallels supports the conclusion, essential to the appropriateness of hope, that the new tasks and possibilities described by the idea of a new species maturity are, in fact, developmentally predicted.

These developmental notions draw specifically on the ideas of Creative Systems Theory. Creative Systems Theory proposes an explanation for why we see the particular progressions that we do. It describes how, in each case, the changes that we witness proceed according to the steps that change more generally follows with self-organizing systemic processes in conscious systems.[22]

Besides generally supporting the concept of Cultural Maturity, this examination of developmental parallels will also bring important detail to our understanding of what the maturity analogy refers to. The

---

21   In keeping with the "in-the-trenches" approach, I will begin each threshold task with an extended example that applies it to a front-page–news cultural issue. And, throughout each chapter, I will offer numerous further examples to make it as concrete as possible. Many of these examples will be familiar to people who have read other books of mine—there are a handful of examples that capture both the necessity of Cultural Maturity and the specifics of its changes particularly well. Here, more than with other writings, I will fill out examples conceptually and give special attention to their implications for the tasks of future leadership.

22   I refer here to change of an extended sort; for example, what we see over the evolution of a creative project, over the course of a relationship, or with the growth of an organization.

concept of Cultural Maturity takes as its reference a very specific kind
of "growing up,"[23] not the fresh freedoms of adulthood, but rather the
greater perspective and sense of proportion that comes with successfully engaging second-half-of-life developmental tasks. Appreciating
this difference clarifies that the expected outcome of Cultural Maturity
is not just greater knowledge, but also new wisdom—and wisdom of a
particularly hard-nosed, practical, and gritty sort.

The third kind of evidence, addressed in Chapter Eight, includes a
series of Creative Systems Theory topics that bring important theoretical rigor to the concept of Cultural Maturity. Of particular significance,
the chapter examines an observation that is key to what makes Cultural Maturity's changes different from those of major change points
of times past. We will look at how the basic direction that has defined
human advancement to this point can't work into the future, and not
just because onward-and-upward progress could result in dangerous
choices. There is an important sense in which continuing on history's
past trajectory would violate who we are. Doing so would sever us from
essential aspects of our natures. We will look closely at how Cultural
Maturity's changes offer a way past this circumstance that might otherwise be the end of us.[24]

Chapter Eight also brings a finer lens to the underlying cognitive
processes that produce the changes in thinking and relating that we
see with Cultural Maturity. Making comparison with the leap in perspective that took us beyond the superstitions and narrow ardencies
of the Middle Ages and gave us our Modern Age worldview helps us
appreciate the fundamental nature of these changes. The new cultural
stage ushered in by the seventeenth-century conceptual innovations
of Isaac Newton and René Descartes, and before that in the fifteenth
century, the fresh artistic vantage of Michelangelo and Leonardo da
Vinci, involved changes not just in what we believed, but in how we
understood. We gained a newly objective, "from-a-balcony" kind of
perspective. We can likewise make sense of everything about Cultural

23 For this reason, while the phrase "growing up" is initially helpful, I will
    always put it in quotes.

24 Creative Systems Theory calls this circumstance the *Dilemma of Trajec-
    tory*.

Maturity's collective "growing up"—what it asks of us, why it does so, and why the changes it describes are things we might expect—in terms of a further, just as readily delineated set of changes in the mechanisms through which we make sense of ourselves and the world around us. Chapter Eight describes how the cognitive changes that produce culturally mature perspective not only redefine understanding in ways that are just as significant as those that have reordered understanding in times past, in the end, they do so in ways that are even more fundamental and consequential.

The fourth kind of evidence—again with its own chapter—is comparative. Chapter Nine contrasts the conclusions of the preceding chapters with other social perspectives and views of the future— for example, the more common views of futurists, the conventional beliefs of the political left and right, New Age wishful thinking, and postmodern social critique. The concept of Cultural Maturity helps us separate the wheat from the chaff in our thinking about what lies ahead. Culturally mature perspective helps us tease out underlying beliefs and recognize when our assumptions keep us from the needed new sophistication in our thoughts and actions. This ability does not in itself constitute proof, but it does contribute to the argument's persuasiveness.

The remaining chapters help fill out these four kinds of evidence. Chapter Ten adds flesh to the previous chapters' more bare-boned introduction to Creative Systems Theory by looking in greater detail at how cultural understanding has changed over the course of history. It draws on a array of very different lenses to examine this progression— from the history of architecture and of philosophy, to the evolution of how we have thought about the nature of time, the biological world, and the human body. Chapter Ten also examines how we don't need detailed theoretical notions to make many of the kinds of observations Creative Systems Theory makes more conceptually, how everyday language can capture much of what is most important in needed discernments.

Chapter Eleven examines how the ideas developed in previous chapters help us rethink the basic assumptions of particular cultural domains. We will touch briefly on nine spheres—economics/business, science/technology, government, medicine, education, the media, love and the family, art, and religion. With each, we will look at changes we can expect to witness in times ahead and also how the best of thinking in that domain should contribute to Cultural Maturity's broader realization. By demonstrating the practical usefulness of culturally mature concepts in another way, these reflections help further solidify the concept's conclusions.

The book's final chapter begins by summarizing the evidence that I've presented. On first encounter, the idea of a needed collective "growing up" can seem extreme and too far-reaching in its implications. But the four sorts of evidence just described make the concept of Cultural Maturity hard to refute. Our three threshold tasks—reflected in challenges of all sorts, and fundamentally new in what they ask of us—make it clear that our times require us to change and grow in essential ways. The identification of developmental parallels between species maturity and maturity in personal development solidifies our understanding of what the needed changes ask of us. It also supports the conclusion that these needed changes are possible. The recognition that culturally mature perspective helps us get beyond seemingly end-of-the-road conceptual roadblocks, combined with a deeper understanding of Cultural Maturity's cognitive mechanisms, makes the concept of Cultural Maturity even more specific and solid. And the way that the idea of a newly possible human maturity provides an overarching vantage for understanding competing views of the future adds to the argument's persuasiveness—and gives its conclusions a satisfying elegance.

The book's final chapter concludes by looking more specifically at the evidence for hope—for whether hope as we look to the future is warranted, and if so, why. The kind of hope that the concept of Cultural Maturity points toward is not that of an ideal world, but rather hope of a more down-to-earth sort. And it offers no guarantees. These concluding reflections look at why resistance and denial with regard to the tasks ahead is expected and already seen. They also examine several scenarios in which failure could happen easily and dramatically—with cataclysmic consequences. Possibility is not destiny, and even if we successfully address Cultural Maturity's challenge, it is very likely that we will often stumble on the way, inflicting pain on ourselves and other species in the process. But Cultural Maturity provides both solid guidance and real hope.

While Cultural Maturity's picture for the future could be wrong, the evidence I will present in this book suggests strongly that at least the basic contours of its argument are correct. Beyond the evidence that provides this book's structure, for me there is also a more personal kind of confirmation. I find it hard to imagine a world I would want to live in without Cultural Maturity's changes. Actually, such evidence is not just personal. Simple survival may not be possible without these changes. If the concept of Cultural Maturity as I describe it is correct, it becomes, in effect, the only game in town.

Views of the Future

I've chosen to make this introduction considerably longer than is found in most books. Because Culturally Mature understanding is new—and also because initially Cultural Maturity can easily be confused with things it is not at all about—it is important that the reader have a solid foundation from which to proceed. Think of this Introduction's reflections as a preview of coming attractions for the book as a whole.

Throughout the book, I will reflect on how Cultural Maturity compares and contrasts with other views of the future. In Chapter Nine, we will examine the main differences in some detail. At this point, briefly noting some of these contrasting viewpoints will help us avoid going off in unhelpful directions by assuming more familiar conclusions or reacting against conclusions that Cultural Maturity does not suggest.

Popular culture, academic discourse, religious belief, and the writings of futurists provide a wildly diverse and often contradictory array of predictions for what the future will require and what it may hold in store. We also all hold beliefs about the future—whether we are aware of them or not—embedded in our assumptions about how things work. What may seem small differences in initial assumptions can result in dramatically different choices—and ultimate consequences.

A quick glimpse of the five "scenarios" (to use the language of futurists) that we will examine in Chapter Nine follows. With each scneario I've made brief comparison to Cultural Maturity.

Many people don't see the future as much different, at least fundamentally, from the present. They assume that our times reflect ultimate truth, as most people through history have done with regard to their particular truths. Sometimes people reach this conclusion simply because they haven't thought much about the future, but others hold to it more overtly. Advocates of such "we've arrived" conclusions assume that current institutions and ways of thinking—political, religious, scientific, or economic—at most need some further polishing. Cultural Maturity strongly affirms the achievements of the Modern Age, but at the same time, it argues that there is no more reason to assume that we've arrived at some culminating truth in our age than in any age previous, and every reason to hope that we have not.

Certain other people believe almost the opposite—that in some fundamental way humanity has failed, gone astray. We find extreme forms in millennialist religious warnings that the end is near, and milder versions in the more pessimistic of liberal/humanist and environmentalist positions (where concern can devolve into an "it is all going to hell in a handbasket" cynicism). Such milder views often call, either explicitly or by implication, for going back to earlier times that they perceive as somehow more ideal. Cultural Maturity affirms that modern times often find us in denial about much that desperately needs attention. Indeed, it supports that important truths— for example, about nature, about the sacred, about community, and more—have been "forgotten."[25] But it proposes that the future holds great possibility. And it makes clear that going back is not the answer if we wish to have a healthy and vital future, and not even if we wish to retrieve things we perceive to be lost.

A third common view assumes that inventions yet to come hold the answers to humanity's problems, and pictures a future defined by ever more wondrous technological advancement. The concept of Cultural Maturity affirms the importance of invention and describes how inventions of the future can support Cultural Maturity's changes. But it also emphasizes that technological solutions without changes in ourselves cannot get us where we need to go. The best of technology-focused views include the recognition that new technologies tend to bring with them new ways of thinking. But, as you shall see, a technological gospel, even if we include the changes in thought that new invention helps stimulate, ultimately stops short of a narrative able to provide reliable guidance. We find a particularly simplistic—

25   See "Progress and the Dilemma of Trajectory" in Chapter Eight.

and dangerous—version in the techno-utopian thinking that often accompanies our modern digital age.

"Postmodern" thought—with its emphasis on our times' loss of familiar cultural handholds—provides a fourth way of thinking about our time and what may lie ahead. Advocates of postmodern perspective emphasize today's loss of familiar absolutes and the importance of taking new responsibility in our lives. They argue that we "construct" the realities we live in, and they see the defining task of the future as doing so more consciously. Cultural Maturity views postmodern thought as providing a useful first step. But it proposes that surrendering cultural absolutes can only be a beginning. Too often, the idea that we construct our truths collapses into an empty relativism. And we will examine how, particularly with the more extreme of interpretations, postmodern thought's common aversion to overarching conception can leave it with little to replace what it so insightfully observes has been taken away. Cultural Maturity makes clear that along with letting go of old absolutes, we must learn to relate and think in different, more dynamic and complete ways.

A last viewpoint frames changes in the language of "changes in consciousness" or "new paradigms" of understanding. The concept of Cultural Maturity is similarly about changes in ourselves, but again, most often we find fundamental differences. We encounter ideas framed in the language of changing paradigms that are quite consistent with culturally mature perspective. But the greater portion of views that see the future in terms of personal and cultural transformation, particularly ideas of a specifically spiritual or philosophically idealist[26] sort, are not really new at all. Rather, they draw on ideas of times well past, and often in distorted ways.[27] Whether they do or not, most such views

---

26 The term "philosophical idealism" refers not to having ideals (which can be of many sorts) but to a specific kind of worldview. Analysis rooted in philosophical idealism views history as progressing toward some final ideal—sometimes political, other times more spiritual.

27 The obviously simplistic spiritual conclusions of popular "New Age" thought provide the most glaring examples. But more serious philosophically idealist thinking in the end reflects a related kind of misconception. Because such thinking can use terms such as

reflect wishful thinking more than anything that is possible in our time. More pointedly, often as not, such utopian pictures of change, even if they were possible to realize, imply realities and consequences that we would not want.[28]

Besides helping us tease apart essential differences from the alternative views I've touched on in this section, culturally mature perspective also provides an encompassing vantage that is able to put such differences in perspective. It sees the alternatives I've noted as the conclusions we would predict when the world is observed through particular lenses. In the chapters ahead, you will see how Cultural Maturity's larger perspective both avoids traps common to these various views and provides ways to address essential questions that none of them, alone or even together, can get at.[29]

Developmental/Evolutionary Perspective

I've described how the concept of Cultural Maturity requires that we put how we think about culture in motion. As framed by Creative Systems Theory, it requires that we put our understanding of culture in a very particular—specifically "creative"— sort of motion. Recognizing the way in which this kind of change is particular is key

---

"systemic" or "integral" that can initially be confused with the wholly different conclusions of culturally mature perspective, this recognition is particularly important to appreciate. See "A Ready Confusion" in Chapter Eight, and "Scenarios for the Future" and "Polar Traps" in Chapter Nine.

28   In most cases, they are just as ideological as absolutist ideas they may claim to take us beyond. A characteristic shared with each of these five scenarios gives this away. Such thinking tends to have special appeal to people of particular personality styles. It makes one's own kind "chosen"—in this case spiritually chosen. See "Scenarios for the Future" and "One 'Crayon' and Another" in Chapter Nine.

29   Certain versions of these five "scenarios" are most vulnerable to being initially confused with Cultural Maturity. I think in particularly of liberal/ humanist, Information Age, postmodern constructivist, and spiritual/ transformational interpretations. By the book's conclusion, it should be clear how each of these views differs from culturally mature perspective in fundamental and critical ways.

to understanding Cultural Maturity, and in a further important way helps us avoid confusion as we venture forth.

The basic idea that culture might evolve, certainly in ways that we can clearly describe, is not just foreign to some people's thinking as noted earlier, it can arouse immediate suspicion in certain circles—and for good reasons. Historically, thinking that views societal change in evolutionary terms has been used to justify all kinds of misleading and dangerous conclusions.[30] We will examine closely just what is missing in thinking that can produce such misleading conclusions. We will also look at how the existence of evolutionary change—cultural change of a deep sort that has identifiable stages—becomes, with close examination, extremely hard to refute.

The book's second half examines in detail the developmental processes that give us Cultural Maturity's changes.[31] At this point, it is enough that we observe some characteristics that help us distinguish the general kind of perspective we will draw on from other ways of thinking about cultural change. I will call Creative Systems Theory's specific kind of evolutionary thinking "developmental/evolutionary."

Distinguishing what is different starts with the obvious but necessary recognition that our concern is evolution of a cultural sort. People can use

---

30 Because of this, many academic thinkers dismiss such ideas out of hand. Most often cited are Georg Hegel's philosophically idealist formulations, which cast a mythically elevated Prussian state as culture's culminating expression (and purportedly later influenced the thinking of Adolf Hitler). I've described how philosophical idealism views history as progressing toward some final cultural ideal. One result is that such thinking can be readily used to justify the elevation of one's own kind and the denigration of others.

31 You could begin your exploration of Cultural Maturity by examining this detailed developmental/evolutionary picture and how Cultural Maturity's changes are its result. That is the approach I apply in my more theoretical book, *Quick and Dirty Answers to the Biggest of Questions*. If it is your preference, at any time you can turn to Chapter Seven. But as a place to start, for most people, that approach would imply conclusions that are best more solidly established first. This book's initial, more in-the-trenches strategy lets you first build your Cultural Maturity muscles by leaning about and applying the new capacities that the various threshold tasks make possible.

an evolutionary argument to justify the conclusion that the new capacities that a vital human future will require are really not humanly possible. They might claim, for example, that "we've evolved to be warlike, and that will never change." In making this argument, people miss the fact that evolution has two meanings. There is biological evolution, and on that front we are unlikely to see much change that will help us, certainly not anytime soon. But there is also cultural evolution: the ways in which social systems grow and evolve over time. Cultural evolution—certainly as framed here—supports some very different kinds of conclusions.

Creative Systems Theory's approach also represents a particular way of thinking about cultural evolution. Most immediately, it is more encompassing in how it sees the mechanisms of change. Conventionally, if people have thought of culture as evolving at all, they've mapped human progress in ways that related specifically to invention—a time of hunter-gatherers, an age of agriculture, a modern industrial age. And they see invention as driving change. With the concept of Cultural Maturity, our interest lies more specifically with changes in how we humans *think* and *behave*. This includes changes throughout our history, and in particular, further changes we see today. And invention becomes only one aspect of what produces the changes that we see.[32]

But even among views that give primary attention to changes at the level of understanding, Creative Systems Theory's perspective is distinctive. As you will see, its developmental approach is unique with regard to how it frames the generative mechanisms of change over time. And of special importance for our inquiry, it is unique in how it frames current changes, the particular way it sees them not just as a next chapter in culture's story but one of specific and pivotal significance.

I will fill out this further critical difference gradually over the course of the book, but further simplifying the alternative "scenarios" presented in the previous section provides a glimpse. We can think of each as reflecting in different ways one of two basic ways of picturing the future "trajectory" of cultural change.

---

32   Over the course of the book, we will examine how the relationship between cultural reality and invention is co-causal. Culture provides the defining context for invention, and invention, in turn, supports the further evolution of culture.

On one hand, we find views that affirm the ongoing viability of the direction of growth that got us here, that advocate a continued "onward-and-upward" trajectory. Here I include beliefs that elevate our current worldview and see the future only as some refinement of the present, and also beliefs that reach a similar kind of result by positing a future defined by ever more dramatic technological progress. Contrasting this, we find various beliefs that consider our present condition to be in some way broken. Some may view it as irretrievably so, in which case collapse becomes the inevitable result. Others may romanticize earlier times and in the process imply that the answer lies in some form of going back. And some claim that change of an all-transforming sort is the only solution.

In later chapters, we will look at how these two opposite sorts of interpretations each have problems that make them ultimately untenable—certainly in their extremes, but also in their more tempered expressions. The key point for now is that the concept of Cultural Maturity represents a third, wholly different sort of interpretation. It is not so easily understood or so readily visualized as images of "onward-and-upward" progress on one hand, or collapse, romantic return, or idealized possibilities on the other,[33] but it gets us where we need to go.

We can think of what results as at once more dramatic and more ordinary than the other two kinds of interpretation. It is more dramatic in that it offers us a chance to successfully address today's complex new challenges with their often God-like implications. But there are also ways in which Cultural Maturity produces a humbler and more basic kind of result. In the end, culturally mature perspective is simply about setting aside ways of understanding that have protected us from realities that before would have overwhelmed us, but that have also protected us from much that is ultimately most important about being human. It is about thinking in ways that better include all that needs to be considered. The result is advancement of a more down-to-earth sort.

Later we will examine how the developmental/evolutionary picture, on which the concept of Cultural Maturity is based reflects how change in human systems inherently works. We will also look

---

33   See "The Dilemma of Representation" in Chapter Three.

at how, in the way it effectively takes us forward, Cultural Maturity, or at least something akin to the "growing up" it describes, becomes the only real option. For now it is enough to note that of the three kinds of interpretations, Cultural Maturity is the one most consistent with hope.

The simple fact that the idea of a collective "growing up" articulates a practical story of possibility by itself supports hope. There is also the way in which this developmental/evolutionary picture lets us be very precise about the kinds of skills and capacities needed for times ahead and how they might be realized. And there is a critical further implication when it comes to hope that I suggested earlier. The fact that the needed new ways of thinking, acting, and relating represent developmental tasks implies that the capacities we need if we are to have a stable, healthy, and creative future are—at least as potential—built into us.

This added piece is critical. If we needed to invent the changes that the concept of Cultural Maturity describes from whole cloth—make them happen simply because they obviously need to happen—it would be hard to argue that optimism is warranted. But if the seeds of the needed new capacities lie in our makeup, the implications become very different. What our time asks of us comes to have less to do with radical invention than with garnering the insight and courage needed to make our inherent potential manifest. If, too, we are not just potentially capable of what the needed new human maturity asks, but are already beginning to make it manifest, as you will see is the case, there is more reason to hope. While this developmental explanation does not guarantee our safety, it does paint a very different sort of picture, both more realistic and more ultimately hopeful.

Later chapters will look at how developmental/evolutionary perspective is needed not just to understand our times and conceive of the future, but also if we want to usefully understand our past and fully appreciate what it means to be human. Such perspective also helps us understand our world more generally. We will examine, for example, how effectively addressing terrorism becomes almost impossible without such perspective, as does any at all useful understanding of conflict that involves countries and ethnic groups that reside in different cultural stages.[34] Functioning effectively in a global economy similarly demands it. The important recognition as we get started is that if something like what this developmental/evolutionary picture proposes is not basically correct, it is hard to imagine a sane and vital—or perhaps even survivable—future.

Necessary Demands

When people begin to engage Cultural Maturity's more complex new realities, they may find, paradoxically, that the result seems simpler and more straightforward than they have anticipated. But culturally mature perspective also necessarily stretches us, and in fundamental ways. If we are to stay the course through the whole of this inquiry and fully garner its rewards, we should take a moment before proceeding to highlight the considerable demands that it will necessarily make.

For many people, the greatest demand will come from how the concept of Cultural Maturity often brings favorite assumptions into question. The needed "growing up" inherently puts ideological sacred cows of all sorts in peril. The concept of Cultural Maturity does not set out to attack sacred cows. Rather, the more complete kind of perspective it draws on inevitably produces this result. But the fact that the intent may be benign does not make the result any less a threat to familiar beliefs.

The developmental nature of what we seek to understand will also add to this inquiry's demands. It means that our observations will often have to be made "through a glass darkly." With developmental processes it can be very hard to make sense of what may lie ahead until we have ventured well into them. And this is not just because we aren't there yet. Even more it is because we lack the needed equipment for understanding. (For example, if you talk about what it is like to be fifteen with a seven-year-old, or to be seventy with a forty-year-old, what you describe will seem not just unfamiliar, but in important ways nonsensical.) This foresight dilemma is significantly amplified when looking ahead requires peering across discontinuities, when our descriptions need to make understandable new developmental chapters

---

34   See "Leadership and Developmental/Evolutionary Perspective" in Chapter Seven.

(as would be the case for both our seven-year-old, given adolescence, and our forty-year-old, given midlife), and it is amplified even more dramatically if, as I've proposed is the case with Cultural Maturity's changes, we confront developmental discontinuities that challenge us in particularly deep ways. Our inquiry must be done always with humility to what we cannot yet know.

The particular way in which Cultural Maturity alters how we think as well as what we think will also make significant demands. Cultural Maturity's cognitive reordering propels us an important step forward in the larger story of understanding. A simple way to describe the necessary changes in how we understand is to say that Cultural Maturity's cognitive changes make our thinking more explicitly systemic. We must take much more into account than we are accustomed to doing, and hold considerations in more conscious and encompassing ways.[35] Whatever the concern, we must more consciously engage the whole ball of wax.

In fact, as we will examine, the systemic challenge goes further. Culturally mature understanding requires a more dynamic and complete kind of systemic thinking than we find with the past's mechanical—engineering—sorts of systemic formulations. We will look at how the critical challenges ahead of us are almost all questions of life, and more than this, questions that concern the very particular kind of life we are by virtue of being human. Creative Systems Theory describes how truth, identity, and interrelationship in human systems of all sorts must be addressed in more dynamic and encompassing *Whole-Person/Whole-System* terms. You will see how addressing any of the three threshold tasks I've noted confronts us with this new conceptual challenge.[36]

---

35   This recognition provides perspective for understanding why sacred cow beliefs become so immediately vulnerable. We will examine in detail how favorite beliefs, particularly those that attract significant followings, tend to take one part of truth's larger systemic complexity and make it a final answer.

36   The need for systemic perspective will influence not just the book's conclusions, but also its approach. Certainly, the book will engage in more broadly expansive inquiry than we commonly encounter. There is almost no sphere I will not touch on at least briefly. The most important

Examining the particular nature of today's systemic challenge will bring important focus to the significant contribution made by Creative Systems Theory's point of departure—the idea that reality (at least the reality of human experience) is, in the end, "creative."[37] We will examine how a creative frame offers a provocative answer to what is arguably our times' most fundamental and critical philosophical/conceptual question: What is to replace Descartes' defining Modern Age notion that reality is, in the end, a "great clockworks," a great machine (a conclusion that follows directly from modern, from-a-balcony perspective)?

An additional demand is directly related. It follows from what this needed more dynamic and complete kind of systemic understanding necessarily involves and the cognitive changes that make it possible. Unlike in the past, the critical questions before us today require that we draw consciously on all of the multiple aspects of our intelligence—not just our rationality, but also more "subjective" sensibilities such as our emotions, our imaginations, and the intelligence of our bodies (each becomes part of substantive understanding). Put in systems terms, the

---

questions ahead for the species all demand inquiry that spans traditional bounds. And the ultimate question of a new cultural narrative certainly does. Culture's new story can't be just about government, economics, medicine, religion, or art. It must be about what these diverse spheres of endeavor are together, and about who we are as the uniquely creative beings who would conceive of them.

A further consequence of this systemic picture is that both in footnotes and in the text I will do more referencing back and forth than is customary in a book. Books being a linear means of expression, the communication of systemic ideas requires the fabricating of a certain "false linearity." This is fun to try to pull off—it's a challenge any storyteller confronts at some level. But every now and then, inevitably, this method is going to fail to provide the solid linkage of ideas that the clear communication of systemic concepts requires—thus the more than customary back and forth.

37   It is important to emphasize that Creative Systems Theory applies the word "creative" in a very specific way (or I could equally well say an unusually general way). The term in this context concerns science as much as art, and the everyday as fully as things of the imagination. Specifically, it refers to how human systems of all sorts grow and develop.

kind of systemic perspective that is our concern requires that we apply the whole of ourselves as cognitive systems. This recognition that our intellects alone can never quite get us where we need to go can at first be unsettling, but it is key to appreciating what today's new challenges require of us. We will examine how it applies to culturally mature conclusions of every sort.[38]

In the end, just the depth of our engagement with the future that this inquiry will involve requires something new of us. All of us have studied the past in history classes, but few of us have ever had classes that address what may lie ahead—even though the future is when we will live our lives and is, in the end, the only thing we can affect. Understanding Cultural Maturity's changes requires that we look to the future—and often our long-term future—with a new kind of unflinching directness. The greater responsibility and systemic perspective that comes with Cultural Maturity is making this possible.

A Bicycle We Can Ride

Culturally mature perspective's considerable demands acknowledged, I need to reemphasize that where Cultural Maturity's changes take us is not obscure, just not familiar. Once we begin to step over Cultural Maturity's threshold, it is the understandings of times past

---

38   See "Truth and Intelligence" in Chapter Six. We find an example of particular importance for this inquiry in how this conclusion applies directly to the developmental/evolutionary perspective that underlies Cultural Maturity's argument. If we limit ourselves to the kind of rational analysis that has defined last-word truth in our Modern Age, this more creative picture doesn't make a great deal of sense. At certain stages in culture's evolution, other aspects of intelligence—the emotional, the intelligences of imagination or of the body—have most defined people's experience. (Think of the primacy of myth and symbol in the beliefs of ancient Egypt or Olympian Greece.) I will argue that we really can't make sense of either the past or the future without a newly mature engagement with the whole of our cognitive complexity.

This need to apply more of our intelligence's multiple aspects, like the more general need for systemic perspective, will influence how I choose to communicate in these pages. For example, I will use metaphors, analogies, images, and figures of speech more often than might be expected with ideas that are this conceptual.

that then seem odd and complicated. Again, in the end, what we encounter is common sense.

Importantly, it is not necessary for us to fully understand Cultural Maturity's changes to experience this new common sense. It is in the nature of developmental processes that we don't need to recognize that new possibilities are happening for them to begin to take place in us and to affect how we think and act. What we see today supports the conclusion that Cultural Maturity's new kind of possibility defines what our times must be about. Victor Hugo famously observed that there is nothing more powerful than an idea whose time has come. We will look closely at the evidence that, when it comes to Cultural Maturity's changes, that time is now.

A playful image helps capture the common-sense nature of taking on Cultural Maturity's new responsibilities and complexities. The fundamental task of our time may be not unlike that of a bicyclist who, in learning to ride, at a certain point sets her training wheels aside. Initially the bicycle feels less stable. And indeed much more can happen, both good and bad. But if the cyclist has done sufficient preparation and the time its right, setting training wheels aside is only in the most limited sense about instability. It is about discovering a new, more complex and dynamic kind of stability—and much greater ultimate possibility.

When I was eating dinner at a local restaurant recently, a neighbor couple who know me only casually—he is a construction worker, she a teacher—asked me what the subject of my current book was. When I said "Cultural Maturity," he responded immediately: "Boy, that is what we need." She nodded her head in agreement. Thirty years ago, when I first coined the term, most people thought it at best a rather boring phrase.

Do we face an "end to civilization," as my friend proposed might be the case? We do in the sense that familiar ways of thinking about who we are, what matters, and how the world functions are ceasing to work. And if we can't soon make good further progress toward the collective "growing up" that this book is about, the decades immediately ahead will often be difficult and unpleasant, and perhaps worse. But as we increasingly recognize that an important further chapter in the human story potentially lies ahead, we can get on with the job of understanding just what the needed new ways of thinking and acting involve and what will be required to get there—our project in these pages.

There is no way for us to know for sure whether we can successfully meet the critical challenges ahead—whether this is a bicycle we can ride. My argument in this book will be simply that we have a chance of success only if we, together, can manifest the maturity of thought and action needed to engage new challenges effectively. Everything depends on this new maturity—how quickly and fully we can make it manifest. I write this volume to contribute to this essential effort.

At the book's conclusion, I've included a series of appendices that certain readers may find helpful. Some people may want to turn to the first two at this point as a way to engage the chapters ahead on the most solid footing. Appendix A presents a simple exercise for identifying new questions and appreciating what makes them new. Appendix B presents a "frequently asked questions" synopsis of the concept of Cultural Maturity. (If you get at all lost in the course of the book's more fine-grained observations, you can return to the FAQ synopsis to get back on track.) Appendix C provides a synopsis of Creative Systems Theory concepts. And Appendix D provides an examination of the Creative Systems Personality Typology (introduced in Chapter Nine) with special attention given to the particular challenges that culturally mature understanding and leadership present to people of different temperaments.

Task #1

Addressing Complexity

CHAPTER ONE

Beyond Easy Answers— Making Our Way in a Complex World

It may seem melodramatic to say that the United States and Russia represent Good and Evil, Light and Darkness, God and the Devil. But if we think of it that way, it helps clarify our perspective in the world struggle.

RICHARD NIXON

OUR PREVIEW-OF-COMING-ATTRACTIONS LOOK at needed new human capacities described how crossing Cultural Maturity's threshold requires that we confront three related tasks: better addressing life's complexities, acknowledging limits, and rethinking the bottom-line measures we use to make our choices. While each of these three threshold tasks in different ways challenges us to get beyond the seduction of simplistic answers, the first does so with particular directness.

Here we examine how our times challenge us to think in ways that better appreciate how complicated life can be. The fact that life is big and often confusingly multifaceted easily overwhelms us. While this has always been the case, in earlier times ideological beliefs have protected us from much that is most demanding in life's complex picture. The fact that our world is becoming ever more complicated, combined with today's new questions with their often God-like implications, make it increasingly essential that we find ways of thinking, acting, and relating that more directly engage life's complex bigness. Ultimately, we must find ways to embrace that complex bigness, make it our friend.

With this chapter and the next, we will delve into the way Cultural Maturity's changes help us better tolerate complexity and, more, how culturally mature perspective helps us think in ways that more directly acknowledge complexity and better manage complexity's implications. We will look at how Cultural Maturity's changes help us think with a systemic—multiplicity-embracing—kind of sophistication that has not before been humanly possible. And we will also examine how the resulting more whole-ball-of-wax picture helps us live all parts of our lives in ways that are, if not simpler, at least more pragmatic and straightforward than what we have known.

This chapter gets us started by establishing how traditional belief systems have shielded us from complexity's implications. It goes on to examine modern instances in which individuals, leaders, and countries have effectively addressed them—a few post-ideological "success stories." With the next chapter, we will look more closely at why, today, we are seeing changes in our relationship to complexity, and also why those changes alter how we think and relate in the specific ways that they do.

Complexity's Challenge—Insights from Politics and the Media

I used the most obvious—and obviously dangerous—example of ideological belief protecting us from complexity in introducing the first threshold task in the book's Introduction: what we see with "chosen people/evil other" dynamics on the world stage. Richard Nixon's words at the beginning of this chapter provide a stark reference. Today we appropriately give thanks that the consequences of such Cold War sentiments were not much worse.[1] But we see such polarized us-versus-them belief systems play out in many different parts of our lives, often with consequences that are in their own ways as deleterious.

Certainly we encounter a related kind of reactive polarization with racism, sexism, and religious intolerance. We also recognize something similar, if not so obviously bigoted, between strongly contrasting view-

---

1   Several times we came frighteningly close to the use of nuclear weapons.

points within most any realm of understanding. While we may act as if conflicting viewpoints reflect logically arrived at conclusions, the intensity of emotions that people can feel toward those with opposite opinions makes it clear that deeper dynamics also commonly play a role. It is in our human natures to divide experience into us-versus-them worlds of "chosen people" and "evil others"—or at least, it has been. The concept of Cultural Maturity argues that it need not be so in the future, and that it can't be if we are to safely and effectively advance in times ahead.

The extended example I will use to introduce our first threshold task's reflections comes from a sphere that impacts each of our lives: the world of government and governance. It is a realm where polarized opinion is common. It is also a realm where the presence of polarization increasingly raises concern. Partisan pettiness more and more often today substitutes for real debate. We can take such pettiness for granted, assume it is just part of the necessary messiness of the democratic process. But at some level we also know that something very important is not working.

The concept of Cultural Maturity offers important perspective, at least as far as whether something more is needed. It argues that policy questions of all sorts today require systemic solutions—and that in the future this will increasingly be the case. It also argues that us-versus-them thinking, even if the eventual result is compromise, can't get us there. If these assertions are correct, partisan pettiness today not only gets in the way of the efficient functioning of government, it undermines democratic government's ability to offer real leadership.

Besides helping introduce the first threshold task, the example of partisan polarization in the halls of government provides valuable insight into what effective future governmental leadership will require. It also offers insight into what a needed next chapter in the story of governance might look like. A personal story, one that starts in the world of media but quickly turns to the implications of Cultural Maturity's changes for effective political decision-making, helps introduce this essential piece in Cultural Maturity's challenge.

Before journalist Ray Suarez moved to television's *PBS News Hour*, he hosted a daytime interview/current-events program on National

Public Radio.[2] I enjoyed the program immensely and tried not to miss it. Ray would choose a topic—often a current, hot-button concern, but as frequently an issue that was not yet on the cultural radar screen. I remember shows that focused on the digital divide, climate change, and risky mortgage practices well before these were broadly recognized concerns.

His choice of guests for the show was just as important. They represented a broad spectrum of opinion, including its extremes, but rarely were they ideologues. Ray pushed them with hard questions and didn't accept formulaic answers. I never failed to learn something from the show and it was clear that Ray, too, was often stretched by where the interactions led. There were always surprises.

When Ray left, the noon slot at my local NPR station was taken over by a different show with a similar format hosted by a highly intelligent man with a more traditional approach.[3] The commentator chose whatever topic was then at the forefront of the news. He would interview the usual suspects with their politically polarized positions, and the predictable back-and-forth fireworks would ensue. I'm sure that many people—including public radio executives, because the show has remained on the air—considered his program as good as or better than what it replaced. The often contentious and emotion-laden format always left the impression that something of great significance had just taken place. And certainly this program represented "balanced" reporting—the common measure for good journalism.

But I felt a huge loss. Only later did I realize fully how deep a loss it was, and just why. Now I recognize that the difference was that Ray Suarez's program worked as culturally mature journalism at a level that, as yet, we don't commonly see.

This achievement was most obvious with issues that were highly charged politically. Culturally mature perspective doesn't dismiss partisanship. It affirms that polarized advocacy has, in times past,

---

2   *Talk of the Nation* in its early years.

3   *Talk of the Nation* continued on other stations with Neal Conan doing an excellent job.

worked to drive effective political process. And it celebrates vigorous disagreement. But culturally mature perspective makes clear that at least the more simplistic of partisan advocacy cannot continue to serve us going forward.

The reason is straightforward, though fully appreciating it takes a degree of stepping back that we are only now learning how to accomplish. Addressing today's most critical policy questions—even just making useful sense of them—demands that we get our minds around any question's multifaceted complexity. Over the course of this book, I will fill out this observation by engaging particular issues— terrorism, health care reform, rethinking economic structures, and more—and also by looking deeply at the underpinnings of current broader changes.

For now a more basic recognition suffices. While we tend to think of political opinions as rationally arrived-at beliefs, even when such positions are well considered, they are not as rational as we have supposed. Nor are they as wholly distinct. At least crudely, the positions of the political left and the political right relate as juxtaposing half-truths within larger systemic realities.

We need only look to the more commonly debated of policy issues to appreciate this more encompassing reality: Are there people who can't put food on the table and who need the support of society as a whole to get by? Yes, certainly. Is it the case that unhealthy dependencies can result if government reflexively provides handouts? Again, yes, certainly.

Is it the case that a nation must stand ready to defend itself and not hesitate to do so when needed? Without question. Is it the case that patience and diplomacy often provide the most effective defense? Again, yes, without question.

Is it true that government is capable of solving problems that private institutions, with their private motivations, are helpless to address? Unquestionably, yes. Is it true that governments tend to grow uncontrollably if given the chance, and that "less is more" is a pretty good principle when it comes to bureaucracy of any sort? I believe so.

With each of these examples, we see opposing positions that reflect aspects of some larger systemic dynamic. Later we will look at how the fact we have not recognized such systemic relationships has in the past ultimately served us. At this point, the important recognition is that for today this lack of overarching perspective has stopped doing so. Without more embracing ways of thinking about these issues, political debate, instead of providing leadership, becomes tediously predictable and wholly unproductive, little more than soap opera.

I think of how often partisan bickering concerned with little more than political advantage erupted in the midst of the 2008-2009 financial collapse. Thomas Friedman put it this way in his *New York Times* column: "We are in the midst of a once-in-a-century financial crisis, and yet we've actually descended into politics worse than usual. There don't seem to be any adults at the top...." For government to work—certainly for government to work in the future—it must function in a way that supports systemically conceived policy.

This is not to advocate for greater agreement or niceness in debate. Culturally mature perspective emphasizes the importance of greater diversity of opinion and greater courage and forthrightness in debate. But culturally mature perspective does very much call for greater maturity both in how we understand and how we work together. This means recognizing that familiar "half-truths," even if we include both halves, simply can't get us where we need to go. We have to better step back and engage the often contradictory-seeming complexities of our concerns—hold tensions generously and attempt to get our minds around the larger processes they represent.[4] Doing so necessarily stretches us beyond traditional ways of thinking. But the potential result is a maturity and creativity in our decision-making that before now has not been an option.

The claim that getting beyond the pettiness of traditional partisanship will be essential can easily evoke a cynical response. People may see no way for this to happen. But while leaving past reactive animosities behind us may not be broadly possible right away, if the concept of Cultural Maturity is accurate, making progress toward this end will

---

4   I'm not at all suggesting that the Left and the Right always contribute equally. In proposing that issues require systemic solutions, I'm saying only that the underlying sensibilities that inform the Left and the Right—Left and Right at their best—are each somehow going to have pertinence. At any particular moment, either the Left or the Right can contribute greatly or offer little, if anything, of significance.

be both increasingly important and increasingly an option. Cultural Maturity's systemic vantage supports more mature and nuanced political engagement. More, it suggests that, at least given time, such increasingly sophisticated engagement will be seen as a key part of our species' inescapably necessary "growing up."[5]

The next chapter will look in more detail at how the greater capacity for systemic perspective that comes with Cultural Maturity's changes should alter political decision-making. You will then have the basic notions needed for such perspective to make sense—and also for you to appreciate some fascinating surprises. For now, a more basic recognition is sufficient. Today's increasingly complicated world requires a more mature, complexity-embracing kind of leadership from both the political and journalistic spheres—and ultimately from all of us. The concept of Cultural Maturity proposes that this kind of sophistication is becoming newly possible.

Complexity and Ideology

The fact of increasing complexity touches every part of our lives. Certainly it affects us societally. With globalization, locales we may not have even heard of—Chechnya, East Timor, South Ossetia—suddenly become front-page news. The growing potential for environmental catastrophe means that we have no choice but to better take into account nature's complex interrelationships. Diversities within culture that in times past we readily ignored, dismissed, or demonized—such as ethnicity, religious beliefs, temperament, gender, and sexual orientation—suddenly clamor for their place on life's stage. And new technologies consistently prove to be at once startlingly wondrous and often just as startlingly beyond our ability to effectively understand and manage.

With the loss of past cultural guideposts, complexity confronts us just as inescapably in our personal choices. Moral questions of all sorts today require that we know ourselves with a depth that was previously

---

5   Later, I will touch on some of the factors that likely contribute to today's unusually marked pettiness and polarization in the political sphere. (See "Success with Leadership" in the "Post-Ideological Success Stories" section of this chapter, and "Transitional Absurdities" in Chapter Eight.)

unnecessary. Living happily as a man or as a woman means addressing questions of gender and identity with a subtlety that in any previous age was not a concern. And what necessarily goes into the definition of meaningful work—and meaning more generally—includes an ever-greater array of options.

Whether our concern is complexity of a more societal or more personal sort, everything today points toward a future that is ever more multifaceted in its demands and kaleidoscopic in its workings. This might seem to be a problem. More accurately, as we will examine, it presents both problems and opportunities. But in our common response to complexity, we confront what has become unquestionably a problem—and one of immense consequence.

In spite of finding new complexities everywhere we look, only rarely do we engage our worlds with the needed nuance and complexity of perspective. Sometimes the reason is just that new complexities have snuck up on us; we haven't had time to adjust to new factors. But commonly the cause is more basic, and more specifically a reflection of ourselves: Our thinking gets kidnapped by ideology.

A key function of ideology through history has been to keep complexity at bay. Us-versus-them antagonisms between nations provide the most readily grasped example. Ascribing all blame to others has kept us safely protected both from our own complexities and the complexities of people we might condemn. But more commonplace ideological identifications—such as those that divide the political right and the political left—have just as much offered the reassuring simplicity of readily identifiable polar beliefs. And more particular opinions that may not look contentious at all on the surface can just as effectively protect us from how bewilderingly complex life can be. One person may view technology as our savior; another may think of technology as the source of all our difficulties. One person sees nature as something to defeat and exploit for human benefit; another views humanity as the problem and all things "natural" as the ultimate good. More everyday absolutes, such as culturally specific moral codes, in a similar way have reduced a multihued complexity of options to a more manageable black-and-white world (or if it is more our inclination, shades of gray).

Cultural Maturity's developmental interpretation doesn't condemn ideological conclusions. During our long human history, ideological beliefs have served us well. Beyond protecting us from being overwhelmed by complexity, shared beliefs have helped us feel connected, and that is good. Ideological assumptions have also brought confidence and clarity (though at the expense of accuracy) to our conclusions. But if the concept of Cultural Maturity is right, leaving ideology's self-affirming simplifications behind us will, in the future, prove increasingly essential—the kinds of questions we confront give us no other choice.

In observing that a key function of ideology has been to keep complexity at bay, I apply the word "ideology" in a specific way that goes beyond how we might commonly use the term. At the least, how I apply the term requires that we be more conscious of just how ideology works. From multiple angles, we will examine how what ultimately defines ideology is the way it takes one part of a systemic complexity and makes it the whole of truth.

Later in the chapter, I will turn to a specific awareness that is essential to understanding ideology's relationship to our task in this book. A simple way to put it is that ideology has both here-and-now and temporal aspects. Ideology includes the more generally recognized, my-side-versus-yours claims we see with narrow nationalistic, political, religious, and philosophical allegiances. But I also include in how I define ideology kinds of absolutist beliefs that populations more generally agree on at particular times in culture—a period's generally accepted cultural mores, ways of thinking about identity and human relationships, assumptions about how institutions should function, and basic notions about what makes something true. With later reflections, we will also look at how these two aspects of ideology—that of a more here-and-now, us-versus-them sort and that which reflects the generally accepted, "consensus reality" of any particular time in culture—interplay as aspects of a single dynamic.

Projection

But before we turn to these necessarily detailed observations, we should first get a better sense of the basic mechanisms through which ideology has protected us from complexity. Besides helping us more deeply understand ideology, appreciating underlying mechanisms provides important support for the claim that Modern Age assumptions don't represent the end point we tend to associate them with. It also offers valuable insight with regard to what may lie ahead.

We shouldn't expect this kind of understanding to come too easily— part of the job of ideology has been to shield us from knowing that these mechanisms, and certainly the aspects of our complexity that they hide, even exist. But at the same time, consistent with Cultural Maturity's predictions, these mechanisms and the roles they have played are more and more commonly recognized.

Here I will touch on a couple of related mechanisms. The first concerns how, in times past, we've tended to attribute aspects of our personal and collective selves to other individuals and larger systems— "given parts of ourselves away." The second involves how this "giving away" has almost always been accompanied by distortion. I will use the terms "projection" and "mythologizing" to describe these two dynamics. Projection and mythologizing are related—aspects of a single mechanism—but treating them separately helps keeps things simple.

Psychology provides our language for the "giving parts of ourselves away" aspect of ideology, at least for how it manifests personally. When we "project," we act as if elements in our inner workings were in fact characteristics of people or groups outside of ourselves. Projection is an unconscious mechanism seen with immature behavior of a personal sort all the time. When a person is said to be acting like an adolescent, being reactive, or blowing something out of proportion, projection al- most always plays a role. The person attributes to the world threats and possibilities that have more to do with him or herself.

We are not so used to recognizing that projection manifests in our collective behavior—and we are certainly not good at catching it when it does. In part this is because of how inextricably tied cultural projections have been to consensus realities. When it seems that everyone around us believes a certain "truth," it can be hard to get a wider perspective. But it is also because the ability to recognize such projection is something that is only now becoming a human capacity.

In fact, projection does very much play out at a cultural level—and continues to hugely affect beliefs and behaviors in our time. We find the easiest to recognize kind of cultural projection in us-versus-them dynamics like those I've described with "chosen people/evil other" relations between nations. We retain the light and deny any part of our darkness, projecting it instead onto others. In the book's Introduction, I observed how, while such sentiments have always before been necessary to the experience of social identity, we also see evidence that we are beginning to move beyond them. Certainly, any possibility of a peaceful world depends on the realization of more mature relationships between the world's peoples.[6]

A related handing of the less savory parts of ourselves to others for safekeeping has, in times past, played a role in almost every part of our collective lives. How much progress we see varies. We more often to-day question the past knee-jerk projections of racism, religious intolerance, and homophobia. And at the same time, many more everyday us-versus-them assumptions such as those that we see with partisan pettiness often remain the norm.

We find a somewhat different sort of cultural projection in the traditional dynamics of leadership. Here, rather than projecting our demons, we project the best in ourselves. At the least, we project our power onto leaders. Like with us-versus-them projections, the idealized projections of traditional leadership have served us by providing a sense of safety and order.

This further projective mechanism is most obvious with pharaohs and kings, who were seen, if not as gods, certainly as god-like. But this same mechanism has continued to work in our time, hidden beneath our "final ideal" beliefs about modern democracy. When people in their minds made Ronald Reagan the kindly father figure, or applied the fantasy imagery of Camelot when picturing John and

---

6   It is important to distinguish culturally mature perspective from simplistic conclusions we can reach about world peace. Cultural Maturity is not about some siding with peace against war—yet another example of polarized thinking. If we want ultimately peaceful outcomes, we need good defenses and a willingness to fight courageously when necessary. Cultural Maturity is also not about ignoring human differences, imagining we should simply celebrate our ultimate commonality. Culturally mature perspective helps us recognize—and find significance in—just how different from one another we can be. Peace, from the perspective of Cultural Maturity, is a systemic notion. In the end, neither the Left nor the Right effectively captures either what peace requires or ultimately what it looks like. (See "Polar Traps" in Chapter Nine)

Jackie Kennedy, their conclusions were as much products of projection as real-world reality.

Recognizing how this has been so has direct implications for rethinking leadership in our time. It also further supports the claim that Modern Age belief can't be the last word. Today, we witness a major crisis of confidence in leadership. We find significantly less trust in leadership today than at the height of anti-authoritarian rhetoric in the 1960s. Not only have old forms of leadership in almost all fields stopped working, they feel less and less like leadership to us at all. I suspect that the need for more Whole-Person/Whole-System authority plays a major role in today's crisis of confidence.

Good future decision-making will require an essential "growing up" in our relationship to leadership. Just as with the demonic imagery of us-verus-them, "evil other" projections, such leadership-related projections are ceasing to benefit us. Stripped of the idealized parental projections of times past, the leader's role becomes necessarily more humble—that of a good and smart person doing a difficult job. But, in the process, it also becomes more powerful. A big part of the reason for this is that mature leadership is better able to tolerate and manage complexity. It thus produces more sophisticated decisions and is capable of ultimately more potent effect.

It is important to appreciate that we have made significant progress here too. Over the last half-century, leadership relations of all sorts—teacher and student, doctor and patient, minister and churchgoer, president and populace—have become decidedly more dynamic and two-way.[7] Such progress can be obscured by the fact that we reside at an easily disturbing, awkward in-between time in leadership's changes (a topic to which we shall return). But leadership changes that have already taken place have had major impact in most every cultural domain.

---

7   We must take care not to fall for a kind of trap similar to the one I just noted in observing the importance of not confusing a siding with peace against war with culturally mature policy. We can confuse the needed new kind of leadership with somehow making leaders and followers the same, or with making leadership somehow "bottom-up" instead of "top-down." In the new leadership picture, the relationship is more explicitly two-way, but the result is ultimately a more powerful kind of leadership influence. (See "Polar Traps" in Chapter Nine.)

We find further examples where projection comes into play with societal dynamics that manifest more personally. The topic of love might strike some people as out of place in this discussion, but it presents a particularly useful illustration. Certainly, it helps us appreciate how broadly Cultural Maturity's changes manifest—no part of our lives is left untouched. Love's changes also further affirm how our current cultural chapter is not the end of the story. And they provide important additional insight into the demands of new leadership, in this case in our personal lives (and ultimately into the demands of leadership more generally).

In my work as a psychiatrist with individuals and couples, I am continually struck by how fundamentally the realities of love are changing—and not just what it takes to make love work, but how love itself works. The Modern Age gave us the advent of romantic love. We celebrate this kind of love—symbolized by Romeo and Juliet—as a kind of final realization. We think of it as love based on individual choice. But while romantic love did represent a profound step—it took us beyond bonds that were determined by family or a matchmaker—it was not yet about individual choice, at least not in today's needed more Whole-Person sense. As has remained the case with national allegiances and formal leadership, our romantic vision of love is based on projection. I unconsciously ascribe feminine aspects of myself to you; you, likewise unconsciously, ascribe masculine aspects of yourself to me.[8] With romantic love, we make the object of our affection our brave knight or fair maiden. Romantic love is two-halves-make-a-whole love.

While in its day, romantic love brought profound new possibility, today we witness changes in love that are even more profound in their implications. Whole-Person love is fundamentally different. It requires that each person acknowledge a more complex and complete picture of human identity—both their own identity and the identity of the person they love.[9] At the heart of these changes is a greater ability to

---

8   The projections are always more complex that just this. The important point is that romantic love, in the end, stops short of love that is about two whole people choosing to share their lives.

9   See "A Powerful Surprise: The Myth of the Individual" in Chapter Two.

acknowledge projection when it is happening, and a greater interest in finding ways to love without projection's past defining influence.

We recognize the beginnings of this "growing up" in our relationship to love in our modern questioning of traditional gender roles. At its best, what we encounter with such questioning is more significant than just new behavioral options. We glimpse the possibility of loving another person more fully as themselves rather than for who we unconsciously need them to be. What we encounter is also very different from making men and women the same—a unisex ideal. Indeed, the outcome is, in an important sense, almost the opposite. It is to offer, really for the first time, a chance for us to relate as wholly embodied men and women. As with mature relations between nations or between leaders and citizens, relating in this way is at once more humble and more rich (and profound) in its possibilities.

With each of the examples I've noted—with us-versus-them, "evil other" dynamics, with leadership, and with love—we see how the projection-based realities of Modern Age belief have, like related beliefs of earlier times, provided protection from life's full complexity. With each of these examples, we also recognize wholly new realities that involve leaving behind the projections of times past and holding reality in more whole-ball-of-wax ways. With each we see how we are coming, at least a bit, to think and act in more complete—and with this more complex and nuanced—ways. On all these fronts, not only are we confronting the importance of stepping beyond the ready projections of times past, we see such projections fading in their influence.

The relationship between projection, ideology, complexity, and culturally mature perspective in each of these examples is the same. Projection protects us from complexity by creating an illusion of order—of static predictability. It keeps us safely sheltered in an either/or, black-and-white reality. Stepping beyond projection makes possible more demanding, but also ultimately more encompassing and coherent understanding. In the process, it propels us into a more multihued and more potential-filled world of experience.

Mythologizing

Projection's complementary mechanism—mythologizing—has been just as key to the unquestioned power of past belief. When we mythologize, we give something magical importance (whether in a deified or demonized sense). Projection and mythologizing commonly work together. With "evil-other" projections, and also with the idealizing projections of leadership and of love, in times past, we've not just given parts of ourselves away, we've also given the disowned parts symbolic significance. The basic idea that culture might have "parental" significance reflects this mechanism at a most encompassing scale.

When we project, we do three things. We split some whole into two parts—for example, good and evil, leader and follower, masculine and feminine. We give one half to the other for safekeeping. And more often than not, we also mythologize each part. When we project, not only do we attribute what we project to some locale outside of ourselves, we ascribe to the projected part—and, in so doing, to ourselves—inflated importance.

Individual development provides insight into how mythologizing has served us and points toward the evolutionary nature of these changes. The relationship between a parent and a child is always at some level symbolic. The parents of a two-year-old are more than simply people. To her they are all-knowing and much larger than life. It is critical that she see them this way. She needs her parents to be deities if she is to find the courage to venture forth into an as-yet foreign and easily confusing world. This need to deify her parents alters and distorts what she sees. But considering her stage in development, it does so in ways that are helpful, indeed essential.

In a similar way, through time and across continents, our cultural beliefs have provided us with elevated—mythologized—images. Our particular county's flag affirms our country's divine status, and, by implication, our own special status—however tenuous such status must be in a global world. We've likewise symbolically elevated experts of all kinds—political leaders, professors, ministers, and renowned scientists—giving them a standing and a perceived level of knowledge beyond that of the mere mortal. And we've related to our own culture's beliefs about what is morally right—however disparate such beliefs may be from one culture to the next—with an emotional charge that makes obvious that these beliefs are much more significant to us than mere conventions of behavior.

Mythologizing necessarily distorts reality. But when such distortion is timely, it benefits us. Specifically, working in combination with projection, mythologizing has helped keep complexity within manageable bounds. In reflecting on mythologizing and its historical function, I'm drawn back to my training in medical school. Much that we did—from the wearing of white coats to thirty-six-hour ritual stints in the emergency room—in the end had more to do with the assumption of a ceremonial role than the learning of medicine. I was initially critical of this. But experience helped me recognize its historic purpose. I remember once wondering, as I watched a surgeon cut into the jello-fragile tissue of a young woman's brain, whether he still could have carried out this task—there with life or death balanced on the tip of his scalpel—if he had not had medicine's mythic trappings to protect him from the full responsibility and uncertainty of his craft.

Over the last few decades, physicians have made significant strides toward setting aside past deific imagery and approaching their work more as ordinary human beings with demanding roles to play. These changes in the physician's posture hold important rewards. Working from a place of deeper humility ultimately translates into greater effectiveness and subtlety. But it also requires a willingness to hold life more complexly, and with a much fuller cognizance of how much we do not, and often cannot, know.

Mythologizing compounds projection's ability to protect us from aspects of complexity we are not yet ready to embrace. Joseph Conrad observed that "every age is fed on illusion, lest men should renounce life early and the human race come to an end." Mythologizing is a primary mechanism of such protective illusion. But mythologizing today, like its partner, projection, leads ultimately to narrowly simplistic answers, whether the issue at hand is religious, intellectual, political, or moral. I like how Ralph Waldo Emerson described the problematical role of mythologizing in national allegiances: "When a whole nation is yelling patriotism at the top of its lungs, I am fain to explore the cleanliness of its hands and the purity of its soul."

The absence of such emotional/conceptual "cleanliness" puts us at risk in ways it has not before. Certainly, it keeps us from questioning institutional structures and practices that badly need reexamination. For example, we could not have had widespread, yet unchallenged, sexual abuse by clergy without this "protective" mechanism. More personally, it blinds us to uncertainties and complexities that might seem harsh at first blush, but that ultimately provide keys to a vibrant and mature life.

Certain of our mythologizings, and indeed some that could most easily lead us astray, are particularly easy to miss. I think of how we mythologize ourselves as a species. We become God's special children set in opposition to a natural world that is at best a realm of mindless reflexes, at worst dangerously untamed. Either view makes for ultimately unsatisfactory choices that in the end put not just nature, but also ourselves as inextricable parts of it, at risk.[10] Later we will look at how, in a related way, we mythologize conscious awareness and human will.[11] Doing so was central to the great successes ushered in by Modern Age "Enlightenment" understanding. But the kinds of questions we face today call for a more humble, but also ultimately more powerful, approach.

Given the dangers presented by mythologizing, it is appropriate to ask just where we are in our efforts to get beyond this once helpful, but now limiting, mechanism. With the majority of the challenges we face, in fact here too we have made at least a solid beginning. I am not claiming that we have somehow moved beyond mythologizing experience. In fact, with the the front-page notoriety given to the tabloid lives of Hollywood "superstars" and multimillion-dollar salaries paid to modern sports heroes, a person could argue that mythologizing has never been more prominent. But if we examine the dynamics of more everyday personal and cultural decision-making—such as those that we looked at with global relations, leadership, and love—we see that mythologizing, like projection, today has ceased to serve a creative cultural function—and, for a growing number of people, has diminishing appeal.[12]

---

10 In an opposite, and in its own way just as unhelpful, kind of mythologizing, we can idealize nature and make humanity the "evil other." (See "The Fact of Real Limits" in Chapter Three.)

11 See "Integrative Meta-perspective and the Workings of Awareness" in Chapter Eight.

12 In later chapters, we will look at how this seemingly contradictory picture—the simultaneous appearance of new possibility along with amplified manifestations of old arguments—is predicted. (See "History—and

Ideology, Complexity, and the Tasks of New Leadership

I've promised to more closely examine the two aspects of ideology noted earlier—that of a more here-and-now, us-versus-them sort, and that which reflects the generally accepted, "consensus reality" of any particular time in culture. These reflections on the roles projection and mythologizing play in the workings of ideology provide the needed preparation. The topic is essential to fully understanding Cultural Maturity and what its changes ask of us.

I've described how ideological belief as we most commonly think of it reflects contrasting positions at a particular point in time. It identifies with one slice of the pie in that particular time's systemic complexity and sets it in opposition to others. Ideology of this first sort protects us from life's bigness in a couple of ways. First, it takes one aspect of a multifaceted picture and makes it the answer (one slice wins). Second, it makes an evolving reality static (one slice not only has the truth, this is final, once-and-for-all truth).

We are less likely to use the word "ideology" to describe the generally accepted, "consensus reality" beliefs of any particular point in culture, but in the sense that traditionally they, too, have protected us from complexity, the term remains helpful. Shared cultural absolutes—moral codes, gender roles, culturally specific assumptions about how social institutions should function—have protected us from life's bigness by creating unquestioned order in a world that otherwise would have had an overwhelming multiplicity of options.

We can accurately think of the first kind of ideology as a subset of the second. The tendency in times past to pick and choose between aspects of systemic complexity and divide experience into mythologized worlds of us versus them is something we see with every cultural stage. At any past stage in culture, these two basic sorts of ideology have worked together to keep complexity within manageable bounds.

Cultural Maturity's changes directly challenge both aspects of this ideological picture and help us move beyond them. As we come to appreciate a more encompassing picture, increasingly we find polarized perceptions limited and limiting. We also better appreciate how absolutes have never been absolute, how instead they have been the truths of particular points in time.

Life—as a Creative Narrative" in Chapter Seven and "Transitional Absurdities" in Chapter Eight.)

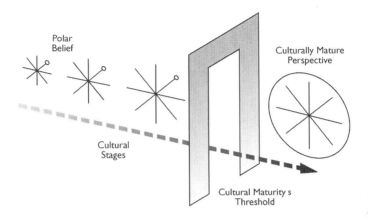

Polar
Belief

Culturally Mature
Perspective

Cultural
Stages

Cultural Maturity s
Threshold

Identification with the realities
of particular cultural stages, and
within them, particular aspects of a
question's multiplicity.

Identification with the whole of
systemic complexity as an evolving
process.

Fig. 1-1. Ideology and Complexity[13]

The diagram in Figure 1-1 brings together our two kinds of ideology
and relates them to Cultural Maturity's changes. Ideology in the here-
and-now, us-versus-them sense is represented by how the sequence of
images on the left side of the diagram gives truth to but one part of
systemic complexity. We see the same basic kind of systemically partial
mechanism with each cultural stage to this point. The image on the
right depicts how stepping over Cultural Maturity's threshold results in
a more complete, more whole-ball-of-wax picture.

A recognition implied in the diagram is central to this book's
argument: The two-part ideological picture I have described has

13   The intersecting lines on the left side of the diagram represent various
       polar juxtapositions as they exist at a point in time. The small circles
       represent the particular aspect of the systemic picture that we identify
       with. On the right side of the diagram, the larger circle represents
       culturally mature perspective's more systemically encompassing kind of
       worldview.

played as essential a role during our most recent stage in culture's story as at any stage previous. The observation that ideology has served the same kind of protective function with Modern Age belief that it has with the beliefs of times previous provides important support for the conclusion that Modern Age belief is not a last word, and could not be.

It is important to appreciate how deeply this observation runs counter to common assumptions. In part it does for the same reasons that people in every previous cultural stage have assumed their reality to be culminating. But it also collides with beliefs that on the surface can seem quite logical and difficult to refute.

For example, there is the way we commonly describe Modern Age institutions in terms of an ultimate realization of the individual. We think of representative democracy as an ultimate manifestation of individual determination. In a similar way, we view market capitalism as a final expression of individual initiative. Likewise, we tend to look on modern religion as a culminating demonstration of the specifically personal relationship with one's God that was first introduced with the Reformation. It is hard to imagine that anything further could lie beyond these achievements.

How we commonly think about modern understanding could similarly appear to support such convictions. The objectivity and clarity that has given us today's great technological and scientific achievements is celebrated as an ultimate expression of the Enlightenment's grand goal of bringing all of understanding into the light of pure reason. What more could exist beyond this?

Over the course of the book, I will provide evidence that directly challenges both of these quite logical-seeming conclusions. In the book's next chapter, I will introduce the recognition that the kind of individual determination we associate with Modern Age institutions is in fact not about individual determination at all. (We saw hints of this in my observing that neither modern love nor modern leadership reflects individual choice of the Whole-Person sort.)[14] Later, I will also propose that the Enlightenment's grand goal of bringing all of

---

14   See "A Powerful Surprise: The Myth of the Individual" in Chapter Two.

understanding into the light of pure reason cannot be achieved—and also that if it could be achieved, it would not be an appropriate ultimate expression of our humanness.[15]

For now, this chapter's reflections on ideology provide solid beginning argument for the conclusion that Modern Age truths can't be some last word. While ideology of the my-side-versus-yours sort has taken evolving forms through the last few hundred years, it has only recently ever been absent. And cultural absolutes have continued to play their essential role in establishing cultural order and coherence well into modern times. Cultural guideposts losing their historical reliability is a phenomenon only of the last one hundred years (and a defining phenomenon only of the last fifty years).

Reflections on the mechanisms by which ideology has protected us from complexity's magnitude provide additional confirmation. If, as I have proposed, the important questions ahead require that we engage complexity without the protection that projection and mythologizing have before provided—including in our time—then viewing Modern Age belief as some kind of cultural ideal and end point is certainly not justified. This can't be the end of the road—or if it is we are in deep trouble. The observation that Cultural Maturity's changes offer the possibility of more systemically encompassing, post-ideological perspective supports that it need not be.

Narrative and Cultural Maturity

An important topic touched on in the Introduction—that of narrative, the stories we tell—sheds important further light on the relationship between complexity and ideology. For this inquiry, it has special significance because it helps bring finer focus to the particular changes that define our time. It establishes valuable language we will draw on in later reflections.

If we look at the evolution from Modern Age belief into current times through the lens of cultural narrative, we encounter a consistent sequence of stories (see Figure 1-2). Traditional Modern Age beliefs

---

15 See "Cultural Maturity's Cognitive Reordering" in Chapter Two, and "Integrative Meta-perspective and the Workings of Awareness" in Chapter Eight.

juxtapose heroic or romantic narratives. Heroic narratives describe the overcoming of obstacles to realize some ultimate achievement. Romantic narratives describe some meeting—either personal or more encompassing—that results in emotional or spiritual completion. Heroic and romantic narratives can work alone or together.

Fig. 1-2. The Modern Evolution of Narrative

Both heroic and romantic narratives are in the end ideological. Each involves projection, mythologizing, and a promise of final fulfillment and last-word truth. Each of the more conventional narratives I referenced at the book's beginning—the American Dream, opposing political worldviews, the traditional beliefs of our various religions, progress's promise of ever onward-and-upward scientific discovery and technological advancement—are of this heroic/romantic sort.

Following heroic/romantic narrative we find stories of a more transitional sort, stories that straddle Cultural Maturity's threshold. Such narratives recognize the limitations of ideological absolutes, but are capable of only a beginning grasp of what—if anything— may lie beyond such belief. I've used the word "postmodern" as a catch-all term to describe this kind of story. In later chapters, we will examine the beginnings of postmodern perspective with existentialism and social constructivism, postmodern thought's prominent role in academic thought during the later years of the last century, and how today postmodernism's influence pervades the popular arts. Postmodern narrative at its best alerts us to how once-and-for-all truths now fail us, the fact of multiple viewpoints, and the importance of taking final responsibility in our choices. At its worst, it reduces to a different-strokes-for-different-folks arbitrariness and a confusion of irony and contradiction with significance that becomes, in effect, but another kind of ideology (and, as you shall see, a kind of ideology that is particularly tedious and difficult to counter). Such is the expected dual fate of such "straddling" belief.[16]

Cultural Maturity's new narrative offers that we might proceed more fully beyond ideology by leaving behind both absolutist belief and tendencies to elevate the absence of belief. It takes the best of postmodern insight and then moves beyond it. It describes the possibility of engaging experience more consciously and fully from the complex whole of who we are as systems, and in the process more fully and deeply confronting the complexities of the world around us.

We can summarize the relationship between ideology, narrative, and Cultural Maturity by reflecting on how culturally mature perspective alters how we experience complexity. We can think of how it does so as a series of steps. First, by bringing attention to the dangers that narrow ideological assumptions and outdated cultural narratives today present, culturally mature perspective helps clarify just why getting beyond them has become so important. Second, such perspective's more encompassing embrace helps us feel more comfortable in complexity's presence. Third, culturally mature perspective helps us recognize mechanisms such as projection and mythologizing and, in the process, to appreciate aspects of life's complexity that ideologies and outdated narratives have before kept out of sight and out of mind. And finally, such perspective helps us think in new, more nuanced and complex ways. It offers the possibility of whole new kinds of understanding that better acknowledge and address life's bigness. We now turn more specifically to this last step.

Ideology, Complexity's Newly "Complex" Picture, and the Challenge of Culturally Mature Systemic Perspective

This picture of how complexity, ideology, and the question of narrative come together has an important additional implication when it comes to leadership that can at first make complexty's challenge seem even more daunting. But understanding it is essential if we are to effectively make sense today's new questions. In particular, understanding it is

---

16   See "Truth, Responsibility, and the Postmodern Contribution" in Chapter Five and "Postmodern/Constructivist Scenarios" in Chapter Nine.

essential if we are to make sense of the new kinds of thinking needed if we are to effectively address today's new questions. We live in a world that is not just more complex, but that requires new, more mature and complete conceptions of just what complexity is about.

Our concern with complexity today is more demanding and significant than just that things are complicated—that there are more pieces to consider. At the least, today's complexities most often involve ourselves, our humanness, along with other factors that are more adequately addressed in more traditional terms. But even when the complexities we wish to describe are not directly about us, they still often require us to think differently.

This further recognition will have a pivotal role in this inquiry. It will provide important insight into the nature of new possibilities. In addition, it will help us better appreciate needed new steps in how we understand. In the book's Introduction, I proposed that today's new questions not only require more systemic understanding, they require systemic understanding of a fundamentally new sort. This additional recognition helps us make sense of just what necessarily becomes different.

Observing some of the characteristics commonly found in today's new complexities helps us better appreciate the full magnitude of the challenge that complexity presents—both to our ability to tolerate it and to conventional understanding. While we tend to think of complexity as having to do only with a greater multiplicity of parts, the kind of complexity that is ultimately our concern is about much more than just this.

A first additional ingredient is uncertainty. Life has always been uncertain. I'm reminded of D. H. Lawrence's admonition that we must never lose touch "with that which laughs at all our knowing." But in today's ever more complex world, the law of unintended consequences can punish us with a quickness and severity not known before. We must acknowledge this and better factor in uncertainty.

A second additional ingredient is the critical fact of change. It has become a cliché to say that change is our time's only constant, but that doesn't make the essential recognition less true. And change today is often confusing in its workings, even paradoxical. It is becoming increasingly important that we learn not just to better tolerate change, but to more deeply understand it, both so that we can better manage it and so that we can best support the changes that are needed.

The developmental perspective that underlies this inquiry illustrates thinking that effectively addresses this second additional ingredient.

Another ingredient is the growing importance of appreciating not just detail and difference, but also how things connect. John Muir once observed, "When we try to pick out anything by itself, we find it hitched to everything else in the Universe." Ours is not just a more diverse world, it is a more interconnected world. It is not just that ecosystems are complex, it is that they are, in fact, systems. And it is not just that we have more choices, but that it has become increasingly important that we address what makes a choice meaningful. It is also increasingly essential, if our answers and decisions are to be ultimately effective, that we address questions in ways that serve not just self-interest—whether it is the self-interest of individuals or of individual groups or countries—but that also take into account larger benefit.

In Chapter Four, we will look more closely at these various aspects of complexity and how they work together. One thing we will look at is how the kind of understanding we have interest in requires not just that we rethink complexity as a whole, but that we also think about each of these ingredients in new ways. We will look at how the kind of complexity that we confront when we re-own projections and step beyond the mythologizing of experience not only includes all of these additional aspects, it does so in a way that requires that we stretch how we would usually think about each of them.[17]

For now a basic observation made in the Introduction points toward why complexity's more complete picture is important to understanding and where it takes us. I've proposed that today's new questions require that we think in ways that better reflect our living human natures. While we can adequately describe the simply complicated in machine language, when our concern is the kind of complexity we find with today's new challenges, this stops being sufficient. Engineering language fails us totally with any of the concerns we've begun to address with this chapter—such making sense of global relations without the us-versus-them assumptions of times past, reconceiving leadership such that it can effectively serve us going forward, or helping us understand the implications of Whole-Person love.

---

17   See "Limits and Complexity's New Picture" in Chapter Four.

Appreciating complexity's more complete picture becomes particularly important when we confront the task of developing conceptual approaches that can effectively address future challenges. I've observed that the language of systems takes us a long way toward the needed new kind of thinking. Systems thinking emphasizes the need to consider all the pieces; that connections are as important as differences; and how, when what we are considering is in fact a system, the whole ends up being greater than the sum of its parts.

But I've also emphasized that today's new questions require more than systems thinking as it is most commonly conceived. A good way to summarize what more is needed is that systemic understanding able to help us make our way in a culturally mature world must successfully address this more vital and complete picture of complexity.

The importance of thinking systemically is not in itself a new kind of recognition. The familiar story of the blind men and the elephant describes the application of systemic perspective at least at a personal scale. And we could effectively extend the image to frame systemic challenges presented by contemporary cultural issues. In the recent economic collapse, too readily we paid attention only to the health of the elephant's parts—one leg a bank, the tail Wall Street, an ear a mortgage holder—without realizing that the elephant as a whole was sick and in trouble. Likewise, in formulating culturally mature ecological policy, we must take into account all the interrelated aspects of the ecosystem and all of the stakeholders involved—again, the whole elephant.

But while most traditional approaches to systems thinking do a good job of describing intricacies and basic interconnections, the assumptions are most often those of a machine world. Even when the system of interest is a human body or an ecosystem teeming with organisms, the language has remained that of a good engineer—hydraulics and forces, gears and pulleys. Given that our interest ultimately is the more complete—uncertainty-, change-, and interconnectedness-permeated—kind of complexity that I have just described, most systemic thinking to this point leaves us yet short of what effectively addressing the critical challenges ahead will require of us.[18]

---

18   This is not the only way systems thinking can fall short. For example,

At the very least, we need to get beyond engineering-language assumptions if we want to effectively address ourselves as systems. This is true equally if our concern is the inner complexities of our psyches, the complexities inherent to personal relationships, or the complexities of global relations. Later we will examine how the importance of bringing to bear a more encompassing and complete kind of systemic perspective in fact applies to understanding of every sort—that concerned, also, with the simply biological or the purely physical. Effectively understanding any living system, at least if we want to do so in a way that reflects that it is alive, in a similar way requires a more complete picture of complexity's workings. (Biologists find themselves in the curious circumstance of making life their topic of study while most often using models that leave them unable to explain it.) And as the best of thinking in physics has demonstrated, engineering assumptions ultimately fail whatever we wish to consider, even when it comes to questions for which engineering solutions might seem most apt.[19]

Recognizing where the need to address complexity's more complete picture takes us helps put our time's task with regard to understanding in historical perspective. The key insight that took us beyond the worldview of the Middle Ages was the recognition that we could stop regarding reality as an interplay of mystical forces and think of it instead as like a great machine. (I've noted René Descartes' famous assertion that existence ultimately functions like a "clockworks.") If the issue with complexity were only that life is complicated, familiar Modern Age engineering solutions would be sufficient for us to address the challenges ahead and none of this inquiry would be needed. These reflections on complexity and systems at least make clear that machine models alone are not enough, that further steps in our understanding must lie ahead. The needed next step in how we think must somehow address the more rich, vital, and encompassing picture of complexity and its workings that is increasingly making itself apparent.

---

more popular versions can confuse simple connectedness with the needed more dynamic understanding of complexity. See "The Dilemma of Differentiation" in Chapter Five.

19   See "Limits and Complexity's New Picture" in Chapter Four, and "Who We Are and What It All Means" in Chapter Eight.

I should note a paradoxical-seeming result that we find with understanding that successfully addresses complexity in this more complete sense, an outcomes that I suggested in the Introduction. Such understanding helps us think and act in ways that, while not ultimately simpler, can, in our experience of them, seem so. Culturally mature perspective helps us better appreciate how life and truth are multifaceted, but, at the same time, it produces understanding that is more direct and straightforward. The latter result is in part because of how such understanding helps us better ask the right questions—and only when we ask the right questions can we come up with useful answers. But, as we will examine, it is also a product of how culturally mature perspective draws on the deeper complexities in ourselves that are needed to effectively engage complex questions. One outcome is more nuanced and detailed discernment. But another, because those deeper complexities better reflect who we ultimately are, is an ability to more directly grasp the simple whole of things.

Throughout this book, I will reflect in different ways on this perhaps unexpected result. It does not at all deny complexity—as you will see, this outcome further affirms complexity's demands. For now we can note these words of Oliver Wendell Holmes: "I would not give a fig for the simplicity this side of complexity, but I would give my life for the simplicity on the other side of complexity." This is the sort of simplicity we have interest in.

How do we best talk about the needed more multifaceted kind of systemic understanding? We lack good terms within our usual ways of thinking. I've spoken of it as "dynamic," reflecting where a more encompassing picture of complexity takes us. But in more limited ways, mechanical systems can also be highly dynamic.[20] I've also spoken of it as more "complete"—in the sense of being more inclusive of all that needs to be considered. In Chapter Six, I will describe how Creative Systems Theory uses a creative frame to address this more "dynamic

---

20   The mechanical workings of a computer can be too complex for our minds to follow. And what are often called the "sciences of complexity" (chaos theory being the most familiar example) study systems that can be even more dynamic while remaining ultimately mechanistic. (See "Limits and Complexity's New Picture" in Chapter Four.)

and complete" picture of complexity.[21] We will look at how the recognition that human experience organizes creatively offers a way to engage the essential task of new understanding in a way that is not just conceptually precise, but that also allows us to bring important detail to how we think about ourselves and the world around us.

The important recognition for now is that our interest lies with understanding that can address systemic complexity of more than just a mechanistic sort. And there is one further recognition that should at least be touched on. The concept of Cultural Maturity proposes that not only are we, in fact, quite capable of engaging existence more complexly than we do, our brains are natively wired for this more nuanced and dynamic kind of understanding. We will examine how such complexity is what makes us who we are. In the end, the question becomes not whether such understanding is possible, but rather how quickly we can step forward and manifest the maturity of perspective needed to effectively make sense of and address such complexity, in ourselves and in the world around us. In later chapters, we will look more closely at both the requirements of culturally mature systemic perspective and how those requirements mirror the way human cognitive processes ultimately work.[22]

Post-Ideological Success Stories

The next chapter will look more conceptually at how Cultural Maturity's changes help get us beyond the easy simplifications that accompany projection and mythologizing—and ideology more generally—and think in ways that better honor the fact of complexity. I will introduce how this result follows from the developmental nature of cultural change. I will also describe how Cultural Maturity's cognitive reordering inherently produces this outcome.

But before we go there, it makes sense to take some time with concrete examples of advances consistent with the kinds of changes I've described—a few post-ideological "success stories." Besides helping to link

---

21   See "Creative Systems Theory Patterning Concepts."

22   See in particular "The Dilemma of Differentiation" in Chapter Five and "Truth and Intelligence" in Chapter Six.

abstract principles to felt experience, examples also help counter both cynicism and misinterpretation. I've stressed how important it is for us to recognize how far we have already come. While we do need to be careful of misplaced self-congratulation, arguments that dismiss the changes we have already realized not only shortchange the past, they also most often misrepresent where we need to go.[23] I grow wary whenever advocates of cultural change imply that everything has yet to change, or even when people express frustration that movement is happening slowly—though I can share their frustration. In fact, we see the beginnings of Cultural Maturity's changes as far back as a hundred years ago.

I will include some such historically important examples here, but I will give greater emphasis to more recent accomplishments. When we look around us today, we witness both increasing tolerance of complexity and many examples of shaping our worlds in complexity-acknowledging ways. Today's endlessly multifaceted realities can overwhelm us. But our ability to engage a creatively rich and demanding world is dramatically greater than it was just a few decades back.

Inherent limits exist to this section's approach. Certainly, examples we have to draw on are going to reflect only first "baby steps" into culturally mature territory. It is also the case that we will often need reflections from later chapters—and in some instances understandings that we are not yet capable of—for the full significance of particular examples to make full sense. And of course this can be but the quickest of samplings.

But, limitations noted, each of these examples in some way illustrates both the confronting of ideology and a new willingness to leave behind assumptions based on projection and mythologizing. Each also points toward the possibility of more nuanced, complex, and sophisticated perspective. (Understanding that reflects the more dynamic and complete kind of systemic thought I've pointed toward is suggested in some of these examples, but not all of them.)

Success on the World Stage

Given the pervasiveness of conflict on the evening news, we might miss that anything has changed with regard to our past ten-

---

23   Such arguments alert us to predictably limited belief systems. See "Scenarios for the Future" in Chapter Nine.

dency to demonize others in relationships between nations. But when we compare attitudes today with those from only a generation ago, in fact much is different, especially at the level of superpower relations. In the Introduction, I made reference to the fall of the Berlin Wall. Beyond the significance of that singular event, we can also look at what has happened—or has not happened—since. With the fall of the wall and the end of the Cold War, "evil empire" animosities between the United States and the former Soviet Union transformed with unprecedented quickness to a relationship of mutual, if often begrudging, respect. And we have not seen major polarization between world powers since (though we must keep our fingers crossed).[24]

I suspect that globalization—paired with ever more available and dangerous weaponry—would have produced catastrophe by now if we had not already made beginning steps toward greater maturity on the world stage. Globalization often *has* produced less-than-positive outcomes. I see the collision of cultures that up until now would have had little contact with one another as a major cause of modern conflict—particularly the kind that we see with terrorism. Globalization also contributes to the destabilization of governments and social structures. But globalization has thus far, for the most part, served as a creative force rather than a destructive one, both economically and as a vehicle for expanded understanding.

We see important related successes with regard to terrorism. I refer to a kind of success that has more to do with ourselves than with terrorism's perpetrators. The possibility of more events like the 9/11 World Trade Center attacks is very real. In the face of this frightening specter, the modern West could very easily make terrorism the new communism and, in the process, undermine any possibility of effectively addressing it (or worse, turn predicted new complexities into a clash of civilizations). But while leaders have sometimes played the demon card and been slow to recognize the necessary larger picture, to a remarkable degree average citizens have not taken the bait. Most people today

---

24 A person could argue that the reason that we haven't witnessed major polarization is because only one superpower remains. But this is changing rapidly, and thus far we have not seen polarization of the old rabid sort.

view terrorism as complex and dreadful, but not as a product of people who are themselves evil.[25]

Success with Leadership

I've described how leadership that is able to effectively address modern complexities must be of a new, more humble, but also more powerful, Whole-Person/Whole-System sort. We can see aspects of this more sophisticated kind of authority in the best of leadership today. I've described how leadership relationships of almost all sorts—from teacher and student, to minister and congregation, to political leader and populace—have become more dynamic and participatory.

A quick listing of characteristics we can see today with exceptional nation-state leadership provides illustration. Each of these characteristics can be understood to follow from the more systemic picture that results when we take back parts of ourselves that we've projected and leave behind the mythologized perceptions of times past. Such leadership acknowledges that questions are often complex and attempts to provide clarifying perspective. In making hard choices, it seeks to avoid polarizing and the unnecessary making of enemies. It inspires when possible, while also acknowledging real uncertainties and the limits to what we can sometimes achieve. It sincerely strives to get beyond partisan pettiness; and it is as concerned with the long-term as with the immediate.[26] Nation-state leadership that succeeds on all these counts is rare. But it is the case that political leadership that succeeds on many of them is becoming increasingly common.

Certainly we witness some striking individual instances of culturally mature leadership. Nelson Mandela's remarkable accomplishments evoke personal memories. A year before the fall of Apartheid I was invited to visit South Africa in a consulting role. The people who sent me there wanted answers to two questions: Was change really happening? (Hopes had been brutally dashed so many times in the

25 Chapter Seven's extended example examines the challenge of crafting culturally mature policy in response to terrorism.

26 You will be able to better understand the changes reshaping formal leadership with the closer examination of Cultural Maturity's cognitive reordering in chapters to come.

past.) And if it was, did any way exist to have change happen without major violence and bloodshed? I was in South Africa for over a month, talking with opposition leadership, academics, government officials, and people in the streets. My answer was split. I came away convinced that real change was indeed possible—and happening. But in spite of all the brilliant and committed people I spoke with and my own background in understanding systems, I could not see a way for change to happen peacefully.

I was right on the first count, but proven quite wrong on the second. I had not factored in the person of Nelson Mandela, who was at that time still imprisoned. I am not one to give leadership more than it is due. Change is as often a product of circumstances as it is a result of the people we associate with it. But I see Nelson Mandela's efforts in a special light. We need only contrast South Africa's recent history with events in neighboring Zimbabwe to appreciate the sophistication of leadership Mandela brought to bear—and how different things could have been without him.

Once Mandela was freed, it would not have surprised the world if he and his supporters had fallen back on polarization—and righteous revenge—given South Africa's past and Mandela's years of imprisonment. Instead, we saw something that went beyond even just personal wisdom. His was a wisdom that embraced South Africa as a whole, and beyond. His vision—and his stature in holding it—produced changes that others, including myself, could not then readily imagine.[27]

Have we made progress with the leadership challenge that introduced this chapter's reflections—getting beyond partisan pettiness in the political arena? The extremes of current childishness can certainly

---

27　I do not mean to imply that Mandela was the sole factor in what transpired in South Africa's relatively peaceful transition. Many critical, behind-the-scenes meetings took place between representatives of the Apartheid government and the African National Congress in the years before Mandela's release. (The Masterpiece Theatre production *Endgame* depicts these meetings.) Later, Desmond Tutu's Truth and Reconciliation Commission played a key role in supporting a smooth transition.

make progress hard to see.[28] But I think in fact that we do see the beginning of change here, also. Certainly the general public expresses growing disgust with current intractableness. The fact that few people question the importance of getting beyond petty bickering is of no small significance. We also find political thinkers at their best attempting to articulate a more post-partisan vision. It can often be hard today to hear more mature voices above the partisan din, but they are there. And the concept of Cultural Maturity predicts that, given time, more mature voices will have a growing influence.[29]

---

28   And the "experts" don't help. Pundits are quick to point out whenever the possibility of greater bipartisanship is raised, that a look at history proves that successful bipartisan efforts are extremely rare. But such assertions only reveal the pundit's lack of culturally mature perspective. From a developmental/evolutionary vantage, a lack of success in this regard is exactly what we would expect to find when we look back historically.

29   Today's extreme polarization in the political sphere presents fascinating questions. I suspect it has multiple causes. Much may not have any real big-picture significance. What we see, though unusual in its severity, is not unique in history. But some of the pettiness we encounter may very well have larger significance. It may reflect our beginning to move beyond the time in culture when the chapter in the evolution of government that has served us so well in recent centuries can continue to do so.

   Much of what we need for this explantion to make useful sense must wait (see "History—and Life—as a Creative Narrative" in Chapter Seven and "Transitional Absurdities" in Chapter Eight), but a couple of pieces are directly pertinent to these reflections on complexity and are worth mentioning briefly. One piece follows directly from Cultural Maturity's demands. I've described how culturally mature perspective requires not just new answers to our questions, but that we ask our questions in new, more mature—more systemic and complete—ways. If we persist at asking questions that now miss the point, we get increasingly unhelpful—in this case polarized—answers. Another piece we will touch on later (see "Capacitance" in Chapter Nine) notes that systems pushed beyond what they can handle polarize as a means of self-protection. The specific challenges we face in our times are commonly taking us beyond what we can easily manage. And Cultural Maturity's changes themselves can easily overwhelm us. Given these demands, we are seeing what we would expect to see in our times—both inspiring illustrations of mature perspective and particularly extreme examples of childish polarization.

To fully appreciate leadership-related changes, we need to recognize a fact that can amplify the dangers, or at least the confusion, as we step forth. We reside in an awkward, in-between stage with these transitions. We see this reflected in efforts at post-partisanship, and also with attempts to apply culturally mature leadership more generally. Post-partisan advocacy is, often as not, rewarded by attacks from both political extremes. And while we may say that we want our leaders to get off their pedestals—and increasingly knock them off if they will not step down voluntarily—we often respect them less when they do. A political leader today must negotiate the line between the mythic and the mortal like a tightrope walker if he or she wishes to be elected, much less stay in office. And the transitional nature of new realities in every sphere makes the posture of anyone in authority (and indeed any exercising of authority—even the most personal) equally precarious.

Success with Rethinking our Human Natures

We encounter some of our time's most important complexity-related advances in fresh understandings that have to do with who we are and what makes us tick—with changes we see in how we think about intelligence, identity, interpersonal relationships, and interactions between social groups.

Changes taking place in how we think about intelligence and identity began early in the last century. Modern psychology and psychiatry—most notably with the recognition of unconscious forces—replaced the Enlightenment picture of human awareness and human will as objectively understandable with a much richer and multifaceted conception of our inner natures.[30] Changes in how we think about who we are, today, are fundamentally redefining the human experience. Social critic Walter Truett Anderson put it this way: "The modern self is dying amid the turbulence of the present era and a new global, postmodern self is being born—a sense of the person as multidimensional, mobile, and changeable, a member of multiple communities, in some ways highly individualistic, in other ways scarcely an individual at all." Chapters

---

30   See "Integrative Meta-perspective and the Workings of Awareness" in Chapter Eight.

ahead will look at ways of understanding that not only affirm this more complex picture, but that also bring detail to its workings.

We encounter changes that are just as striking with interpersonal relationships. I've described how learning to relate without the idealized projections of times past is redefining what it means to love. A parallel new capacity for more Whole-Person/Whole-System relating today permeates interpersonal bonds of all sorts—in friendships, in families, in communities. This evolution reflects changes as foundational in their implications as the world of human relationship has ever seen.

At the level of broader social interrelationships, progress we've made toward better acceptance and understanding of diversity deserves particular note. At least in the modern industrialized world, bigotry—a product of projection combined with demonization—is gradually becoming less of a defining social force. It is essential that we not deny how far we have yet to go. But the election in the U.S. of a black president in our time is something truly remarkable. And in the same election we could have just as easily seen the first woman assume the Oval Office (and with the next election, we very well might). Few gay people I know would have predicted that we would so soon see today's increasing level of acceptance toward both gay marriage and gays in the military.[31]

Some of the last century's most dramatic descriptions of how deeply complex we are have come from academia and more formal thought. Modern anthropology and sociology, for example, consistently remind us not just of our common humanness, but also of the depths of our differences. They don't let us forget that human truth always exists in a

---

31 Equality in the sense of equal rights by itself does not culturally mature capacities. This result is best thought of as a culminating
expression of the Modern Age's thrust toward individuality and individual freedom. But equal rights along with a deep appreciation for
human differences, and in particular how directly such differences can
benefit us, does require such capacities. Chapter Six looks at how recognizing the creative power of diversity requires Cultural Maturity's
more systemic sensibilities.

context (a topic to which we shall return[32]). In a related way, the best of thinking in education about learning style differences (and in the most sophisticated formulations, deeper personality style differences) describes a world in which my experience may be different from yours at levels we have not before seriously considered. (This is another topic we will return to.[33])

In medicine, we encounter a particularly striking new recognition of not just our complexity, but also the dynamic nature of our living complexity, in the growing appreciation of the intimate relationship between mind and body. Not long ago, medicine confidently treated mind and body as if they resided on opposite sides of an unnavigable moat. Today, we recognize how an intricately interwoven array of neural pathways and communications molecules join the moat's banks. New mind/body understandings have played essential roles in the biotechnology revolution, reshaped thinking about the nature of the psyche, and will be increasingly critical to crafting good health care policy.[34]

We witness important complexity-related advancements in the social sphere, too, in the ways in which we are rethinking organizational functioning. The best of new organizational theory emphasizes the importance of appreciating complex systemic relationships. That includes both systemic relationships within organizations, and particularly with globalization, how organizations relate systemically to the world around them.

Most new organizational formulations focus on familiar institutional spheres—business, government, or education—but some have more unexpected origins. Recent rethinking of U.S. military strategy provides an example that is fascinating both because of where we find it and how rapidly changes have taken place. Modern military training has focused on using overwhelming force to kill enemies. But in 2007, U.S. military strategists for the Iraq War began to recognize that the "successful" use of force was in fact only creating more enemies. Commanding General

---

32   See "Truth's Multiplicity" in Chapter Five.

33   See "One 'Crayon' and Another" in Chapter Nine.

34   Particularly where prevention comes into play.

David Petraeus met in Fort Leavenworth, Kansas, with others who would not normally be in such a conversation—not just military thinkers, but journalists, academics, and human rights activists—to develop a new counterinsurgency strategy. The resulting new field manual emphasized community-building operations in equal balance with combat, and the importance of cultural understanding and negotiating with regional leaders. The result, in a remarkably short time, was not just different tactics, but the beginnings of a new military mentality.[35]

One of the places where we most often find examples of organizational practices that successfully support complex systemic processes today is the world of high tech. I think immediately of Apple Computer in its years under Steve Jobs. Apple's design team took as its point of departure a specifically more encompassing—more systemic—kind of referent than we tend to see in the business world. Rather than focusing from the beginning on profitability, the design team members asked what kinds of devices they personally would most love to have. They also executed their imaginings with a deep commitment to quality, beauty, and the experience of the user—to making every aspect of each of their products, as they described it, "insanely great"—a choice even more radical in its systemic implications.[36] In doing so, Jobs's design team gave art, the social sciences, and the hard sciences equal roles in the design process.[37]

---

35   This kind of rethinking is just in its infancy. Military training is still for the most part about killing bad guys. And just how broadly applicable modern counterinsurgency approaches can be is roundly—and appropriately—debated. Certainly their ultimate effectiveness in both Iraq and Afghanistan is appropriately questioned. In Chapter Seven I will propose that such limited success had more to do with the fact that these wars were engaged in without an appreciation for cultural stage difference than with the particular strategies employed. My point here is only that the fact that we see such rethinking at all is significant. (I also need to emphasize that these observations are not meant to in any way suggest that the decision to invade Iraq was culturally mature. See "Terrorism—Getting It Right" in Chapter Seven.)

36   See "Truth's 'Crux'" in Chapter Six for a look at the importance of applying this more encompassing and ultimately creative sort of referent.

37   Apple did something else that reflects a rare degree of systemic

Success in Science and Technology

Advances in the world of science provide multiple provocative examples for this listing. A person might be surprised to find this to be the case. We tend to think about scientific advancements as having to do with pure discovery, not societal change. Certainly we would not expect dynamics like projection and mythologizing to come into play. But even with the most "objective" of pursuits, we witness a related evolution and, as later chapters will explore, for related reasons.[38]

Cutting-edge thought in both the biological and physical sciences through the last century has presented a newly rich and multifaceted (and often deeply perplexing) picture of our nonhuman worlds. Of particular importance is the way this picture has challenged the mechanical assumptions of classical science and forced us to think in more dynamic and systemically encompassing ways.

Ecological thought provides the example with the most obvious application to decision-making. For much of the twentieth century, the discipline of biology treated ecology as a poor cousin. Today, complex ecological formulations drive many of biology's—and modern social policy's—most important conversations. Ecological thought

---

sophistication. Rather than focusing resources on one part, or a few parts of the company, it brought Apple's innovative culture to every aspect of its efforts—not just hardware and software design, but also supply chain management, marketing, and distribution, both online and through the Apple stores. Everyone became part of the creative picture. In Apple's example we see an important model of what American industry can be, and must be, if it is to continue to provide world leadership. (See "Limits and Culturally Mature Leadership" in Chapter Four for a look both at limits to where the modern West can continue to provide leadership and where the modern West can, and must, provide exceptional leadership going forward.)

38 If we define ideology as belief that is systemically partial, certainly our modern technological gospel, but also, as we shall see, the assumptions of traditional mechanistic science, are appropriately thought of as ideological. This is not to in any way diminish the accomplishments of either science or technology, just to place their underlying belief systems within a larger historical perspective. (See "Values, Cultural Domains, and the Future" in Chapter Seven, and "Science and Technology" in Chapter Eleven.)

challenges us to address ecosystems as systems—as integrated wholes. Early biologists focused almost exclusively on individual organisms. Today, ecology combines with biological subdisciplines that focus more on change—such as evolutionary biology, embryology, and genetics— to produce an ever more complex, dynamic, and intricately interwoven picture of life.

The hardest of the hard sciences, physics and chemistry, have thrown us with particular inescapability into complexity's multifaceted and sometimes wonderfully baffling world—in this case, a world of gal- axies upon galaxies, of subatomic particles that forever reveal smaller particles, and of apparent rabbit-out-of-the-hat outcomes that defy tra- ditional explanation. I am reminded of Werner Heisenberg's famous description of existence as seen through the eyes of quantum mechan- ics: "The world thus appears as a complicated tissue of events, in which connections of different kinds alternate or overlap or combine and thereby determine the texture of the whole."

This picture predicts something else that we also see: technologies that are similarly dynamic, complex, and richly networked. History teaches us that while invention drives understanding, the opposite is also true: what we can invent follows from how we are capable of understanding. The Industrial Revolution could not have happened without the Enlightenment's newly rationalistic and mechanistic picture of truth's workings, and a look through history reveals a similarly interlinked causality every step of the way.

We can legitimately debate why we witness the advances we see to- day. But certainly we recognize all around us much that is consistent with complexity's new, more systemic picture: the Internet's ever ex- panding, intricately interlinked, and dynamically interactive presense; discoveries that tap the multileveled, ever-evolving structures of the hu- man genome; nanotechnologies that engage Lilliputian-scale complexi- ties that forever surprise us in their implications; and more. Whether such defining inventions prove to be "advances" will depend on the wisdom we bring to their use. But it is highly unlikely that we could have invented them before now. And if somehow we did, we might very well not have recognized them as having any great significance.[39]

---

39   Given our fondness for 20/20 hindsight, this statement might seem an

Stepping Back More Generally

I could easily go on. For instance, complexity-related changes in the world of aesthetics provide examples that are no less striking than those I've just reviewed, and arguably no less significant. Art not only mirrors broader changes, it often anticipates what we will later understand consciously. We find the most familiar example of this "anticipatory" function of art in how Renaissance aesthetics presaged the later social advances of the Reformation, democratic governance, and the Industrial Age. The cubism of Pablo Picasso and Georges Braque, with its multiple, counterpoised perspectives, communicates the new, more complex picture with provocative immediacy—both in what it asks of viewers and in how perplexing it can seem. We see something related in how the best of postmodern architecture draws simultaneously of multiple aesthetic traditions.[40]

And we could turn as readily to the spiritual realm. We are becoming much more comfortable with religious diversity and are much more likely to be curious about traditions different from our own than we were just a short time ago. Today, a growing number of people refer to multiple traditions when speaking about what informs their religious/spiritual beliefs. In times past, this would have been a most rare occurrence.[41]

As the maturity of our collective worldview deepens in years to come, we should find ourselves not only approaching particular spheres of understanding in ways that are more complex and nuanced, but also getting better at thinking in more encompassing ways about reality more generally. We see the beginnings of this with the growing influence of hybrid disciplines—behavioral economics, medical anthropology, sociobiology, educational psychology, bioengineering, and more.

---

exaggeration. But history teaches that it is not—even very recent history. I think of how Xerox passed on developing the personal computer even though it had done much of the early innovation that made the personal computer possible. Executives couldn't grasp that it might have sufficiently broad application.

40 See "The Arts" in Chapter Eleven for a closer look at art's anticipatory function and its implications for the future.

41 See "Religion and Spirituality" in Chapter Eleven.

And in spite of how the walls of academia have historically hindered interdisciplinary reflection, we recognize in education of late a growing appreciation for the importance of more broadly embracing inquiry.

I find fascinating the ease with which people today, often in the most unexpected of contexts, make leaps and linkages in their thinking that give direct expression to the more complex picture predicted by the idea of a new human maturity. In a 2009 piece for *The New York Times*, conservative columnist David Brooks challenged politicians and economists with these words: "Mechanistic thinkers on the right and the left pose as rigorous empiricists. But empiricism built on an inaccurate view of human nature is just a prison." In making his argument, he drew for comparison on changing models in the sciences. "Once there was just Newtonian physics and the world seemed neat and mechanical. Then quantum physics came along and revealed that deep down things are much weirder than they seem. Something similar is now happening with public policy." Political right meets political left, and politics and economics meet the cutting edge of hard science, all in a new, more dynamic and complex—and weird but also wonderfully intriguing—picture of reality's workings.

As I've emphasized, these advances represent only baby steps. These are baby steps into a new territory of experience and understanding that will take the next fifty to a hundred years to makes solid sense to us. And that new territory of experience will be teaching us new things for hundreds of years more into the future. The important recognition for now is simply that each of these examples presents a picture of possibility that is newly rich and complex in its workings—and not just a picture of potential, but possibility that is being made manifest today.

I've also noted that this chronicling of cultural advances gets us a bit ahead of ourselves conceptually. The next chapter makes a start toward this greater conceptual sophistication by looking more closely at how Cultural Maturity alters our relationship with complexity and just where, ultimately, those changes take us.

CHAPTER TWO

Post-Ideological Perspective— What It Takes and Where It Take Us

Things should be made as simple as possible, but no simpler.
ALBERT EINSTEIN

YOU SHOULD NOW HAVE A GOOD GENERAL SENSE of the way ideological beliefs protect us from life's bigness—specifically from its complexity. And you've now seen how we are taking at least first steps toward viewing our worlds with greater nuance and maturity. But we are left with important questions when it comes to our first threshold task. The first chapter provided only the most beginning sense of what generates the possibility of these changes or the mechanisms by which they take place. It also offered only a most general understanding of where Cultural Maturity's post-ideological changes take us and just how the result is different from what we have known in times past.

This chapter engages these additional concerns. First, to gain further insight into the challenge presented by complexity, we will look into the origins of today's often overwhelming complexity. Next, in order to better grasp how that challenge can be addressed, we will more closely examine the analogy with personal maturity that gives the concept of Cultural Maturity its name. And then, to more deeply understand what gives us Cultural Maturity's new capacities, we will more specifically address the cognitive reordering that produces its changes.

With the later sections of the chapter, we will turn our attention to a series of topics that provide particular insight into the broader "where it takes us" question. We will examine how the role of polarity in how we think—and how that role is changing—provides key insights into how Cultural Maturity alters our relationship to complexity. We will touch briefly on how complexity's new picture informs our understanding of human identity and human relationship. And we will look more specifically at the implications of this new picture for the future of leadership.

Each of these approaches will support and fill out important previous observations. Each confirms both that Modern Age assumptions can't be an end point, and that there is no reason to think that they should be. Each also further substantiates the conclusion that Cultural Maturity's changes provide a possible next chapter in the human story, one that is predicted if we are to effectively take on its challenges. And each gives further credence to the claim that this next step in the evolution of culture potentially offers not just new options, but options of particular significance.

The Origins of Modern Complexity

The topic of complexity confronts us with an obvious question: Why, today, do we encounter such endless and often endlessly confusing complexity? The answer helps us appreciate the often God-like nature of the challenges we face. It also helps us better understand the importance of leaving behind the projections and mythologizing of times past and the consequences of doing so. And, of more general significance for this inquiry, it helps us begin to flesh out our bare-boned, first-glimpse understanding of Cultural Maturity's mechanisms.

Modern complexity is in part a simple product of our great success as a species. Technological advancements—global communication and transportation, ever-growing industrial might, the advent of modern computers, new medical technologies—have produced a world with a lot more that we must take into account. And increasing world population—a reflection at least of our success at reproducing—contributes to a growing list of complex challenges.

But a couple of additional contributors are just as important, and for our larger purpose in this inquiry, of particular significance. Each requires that we turn our attention from specific complexities we might want to consider to ourselves, the ones doing the considering. Cultural Maturity's changes play a direct role with each of them.[1]

The first additional contributor is the way that generally agreed-upon cultural guideposts are becoming less reliable. For good or ill, the diminishing power of cultural dictates makes life markedly more complicated. I've described how we need Cultural Maturity's changes to fully make sense of this loss of guideposts. Globalization—at least in part a simple product of advances in transportation and communication—explains some of what we see, but not the aspects of these changes that have greatest consequence.[2] More deeply, Cultural Maturity's "growing up" alters the relationship between the individual and culture.

While culture and the individual have related in specifically different ways with each new stage in culture's evolution,[3] culture's symbolic role as parent in the lives of us mortals has remained constant. Part of what has made this parental relationship essential is that it has served to protect us from life's complexities. The rules and roles of culture, like those of a family, have coordinated behavior and spared us from having to deal with questions that were more complex and demanding than we were yet ready—sufficiently mature—to address. With the modern "age of the individual," we prefer to think of ourselves as above needing such childish crutches. But, as should now be clear, this parent/child mechanism has been no less present in modern times than it was in ages past.

The combination of our success as a species and this loss of traditional cultural guideposts might seem like sufficient explanation for complexity's new demands. But, in fact, we've yet to touch on

---

1   Cultural Maturity is in fact also pertinent to technological advancement's contribution. As I've described, while invention drives cultural change, it is just as much the case that changes in what and how we understand are key to making new invention possible.

2   In fact, globalization itself is not fully explained by the greater contact that comes with global transportation and communication. Remember Robert Frost's assertion that "good fences make good neighbors." Globalization, by itself, would only bring people's differences into greater proximity and, if anything, *increase* the ideological rigidities that keep us separate.

3   See "History—and Life—as a Creative Narrative" in Chapter Seven.

the piece that most informs this inquiry. What we have considered thus far doesn't fully explain the extent of complexity we see, and more importantly, it doesn't explain the new forms that complexity often takes. It doesn't explain complexity's new, more dynamic and complete picture, and a critical outcome related to it—how leaving behind culture's past parental role might result in anything more than postmodern aimlessness.

The critical additional ingredient is a direct product of the cognitive reordering intrinsic to Cultural Maturity. Because of changes in the way we think, quantities of complexity that until now would have been too much to handle, along with kinds of complexity that would before have been beyond us to make sense of, are becoming newly tolerable and newly understandable. The greater ability to recognize when we project and mythologize described in the previous chapter is a product of this additional ingredient. Such recognition thrusts us into realities that are decidedly more multifaceted and demanding in their implications, whether our concern is the requirements of good leadership or the future of love. We've looked at how ideological beliefs have always before shielded us from complexity. Culturally mature perspective reveals a world that is dramatically more complex, and complex not just in the sense of being complicated, but complex also in the more dynamic and complete sense we encountered in the previous chapter.

The reader might reasonably respond, "Hey, wait a minute. Haven't you claimed that Cultural Maturity provides an antidote to modern-day complexity?" I have, and this remains very much the case. Without Cultural Maturity's changes, today's new complexities could very well be the end of us. But Cultural Maturity's changes also contribute to that complexity. And they do so in particularly consequential ways.

The recognition that Cultural Maturity has a dual significance when it comes to complexity is essential to making sense of our times and what they ask of us. Cultural Maturity's changes directly contribute to complexity. Stepping beyond the protective shields of ideology—whether the ideological conclusion reflects us-versus-them assumptions or shared, Modern Age cultural beliefs—makes the fact of life's dynamically multifaceted complexities increasingly inescapable and obvious. At the very least, doing so reveals a greater variety of options. But at the same time, culturally mature perspective's more encompassing vantage allows us to be more comfortable with complexity—whatever its kind and source. And Cultural Maturity's cognitive changes offer that we might learn to understand in more complex and sophisticated ways that allow us to more effectively make our way in complexity's presence. Cultural Maturity opens the door to new, more rich and sophisticated—more complex, but also in important ways simpler—approaches to thinking about identity, relationship, and understanding as a whole.

This dual result—at once contributing to complexity and making complexity more understandable and manageable—is critical to the prospect of a future that could be both intriguing and tolerable, and thus a future we might celebrate. The fact that Cultural Maturity's cognitive changes reveal a more complex world is much of what makes a culturally mature future fascinating and something we appropriately anticipate. And the fact that those same changes make possible more complete ways of being and understanding is what makes such a future something we can safely and creatively navigate.[4]

Personal and Cultural Maturity

Because the kind of change Cultural Maturity represents is new and because what we encounter doesn't follow at all obviously from what

---

4   Another contributor to modern complexities—one not to be celebrat-
     ed—is the way outdated ideological views (that have before protected
     us from recognizing complexity) have interfered with or delayed neces-
     sary decisions and in the process produced new, and often particularly
     dangerous, complexities. The complexities we face with climate change
     provide a good illustration and also an example of where causes often
     overlap. Global warming is exacerbated by the simple fact of increas-
     ing world population (a reflection of our success as a species). But it is
     also more particularly a product of the Industrial Age's once helpful, but
     now increasingly problematic, growth-is-always-good worldview. And
     that today we often ignore the implications of climate change can have
     origins in more specific outdated narratives—from a religion's denial of
     scientific evidence to the technological-gospel assumption that a pain-
     less solution can always be found. Addressing climate change effectively
     requires ways of thinking that take us beyond ideological assumptions
     and help us think in more mature and complex ways. (See "Limits and
     New Capacities: Assessing Risk" in Chapter Four for a closer look at the
     climate change challenge and its relationship to Cultural Maturity.)

has come before, it helps to have a more solid sense of why we might witness such changes in the first place. Shortly we will turn to the cognitive reordering that helps us get our minds around complexities of all these sorts and, in potential, apply them to positive ends. But the developmental analogy that gives Cultural Maturity its name provides valuable introductory insight.

We find that we encounter related changes—of a more circumscribed sort—with maturity in individual psychological development. Personal development–related dynamics that I noted in the previous chapter support this observation. I described how both projection and mythologizing come part and parcel with being young. In a related but more limited sense to what we see today at a cultural level, such protective mechanisms are tested and challenged by the developmental tasks of individual growth's more mature stages.

Later in the book, I will describe how the relationship between personal maturity and the maturity our species must bring to the tasks of our time reflects something fundamental in how human systems grow and evolve more generally. We will look at how we encounter related dynamics with human developmental processes of all sorts— for example, in the changes that order relationships, the life of organizations, and simple creative processes.[5] But for now, this more basic developmental parallel will suffice.

For the analogy to help us, we need to first solidify an essential distinction noted in the Introduction. People use the word "maturity" in two different ways in reference to human development. There is maturity in the sense of becoming an adult—leaving behind our childhood and adolescent years and acting in more grown-up ways. And there is the "more mature" maturity that comes with taking on the developmental tasks of life's second half. Maturity in the later, second-half-of-life sense—not just becoming an adult, but becoming a mature adult— provides the defining metaphor for the concept of Cultural Maturity.

We find direct parallels to changes that come with such second-half-of-life maturity in changes that I've described now happening for us as a species. For example, I've described how Cultural Maturity challenges our past "parental" mythologizing of culture. With personal maturity

---

5   See "History—and Life—as a Creative Narrative" in Chapter Seven.

in the first sense, simple adulthood, we leave our home and parents physically; with second-half-of-life maturity, we do so in a more psychological and ultimately more fundamental sense. Up to this point in personal development, mythologizing our parents—whether this has taken the form of seeing them as ideals or as the ultimate source of our problems—has protected us from the full impact of a mature life's responsibilities and complexities. With second-half-of life maturity, we really "grow up"—we begin to re-own our projections and leave such mythologized parental imagery in the past.

Such maturity in our personal lives marks a unique point in individual development. We commonly see a new willingness to question past assumptions—our more personal-level "ideological" beliefs. We also manifest a new facility for doing so. We find ourselves examining both where pieces in our self-understanding may be missing and where we may have distorted (idealized or demonized) those pieces that we do recognize. Not everyone reaches this stage of greater reflectiveness. Our later years can instead produce a "hardening of the categories" in which we cling even more strongly to old prejudices. But if we successfully engage the timely developmental tasks of life's second half, the result is an expanding and maturing of perspective and a gradual emergence of a more nuanced, even wise, worldview.

It is important that we appreciate the depth and dynamism of the process that produces this expanding and maturing of perspective. Certainly the accumulated experience of a life well lived contributes to what we see—such experience makes it less likely that we will fall back on simple-answer solutions when new questions crop up. But changes inherent in the developmental process itself also make newly encompassing and sophisticated perspective increasingly possible for us. One of the most striking aspects of midlife is how it confronts us with aspects of our psyches that prior to that time we have kept hidden, even from ourselves. While we may not fully recognize what is happening consciously, this mechanism is key to the developmental tasks of life's second half. A closer look lets us be more concrete.

In my work as a psychiatrist, I find this confrontation with our personal complexities to be one of personal maturity's most obvious and defining characteristics. A person who has been highly extroverted may suddenly begin paying attention to more inner aspects, or an introvert may suddenly discover her more gregarious side; a person who has been more intellectual may become more attentive to feelings, or vice-versa. Parts that before have been dismissed and often projected onto others become newly acknowledged. Such newly recognized parts may at first seem to conflict with the elements in ourselves with which we've most strongly identified. But central to mature perspective is learning to accept, and even appreciate, such greater complexity.

Various people respond differently on first encountering a previously neglected part. One person may vigorously push the new part away—for example, a very logical person may find new, more emotional impulses a threat. Or we can see just the opposite. The person may idealize the new part—a very down-to-earth, nuts-and-bolts sort of person might make newly felt spiritual inclinations the answer, the new all-encompassing truth in his life. In time we recognize that it is not choosing between parts, but rather holding a larger picture, that is being asked of us—acknowledging and embracing our contradictions and multiplicities. The result is a deepened and, paradoxically, more solid and coherent experience of identity. If anything defines maturity, it is this more complete embrace of our inner narratives. I like the words of Walt Whitman in "Song of Myself": "Do I contradict myself? Very well then, I contradict myself; (I am large—I contain multitudes.)."

The recognition that at this point in human history we find changes similar to those that come with second-half-of-life personal development assists us in multiple ways. Most obviously it helps us understand why it is that today we might see the complexity-related changes I've described—Cultural Maturity is, in a related way, about getting our arms around the whole of our complex natures, but here at a species scale. Our developmental analogy also helps us better understand where these changes take us—Cultural Maturity similarly produces a more encompassing, at once more detailed and more integrated picture. In addition, our developmental analogy provides hope as far as whether Cultural Maturity's changes can be achieved. It supports the conclusion that Cultural Maturity's changes are not just possible, they are inherent—at least as potential—in our natures.

We can also take this basic recognition of complexity-related parallels an important step further, one that links back to reflections in the previous chapter about the dynamic nature of the complexities we face, and in particular, of our human complexities. The fact that personal maturity's changes can seem pardoxical gives it away. At personal development's more limited scale of perspective, we engage complexity that has to do with more than just things being complicated. We more consciously connect with the particular kind of complexity that makes life alive—and, when we are the focus of attention, alive in the specific sense that makes us human.

As with Cultural Maturity, this outcome at the scale of personal identity is a product of the more dynamic and complete engagement of our inner and outer realities that comes with mature perspective. It is this more wholly encompassing engagement that invites the kind of understanding that in our later years produces not just knowledge, but also wisdom.[6]

Besides helping to fill out where Cultural Maturity's complexity-related changes take us, this additional recognition also helps clarify just how I use the word "wisdom" in talking about Cultural Maturity's changes—a word that is easily misinterpreted. In our time, we tend to misconstrue what the second half of life is about in one of two opposite ways. We may miss that it has to do with anything positive—view it as about being increasingly "over the hill." Or we can use a word like "wisdom," but romanticize the term, making it about the spiritual or poetic side of things rather than the kind of systemic maturity that is our concern, a misperception that ultimately cheapens what wisdom is about.

Real wisdom is what results when we take on "second-half" devel-opmental challenges. Such wisdom—as found in a more limited sense in personal development, and more deeply with Cultural Maturity—is about better grasping the big picture, recognizing its demanding

---

6   While the underlying mechanisms of personal maturity and Cultural Maturity have important parallels, these two scales of maturity also have fundamental differences, both with regard to what they involve and where they take us. Chapter Seven (see "Personal Maturity, Cultural Maturity, and the Mechanisms of Wisdom") examines important distinctions. If we miss essential differences, we become vulnerable to conceptual traps.

intricacies, and finding delight in understanding that captures the complex in particularly elegant ways. [7]

With "second-half" maturity, whatever the developmental scale, we come to better recognize our inner complexities and also to better acknowledge complexities of all sorts in the world around us. In the process, we become more sophisticated in our discernments, and more intelligent—and possibly more wise—in our choices. If we as a species successfully take on our time's developmental challenges, Cultural Maturity's changes should bring a new appreciation for the rich—at once wonderful and often overwhelming and befuddling—complexities that are intrinsic in existence. Cultural Maturity is about appreciating how life, wherever we find it—to again borrow Whitman's words— "contains multitudes."

Cultural Maturity's Cognitive Reordering

Let's now take a big-picture look at the cognitive reorganization that produces these changes. The new picture of reality that comes with Cultural Maturity reflects not just changes in *what* we think, but in *how* we think—in the mechanisms of cognition. We can recognize these same changes, but in a more circumscribed form, with second-half-of-life changes in personal development. With Cultural Maturity they manifest in a way that includes every aspect of our personal and collective experience. Later I will expand on these observations.[8] For

---

7   To fully appreciate how wisdom and maturity relate, we need to distinguish between intellectual speed and facility (which decline somewhat in our later years) and wisdom. A provocative study published in the proceedings of the National Academy of Sciences (psychologist Igor Gross at the University of Michigan is its lead author) concludes that older people excel in wisdom-related dimensions such as recognizing that the world is always changing, seeing events from the perspectives of the people involved, appreciating the limits of knowledge, and having a tendency to search for ways to resolve conflict. (Actually, intellectual speed and facility in most people decline less than we used to think. Old studies lumped people with degenerative processes such as Alzheimer's disease together with healthy subjects.)

8   Chapter Seven examines how similar changes reorder understanding not just with personal development, but at the midpoint of formative processes of all sorts. Chapter Eight takes a closer look that gives special at-

now it is enough that we appreciate how Cultural Maturity's cognitive reordering alters our relationship to complexity.

It helps to think of Cultural Maturity's cognitive reorganization as a two-step process.[9] The first step is new in the sense of how fully it involves the whole of who we are. The second step is new in an even more fundamental sense—it represents a kind of process we have not seen in any of the previous stages in culture's evolution. Each step reflects not just changes that we might hope for, but changes that are predicted by how developmental processes work—and steps that we are beginning to witness. We need both steps if we are to effectively understand complexity and successfully make our way in our ever more complex world.

The first step in Cultural Maturity's cognitive reordering involves a new more complete kind of stepping back. It produces a new expansiveness of vantage. What we step back from has multiple aspects. Of most obvious significance, we step back from ourselves as cultural beings. It is this that gives us perspective on culture's past parental function—we begin to glimpse how individual human experience and human culture may together reflect a larger reality.

We see another aspect of what we step back from reflected in the previous chapter's observations about the importance of leaving behind the projective mechanisms that in times past have defined so much of how we have interpreted our realities. We become better able to step back from and recognize our projections, both those that idealize and those that demonize. Culturally mature perspective involves a new, more complete kind of stepping back from our complex natures.

One particular aspect of our human complexity that Cultural Maturity's new expansiveness of vantage helps us better recognize will provide especially important insight for this inquiry. It makes clear that what we are dealing with ultimately is change of a cognitive sort. It also

---

tention to how these changes alter the workings of conscious awareness, and with this, how we both conceive of who we are and understand what makes something true.

9   In fact, these two steps represent parts of a single mechanism. But because each step by itself can be tricky to grasp, they are best taken one at a time.

helps distinguish Cultural Maturity's vantage from our more familiar Modern Age, Enlightenment perspective. In the book's Introduction, I described how culturally mature understanding requires that we draw consciously on all the multiple aspects of intelligence.[10]

With Enlightenment perspective we stood back from the more mystical sensibilities that ordered medieval belief. But in order to do so, we made one aspect of intelligence—rationality—the new arbiter of truth. With culturally mature perspective, we stand back from intelligence in its entirety, including the more rational aspects that have most recently reigned supreme. The result, in a critical way, takes us beyond the kind of stepping back that gave us Modern Age, from-a-balcony objectivity, the analogous defining gift of Age of Enlightenment perspective.[11]

The second step in Cultural Maturity's cognitive reordering is as essential as the first—without it the more complete stepping back I've described would not provide great benefit. It produces an almost opposite result. At the same time that Cultural Maturity's changes allow us to step back and obtain a more encompassing perspective, they also make possible a new and deeper engagement with all that we have stepped back from. Cultural Maturity's cognitive reordering is simultaneously about a more expansive vantage for appreciating our complexity and a more direct—more embodied—connectedness with all of who we are as complex beings.

This second, deeper-engagement step is wholly new. It involves a kind of process that at a cultural scale we have not witnessed before, one that is essential to what makes Cultural Maturity's changes different from what we have seen with fundamental changes of times past. We will need reflections in later chapters for the distinctions I will make here to be fully understandable,[12] but a further contrasting with

---

10   See "Truth and Intelligence" in Chapter Six for a closer look at intelligence's multiplicity.

11   This is not to say that we haven't before been able to step back from our rationality—philosophy is quite specifically about doing so. But philosophy's tool of inquiry is this same rationality. See "A Creative History of Truth" in Chapter Ten.

12   See "History—and Life—as a Creative Narrative" in Chapter Seven

Enlightenment objectivity provides a basic feel for this second step and its particular significance.

We tend to assume that Enlightenment perspective's from-a-balcony vantage lets us see everything with unobstructed clarity. But, in fact, the less rational parts of our functioning (ultimately the much larger part of human complexity) have remained largely unconscious—safely out of sight and out of mind. Think of looking out from a mountaintop, but with clouds obscuring the larger part of the view below. What I've described as the first step in Cultural Maturity's cognitive reordering offers no respite from this limiting circumstance—indeed, by itself it would only create further distancing. Greater awareness without our second step's complementary greater depth of engagement would leave us trying to make our way in a world in which truth becomes at best "an inch deep and a mile wide," or worse, essentially random. For now, we can observe that this outcome represents a not-unfamiliar circumstance in our contemporary world.[13]

With the second step in Cultural Maturity's cognitive reordering, the greater awareness produced by the first step comes to have real significance through a newly possible depth of connection with all that we have stepped back from. It is not that the clouds just part—later we will look closely at how culturally mature perspective is about something very different from, and also much more interesting than, the unconscious world suddenly becoming conscious.[14] Put simply for now, the second step in Cultural Maturity's cognitive reordering produces a new depth of systemic engagement with all of who we are.

To appreciate the importance of this second step and some of where it takes us, we can again turn to intelligence and its workings. A key

---

along with "Creative Reengagement" in Chapter Eight.

13   See "Transitional Absurdities" in Chapter Eight and "Postmodern/ Constructivist Scenarios" in Chapter Nine.

14   We catch a glimpse of this more significant outcome with the earlier observation that culturally mature leadership, while more powerful, is also more humble. At the same time that culturally mature leadership involves this deeper engagement with our complexity, it also involves a loss of awareness' past exalted status. See "Integrative Meta-perspective and the Workings of Awareness" in Chapter Eight..

way the second step manifests is in a deepened connection with the whole of human intelligence. With the first step, we more fully step back from intelligence's multiple aspects— rationality, and also cognition's more emotional, imaginal, and bodily dimensions. With the second step, we engage all these diverse ways of understanding with a depth that before has not been possible. The result is key to all the observations this book is about. With regard to complexity, our more dynamic and complete picture of complexity can make useful sense only with this ability to more directly draw on intelligence's multiple aspects. Certainly, the ability to do so is key to developing the more mature systemic formulations needed to address such complexity.

Just as our multiple intelligences represent only one part of what we newly step back from, they also represent only one aspect of what we more deeply engage with the second half of Cultural Maturity's cognitive changes. For example, aspects of ourselves that we have before projected again have a role. With Cultural Maturity's cognitive reordering, we don't just become more aware that projection—and the mythologizing that commonly accompanies it—has occurred; we actively reincorporate past projections and apply the energy that has gone into mythologizing to more useful ends. In so doing, we directly engage with aspects of our complexity that we previously didn't consider parts of ourselves at all (or at least that we interpreted in distorted ways that protected us from their full implications).

Creative Systems Theory calls the results of this two-part change process *Integrative Meta-perspective*. Integrative Meta-perspective is a mouthful of a term, but it quite precisely captures what becomes different. The diagram in Figure 2-1 depicts this cognitive reordering. To keep things simple, the diagram focuses on intelligence-related changes.[15] But even in this simplified form, the diagram supports the general observation that Cultural Maturity's changes produce a more encompassing kind of perspective and, with this, a newly systemic and complete kind of "objectivity."

---

15   And it makes full sense only with the developmental progression presented in Chapter Seven. For example, the sizes of the circles have specific significance, and Transition refers to not just to a general time of change, but to a distinct period with particular characteristics.

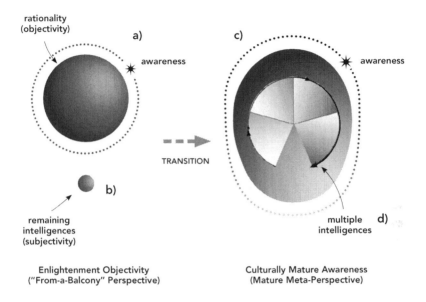

a) Rational intelligence (allied with awareness to produce from-a-balcony objectivity)

b) The subjective (all remaining intelligences as experienced in Modern Age reality)

c) < --------- * --------- > Culturally mature awareness in its various more and less conscious permutations

d) Multiple intelligences (made newly explicit with culturally mature perspective)[16]

Fig. 2-1. Cultural Maturity's Cognitive Reordering

There is an important further aspect of complexity essential to Integrative Meta-perspective's more complete picture that

16   See "Integrative Meta-perspective and the Workings of Awareness" in Chapter Eight for an examination of how being maturely aware is not at all the same as being conscious of everything, and also how different intelligences require different degrees of conscious involvement.

will require more thorough stage-setting to make ultimately useful sense,[17] but I can touch on it here briefly. We more fully step back from, and more deeply access, aspects of experience that we knew intimately at earlier cultural times but that we have since, for developmentally appropriate reasons, put behind us. We catch a glimpse of this additional piece in how it manifests in relation to our most recent cultural stage.

At first, what takes place as we move beyond Modern Age cultural realities might seem less fundamentally new and more like something we necessarily do with each new chapter in culture's story—we leave behind the defining beliefs of our most recent cultural stage. Today these beliefs are the Modern Age's rationalist, materialist, objectivist, and individualist assumptions. But here on the threshold of Cultural Maturity, in another way we witness something fundamentally different. Always before when we've passed from one stage to the next, we've not only set aside beliefs that no longer serve us, we've actively pushed them away—we've distorted and demonized past beliefs so that we might gain needed distance from them. The new cultural stage came to view the previous worldview as backward and ignorant—or worse.[18] This time, we don't see this same active pushing away. We just as decisively step beyond familiar ways of understanding, but we do so in a way that is also integrative.[19]

This distinction has essential implications for more deeply engaging complexity. Beyond Cultural Maturity's threshold, Modern Age

---

17   See "Progress and the Dilemma of Trajectory" and "Creative Reengagement" in Chapter Eight.

18   In the first half of personal development, we similarly push away the realities of previous developmental stages. Creative Systems Theory describes how amnesias insert themselves between developmental stages. For example, while we might expect adolescents to be experts on childhood (since they've just left the childhood world), in fact, adolescents tend to find the behavior of children quite nonsensical. Young adults can find the thoughts of adolescents equally baffling.

19   In Chapter Eight, we will examine how maturity in individual development involves a related kind of integration in time.

sensibilities, rather than being forgotten, become part of a larger multiplicity of perspective. We recognize them as aspects of the needed, more systemic, more whole-ball-of-wax understanding. In Chapter Eight, we will examine how something similar applies to the beliefs of past cultural stages more generally.

I will often address these various pieces—drawing on our multiple intelligences, reincorporating projection, and reengaging past sensibilities—separately in these pages. Each provides particular insights. But, in the end, they come together as aspects of a larger process. Put in the language of complexity, Cultural Maturity's cognitive changes involve at once stepping back from and newly engaging the fullness of our uniquely complex human natures. Later I will describe how we can think of these various pieces coming together as the generative mechanism that makes us creative—toolmaking, society-making, meaning-making—beings.

At this point, the important recognition is that the resulting Integrative Meta-perspective lets us think with the needed completeness—and completeness not just in the sense of better including lots of pieces, but in the sense that gives us the new kind of systemic sophistication that questions of all sorts will more and more require. Integrative Meta-perspective makes it possible not just to better acknowledge complexity, but also to address the more dynamic and complete kind of complexity—permeated by uncertainty, change, and interconnectedness—that will increasingly define the human experience.[20]

An appreciation for Integrative Meta-perspective's mechanisms helps make understandable much that might otherwise seem baffling

---

20   There is also a more general change process that helps make Integrative Meta-perspective possible: an expanded ability to hold and tolerate experience. (See the concept of Capacitance in Chapters Four and Nine.) This additional contribution is not specific to Cultural Maturity's changes like the others I have mentioned. Rather, it is a simple product of development—any growth produces this result. But it is specifically necessary for new developmental chapters. New developmental stages require an expanded abilty to take in experience. To get our arms around all that Cultural Maturity involves requires that our arms have sufficient reach.

in Cultural Maturity's new picture. For example, it clarifies a paradoxical seeming result that I've suggested and that will be a recurring theme—how Cultural Maturity's changes produce outcomes that are at once profound in their implications, and in important ways quite ordinary.

We can describe where Integrative Meta-perspective takes us in dramatic terms if we wish. Drawing on the last section's developmental observations, we can quite accurately think of our two-part cognitive restructuring—stepping back from our complexity while at once more deeply engaging these various pieces—as a "device" for producing wisdom. Yet, at the same time, there is a way in which the result could not be more striaghtforward. Certainly, it is nothing esoteric. No longer mythologized, our beliefs come to more accurately reflect what actually is. Our understandings, now better able to take in complexity's full implications, come to more fully acknowledge both the whole of ourselves and the whole of the world around us. Our pieces come together in our new, now more mature and fully reality-embracing kind of common sense.

Cultural Maturity and Polarity

We now have a good basic answer to the question of how it is that Cultural Maturity might alter our relationship with complexity. We can understand Cultural Maturity as a set of predictable developmental changes that reflect a specific sort of cognitive reorganization. This new cognitive picture begins to make life's complexities more recognizable, more understandable, and more tolerable.

But we will benefit from having conceptual tools that can help us make better sense of just where complexity's new picture takes us. The next few sections draw on one of the most useful. I implied its importance in the previous chapter with my observation that ideological beliefs commonly reflect contrasting positions within larger systemic realities.

Needed new understandings of every sort require that our ideas link experiences that we've regarded not just as different, but as opposite—as polarities. Integrative Meta-perspective helps us appreciate how polarities reflect counterpoised aspects of larger systemic processes. It also helps us think more directly in terms of those larger processes. Creative Systems Theory speaks of "bridging" traditional polar assumptions.

The concept of "bridging" is not as simple a notion as it might first appear. As we will examine, the result is no at all the same as what we find with more familiar notions such as adding, averaging, or joining—and certainly it is different from simple oneness, what we often find with more spiritual interpretation.[21] But once the basic idea has been grasped, it proves very useful. For example, with regard to reflections to this point, the concept of bridging provides important further insight into how post-ideological perspective might be possible. It also furnishes a solid starting point for making sense of the more dynamic and complete kind of systemic understanding that results when we succeed. In fact, the various ways in which bridging can be misunderstood also prove useful. We will look at how we can use them to help us identify when our thinking falls for common conceptual traps.[22] For now, making initial acquaintance with this concept will suffice.

F. Scott Fitzgerald proposed that the sign of a first-rate intelligence (we might say a "mature intelligence") is the ability to hold two contradictory truths simultaneously in one's mind without going mad. His reference was to personal maturity, but this capacity is such an inescapable part of culturally mature perspective that we could almost say that it defines it. The needed new kinds of relating, values, and understanding don't require that we consciously recognize that bridging is taking place, or even that polarities are involved. But they do require that we somehow get our minds around a larger picture and act from it. Certainly wise decision-making does.[23]

---

21 I will often put the term in quotes to emphasize its very specific meaning.

22 See "Polar Traps" in Chapter Nine.

23 My 1992 book, *Necessary Wisdom*, uses this simple observation as a lens to examine a broad array of contemporary issues.

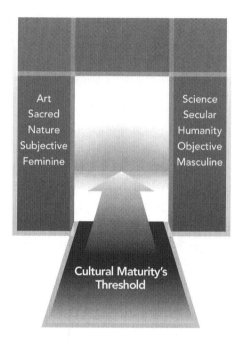

Fig. 2-2. "Bridging" and Polarities

We can use the Introduction's doorway image to help us grasp polarity's relationship to Cultural Maturity. Think of the columns on each side of the doorway's threshold as representing the opposites of polarity (see Figure 2-2). The act of stepping up to the threshold begins to bring into question the usefulness of polarized advocacy (what we see, for example, with postmodern perspective's challenging of past absolutist beliefs). When we proceed forward and over Cultural Maturity's threshold, polarized assumptions are replaced by Integrative Meta-perspective's more encompassing vantage. We find ourselves in Cultural Maturity's more systemically ordered territory of understanding and experience.

We witnessed bridging in this expressly systemic sense with my description in the previous chapter of how effective global policy requires seeing beyond past us-versus-them assumptions and recognizing a more complex and nuanced picture of relationships between nations. In the end, mature leadership on the global stage requires bridging not just ally and enemy, but also the polarity of leader and follower, and even usual ideas about war and peace. (Nelson Mandela's influence in helping to end Apartheid involved much more than just some "siding" with peace. He did not shy away from the hard realities that governing in a multiethnic society with a difficult history would involve.)

At a more personal level, culturally mature gender identity and love each require a bridging of masculine and feminine aspects within ourselves. Later in this chapter, we will see how culturally mature perspective requires us to rethink individuality in a way that bridges the polar assumptions of times past.[24]

The change that most defines Cultural Maturity provides a prime example of bridging: Cultural Maturity bridges ourselves and our societal contexts (or, put another way, ourselves and final truth). With this most encompassing bridging we leave behind society's past parental function. Besides providing a context for understanding more specific bridgings, it provides good illustration of what bridging is and is not. What results is not some simple joining—with Cultural Maturity, culture's role doesn't disappear—but, rather, the appreciation of a more complexly systemic picture. We come to better recognize how the individual and culture creatively relate—how, through our thoughts and actions, we produce culture, and how in an ongoing way, personal and cultural realities each creatively inform the other.

Beyond this most overarching linkage, we find a multitude of more local bridgings. Nothing characterized the previous century's most important conceptual advances more than how their thinking linked previously unquestioned polar truths. For example, physics' new picture provocatively drew a circle around the realities of matter and energy, space and time, and object with its observer. New understandings in biology linked humankind with the natural world, and by reopening timeless questions about life's origins, joined the purely physical with the organic. And the ideas of modern psychology, neurology, and sociology have provided an increasingly integrated picture of the workings of conscious with unconscious, mind with body, self with society, and more.

Recognizing the fact of polarity is not by itself new. Our familiar Cartesian worldview is explicitly dualistic. And the idea that

---

24   See "A Powerful Surprise: The Myth of the Individual."

getting beyond thinking based on polarity might be important is, in a specific, more limited sense, a quite ancient recognition.[25] But in modern times, even if we have acknowledged the basic fact of polarity—and often we have not[26]—we've missed how it is that polar opposites might relate in ways that produce today's needed more mature and complex picture. We've assumed that it is right to think of minds and bodies as separate, even though daily experience repeatedly proves otherwise. And we've accepted that a world of allies and "evil empires" is just how things are, even as one generation's most loathed of enemies has become the next generation's close collaborator.

It is important to emphasize that the "problem" presented by a lack of more encompassing perspective is not an intrinsic difficulty, but rather an expression of where we reside in the story of understanding. In times past, polarity worked. The polar tensions between church and crown in the Middle Ages, for example, were tied intimately to that time's experience of meaning. With our Modern Age—and just as right and timely in their contributions—we saw Descartes's cleaving of truth into separate objective and subjective realities, along with the competing arguments of positivist

---

25   We see it tied to wisdom in "perennial philosophies" of all sort. Epictetus observed that "Every matter has two handles, one of which will bear taking hold of, the other not." We also recognize it with the Yin and Yang of classical Chinese belief. Later, we will examine how, while what we see in these examples might seem similar to Cultural Maturity, the result is fundamentally different. Critical distinctions involve both the fact that the wisdom reference with such early utterances was to personal rather than cultural maturity, and also the stage-specific cultural realities that give us such utterances. (See "Personal Maturity, Cultural Maturity, and the Mechanisms of Wisdom" in Chapter Seven.)

26   For ideologically predictable reasons. The more extreme of positivist views, for example, regard the subjective hand of experience as having no ultimate significance. (See "Polar Traps" in Chapter Nine.) Spiritual interpretations can, in an opposite way, dismiss the material world as "illusion." (Again see "Polar Traps" in Chapter Nine.) And dynamics specific to our current time can in a more general way make one half of polarity seem at least inconsequential. (See "Progress and the Dilemma of Trajectory" in Chapter Eight.)

and romantic worldviews. And while here I've strongly emphasized the outmodedness of petty ideological squabbles between political left and political right, I am just as comfortable proposing that such squabbles, in their time, were creative and essential. In times past, polarized positions drove the important conversations. Later we will look closely at how polarity has been critical to the mechanisms of change in human developmental processes of all sorts.[27] The problem is not with polarity itself, but with polarity's inability in our current time to effectively generate truth and meaning.

Polarity's relationship to complexity helps tie the concept of bridging to previous reflections and also helps to fill out our understanding of what we have seen with regard to polarity to this point culturally. The fact that prior to now in history we could miss that polar understanding might limit us could at first seem odd. Why would we assume that reality is anything but whole? It turns out that there have been good reasons for missing this larger picture. The way polarity has been necessary to the mechanisms through which culture has grown and evolved lies at the heart of it. But embedded in those mechanisms is a related reason that ties directly to our first threshold task. Thinking in polar terms has protected us from life's easily overwhelming complexities. When timely, polarity, like the ideological beliefs through which it often takes expression, has helped keep complexities that otherwise would have been too much to tolerate at arm's length.

This observation takes some further reflection if it is to fully make sense. There is an important way in which polarity is a direct expression of complexity. Certainly it is what gives us the alternative options (us versus them, thoughts versus feelings) that we tend to associate with difference. A person might reasonably ask how things could be more complex than this. But part of polarity's function has also been to shield us from complexity. Questions of significance almost always involve a multiplicity of aspects. Polarity has reduced this multifaceted complexity to a more manageable two. And those two aspects are not as different as we tend to suppose. Like creatively

---

27 See "History—and Life—as a Creative Narrative" in Chapter Seven for an extended historical examination.

related sides of a single coin, they have been at once opposites and necessary to each other's existence.[28]

We can similarly understand the fact that polarized perception is today ceasing to serve us in terms of complexity. We've seen how Cultural Maturity's cognitive changes make it possible to more directly engage our own complexities and in the process be more comfortable with in-the-world complexities that before would have overwhelmed us. Integrative Meta-perspective's two-part process is quite specifically about bridging. We step back from and at once more deeply engage polarities of all sorts. One result is that we less and less need the protection from complexity that polarized understanding has before provided.

Observations in the preceding chapter about the role that projection has historically played in human understanding in another way help make the connection. Projection requires polarity. We've examined how projection has had both a protective and a developmental purpose, and also how maturity's changes help us get our minds around systemic relationships that projection has previously kept us from recognizing. Mature thought in our individual lives does this in an important but circumscribed sense; culturally mature thought does it with regard to understanding more generally.

The observation that culturally mature perspective brings with it the bridging of familiar polar assumptions provides a practical tool with broad application. We can readily apply it to specific problems or challenges where thinking in more systemic ways might be of value. Here is a simple formula: First, identify the issue's underlying polar assumptions. Next, see if you can hold the polarities you have identified in ways that reflect a more encompassing vantage. Finally, reflect on how that more encompassing vantage alters what you see and note any new kinds of options it makes visible. Follow these steps, and newly creative responses, or at the very least, much better questions, will result.[29]

---

28 Later we will examine how the fact that polar opposites are not opposite in the sense we assume has essential implications for this inquiry. See "Polarity's Underlying 'Procreative' Symmetry" in Chapter Six.

29 See "Cognitive Rewiring" in Chapter Nine for a more detailed explanation of how it is that following this formula produces this result.

We can also use the concept of bridging to help us reframe whole domains of understanding. When I work with groups interested in the future of some particular cultural sphere—education, religion, medicine, or government—I will often start by having participants list polarities that have before defined that domain's assumptions (see Figure 2-3). Our discussion will inevitably come back to how these various polarities might be bridged, and how together they help us understand that domain as a whole more systemically.

Fig. 2-3. Juxtaposing Domain-Specific Polarities

A Threshold Lesson: Whether in the workings of our individual psyches or in the more encompassing workings of culture, polarized perception has protected us from being overwhelmed by complexity. Integrative Meta-perspective lets us both step back from polarized perceptions and more consciously and deeply engage the larger systemic realities that underlie them. The more encompassing understanding that results "bridges" the polar assumptions of times past. Just how it does provides a powerful tool for addressing critical challenges before us.

"Bridging," Complexity, and Systemic Understanding

Later chapters draw extensively on the workings of polarity and the dynamics of bridging. In Chapter Six, I will describe how polarities have predictable symmetry—how we can think of them as having "right" and "left" hands—and how an appreciation of this symmetry is key to understanding where Cultural Maturity's changes take us.[30]

30   See "Creative Systems Theory Patterning Concepts."

In Chapter Seven, I will delineate how any human formative process organizes as a predictable sequence of polar relationships. I will also closely examine the essential role bridging plays in the mature stages of any formative dynamic.[31] In Chapter Nine, we will look in detail at how an understanding of what bridging is and is not provides one of the simplest tools for separating the wheat from the chaff in our thinking about the future.[32]

At this point, the concept of bridging can help us further flesh out the specific kind of understanding challenges ahead will more and more require of us. I've emphasized that the kind of systems thinking need for times ahead must take us beyond more traditional mechanistic systemic models—how it must reflect not just that we alive, but that we are alive in the particular way that makes us human. Creative System Theory specifically addresses this requirement. But fortunately we don't need detailed conceptual notions to begin to make sense of the needed new kind of systemic sensibility. The concept of bridging provides one of several key notions I will draw on to highlight and represent it.

Bridging, in the specific way I am using the term, not only alerts us to the fact of complexity, it alerts us to the more dynamic kind of systemic understanding that is here our concern. Examine any conclusion that begins to effectively bridge polarities—whether the polarity is ally and enemy, Left and Right in the political sphere, mind and body, objective and subjective, or matter and energy—and we find thinking that is of the needed more vigorous and complete sort.

A basic observation highlights this recognition. Any bridging of polarities produces results that can initially appear paradoxical. Such apparent paradox is most obvious with ideas that are not so much about us—for example, in how cutting-edge notions in physics are perfectly comfortable with something being at once a particle and a wave. But it is just as inescapably present with explicitly human concerns. Mature love makes us both more complete in ourselves and capable of

---

31   See "History—and Life—as a Creative Narrative."

32   See "Polar Traps."

deeper connections; mature leadership is both more powerful and more humble than what it replaces.

Some of the most important observations I've made about Cultural Maturity have taken the form of apparent paradox. I've emphasized how, while culturally mature perspective is dramatic in its implications, at the same time, the conclusions it produces are ultimately common sense. I've also described how culturally mature understanding is more complex, and at once simpler, than what it replaces. In each case, I wasn't just being clever. Paradox provided the most direct way to express a larger systemic truth.

One of the paradoxes I've suggested relates directly to bridging and has particular importance when in comes to the task of developing new conceptual approaches. At the same time that bridging increases our appreciation for how things may relate, it also helps us better grasp authentic difference. Bridge mind and body and we not only better recognize how mind and body work as a whole, we also more deeply grasp the contributions that mind and body each make to that whole. Bridge masculine and feminine, and we not only see that the masculine and the feminine have never been as fundamentally distinct as we have imagined, we also recognize the unique gifts that the masculine and the feminine each contribute with a depth that has not before been possible. No result provides a better test for whether bridging in the systemic sense we have interest in is taking place.

Culturally mature perspective makes clear that such paradoxical-seeming outcomes are not at all products of what we observe being somehow inexplicable, or even ultimately strange. That results might appear paradoxical is a product of limits inherent to how in times past we have understood. When we step back sufficiently, we recognize that what we are seeing, simply, is the more dynamic kind of complexity inherent in a more systemically complete picture of how reality works.

A related observation in a further way helps clarify how bridging ties to the needed new kind of systemic understanding. It has to do with what it takes to effectively represent such understanding. In the next chapter, we will examine how culturally mature concepts by their nature defy usual approaches to either verbal or pictorial depiction. Creative Systems Theory calls this outcome the Dilemma of Representation.[33]

The Dilemma of Representation inescapably confronts us when we attempt to depict where the bridging of any polarity takes us. Note how the term "bridging" by itself tells us very little about what happens when bridging actually takes place. It describes quite well what we must leave behind—the kind of polarized thinking that underlies ideology and the now-limiting assumptions of Modern Age belief. But as far as what lies ahead, unless we infer much more than the word explicitly communicates, the word doesn't tell us much at all. At best the term "bridging" alerts us to the fact that future ways of understanding must be more multifaceted—and that only by inference.

A closer look at Figure 2-2 (the threshold diagram with polarities added) highlights this representational quandary. It effectively represents bridging only by virtue of a certain visual trickery. The word "bridging" might seem to describe joining the columns, what the doorway's lintel would represent. But this action would only produce adding, averaging, or oneness depending on how we did the joining. Bridging in the sense that produces culturally mature understanding involves a wholly different sort of action: approaching the doorway's threshold and stepping over it (and even this tells us little about the specifics of the territory beyond).

One additional polarity-related observation further substantiates the connection between bridging and the needed more dynamic and complete kind of understanding in a particularly consequential way. We reasonably ask how we understand polarity at its most basic. We might think that polarity at its most basic would contrast opposites like good versus evil or perhaps objective versus subjective. But more accurately, it juxtaposes separateness (difference) on one hand with unity (relatedness) on the other. In philosophy, it is this polarity that underlies the ever-conflicting views of understanding's great opposing camps: rationalist, reductionist, and positivist sorts set against people of more romantic, idealist, or spiritual inclination.

Note that this answer relates directly to the paradox that I just gave special emphasis, how bridging increases our appreciation for both

---

33   See " The Dilemma of Representation" in Chapter Three.

difference and relatedness. It also dramatically affirms the importance of culturally mature perspective by highlighting the depth and fundamental significance of the questions it can help us address.[34]

In his widely enjoyed book, *Zen and the Art of Motorcycle Maintenance: An Inquiry into Values*, Robert Pirsig describes this most fundamental of polarities—and emphasizes the importance of a new relationship to it for today—using a simple image. He proposes that we can think of the world as a handful of sand arranged in separate piles. In Pirsig's description, "classical understanding is concerned with the piles and the basis for sorting and relating them," while "romantic understanding is directed toward the handful of sand before the sorting began." Pirsig proposes that, "what has become urgently necessary is a way of looking at the world that does violence to neither of these two kinds of understanding and unites them into one." He is, of course, far from the first to pose this problem[35]—but the answer has always seemed just out of reach. And the fact that it has eluded us is of no small consequence. Among other things, our past inability to address it effectively leaves science and religion appearing to venture in wholly different worlds.

The fact that the best of contemporary understanding bridges polarities suggests that we are getting closer at least in application, if not on a more abstract level. It follows from the concept of Cultural Maturity that in time we should also see approaches to understanding that succeed more conceptually—and at an overarching, all-encompassing scale.

For now we can draw on the concept of bridging to at least approach the task in a way that can bring us closer to useful answers. Framed systemically, extremes like positivism and romanticism or

---

34 Some of the most fascinating insights that come with culturally mature systemic perspective's picture of complexity have to do with really big-picture questions. We find that Integrative Meta-perspective lets us address questions that previously have left us baffled. (See "Unexpected Rewards" in Chapter Eight of this book, and the whole of the companion volume *Quick and Dirty Answers to the Biggest of Questions.*)

35 Numerous others, from Immanuel Kant to Martin Heidegger, Thomas Kuhn, and Ludwig Wittgenstein have done so. (Eastern philosophy has also examined the issue, though more at the level of personal maturity.)

science and religion become, instead of warring polar answers, complementary voices in larger systemic conversations. Neither those who hold to a narrow religious belief nor those who hold a similarly absolutist view of science will like this more systemic picture. But, as we shall examine, understood deeply it offers not just that the beliefs of science and religion can be reconciled, but that we can rethink these two most ultimately defining of past human narratives in ways that make each more rich and significant.[36]

This chapter's reflections on complexity, polarity, and systems translate ultimately into the possibility not just of such sweeping, overarching reflection, but also of the development of conceptual approaches that can provide the nuanced understanding necessary if we are to effectively go forward. Creative Systems Theory proposes that answering three simple polarity-related questions gives us almost all that we need to do so: Why do we humans tend to think in the language of polarity in the first place? Why have we now begun to see understanding that bridges polar assumptions? And how do we best think about what happens when we do bridge polarities? In Chapter Six, we will examine how a creative frame effectively answers each of these questions and provides the basis for a "pattern language" approach able to help us address complex questions with the needed dynamism and detail.[37]

The Whole Box of Crayons

I've cautioned that we can confuse "bridging" as I use the term with wholly different kinds of results—such as adding or averaging, or simple oneness. Increasingly I draw on a metaphorical image that captures what the concept of bridging points toward in a way that is both more detailed and less vulnerable to misinterpretation. Take a box of crayons (see Figure 2-4). We can think of addressing human complexity with the needed greater awareness and depth of perspective as akin to consciously and effectively using the whole box of

---

36 See "Science and Religion" in the "Unexpected Rewards" section of Chapter Eight. Also see Chapter Eleven's sections on the future of science and the future of religion.

37 See "Creative Systems Theory Patterning Concepts" in Chapter Six.

crayons. The box represents the needed more expansive awareness; the crayons' multiple colors signify the new and deeper engagement with human complexity's multiple aspects.

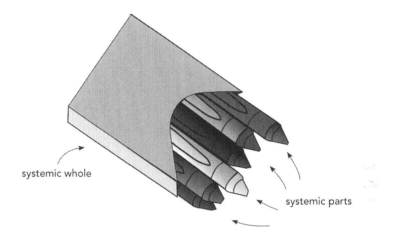

Fig. 2-4. Whole-Box-of-Crayons Systemic Understanding

The image is significant for how explicitly it represents Integrative Meta-perspective and the multifaceted, inherently generative, kind of engagement with experience that it produces. Whole-box-of-crayons perspective takes us beyond black and white—and even shades of gray—and draws consciously on the whole rich complexity of hues we manifest by virtue of being human. Cultural Maturity's cognitive changes make such whole-box-of-crayons perspective newly possible. With time they make it common sense.

As with the doorway image, the success of this box-of-crayons picture hinges on representational sleight-of-hand. The fact that each crayon is simultaneously a crayon and has its specific hue helps communicate the way parts in human systems are at once deeply interconnected and distinct. And the implied use of the crayons to draw suggests the underlying creative relationship that gives parts in human systems significance.

The box-of-crayons image provides a compact way of tying together this chapter's observations about systemic understanding and previous reflections about complexity and ideology. Ideology becomes what we get when we take one crayon (or a particular juxtaposition of crayons) in our creative systemic box and make it the whole of truth. That can be any sort of crayon—political, religious, gender- or temperament-related, or philosophical. And, as we shall see, that can be crayons as they take expression in here-and-now, us-versus-them ideological beliefs, or that manifest in the time-specific beliefs of cultural stages. Giving one crayon (or several crayons together) elevated status in this way distorts reality. But it also protects us by keeping complexity's larger and potentially overwhelming picture at arm's length.[38] What Cultural Maturity ultimately asks of us is that we learn to think, act, and relate from a place that draws on the entirety of our whole-box-of-crayons inner makeup—and engage in and understand the world with a similar kind of systemic completeness.

The box-of-crayons image also helps further clarify how "bridging" as I use the term differs from other outcomes we might confuse it with such as averaging, compromise, or simple oneness. Simple oneness involves siding with a crayon that identifies with unity. With averaging or compromise, we split the difference between two crayons, with the result being a mushing together or blurring of hues. None of these results require—or involve—the box's larger vantage. With culturally mature whole-box-of crayons perspective, the capacity to hold the system's larger complexity represented by the box provides defining leadership.[39]

A litmus test for this result highlights just how fundamentally different this outcome is and brings emphasis to its importance. We might expect that crayons that no longer get to be in charge might find whole-box perspective a threat and rally again it. But, at least with time, this proves not so. Certainly the system as a whole becomes more vital. But it is also the case that while particular crayons lose their past

---

38   When we project, we hand one crayon to some other system for safekeeping (generally in distorted form), and we ourselves become, in the process, that crayon's (equally distorted) opposite.

39   Concepts developed in later chapters will help further clarify these essential differences. See 'Parts Work' and 'Cognitive Rewiring' in Chapter Nine.

ability to run the show, at once each crayon's hue becomes itself more full and vibrant.[40]

That a box of crayons has a specifically creative purpose adds to the image's appropriateness. Creative Systems Theory uses the word "creative" to describe the way complexity's various aspects—including uncertainty, change, and interconnectedness—come together. Creative Systems Theory also proposes that parts of all sorts in human systems are creatively related. The box-of-crayons image provides a visual representation of how this works. We can think of it as a first-cut example of the specifically creative sort of "pattern language" concept that is Creative Systems Theory's contribution.

> A Threshold Lesson: When addressing complex problems or challenges we can make a good start toward the needed new post-ideological understanding by identifying not just pertinent polarities, but also the "crayons" that make up that particular system's multiplicity. These could be stakeholders in a watershed, departments in a university, different personality styles in a group, or worldviews in a global conversation. And we can learn even more if we can understand systemic parts not just as mechanically linked (where just adding parts together would suffice to describe the larger picture) but as aspects in dynamic—"creative"—relationship. Doing so alters both the answers to our questions and the questions we are able to ask in the first place.

A Powerful Surprise: The Myth of the Individual

Cultural Maturity's new whole-box-of-crayons systemic picture is in the end about nothing more than seeing in more encompassing ways—our needed new common sense. But while ultimately straightforward, as we shall see, it holds in store some significant surprises. One surprise with particularly dramatic implications concerns how we think about individual identity. Besides helping us more deeply understand who

---

40   Note the relationship between this result and my earlier polarity-related "paradoxical" observation that bridging increases our appreciation for both difference and relatedness. With any polarity, bridging in a similar way enhances each pole's vibrancy and significance.

we are, it helps make understandable what needed changes in how we relate to one another both personally and more collectively in institutions involve. It also provides some of the best evidence that a further chapter in culture's story is needed and possible.

It turns out that the way we have tended to think about identity is far from complete. The Modern Age concept of individuality is based on an ultimately partial way of understanding. Creative Systems Theory calls this misconception the modern *Myth of the Individual*. The Myth of the Individual has three parts. Our recognition of each part in different ways adds to our systemic picture of understanding and further ties it to a needed next chapter in our human story.

First is the assumption that in modern times we have in fact been individuals. I've described how we have before thought of both modern leadership and romantic love as expressions of individual choice. Indeed, we've thought of a new freedom for the individual in each instance as what most defined what was different from what we had known. With the beginnings of history's Modern Age, a world in which love's determinations were made by family or matchmaker and more authoritarian forms of leadership gave way to a reality in which we experienced—indeed celebrated—choice as laying increasingly in our hands. But, as you've seen with both love and leadership, this realization of the individual was illusionary, or at least partial and preliminary. In each case, what we had was two-halves-make-a-whole relationship. Being half of a systemic whole is not yet about being an individual, certainly not in any complete sense.

The second part of the modern Myth of the Individual concerns the common assumption that individuality as we have thought of it represents an ideal and end point. Because such "individuality"—the kind we saw with romantic love and heroic leadership—leaves us short of the sort of relating we need for the future, clearly it doesn't represent either. Being an individual takes on a fundamentally different meaning with Cultural Maturity's changes. Individual identity becomes about more consciously holding the whole of our human complexity.

The third part of the modern Myth of the Individual concerns a more specific way in which how we have thought about individuality ultimately falls short. It would be reasonable to assume that individuality, when fully realized, would be about finally becoming wholly distinct. A capacity for greater distinction is indeed very much part of what culturally mature identity gives us—culturally mature love and leadership each involve the ability to stand more wholly separate. But, as I've described, this capacity for great distinction is in fact only half of what we find. More consciously engaging the whole of our multifaceted complexity also alters identity in the sense that it deepens our capacity for connectedness. Whole-Person love offers the possibility of more complete and enduring love. And Whole-Person/Whole-System leadership in a similar way offers the possibility of deeper and more authentic engagement between leaders and those the leader represents.

The deeper connectedness that comes with Cultural Maturity's changes is in part a product of the fact that we bring ourselves more wholly to the task of relating—and are thus capable of engaging in fuller ways. But there is a further factor that expands on earlier observations about where Integrative Meta-perspective takes us. Along with heightening our capacity for difference, Cultural Maturity's cognitive changes offer that we might draw more consciously on parts of ourselves that appreciate that to live is to be connected—to others we care about, in community, with nature, and with existence more generally. (Later we will examine how the more nonrational parts of intelligence bring greater attention to the importance of connectedness.) This deeper capacity for connectedness cannot happen without first recognizing our fundamental distinctness. But this additional contribution is essential to fully realized Whole-Person identity and relationship.

The Myth of the Individual has pertinence not just to how we think about relationships and individual identity, but also to how we conceive of human institutions—of all sorts. Common assumptions about government as we know it make a good point of reference. We've tended to think of modern representative government—as with Modern Age institutions of all sorts—as final destinations. Part of the argument for this conclusion (if we need an argument—people at every cultural stage assume their particular reality is complete and culminating) is that modern institutional democracy is "government by the people." By this we mean government as an expression of individual choice.

But while certainly it is the case that Modern Age democracy involves greater choice than the governmental forms of any earlier cultural stage, the Myth of the Individual suggests that what we have seen thus far is individual determination only of a limited sort. We have not yet witnessed government by the people, at least not in the Whole-Person/Whole-System sense that the concept of Cultural Maturity proposes is now becoming necessary and possible.

Democracy in the sense of whole people taking full responsibility for their choices requires a further step in our evolution as choice-making beings. Previously I've observed several different Cultural Maturity–related changes that could contribute to a next chapter in government. I think specifically of stepping beyond seeing nation-states (and their institutions) as mythic parents, setting aside ideological polarization and partisan pettiness, and leaving behind mythologized concepts of leadership. We can now add one more that in an important way brings all the others together: Culturally mature governance becomes more authentically government by the people, government as an expression of human identity in its fully mature manifestation.

Culturally Mature Leadership: Further Surprises, Additional Paradoxes, and Why Any of It Matters

This chapter and the one previous have provided good beginning language for addressing where culturally mature leadership's new picture takes us (keeping in mind the inherent limits of both words and pictures). We can talk about the needed more sophisticated leadership in terms of a new relationship to complexity—as long as we remember that our interest lies with complexity of the more dynamic and encompassing sort, not just the mechanical complexity of interacting parts. We can speak of it in terms of thinking systemically, as long as we appreciate that our concern is the kind of systemic understanding that becomes common sense with Integrative Meta-perspective. We can speak of it in terms of bridging polarities—as long as we stay cognizant of what "bridging" is and is not. And we can speak of it as whole-box-of-crayons understanding, as long as we fully appreciate what the "whole box" entails and don't in some way confuse our favorite ideological crayon with the needed completeness.

But if we are to effectively apply this new picture to the tasks of new leadership, we benefit from some further, more specific observations. The most basic of complexity-related leadership questions gets us started: Just why is it so important that we get beyond ideology and think and act in more systemic—whole and nuanced—ways? We might easily assume that no explanation is needed. Getting beyond ideology would just seem something we should naturally desire. Who would not want a world in which leaders make more intelligent, and even wise, decisions? But things aren't so simple.

I've described how culturally mature perspective puts sacred cows of all sorts in jeopardy. And while we might think that conflict between ideologies is something we would inherently want to avoid, historically we've not had problems with either ideology or conflict. Countries that have traditionally been adversaries have derived identity and meaning from their animosities. And partisan adversaries in the political arena have commonly found self-righteous demonization, if not explicitly enjoyable, at least self-affirming. The end of ideology is no small thing, so much so that we can find it hard to imagine its possibility.

The most obvious answer to the question of why we should want to think and act more systemically simply acknowledges the risks we face if we don't get beyond the projections and mythologizings of times past. A lack of needed maturity in the face of today's often decidedly dangerous new complexities could very well be, if not the end of us, certainly the source of profound and unnecessary suffering—for decades, and perhaps centuries, to come.

We also face an ironic circumstance that comes part and parcel with where we stand in relation to Cultural Maturity's changes. With growing frequency, our supposedly protective ideological easy answers make our lives not less complicated, but more—and often dramatically so. The political sphere provides a ready example. I've proposed that today's knee-jerk partisan thinking both leaves us short of needed answers and undermines our ability to fully recognize the questions that we should be asking. One result is that critical decisions, especially those that involve really hard choices, get kicked down the road—setting us up for a future full of ever more difficult circumstances. And such unnecessary complexity is not just reserved for future generations; we also create it for ourselves in the present. Discourse that is based on ideology today more and more often gets tedious and convoluted in ways that share more with the melodrama of a TV soap opera or reality show than real governance.

Later, we will look at increasingly pervasive and dangerous complexities that are products of more general ideological blindness—not of partisan allegiances, but of simple-answer beliefs that most people share (we made a start with the footnote on climate change earlier in this chapter). In Chapter Three, I will describe how the gridlock that defines today's health care delivery debate has it origins less in policy differences than in shared ideological beliefs about health, and ultimately about life and death. In Chapter Seven, I will suggest that the second Gulf War would not have been instigated—or certainly would have been engaged with very different expectations—if our thinking, from both Right and Left, had not been limited by ideology, both nationalistic ideological beliefs and specifically Modern Age beliefs about how change works at a cultural scale. In Chapter Seven, I will also describe how the recent deep and prolonged economic crisis that put financial institutions and personal resources dangerously at risk didn't need to happen—how its origins lay with broadly held ideological beliefs about the nature of economies and, in the end, about money itself. With each of these examples, ideological assumptions that in times past helped simplify a complex world today make life more complicated—and in increasingly problematic ways.

While such concrete dangers provide the most readily grasped rationale for getting beyond ideology and thinking and acting in more sophisticated ways, there is also a more basic—and ultimately compelling—reason for doing so. Beyond the fact that the consequences will be dire if we fail to think more complexly, there is the fact that this is change "whose time has come."

It would be reasonable to ask, given the immense demands that come with culturally mature leadership, whether it might be best to hold off addressing some of the kinds of new complexity I've noted. The possibility of nuclear Armageddon or environmental catastrophe if we don't choose wisely certainly warrants immediate concern. But other changes—such as those I described in the previous chapter that relate to how we think about love, or the ways we experience art or the sacred—would seem to have less to do with dangerous consequences than with the simple fact of new possibility. Couldn't we do without these additional changes, at least for a while? We have a lot on our collective plates, and these further changes also make considerable demands.

But such picking and choosing is really not an option, however much we might want it to be. The reason is that these less obviously critical post-ideological, complexity-related changes form parts of the complete "idea-whose-time-has-come" package. I've spoken of the ultimate crisis of our time as a crisis of story, in the end a crisis of purpose. What it takes to make things work is changing. Equally, and inextricably related, what it takes for something to feel like it *matters* is changing. A big piece of what is new—and newly exciting—in today's advances is our ability to better acknowledge the fullness of our own complexities, and the rich complexities of the world around us.

In the end, what makes achieving a more mature relationship to complexity truly significant—significant at the level of ensuring a healthy and vital future—is the possibility of better getting our arms around not just specific concerns, but the larger whole of human experience. In doing so, we confront the ultimately defining challenge of revisiting our human narrative, of crafting a new, and newly powerful, cultural story. Any time we ignore or hide from timely possibilities, and particularly when we hide from such species-scale possibilities, we put ourselves in peril—such is our human nature. Deny an idea whose time has come for long, and not only do we lose out on opportunity, we do damage to our souls. Here we risk doing so in a quite ultimate way.

A Threshold Lesson: Maturely engaging complexity both helps us address otherwise overwhelming and dangerous circumstances and contributes directly to the broader evolution of culturally mature sensibility.

In confronting today's complexities, the culturally mature leader will encounter important new realities—many at first surprising—that each in its own way contributes to the argument for Cultural Maturity's changes. Here I'll note just a small handful. Each applies ultimately to dealing with new complexity wherever we find it, but I'll give particular attention to the topic I used to introduce this first threshold task: the importance of getting beyond partisan pettiness if government is to continue to serve us. I promised we would get back to the topic after we had more basic complexity-related concepts under our belts.

Additional Surprise #1:

For many people, the most surprising outcome with the challenges we have looked at is the whole notion that getting beyond the projections and mythologizings of times past might be an option. In the political sphere, given the extreme ideological pettiness we see today, the idea that greater maturity is something we might anticipate could seem particularly suspect.

But by this point in our inquiry, such maturity should at least seem a goal worth contemplating. It should also begin to seem a goal that could be realized. If political left and political right are appropriately seen as a systemic polarity, as I have proposed, then we find conceptual support for this conclusion from both our look at developmental mechanisms and our examination of Cultural Maturity's cognitive reordering. And we get more concrete support from systemic relationships of other sorts.

Fifty years ago, few people would have imagined that we would see the progress we've witnessed in rethinking polarities such as masculine and feminine in the politics of gender, mind and body in medicine, and us versus them on the global stage. If the bridging of traditional polar assumptions we see today is a reflection not just of specific insights, but of a broader cultural reordering, then we should be as likely to find that evolution happening with the polarities of political partisanship as with any of the other systemic relationships we have considered.

Additional Surprise #2

The next new reality—and further surprise—follows directly from the first and has particularly important implications for the tasks of culturally mature leadership. It has to do with how polarities relate. The important point with regard to opposing ideologies is not just that people with differing beliefs may better get along in the future, but that we will better recognize how it is that opposing beliefs can add one to the other. A related recognition can be even more of a surprise. In fact, such complementarity is nothing new.

I've proposed that polarity has always been part of understanding. Later we will look more closely at how it comes with the way cognitive processes work and how it has evolved in predictable ways over time. If we apply this generative picture of polarity's workings to the political sphere, we see how the relationship of political extremes has all along been something of an (unwitting) conspiracy. The new ingredient that comes with Cultural Maturity is not the fact of complementarity, but the necessity that we recognize it—this along with the capacity to do so. Culturally mature perspective frames positions in ways that allow complementary insights to result in fruitful policy.

This observation provides important insight into what decision-making on the other side of petty political polemics might look like. If we recognize that opposing positions reflect alternative systemic vantages[41]—even if at times we can barely grasp this fact—it is possible for debate to take on a more collaborative tenor. As a consequence, the recognition of new creative options becomes much more frequent, and effectively moving forward becomes much more common.

Additional Surprise #3

The third new reality provides an almost opposite recognition. It draws on this chapter's key observation that culturally mature systemic perspective, by its nature, increases our appreciation for both commonality and difference. Culturally mature perspective not only makes differences of opinion more tolerable, it makes actual difference of opinion newly recognizable. The consequences might seem even more surprising.

We can again draw on the political realm to illustrate. I've suggested that differing political opinions have never been opposite in the wholly distinct sense we have imagined them to be. In fact, it is when ideas are most vehemently at odds—when positions are most polarized and mythologized—that the least real difference exists. Positions then come to resemble two sides of a single coin in the most trivial sense. Know the position of one side of the coin, and the position of the coin's other side becomes totally predictable.

Note an important implication for debate: While we easily associate culturally mature perspective with simply being more respectful of differences, the result is, in fact, much more significant. When we cross Cultural Maturity's threshold and "bridge" political left and political

---

41 This conclusion applies only if opinions are conceived with basic integrity. Opinions that are meant only to thwart or demean have different implications.

right, we not only better see what we have in common, we also come to better recognize actual, real difference. Culturally mature perspective helps us appreciate how different political positions—at their best—can represent authentically different elements within the systemic whole of political inquiry and advocacy. Those who make a rallying cry of how different their views are from those of their political opponent should take notice of this important outcome. If you want real difference, you need to "side" with culturally mature systemic perspective.

This further surprise provides important support for my earlier claim that getting beyond political pettiness is not at all about political discourse becoming less animated, or even less contentious. Often the result is quite the opposite, in fact. What getting beyond petty polarization *is* specifically about is the political process becoming more consciously systemic, and through this, more overtly creative.

Additional Surprise #4

A last new circumstance should now be familiar, but because it adds a particularly consequential piece to the "why any of it matters" argument, it is worth highlighting. (And you may still find it surprising.) It follows from an outcome of Cultural Maturity's cognitive changes that I've emphasized repeatedly—how in the end the result is "common sense." Culturally mature perspective makes decision-making if not simpler, at least more direct and pragmatic. This is an essential result if present and future complexities are not to overwhelm us. And when we get beyond Cultural Maturity's threshold this is what we see.

This outcome follows from how Cultural Maturity's cognitive changes help us better get our minds around complexity. In particular, it follows from how culturally mature perspective helps us more deeply engage the specific kind of complexity that as humans makes us who we are. At least such complexity comes to seem less a foreign presence, more ordinary—"just the way things work." Culturally mature perspective also lets us engage and manage that complexity in more straightforward—and thus, in the end, simple—ways.

The box-of-crayons image helps fill out previous ways I've spoken of this result. When we conceive of identity, relationships, and truth from a Whole-Person/Whole-System perspective, we make our choices from the vantage of the whole box. Doing so requires that we "hold life large" and take more factors (crayons) into account. It is thus more demanding. But it is not complicated in the entangled and entrenched sense we so often find when such perspective is lacking.

When we identify with particular crayons, and in particular when crayons we identify with attempt to engage the crayons of other systems, simplicity abandons us. Experience becomes quickly convoluted and drama-filled, and we lose any possibility of useful solutions. This is the case equally whether we are attempting to make good planetary-scale decisions, seeking to provide leadership in our communities, or working to have healthy and fulfilling personal relationships. Whole-box-of-crayons perspective brings an elegance to understanding that has not before been an option.

Later, we will look at another way in which Cultural Maturity's cognitive changes support simplicity. I've introduced the importance of better appreciating pattern in complexity and how Cultural Maturity's changes make the needed new kind of pattern recognition possible. Such recognition of pattern provides new, more compact ways of thinking able to take great complexity into account.

Complexity, Ideology, and Culturally Mature Perspective— A Threshold Summary

Let's summarize where the first "threshold task" has taken us. Over this chapter and the last, we've seen how ideology has always before protected us from life's easily overwhelming complexities. We've also seen how, if we are to make good future choices, we must learn to step beyond ideological easy answers and better get our minds around complexity. In addition, we've begun to see how Cultural Maturity's changes make that possible. They provide the option of understanding and acting in more nuanced and complex—post-ideological—ways. We've witnessed how culturally mature perspective makes us better able to tolerate complexity and also helps us apply what we then experience toward positive ends.

I've emphasized that these results may not be immediately celebrated. Cultural Maturity's more systemic, post-ideological picture makes severe demands. But I've also emphasized that we really don't have a choice—the price for clinging to the protective assumptions of times past is too large. Cultural Maturity's more embracing acknowledgement of complexity will be necessary if we are to avoid cataclysmic global discord, adequately address the dangers of environmental destruction, establish effective global economic structures, or develop our increasingly networked informational capacities in ultimately beneficial ways. And it is just as imperative that we bring more maturely complex perspective to bear if we are to succeed with the most personal of human connections—whether with love and the family, in our communities, or internally, between the diverse elements that make up our individual identities.

We've also seen how the rewards go deeper than just helping us to choose more intelligently—or even wisely. A mature understanding of complexity helps us make fuller sense of order and meaning in every part of our lives. It helps us find wonder in our own personal intricacies and increasing fascination with the complexities of the world around us, even in the face of contradiction and apparent incompatibility. It also provides critical insight for addressing the essential task of rethinking our human story. A culturally mature relationship to complexity reveals how the diverse challenges that lie ahead for us reflect aspects of a compelling, even inspiring, picture of human possibility.

I return to my friend's question from the Introduction: Are we seeing the end of civilization? If we mean civilization in the sense of God-given ideological answers and "chosen people" identities, then yes, we confront the end of civilization. If we cannot leave such beliefs in the past, we will certainly suffer greatly as a result. We have no choice but to think more complexly. Complexity—and of the more dynamic and complete sort—is just how things work. It always has been. But before now we've not been capable of handling the depths to which this is so. Today our well-being, and perhaps our survival, is dependent on our ability not just to accept this more full and complete picture, but to embrace it.

The first of our threshold tasks has provided important supporting evidence both for the concept of Cultural Maturity and for the importance of the developmental/evolutionary kind of thinking on which the concept is based. You've seen how the degree of complexity we encounter today might seem beyond us to tolerate, much less to manage. I don't know of other ways of looking at what our times are about that so effectively explain how moving forward in the face of today's easily overwhelming complexities might be an option.

This first of our three tasks also provides valuable encouragement for those working to further culturally mature change. Certainly these observations have supported the conclusion that such efforts are in alignment with results that are possible, and that matter—deeply. But they also support the idea that even the smallest of efforts are not made in vain. While culturally mature perspective is needed to fully embrace complexity, it is also the case that each time we effectively take on complexity's challenge, our actions help take us beyond Cultural Maturity's threshold. This result applies to whatever complexity is our concern, but it also applies to understanding as a whole. Grappling with any particular complexity becomes a hands-on "technique" for addressing the tasks of Cultural Maturity more generally.

We now turn to the second threshold task and the importance of a new kind of relationship to limits.

Task #2

Confronting Limits

CHAPTER THREE

Recognizing the Power of Limits

Do not try to live forever. You will not succeed.
GEORGE BERNARD SHAW

THE SECOND THRESHOLD TASK confronts us with the fact of real limits. Like it or not, today we face a growing number of constraints that we can neither hide from nor transcend, no matter how clever or diligent we might be. Our times require that we bring a sophistication to how we relate to limits that before now would have been beyond us to understand, much less to realize.

Some of these limits involve inescapable physical realties—for example, limits to energy resources and limits to how much of the effluvium of civilization the planet can absorb. But many of the new limits we confront today are as much about ourselves: limits to what we can safely do in our ever more complex world; limits to what we can be for one another, whether as leaders or lovers; or limits to what we can control, and often simply understand.

In times past, we've tended to deny the fact of limits—for understandable reasons. Doing so has protected us from their often disturbing implications. But denying limits has also distorted our vision. Today, ignoring real limits has stopped being an option. The price we pay for doing so is more and more often simply unacceptable.

Effectively engaging limits might at first seem to involve a wholly different sort of challenge than that presented by the first threshold task. But in the end, what this second threshold task confronts us with, and also what engaging it successfully requires, is intimately related to what we've examined over the previous two chapters. In a similar way to what you've seen with how ideology has before protected us from complexity, ideology in times past has kept the fact of real limits safely at arm's length. And in a related way to how Cultural Maturity's changes help us engage complexity, culturally mature perspective allows us to more readily acknowledge and address inescapable limits.

Appreciating just how this works again requires that we step beyond usual ways of understanding. Indeed, effectively engaging limits challenges familiar assumptions in ways that can be particularly unsettling. Often it is unclear what should be done in the face of such limits—or if there is ultimately anything useful that can be done. Of the three threshold tasks, confronting limits most directly evokes fears that the end of civilization in a literal sense might be upon us.

But successfully grappling with the quandaries that the fact of real limits presents produces essential rewards. In the end, doing so makes it possible for us not just to better tolerate limits, but also to engage them in ways that can produce positive, indeed creative outcomes. It also offers one of the best ways to learn about the new, post-ideological common sense that comes with Cultural Maturity.

This chapter looks at the nature of new limits and what they ask of us. The next chapter examines how effectively confronting limits not only results in more intelligent choices, it reveals options that are otherwise not possible to recognize.

Health Care Limits

The second threshold task's extended example turns to the world of health care. The current health care delivery crisis presents a particularly good limits-related example, one that for me as a physician touches especially close to home.

We tend to frame the health care delivery crisis as a battle between approaches—such as single-payer versus free-market—and evaluate potential approaches by contrasting solutions used in other countries. But the fact of the matter is that no kind of approach, however and wherever it is applied, will work unless we are willing to more deeply confront limits. Over the last decade, health care costs in the U.S. have increased at five times the rate of inflation, and there is no natural end in sight. Health care expenditures threaten to bring down health care systems of every sort, all over the world.

Spiraling costs aren't really anybody's fault. The dramatically increasing expenditures we see are primarily a product of modern medicine's great success.[1] Early medical innovations—such as sterile technique and penicillin—were relatively cheap. More recent advances—such as sophisticated diagnostic procedures, exotic new medications, transplant surgeries, and more—have been increasingly expensive, and future advances promise only to get more so. But whatever its cause, this trend of escalating costs obviously can't continue indefinitely. It threatens not just the future of health care, but also the long-term viability of economies.

So how do we effectively address the health care delivery crisis? The answer is straightforward, but it's not something that we want to look at. Unless we are willing to spend an ever-expanding percentage of national resources on health care, we have no choice but to restrict available medical services—or, if we wish to be more blunt and provocative in our language, we must ration care. And we really have to do it. We can start with getting rid of procedures without demonstrated efficacy. But eventually we will also need to limit the availability of procedures that have real value. This is not just a matter of choice. Given time and ever more expensive future advances, the need to limit even care that provides demonstrable value becomes inescapable.

Rationing care puts before us a whole new order of ethical challenge. At the very least, not providing care when we have effective care to offer calls into question modern medicine's defeat-disease-at-any-cost heroic mythology. But the challenge is deeper. Restricting care demands a new relationship with life's ultimate limit—with death. Medicine has always been about life-and-death decisions. But limiting care demands that we consciously, in effect, choose death—at least in the sense of withholding care that might delay death's arrival. In the end, effective health care policy will require a maturity in our relationship with death that has not been necessary—nor, I would argue, within our human capacity—until now.

---

1   This is not to say that inefficiencies and the excesses of drug companies, insurance companies, doctors, and hospitals have not played roles. But such factors have not been the primary drivers, and addressing them, while essential, cannot by itself solve the health care delivery crisis.

One of the reasons I like health care delivery as an example is that it so pointedly illustrates how the conundrums we face in confronting ultimate limits are rarely just a product of external circumstances. More ultimately they are about ourselves. The health care delivery crisis is a crisis of resources, but as much it is a moral crisis and a challenge to what we believe. It is, in the end, a product of policies based on outdated ways of thinking—on our ideologies, if you will. The solutions consequently must come from changes in what and how we understand.

I have met few people—and in particular, few people involved in political decision-making—who recognize the full implications of the health care delivery crisis.[2] Current efforts at health care reform emphasize providing better coverage for the uninsured, giving greater attention to preventive care, putting medical records in electronic form, and conducting effectiveness studies for medical treatments. These are all good short-term goals. But the savings that might be accrued by these implied cost-cutting measures are much less than most people imagine. Eventually, we must confront more ultimate limits. What doing so asks of us will make other death-related policy issues such as abortion, assisted suicide, and capital punishment look like child's play.[3]

---

2   This includes people who take this crisis very seriously. Hilary Clinton's miscalculation of its difficulty resulted in a major failure at the beginning of her husband's presidency. Barack Obama managed to pass legislation, but it took much more political capital then he expected to do so, and I expect that the legislation's ultimate effect on costs will be limited at best.

3   The health care debate in the U.S. became particularly rabid and irrational during the 2009 efforts at reform. Conservatives at town hall meetings raged that liberals wanted not just a government takeover of medicine, but to "kill Grandma" (a reference to funding that encourages end-of-life directives, a most benign inclusion). The liberals adamantly argued that their proposals did not involve rationing. They were right—unfortunately—which only made obvious that they were just as much in denial about the limits we have to face. In fact, any proposal that achieves significant cost containment must include rationing. Notice that the extreme vitriol cannot be explained simply by partisan differences, however contentious political discourse today has become. Rather, this is the kind of blood-hungry fanaticism we encounter with other no-compromise, death-related issues like abortion and assisted suicide.

The questions presented by confronting health care limits are not just harder than we yet recognize, they are harder than we have been capable of recognizing up to this point in our development as a species. But they are the questions we need to ask if future heath care decisions are to serve us. The courage to ask such questions also supports the new and deeper—complex and wise—understandings that the future requires more generally.

In Chapter Four, with this chapter's big-picture limits-related reflections then under our belts, I will return to the health care delivery crisis. There I will describe how grappling with health care limits can result not just in more intelligent decisions, but also in a more vital and life-affirming relationship with the whole health care endeavor.

The Fact of Real Limits

We like to imagine that life is limitless. This is particularly true today. Television ads and popular culture announce that ours is a time "without limits." But while it is true that more is possible today than ever before, it is also true that never before has it been more essential for us to make sense of and respect limits. Our well-being—and perhaps even our continued existence—depends on it.

Confronting limits is nothing new. We could rightly say that doing so is exactly what the human story has been about. In first becoming human, we stood, defying the limitations of gravity. Later, we grew crops and built cities, confronting the limitations of scale presented by our hunter-gatherer beginnings. In the Middle Ages, we constructed grand cathedrals that reached toward the heavens. Today we send people into space, transcending the very bounds of earthly existence.

But what our time asks is often very different. A growing number of contemporary limits—limits to planetary resources, limits to ways of acting that in today's world become unacceptably dangerous, new economic limits, limits to what we can predict and control—are not conquerable, at least in the old sense. In times past, our task when we encountered constraints was to do battle. Today, we increasingly face limits that neither force nor cunning can defeat.

Successfully coming to terms with real—inviolable—limits will be essential to any future we would want to be a part of. Recognizing such limits and better understanding their implications should also play an increasingly central role in catalyzing the broader maturity of thought and action that the future demands. For many people, it is limits that first make the depth of the challenges we face inescapable—and the need for something like what the concept of Cultural Maturity describes impossible to ignore. Parts of the message are hard, sometimes very hard. Other parts can be surprising in the unexpected rewards they reveal.

I find it helpful to think of how Cultural Maturity's changes alter our relationship to inviolable limits in terms of a sequence of recognitions. First, by helping us step beyond protective beliefs, Cultural Maturity's changes help us acknowledge that such limits do indeed exist. Just this first piece is significant. We have a great capacity for denial, even in the face of irrefutable evidence. This is particularly so if the consequences of our decisions may not be immediate. It is also the case that many of the most important inviolable limits intervene at deeper levels than even the best of thinkers commonly recognize—as we see with health care limits and the ultimate need for a more mature relationship with mortality. Simple acknowledgement often gets us much of the way to needed solutions.

Second, culturally mature perspective helps us recognize that inviolable limits are not the adversaries we might at first assume them to be. When we hold life large—when we affirm life's bigness and complexity—we recognize that ultimate limits come with how things work. We would not have life without limits (cells need their limiting cell membranes); nor would we have almost anything we call beautiful (every painting has a frame, or at least a limiting boundary). Culturally mature perspective helps us appreciate that while dreams of limitlessness may help fire youthful enthusiasm, such dreams are fantasy and cannot serve us going forward. With the recognition that limits have a necessary role in anything that matters, we are less likely to run from their implications. We become more willing to acknowledge limits and seek ways to engage them creatively.

The third recognition is least obvious and takes several steps into culturally mature territory to fully make sense. Culturally mature perspective reveals how important possibilities—sometimes profound possibilities—can lie beyond seemingly impenetrable constraints. The book's next chapter will look more closely at this result, but the explanation is, in fact, familiar from the first threshold task. Put simply, we recognize new possibilities when we successfully address inviolable limits because they come part and parcel with the more culturally mature territory of experience that is revealed when we do so. Stepping into this new territory confronts us with a more demanding world. But doing so also presents new options—for the simple reason that what we encounter is more complete.

With this last recognition, our first two threshold tasks come together as aspects of a single challenge. Limits invite us to understand in the new, more systemic and, in the end, more option-filled ways that culturally mature perspective makes possible. Recognizing today's necessary nos makes newly comprehensible—and realizable—tomorrow's most important new yeses.

Acknowledging Limits

Given that acknowledgement is where we necessarily start, let's step back and identify a few significant inviolable limits as examples. My purpose with this listing is not to be comprehensive, only to give a basic feel for the variety of new limits. I've divided today's new limits into five broad categories: physical/environmental limits, economic limits, limits related to government and governance, social/psychological limits, and limits inherent in our modern definition of progress. These are crude groupings—they overlap each other and each includes limits of multiple kinds. But they provide a basic order.

Most of the limits we will examine are not in and of themselves new. Rather, for various reasons, they have now become inescapably important. Some of these limits have existed in potential, but we have only now reached the point at which they directly come into play. This is the situation with environmental limits and with economic limits of the sort we see with the health care delivery crisis. Others have always played roles in human experience, but gain full significance only with Cultural Maturity's changes. We find a good leadership example in inherent limits to what a leader can know and control.

With these brief descriptions, I will often make reference to beliefs that in times past have protected us from acknowledging particular limits. Later we will look at how it is in the nature of ideological beliefs that they make claims for limitlessness. We will also look at how the recognition of pertinent limits-related ideological assumptions helps us better appreciate what it means to address the challenge a particular limit presents.

It is important to again recognize that limits are rarely at first seen positively. Even this short list may leave some readers feeling that the wind has been taken from their sails, certainly that hope for the future has been called into question. These are important feelings to acknowledge and learn from. Later we will examine how each kind of limit, with further reflection, holds within its seemingly inescapable constraints the seeds of further possibility. But the place we appropriately start is simple acknowledgment—which means looking unflinchingly.

Physical/Environmental Limits

Physical/environmental limits are not themselves new, nor are the consequences of exceeding them new. They were, for example, the cause of the end of human habitation on Easter Island and the reason for many past human migrations. What is new to our time is the extent and severity of potential damage. The world's growing population,[4] combined with the fact that the larger portion of that population is just now becoming industrialized, dramatically amplifies dangers. Limits to resources—energy, clean air and water,[5] adequate food supplies—present some of today's most readily recognized obstacles to a healthy future. Diminishing resources undermine the health of societies. They also put economies at risk. And increasingly, they place nations that otherwise might peacefully coexist dangerously at odds. Biologist Edward O. Wilson put the situation with environmental limits bluntly in his book, *The Future of Life*. In his words, "An Armageddon is approaching at the beginning of the third millennium. But it is not the cosmic war and fiery collapse of mankind foretold in sacred scriptures. It is the wreckage of the planet by an exuberantly plentiful and ingenious humanity."

---

4   World population is predicted to increase by nearly a third—the equivalent of two Chinas—by 2050.

5   Many experts consider water availability to be the physical limit–related crisis that will most define this century.

The potential negative consequences of ignoring particular physical/environmental limits can be immense, and there is also the risk that specific limits will compound with others to produce truly catastrophic outcomes. For example, climate change due to greenhouse gases could result in widespread drought, with frightening shortages of arable land and all manner of social upheaval as consequences.[6] And it is not just ourselves who will suffer if we ignore limits. Like it or not, our success as a species has made us not just a particularly interesting product of the planet's evolution, but, at least for this brief period in creation, responsible for the continued vitality of that evolution. Over the last fifty years, we humans have changed ecosystems more rapidly and extensively than in any comparable time in our history. Wilson, in that same book, went on to propose that the extinction of species is the tragedy that future generations will be least likely to forgive.[7]

Part of what we see is a simple product of our success as a species, but much is also more specifically ideological. When we combine an Industrial Age "growth is good" mindset with Modern Age beliefs that cast us as wholly separate from nature and with appropriate dominion over it, what we witness today is a predicted outcome. Whatever the origins of this result, it is clearly time to get our planetary house in order—if there is time.

In observing ideology's role in blinding us to environmental limits, it is important to note that ideological beliefs can also get in the way in our efforts to preserve the environment. Stewart Brand, one of the early leaders of the environmental movement, in his book, *Whole Earth Discipline*, calls environmental leaders to task for too often being anti-technology and for an ideological narrowness that can cause them to

---

6   Current estimates suggest that even with the best of policies, greenhouse gas emissions could double by 2050. I'm comfortable acting on the assumption that global climate change is real and in largest measure a product of human activity—this in spite of the inability to know for sure (an additional inescapable limit). I will describe why I am comfortable doing so in the next chapter. The answer has nothing to do with whether we can be certain about global warming. It concerns instead how we best make use of data when we face limits to what we can know.

7   Over a quarter of the planet's species of mammals, reptiles, and amphibians are currently threatened with extinction. Current trends would result in the loss of one third of the world's species by the end of the century.

miss important big-picture implications of their advocacies.[8] He argues for a new "ecopragmatism." In their own ways, the political right and the political left each can deny physical/environmental limits, at least when it comes to what effectively addressing them will require of us. (This is a topic we will return to in the next chapter.)

Economic Limits

Economic limits take multiple forms, but they start with simple limits to what we can afford—as with the health care example. It should be increasingly obvious that our past "there will always be more where that came from" mindset cannot serve us as we go forward.

We also face economic limits tied to how economic systems work. The 2008-2009 financial collapse shone a revealing light on a handful of key examples. Most broadly, it brought into question the common belief that free markets could somehow regulate themselves. It also confronted us with a couple of more specific economic limits. We witnessed firsthand how perverse incentives lead ultimately to calamitous outcomes——something even the most rudimentary of systemic thinking teaches us. The financial meltdown was commonly attributed to investment bankers taking unwise risks. But from the bankers' perspective, their actions often really weren't risks at all—bankers would profit no matter what transpired.[9] We also experienced the inevitable

---

8   Luddite views toward technology along with the moral righteousness often seen with take-no-prisoners environmental positions (its extreme illustrated in the more vehement of animal rights advocacy) tend to represent more a flipping of the Modern Age man/nature polarity (which claims appropriate dominion over nature) than anything that supports the mature systemic perspective needed for good future environmental decision-making. (See "Polar Traps" in Chapter Nine.)

9   When banks were self-contained entities, bankers were conservative folks; if loans failed, bankers paid the price. Today, financial instruments that place the risks outside of the banks entirely make the incentive picture ludicrous and destined for the kind of consequences we saw. Perverse incentives are not limited to the banking realm. For example, they represent another major contributor to spiraling health care costs. Providers are generally compensated for quantity of treatment rather than quality of outcome. Given how feedback mechanisms work, the natural result is runaway costs.

consequences of allowing institutions to become "too big to fail." A basic understanding of systemic risk assessment makes it obvious that "too big to fail" should mean "too big to exist."[10]

Such flaws in past practices and assumptions raise a more encompassing and particularly provocative ideology-related question that we will later examine more closely. Let me raise it briefly now: It is reasonable to ask how such risks could have eluded our attention until it was too late given that we would have needed only the most basic grasp of systemic principles to recognize them.[11] I will argue that the reason has as much to do with ideology as with ignorance.[12] Here I mean ideology less in the sense of conflicting viewpoints than how our time's defining narrative mythologizes the monetary realm. How else do we explain the inability of the best economic minds to recognize what in hindsight were inescapable house-of-cards realities?

Limits Related to Government and Governance

We've previously touched on a number of important governance-related limits. We've looked at the dangers that come with "chosen people/evil other" beliefs on the world stage, and seen how the mythologizing of leadership and institutions—including the institution of government—distorts reality and can put us at risk. We've also

---

10   Along with banks that were too big to fail, we saw deregulation putting all sorts of entities that were also too big to fail into the banking business with little oversight. We confront related dangers, today, with corporations whose influence makes them functionally too big to regulate.

11   All a person would have needed to ask was, "What would happen if the price of housing fell 20 percent?" This is an obvious question to ask, given that housing market fluctuations greater than this have occurred in recent decades (in California and Japan, for example). What transpired follows predictably from how "positive" feedback loops (the kind of feedback that produces runaway systemic processes) inherently work. A housing price fall of less than 10 percent was enough to start the house-of-cards collapse (and eventually the fall exceeded 40 percent).

12   Or even with greed or deceit, though such ideology makes greed and deceit more acceptable. See "Values, Cultural Domains, and the Future" in Chapter Seven for a closer look at the ideological underpinnings of the economic collapse.

examined how the beliefs of both the political left and the political right fail the systemic test, and thus alone, or even together, leave us short of the sophistication needed for devising good future policy.

A couple of more specific limits-related issues will present critical global leadership challenges in the decades immediately ahead. The first has to do with the availability of weapons of mass destruction—chemical, biological, and nuclear. Efforts at disarmament are important and must be pursued. But they are very unlikely to result in some final elimination of weapons. More likely, at least in the short term, we will see continued proliferation, with deadly weapons increasingly in the hands not just of governments, but also of ethnic factions and terrorist groups. We have to accept that the world is often not going to be as safe a place as we might wish. Deny this, and we become vulnerable to reactive responses that in the end would make us even less safe.

The second issue concerns the inability of any government to effectively go it alone in the future. Major human challenges will be, with growing frequency, planetary challenges. Establishing effective global economic structures, confronting terrorism, addressing environmental destruction, or responding successfully to the threat of pandemic disease represent only a few examples from a very long list. Such planetary-scale challenges remind us that "no man is an island" at a whole new order of significance. Limits to going it alone gain additional significance with the humbling recognition that, at this point, we have barely a clue as to how to effectively carry out decision-making at a global scale.

Social/Psychological Limits

Many of the most important of limits we now face involve not so much what we do, but who we are. Limits to what any kind of system can be for another system provide some of the most striking examples. Limits of this sort are themselves not new, but Whole-Person/Whole-System relationship[13] makes a level of conscious ac-

---

13   I've defined Whole-Person/Whole-System relationship as what we get when two entities relate not through projection and mythologizing, but as systemic wholes.

ceptance of such limits necessary that we could not have handled before now. This is true equally with love (as seeing another person as the other half that completes us more and more often gets in the way of the experience of love), for leadership of all types (as we surrender parental images of authority), and for broader social bonds (as beliefs that mythically elevate our own kind suddenly make us less safe instead of more).

A primary function of mythologized interpersonal bonds, regardless of whether bonds are elevating or denigrating, has been to protect us from ultimately inescapable limits to what we can be for others and to what others can be for us. The successful realization of Whole-Person/Whole-System identity requires an acceptance of fundamental limits. I've described how the kind of authority we need if we are to address future tasks of all sorts must be more powerful, but also more humble. Part of what makes it more humble it is that it acknowledges the fact of real limits. That includes not just authority as we exercise it in the world, but just as much authority as we exercise it in ourselves.

Some of the most important social/psychological limits have to do with what we can control and predict. Again, such limits are not new, but they will have growing significance in a world where small missteps can more and more often have dire effects. At the very least we need to better acknowledge basic human fallibility. Like it or not, we human creatures, who pride ourselves on our insightfulness, frequently do dumb things—very bright people and trusted leaders included. In the end, it is much less likely that the human experiment will come to an end from an act of malevolence than from an act of ignorance or self-deception. Effective risk assessment is impossible without the acceptance of fundamental limits to what we can control and predict. Deny such limits and we will fail to ask the basic questions that a safe and healthy future will require.

We also confront more fundamental limits to what ultimately we can know. I hinted at this kind of limit when I made uncertainty one of the defining characteristics of the kind of complexity that we must now learn to get our minds around. This kind of limit was also suggested in my description of how Integrative Meta-perspective takes away our old objectivist, arms-length picture of knowledge. My assertion that the answer to the health care delivery crisis lies with a newly mature relationship to death provides a more concrete example of this kind of limit. To accept death is to accept also that it lies forever not just beyond our control, but also beyond our comprehension.[14]

Many theorists would make knowing's limits absolute. Physicist Max Planck expressed the extreme interpretation this way: "We have no right to assume that any physical laws exist, or if they have existed up to now, that they will continue to exist in a similar manner in the future." We could debate whether going that far makes sense (Creative Systems Theory suggests it does not[15]), but appreciating limits to what we can know will become increasingly important in the future if we are to make good choices, as individuals and as a species.

Limits Inherent in our Modern Definition of Progress

A final sort of limit is pertinent to each of the others, and particularly pertinent to our inquiry. We confront limits inherent in modern notions of what going forward entails. All previous cultural narratives have in their own ways proclaimed the absence of limits. Certainly they have regarded their own truths as final and determining. But our Modern Age cultural story has been particularly strident in its argument for the end of limits. Its key motifs—individuality, objectivity, democratic determination, religion based on a personal relationship

---

14   Religious beliefs through time have all provided us with answers to the question of what death brings. So has science, though what it offers— that our ending is just that—rather lacks poetry. But, ultimately, we don't get to know (or at least we have to wait to the end to know). Actually, if the previous chapter's conclusions about polarity and systemic understanding hold up, we can go a bit further. We can surmise that the question is in the end more interesting than just whether religion or science will ultimately prove correct. Culturally mature systemic perspective suggests that the explanations put forward by both religion and science likely each stop short of fully capturing death's significance—certainly to us.

15   At least functionally. The theory argues for the importance of understanding order in new, more systemic ways. Such order embraces uncertainty—indeed—ultimate uncertainty. But it is order in the sense that it supports useful prediction.

with one's God, the freeing of economic markets—all in different ways proclaim the throwing off of the limiting shackles of times past.

Our modern concept of progress is a direct expression of this specifically limits-challenging worldview. We tend to think that progress as we commonly describe it is an obvious and wholly rational notion. But as should become clear with later reflections,[16] our idea of what constitutes advancement is specific to our time in culture's story. And it is just as ultimately ideological as the defining beliefs of any time previous. Here, too, we confront limits, and of a particularly consequential sort.

I draw again on Thomas Friedman's thoughts on recent economic instabilities. In a related *New York Times* piece, he wrote, "Let's today step out of the normal boundaries of analysis of our current economic crisis and ask a radical question—What if the crisis of 2008 represents something much more fundamental than a deep recession? What if it's telling us that the whole growth model created over the last 50 years is simply unsustainable economically and ecologically and that 2008 was when we hit the wall—when Mother Nature and the market both said: No more." This dynamic may not have been a major factor in this particular downturn, but if the concept of Cultural Maturity is correct, it will be a factor eventually.

We can come at making sense of this particularly encompassing limit from multiple angles. Modern progress' onward-and-upward picture confronts limits most obviously with physical/environmental constraints. With the larger portion of the world's population just becoming industrialized, somehow we must create a new story that is physically sustainable in a way that past narratives were not. Economic limits understood broadly provide a further layer to the argument. We've come to measure social and individual well-being almost wholly in economic terms—such as individual "net worth," and rising GNP. Today we are better recognizing that a solely material yardstick is inadequate for measuring either personal worth or the health of societies—or even the stability of economies. This is not to call for some opposite, "small is beautiful" advocacy. But it is to call loudly for rethinking wealth and advancement in ways that more fully take

---

16   See "History—and Life—as a Creative Narrative" in Chapter Seven.

into account all that creates human meaning (and, more specifically, all that human meaning asks of us in our time)—an important future topic.[17] Later we will examine how continuing to cling to the past's "onward-and-upward" narrative would present a more fundamental problem: It would sever us from aspects of ourselves in ways that could have only disastrous consequences.[18]

Clearly there must be something important missing in how we have thought about advancement. I hinted at this in first introducing developmental/evolutionary perspective. Conventional thought limits our options for the future to going forward as we have, collapsing, or going back. But none of these options can produce vital and healthy outcomes. For now it is enough to note that Cultural Maturity's evolutionary picture provides a further kind of option. We have to think in quite new ways for where it takes us to be fully understandable. But when we do, what we see reframes not just the task of going forward, but our ultimate relationship to inescapable limits.

This collection of limits is sufficiently wide-ranging that a person could legitimately question whether I should be listing them in one place. But our various limits share three critical characteristics that make considering them together both appropriate and rewarding: First, we don't have the option of ignoring any of them. Second, all of these limits are inviolable—they offer no obvious way forward. And third, Cultural Maturity's cognitive changes make effectively engaging them now possible.

Clarifying the Task

To understand limits and the nature of the constraints they present, we need to start by distinguishing two kinds of limits with wholly different implications. When our response to limits proves unhelpful, often the reason is that we have confused one kind of limit with the other. The depth of disillusionment we can feel today in the face of limits commonly has this origin.

---

17   See "Truth's 'Crux'" in Chapter Five.

18   See "Progress and the Dilemma of Trajectory" in Chapter Eight.

Some limits are made to be challenged and transcended. Roger Bannister broke through the mile's previous four-minute barrier. The Wright brothers revealed that we might, like birds, escape earthly constraints. Limits such as these—to how fast we can currently run and to our options in the face of gravity's might—call for a heroic response. They are adversaries to be overcome. We appropriately celebrate if we succeed, and see ourselves as failing if we do not. This first sort of limit has a proud heritage. But it is not our concern here.

Our interest lies with inviolable limits. Inviolable limits are inherent in how things work and thus cannot be overcome. They have fundamentally different implications. A response that for the first kind of limit—the kind Roger Bannister and the Wright brothers shattered—would be bravery, for an inviolable limit becomes bravery's opposite: at best ignorance, and at worst, denial and cowardice.

This distinction noted, we are left with an essential question: If a heroic response is not appropriate to a particular limit, just how are we supposed to respond? The question is critical and the answer is not as clear and obvious as with limits of the first sort. Our cultural stories up to this point in history have been heroic, and our Modern Age heroic story—or it might be better to say "heroic/romantic story," to include both polar halves of its limits-denying picture[19]—has been particularly adamant in its claims for limitlessness.

Left to a heroic worldview, we can easily end up only depressed and cynical. A heroic worldview offers only victory and defeat as possible outcomes, and the fact of inviolable limits takes away the possibility of victory, at least as we conventionally think of victory. We can easily feel that we have no options. I suspect that the growing inescapability of inviolable limits, combined with our lack of historical guidance for engaging them, contributes significantly to our modern crisis of purpose. In a very deep way, many people today feel defeated.

The good news is that we do have options that can carry us forward, options that become increasingly recognizable as we step over Cultural Maturity's threshold. When we acknowledge inviolable limits, our relationship with them begins to change. Certainly, we better appreciate

---

19 Philosophically romantic beliefs, like heroic beliefs, imply limitless possibility.

that responding to such limits intelligently—factoring them into our decision-making—could help us avoid some of the worst of potential outcomes. We also begin to realize that limits come with the territory when we hold life large. And there are more specific rewards—rewards of major importance—that we may at least begin to recognize.

The analogy between Cultural Maturity and maturity in individual development again provides assistance. It helps us make sense of these further kinds of options and the possibility of more creative results. An individual life's first half is appropriately heroic.[20] With most limits we then face—those presented by limitations of strength or knowledge, those that manifest in self-doubts or emotional failings—our task is to defeat them if at all possible. But with second-half-of-life developmental tasks, this picture changes. A new and greater ability to appreciate what is possible and what is not is key to fulfillment in a lifetime's second half. The lessons we learn when we run up against absolute limits are often not initially celebrated. But such lessons are essential if our lives are to continue to be healthy and purpose-filled.

No theme more pointedly defines life's second half than the inescapable fact of limits, and limits that cannot be overcome in any traditional sense. Midlife, and the second half of life more generally, present layer upon layer of new constraints. We face new physical limits—to our strength and agility, to how young and beautiful we can appear. Life demands that certain of our dreams, often dreams closely tied to our sense of identity, be surrendered, or at least tempered. And ultimately of greatest consequence, midlife places before us, with an immediacy that would have overwhelmed us prior to this moment, the fact of our mortality. Most of us have before reflected on death, but midlife is the time when we first really "get it," first fully grasp our own death's inescapability.

This sudden barrage of new limits can seem to present no good options. If we deny that such limits exist, our lives become increasingly absurd—thin caricatures of youth. But if we do the opposite—give up life's good fight—the result is no better. To do that is only to become defeated and cynical. Neither side of the hero's traditional story—victory or surrender—captures the response that these limits require.

---

20   Heroic/romantic.

As with cultural limits in our time, it can be difficult to find words for what the inescapable limits so prominent in life's second half ask of us. But here are a few phrases that touch on aspects of what the needed more mature kind of courage involves: a more ready willingness to confront hard realities, an expanded sense of proportion and perspective, a new humility to what is possible and what is not, a fresh appreciation for contradiction, a deepened connection with the unfathomable, and a greater sense of what really matters and a fuller commitment to it.

What we can know for sure is that when we maturely engage such limits, life comes to feel more full and complete. We can also know that when we do so we begin to recognize that continuing onward offers further possibility—indeed, possibility with deep significance. Personal maturity's new limits can at first feel not at all welcome (and many never do). But if we can meet such limits creatively, addressing them clearly makes us more than we were. Confronting limits to our physical strength teaches us about using our strength in more subtle ways, and about ultimately more important kinds of strength. Confronting limits to youthful beauty reveals to us more enduring kinds of beauty. And confronting what may not be possible reminds us about what is essential. I've proposed "wisdom" as the term that best captures the task of life's second half. In limits, we find wisdom's greatest teachers.[21]

Although people in our time often struggle against the thought, the second half of life is as much as or more about growth than the first, and it is limits that often lead to the greatest growth.[22] Later we will look at how we can extend these observations to the way human

---

21 Death represents life's ultimate teacher of wisdom. Ask a simple question: When you get to the Pearly Gates—or whatever we get to—what will you most want to say about your brief time on this planet? No question more quickly reveals where meaning lies and better puts life's choices in perspective.

22 In contrast to how we revered elders in times past, we tend, today, to idealize youth and discount second-half-of-life contributions. Creative Systems Theory provides an explanation for this difference. (See "Personal Maturity, Cultural Maturity, and the Mechanisms of Wisdom" in Chapter Seven.)

formative processes work more generally.[23] We witness similar limits-related changes with the mature stages in human change dynamics of all sorts—in a simple creative process, with organizational change, in the common steps through which love grows and matures. Of particular importance for our inquiry, we witness them too at the level of human culture and its evolution. The mature stages in any human formative process bring a new kind of relationship to ultimate limits. Inviolable limits become more consciously accepted. Eventually, they become embraced.

Mature perspective—wherever we find it—reminds us that inviolable limits always have much to teach us, and not just with regard to the particular issues those limits relate to. Certainly, inviolable limits teach us about humility, reminding us with Wordsworth that "wisdom is often nearer when we stoop than when we soar." A bit more deeply, they teach us about proportion. I am reminded of Reinhold Niebuhr's often-quoted prayer: "God, give us the grace to accept with serenity the things which cannot be changed, courage to change the things that should be changed, and the wisdom to know the difference." More deeply still, inviolable limits help us see a bit more clearly what reality is about, and in an important sense what it has always been about—at least as far as seeing is possible through our human eyes.

A Threshold Lesson: Before responding to a limit we encounter, we need first to tease apart whether the limit calls for a heroic response, or if it is instead inviolable and thus requires a more mature kind of engagement.

Confronting Inviolable Limits

Grappling with any particular inviolable limit takes us through a predictable sequence of experiences. Appreciating this progression provides important guidance and also helps fill out our understanding of the ultimate implications of inviolable limits.

First, we tend to deny that a limit exists, or at least that addressing it will require anything new. Second, we may acknowledge its presence, but we tend to feel frightened and disturbed by what we encounter.

---

23   See "History—and Life—as a Creative Narrative" in Chapter Seven.

Third comes more overt acceptance. At least we recognize that ignoring a limit could have dangerous consequences. Later we begin to grasp how the existence of that limit, rather than being itself a problem, is inherent in how things work. Finally, we begin to appreciate how, if engaged maturely, that limit holds in its constraints the potential for options we have not previously recognized.[24]

Let's look at some examples that illustrate this sequence of experiences. Since environmental limits so obviously impact all of us, they make a good place to begin. Until recently, most people kept the challenges presented by our natural world's physical limits far out of sight and mind—in spite of ample evidence for such limits' inescapability. Even if people didn't ignore the existence of environmental limits, they assumed that future inventions would make the perceived limits irrelevant.

Today we tend most often to see the second kind of relationship to limits when it comes to the environment. People recognize such limits, but relate to them primarily as realities that diminish us. The fact that we acknowledge environmental limits represents a start, but ultimately more is required of us. If we see the task only as learning to do with less, we remain well short of a solution. Because most people find "doing with less" uncompelling as an ultimate solution—and appropriately so—even when warnings about environmental limits are heard, too often the warnings are not heeded.

Further recognitions are needed—ones we are starting to appreciate. At the least we need some version of the third kind of recognition, how environmental limits are less problems than inescapable aspects of how healthy systems work. In the end, we also need at least a bit of the final kind of recognition. We need to appreciate how confronting such limits head-on enhances the purpose and potency of our human experience.

This last kind of recognition fundamentally alters the conversation and reveals choices that before we might not have considered. It begins with the observation that thinking of resource limitations in terms of

---

24 Not surprisingly, this sequence follows the steps we commonly go through in grieving an important loss. Acknowledging limits always in some way involves the death of a once-cherished heroic/romantic dream.

"doing with less" captures only part of the picture. Confronting such limits challenges us to understand "more" in fuller ways. Certainly the mature acknowledgment of limits makes for a healthier planet, and that benefits everyone. But questions of resource sustainability (fulfilling one's needs without diminishing the options of future generations) also lead us toward issues at the heart of our modern crisis of purpose—questions about the nature of abundance (about when enough is enough). Such questioning provides a critical antidote to times in which what often most defines us, and links us, is how much we consume. The result is a new and deeper appreciation for the diversity of factors that make a human life rich.

This might seem like an idealized picture. But it is essential that it not be. If this picture is wrong, it becomes hard to justify being positive about the future. And in my experience, it is not wrong. People who choose to live more environmentally friendly lives most often, in the process, also choose to live more personally healthy lives, physically and psychologically. If they stick with their choices, they rarely describe feeling deprived. In fact, most feel quite the opposite.

We find the same progression when engaging limits to what one person (friend, lover, or leader) can be for another. Let's use love as an example. When people first hear of the possibility of more Whole-Person/Whole-System love, at first the notion may not make much sense—or if it does, it may still not seem particularly appealing. Initially, Hollywood's stereotyped picture of romance can appear much more attractive. Later, people begin to recognize the dangers that accompany making another person the answer to one's life—one's "other half"—but still struggle with the implications of leaving what they have known behind. They may grieve the loss of the romantic dream and the wonderfully comforting hope that they will one day find someone who will understand them completely. Eventually, they experience such loss as simply clarity and embrace it as an entry point to mature love. In doing so, they begin to appreciate possibilities that before they could not have recognized, much less realized. The old dream remains as a source of reminiscence, but only that.

We again see this sequence in how people commonly respond to today's more general need to surrender cultural absolutes and mytholo-gized beliefs. Initially it can be hard for us to acknowledge this loss of familiar social guideposts—and certainly to recognize the possibility that no new ones, at least of the absolute sort we have known, will appear to replace them. People often fall back on denial. But with time, we realize that what we witness is in fact the loss of a surety that never really was—the death of once necessary illusions. This may at first evoke only fear or despair. But as we step over Cultural Maturity's threshold, we see that what these changes ultimately mark is the possibility of more nuanced and embracing truths—ways of understanding that better speak from the fullness and wonder that comes with being human.

A Threshold Lesson: We gain important information when confronting limits-related challenges by noticing how far along we are in our relationship to the limit that is our concern. And we gain important information for confronting Culturally Maturity's broader challenge by noticing where we are in our relationship to inviolable limits more generally.

Cultural Maturity, Ideology, and Limits

How is it that Cultural Maturity's changes alter our relationship with limits in such fundamental ways? We can come at answering the question from several now-familiar directions. Earlier in the chapter, we looked at how our developmental analogy supports this general sort of change. With second-half-of-life maturity, limits take on whole new kind of significance.

Cultural Maturity's cognitive reordering similarly provides insight. We've examined how the result of Cultural Maturity's cognitive changes is a more complete, more fully systemic kind of perspective whatever the question we wish to consider. A more complete picture is going to incorporate limits for the simple reason that limits come part and parcel with the kind of system we have interest in. Limits are intrinsic to life, and certainly to existence as the specific sort of life we are by virtue of being human.

We can also turn again to the fact of ideology and ideology's function in the human endeavor. With the first threshold task, you saw how ideology has protected us from needing to deal with more complexity than we could before have tolerated. A related function of past worldviews has been to protect us from the maturity-demanding fact of real limits. A simple observation sums up how this works: Ideologies hide myths of limitlessness. Ideological beliefs, by their nature, argue that limits are illusory.

Recognizing this dynamic gets us a long way toward understanding how successfully engaging inviolable limits might produce the results that we see. It also helps bring together the book's first two threshold tasks and further clarifies how they represent aspects of a single challenge.

Ideology's limits-denying function is most explicit when ideological conclusions directly reflect culture's past role as symbolic parent—when they take the form of a time's generally accepted cultural absolutes. Parentally conceived truths are presented—and experienced—as omniscient and omnipotent truths. Whether manifest in culturally specific moral codes, my-country-right-or-wrong nationalism, or a view of technology that becomes its own kind of gospel, such beliefs imply an ultimate, and thus ultimately limitless, seat of truth.

We can also look to the heroic and romantic narratives of our most recent past to recognize this denying of limits. I've described how both kinds of narratives are, in the end, ideological. We can also recognize how each derives much of its narrative power from the way it keeps the fact of ultimate limits at arm's length. Heroic narratives are, in effect, defined by the conquering of limits. Romantic narratives take us beyond limits by providing magical solutions that eliminate obstacles and differences.

With postmodern narratives, we again straddle realities. Postmodern ideas, in their claim that truth is constructed rather than given, specifically challenge claims for limitlessness. They bring into question both parentally conceived absolutes and more specific limits-denying narratives, whether heroic or romantic. But postmodern ideas can also become their own kind of ideology—and claim for limitlessness. When we reduce the recognition that truth is multiple and relative to a picture that makes truth essentially arbitrary, the result is an argument that is limitless at least in its ability to get the last word—there is really no way to counter the conclusions of an all-doubting worldview. To the suggestion that further chapters in culture's story may lie ahead, the extreme postmodern advocate need only assert that this claim, too, is "only a construct."[25]

---

25 Which is of course true, but also irrelevant. The question is not whether a particular assertion is a construct—which every assertion is—but whether it is a useful and timely construct.

The previous chapter's reflections on polarity and complexity provide a more general way to think about how ideology protects us from the fact of real limits. We find myths of limitlessness whenever we confront ideological conclusions of a more this-versus-that sort, whatever the defining either/or may be—political left versus political right, masculine versus feminine, mind versus body, material versus spiritual, or good versus evil. Such belief always in some way proclaims that if we ascribe to the correct polar conclusion and try hard enough, all obstacles can be surmounted.

Sometimes the source of the idealized conclusion is a belief that the pole opposite to the one that we identify with is an enemy to be defeated—succeed and all will be eternally well: Good defeats evil and we enter the kingdom of heaven (at least if this is our particular religion's definition of good). Political left defeats political right—or the reverse—and ideological purity conquers all.

In other instances, the source of the perceived limitlessness is precisely the opposite. Instead of projecting our demons, we project images of ultimate truth. When we put leaders and lovers on pedestals, we are saying we believe that they have the power to make us ultimately safe and ultimately happy—however ultimately absurd this conclusion may be.[26]

Our box-of-crayons image provides a more multiplicity-acknowledging way to get at this more general relationship between ideology and limits. I've described how ideological beliefs take one aspect of some systemic entirety and make it the whole of truth. Ideological beliefs identify with but one or a few crayons in the systemic box. When a red, blue, or yellow crayon claims to ultimately define truth, it is also claiming that its significance is limitless—and by implication, that what it can make happen is limitless.

This close relationship to ideology and how we interpret limits has critical implications for leadership. When we find ourselves needing to

---

26 Our polar assumptions can also be more specifically dualistic—in the Cartesian sense—with each pole seen as having a part of the truth. Mind and body, or material and spiritual, depending on how we think of them, can each represent this kind of polar relationship. But here, too, at the least we remain in deterministic worlds (in which final outcomes are in theory predictable). And not uncommonly, one pole, or both poles simultaneously (however logically contradictory this might seem), get last-word-truth status. Here, too, myths of limitlessness, in the end, prevail.

confront inviolable limits, most often, too, we find ourselves needing to confront ideology. And when we don't recognize hidden belief-related contributions to the ways we experience limits, our efforts as leaders to address issues easily become ambushed by ideology.[27]

Appreciating how ideology and limits relate also helps us to more fully grasp where engaging limits ultimately takes us—and in the process why engaging limits is something we might want to do. I've suggested that what meeting limits head on ultimately does is make possible a more systemic holding of experience. We've also seen how culturally mature systemic perspective not only helps us better address critical questions, it reveals possibilities that are otherwise not visible.

The particular nature of Modern Age ideology adds an important further layer to the implications of ideology's role as we confront inviolable limits. I've described how ideology in our time makes particularly strident claims for limitlessness. This is the case whether the focus with Modern Age belief is individual freedom, unfettered markets, or technological advancements as our saving grace. Such belief, more than the beliefs of any time previous, specifically identifies with a human transcendence of limits.[28] One result is that our Modern Age story has protected us from limits with particular effectiveness. Another is that it has often directly pushed us toward the circumstances that make the need to address inviolable limits impossible to escape.

Previous reflections on the health care delivery crisis provide a good example. We looked at how health care's inevitable confrontation with limits is largely a product of increasingly expensive treatments. But we also saw how we find an equally important contributor in modern medicine's

---

27   Inviolable limits are not always hidden by ideology. Inviolable limits of endless sorts come with daily life, and most often we just take them in stride. When you leave the room you are in, you will likely not try to exit by walking through a wall. Instead, you will choose the door and not feel any the less for making this limits-acknowledging choice. But in times past, we have almost always seen (or more accurately, not seen) inviolable limits of any significance through the eyes of ideology.

28   Arguably, the beliefs of previous cultural stages even more directly identified with a transcendence of limits. But then it was gods and kings, not mere mortals, who had the transcendent power.

heroic mythology and the way it has made defeating death and disease—no matter what the cost—health care's ultimate calling. Such belief has at once hidden inevitable limits from us and hastened their arrival. It has pushed us ever more quickly beyond what we can afford.

We can recognize something similar with environmental limits. The need to address such limits follows in part from the fact of physical limits colliding with our audacious success as a species. But the environmental crisis is just as much a product of our Modern Age cultural narrative. We've comfortably treated the natural world as a resource that exists to serve us. Beyond how such belief has protected us from recognizing limits, it has also pushed us to the edge of environmental limits. I've described how our present circumstances—of dangerously diminishing resources and species in peril—given time, were inevitable.

In a similar manner, current economic difficulties are products not just of new economic complexities, but also of ways of thinking about human worth and human advancement that have stopped working. Certainly past ways of thinking have protected us from recognizing limits-denying blindnesses in our economic assumptions. But they have also pushed us to the brink in our application of those assumptions. Continued economic well-being hinges not just on better economic policy, but also on a more limits-acknowledging definition of the kind of advancement that we want effective economic policy to produce.

Modern Age ideology's dual role in relation to limits—how it has both protected us from the fact of limits and also driven us toward present circumstances—highlights the inescapable necessity of Cultural Maturity's changes. Certainly it supports the conclusion that the "antidote" when we confront limits of whatever sort is the same—the greater capacity to hold life large that comes with culturally mature perspective. But these observations also confirm that Cultural Maturity is not just something we may choose, or not, as we wish. There is really no fork in the road. In another way, Cultural Maturity—or something that accomplishes similar ends—becomes the only real option.

The Dilemma of Representation

Limits to what we can know have particular pertinence to the task of developing culturally mature approaches to understanding. One such limit noted earlier, what Creative Systems Theory calls the

Dilemma of Representation, highlights a key reason that culturally mature ideas can be challenging to articulate and to grasp. It turns out that conventional approaches to both pictorial depiction and to language fall short when we try to depict Cultural Maturity's cognitive changes and where they take us.

In part, the reason we confront the Dilemma of Representation is just that Cultural Maturity's new reality is truly new—old images and words aren't going to help us. But even more important is *how* it is new. Like it or not, culturally mature territory is not so readily described. Not only does the required new understanding not translate into familiar images and words, it doesn't translate well into images and words at all.

The fact that we encounter the Dilemma of Representation has nothing to do with the results of Cultural Maturity's changes being mysterious. Quite the opposite—it is a product of the necessary precision. But the Dilemma of Representation is very real, and essential to understand if we are to effectively address the challenges ahead. It intrudes whenever we wish to describe culturally mature concepts or results.

I made reference to the Dilemma of Representation in Chapter Two with each of the two images I drew on to depict culturally mature understanding. In using the doorway image to describe "bridging," I emphasized that the image necessarily involves representational trickery. We saw how while bridging might seem to be best represented by joining the two sides of the doorway's frame, bridging of the sort we have interest in requires something very different—stepping between the columns and into the new territory beyond. We saw, too, how the box-of-crayons image employs a related sleight-of-hand. The crayons' differing hues, along with the implied presence of the artist's hand, are what make the representation work.

Creative Systems Theory calls images that succeed in this way "three-plus" representation. They use two dimensions (that imply three) to depict phenomena that three dimensions alone cannot capture. Good three-plus images are rare. I am always delighted when I find one that works.

Philosopher and semanticist Alfred Korzybski pointed toward the related conundrum when it comes to language early in the last century and tied it specifically to the demands of systemic understanding. In his words: "Any organism must be treated as-a-whole.... It is seemingly little realized, at present, that this simple and innocent-looking statement involves a full structural revision of our language."

A good way to recognize how the Dilemma of Representation applies to language is to try to verbally articulate any conclusion that bridges polarities. We can effectively use words to speak about how we have traditionally thought about the mind or the body, about leaders or followers, or about the political left or the political right. But attempt to talk about minds and bodies, leaders and followers, or political extremes more systemically and conventions of language quickly break down. We can talk of having "mind/bodies" or applying "participatory leadership," but the messy vagueness only serves to emphasize the inadequacy of conventional language for the task at hand.

Voicing any culturally mature concept or conclusion requires careful attention to how we use words. The most obvious reason follows from the cognitive complexity—the interplay of intelligences—that culturally mature thought necessarily draws on. The world as seen through intelligences other than the rational does not so readily translate into words (though poets often do admirably well). The particular challenge that Integrative Meta-perspective presents with regard to intelligence—how it requires that we engage experience with the whole of human sensibility applied in a conscious and systemic fashion—produces results that even more fundamentally confound conventional discourse. (Here poets and pundits are left equally in a quandary.)

The common structure of language further highlights the representational difficulties words can present. Conventions of grammar are products of their times in culture, and this is no less true with modern usage. A prime example concerns sentence structure. We have two basic kinds available to us, each of which implies a certain kind of causality. "Active" constructions imply mechanistic causalities (the cue strikes cue ball and drives the five ball into the corner pocket). We also have "passive" constructions that emphasize simple connectedness (a rose is a rose). The causalities that order complexities of the dynamic, systemic sort we have interest in here can't be fully captured by either kind of description.

The Dilemma of Representation has influenced the writing of this book in multiple ways, often behind the scenes. Besides the specific use of three-plus depiction, I've taken great care with how I have used language, often phrasing statements in unusual ways. I've been careful that my style of writing doesn't suggest relationships and causalities that run counter to what I am trying to communicate.

I've also drawn more extensively on metaphors and figures of speech than one would expect in a book that is this theoretically rigorous—for example, in using phrases like "the whole ball of wax," "holding life large," and "getting our minds around a question's complexity" to imply systemic understanding. Because metaphors and figures of speech draw on multiple intelligences, common language can sometimes communicate better than we might think. But just as with language more generally, we have to choose our metaphors and figures of speech well and apply them precisely. Those that work most effectively in some way imply three-plus representation.

Earlier, in making reference to the familiar story of the blind men and the elephant as a way to introduce systemic understanding, I implied that it most reflected systemic perspective of the more traditional sort. Actually, it does more than this. The story makes reference to multiple systemic aspects—an ear, a trunk. But it is the fact that these are aspects of a living organism—and a dramatic one that moves—that ultimately makes the image work.[29] The "bicycle" metaphor I used in the introduction works not just because we are familiar with the function of training wheels, but also because of the almost magical way centrifugal force keeps a bicycle upright.

One of the approaches I've used to get around the Dilemma of Representation is particularly pertinent to making sense of where Cultural Maturity's changes takes us. I've frequently drawn attention to how culturally mature understanding confronts us with apparent contradiction. I've described how culturally mature conclusions can be thought of as both more complex and simpler than what they replace, noted how Cultural Maturity's changes increase our appreciation for both difference and connectedness, and observed how culturally mature perspective makes us at once uncompromisingly respectful of real limitation and also able to see beyond such constraints. Recognizing such apparent contradiction doesn't eliminate the Dilemma of Representation. But it points toward the

---

29   Squares on a checkerboard would not work nearly so well.

existence of a more encompassing picture. It also helps us make our way without giving one side of a particular apparent contradiction undue influence.

Along with further highlighting the conceptual stretch that culturally mature understanding requires, the Dilemma of Representation also provides a useful tool for evaluating the success of efforts toward such understanding. Mechanistic formulations can be complicated, but we don't have any problem representing them as long as our depictions have sufficient detail. Ways of thinking that emphasize connectedness and ultimate oneness can't be represented, but the reason is wholly different from what we encounter with culturally mature systemic conception—making mystery primary makes ultimate truth invisible. Culturally mature truths defy representation not because they are invisible, but because they are more inclusively substantive than conventional representation can depict. It is important to learn to distinguish these two very different kinds of representational difficulties, and with a little practice it is not hard to do so.

The Dilemma of Representation can't be escaped. And it comes into play not just when we wish to depict human systems. For example, biology confronts it when it when it fails in its attempts to articulate just what makes life alive. And we face this same quandary in physics with the impossibility of conventionally representing the concepts of Quantum Mechanics. Does the Dilemma of Representation then represent something inherent in existence? What we can know for sure is that this difficulty inherently accompanies how we are coming to understand—though we would hope that changes in how we understand are taking us at least a bit closer to thinking in ways that reflect how things actually work.

We could easily think of the Dilemma of Representation as a problem. Certainly it makes both understanding and communication more difficult. But in the end, what the Dilemma of Representation does is alert us to the more sophisticated kind of thinking we have interest in. Limits to articulation, both verbal and pictorial, remind us how much such thinking necessarily stretches us. But they also remind us how much stepping forward into Cultural Maturity's new world of experience offers in return for our effort. The Dilemma of Representation affirms just how remarkable life's complexities can be.

It also affirms the significance of the kind of new understanding needed if we are to effectively address the often overwhelming and frequently contradictory, limits-permeated challenges the future presents.

What Limits Ask of Us

The relationship between Cultural Maturity and limits should now make basic sense. So should what confronting inviolable limits demands of us and, at least a bit, where doing so ultimately takes us.

When we approach Cultural Maturity's threshold, we begin to better appreciate the fact of real limits. At first, on recognizing this result, we are unlikely to celebrate it. But as we proceed forward, at least the fact that ignoring limits is not an option becomes clear. It also becomes clear that the existence of limits is not by itself a bad thing. Cultural Maturity's more encompassing vantage helps us understand how limits play essential roles in most anything that matters to us.

With time, culturally mature perspective provides the subtlety of understanding required for us to effectively make our way in a world with real limits. It helps us think in ways that take real limits into account. And that same subtlety of understanding makes possibilities recognizable that were not previously there to see.

Beyond Cultural Maturity's threshold, it is our old ways of thinking with their implied dreams of limitlessness—however modern and cutting-edge they might have seemed—that become limiting.

CHAPTER FOUR

The Wisdom of No—Celebrating Mature Possibility

The universe is full of magical things,
patiently waiting for our wits to grow stronger.
BERTRAND RUSSELL

THE MOST BASIC OF THE NEW LIMITS-RELATED RECOGNITIONS that come with Cultural Maturity's changes become pretty self-evident with reflection. Certainly this is the case with the importance of getting beyond denial and acknowledging the fact of inviolable limits. We will obviously pay a high price if we do not acknowledge limits intrinsic to our planet, to our technologies, and to ourselves. The recognition that inviolable limits are less adversaries than just part of how things work may at first make us pause, but it, too, in the end is straightforward. Fantasy and wishful thinking ignore limits, but conclusions derived from such beliefs are trivial at best. To reach truth in any situation—the real stuff—we must include the fact of life's ultimately inescapable constraints.

The final recognition—how effectively confronting inviolable limits can reveal new possibilities—should now begin to make sense, but it could still cause confusion. Certainly, it can seem contradictory. The fact of limits would seem to restrict possibility—that is a big part of the reason that historically we've preferred not to acknowledge them. Shouldn't engaging limits, then, only make such restrictions more obvious?

My intent with this chapter is to make the fact that successfully confronting inviolable limits increases possibility more clearly understandable.

It is essential that this outcome make sense to us. The promise of new possibility is important ultimately to our willingness to acknowledge inviolable limits in the first place. We must have good reason to engage inviolable limits if we are to make the effort, and we find a particularly compelling reason in such new possibilities.

I will begin these additional observations by reflecting a bit more deeply on how new possibility is a direct product of Integrative Meta-perspective and the more systemic picture that comes with Cultural Maturity's changes. Then, to more fully flesh out the nature of such new possibility, we will venture more directly into Cultural Maturity's world of experience. I find it helpful to think of the new possibilities that come with confronting inviolable limits as an unfolding sequence. Most immediately, confronting limits helps us think more clearly and intelligently, whatever our concern. Step a bit further over Cultural Maturity's threshold, and we start to be not only smarter in our decisions, but also more creative, to recognize options that previously were not there to see. Step further still and we begin to bring more overarching perspective, and even wisdom, to our choices. We will explore examples that reflect each step in this sequence.

I will then return to a topic touched on earlier that provides particular insight into how a culturally mature relationship to limits increases possibility. In Chapter One, I noted that the kind of complexity we have interest in requires that we take into account not just a lot of parts, but also uncertainty, change, and interconnectedness. I also promised to later examine how each of these additional aspects of complexity itself needs to be understood in new, more dynamic and complete ways. Here I will describe how each of these aspects of complexity confronts us with inherent limits to understanding. I will also describe how, when we put these aspects together, the result is not just a more complete picture of how things work, but a more possibility-filled, specifically creative picture.

Finally, we will examine some of the implications of the book's limits-related reflections for future leadership. Culturally mature leadership requires a keen sensitivity to limits. We will give special attention to how such sensitivity becomes particularly important when our leadership task involves not just good decision-making, but also advocating for culturally mature changes in the world around us.

Limits, Complexity, and Possibility

The previous chapter's observations supported the conclusion that positive outcomes, at least, are a reasonable expectation when we confront inviolable limits. A more sustainable relationship to either physical or economic limits obviously benefits us, as does a more accurate sense of our own limits when we are making decisions. And the fact that new possibilities might be a consequence was certainly implied. For example, we looked at how the Whole-Person/Whole-System kind of relating that becomes an option when we are able to accept limits to what we can be for others—and what they can be for us—results in the possibility of more sophisticated kinds of human connections, whether between lovers, between leaders and followers, or between nations.

We also caught at least a glimpse of why we might see new possibility. The explanation follows from the assertion that makes limits an appropriate concern of this book: Confronting inviolable limits challenges us to engage Cultural Maturity's threshold and to begin to step over it. When we do, we start to recognize the further possibilities inherent in a culturally mature world.

Linking reflections from previous chapters about systems thinking, ideology, complexity, and limits helps add conceptual refinement. We find that the "contradictory" fact of new possibility becomes perfectly logical—as long as we recognize that we need the logic of systems for such new possibility to fully make sense.

For example, we've examined how ideology not only restricts our ability to recognize complexity, it also makes claims of limitlessness. We might think that dreams of limitlessness would increase possibilities. But when ideology hides some limit from us, it also hides from us the more systemically complete reality in which that limit is embedded. In doing so, in addition it hides from us the greater possibility that accompanies that more complete reality.

The way our understanding of complexity changes once we step over Cultural Maturity's threshold hints at how we should encounter not just new possibility, but often intriguing surprises. We've seen how our interest ultimately is not just complexity in the sense of many parts to consider, but complexity of a more dynamic and complete—indeed, ultimately creative—sort. When we effectively confront inviolable limits and begin to better appreciate possibilities that were before hidden by past distorting stories, often we discover that these are possibilities that before now would have made no sense to us.

The concept of bridging provides support for this possibility-affirming—and surprise-affirming—picture. I've described how polarized beliefs protect us from limits. When we bridge any polarity, we bridge not just opposing positions, but two opposing claims of limitlessness. Often what first alerts us that something is missing in our thinking is the recognition that some such implied claim doesn't hold up—for instance, the claim that a leader has all the answers or that an enemy is the cause of all our problems. If we continue our questioning, the result is a more systemic picture that reveals the claims for limitlessness implied by each side of our original polarity to be groundless. The resulting more systemic picture also invites a new, more dynamic, rich—possibility-filled, and often surprise-filled—kind of understanding.

The box-of-crayons metaphor provides a bit more detail. Any "crayon" in isolation, whether it reflects half of a polarity or one aspect of a more multifaceted systemic complexity (such as one of the various stakeholders in a watershed), may claim limitless significance for its particular vantage. With whole-box-of-crayons understanding, we acknowledge the limits intrinsic to any single-crayon perspective and also come to better appreciate limits more generally. In doing so, because we are better able to see complexity without the distorting lens of mythologized belief, we recognize new, more intelligent choices. And because whole-box-of-crayons systemic perspective allows us to appreciate complexity of our more dynamic and complete sort, we become newly able to recognize options that are not just more intelligent, but more explicitly creative, and, in potential, also more wise.

The way our Modern Age narrative, with its particularly adamant limits-transcending claims, elevates the word "freedom" points toward a simple way of understanding the new possibility that commonly lies hidden beneath inviolable limits. Freedom is a great word and historically has provided important inspiration. Few words are at once so heroic and so romantic in their implications. And few words seem to so obviously be about achievement of an ultimate sort.

But, more often than not, we use the word in a way that is, in the end, ideological—we identify freedom with the absence of constraining limits.

Certainly this is the case when "freedom" becomes a rallying cry. More accurately, freedom in the sense of the absence of constraint is one half of a polarity—freedom on one hand juxtaposed with limitation on the other.

While it is very much the case that we have more options today than at previous cultural stages, if freedom is to continue to be a useful concept, we must learn to appreciate how the real thing always exists within an array of context-related limits—indeed, freedom makes no real sense separate from such limits. In the end, the common ideological use of the word "freedom" falls short in the same sense as our Modern Age concept of the individual falls short. We could similarly speak of a Modern Age "myth of freedom," and the need for a newly mature and systemically complete grasp of what freedom is ultimately about.

In an important sense, this chapter's reflections on limits and new possibility are about redefining freedom, about understand freedom in a way that can again make it a useful concept. With Cultural Maturity, freedom increases. But it is freedom in the specifically creative—and newly wise—sense that becomes greater when we effectively confront inviolable limits.

Limits and New Capacities: Assessing Risk

The sequence of new possibilities noted earlier starts with how confronting inviolable limits helps us to think more clearly and thus to make more intelligent choices. Mythologized perceptions may titillate and provide reassurance, but they also distort what we see. When we confront inviolable limits, we also come to see more accurately.

The importance of effectively evaluating risk—and the way in which a more culturally mature relationship to limits helps us do so— provides a good illustration. Effective risk assessment requires that we acknowledge limits of the more obvious, physical sort—such as limits to the ability of a building or a bridge to withstand an earthquake. It also requires that we confront limits that are more about ourselves, such as limits to what we can control or to what we can know in advance. Culturally mature perspective helps us evaluate risk free of ideological beliefs that in times past have served to protect us from fully acknowledging real limits of all these sorts.

Distorted interpretations of risk cause problems in two opposite ways. They can cause us to underestimate risk and not take needed action.

Or, just as readily, they can cause us to overblow potential dangers and take unnecessary, and perhaps even dangerous, actions.

We witness an example of the first kind of result today with climate change. A person makes the accurate, limits-related observation that we can't know with absolute certainty that global climate change is real and then uses it to justify not responding to the threat. I often ask people who resort to such logic what they think the odds are that human-caused warming of the planet is happening and could have dangerous consequences. I make them commit to a number. I then ask them how they would feel about their children playing Russian roulette. Few people are willing to claim that the odds of global warming being real and significant are less than Russian roulette's one in six. And the few who might maintain this claim have a hard time escaping the recognition that their conclusion has more to do with ideology than carefully considered evaluation.

Distorting risk in the other direction—overblowing its significance—can get us into just as much trouble. We see this tendency today with terrorism. Terrorism-related content is ever-present in the news, and terrorism-related fears commonly determine social policy. Yet an individual in the U.S. is hundreds of times more likely to be killed by a car when crossing the street than by a terrorist. This is not to make light of terrorism; terrorism should become an increasing concern as globalization brings diverse peoples into ever closer proximity. But we need to take great care when we observe such distortion of perspective. Fear makes us extremely vulnerable to poor decision-making and manipulation.

Calamitous events such as the 2011 nuclear accident at the Fukushima Daiichi nuclear power plant following the earthquake and tsunami in Japan, and the 2010 Deepwater Horizon oil disaster in the Gulf of Mexico highlight the growing importance of accurately evaluating risk. In each case, safety concerns were overlooked that could have made the results very different. The Fukushima and Deepwater Horizon events also bring attention to a broad arena—the energy crisis—that in times ahead will require immense responsibility and particularly sophisticated systemic assessment.

The energy crisis presents an especially complex and tricky array of risks and benefits. We have to take into account not just the physical risks and direct costs associated with various energy sources—fossil fuel, wind and solar power, hydropower, nuclear power, and more—but also the effects that moving faster or slower in developing them might have on the health of economies (which in turn affects our capacity to devise new energy technologies and to mitigate environmental damage). And ideological beliefs of all sorts come into play—and not just those that may deny the more obvious kinds of limits. For example, it is becoming increasingly apparent that we must take seriously the idea that nuclear power needs to be a part of the solution, at least short-term—a conclusion that few environmentalists happily acknowledge.[1]

The future will require us to make intelligent choices in the face of a growing array of human activities that involve both significant uncertainty and very real danger. We must learn to always ask two kinds of limits-related questions: First, could failure produce a level of carnage beyond the acceptable? (We need to examine worst-case scenarios and be sure that moving forward at all is wise.) Second, if we choose to move forward, what can we do to minimize the risk of failure and to lessen consequences if failure occurs? Given the potential for both great harm and great benefit that comes with so much of modern advancement, making sure that both kinds of questions are always asked (and that the influence of money does not get in the way of thorough assessment) has become an inescapable human responsibility.

Culturally mature perspective, along with making us more able to evaluate systemic risk, also makes possible new kinds of limits-related concepts that support us in doing so. Later we will look at one example, the Creative Systems Theory concept of *Capacitance*.[2] Capacitance describes the amount of complexity we as systems can tolerate—think of a balloon that, if filled too full, risks bursting. The concept offers us a

---

1   Including myself. Earlier in my life I helped lead efforts to stop nuclear power plant construction. I think it would be wonderful if renewable energy sources by themselves could be sufficient. But the numbers make clear that this result will be very hard to achieve any time soon. The nuclear power conversation is at the very least an important conversation to be having.

2   See "Creative Systems Theory Patterning Concepts" in Chapter Six, and "Capacitance" in Chapter Nine.

generic way to think about human limits that makes a wide array of psychological behavior more understandable and provides important guidance for living healthy lives. Attention to Capacitance is also per-tinent to leadership in larger systems. When any system gets pushed beyond its Capacitance, culturally mature decision-making becomes essentially impossible.

A Threshold Lesson: Recognizing limits, particularly limits to what we can know, control, and tolerate, is essential to choosing intelligently between options.

Limits and Newly Creative Possibilities: Rethinking Health Care Delivery

We next turn to how acknowledging limits not only helps us choose more intelligently between options, doing so helps us recognize more creative and ultimately helpful options. I've previously implied this fur-ther result in describing the way limits often have important lessons to teach—for example, how physical/environmental limits teach us about sustainability, how the recognition of psychological/social limits to what we can be and do encourages deeper levels of self-reflection and self-understanding, and how limits to going it alone in the face of global-scale leadership concerns remind us that "no man is an island."

The reason that confronting inviolable limits reveals new, more creative options is in the end the same as the reason that it supports choosing more intelligently between familiar options: Culturally mature perspective allows us to more fully draw on ourselves as complex systems. We become able to recognize more systemic options, and because such options are more complete, often they are also more creative. Once we've progressed a solid step into culturally mature territory, such more creative options become obviously important, increasingly intriguing to consider, and more and more available to act on.

The health care delivery example provides a particularly good illustration of how this works. Previously, I described two related kinds of inviolable limits that are inextricably tied to the health care delivery crisis: economic limits, and life's ultimate limit—the fact of our mortality. If we are to deal with spiraling costs, we need first to acknowledge that economic limits are inescapable. We also need to recognize that addressing economic limits will require that we find a more mature alternative to modern medicine's traditionally heroic relationship to death. I've proposed that neither more centralized, managed care structures nor more free-market health care approaches will work if we don't confront these two fundamental constraints.

The larger, more complex picture implied by a deep acknowledgement of health care limits requires much more of us than do the steps that we today most often emphasize in addressing the health care delivery crisis. We need to address inefficiencies wherever we can find them, certainly. We also need to curb the more egregious of health care excesses. But there is very much a larger picture. And while that larger—more systemic—picture greatly expands the challenge, it also reveals some of the greatest rewards.

One of the best ways to see such rewards is to examine the way in which confronting health care limits leads to addressing concerns that go beyond health care delivery per se. Confronting health care limits should contribute to increasingly mature and empowering insights regarding not just access to care, but also what it takes to be healthy, what it means to heal, and, more broadly, the requirements of a healthy society.

A health-care-limits exercise I've done with leaders at the Institute for Creative Development predictably produces this kind of expanded perspective. The exercise starts with me giving the group I'm working with a budget along with a handful of patient biographies. The biographies include information not just about age and presenting illnesses, but also about the patient's family and work history, self-care variables such as smoking and exercise, and more general observations about what the person has done with his or her life. I lock the group in a room for a couple of hours with instructions to come back with a breakdown of how they will spend the budget, and also with descriptions of how they reached their decisions. I emphasize that the wrenching predicament I have put to them is more than just some interesting exercise, that it reflects the inescapable choices we face as societies if we are not in total denial (and which we face covertly even if we are in denial).

The exercise never fails to prove both agonizing and ultimately enlightening. Participants have to make decisions that not only directly affect other people's well-being, but that often, in effect, involve choosing death. Participants also have to determine on just what bases such decisions should be made. For example, should they consider, along with a person's disease, also his or her age, or perhaps whether that person has children who are dependent on him or her?[3] In addition, participants have to confront the question of just what kinds of decisions we humans are capable of making—whether certain considerations, while perhaps appropriate-seeming in a situation, may present moral slippery slopes that will always be too slippery for our human capabilities.

After the exercise is complete, the conversation inevitably turns to health care more generally—to what ultimately health care should be about and where health care dollars are ultimately best spent. As it does, questions come to the fore that expand the health care picture dramatically. For example, participants might ask, "Wouldn't it make sense to spend more of our money on prevention?" And then, "If prenatal care is valuable prevention, what about good nutrition?" And we can go on. "If good nutrition is important, what about cleaning up toxic chemicals in the environment?" And if that too is part of health care's larger picture, what about the effects of poverty, and lack of housing—and today's larger crisis of purpose?

All that may take the systemic analysis too far, at least further than we can now readily put into practice. But additional important "bridgings" beyond those that pertain to polarized policy positions and the ultimate polarity of life versus death clearly now come into play: doctor and patient (in how a more empowered doctor/patient relationship has clear advantages when it comes to prevention); mind and body (in the degree that all aspects of the person—physical, psychological, spiritual—assume roles in the most effective care); and personal and societal (in the impossibility, ultimately, of separating questions of individual health from those of larger social well-being).

Acknowledging economic health care limits leads in the end to rethinking health care fundamentally. The needed, more whole-box-of-crayons systemic picture of both health and health care delivery increases demands all the way around. But it also results in us doing

---

3   And what about the lifestyle choices a person has made, both negative— whether the person smoked, for example—and positive—how much the person's life has made a contribution to the well-being of others?

a better job of asking the important questions. Today, that translates into taking a fresh, really big-picture look at the whole health care endeavor. One result is the recognition of options that are more nuanced and creative than we could have considered before.

A Threshold Lesson: Addressing limits alerts us to the importance of more systemic ways of thinking, whatever our concern. The deeper engagement with our own complexity that results makes the recognition of more creative options increasingly something we are capable of.

Limits and Wisdom: Rethinking Wealth

We can go an important step further with this examination of ways in which confronting inviolable limits can produce new possibility. Besides helping us to make more intelligent, less distortion-influenced choices and to appreciate new, more creative options, maturely addressing limits also helps us recognize options that are more wise—certainly more purpose-filled. The health care example provides a hint at this further kind of possibility. I've proposed that the greatest teacher of wisdom in individual psychological development is the fact of our mortality. The health care delivery crisis, by challenging modern medicine's traditionally heroic narrative, presents a related confrontation at the scale of societal/species development.

The following example—and the personal story its contains—helps illustrate both what I mean and what I don't mean in suggesting this further kind of possibility. It concerns learning to handle money—and, more ultimately, the nature of wealth. The example nicely summarizes where we have come to with this chapter's reflections by bringing together the various sorts of new possibility. It also provides a link between this, the second threshold task, and the final threshold task: rethinking the guideposts we use to make our choices. It draws most specifically on the dynamics of personal maturity, but we can extend it to address bringing needed wisdom to future cultural decision-making.

As children, when it comes to money, we tend not to think much about limits. We assume "there is more where that came from" (in this case, generally our parents). Later, we realize that real limits exist and that there are consequences for spending money that we do not have.

We learn to budget, or to at least be a bit smarter in our spending. This is a good and positive thing. Certainly it helps us avoid unfortunate consequences. It is a kind of lesson most of us learn whether we like it or not. And it is essential. It takes us beyond denial, both denial in the sense of pretending we can spend what we don't have, and denial that manifests in clinging to some new dream of limitlessness, like winning the lottery.

But a fully mature relationship to monetary limits involves more than just "growing up and being responsible," even if our concern is only personal maturity, not the cultural sort of maturity that is our interest in this book. Ultimately, our learnings must help us take further steps. At the least, we need to get to a place where monetary limits start feeling more simply like attributes of life, rather than constraints imposed on us. With this additional step, we become able to more consciously and comfortably ask just what is important enough to spend our limited resources on.

And there is more. We might at first think that asking about what is important enough to spend our resources on is only about priorities. But if we engage such questioning with real depth, we discover more significant lessons—indeed, the most essential of lessons. We begin to ask what, uniquely for us, is ultimately important. It can be scary to look at this question squarely.[4] But doing so is, in the end, necessary if we are to have fully purposeful and rewarding lives—lives that are "rich and prosperous" in the fullest sense. The answers we get from such questioning result not just in more intelligent choices, but in a more authentically wise relationship to money—and also in greater wisdom in our relationship to ourselves and to life more generally.

When I was in my teens, we had a family friend, an artist, whom I greatly admired. I was struck by how smart—even wise—he was with money. He didn't have a great deal of it. But I never felt in him any of the common "starving artist" sentiment. I once asked him how he thought about money. Looking back, I realize now that my curiosity came from the fact that I could not yet get my young mind around how

---

4   One could argue that it represents the most taboo topic at a cocktail party. We are much more comfortable talking about politics, or even religion.

he so effectively dealt with real limits. His response was simple and direct. He said there was really only one rule: "Always have enough money to buy paint."

I often share this story when working with clients who are dealing with values-related questions in their lives. I conclude by proposing that if they want to be truly "wealthy" in life they need only ask two questions: First, what, for you, is "paint"? And second, what do you want to use the particular "paint" that is important in your life to create? Answer these two questions deeply, and guidance of an ultimate sort is the result.

The kind of perspective this money example describes doesn't require Cultural Maturity. It really doesn't even require personal maturity in the sense of second-half-of-life developmental tasks—we can learn to be wise about money at any age. Most specifically, it is about maturity in the learning/creative task of managing money. But both personal maturity and Cultural Maturity do dramatically increase the likelihood of an ultimately wise relationship to money.

We can readily tie this story to Cultural Maturity's broader challenge. The same two questions apply directly to the task of writing a new cultural narrative—certainly to the importance of rethinking wealth and progress as noted in the previous chapter's listing of new limits. Here we might reverse the order. The query "What do we want to use our paints to create?" presents the big-picture narrative question. I've proposed as an overarching response that we want to create a culturally mature world. The query "What, for us, is paint?" challenges us to understand what we need if we are to effectively address this challenge. My proposed answer, at least as a starting point, is captured by the three "threshold tasks" we are in the process of examining. We can think of them as primary colors in the needed creative palette of hues.

A Threshold Lesson: Effectively engaging inviolable limits not only helps us think more intelligently and creatively, it can also bring more overarching perspective to our lives and greater wisdom to our personal and collective choices. In fact, it is in confronting particularly difficult kinds of limits that this is most likely to be the case. When we maturely engage the most demanding of "nos," our reward is not uncommonly "yeses" of particular significance.

Limits and Possibility: Where Limits Take Us

We should acknowledge a possible objection to these reflections on limits and possibility. A person might appropriately think that what I have proposed is a bit too cheery. Certainly it is true that I have put particular emphasis on how inviolable limits need not be the end of the road. I have emphasized possibility in part because, in the face of inviolable limits, we so easily get trapped in cynicism and hopelessness. But I have also done so because the new possibilities that accompany effectively addressing limits have so much to teach.

My hope is that the tack I have taken has at least helped clarify how the new human sophistication that comes with Cultural Maturity makes limits a more interesting concern. If such clarity helps a person move more creatively in a world where real limits are inescapable, then the approach I have taken is further justified. I find it of no small importance that confronting inviolable limits can make newly vivid both the richness of ourselves and the richness of the complex world around us.

It is important to emphasize that nothing in what I have described in any way protects us from the fact of real limits. With each of the examples I have cited, limits remain limits. Culturally mature perspective doesn't look for a way to make inviolable limits less formidable. It isn't about finding some magical way around limits, discovering some new, more enlightened kind of heroic/romantic, limits-denying story. It specifically highlights limits' ultimate impenetrability. What culturally mature perspective does is alter our felt relationship with real limits, and, through this, the possibilities we are able to entertain.

It is also important to again clarify that none of the encouraging—and perhaps surprising—outcomes that I have suggested are ultimately mysterious. As with better understanding complexity, learning to better recognize limits and appreciate the new options that come with doing so is, in the end, only about engaging reality with greater subtlety and a new expansiveness of embrace—and in the process, seeing things more accurately.

Philosopher George Santayana observed that, "wisdom comes by disillusionment." Disillusionment is what first acknowledging any inviolable limit can feel like, and the word accurately describes a common experience when we first appreciate how deeply such limits define our time. But as Santayana recognized with disillusionment of a personal sort, the kind of disillusionment we experience today culturally need not diminish us. In the end, it is only about setting aside once helpful but no longer timely illusions and simplifications. In doing so, we see more realistically. We also become able to recognize new, even more fulfilling—and often surprising—possibilities that have before been hidden by our protective beliefs.

A successful response to the challenge of limits makes existence newly possibility-filled only because existence *is* possibility-filled. The new possibilities we encounter in confronting inviolable limits are simply those that inherently accompany the more full and vital, whole-box-of-crayons view of reality we find on the other side of Cultural Maturity's threshold. In another way, we encounter our new common sense.

Limits and Complexity's New Picture

Earlier, I proposed that the kind of complexity we have interest in— and the kind that Integrative Meta-perspective helps us now get our minds around—requires that we consider not just detail and difference, but also uncertainty, change, and interconnectedness. I also introduced the observation that we need to understand each of these multiple factors in new ways and promised to return and examine this assertion more closely. It turns out that fully grasping any of these three further aspects of complexity itself presents limits to usual understanding.

A simple way to recognize the fact of such limits is the way each of the three additional aspects of complexity, when fully grasped, "bridges" usual assumptions. I've described how notions that bridge polarities ultimately confront not just limits to representation, but to understanding of any conventional sort. A brief look at ways these additional limits come into play helps further highlight how the challenge presented by the fact of real limits and that presented by complexity are in the end aspects of a single challenge. It also provides important further insight into the new kind of thinking needed for the future—at the least what it must be able to accomplish.

The uncertainty-, change-, and interconnectedness-infused—and now limits-infused—picture of complexity's workings I've begun to describe applies to every kind of human complexity. And ultimately, it applies at some level to complexity almost anywhere we find it. Indeed, it is with the non-human that much of the greatest progress has been made in fleshing out this more limits-acknowledging picture of the more dynamic and complete kind of complexity that is our concern. Here I will often highlight examples from the physical and biological sciences.

Let's start with uncertainty. In a sense, any limit to understanding is about uncertainty. But uncertainty is also legitimately its own topic. The recognition that we need to better acknowledge uncertainty has already had an important, at least implied, place in these reflections. I've described how parentally defined truths, and ideologies more generally, have, from our beginnings, provided reliable absolutes. A primary function of past belief systems has been to limit our experience of uncertainty.

An important consequence of culturally mature perspective is that it makes us more accepting of the fact of uncertainty. At the very least, this means being more comfortable in the face of uncertainty. It also means being better able to respond to uncertainty, depending on the circumstances, in the most creative ways. In designing a bridge, we want to reduce uncertainty as much as possible—anticipate potential problems and do everything that we can to eliminate them. In other situations, we may choose to do the opposite—to increase room for uncertainty. In brainstorming, in love, or just in how we live our daily lives, it is often constraints to uncertainty that most limit possibility. When we make uncertainty our friend, we become more intelligent—and wise—in our determinations.

In the end, Cultural Maturity's cognitive reorganization not only makes uncertainty more tolerable and manageable, it also fundamentally alters how we understand uncertainty. Making uncertainty our friend is about more than just acceptance; it also pertains to how we see uncertainty's relationship to truth. In several different new ways, uncertainty becomes a "bridging" notion.

Most immediately, uncertainty in the new picture, rather than being something we think of as almost the opposite of truth, becomes an inherent aspect of truth that works. Over the course of the last century, uncertainty has gained an increasingly accepted role in conceptual formulations—and not just when the topic is ourselves. We find the most well known example in Werner Heisenberg's Uncertainty Principle, with its assertion that we cannot determine a particle's position and momentum simultaneously. The increasingly acknowledged "sciences of complexity" similarly make uncertainty inescapable (here by demonstrating how even simple mathematical equations can produce impossible-to-predict results).[5] And statistical analysis is helping us better appreciate uncertainty's role in the working of systems of all sorts—for example, with how uncertainty can intercede not just without warning, but also in dramatic "tipping-point" fashion.[6]

Equally pertinent to this inquiry is how we are more directly acknowledging uncertainty's role not just in what we understand, but also in how we understand. The best of scientific conception today includes the recognition that we are always participants in any act of knowing—a fact that makes ever knowing something for sure impossible.[7] Constructivist ideas in philosophy and education have brought particular emphasis to the fact that what we think we know is always as much a reflection of ourselves as what we claim to understand—and in the process have made uncertainty's contribution when it comes to understanding human systems particularly explicit.

In both of these ways, uncertainty becomes a bridging notion. It becomes intrinsic both to how we think of truth and to the processes

---

5   Early I noted the formulations of chaos theory. Such formulations remain mechanistic, but they are not deterministic. Uncertainty is intrinsic to the workings of "chaotic" systems.

6   Tipping-point phenomena are most easily recognized in human systems. For example, they are readily seen in the behavior of crowds. But such phenomena are not limited to human systems. Some of the most frightening scenarios with regard to global climate change involve such tipping-point uncertainties. Scientists postulate that we might see a sudden massive dying off of tropical rainforests (with both a dramatic loss of their carbon dioxide buffering capacity and further release of carbon into the atmosphere from their breakdown). Temperatures could escalate rapidly. Other scientists conjecture about the possibility of sudden dramatic changes in ocean currents causing a similar rapid escalation.

7   See "Integrative Meta-perspective and the Workings of Awareness" in Chapter Eight for a closer look at ways in which understanding has become newly "participatory" (and also ways in which it has not).

through which we come to understand what is true. We see this result, in a way that ties directly to task of developing culturally mature systemic conception, in how needed new ways of understanding challenge equally the certitudes of determinism and views that identify with the ultimate impossibility of knowing. Certainty and uncertainty become opposite aspects of a larger systemic relationship.

Uncertainty's new picture explicitly challenges Modern Age mechanistic/objectivist determinism. Descartes reminded us that "if you want to be a real seeker after truth, you must at least once in your life doubt, as far as possible, all things." Today Descartes would have to accept that such questioning includes the mechanical assumptions of a Cartesian worldview. But with equal directness, culturally mature perspective challenges views that in various ways identify with the impossibility of ever really knowing. We find this kind of identification with postmodern noncommittalness, with the reflex doubt often found with liberal cynicism, and with spiritual views that identify with mystery.[8] Such views in effect make uncertainty itself truth. Earlier I proposed that culturally mature perspective challenges Max Planck's assertion that we have "no right to believe that physical laws exist." (He is correct, but his conclusion is readily interpreted in less than helpful ways.) Identification with uncertainty is one of the best ways to protect oneself from real uncertainty.

Korzybski again provides useful insight. In his words, "There are two ways to slide easily through life, to believe everything and to doubt everything. Both save thinking." Note how a creative interpretation of uncertainty's role avoids both kinds of traps.[9]

Our second additional ingredient, change, will get its own chapter (Chapter Seven), but some brief reflections help bring it into complexity's new, more limits-affirming picture. The topic of change has inescapable importance for our inquiry. Even if we think of change in quite conventional ways, our times require us to be more attentive to it.

---

8   We can think of traditionally religious views in terms of either half of the certainty/uncertainty polarity. They juxtapose a determinism of divine omniscience with a personal reality based ultimately on faith.

9   Creative Systems Theory uses the word "meta-determinant" to describe this more systemic result.

Today's pace of change, without question, makes life more demanding. Good decision-making requires increasingly that we take change, and often change of a difficult-to-predict sort, into consideration.

It is also the case that effectively engaging change will require, as with uncertainty, that we think about it in ways that bridge familiar assumptions. More traditionally, we've thought of change as what we get when we apply a separate animating force. In this old picture, stability and change stood as opposites. The new picture not only takes change into account, it make change intrinsic in how things work.

We see change's new significance in the many ways we are coming to recognize that what is true at one time may not be true at another. Einstein alerted us to how truth, even at the level of the physical, is relative in time. In later chapters, we will examine how culturally mature perspective helps us better understand what makes periods in history different from one another. Particularly important for this inquiry is the way in which culturally mature perspective helps us understand how the capacities we will need in times ahead are different from what we have known in times past.

Change-infused understanding today finds growing influence—and not just where the focus of interest is ourselves. I think of the increasingly recognized concept of emergence (first coined by philosopher C. D. Broad). Interactions in complex systems can produce outcomes that are not only greater than the sum of their parts, they are not really understandable in terms of their parts—certainly not by just adding parts together. We see such emergent processes in the way a weather pattern can suddenly coalesce to create a cyclone, in the appearance of new biological structures in evolution (such as the first crude eyes), or with how a gathering of individuals can become a community (or a mob).

Emergence is explicitly a "bridging" notion. We need only look to one of the most striking and foundational emergent events—life's origins from a substrate of lifeless chemicals. This view of life's origins challenges equally the beliefs of people with more mechanistic/reductionistic views and with more vitalistic/spiritual inclinations. Emergence in human systems is similarly nondualistic. It is never just top-down or bottom-up, but rather a property of the system as a whole. This is the case whether our interest lies with how new insights arise from the interplay of perceptions in the mind of an individual, or more collectively, with how not just new ideas, but whole new forms of so-cial organization can manifest spontaneously in group interactions. Good leadership in a culturally mature reality becomes about managing highly complex—at once ultimately uncertain and intricately interre-lated—systemically emergent possibilities.

With regard to our third additional ingredient, interconnectedness, we find today, as we do with uncertainty and change, both greater acknowledgement and also new sophistication in our understanding of what it is about We see new attention given to interconnect-edness with most of the best new thinking of the last century. The modern social sciences—particularly sociology and anthropology, but also psychology (for example, with family therapy)—would not exist were it not for a new appreciation for human interconnected-ness. Increasing appreciation for interconnectedness also permeates the hard sciences. The concept of entanglement in physics provides a particularly provocative example. It turns out that particles once joined can influence each other at a distance without any apparent casual link—they can be yards or even miles away and yet act as if they are still connected.[10]

Again, here, as with more systemic understandings of uncertainty and change, a culturally mature understanding of connectedness requires that we confront limits to usual assumptions about what the word implies and expand our understanding beyond how we usually think. Connectedness, too, becomes a bridging notion. I've emphasized that a key defining characteristic of culturally mature understanding is that it simultaneously increases our appreciation for relatedness and for difference. It is connectedness in the sense that is comfortable with this apparent contradiction that is what we have interest in. We are recognizing at ever deeper levels how we can't leave interconnectedness out of our decision-making processes. Whole-box-of-crayons complexity makes no sense without it. But to get where we need to go, this can't be interconnectedness in

---

10   While entanglement makes a great example, in more popular writings it often gets interpreted in ways that make it a simpleminded argument for ultimate unity. It is a much more interesting phenomenon than such conclusions imply.

the sense of simple oneness. It must be interconnectedness of a more difference-acknowledging, limits-acknowledging, maturely conceived sort.

The recognition that uncertainty, change, and interconnectedness each confront limits to usual understanding in a further way confirms how limits and the kind of complexity we have interest in go hand in hand. It also adds additional substance to the conclusion that we are becoming better able to acknowledge the fact of real limits. And with regard to our focus in this chapter, it further supports the essential claim that addressing inviolable limits can reveal new possibility.

Indeed, it adds an important exclamation point—and clarification—to this claim. It highlights how the new possibility that the needed new relationship to real limits reveals is not just any possibility, but rather the specific new sort of possibility required for life in a culturally mature world. The larger portion of the limits-related observations noted in this section involve insights that would not have been available to us within the realities of previous cultural stages.

Earlier, I tied this more filled-out picture of complexity to the challenge of developing approaches to systemic understanding that could take us beyond machine models. I proposed that complexity's various aspects present not just a more complete picture, but also an explicitly more generative—one could say simply "creative"—picture. The word "creative" captures where the needed more uncertainly-, change-, and interconnectedness-permeated picture of complexity takes us in a particularly direct and elegant way. Uncertainty is intrinsic to creativity; creativity is specifically about change; and things creative are inherently interconnected. In later chapters, we will look in detail at how Integrative Meta-perspective helps us think in more consciously creative ways. We will also explore how Creative Systems Theory applies a creative frame to understanding human systems of all sorts.

In fact, we need not stop with human systems in applying a creative frame, at least metaphorically. Nobel chemist Ilya Prigogine beautifully articulated an explicitly generative picture for the physical sphere with these words in his book, *Order Out of Chaos*: "Our physical world is no longer symbolized by the stable and periodic planetary motions that are at the heart of classical mechanics. It is a world of instability and fluctuations, which are ultimately responsible for the amazing richness of forms and structures we see in nature around us."[11]

Appreciating how creativity and real limits are inextricably linked takes us a long way toward understanding how acknowledging limits might produce new possibility. Later chapters will fill out this relationship. At this point, we can note simply that limits to what we can know and do come part and parcel with anything creative. Creativity—the real thing, not just wishful thinking—always includes the presence of inescapable constraints. At the very least, it is not possible to fully anticipate what anything creative will bring—and we would not want to.

> A Threshold Lesson: In the end, effectively addressing limits and reaping the rewards hidden within their inescapable constraints is only about seeing complexity and how it works more clearly. This kind of clarity is only now becoming something we are capable of. But with it, both more vital kinds of understanding and new, more creative possibilities inherently become options.

Limits and Culturally Mature Leadership

At the end of Chapter Two, I reflected on the demands of culturally mature leadership—there with an emphasis on the implications of complexity's new picture. With the contradictory-seeming recognition that acknowledging inviolable limits can result in new possibility now less of a mystery, let's shine the lens of limits more specifically on leadership.

The fact that most immediately stands out is that limits add greatly to the demands of leadership. Much of what will most define good leadership in the decades and centuries ahead is a greater willingness to confront hard realities. In the next section, we will touch on a couple of new leadership challenges where possibility again comes

---

11   In a similar way, creative imagery provides at least a good metaphorical description for what is particular about the cutting edge of modern invention; for example, how the hyperlinked, interactive structures of new information technologies make communication dynamic—and, in potential, creatively dynamic—at levels we've not seen before.

to the fore. But effective culturally mature leadership requires an unflinching willingness to respect the constraints that come with real limits. We can't leave the topic of limits without reacknowledging how inescapably this is the case.

The previous chapter's introductory list of inviolable limits made this necessity of confronting difficult truths clear. I suggested that many readers would feel deflated by the end of it. The culturally mature leader lives every day all too cognizant of this limits-infused picture and how limits of multiple sorts will affect every choice he or she makes. I've spoken of culturally mature leadership as at once more powerful and more humble. Limits play a key role in making culturally mature leadership often a less grand sort of endeavor than we might prefer.

Along with leadership demands that come with how limits intrude in any act of leadership, we also encounter the effects of more specific limits that make themselves felt when we attempt to advocate for culturally mature understanding. We can't escape the fact that communicating about culturally mature perspective and its applications is rarely as easy as we might hope. I will begin with such advocacy-related limits.

The most obvious such limit has been a repeated topic. Because culturally mature systemic perspective is going to challenge ideological sacred cows, it is often not going to be as readily accepted and applauded as we might wish. But there is also a related kind of limit that in a less explicit way produces the same result. In the book's Introduction, I observed that we tend not to think of maturity as a terribly "sexy" word. The issue is not just the word. What culturally mature conclusions are actually about may not initially seem as edgy or dramatic as what they replace.

We can frame the difficulty equally well in terms of either of the first two threshold tasks. As far as complexity, the basic fact that culturally mature conclusions are systemic—and thus multifaceted and nuanced—means that they can initially seem less exciting. Polemical argument tends to be charged with adrenalin. Rarely do culturally mature conclusions have the same kind of bread-and-circuses entertainment value. The role that limits inherently play in culturally mature conclusions further highlights this circumstance. Heroic/romantic claims with their implications of limitless, possibility are going to have more immediate visceral appeal—at least with an audience not accustomed to culturally mature reflection.[12]

In the end, culturally mature advocacy is more compelling—much more so—because it directly acknowledges the largeness of life, asks the right questions, and better gets at what is ultimately significant. But unless an audience is capable of tolerating the complexity and the fact of real limits, mature perspective's greater significance may not be obvious. Culturally mature leaders must stay always attentive to how easily even the most important and timely of culturally mature proposals can get lost in the din of more ideological assertions.

A related limit that affects how readily culturally mature opinions and processes are accepted and applauded concerns where we are in relation to Cultural Maturity's changes. I've described how we are taking but first baby steps. The implications can be particularly pronounced when engaging a group. It is yet rare, today, to find contexts where culturally mature perspective is the norm. Groups tend to come together around shared belief systems and, at this point, those are almost always belief systems of an ideological sort.[13] Given this fact, even the most insightful and ultimately helpful of observations will, often as not, encounter resistance—or worse. The culturally mature leader must always be attentive to where his or her actions will confront ideological limits.

Culturally mature leadership also confronts limits when it comes to communication and advocacy that have nothing to do with an audience's limitations. Remember the Dilemma of Representation. Limits

---

12   Much that we encounter in the media is attractive precisely because it protects us from what our time demands of us. Soap opera/roadkill journalism, for example, produces a seductive illusion of substance, though little real significance is present. (The lead example in Chapter Five examines such "selling of pseudo-significance.") Those interested in communicating about and advocating for culturally mature conclusions need to appreciate these limitations.

13   See "Comparison and Advocacy" in Chapter Nine for a closer look at this circumstance.

to usual approaches to expression mean that finding ways to effectively communicate culturally mature conclusions will often, by themselves, present significant challenges.[14]

> A Threshold Lesson: Effective culturally mature advocacy must start with an appreciation of limits to what may be possible to communicate. These limits can be considerable.

Another important kind of limits-related leadership recognition turns the lens back on ourselves. It is simply the case that culturally mature advocacy requires an unusual degree of self-awareness. The exercising of culturally mature leadership leaves little room for error.

I don't mean error in the sense of simply making mistakes—culturally mature perspective often makes us more tolerant of simple mistakes. But we don't have the luxury of being very far off with regard to whether our assertions succeed at being culturally mature. If the leader misses the mark and doesn't realize it, his or her actions are not just going to be of less help than hoped, they are going to undermine any reason for acting in the first place. Given the baby-step nature of even the best of culturally mature understanding, this can happen much more readily than we might assume.

For example, a person's biases might lead them to fall for the trap of confusing more systemically conceived leadership with being more inclusive and nonjudgmental. Remember the first chapter's extended-example challenge to the media to get beyond the supporting of partisan pettiness. I emphasized that while news based only on polemical views no longer serves us, "balanced reporting" remains just as short of what the future requires. This added distinction might seem like hairsplitting. Certainly, just good balanced reporting can be hard to find. But with culturally mature perspective's critical importance, and with the greater portion of what we see in the media and in the political arena being

---

14 Later we will examine an additional factor that can add to the difficulty of culturally mature advocacy. Our specific point in the evolution of culture can leave us particularly distanced from essential sensibilities needed for culturally mature understanding. (See "Progress and the Dilemma of Trajectory" and "Transitional Absurdities" in Chapter Eight.)

far from culturally mature, such apparently subtle distinctions come to have make-or-break significance. Balanced reporting is not about "bridging." At its weakest it doesn't recognize the existence of anything beyond adding or averaging.

Beliefs that would seem to be explicitly about limits can include assumptions that directly undermine the kind of understanding that culturally mature leadership requires. The political right and the political left each have their versions. For example, on the Right we hear calls for more limited government. At its best, this is a call simply to cut back governmental spending where possible—a good idea, given economic constraints. But hidden beneath such calls we commonly find ideological beliefs that contrast an idealized image of small government with a demonized image of big government—a picture that at its ideological extreme makes the very fact of government the problem and makes useful reform impossible.

I made reference earlier to a limits-related trap common with the Left. Advocates for environmental sustainability can miss the presence of ideological assumptions that, in the end, make effective environmental policy much less likely. It is a kind of trap I've fallen for. Growing up in the Pacific Northwest, the out-of-doors has always had a special place in my life. In my youth, I remember feeling opposed to logging—massive clear-cuts and the decimation of old growth forests in particular were just too painful for me to witness. But I had to acknowledge that I lived in a wooden house. And over time I saw that logging at its best is a sustainable enterprise and came to appreciate how the logging industry is a rich part of Northwest tradition. I am still an environmentalist—and I am very much an advocate for wise and sustainable logging practices. But getting older has brought a more complex understanding of what being an environmentalist must be about.

It is important to recognize that the fact that there is little room for error may have less to do with the specifics of what a leader may say than how he or she "holds" reality while addressing an issue. This fact has both "good news" and "bad news" consequences. A person can be clumsy with words, but if he or she is "coming from the right place," what needs to be communicated can often come across quite adequately. In a less encouraging kind of surprise, words that work wonderfully one day can fail miserably the next because we have somehow lost our felt connection with the needed fullness of perspective.

Besides requiring awareness in the sense of understanding oneself, culturally mature advocacy also requires a keen sensitivity to one's audience. Even if our assertions are generally on target and we are coming from the right place, misreading one's audience can easily result in misunderstandings—and not just minor misunderstandings. Misunderstanding one's audience is easy to do. I've noted the important fact that it takes culturally mature capacity to fully grasp culturally mature capacities. The most immediate kinds of audience feedback can often be less than helpful. Later I will describe how people of multiple ideological persuasions could read what I've written in this book about the three threshold tasks and believe that they agree with all that I've said. (Actually, they would be unlikely to fully read what I've written because they would conclude I'm saying nothing new and get bored with all the details.) [15] The needed leadership sensitivity must include careful attention to where an audience is in relationship to what one might be saying.

An ironic circumstance puts added emphasis on the need for this kind of attention. It is a circumstance that without perspective to understand it can seem rather unfair. We might assume that if we are relatively articulate and "come from the right place," communication will be successful—or at least that we've maximized the likelihood of effective communication. The opposite can be the case. I've briefly introduced the concept of Capacitance. If we engage an audience from a place that is significantly beyond their Capacitance, at the very least we will not be understood. Often it is then that we encounter the most vehement of polarized reactions (sometimes from both sides of an issue at once). [16]

A Threshold Lesson: Culturally mature leadership requires vigilant and ongoing self-reflection. It is possible to miss the mark and not realize it—even when emphasizing the importance of

---

15   See "Polar Traps" in Chapter Nine.

16   See "Capacitance" and the concept of *Creative Symptoms* in Chapter Nine.

acknowledging limits. It is also possible to be right on the mark, and if one is not attentive to circumstances, still be ineffective.

Easily the most disconcerting limits-related leadership observations concern limits to what culturally mature leadership can actually accomplish. While we can legitimately think of Cultural Maturity as an overarching "answer" to current problems, even the most effective of culturally mature change efforts commonly require humility with regard to what is possible.

Certainly they require humility with regard to how long results can take to happen. They also commonly require a willingness to replace ideas we might have of ideal and final outcomes with approaches of a more "good enough" sort. In the end, "good enough" can translate into something better than our ideal images might promise (as we saw with our health care example). But in starting out, it may not be at all obvious that positive possibilities exist, or if they do, just how they might manifest.

We confront some of the most disturbing constraints to what we can accomplish with limits to our ability to solve pressing world problems— even with the best of solutions. We might appropriately assume that if we can just apply culturally mature leadership and culturally mature policies, vexing problems can be eliminated. But often it is limits to how much we can change things—or at least to the speed and directness with which change can happen—that culturally mature perspective makes most apparent.

Transition to a carbon-neutral economy is essential and possible. But it won't happen overnight, and significant damage will certainly take place before we can achieve appropriate greenhouse gas levels. Likewise, the elimination of nuclear weapons is not an absurd hope. But we will probably first see an expansion of the number of states with such weapons, and quite possibly the use of such weapons, again, somewhere in the world. And while world population must and can stabilize, we will have to absorb further significant increases before numbers level off.

With each of these examples, it may be possible to accomplish the objective, but real limits exist to just how quickly we can do so, and also to the extent that simple policy can produce the desired results.

We find a particularly poignant example of how limits constrain even the best of culturally mature leadership in efforts to address conflict.

There are places in the world where conflict can seem never-ending—for example, in parts of Africa and the Middle East. The consequences are commonly horrific. It would seem reasonable to expect that culturally mature leadership could bring an end to such carnage.

Instead, what culturally mature perspective often most teaches us about is limits to what we can do. When conflict is based on ongoing "evil-other" projection, and where there is little culturally mature perspective available within the systems themselves, intervention can as easily make things worse as better. This does not mean that efforts are not sometimes well rewarded. But peacekeeping is hard enough. The establishing of peace through outside intervention can be nearly impossible. We must be willing to assist to the degree that we can. But, in addition, we have to stay humble to what is in fact possible to effect. We also have to stay sensitive to unintended consequences that can result from shortsighted attempts to be helpful.[17]

Even when change is happening—and change that is allied with what culturally mature perspective suggests we would want to have happen—we remain limited. Certainly this is the case with predicting just what will happen. But we are also often profoundly limited, too, in terms of how much we can help. In the book's Introduction, I made reference to current reform movements in the Middle East and suggested that they have evolutionary/developmental roots. As we watch events unfold, we can be relatively certain that in the long term these changes will bring benefit. But in the short term, we should also see new forms of authoritarian rule—secular or religious—and even regression in the face of disorder. And while outside assistance can sometimes help, often, even with the best of intentions, it will ultimately hinder. Any leadership assistance we can provide will often, again, necessarily be of a more humble sort than we might prefer.

A Threshold Lesson: Culturally mature leadership can often accomplish less than we might hope. This is so even if we bring to bear the most sophisticated of understanding and the greatest purity of intent. Limits remain limits.

---

17   See "Terrorism—Getting It Right" in Chapter Seven for a look at some of the implications of these limitations when it comes to fighting terrorism.

Leadership and Big-Picture Possibility

Let's conclude with a couple of limits-related leadership observations that juxtapose constraints and possibilities in particularly interesting ways. The first turns to possibilities ahead specifically for the modern West. The whole topic of possibility makes sense only if we accurately understand current circumstance—and often today when we in the modern West look toward the future, we do not. If modern societies are to provide useful leadership going forward, we will need to more clearly recognize where we reside in culture's story.

This "what time is it" question has direct implications for a more commonly asked question. In my speaking engagements, people sometimes ask me whether I think industrialized nations such as the United States and the countries of Western Europe can compete in the long term in the world's increasingly global economy. I answer yes and no. If we mean competing in the sense of industrial growth I think not—at least not in the decades immediately before us. Too many places in the world—China, India, Brazil, and more—are just now moving fully into their industrial ages. These new powers combine the developmentally "youthful" fervor that naturally accompanies this stage in culture with huge populations and economies that offer, at least for now, more cost-effective production. For the U.S. and Western Europe, that means they have advantages that will prove difficult to counter. Writers often propose that our salvation lies in today's new information economy, where knowledge and speed of technical innovation provide the needed competitive advantage. But much of the world is quickly catching up there as well.

But I think the answer is very much a "yes" as far as whether the U.S. and Western Europe can provide world leadership—and that yes is of huge importance. The modern West is positioned to lead in Cultural Maturity's changes. That means leading in the greater creativity and capacity for collaborative engagement that Cultural Maturity's changes make possible. It also means leading through a more general modeling of culturally mature perspective and values. Not only is such leadership an option, the planet's well-being in the decades before us depends on it.

A Threshold Lesson: The modern West has an essential leadership role going forward. But it is a role that requires first that we take leadership in our own cultural evolution.

The second additional limits-related leadership observation is more philosophical, but important not to overlook. It concerns how the ways we think can limit the kinds of possibilities we are able to contemplate. It takes us back to the fact of uncertainty and uncertainty's relationship to the particular kind of new possibility that culturally mature perspective reveals.

Traditional mythologies—either heroic or romantic—have unknowable outcomes in the sense that we cannot know ahead of time whether we will succeed or fail. But within them, we do have a general image of what success or failure should look like. Hopefulness and possibility in the context of such mythologies appropriately hinges on whether we see such success to be likely.

In contrast, while culturally mature success is of a more humble sort, it also inherently involves potential outcomes beyond what we can anticipate. Or, more accurately, we can't anticipate the particulars. What we can anticipate is that what transpires will reflect the more rich and complex, whole-box-of-crayons understanding that comes with culturally mature perspective.

This particular kind of possibility has fascinating implications when we apply it to our long-term human future. Given how forcefully Cultural Maturity alerts us to the limits inherent in past images of ever-onward-and-upward material advancement, it is understandable that we might reflexively replace such outmoded images with the simple hope that we might have a sustainable and survivable future. Social collapse and a dystopian future of the sort often depicted in popular media is not wholly out of the question. But if we are to fully embrace the possible, we need always keep in mind how deeply limits to what we can know and predict play roles in our ability to even imagine what lies ahead.

The appropriate expectation—if the kind of evolutionary picture we have been contemplating holds—is not just a more sustainable and survivable future, or at least not this alone. More appropriately, we hope and plan for a world that is creative—and potentially rewarding—in ways that we cannot yet imagine. We can turn to philosopher Bertrand Russell's words that introduced this chapter. The more appropriate "expectation," if we can fully meet Cultural Maturity's challenge, is that we will encounter "magical things [that have been] patiently waiting for our wits to grow stronger."

A Threshold Lesson: Acknowledging limits to what we can know and predict, along with helping us recognize naïve expectations, also alerts us to ways in which our beliefs can limit the full wonder of creative possibility.

Confronting Limits—A Threshold Summary

The second of our threshold tasks has alerted us to a simple fact: many things that we might wish to be options are not. Sometimes we face inviolable limits because of basic physical realities, as we find with environmental limits. Sometimes limits are of a more economic sort. And some of the limits we confront are simple facts of being human. For example, we must face that rarely can we be as in control of situations as we might desire. It is also not possible to be the kind of answer for other people that we might wish (whether in love, leadership, or relations between nations), and neither is it possible for them to be that kind of answer for us. We must also recognize that no truth will ever have the certitude of our cultural truths in times past.

We've seen how we really don't have a choice but to acknowledge and take on these and other equally stark constraints. The consequences if we fail to do so are simply unacceptable. If we deny physical limits, the earth will cease to be a place we would wish to live on. If we ignore economic limits, we undermine the well-being of societies. If we deny limits to what we can control, we will find ourselves less and less capable of controlling in ways that can serve us. If we refuse to see limits to what we can be for each other, we will find ourselves without the skills needed to make relationships work. And if we deny limits to what we can know for sure, we will necessarily be left short of any kind of workable knowing going forward.

But we've also seen how this limits-infused picture brings good news along with its considerable demands. Indeed, the rewards for meeting limits honestly are immense. Doing so helps us see with a maturity and completeness not before possible. In addition, it helps us recognize important new options. In the end, confronting inviolable limits directly engages our time's crisis of purpose. When we face what may not be possible, we better recognize what is essential. We also begin to glimpse a fuller and even more potential-filled picture of who we are—as individuals and as a species.

We can return to my friend's question: Are we seeing "the end of civilization?" The fact of inviolable limits can ignite fear that this is the case. If we mean civilization in the sense of the Modern Age dream of limitless material progress and final dominion over nature, our bodies, and life's great mysteries, we are seeing an end. And if we do not engage limits with the needed maturity and creativity—and soon—the results will at least be most unpleasant. But what inviolable limits ultimately mark is the end of one grand narrative—great in its heroic triumphs—and the beginning of another, only starting to reveal its rewards, that is, in potential, even more grand.

As with our first threshold task, these limits-related observations, in offering a way forward, also provide important supporting evidence for the concept of Cultural Maturity itself. When we initially encounter inviolable limits, a reasonable first response is that they offer no good options. Or if we do recognize options, it can be hard to imagine that humanity is up to what taking advantage of them will require. The developmental/evolutionary thinking that gives us the concept of Cultural Maturity explains how successfully moving forward in the face of such limits is possible. I don't know of any other big-picture way of looking at the future that does so effectively.

These limits-related observations also again provide encouragement for those working to support culturally mature change. While culturally mature perspective is needed to fully embrace limits, it is also the case that each time we courageously confront inviolable limits, our actions help take us beyond Cultural Maturity's threshold. This result applies to whatever limit is our concern, but it also applies to understanding as a whole. Grappling with any particular inviolable limit becomes a hands-on "technique" for addressing the tasks of Cultural Maturity more generally.

We turn now to how Cultural Maturity alters not just the questions we ask and what might be possible, but where we go to find truth.

Task #3

Rethinking Guideposts

CHAPTER FIVE

What Matters and Why—Responsibility, Values, and Culturally Mature Choice

The aim of art, the aim of life, can only be to increase the sum of freedom
and responsibility to be found in every man and in the world.

ALBERT CAMUS

OF OUR THREE THRESHOLD TASKS, the third most directly addresses where successfully stepping beyond the simplistic answers of ideological belief takes us. With the first threshold task, we examined how ideology's one-size-fits-all, once-and-for-all absolutes have protected us from being overwhelmed by life's great complexity. With the second threshold task, we looked at how ideology has helped us tolerate reality's magnitude in another way by keeping the unsettling fact of real limits safely at arm's length. The third threshold task concerns where we go to find guidance once ideology's complexity-avoiding, limits-denying measures stop doing the trick.

It asks a simple question: When we step over Cultural Maturity's threshold and familiar guideposts abandon us, on what then do we base our choices? We could make the question, "What values should then determine our choices?" but, as we will examine, our concern is more basic. Ultimately our interest lies with what, in a culturally mature reality, makes something true. No question could be more important as we look to the future. Without a good answer, we lack a North Star with which to make our way.

It is essential that we appreciate how effectively answering this most basic of questions makes demands that we have not known before.

Cultural Maturity's changes alter both where we go to find useful guidance and just what useful guidance—truth that can help us—looks like. With this chapter and the next, we will look at how culturally mature decision-making requires that we question familiar truths of every sort—not just our ideas, but also conclusions embedded in our emotional responses, our imaginings, and our bodily impulses. We will also look at how Cultural Maturity requires that we not only entertain new truths in the sense of being open to new answers, but also that we fundamentally rethink what truth itself is about. In addition, we will look at how it requires that we develop new kinds of truth concepts, and also make a start at examining just what such new truth concepts might look like.

Why do we see such fundamental changes in how we understand truth? Most obviously new, and wholly new—new in a sense that has never before been part of our experience—is the way in which truth's new picture reflects leaving behind the parent/child dynamics that historically have defined the relationship between culture and the individual. But that is only a start. Beyond this shift, we encounter the cognitive reordering inherent in Cultural Maturity's changes—Integrative Meta-perspective's essential dual task of more fully stepping back from our human complexity and at the same time engaging all of who we are with a not-before-possible depth and completeness. The result is not just a next step in the evolution of understanding, but understanding of a whole new sort.

Of the three threshold tasks, the third requires most explicitly that we step back and be the philosopher. This doesn't necessarily mean venturing off into rarified discourse. I've emphasized that culturally mature perspective produces results that, while more challenging than what they replace, are not esoteric. But when we ponder truth-related questions, we necessarily engage with issues that in times past would have been more the purview of philosophy. It is also the case that our third threshold task necessarily involves bringing additional theoretical nuance and rigor to our considerations. Teasing apart just how truth becomes different with Cultural Maturity's changes will thus require some committed reflection.

This chapter starts by examining how culturally mature decision-making requires taking a new, more conscious responsibility not just for the choices we make, but also for the truths we draw on in making them. Then, to help clarify the implications of this result, we will compare what this new responsibility demands of us with the responsibility demands we find with postmodern thought. We will then more deeply address the general way of framing what is new that I've proposed is most useful. I've observed that Cultural Maturity's cognitive changes produce ways of thinking that by their nature are systemic, and more specifically, that are systemic in a new, more dynamic and encompassing sense. Here we draw on a key conceptual quandary to help fill out the implications of this observation for our new truth task.

We will then, as a first step toward developing new truth concepts, turn to one particularly important specific new-truth characteristic: how culturally mature perspective requires that we reexamine the basic categories in which we place our truths. With culturally mature truth, we necessarily address two new broad kinds of truth. First, in a wholly new, more systemic sense, culturally mature truth involves getting at the "crux" of truth. We have to strip away cultural assumptions and get at what matters in ways that are both more bare-boned and more complete. Second, culturally mature decision-making requires that we better recognize truth's "multiplicity"—that in a new and deeper sense we appreciate interrelationship and pattern. We will closely examine an observation key to such pattern recognition: In the end, truth always exists in a context.

Chapter Six turns more specifically to the task of crafting needed new truth concepts. It introduces approaches to understanding that engage truth with the needed maturity of perspective, "pattern language" tools that can effectively guide us as we confront the challenges before us.

While our third threshold task makes some particularly challenging demands, there are also ways in which, as with our previous threshold tasks, it is ultimately straightforward. All of the observations in this chapter and the next follow directly from Cultural Maturity's cognitive changes. At the least, why we need to engage this third threshold task is straightforward. But so is the fact that effectively engaging it is an option. From Integrative Meta-perspective's more complete vantage, Cultural Maturity's necessary new kinds of truth, with familiarity, can come to seem quite ordinary, even simple. In another way we encounter our new common sense.

The Selling of Pseudo-Significance

Our third threshold task's introductory example begins in the world of information and media but quickly turns to more fundamental concerns. When I talk to groups about the future, I am often asked where I think the greatest future technology-related dangers lie—an apropos question given that we always find double-edged potential consequences with even the most promising of technologies. My answer surprises people: The greatest area of danger is also where the greatest possibilities lie—the information revolution.

No sphere of technical advancement is likely to better support Cultural Maturity's changes. Emerging information technologies are increasingly interactive and systemically linked. And their combined use of text, sound, and image allows us to communicate with greater depth and creativity than ever before. In an important sense, we could not ask for more. But at the same time, if new information technologies are not used wisely, they have the potential to do great harm, indeed to fundamentally undermine the human experiment.

Understanding these changes starts with the basic recognition that much that we find in media of all sorts today—from television to video games and social media—has little to do with communication. I mean something very specific in making this assertion. Most people recognize that much that gets called communication provides little in the way of useful information. But my point is different. Often the result is, in effect, information's opposite. What we see has more to do with a selling of pseudo-significance than a conveying of anything that benefits us.

We recognize this result when movies and television substitute shootings, car chases, and quick-flash images of erotic titillation for substance, for anything real. We also recognize it with "if it bleeds, it leads," sensationalism-based journalism. With digital media, the dynamic can be even more striking. Video games often function as little more than Skinner boxes[1] with explosions being the reward. And while social media can serve valuable functions, often it provides but the shallowest of substitutes for real human interaction.

---

1   The experimental apparatuses used to demonstrate how rewards produce the repetition of behavior—a pigeon gets a morsel of food for pecking in the correct place.

Should this situation concern us? If we are only seeing triviality when we might hope for something better, then it would be neither new nor of great consequence. But when we look deeply and place what we witness in the context of the challenges that will most define our future well-being, this trend very much becomes a concern. What we witness takes us beyond the simply superficial toward something more ominous—the substitution of artificial stimulation for substance. Much of what I described in the previous paragraph works ultimately at this level.

Fully appreciating why this is a problem requires an understanding of what makes pseudo-significance—and most particularly the substitution of artificial stimulation for significance—attractive. Pseudo-significance mimics the mechanisms of addictive drugs. I'm drawn back to an experiment that introductory psychology texts often reference to illustrate the dynamics of addiction. Wires are inserted into excitement centers in a rat's brain and then attached to a depressable pedal in its cage. Eventually the rat steps on the pedal. Once the rat discovers the connection between pressing the pedal and the feeling of excitement that results, the rat presses the pedal with growing frequency. In time, the animal neglects other activities, even eating, and dies. Addictive drugs, in a similar way, hook us by providing the feedback our bodies use to let us know when something matters—arousal, release, pleasure, or magical/spiritual experience— without us having to do any of the work, learn any of the lessons, or take any of the risks that real significance requires. The selling of pseudo-significance as substance involves the same mechanism. And the closer the artificial substitute comes to being little more than bare excitation—stimulation with only the illusion of content—the more powerful the result.

This picture raises some scary questions about the future. While tomorrow's new communications technologies will have the potential to keep us more richly and creatively informed, they will also have the potential to produce ever greater and more highly targeted artificial stimulation—to function as increasingly powerful "designer drugs." Add to this dynamic the way in which such exploitation can generate great profit and also how today's crisis of purpose makes us particularly vulnerable to this kind of manipulation, and we get an exceedingly dangerous situation.[2] The information revolution could be an essential part of what saves us—or a direct contributor to our undoing.

We are left with the question of whether there is any effective way to respond to the selling of addictive pseudo-significance. We can say for sure that there must be if our future is to be at all healthy and sane. We can also say something about just what an effective response depends on. Effective action hinges on learning to better distinguish when fake significance masquerades as the real thing.

This observation ties in a critical way to the third threshold task. Distinguishing when fake significance masquerades as real significance ultimately depends on a more general capacity that we will shortly look at more closely: the ability to determine significance in a way that is more direct and bare-boned—distinct from truth's cultural trappings— and also more complete. This more general ability can be realized at all deeply only with Cultural Maturity's changes. It will become increasingly essential in times ahead—and not just when it comes to making good media choices. It will be critical to making good decisions of all sorts without the ideological assumptions of times past.

The great significance of this needed capacity puts the importance of effectively addressing the media question in high relief. The reason the substitution of artificial stimulation for significance presents enormous danger is only in part that the results can be addictive. Of more ultimate importance, the exploitative use of media does direct damage to this essential new capacity. The selling of artificial stimulation as substance destroys the feedback mechanisms we will more and more need if we are to effectively make our way. It undermines the truth-discerning abilities on which our future will ultimately depend.

The digital revolution also alerts us to a further truth-related imperative beyond this need to discern what matters more directly. We most easily recognize it in relation to a more generally acknowledged

---

2   Our specific point in the evolution of culture makes us both particularly prone to confusing surface excitation with significance and especially vulnerable to the seduction of artificial stimulation. See the concept of Transition in "History—and Life—as a Creative Narrative" in Chapter Seven and "Transitional Absurdities" in Chapter Eight.

Information Age conundrum: Even when information is not used exploitatively, its sheer quantity threatens to overwhelm us. Part of the antidote to information overload is precisely what I have described—we need to get better at discerning where substance lies. But we also need something more. We need ways of thinking that help us recognize pattern in information—that help us discern useful knowledge within information, and, beyond this, that can assist us in the wise use of that knowledge.[3]

Culturally Mature Truth

The question of what remains to guide us as past absolutes—culturally specific beliefs, mythologized projections, and the underlying stage-specific truth claims of our Modern Age—lose their historical potency could not be more significant. Psychiatrist Victor Frankl summed up what is most obviously different today in his book *The Will to Meaning:* "Unlike an animal, man is not told by instincts what he must do. And unlike man in former times, he is no longer told by tradition what he should do." Psychologist Mihaly Csikszentmihalyi, in his book *The Evolving Self*, put the essential difference more specifically in terms of belief and understanding: "The passing of traditional belief is a dangerous time…. For a short while those who reject the entire worldview feel liberated and exhilarated to be in a new land without rules or restrictions. However, it soon becomes obvious that to live in absolute freedom is neither possible nor desirable…. But where does one find a faith we can believe in in the third millennium?" Better we might ask, simply, where do we find truths we can rely on?

A person could take issue with my use of the word "truth." We could perhaps speak more appropriately of "what ultimately matters"; what for a particular task best measures success; or perhaps better, what values must underlie our choices. But while new ways of thinking about success and about values more generally come with Cultural Maturity, in the end they reflect more basic underlying changes in how we understand. With this recognition, truth—at least how we make

---

3   I am a strong advocate of media literacy classes in the schools. In Chapter Eleven I examine some of the particular challenges that media literacy presents in a digital world. (See "The Media.")

sense of it—becomes ultimately what we are talking about. The notion of a needed new human maturity makes it inescapable that new, more precise and complete ways of thinking about what makes something true have today become essential. It also helps us understand what such new ways of thinking about truth must look like and how they might be possible.

In the broad sense that I am using the word "truth," we could accurately say that truth has been our basic concern in this book from the beginning. Each of our previous threshold tasks has at least set the stage for us to rethink assumptions at this most basic of levels. We've examined the way in which stepping over Cultural Maturity's threshold requires that we leave behind past ideological distortions and polemical half-truths. And we've seen how, when we do so, we become capable of thinking in more complete ways. We've also looked at how a mature engagement with limits thrusts us into a world in which greater conceptual sophistication becomes inescapably necessary—and offers essential rewards.

We've also encountered recognitions that help place this third threshold task within a larger historical and conceptual perspective. For example, I've described how past truths have been not just societally specific and mythologized, but also tied to the underlying realities of particular stages in culture. And I've attempted to make clear that while we have preferred to think of our modern cultural truths as rational and objective, they have been no less linked to their time than those of any stage previous. There is also how the new insights that come with new stages in culture are products not just of fresh knowledge, but changes in how we understand, identifiable cognitive changes. This has been the case with each previous new chapter in the story of understanding, and certainly this recognition applies as well to the changes reordering truth in out time.

In fact, this recognition applies with particular audacity to the new truths that become necessary—and that increasingly seem like common sense—past Cultural Maturity's threshold. We've seen how Integrative Meta-perspective offers that we might both more fully step back from our human complexity and engage all of who we are with a not-before-possible depth and completeness. The result is not just a fundamentally more encompassing view of current truths than before would of have been an option, but also the ability to understand the truths of times previous with new clarity and sophistication. Culturally mature truth asks: What gets us where we need to go in this new, more challenging, but also more possibility-filled perceptual/conceptual landscape?

Responsibility and Culturally Mature Truth

Truth's new picture starts with responsibility. Like the word "maturity"—and also terms like "complexity" and "limits"—responsibility is a word we may not initially find worthy of celebration. But inescapable responsibility is one of culturally mature truth's most defining characteristics. Culturally mature truth requires of us greater responsibility than the truths of times past. In the end, it requires of us whole new kinds of responsibility.

Today's most obvious new responsibilities concern how we act. Our earlier look at limits examined how our human well-being today lies more directly in our own hands than ever before. Indeed, responsibility for the well-being of much of life as a whole has come to lie in our hands. But a further kind of responsibility is more central to our effort in these pages. Success with more concrete responsibilities depends on it. Cultural Maturity's changes make us newly responsible for the truths on which we humans base our decisions.

In a more rudimentary sense, we have always been responsible for the truths we apply. Responsibility follows from the fact that we are conscious beings, creatures capable of choice. In the words of Antoine de Saint-Exupéry, "To be a man [a person] is, precisely, to be responsible." And because each chapter in culture's story has conferred greater freedom of choice—the age of kings more than that of god-kings, and our modern age of the individual more than that of royal rule and decree—each stage of culture's evolution has increased such responsibility. The greater the freedom we bring to our decisions, the greater the responsibility.

But what our times ask of us is different. Cultural Maturity's changes make a fundamentally more demanding sort of responsibility necessary—and newly possible. Every kind of responsibility today has become a double responsibility. Along with being responsible for our choices, we have become newly responsible for determining just what choosing responsibly means. In a new, fundamentally deeper sense, we are becoming responsible for defining the truths we use to shape our lives.

The most immediate contributor to today's responsibility-twice-over imperative is that loss of cultural guideposts. Previous to now, once-and-for-all cultural absolutes have provided our bottom-line truths, and in the process shielded us from magnitudes of responsibility that before now we could not have endured. But, as we've seen, this loss of guideposts can only be a first step toward the new kind of understanding required of us. We also become responsible for the deeper kind of engagement that comes with Cultural Maturity's cognitive changes. To say only that decisions are now "our call" would, in the end, abdicate responsibility's challenge.

This needed new double responsibility applies to truths of every sort. It is easiest to see with personal choices. Effective moral decision-making today involves more than just thinking through more options. It requires getting more directly at what for us makes a choice moral. Similarly, a rewarding life as a man or a woman requires not just a willingness to question past gender dictates, but also a new and deeper relationship to ourselves as gendered beings. Engaging love at all usefully has come to require rethinking assumptions and allowing new possibilities, certainly. But it also demands a deeper and more direct appreciation for the needs that love fulfills (companionship, intimate bonds, parental cooperation, and the rest). In a related way, a fulfilling sense of identity requires not just that we challenge past cultural expectation, but also that we bring to bear a more personal and fully embracing relationship to the question of what creates worth. If our individual choices are to serve us, we must start by asking in a way not before necessary or really acceptable, just what for ourselves is true.

The situation is the same with more collective human choices. Leadership of every sort today requires that we address the measures we use to determine right action with a not-before-possible directness. And earlier observations about how we are better recognizing the way we are always participants in any act of knowing point toward how, in the end, this recognition applies also to understanding our physical and biological worlds.[4]

---

4   See "Integrative Meta-perspective and the Workings of Awareness" in
     Chapter Eight provides a more detailed examination of this important
     recognition .

Responsibility's new double challenge also pertains directly to that most encompassing of decision-making tasks, articulating a new, more complete and wise human narrative. Doing so demands that together we take on a more mature and conscious storytelling role. In the end, doing so requires that we fundamentally rethink what it means to be human—as individuals, in our relationships with others, and in our larger relationship with life in its entirety. This need to articulate a new human narrative describes our ultimate new human responsibility, and our ultimately most defining new-truth task.

Truth, Responsibility, and the Postmodern Contribution

It is important to appreciate how fundamentally different the result of this double responsibility is from other kinds of outcomes. Certainly it is different from what we find with the traditional Modern Age picture of truth. In modern times, we've tied our understanding of truth to images of objectivity and unfettered free choice. But as I've described, culture has maintained its parental function throughout the Modern Age. And our thinking has remained polar and mythologized. If our truth concepts are to serve us, we need to start with the recognition that Modern Age objectivity has not been as objective as we have liked to believe,[5] nor, in the end, has free choice been quite so free.[6] Cultural Maturity's double responsibility, in keeping with the culturally mature leadership through which we give it expression, results in a more humble—and also, in the end, more powerful—kind of truth.

The outcome is also fundamentally different from some ultimate expression of the extreme individuality that so often guides choice in our time. Individuality as we commonly think of it might seem to represent a final acceptance that truth lies in our hands—and is thus our responsibility. But as we have seen, this kind of individuality is not at all the same as the Whole-Person kind of individual identity that comes with Cultural Maturity's changes. Extended beyond its usefulness, individuality in this sense leaves us estranged even from ourselves. Ultimately,

---

5   For a closer look at this result, see "Integrative Meta-perspective and the Workings of Awareness" in Chapter Eight.

6   See "Free Will and Determinism" in Chapter Eight.

it translates into an abdication of responsibility—certainly of the kind of responsibility our future requires.[7]

Integrative Meta-perspective also propels us beyond kinds of belief that have more recently become fashionable, but which, in their own ways, can be even more absolutist. For this look at changes in how we understand truth, postmodern thought provides a particularly important example. Appreciating how the new kind of responsibility required by culturally mature truth is fundamentally different from the kind emphasized in postmodern interpretations is worth some more focused reflection.

I've described how postmodern perspective has a specific developmental relationship to Cultural Maturity. Postmodern understanding specifically challenges our Modern Age heroic/romantic narratives. But it also, even at its best, only "straddles" Cultural Maturity's threshold. Postmodern thought's historical contribution brings attention to the importance of the first step I've noted—leaving behind familiar guideposts. But at the same time, it leaves us hungry for something more.

Postmodern is an imprecise term—not just with regard to its definition but also with regard to what and who we should include in its purview. For some, the term refers most simply to a time (roughly the last half of the twentieth century); for others to a broad social and aesthetic movement (I've made reference to postmodernism in architecture); and for others to particular schools of philosophy. Indeed, there is debate about what time we are talking about. In philosophy, social constructivism is unquestionably postmodern. But existentialism, with its roots a hundred years previous, is often given similar status.

However we resolve the inclusion debate, those two threads— existentialism and social constructivism—provide good reference for comparison with how Cultural Maturity's perspective alters truth.

I've described how the key difference lies with the fact that postmodern thought gives us little to replace what, with its recognition that traditional guideposts have stopped serving us as before, it insightfully observes has been taken away. In the end, almost nothing of what we have examined in truth's new picture makes real sense from the assumptions

---

7   See "Transitional Absurdities" in Chapter Eight.

of postmodern belief—and not just the specifics, but simply the need for such examination. Existentialism and social constructivism help fill out what is missing from slightly different angles.

Existentialism, most influential in the late nineteenth and early twentieth centuries (in Europe, and in the middle of the twentieth century in the United States) questioned the existence of objective truth of all kinds—philosophical, religious, social, and scientific.[8] Its thinkers proposed that meaning is to be found not in the discovery of answers, but in the courageous engagement of a world without guidelines. I think of Jean-Paul Sartre's famous assertion that "man is condemned to be free."

The recognition that postmodern thought "straddles" Cultural Maturity's threshold explains both the richness of existentialism's contributions and its limitations. Existentialist thinkers describe with particular eloquence the psychological precipice we stand at with the loss of familiar absolutes. They also begin to bring emphasis to the new responsibility required of us if we are to effectively make our way. The shortcomings of existentialist thought derive from its inability to help us in more than the most limited way with making sense of what may lie beyond that surrender of absolutes. Given their time in history, existentialists have been predictably better at critique than illumination, better at articulating what no longer is adequate than what may lie ahead.

Social constructivism, a loose body of work that gained prominence in the 1970s and 80s,[9] emphasizes the dependency of beliefs on cultural context. A constructivist perspective replaces the idea that truth is an objective "out there," something to be discovered, with the idea that we, as individuals and together as social beings, "construct" truth. Depending on the absoluteness of the view, truth can mean primarily personal belief and social convention or can refer to everything—including the chair on which you sit. Constructivist thinkers emphasize the existence

---

8   Existentialist ideas were foreshadowed in the thinking of Friedrich Nietzsche and Søren Kierkegaard and made explicit in the writings of Jean-Paul Sartre, Martin Heidegger, Karl Jaspers, Albert Camus, and others.

9   With the ideas of Michel Foucault, Jürgen Habermas, Jacques Derrida, Richard Rorty, Jean-Francois Lyotard, and others.

of multiple worldviews, and talk about there being not one truth but many. Social constructivists tend to be immediately skeptical toward anything that might look like overarching conception (even though one might argue that theirs is such), a characteristic that Jean-Francois Lyotard described as an "incredulity toward meta-narratives."[10] From a constructivist perspective, there are no universal theories, only local theories, truths specific to particular times and places.

In this fundamental skepticism we find the source of much of social constructivism's usefulness. Constructivists eloquently articulate how we mapmakers are never wholly separable from our maps. Their ideas also shed important light on the value to be gained from appreciating the contrasting perceptual and conceptual realities embedded in differences such as gender, age, and cultural background.

But that same skepticism also produces major blindnesses. The claim that truth is constructed often comes dangerously close to an assertion that truth is arbitrary. People's beliefs can become inventions born from little more than whims of power or shifting tastes. The best of constructivist thinkers do not suppose that one reality is as good as another and are careful to point this out. But as seen from a culturally mature perspective, social constructivism is deeply limited by that "incredulity toward meta-narratives."

Social constructivism's suspiciousness toward big-picture ideas has admirable roots—getting beyond cultural absolutes is no easy task. But its knee-jerk dismissing of such ideas easily discards the baby with the bathwater. It rejects the guidance that overarching perspective can offer exactly when it is needed most.

Postmodern thought holds a respected place in Creative Systems Theory's developmental/evolutionary picture. But while the postmodern contribution brings us up to Cultural Maturity's threshold—and in the argument for finding purpose in a world without obvious meaning and an eclecticism of aesthetic, sometimes a small step beyond it—by itself, it can only be a beginning. Yes, truth is our responsibility. But that doesn't mean it is willy-nilly "our call." And yes, truth is "constructed." But beyond this recognition, it is essential that we better understand why we have constructed truth in the particular ways we have. Most important,

---

10   Richard Rorty proposes, "There is no big picture."

we need to understand how to construct truths sufficient to the tasks now before us, to appreciate, as here, both the criteria such truths must meet and some of the ways that meeting those criteria can be achieved.

In reflecting on the gifts and limitations of postmodern perspective's evolutionary contribution, I am reminded of a concert I attended some forty years ago. It showcased the music of John Cage. Cage's compositions eloquently expressed postmodern aesthetics. In one well-known piece, each musician in the orchestra is given a single sheet of music on which is written a sequence of musical measures. Everyone starts at the beginning, but how many times each musician plays each measure is open to his or her whims on that particular evening.

The piece's presentation lasted about forty-five minutes. I suppose it could have lasted many hours if the musicians had been more perversely inclined. As an aesthetic experience, the piece was meager at best, but philosophically and psychologically, at that time, it struck me deeply. It challenged me to examine questions that had become newly provocative: How do we as individuals and social beings derive meaning out of our experience? What is the relationship between order and randomness? What makes something beautiful?

But after I had spent a half hour immersed in reflection on such questions, my mind began to wander. I found myself wanting Cage to get on with it. Music needs to be more than just philosophy and psychology. And I wanted him to do more than just offer up questions, to commit himself to something, to at least take a shot at creating truth or beauty, whatever those words might mean to him.

In one sense he was doing just that. Earlier I spoke of how the arts have an "anticipatory" function in culture.[11] By that definition, Cage's composition was valid and important art. It very much pushed at the creative edges of cultural understanding and experience. Still, no one got up to dance. And today, its creative timeliness now decades in the past, it would be unlikely to generate much of a response at all.

In a similar way, postmodern social theory has been timely and provocative. But it, too, has tended to remain disembodied. It does not

---

11   In Chapter Eleven (see "The Arts"), I will propose that the ultimate purpose of art is to somehow give voice to just-emerging cultural sensibilities.

inspire us to dance.[12] And the creative edge of culture's challenge has moved sufficiently beyond it that its significance is largely historical.

Returning to the double responsibility necessary to a culturally mature relationship to truth, the critical recognition with this brief look at the postmodern contribution is that any new way of thinking must do something more interesting and consequential than just turn what before were dictates into choices that are now "our call." While postmodernism's picture might seem to suggest ultimate freedom from constraint, at its weakest it only begs freedom's question.[13] The needed double responsibility requires not just that we choose between more options, but that we think in new and deeper ways about what it means to have options.[14]

Cultural Maturity's cognitive changes directly address this further challenge. Integrative Meta-perspective provides greater choice. But it also brings new awareness, new responsibility, and a newly possible depth and complexity of perspective to how we understand. In addition, it offers ultimately that we might draw on more nuanced, multifaceted, and encompassing kinds of truth.

----

12   There are exceptions. We sometimes see new contributions described in postmodern language that capture some of the deeper vitality the future will require. At first, postmodern architecture tended only to replace the glass and stainless steel sterility of the height of modernism with a hodgepodge of aesthetics. Today, we often see postmodernism aesthetic translated into a richly inspiring and organic vision. I think of Jørn Utzon's Sydney Opera House and Frank Gehry's masterwork, the Guggenheim Museum at Bilbao. We've also seen increasingly mature constructivist thinking in education, thinking that looks deeply at what it means to emphasize the student's process of inquiry.

13   To quote from "Me and Bobby McGee," the Kris Kristofferson song made famous by Janis Joplin, such freedom is "just another word for nothing left to lose." Later we will examine how conclusions drawn from such a picture can result in decisions of a particularly absurd sort and contribute directly to our time's crisis of purpose. See "Transitional Absurdities" in Chapter Eight.

14   See "Postmodern/Constructivist Scenarios" in Chapter Nine for further reflections on postmodern thought—both its contributions and its limitations.

The Dilemma of Differentiation

At least at the collective level, Cultural Maturity's new truth-related responsibilities involve more than just the double responsibility of determining our choices and also discerning what we should base our choices on. Today's new questions make us responsible for developing new kinds of truth concepts. I've spoken of the importance of addressing our human complexity in ways that are more "dynamic and complete." I've also claimed that the language of systems provides the best way to accomplish this—with one very large caveat. I've emphasized the importance of addressing living systems—and in particular ourselves as systems—in ways that better reflect that they are alive.

I've also noted the significant difficulties we encounter when we attempt to do so. Ideas that effectively acknowledge life require not just more inclusive understanding, but a fundamentally new kind of understanding.[15] It is important, before we turn our attention to the practical task of crafting needed new kinds of conceptual frameworks, that we have a solid grasp of what systemic truth concepts that are new in this sense ask of us. We also need to more fully grasp the essential implications of ideas that succeed.

To this point, I've given greatest attention to how the type of systems thinking that can help us must get beyond the engineering language common with more formal systems conception. But systemic understanding is unusual for the diverse, even opposite, worldviews it can be used to justify. A puzzling question embedded in the challenge of addressing living systems in life-acknowledging terms helps clarify common ways that systemic thinking can fall short: How do we think about difference if our ideas are to honor the fact that we are alive?

Creative Systems Theory calls this conundrum the *Dilemma of Differentiation*. The simple fact that culturally mature truth requires that we make distinctions puts us immediately in a pickle. Differentiation, the ability to say "this as opposed to that," is ultimately what makes thinking work. But usual ways of describing difference can't address the required dynamism.

The Dilemma of Differentiation alerts us to two opposite sorts of

---

15   Physicist Erwin Schrödinger articulated the life conundrum particularly well in his classic book *What Is Life*.

traps. Each of them can be found in popular expressions of systemic thought. The most obvious trap is the one I've emphasized. A person depicts difference in traditional engineering terms—that is, in terms of parts that interact in a mechanistic manner. Systemic formulations that reflect this trap can be highly detailed, but no matter how subtle and sensitive the delineations, when we put the parts together, we end up back in an engineering, machine world.

Less frequently we encounter an opposite, yet just as deadly, kind of trap. Many popular writers who use systems language—particularly writers of a more humanist or spiritual bent—often largely ignore parts and focus only on relationship. Commonly the result is ideas that reduce to little more than elaborate ways of saying "all is one." Recognizing connectedness can be comforting—and it identifies a truth that is just as important and accurate as the "all is many" claims of mechanistic belief. But ignoring the question of parts makes for impoverished conception at best. Worse, it makes for misleading conception. Real relationship (connectedness in the systemic sense that we have interest in)—whether personal or conceptual—requires difference. Certainly life requires it.

A defining characteristic of culturally mature systemic truth is that it reconciles—finds a way past—the Dilemma of Differentiation. Ideas that are systemically complex in the sense of simply being complicated, and those that arise from notions that in the end collapse complexity into a reassuring oneness, each fail to address the Dilemma of Differentiation.

We could say that each view is simply wrong, or we could frame the challenge more developmentally. The fact that we might encounter these opposing kinds of systemic formulations is exactly what we would expect given how we have before understood. Chapter Seven examines how each stage in culture is most defined by a particular kind of polar juxtaposition.[16] I've spoken of how Modern Age truth juxtaposes more rationalist/reductionist/positivist truth claims on one hand with more romantic/idealist/poetic beliefs on the other. We can think of the two kinds of systemic formulations I've just described as vestiges of our most recent contrasting assumptions about what ultimately makes something true.

---

16   See "History—and Life—as a Creative Narrative."

Note that we could frame how each falls short in terms of polarity at its most bare-boned. I've described how polarity at its most basic juxtaposes separateness (difference) on one hand and unity (relatedness) on the other. Systems ideas that emphasize parts, and systems ideas that posit that final truth lies with interconnectedness, reflect identification with these most fundamental polar extremes. Engineering models bring emphasis to difference. And oneness-focused interpretations bring attention to relatedness. With culturally mature systemic perspective, these two more limited systemic approaches become opposite-hue crayons in the larger systemic box.

A result that we always find with Integrative Meta-perspective, one to which I've given special attention and which follows directly from bridging this most basic of polarities, helps affirm the importance of systemic thinking of this new sort. I've described how culturally mature understanding not only acknowledges both difference and relatedness, it simultaneously increases our appreciation for each of them. In challenging polarized thinking, culturally mature perspective always, in the end, does the claims of each pole one better—and precisely with regard to what that pole has before argued was most important to consider. With culturally mature systemic perspective, difference and relatedness—polarity at its most fundamental—each win, and in much more than some both/and sense. Each gains new emphasis and also derives a new, more vital and creative definition.[17]

While the needed new, more dynamic and complete kind of systemic truth requires more of us, for now-familiar reasons it need not be as demanding to grasp as we might imagine—at least when we are ready for it. I've described how the ability to think systemically in ways that

---

17 In Whole-Person relationships, we better appreciate our separateness and also become capable of a new depth of connectedness. We see something similar more conceptually with a developmental/evolutionary framing of cultural stages. We are able to grasp more deeply how periods in culture differ from one another and, at the same time, we come to better appreciate how those differences reflect a larger coherence. In each of these examples, difference and relatedness are not just both honored, they come to reflect new, more dynamic and systemically complete kinds of concepts.

are more sophisticated is a natural result of Cultural Maturity's cognitive changes. Such truth is a simple product of thinking that more consciously and deeply draws on the whole of our cognitive complexity. This is not to diminish such truth's significance. I've suggested that the new kinds of understanding that Cultural Maturity's cognitive reordering produce are as transformative in their implications as the theories of Newton and Descartes were in their time. In an important sense, they are more so. The kind of systemic truth that results from Cultural Maturity's cognitive changes represents not just a next step in truth's evolving story, but a unique step with wholly new consequences. It is only to once again emphasize that what is being asked of us is ultimately straightforward.

Cultural Maturity's more whole-box-of-crayons systemic-truth picture is most directly pertinent to ourselves, and the human is where our interest with this inquiry primarily lies. But Cultural Maturity's cognitive changes alter not just how we see ourselves. They also alter how we interpret the world around us. I've noted specific examples. In fact, much of the best of systemic thinking throughout the last century has focused on the biological and the simply physical.

A handful of contributions are particularly pertinent to the evolution of the needed more dynamic and complete kind of systemic thinking. These include the organicism of J.B.S. Haldane and E.S. Russell, the General Systems Theory of Ludwig von Bertalanffy, Norbert Wiener's cybernetic notions, Gregory Bateson's biological concepts, the sciences of complexity, and in the human sphere, various organizational and family systems models. Each of these contributions is limited—either by being ultimately mechanistic (both cybernetics, and in most all instances, the sciences of complexity), or particularly when it comes to human systems, by lacking the detail and nuance needed for wide practical application. But each reflects an effort to address the new challenges that the kind of systemic understanding that can work for times ahead present.

Two Kinds of Truth

The next chapter will turn to the specific approach to systemic conception used by Creative Systems Theory. We will look at how a creative frame makes possible understanding that from step one reconciles the Dilemma of Differentiation. We will also look at how we can use a creative frame to develop detailed truth concepts able to help us make our way in the territory ahead.

But to go there immediately would get us ahead of ourselves. We need an additional systems-related recognition if we are to fully appreciate the implications Cultural Maturity's changes have for understanding human systems. Beyond altering the particular truths we might draw on, Cultural Maturity's cognitive reordering also changes the basic categories we use to define truth.

This additional kind of change is as radical in its significance as the more general needed new kind of systemic thinking. We must understand it if we are to lead effectively, whether in our personal lives or when making major collective decisions. And certainly we must understand it if we are to successfully craft comprehensive new-truth frameworks that can serve us as we go forward.

Two new kinds of discernment—each systemic in our new, more dynamic and complete sense—are critical to effective culturally mature decision-making. In a way, each reflects a kind of distinction that we humans have always made. But with Cultural Maturity, we necessarily engage each kind of discernment in a manner that fundamentally alters what it is about. Truth comes to reside in two wholly new conceptual groupings. To keep concepts simple, I will refer to them as the "crux" and "multiplicity" aspects of culturally mature truth.

This fact of new-truth categories can initially seem tricky to make sense of, but for the same reason we've seen with other Cultural Maturity–related recognitions, ultimately it is not that complicated. When we step over Cultural Maturity's threshold, these categories are what we find. They come part and parcel with culturally mature perspective's more encompassing systemic picture. The first new kind of truth is a product of the new ability to at once step back from and more deeply engage the whole of our internal complexity that comes with Integrative Meta-perspective. The second is a product of the analogous new ability to more accurately discern the various aspects of that complexity—to see them without the distorting lenses of projection and mythologizing.

Some historical perspective helps clarify both what our new discernment categories describe and just what is new. In what might at first appear to be a related phenomenon, since the beginnings of human understanding we have placed our truths in two worlds. We've spoken of this two-part picture in a variety of ways—truth's essence as opposed to truth's particulars, inner truth as opposed to worldly truth, spiritual truths as opposed to material truth. At various times in culture's story we have given one half or the other of this basic juxtaposition greater emphasis. Plato, in contrasting eternal "forms" with their projected shadows on the cave's wall, gave ultimate credence to the more inner dimensions of truth. Descartes, in contrasting objective and subjective worlds, made an almost opposite claim. But wherever we look, up to this point in culture's story we encounter a related two-part basic division of truth.[18]

But I strongly emphasize that phrase, "up to this point." Culturally mature crux and multiplicity discernments represent wholly new kinds of concepts, new not just in the sense of next chapters in a continuing story, but fundamentally new. Two things change in what before has been a consistent picture. First, again, each kind of truth loses its parental trappings. Each, in a new sense, must be engaged unadorned. Second, because each now reflects Integrative Meta-perspective's more encompassing picture, each becomes expressly systemic, and systemic in the new, more dynamic and complete sense that we examined in the previous section.

We already have a couple of simple conceptual tools that can take us a long way toward capturing both new kinds of truth. The concept of "bridging" captures both kinds of truth at the basic level of polarity. Any polarity, when we effectively draw a circle around it, defines a crux discernment. The polar aspects, once bridging has taken place, reflect distinctions of the multiplicity sort. The box-of-crayons image provides a more detailed conceptual tool (see Figure 5-1). We can think of culturally mature crux discernments as what we get when we give primary attention to the perspective of the encompassing box. Culturally mature multiplicity discernments describe what the world looks like when we

---

18   See "A Creative History of Truth" in Chapter Ten for a look at how the aspects of this two-part picture that take precedence at any given time follow a predictable historical progression.

draw on the sensibilities of particular crayons (while not losing the box's encompassing vantage[19]).

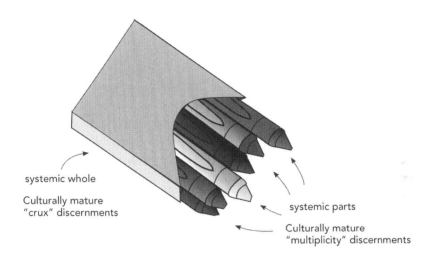

systemic whole

Culturally mature "crux" discernments

systemic parts

Culturally mature "multiplicity" discernments

Fig. 5-1. Culturally Mature Crux and Multiplicity Discernments

Once we step over Cultural Maturity's threshold, culturally mature crux and multiplicity discernments become critical in every part of our lives. They are equally essential to making the most everyday of personal choices and the most consequential of collective determinations. Of particular importance for our inquiry, culturally mature crux and multiplicity distinctions form the necessary foundation for the more formal and detailed kinds of "pattern language" formulations that will become increasingly critical if we are to effectively make our way in times ahead. When we successfully apply culturally mature crux and multiplicity discernments, they make possible both a nuance of distinction and a compactness of conception that is wholly new and that will be increasingly essential.

---

19   If we lose the box's defining presence, we end up back in our old definition, and ideology once again rules.

Truth's "Crux"

Culturally mature crux discernments are where culturally mature perspective's responsibility-twice-over task necessarily begins. They are also, when push comes to shove, what we must necessarily come back to in our decision-making processes. They provide the general compass bearing necessary if future choice is to have direction and coherence.

I made reference to the central importance of culturally mature crux discernments in the extended-example look at new media and the dangers of pseudo-significance. I pointed toward a question that must be our point of departure if we are to effectively address the future of human communication: What is it that ultimately makes information information—and even more, what makes it information that matters? Questions of every sort, today, require that we start with such at once spare and encompassing systemic determinations. Think of any particular systemic crux discernment as an arrow that gives us basic guidance as we make our way in Cultural Maturity's newly demanding world.

The need for crux discernments of this fully systemic sort comes most obviously from the diminishing power of parental guideposts. Without predefined cultural references telling us what should matter, we have to somehow more directly get at what makes something significant. But, in the same sense that we saw with more general observations about the new double responsibility that accompanies culturally mature truth, Cultural Maturity's deeper cognitive changes also necessarily come into play. Without them we are left with little more than postmodern whim. The greater awareness and more immediate contact with our human complexities that accompany Cultural Maturity's cognitive changes are what, in the end, make needed more direct and embracing engagement with what matters possible.

Before we turn to examples, it will help if I expand briefly on how culturally mature crux distinctions are different from related concepts of times past. Philosophers, theologians, and poets have always sought to get at truth's crux in the earlier definition I've referred to—in the sense of some "essence" or "core" of truth. But culturally mature crux distinctions are not just about essences. And certainly they are not about timeless essences (which in the past has been the implication). They are what we get when we succeed at taking everything that needs to be considered into account—supposed core, supposed periphery, and everything else.

Drawing on the box-of-crayons metaphor, "crux" in the old sense referred to a single crayon of a more inner—aesthetic or spiritual—sort. Culturally mature crux distinctions consider all that we encounter in the concrete world of particulars to be equally essential. Culturally mature crux distinctions challenge us to hold and appreciate the whole box. Once we step over Cultural Maturity's threshold, effective decision-making requires that we take into account everything that goes into making our choices vital and alive—in ourselves and in the world around us.

Addressing the crux truth task is a key part of the necessary new double responsibility. Certainly this is the case with personal choices. I've described how effective moral decision-making today requires getting more directly at what for us makes a choice moral. Doing so requires that we take into account everything that goes into an act's significance. I've also observed how a rewarding life as a man or a woman requires a new and deeper relationship to ourselves as gendered beings. Such relationship requires that we consider everything that being a man or a woman entails. I've noted, too, how engaging love at all usefully requires that we get more directly at how love adds to who we are. Doing so demands a related deeper and more direct appreciation for all the various needs that love fulfills. And the same principle applies to the task of rethinking identity in our time. Personal questions of all sorts today require that we start with this kind of "whole-box," crux discernment.

In the end, the importance of starting with this more complete kind of crux discernment applies to human choices of every sort. For example, it is as pertinent to the decisions we make together within specific spheres or domains of endeavor (such as government, science, or religion). With any new chapter in culture's story, primary realms of activity acquire new defining truths. But the diminishing of culture's past parental influence combined with the need for more multifaceted understanding means that the ways we conceive of various spheres of human activity can, and must, be more consciously embracing—at once more direct and more systemically complete—than how we have thought of them in times past.

We saw this more complex (and in the end also simpler, more stripped-down) task implied for the field of medicine with the previous chapter's reflections on health care limits. Modern medicine's bottom-line measure has been to defeat death and disease—essentially at any cost. We've seen how this measure, today, has become not just unsustainable, but by itself limited and limiting, and how measures that can work for the future must be of a more encompassing sort. They must somehow acknowledge quality of life along with the fact of life; psychological, social, and spiritual aspects of health and healing in addition to the purely physical; and not just individual health but also larger societal well-being. Health care's new yardstick must address health itself—in the fullest, most complete sense.

The sphere of education provides a good further example. Education's future depends not just on us rethinking educational policy, but also on rethinking what education is ultimately about. We tend to take education's purpose for granted—assume it to be obvious and unchanging. In a sense, it is unchanging—as T.H. White put it in *The Once and Future King*, the purpose of education has been to "learn why the world wags and what wags it." But education's purpose has taken expression in very different ways at various times in culture's story. In the future, education must manifest that purpose in ways that are both more conscious and more encompassing than at any time previous.

Modern "classroom" education had its origins in providing the universal literacy necessary for democratic governance and the Industrial Revolution. Toward this end, it has served us well. But education able to support and teach culturally mature capacities requires a more complete definition. The essential tasks ahead for our species will necessarily involve learnings that are not just different from what we have known, but also often learnings incompatible with education's purpose as we have most recently thought of it.

We can draw on moral decision-making's new demands for illustration. With modern public education, we've taken great care to keep moral concerns out of the classroom—carefully preserving the separation of church and state. Yet we can't escape the fact that any kind of healthy future will require us to confront increasingly complex ethical questions. Later, we will look at the important sense in which concerns of every sort today have become moral/ethical questions.[20] For future education to serve us, it must make learning to address such questions "core curriculum." Effectively addressing the complex challenges before us will require that we recognize a more complete picture of learning and draw on more embracing, bottom-line measures for educational success.

Implied in these examples is a recognition that helps clarify what might have at first seemed contradictory language. I've spoken of truth's "crux" and the box-of-crayons image's encompassing box as analogous notions. We can think of culturally mature crux discernments in two different ways that at first might seem to be almost opposite to one another. Culturally mature crux discernments are about getting at what matters in the most direct, bare-boned fashion. They are thus about truth at its simplest. And, at the same time, because they are about addressing truth in all its aspects, they are about affirming truth's multifaceted complexity. In fact, we must think about them in both of these ways and, in effect, simultaneously, if our discernments are to reflect the kind of systemic thinking required once we step over Cultural Maturity's threshold.[21]

We also need to at least acknowledge a further difference if these initial observations are to fully get us where we need to go. It will take later reflections for this additional difference to make complete sense, but it similarly follows from Cultural Maturity's cognitive changes: Any culturally mature crux discernment, in addressing a specific concern in our time, also at least a bit addresses the more encompassing question that our more time-specific concern through history has engaged. This need not be a conscious process, but it can be. Later we will examine how the more overarching perspective that comes with Cultural Maturity's cognitive changes helps us step back and appreciate the larger story that underlies any particular kind of truth. It also helps us appreciate how today's new truths incorporate that larger story in a way we have not seen before. In an important sense, culturally mature crux distinctions help us get at what "mattering" in relation to any particular kind of question has always been about.[22]

---

20   See "Morality, Life, and Truth" in Chapter Six.

21   Again we encounter our Dilemma of Representation.

22   See "Creative Reengagement" in Chapter Eight.

The developmental analogy—which compares Cultural Maturity with maturity in an individual lifetime—again sheds useful light. Maturity in individual development in a more limited way similarly involves engaging truth's crux in both the systemic here-and-now sense and in this more encompassing temporal meaning. We most easily recognize needed new inclusiveness of the present-tense, "we contain multitudes" sort, but always to some degree it also comes into play in terms of what matters for us more ultimately. Wisdom involves better getting our arms around not just significance in the moment, but also significance as it pertains to the whole of our lives. This more encompassing result asks more of us. But it also lets us engage our personal lives with a new and greater fullness and elegance, and with a more embracing and reliable kind of potency.

We can look back to our list of personal truth concerns to see how this more wholly encompassing picture—encompassing both in the immediate and in the more temporal sense—applies to culturally mature decision-making. Getting more directly at what makes a choice moral, today, very much means what is moral specifically in our time. But, at least a bit, determining what is moral also means better appreciating what at any time has made a choice moral.[23] Similarly, while that new and deeper relationship to ourselves as gendered beings requires acknowledging our very particular here-and-now complexities and contradictions, it also, at least to some degree, means reengaging the more primordial roots of being a man or a woman. In a similar way, while that more direct recognition of the needs that love fulfills refers to what we derive from love in our time, it also means better appreciating the needs that love has fulfilled all along, throughout our human history. And in a related manner, finding the more fulfilling sense of identity possible today requires not just bringing to our internal conversation the more multifaceted picture that defines worth in our time, it also means asking in new and deeper ways about what human worth is ultimately about.

More domain-focused reflections provide a further glimpse of how this more temporal sort of systemic engagement comes into play. We

---

23 Chapter Six examines how morality has always been about actions that, in a particular context, are most "life-affirming."

see this more temporal dynamic at least hinted at with my description of health care's more systemic picture. I described how health care's new yardstick must address health in the fullest, most complete sense. In the end, that means looking not just at health as we think about it in our time, but at least a bit, considering what health is about more fundamentally. This includes engaging sensibilities that have had a less prominent role in recent times. At earlier times in our cultural story, for example, the social and spiritual aspects of health were often, in a more limited sense, viewed as the core concerns of health and healing. We've seen how they now must at least be consciously considered.[24]

We also saw this more temporal dynamic reflected in the earlier brief look at education. I described how the complex challenges before us require that we draw on more embracing measures for educational success. Most immediately, "more embracing" refers to the demands of education in our time. But at least a bit, too, it refers to a more temporal kind of completeness. For example, giving the moral dimension of learning a central place in education is not entirely new—moral decision-making lay at the heart of medieval monastic education. I cannot emphasize too strongly that what I'm referring to here is different, fundamentally, from going back to the education methods of an earlier time. But we very much need to learn how to ask our questions and make our deliberations from a vantage that better appreciates all that goes into making us human.[25]

In the end, engaging our crux truth task—and in a way that incorporates all of these aspects—applies not just to ourselves and to specific cultural domains, but also to the broadest of collective decisions. I've described how our old ways of thinking about wealth and progress—and "more" in general—can't serve us going forward. The concept of Cultural Maturity is an attempt to answer this most encompassing crux-truth question. Any act or idea consistent with the realization of Cultural Maturity becomes "true" in this now most essential sense. Culturally mature truth is about better addressing what most matters right here and right now. And always a bit, too, it is

---

24   See "Medicare (and Health Care More Generally)" in Chapter Eleven.

25   See "Education" in Chapter Eleven.

about stepping back and more fully appreciating what most ultimately matters as a function of being human.

Whatever the concern, whether intimately personal or broadly collective, our time requires increasingly that we confront it at this crux level of significance. In times past, addressing truth in such a stripped-down, yet also more embracing, whole-box-of-crayons manner would have seemed if not nonsensical, certainly dangerous. It would have appeared to be an all-too-slippery-slope enterprise that risked the loss of all we had gained as seekers of truth.

Today we have no choice—and would not want to have it otherwise. We can effectively take on the multilayered new responsibilities on which the future depends only if we start our actions with crux discernments of this newly complete sort. Such discernments are also key to the new kind of conceptual approaches needed if we are to successfully realize new possibilities. Any "pattern language" framework that is at all complete must have concepts that effectively address this crux truth task.

A Threshold Lesson: Whole-box-of-crayons crux discernments provide the basic feedback we use to make our way once we step over Cultural Maturity's threshold.

Missing the Mark

The distinction between how we have traditionally thought of truth's crux and culturally mature perspective's more systemic understanding of truth is of much more than just philosophical significance. If we miss what becomes different with Cultural Maturity's whole-box-of-crayons definition, we end up in conceptual traps that undermine effective action in ways that can do considerable harm.

My field of psychology provides a particularly good illustration of what can happen when our thinking stops short in this way. It concerns opposite ways in which psychotherapeutic schools have framed what is most important to consider—and in the end where "real" truth lies.

Psychologists and psychiatrists prefer not to acknowledge that what they do involves ideological biases, preferring to believe that their practices reflect well-thought-out and demonstrated methodologies. Historically, practitioners who hold to these opposite interpretations have frequently been at odds (often behaving more like members of competing fundamentalist sects than the scientifically objective professionals they claim to be). The contrasting beliefs held by these often warring camps tie directly to earlier reflections on the nature of culturally mature identity. We can think of them as heroic and romantic versions of the Myth of the Individual. Psychotherapists who apply either of these contrasting formulations pay the price of predictable blindnesses and severe constraints to how deeply they, as practitioners, can be helpful.

Let's start with the more romantic side of things, as that is where we most often find confusion with traditional ideas about truth's crux. Certain schools of psychology elevate an "inner self" and equate it with a "true self." This is common with certain analytic, and almost all humanistic, existential, and transpersonal psychological approaches. The formulations of people who think this way commonly identify the feeling side of experience (or sometimes spiritual sensibilities) with truth, and ultimately with identity as a whole. This chapter's reflections should make clear that this is an ultimately partial—systemically incomplete—way of seeing things.

On the other side of the fence, we find behaviorists who see significance only with in-the-world particulars. They view more inner concerns to be of secondary significance at best. Just as much, the picture they draw on is limited, and limiting. And just as much, these polar opposite conclusions about truth and identity can get practitioners into trouble.

The more appropriate truth/identity task—at least if our interest is "self" in a culturally mature, Whole-Person sense—should be clear from this chapter's reflections. It involves getting our arms around the entirety of our complexity—inner and outer aspects equally—and appreciating them as parts of a larger entirety.[26] In a culturally mature reality, self becomes what results with Integrative Meta-perspective— who we are as the whole box of crayons. Deeper engagement with inner aspects can provide useful guidance in cases where a person has tended to identify with more outer, worldly concerns. But it is just as much the case that a person who has identified with more internal sensibilities benefits from developing their more in-the-world capacities. Miss this

---

26   See " 'Cognitive Rewiring' " in Chapter Nine.

larger picture and we end up with ultimately unhelpful conclusions and dangerous errors in our thinking.

Later we will examine a related observation that makes the importance of more systemic ways of thinking about truth, identity, and psychotherapeutic practice particularly inescapable. More inner sensibilities or more outer sensibilities appropriately play the larger role in people with different personality styles. Thus, to make inner truth or outer truth the "real truth" is also to make people of certain temperaments not just superior, but in an important sense "chosen." We will look also at how more inner and outer sensibilities have varying relative significance at different stages in any human developmental process.[27]

These observations about how "the real self" may be experienced in very different ways by different people provide a good segue for our next topic. They involve making beginning systemic "multiplicity" distinctions.

Truth's "Multiplicity"

The second needed new kind of discernment stands as a bookend to the first. With it, we shift our attention from truth's crux to questions of difference and detail, to truth's multiplicity. We could call this truth's complexity, but from a mature systemic perspective, crux discernments are just as much about complexity as multiplicity determinations are. Returning to the box-of-crayons imagery, our attention shifts from the box (representing truth's crux—here with the more encompassing aspects of its two-part definition emphasized) to the multiple hues of the crayons within.

Culturally mature multiplicity discernments are new, and as we examined with the parallel crux truth picture we just looked at, fundamentally so. It is not at all that we haven't before made observations that differentiated this from that—in a similar way to what we saw with

---

27   In Chapter Ten's closer look at body intelligence, and also in Appendix D's look at personality style differences, I will describe how talking in this way about experience and truth as more "inner" and more "outer" is more than just metaphorical, how it reflects different ways in which experience organizes in the body.

truth's crux, multiplicity distinctions are represented historically by a grand lineage. But in times past, such distinctions have taken the form either of mythologized opposites (various manifestations of "us" versus "them") or more detailed, but still cut-and-dried, this-versus-that lists and categories. Effectively addressing the new challenges before us again requires more dynamic and complete ways of thinking—here about complexity's aspects.

The same two basic differences that we encountered with new distinctions of the crux variety apply to what is new when it comes to culturally mature multiplicity discernments. First, culturally mature multiplicity discernments are necessarily made without the benefit of past cultural guideposts. Second, multiplicity distinctions become necessarily of a more consciously systemic sort, and systemic in the now-familiar, newly dynamic and encompassing sense.

The result is something fundamentally different from how we've divided things up in times past. Culturally mature multiplicity discernments allow us to make distinctions that are more nuanced than in times past, and nuanced in ways that more directly reflect our uniquely human natures. Culturally mature multiplicity discernments also offer a compactness of expression we have not seen previously.

The introductory media example, as we saw with crux distinctions, also pointed toward the importance of this more detailed kind of discernment. I proposed that "we need ways of thinking that help us recognize pattern in information—that help us discern useful knowledge within information, and beyond this, that can assist us in the wise use of that knowledge." We've also already had a preview of the power of such discernment. The developmental/evolutionary frame on which this inquiry is based reflects this new kind of pattern thinking.

For now, we can look to a simple, but in fact quite precise, way to think about multiplicity in this sense: Culturally mature multiplicity distinctions describe how truth, in the end, always exists in a context. Time and place—when an act occurs and the locale or system where it occurs—become ultimately as essential to what makes something true as the content of the act. We could say that culturally mature perspective makes truth relative, but this is explicitly not relativity of the casual "different-strokes-for-different-folks" sort. This sort of relativity is about recognizing that if we want to be precise in our thinking, considerations about all that is happening in relation to our specific challenge can be as important as the more obvious sorts of particulars.

Historically, such contextual subtlety really didn't need to be our concern. Culturally specific dictates—whether moral codes, assumptions about appropriate institutional forms, or a people's concept of the divine—provided one-size-fits-all truths. In point of fact, these truths were also time- and place-specific (specific to their particular time and place in humanity's story), but our limited capacity to see outside our own time and place, and especially to see importance outside of it, meant that this was not something we could recognize or needed to recognize. In contrast, truth beyond Cultural Maturity's threshold makes no real sense separate from contextual considerations.

We commonly miss just how relative our perceptual and conceptual worlds can be. They are dramatically so—even at the level of the biological. We evolve not to see, hear, and taste what is true in some absolute sense, but to perceive in the specific ways that will most support our unique approach to survival. The perceptual world of a dog, a bee, a bear, or an amoeba is much different from our own. And while we reflexively assume that our reality is the most sophisticated, if I were lost in the woods with only the scent of my previous steps to guide me home, the perceptual reality of the dog or the bear would provide much more sensitive and useful truth.

We can think of our human contextual relativities as layered. Because we are creatures, such biological relativities always come into play, and not just when our concern is the ways in which we are different from other creatures on the planet. This first layer plays a role, for example, when we ask what factors make men and women different. The "nature" side of the common nature-versus-nurture debate is concerned with this first layer.

Beyond the wholly biological, we find aspects of perceptual and conceptual relativity that are products of learning—the complementary "nurture" side of things. Our immense capacity to adapt, learn, and grow means that to a degree not present with other creatures, what I see and what you see may not be the same. The sources of such conditioning-related differences are endless: differing ethnic or religious backgrounds; gender expectations; birth order; or simple happenstance—a particular teacher who influenced you, or an odd event that is not part of most other people's experience.

A third, more uniquely human layer in truth's relativity, one that is not so commonly recognized, is especially pertinent to our inquiry. The first two kinds of contextual relativity require Cultural Maturity's changes to be understood clearly, but the third requires Integrative Meta-perspective to be recognized at all. We can be different for reasons that are more nuanced and particular than biology as we customarily think of it, and deeper than just conditioning. We often make reference to such difference colloquially. When we talk about "where a person is coming from," it is often this third sort of contextual difference that we are most observing. "Pattern language" discernments of the multiplicity sort draw on this further layer of contextual relativity.

Some of these uniquely human differences are more temporal—about context in the sense of *when* things happen. We see the impact of temporal relativities whenever ongoing change processes come into play—for example, with stages in individual development; with the way relationships change over time; with the steps through which organizations evolve; or with the kind of change we've given particular attention to in these pages, the evolution of cultural systems. The concept of Cultural Maturity is a product of such temporal "pattern-language" thinking applied at a societal level.

Other such contextual differences are of a more here-and-now sort, concerned with context in a spatial sense, with place as opposed to time. Here-and-now, in-this-moment relativities become significant whenever present-time differences with origins deeper than just conditioning come into play. Some examples include how our multiple intelligences variously influence what we see; temperament/personality style differences; contrasting political or philosophical allegiances where the roots are of a differing crayon-in-the-systemic-box sort; and the contrasting views and values of academic disciplines, departments/functions in an organization, or cultural domains. With regard to more here-and-now distinctions, we will give special attention to the effects of our multiple intelligences and to temperament/personality style differences.[28]

---

28 Chapter Six presents a framework for thinking about intelligence's multiplicity, and Chapter Nine and Appendix D examine a particularly useful personality style approach.

We get a provocative illustration of the significance of this third sort of "where we're coming from" contextual relativity if we combine some of the differences it highlights with earlier observations about how moral truth is changing. The Golden Rule—"Do unto others as you would have them do unto you"—makes a remarkably good answer to the question of morality's ultimate bottom line (morality's "crux"). It holds up well no matter what the cultural or individual context is. But notice what happens if we take cultural stage or personality style differences into account. The rule holds, but it has very different consequences depending on the context. We can't escape the fact that different people can want very different things "done unto them."

This kind of recognition will be increasingly pertinent to good leadership in all parts of our lives as we go forward. For example, acknowledging that different people might want different things "done unto them" helps us cut through the bigotries that inherently accompany ideology. Just recognizing the validity of difference immediately weakens bigotry's hold. And if we can appreciate such difference in a way that goes beyond just replacing bigotry with simple acceptance—that fully embraces difference—we can replace a reality of "us" versus "them" with a vibrant and newly multihued interactional world.

A good temporal relativity example relates to a way in which we can misunderstand the implications of Cultural Maturity. If we are not careful, we can end up reducing the concept of Cultural Maturity to ideology—to thinking of it as good in and of itself, as good in some timeless sense. We don't make this mistake if we always keep in mind that we are dealing with a developmental process. Few people would disagree with the statement that expecting mature behavior of a young child is not just misguided, but ultimately a violation. Similarly, when we prematurely expect culturally mature capacities within social systems, we are at the very least unlikely to see successful outcomes. Temporal multiplicity distinctions support the needed sensitivity.

Truth has always been contextual. But our ability to be this conscious of truth's relativities and to recognize just how far their implications extend is new. Cultural Maturity's cognitive changes make truth's relativities at all three levels I've described—the biological, that which is a simple product of learning, and these more specifically human contextual differences—newly tolerable and understandable (even fascinating). Sometimes the answers to our questions require that we take multiple relativities into account. How we experience gender, for example, includes biological differences, simple conditioning, variation that is a product of the predictably different ways various cultural stages view men and women, and how we may respond differently to any of these variables depending on personality style. Cultural differences can in a similar way involve all these levels—ethnicity at the level of the biological, tradition and mores at the level of conditioning (learning), and both cultural stage and locale at the level of our more specifically human relativities.

Effectively addressing the complex questions before us will require increasingly that we be conscious of truth's relativities. We must never forget how what is true in one situation may not be true in another. And we can't stop there. A casual different-strokes-for-different-folks, ecumenical acceptance of truth's relativity leaves us well short of Cultural Maturity's threshold. The needed sophistication of inquiry must be able to tell us something about the specifics of difference, why we see the differences that we do, and how an appreciation of such difference brings new clarity and creativity to our considerations.

A Threshold Lesson: Once we've addressed what lies at a question's crux, we necessarily turn to questions of context. Without the former, we are left without the bottom-line guidance that purposeful action requires. Without the latter, we find useful generalities, but not the nuanced distinctions needed to effectively make our way.

Common-Sense Truth

The ability to make nuanced, culturally mature crux and multiplicity distinctions should prove increasingly critical in times ahead. This is not at all to say that the sorts of discernments I've described in this chapter are the only kinds of truths we will need to draw on once we step over Cultural Maturity's threshold. We will continue to see essential advances of a more purely technical sort. And much of truth doesn't change at all—a door remains a door, and one plus one still equals two. But increasingly we will need facility with these new kinds of discernments. Without such facility we will make badly misguided, often dangerous decisions.

In concluding these initial new-truth reflections, it is important to reemphasize a conclusion highlighted at the chapter's beginning and touched on in limited ways with my descriptions of each of these new kinds of truth concepts—once we step over Cultural Maturity's threshold, these new kinds of truth become straightforward. Given how I've approached these reflections—using abstract language like "crux" and "multiplicity" and with references to philosophical assumptions—we could easily be left wondering whether we are up to all that these newly sophisticated notions require. That we are able to effectively engage them follows from the fact that they are products of developmental/ evolutionary processes. We don't need to consciously know anything about crux and multiplicity aspects of truth, culturally mature or otherwise, to begin making these sorts of discernments. The changes that produce these new ways of thinking about truth come part and parcel with Cultural Maturity's larger changes.

You would not have gotten this far in this book if you were not already making quite subtle crux and multiplicity discernments in many parts of your life. You are probably carrying out daily life decisions with often only a glance to cultural convention. Doing so requires getting more directly at what for you is true (getting at truth's crux). It also means being sensitive to context, both the context of your unique values as a person and the particular contexts in which you are making choices (truth's multiplicity). This more mature decision-making may be happening mostly at a level of personal maturity. But given the context of our time and your interest in reading these words, much too is certainly taking place at a Cultural Maturity level.

Particularly given some of the ideas I will put forward in the next chapter, all this might seem like a startling revelation. There I will address more explicitly how these changes in how we think reflect innovation at the level of truth itself. This would certainly seem the appropriate work not just of a philosopher but, given the significance, depth, and newness of these changes, a philosopher of unusual acumen. But once we step over Cultural Maturity's threshold, these kinds of distinctions start becoming the kind that feel obviously important to make. They become what works. In noticing that they do, we may develop concepts about why they do. And seeing others make similar choices and hearing other people's ideas may help us refine those concepts. But if these are "ideas whose time has come," as I've suggested, it is not always important that we understand what we are doing, or even that we are conscious that anything has changed. These new kinds of distinctions become a further part of our new common sense.

CHAPTER SIX

Rethinking Truth Itself—
Pattern and Possibility

The ultimate metaphysical ground is the creative advance into novelty ....
both God and the world are in [its] grip.
ALFRED NORTH WHITEHEAD

CHAPTER FIVE TOOK US IMPORTANT STEPS in addressing the third threshold task. We've examined how the post-ideological, complexity-acknowledging, limits-affirming kinds of truths we need to address today's new challenges require a whole new order of human responsibility. We've also looked at how such truths are necessarily systemic, and systemic in a specific new sense. And we've reflected on how, at least when it comes to the truths that relate to ourselves, culturally mature perspective alters truth's basic categories.

But more about truth than just its categories become different with Cultural Maturity's cognitive changes. As I suggested with the previous chapter's reflections on systemic understanding, culturally mature perspective alters not just particular truths, but truth itself—or at least how we are able to understand it. In this chapter, we look more closely at this result. In doing so, I will give special attention to how a creative frame provides an effective and practical way to make sense of and apply the new, more dynamic and complete picture of truth that culturally mature perspective reveals.

I will start by drawing on three now-familiar recognitions. The first brings us back to the fact that we need to think in ways that better reflect our living human natures. I will use the example of addressing future moral/ethical concerns to paint a general picture of what thinking in the needed more vital ways entails. More specifically, I will address how thinking in the needed more life-acknowledging ways requires determinations that are necessarily of a more "exploratory" sort than related determinations of times past.

The second recognition returns to how needed new truths "bridge" traditional polar assumptions. We will examine a characteristic inherent in the workings of polarity that is key to appreciating where bridging in the sense I have spoken of takes us—how polarities share an underlying symmetry. We will also take time with the question of why we see polarity in the first place. Each of these topics points us toward the appropriateness and power of a creative frame.

The third new-truth recognition comes back to how culturally mature truth requires that we engage more aspects of intelligence, and in more conscious and integrated ways, than the more limited truths of times past. We will look more closely at how the way in which Integrative Meta-perspective engages the whole of intelligence's systemic complexity alters our experience of what makes something true. In particular, we will look at how this fact supports the conclusion that more creative understandings of truth are not just possible, but predicted.

Finally, we will turn more specifically to how Creative Systems Theory applies a creative frame to understanding, and how nuanced crux and multiplicity truth concepts able to guide us in the territory ahead are a result. These further reflections will set the stage for the next chapter's look at the developmental/evolutionary picture that gives us the concept of Cultural Maturity.

This chapter concludes with a series of observations that help bring our third threshold task's truth-related reflections together. We will look at how culturally mature perspective brings a precision to the truths we use that has not before been possible. I will also expand on an observation noted earlier—how the needed new, more complex kind of understanding can be functionally simpler than what it replaces—here relating it to this chapter's more specifically truth-focused formulations. I will end by describing how the new kinds of truths that come with Cultural Maturity's changes, in themselves, provide antidotes to today's crisis of purpose.

Morality, Life, and Truth

The first new-truth recognition returns to the now-familiar observation that I highlighted in the previous chapter with the Dilemma of

Differentiation: We need to think in ways that better reflect the fact that we are living beings, and more specifically, the particular sort of life that we are by virtue of being human. I've described how Integrative Meta-perspective produces this result and also how culturally mature crux and multiplicity truth notions are each different from what we have know before in ways consistent with it.

But these are abstract, theoretical observations. We are left with the question of just what thinking in ways that better reflect our living human natures looks like. The task of effectively addressing moral/ethical concerns in a post-ideological world helps make tangible what this necessary new step in how we think about truth involves.

I've described how cultural absolutes (whatever a culture's particular versions) have historically provided us with unquestioned guidance for making moral/ethical decisions. I've also described how the diminishing usefulness of past cultural guideposts means that today we have become responsible not just for making good moral choices, but also for getting more directly at what makes something moral. But just what does it mean to get more directly at moral significance? This basic question brings us face to face with the task of thinking in ways that better reflect our living human natures.

I've proposed that postmodern perspective, while it has effectively challenged past moral absolutes, even at its best can give us only limited help with replacing them. (And postmodern belief at its worst, in reducing the ethical dimension to a different-strokes-for-different-folks moral relativism, only gets in the way of the needed greater sophistication.) The concept of Cultural Maturity suggests a more systemic— both life-acknowledging and ultimately human–life-acknowledging— picture of moral/ethical decision-making.

I find it helpful to approach getting there in a series of steps. The first step observes that once we traverse Cultural Maturity's threshold, the measures we use for determining what is moral become, like new truths more generally, at once more bare-boned and more encompassing. Our bottom line becomes not the isolated rightness or wrongness of particular behaviors and thoughts, but the degree to which an act or thought ultimately serves well-being.

That's a good basic answer, but the idea that moral acts serve well-being is too general to provide ultimately useful guidance. To be a bit more precise, we can make our answer quantitative: An act becomes moral when it makes things[1] "more," a more encompassing—and by implication generative—way of describing significance that I have previously made use of.

But a further essential question remains if this more specific response is to help us—"more what?" The word "more" needs something to refer to. The most compact response, given our living natures, is "more alive." Conclusions become morally true in any functional sense (the only sense that ultimately matters) to the degree that they enhance life—or, more precisely, to the degree that they enhance the particular kind of life we are by virtue of being human.

This answer might still seem vague. But in fact it could not be more precise. What might appear to be vagueness is not imprecision. Rather it is the Dilemma of Representation playing its now predictable role in depiction that reflects the needed completeness.

In fact, this kind of feedback—the degree to which what we do supports and furthers human life—is what we have always used, throughout history, to guide us in making moral decisions. Culturally prescribed moral dictates reflect ways in which we've collectively codified thoughts and actions that are likely to be life-enhancing. The difference today is simply that we are becoming able to step back and be conscious that this is what we are measuring. Cultural Maturity's cognitive changes also make it possible to bring a new degree of detail and sophistication to this kind of discernment.

There is an important sense in which this kind of reframing applies to truths of every sort, not just to moral truth. Isaac Newton's laws of motion were a right and timely—at the time, most "alive"—response to right and timely cultural questions, as were the words of Winston Churchill in England's "darkest hour," or the art of Pablo Picasso or Jackson Pollock to the existential contradictions of a postmodern world.

Today the capacity to think about truth in ways that better reflect our particular living natures—and to do so consciously—becomes increasingly essential. In our choices as individuals, in our relationships and families, with our participation in organizations and nations, and

---

1   Pertinent systems.

in our attempts to understand the larger world around us, we want to ask as clearly and directly as possible what ways of thinking will make us more in this fundamental sense. At a species level, we can use this more systemic reframing of truth to define Cultural Maturity itself—certainly what Cultural Maturity ultimately asks of us. Put in the language of systems, Cultural Maturity is about thinking in the ways that, uniquely in our time, become most affirming of what ultimately makes us who we are. It is also about transforming such thought into action.

Note an important implication of this more systemic way of understanding moral truth—and, in the end, truth more generally—that I suggested earlier. In a sense that has not before been the case, it makes every question a moral/ethical concern. In times past, only some questions were thought of as moral. For them we looked to religion for needed answers. Other question, such as the concerns of science or business were considered to be "value-free." But every personal or collective choice we make, whatever its sort, increases or decreases the fullness and vitality of our existence. From Cultural Maturity's more encompassing perspective, every choice becomes a moral/ethical choice. In the next chapter, I will apply this recognition to specific cultural domains.[2]

> A Threshold Lesson: In living systems, truth and life, in the end, ask the same question. With culturally mature perspective we more directly see how the truths we use to make choices must enhance life—and in particular, the specific kind of life we are by virtue of being human.

"Exploratory" Truth

In addition to helping us better understand what makes culturally mature truth new, the observation that we need to think in ways that better reflect our living human natures also points toward the potential usefulness of a creative frame. The basic recognition supports a creative frame in a limited way: The word "creative" suggests a more vital sort of understanding. Creative Systems Theory's approach to thinking about our human natures makes explicit this support for a creative interpretation

---

2   See "Values, Cultural Domains, and the Future" in Chapter Seven.

at least when it comes to ourselves. Creative Systems Theory proposes that what makes us particular, if not unique as creatures is the audacity of our toolmaking, meaning-making—we could say simply, "creative"—capacities.

Shortly we will examine how truth's content becomes more explicitly creative when we step over Cultural Maturity's threshold. But before we go there, we should take a moment to appreciate the creative component inherent in the more process-related aspects of culturally mature truth. Much in how culturally mature truth becomes new has less to do with specific choices—even wise ones—than with how we go about making choices. This is not at all to simply reduce truth to process. Process and content represent another key polarity, and when it is bridged, as we see with all bridgings, our appreciation for how poles are different increases along with our recognition of inherent relationship. But it is true that in a whole new sense content and process cease being separate concerns. With this, process and content each take on new, more dynamic and complete, "creative," definitions.

We aren't used to thinking of truth in process terms. We are more apt to think of truth as almost the opposite of a process—if not fixed and absolute, at least the end product of our inquiries. Cultural Maturity makes it inescapable that what constitutes right choice is ultimately a moving target. It also makes clear that what is most important to know is often permeated by change and uncertainty in ways that the more cut-and-dried truths of times past were not.[3]

One result is that culturally mature decision-making often becomes more exploratory and experimental than what it replaces. I often use exploratory metaphors in my therapy practice—to help people confront questions of basic life direction and also to address specific life choices (with regard to profession, relationships, where to live, values to hold). Such metaphors help people shape their lives in ways that

---

3   If we are to avoid traps in our thinking, we need to recognize that while most often we make the content side of experience what ultimately defines truth, we can fall off of the roadway of culturally mature understanding just as readily by making truth primarily about process. We can see this kind trap with more humanistic and spiritual psychological and organizational approaches.

best honor their unique identity and contribution. In a sense, such concerns have always been exploratory. But in the past, cultural dictates—for both good and ill—have dramatically restricted options.

For people of more rational bent, I might talk about such inquiry as akin to the best of scientific experiments. Well-done experiments engage the experimenter in a sequence of creative responsibilities. The first is responsibility for asking a good question, one worthy of the experimenter's time and focus. Next comes responsibility for crafting experiments and developing hypotheses that might shed new light on that question. Finally comes responsibility for obtaining the most accurate and useful results.

Making good choices in a well-lived life tends to be messier than this. But when external guideposts are limited, we necessarily engage in a similar kind of progression. We start by selecting a worthy creative starting point (if the question concerns work, selecting an endeavor that excites and could prove fulfilling; if it concerns love, choosing someone for whom we feel caring and who could be good for us). And we experiment. We observe and we try things out. And we listen for what brings fulfillment. In the process, we learn about ourselves (and, with love, the other person). And we learn about the shapes that choices might take (how we might approach work, or how to engage love in ways that best reflect two people's unique natures and their growing connection).

When approaching life experimentally, we need to be exceedingly honest with regard to what works and what does not. Like good science, a creatively lived life is only in a limited way about getting the answers we want. With both, the most irresponsible thing one can do is alter data so as to better fit our hopes. The task is to seek out what is creatively true. It is through this that we make choices that are right, and choices that matter.

Science metaphors are likely to get blank stares—or worse—from people of more emotional or intuitive bent. But the metaphor of the artist's creative process works equally well. I might talk about how a composer writes a piece of music or how a painter applies his or her craft. The artist's first responsibility is to discover a worthy creative impulse—a possibility to which one is deeply drawn. Next comes trying out different ways to give that impulse expression. Lastly, there is the task of discerning what works and what does not. Artistic expression is about listening for what is beautiful and exploring different ways to make that beauty manifest. As with good science, eloquent artistry requires incorruptible self-honesty—fudging the results gets us nowhere. And in a similar sense, we cannot know ahead of time exactly where that honesty will lead.

People can object to such use of experimental/exploratory metaphors. For example, some can find them initially a bit heady, too analytical. This is particularly common if the topic is something like love. My response is that consciously engaging love (or life more generally) as a process does in fact require careful discernment—though something ultimately more than analytical discernment. Culturally mature decision-making requires bringing nuanced perspective to all kinds of questions for which simple being, faith, or subjective passion have been the more appropriate kind of engagement in times past.

In an opposite sort of objection, a person might claim that experimental imagery is just too imprecise—too "loosey-goosey." Again, using love as an example, a person might argue that it leaves out the most important ingredient in relationship—commitment. But, in fact, approaching love as a creative process in the end implies greater attention to commitment. Certainly, commitment can be one of the most powerful tools we have for making relationship's creative life possible and sustainable. More, the absence of clear guidelines in a culturally mature reality gives the articulation of commitment and the determination of its forms ever greater importance. Even if the commitment choices we make are very traditional, they need a deeper level of personal commitment to sustain them. What the exploratory metaphor adds to traditional notions of commitment is a better appreciation for how the rules for success in love—and the meaning of commitment—change when we no longer have the luxury of established goals and procedures.[4]

---

4   Exploratory metaphors do run a risk of biasing understanding toward the more unformed and uncertain aspects of formativeness (we tend to associate exploration and experimentation with beginnings). They thus must be used carefully. But because it is the beginning aspects of formative process that in our time often feel most foreign to us (see "Progress and the Dilemma of Trajectory" in Chapter Eight), such metaphors, if used skillfully, can be provocative and powerful.

Exploratory language can be applied just as usefully to decision-making of a more collective sort. The question of how we best manage the often-contradictory potentials of modern invention provides a good example. Because many of our most important advances, along with promising good, also present significant risk, responsible management will be critical. But responsibility in the sense of just doing the right thing can only be of limited help. Often it is not at all clear—except to those of dogmatic persuasion—just what doing the right thing means. Evaluation commonly involves complexly interwoven causal factors, and there is always the possibility of wild-card events. In the words of Freeman Dyson, "If we had a reliable way to label our toys good and bad, it would be easy to regulate technology wisely. But we can rarely see far enough ahead to know which road leads to damnation."

Faced with such uncertainty, how do we best respond? Some people reflexively call for extreme caution. Others may assert that free and open discovery is the only hope we have. And looming over choices with regard to specific technologies is the question of whether responsibly managing human invention and its consequences is really even possible. The drive to be toolmakers may be simply unstoppable, impervious to self-reflection.

The perspective offered by an experimental/creative frame provides at least the beginning of a way for us to get beyond the apparent impasse. It suggests that management as we customarily think of it may not be the right word. In the end, we can't really control invention any more than we can once and for all control the outcome of love, the creation of a work of art, or the results of scientific experimentation—and we would not want to. It also emphasizes that a lack of final control does not save us from responsibility; indeed, quite the opposite. We may not yet know how to most effectively carry out such shared creative decision-making, but we can be sure our well-being will more and more depend on it. When we look back at ourselves in a hundred years, if we are at all successful at devising social structures and mechanisms for making such choices, we will surely regard these as some of our times' greatest achievements.

This exploratory kind of responsibility demands more of us. Certainly it requires that we leave behind narrow assumptions and allegiances. Ideology throws us into a polarized world where the needed creativity becomes very difficult. But with Cultural Maturity, this more exploratory kind of responsibility becomes something we are capable of. And we increasingly see that it is the only kind that can work. We also increasingly recognize that when we consciously move beyond absolutist beliefs and think in more exploratory ways, not only do we make better headway, very often we find wholly unexpected solutions.

One of my favorite examples of this kind of result comes from a think tank on nuclear waste disposal that the Institute for Creative Development convened in 1992. It brought together many of the best nuclear scientists from around the world. The question of how to deal with nuclear waste commonly reduces to an either/or debate, with neither answer being of much help. We can decide to store nuclear waste in such a way that we are absolutely sure it will do no harm for hundreds of thousands of years into the future (which is impossible), or we can pretend it is not a problem (when it very much is a problem). Political persuasions often determine on which side of this debate we find ourselves.

Over days of committed reflection, the think tank members arrived at a different sort of answer. That they were able to do so was a testament to their ability to get beyond polemical assumptions and engage the question as an exploratory process. Participants concluded that the best solution might be to store the waste in a retrievable form for a few thousand years—which we can do with current technologies—and figure out what to do with it at that point. While this might initially seem like just kicking the can down the road, in fact it represents a most practical solution. By the time we retrieve the waste, the more dangerous parts of the radiation will have dissipated. And we will most likely also have come up with good uses for the remaining radioactive material. (I found it fascinating that the solution they arrived at involved thinking about nuclear waste itself more as a process.)

An exploratory framing of choice and truth translates readily to the more encompassing task of addressing our human future as a whole. Addressing the future responsibly requires that we accept that what lies ahead necessarily defies final prediction. Notions like Cultural Maturity and the ideas of Creative Systems Theory can serve as crude maps, but such maps provide only general direction. In ages past, this amount of uncertainty would have been too much to tolerate. Today, nothing more defines the tasks of our time—and the excitement of our time—than the need to take ownership in the exploratory creation of a human future beyond what we can yet imagine.

In this section I've used two terms—"experimental" and "creative"—with subtly but significantly different implications (with the term "exploratory" reflecting a bit of the meaning of each). The difference is important. The word "experimental" adequately describes the basic postmodern task of making our way without familiar guideposts. The word "creative" implies underlying generativity and pattern in a sense that the term "experimental" does not. Creative Systems Theory proposes that "creative" is the more precise term—and that it must be. It argues that if the truths we draw on are not ultimately creative, it would not be possible to effectively make our way—at any time, but certainly now. We will examine how the concept of Cultural Maturity makes sense only within an explicitly creative understanding of human nature and the human endeavor.

Polarity's Underlying "Procreative" Symmetry

The idea that culturally mature perspective draws a circle around what before have appeared to be polar opposite assumptions has in some way contributed to truth's new picture throughout this book. With the first threshold task, I used the concept of bridging to fill out the basic observation that today's new complexities require that we leave behind projection and think in more encompassing ways. With the second threshold task, I described how polar ideologies juxtapose myths of limitlessness, and also the way each aspect of complexity's more dynamic and complete picture—not just multiple parts, but also uncertainty, change, and interconnectedness—is itself a bridging notion.

I also implied the bridging of polarities in the way confronting inviolable limits produces results that can seem paradoxical—for example, how limits can at once constrain us and teach us about new possibility. With the previous chapter's introduction to the importance of new truth categories, we saw how culturally mature "crux" and "multiplicity" truths each bridge the polar assumptions of times past.

The concept of bridging also ties directly to each of this chapter's main recognitions to this point. It offers a particularly graphic way to recognize how culturally mature perspective might help us develop truth concepts that better reflect our living human natures. With any act of bridging, we take either/or assumptions and replace them with a picture that is more vital, dynamic, and multihued in its implications than we could have understood in times past. The concept of bridging informed the previous section's observations about the exploratory nature of culturally mature truth in the way Integrative Meta-perspective makes truth equally about process and content. Not only does culturally mature perspective value content and process equally, every culturally mature concept, being in the end creative in the sense I am using the word, is simultaneously about process and content.

But while bridging as I have presented the concept gets us much of the way toward capturing the new kind of truth we have interest in, we need more if we are to understand at all deeply how bridging works. We also need more if the creative implications of what we see are to make full sense. The way polarity has played a major role in how we think provides one of the most direct ways to understand the power of a creative frame. But an additional observation is required if we are to fully appreciate these creative implications.

We get a bit closer with an important earlier recognition: Polar juxtapositions are always more than just either/ors, simple opposed tendencies like two competing athletes or cars that threaten to run into one another. They exist in systemic relationship—like halves of an apple cut in two. My earlier claim that opposing political ideologies are much less different than we commonly imagine was a reference to this underlying relatedness. I've suggested that recognizing this relatedness at the least points toward a more vital, more complete kind of understanding.

The creative implications become explicit with the addition of a further recognition. We find that polar relationships reflect a particular kind of symmetry. Put simply, conceptual polarities have complementary right and left hands. With polarity's right hand we find harder, commonly more rational and more material qualities. With polarity's left hand we find qualities of a softer, more poetic, and often more spiritual sort. Facts juxtapose with feelings, mind with body,[5] matter with energy, and so on.

---

5   We must be attentive to language when we make such distinctions. For
     example, with mind and body, what is "left" and what is "right" may dif-
     fer depending on how we use words. If "mind" refers to the intellect and
     "body" to our more sensory life, the order in which I listed the terms—

Psychology has terms for these extremes, drawn from the study of myth. It refers to the more concrete side of each pairing as "archetypally masculine," and its softer counterpart as "archetypally feminine." The gender-linked language can cause confusion, particularly today as women and men each seek to make both poles their own, but its sexual connotations are evocative and in a way particularly pertinent to our inquiry. In some fundamental way, the relationship between polar extremes becomes "procreative."

An appreciation for such symmetry assists us most immediately by helping us flesh out systemic relationships of the here-and-now "multiplicity" sort. For example, we can understand a lot about opposing conservative and liberal tendencies in the political arena by thinking of them in terms of juxtaposed archetypally masculine and archetypally feminine tendencies. On the Right we find harder, more difference-biased values—competition in the marketplace, a strong military, the integrity of national borders, and rugged individualism. On the Left we find values of a softer, more relationship-biased sort—identification with the disadvantaged, government as advocate for the common good, environmentalism, and equal rights. It is a simplistic approach that leaves out a lot, but it also provides useful insight.[6]

Later in the book, I will make use of other here-and-now multiplicity observations that similarly draw on this fact of underlying symmetry. For example, I will apply this recognition of symmetry to help us identify and map common conceptual traps.[7] Observations in the previous chapter about how familiar systems notions fall short illustrate this kind of application. I described how systemic understanding as we have known it sides variously with more engineering truth or more

---

mind and body—is consistent with the other polarities mentioned in the sentence. But if we make "mind" that which produces human sentience and "body" simply anatomy, the order is reversed: body and mind.

6   I've heard the Republican and Democratic parties in the U.S. jokingly referred to as the "daddy party" and the "mommy party." This turns out to be a fairly apt shorthand. Chapter Nine (see "One 'Crayon' and Another") and Appendix D provide more detailed reflection by tying this kind of observation to personality style differences.

7   See "Polar Traps" in Chapter Nine.

spiritual and poetic truth. We could equally well talk of these differences in terms of identification with more right-hand or more left-hand aspects of understanding. (We just saw this same juxtaposition of polar traps manifest in another way in how different people can identify truth more with content or more with process.)

The recognition of underlying symmetry also has critical implications when it comes to "multiplicity" discernments of the more temporal sort. While polarities at every cultural stage juxtapose right-hand and left-hand sensibilities, these juxtapositions evolve in predictable ways. For example, over the course of history, we see a gradual progression from times in which archetypally feminine values—connection with nature, tribe, or spirit (values that emphasize oneness)—most defined truth, to a reality in our time in which archetypally masculine values—individuality, materialism, competition, or the logic of science (values that emphasize separateness)—have come to play a much larger role.[8]

In the next chapter, we will examine how this progression helps us make sense of Cultural Maturity as a time in history. It will help us understand how Cultural Maturity's changes fit into culture's larger story, why they involve the new capacities I have described, and why in our time these changes have become essential.[9]

---

8   This progression adds historical refinement to the just-mentioned short-hand for thinking about political parties. The sense in which opposing parties reflect more right-hand and left-hand sensibilities refers to those proclivities as they manifest specifically at our particular point in culture's evolving story. Note that the values both parties represent today are more materialistic and individualistic—more archetypally masculine—than we have encountered at any previous time.

9   Chapter Eight examines a critical implication of this progression that Creative Systems Theory calls the Dilemma of Trajectory. With time, the direction that has taken us to where we are leaves us nowhere to go. Increasingly in today's world, right-hand truth becomes the only real truth, with left-hand sensibilities at best playing some faint decorative function. If more systemic perspective is in fact what today's new questions require, then Cultural Maturity, or something like it that can similarly provide a more integrative picture, becomes the only real option.

Polarity and Formative Process

At this point, we can use this brief look at polarity's "procreative" symmetry to more conceptually set the stage for these later more detailed and culturally specific reflections. To get a basic understanding of Creative Systems Theory's specifically "creative" picture of change and interrelationship in human systems, we need only add a basic understanding of polarity's role in the workings of formative process. In Chapter Two, I described Creative Systems Theory's claim that if we can successfully answer a series of polarity-related questions, we have made it most of the way toward what is needed to develop effective culturally mature conception. Those questions: Why do we humans tend to think in the language of polarity in the first place? Why have we now begun to see understanding that bridges familiar polar assumptions? And how do we best think about what happens when we do bridge polarities? Drawing on polarity's generative implications, a creative frame provides answers to each of these questions.

First, why do we think in polar terms in the first place? Creative Systems Theory proposes that polarity is essential to the workings of formative process. A briefest of descriptions: Creative processes begin in a womb-world—in original unity. The newly created thing then buds off from that initial wholeness, creating polarity in the process. Over time, the newly created thing, and polarity with it, evolves and matures, with polarity manifesting in predictable forms with each creative stage.

The diagram in Figure 6-1 depicts the initial stages of this creative mechanism. The recognition that, at any point in time, the juxtaposed creative poles reflect archeptypally masculine and archetypally femine aspects ties it back to previous reflections in this chapter. The more manifest half of any polar pair (the "newly created form," upper pole in each creative stage) gives expression to more archetypally masculine qualities. The more germinal half of any polar pair (the "creative context," lower pole in each creative stage) gives expression to more archetypally feminine qualities. [10]

---

10   We will later examine how this vertical representation reflects only one way in which polar tendencies manifest with each stage-specific reality, but it is the most readily grasped. Over time in any developmental process, both the relationship between poles and how we experience each pole evolve in characteristic ways.

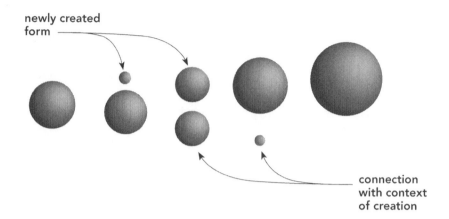

newly created form

connection with context of creation

Fig. 6-1. Polarity and Formative Process

A creative frame similarly provides an answer to the second polarity-related question, why now we might see the bridging of past polar assumptions. Creative Systems Theory describes how bridging plays an inherent role in creative process. We can think of the underlying progression of any formative process as having two halves distinguished by polarity and our relationship to it. The creative stages that bring new creation into being aren't the end of things. Any creative process has a differentiation phase and an integration phase. Once new possibility has become established in a human mind or minds, that possibility reengages with the context from which it was born, becoming part of a newly expanded whole. The person or group then experiences this now-expanded whole as "second nature"—as the new common sense.

Figure 6-2 depicts this two-part progression. This basic progression plays out with creative processes of all sorts. When I myself have a fresh insight, at first I find excitement in its newness. It becomes something separate and distinct. Gradually it becomes more distinct and grows and evolves in the process. Then, with time, I begin to experience it differently. I relate to it now as simply one part of a new, expanded me. When an innovative idea first arises in a culture, it creates excitement and controversy. It is something new and unique. Then, gradually, having been challenged and having matured, the idea can become an accepted part of a now-expanded cultural reality. Creation begins in oneness, becomes manifest through polarity, and then reconciles into a larger, more inclusive entirety. Creative Systems Theory proposes that the fact that we are now beginning to think in ways that recognize larger systemic relationships is a product of this second creative mechanism.

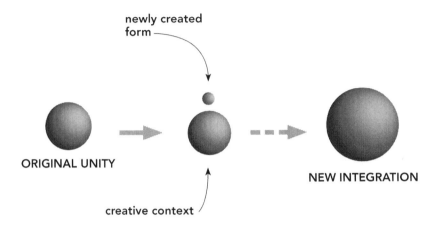

Fig. 6-2. "Bridging" in Formative Process

What Creative Systems Theory calls the *Creative Function* (see Figure 6-3) brings these two depictions together. By representing how polar relationships evolve over the course of any human formative process, it provides a map for delineating change of all sorts—including culture's larger story. The Creative Function makes understandable how the very different ways in which polar opposites have related to this point in culture's evolution reflect an underlying creative mechanism. And it clarifies how the way that relationship is changing in our time has similar origins.

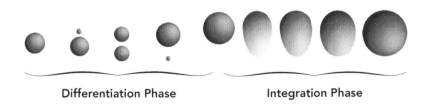

Fig. 6-3. The Creative Function

The answer to the third polarity-related question—what happens when we bridge polarities—has informed all of these reflections on truth. Ultimately, it has been what this book as a whole has been about.

A Threshold Lesson: Recognizing a particular polarity's underlying symmetry provides important insight by making more understandable why apparent opposites take the forms they do. And appreciating the creative mechanisms that underlie any particular polarity helps us understand both why in times past we have thought of it as we have and how the concept of Cultural Maturity provides a more dynamic and encompassing interpretation.

Truth and Intelligence

Our next new-truth topic concerns not so much *what* we might know, but rather, *what we know with*. We again turn our attention to intelligence. I've suggested that the way we think about intelligence is changing. And of particular pertinence to this third threshold task, how we must use intelligence—which of our multiple ways of knowing we must draw on and just how to do so if we are to make good choices—is changing.

Our emerging picture of intelligence provides one of the best ways to understand how culturally mature truth is new. It also provides both some of the best evidence for a creative frame and one of the best points of departure for translating a creative frame into practical conceptual tools. This chapter's next section turns specifically to the creative implications of intelligence's new picture. But before we go there, we should first reflect further on the more general importance of recognizing intelligence's multiplicity.

In introducing the cognitive reordering that produces culturally mature truth, I described how intelligence's multiple aspects represent key elements of our internal complexity. I observed that Integrative Meta-perspective involves more fully stepping back from these diverse ways in which we process experience. It also requires us to embrace our multiple ways of knowing more deeply and apply them in more comprehensive—and ultimately more creative—ways than has before been an option.

In making these observations, I noted one truth-related consequence of these changes that for many people is particularly striking. Culturally mature perspective makes clear that we can rarely make culturally mature choices by using our intellects alone. Culturally mature decision-making requires that we apply our intelligence in the rational sense—indeed, that we do so with new precision—but it also necessarily engages other aspects of intelligence.

This chapter's previous new-truth characteristics each support this conclusion. If we limit ourselves to the rational, the life-acknowledging kinds of understanding needed for good future decision-making will elude us—in isolation, our rationality knows only an engineering world. The need to bridge polarities in our thinking similarly supports the importance of engaging our multiple intelligences. Culturally mature understanding consciously "bridges" facts with feelings, the workings of the imagination with more practical considerations, and observations of the mind with things only our bodies can know. Culturally mature truth requires that we draw on the whole of ourselves as cognitive systems. It is this that produces the possibility of thinking with the needed new kind of systemic sophistication.

The importance of more deeply engaging the whole of intelligence is reflected in the best of contemporary understanding. Medicine is beginning to recognize how mind and body, far from being separate worlds, interlink through a complex array of communications molecules. And educational circles endlessly debate whether IQ adequately measures the whole of intelligence.[11] We hear the challenging of intelligence's traditional picture even in the hardest of the hard sciences. I think of physicist Niels Bohr's famous assertion that, "when it comes to atoms, language can be used only as in poetry."

In a more limited sense, we have always drawn on all aspects of intelligence. When we do a math problem, talk with a friend, or paint a picture, we tap very different parts of our neurology. But culturally mature understanding involves more than just drawing on different parts of ourselves. It requires both a more conscious engagement with intelligence's multiple aspects and a greater capacity to engage that multiplicity in an integrated fashion. The need for this more aware and sophisticated relationship to our multiple intelligences applies

---

11   A popular version of the debate can be found in Daniel Goleman's proposal that we need to also measure EQ—emotional intelligence.

regardless of the concern—whether it is more personal or more collective, whether it is when we engage the softer worlds of art and things spiritual or the harder realities of business and science.

We can draw again on the analogy with personal development. The fact that our thinking in life's later years can become more nuanced is similarly a product not just of how we think, but of what we think with. Knowledge can be articulated quite well by the intellect alone. Wisdom, however, requires a more fully embodied kind of intelligence, one that better draws on the whole of our cognitive complexity. Wisdom results not just because we better include all the aspects of our questions, but also because, when seeking answers, we don't leave out essential parts of ourselves. If the concept of Cultural Maturity is correct, we should expect an analogous result at a species level.

The recognition that rational discourse is not by itself sufficient for culturally mature understanding can at first be disorienting—we like to believe that being smart and thinking hard enough will get us to the truth. And we tend to believe that when we are not wholly rational, we are less exact. But success is a great motivator. We find that when we apply the whole of our cognitive complexity in the needed more conscious and integrative fashion, new, even more precise ways of thinking become available to us. We also become able to grasp answers to questions that before have eluded us. The fact that you have gotten as far as you have in these pages reflects that you have successfully applied multiple ways of knowing at least a bit.

Recent advances in cognitive science have made a good start toward painting today's needed more differentiated (and integrated) picture of intelligence's workings. We see conceptions of intelligence more complexly dividing the pie of cognition in a variety of ways. For example, the neurosciences have replaced old images of a single managerial, rational brain with a view that recognizes multiple quasi-independent "brains"—in one familiar interpretation, a reptilian brain and a mammalian brain, capped with that thin outer cerebral layer in which we humans take special and appropriate pride. Educational theorists offer an array of interpretations, the most well known being Howard Gardner's eight-part smorgasbord of intelligences—linguistic, musical, mathematical, spatial, kinesthetic, interpersonal, intrapersonal, and rational. The popular assertion that we need to think with "both sides of the brain," while neurologically simplistic, draws our attention to how the task is not just to have lots of intelligences at our disposal, but to find ways in which various aspects of how we make sense of things might more consciously work together.

The importance of bringing the whole of intelligence to bear applies equally to crux and multiplicity discernments. With regard to truth's crux, we can get our minds around the larger whole of any systemic truth only if we can engage experience with the whole of who we are. The same applies to more detailed pattern—language distinctions— with the addition that now we draw on the whole of who we are in more differentiated ways. This is easiest to see with here-and-now multiplicity observations. The world looks very different depending on which intelligence holds the larger sway. But as we will examine shortly, it applies to temporal multiplicity distinctions in ways that are particularly consequential for our inquiry. Developmental/evolutionary perspective makes little sense without an appreciation for multiple intelligences and how they shape who we are.

For now, the expanded picture of intelligence introduced in this section at least raises intriguing questions—and about more than thought. Our intelligences represent not just the ways in which we think, but the varied lenses and filters through which we discern and make sense of our worlds (and ultimately ourselves). A more differentiated picture of intelligence asks that we revisit all manner of assumptions that before we have left unquestioned. Our perceptions must suddenly always be understood in relation to the sensibilities through which they are organized and interpreted.[12]

---

12 These reflections on intelligence's multiple aspects highlight an important reason that traditional philosophical thought tends to be of less help than we might hope when it comes to truth's new questions. Classical philosophy's task is to apply reason at the highest levels. But views that identify only with rationality will necessarily confront the limits inherent in any single-intelligence conclusion. Rationality is not where philosophy ends, of course. But assertions that identify instead with rationality's opposite— romantic views, for example—similarly identify with only one aspect of intelligence (in this case, the nonrational, feeling dimension). Because philosophy paints ultimately with a rational brush, views that identify instead with the nonrational commonly suffer philosophy's limits-related fate

A Threshold Lesson: We can learn a lot by noticing the particular sensibilities that we draw on in making discernments. The intelligences we apply affect not just how we reach our conclusions, but also the conclusions themselves.

Creativity and Ways of Knowing

Creative Systems Theory's approach to thinking about intelligence's multiplicity represents only one strategy, but it proves especially useful for our purposes. Creative Systems Theory points out that our toolmaking nature means that human intelligence must, at the least, effectively support formative process. It goes on to describe how human intelligence is organized specifically to facilitate and drive creative change. When combined with previous observations that link polarity and formative process, a creative framing of intelligence's multiplicity provocatively sets the stage for Chapter Seven's examination of developmental/evolutionary perspective.

Creative Systems Theory proposes that we are the uniquely creative creatures we are not just because we are conscious, but because of the particular ways in which specific aspects of our intelligence work and how different aspects interrelate. It describes how our various intelligences—or we might say "sensibilities," to better reflect all they encompass—relate in specifically creative ways. And it delineates how different ways of knowing, and different relationships between ways of knowing, predominate at specific times in any human change process. It ties the underlying structures of intelligence to patterns we see in how human systems change—thereby both helping us better understand change and hinting at the possibility of being more intelligent, and even wise, in the face of change.[13]

---

twice over. Often they are championed with some of the most lengthy and tedious of rational argument. See "Who We Are and What It All Means" in Chapter Eight. for a look at how our answers to key philosophical questions change with culturally mature perspective. See "A Creative History of Truth" in Chapter Ten for a look at how Creative Systems Theory can be used to map the history of philosophical thought.

13   Creative Systems Theory's picture of multiple intelligence is unusual both for its emphasis on change and for the attention it gives to how various cognitive aspects work together.

Let's take a brief look at how this works: Creative Systems Theory identifies four basic types of intelligence.[14] For ease of conversation, I will refer to them here as the intelligences of the body,[15] the imagination,[16] the emotions,[17] and the intellect.[18] Creative Systems Theory proposes that these different ways of knowing represent not just diverse approaches to processing information, but also the windows through which we make sense of our worlds. More than this, they give us the formative tendencies that lead us to shape our worlds in the ways that we do.

Creative Systems Theory also describes how these various intelligences work together in ways that are not just collaborative,[19] but that directly support creative change. Our various modes of intelligence,

---

14 We could break intelligence's picture down further (and Creative Systems Theory does), but four makes a good compromise between oversimplification and unnecessary complexity.

15 Creative Systems Theory calls this *somatic/kinesthetic intelligence*. This is the language of movement, sensation, and sensuality, as well as other aspects of ourselves that we are only beginning to discover. For example, it is increasingly accepted that the immune system is in the broadest sense "intelligent"; it makes subtle discriminations and learns every day to make new ones.

16 Creative Systems Theory calls this *symbolic/imaginal intelligence*. This is the language of poetry, metaphor, dream, and artistic inspiration. In *A Midsummer Night's Dream*, Shakespeare was referring to imaginal intelligence when he wrote, "the lover, the lunatic, and the poet/are of imagination all compact."

17 Creative Systems Theory calls this *emotional/moral intelligence*. This is the language of mood, affect, and the more interpersonal aspects of discourse. It also relates closely with how impulse translates into action.

18 Creative Systems Theory calls this *rational/material intelligence*. This is the language of syllogistic logic, and the more explicit aspects of verbal exchange.

19 To say that our diverse intelligences work in ways that are collaborative is not to say that they don't at times work at cross purposes to one another. Often they arrive at conflicting conclusions—sometimes because they simply do, but also often because conflict is a natural and necessary part of an underlying developmental dynamic. For example, internal wars between thoughts and emotions play an essential role in the developmental tasks of adolescence.

juxtaposed like colors on a color wheel, function together as creativ-ity's mechanism. That wheel, like the wheel of a car or a Ferris wheel, is continually turning, continually in motion. The way the various fac-ets of intelligence juxtapose makes change, and specifically purposeful change, inherent to our natures. The diagram in Figure 6-4 depicts these links between the workings of intelligence and the stages of for-mative process.[20]

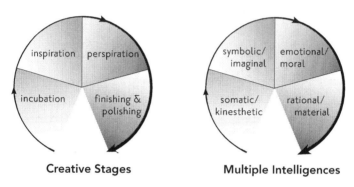

Creative Stages   Multiple Intelligences

Fig. 6-4. Formative Process and Intelligence

A brief look at a single creative process—let's take as an example the writing of a book such as this one—helps clarify this result. In sub-tly overlapping and multilayered ways, the process by which this book came to be took me through a progression of creative stages and as-sociated sensibilities. Creative processes unfold in varied ways, but the following outline is generally representative:

Creativity's "Incubation" Stage (and Body Intelligence)
Before I began to write, my sense of the book was murky at best. Cre-ative processes begin in darkness. I was aware that I had ideas I wanted to communicate. But I had only the most beginning sense of just what

---

20   Chapter Ten provides more detailed descriptions of these four basic kinds of intelligence. It also clarifies how what we see is more interesting that just one stage/one intelligence. While one intelligence predominates with each stage, it is also the case that each intelligence, expressed in a particular way, manifests within in each stage.

ideas I wanted to include or how I wanted to address them. This is creativity's "incubation" stage. The dominant intelligence here is the kinesthetic, body intelligence, if you will. It is like I am pregnant, but don't yet know with what. What I do know takes the form of "inklings" and faint "glimmerings," inner sensings. If I want to feed this part of the creative process, I do things that help me to be reflective and to connect in my body. I take a long walk in the woods, draw a warm bath, build a fire in the fireplace.

Creativity's "Inspiration" Stage (and Imaginal Intelligence)

Creativity's second stage propels the new thing created out of darkness into first light. I begin to have "ah-has"—my mind floods with notions about what I might express in the book and possible approaches for expression. Some of these first insights take the form of thoughts. Others manifest more as images or metaphors. In this "inspiration" stage, the dominant intelligence is the imaginal—that which most defines art, myth, and the let's-pretend world of young children. The products of this period in the creative process may appear suddenly—like Archimedes' "eureka"—or they may come more subtly and gradually. It is this stage, and this part of our larger sensibility, that we tend to most traditionally associate with things creative.[21]

Creativity's "Perspiration" Stage (and Emotional Intelligence)

The next stage leaves behind the realm of first possibilities and takes us into the world of manifest form. With the book, I try out specific structural approaches. And I get down to the hard work of writing and revising—and writing and revising some more. This is creation's "perspiration" stage. The dominant intelligence is different still, more emotional and visceral—the intelligence of heart and guts. It is here that we confront the hard work of finding the right approach and the most satisfying means of expression. We also confront limits to our skills

---

21 Because the imaginal indirectly anticipates final form, there is a sense in which it presages fact. I am reminded of Rainer Maria Rilke's poetic reflection that "The future enters into us in order to transform us long before it happens"—an observation about both creative process and understanding's broader generativity.

and are challenged to push beyond them. The perspiration stage tends to bring a new moral commitment and emotional edginess. We must compassionately but unswervingly confront what we have created if it is to stand the test of time.

Creativity's "Finishing and Polishing" Stage (and Rational Intelligence)

Generativity's fourth stage is more concerned with detail and refinement. Although the book's basic form is established, much yet remains to do. Both the book's ideas and how they are expressed need a more fine-toothed examination. Rational intelligence orders this "finishing and polishing" stage. This period is more conscious and more concerned with aesthetic precision than the periods previous. It is also more concerned with audience and outcome. It brings final focus to the creative work, and offers the clarity of thought and nuances of style needed for effective communication.

Creative Integration (and Integrative/Systemic Intelligence)

Formative process' further stages get us a bit ahead of ourselves. But their existence was implied in our previous look at polarity's role in formative process. Creative expression is often placed in the world at this point. But a further stage—or more accurately, an additional series of stages—remains. These stages are as important as any of the others—and of particular significance to our understanding of culturally mature perspective. This sequence varies greatly in length and intensity. Creative Systems Theory calls this further generative sequence *Creative Integration*.

With the process of refinement complete, we can now step back from the work and appreciate it with new perspective. We become better able to recognize the relationship of one part to another. And we become more able to appreciate the relationship of the work to its creative contexts, to ourselves and to the time and place in which it was created. We might call creativity's integrative stages the time of seasoning or ripening.[22]

---

22   Sometimes this set of stages takes place well after a work has taken expression. When this is the case, its underlying emphasis tends to be more on maturity in the creator's life than on the process of the specific work,

With Creative Integration we engage the second half of formative process (again, see Figure 6-3). Creative Integration forms a complement to the more differentiation-defined tasks of earlier stages. With regard to our multiple intelligences, Creative Integration is about learning to use our diverse ways of knowing more consciously together. It is about applying our intelligences in various combinations and balances as time and situation warrant, and about a growing ability not just to engage the work as a whole, but to draw on ourselves as a whole in relationship to it. Because wholeness is where we started—before the disruptive birth of new creation—in a certain sense Creative Integration returns us to where we began. But just as much, this new place could not be more different. The fact of new creation changes everything.[23]

Creative Systems Theory applies this relationship between intelligence and formative process to human experience as a whole. It proposes that the same general progression of sensibilities we see with a creative project orders the creative growth of all human systems. It argues that we see similar patterns at all levels—from the growth of an individual, to the development of an organization, to culture and its evolution. A few snapshots:

The same bodily intelligence that orders creative "incubation" plays a particularly prominent role in the infant's rhythmic world of movement,

---

or about finding mature expression in a body of work. At other times, especially when the work represents mature stages in the creator's efforts, it may manifest fully as a part of the creative process that brings a work into being. This is particularly likely when the needed maturity is cultural as well as personal. In either case, these stages draw on intelligence as a (now more creatively integrated) whole.

23   Later I will draw on a consequence of this specifically creative picture of intelligence that has important implications for the future. Two facts—that it is inherently generative and that it includes aspects that are as concerned with how we are connected as how we are separatee—means that just by how our cognitive processes work we are moral/ethical beings. We are concerned with betterment, and also with things larger than ourselves along with individual well-being. I will make reference to this consequence in distinguishing human intelligence from artificial intelligence, and also in reflecting on whether we should be hopeful as we look to the future.

touch, and taste. The realities of early tribal cultures also draw deeply on body sensibilities. Truth in tribal societies is synonymous with the rhythms of nature and, through dance, song, story, and drumbeat, with the body of the tribe.

The same imaginal intelligence that we saw ordering creative "inspiration" takes prominence in the play-centered world of the young child. We also hear its voice with particular strength in early civilizations—such as in ancient Greece or Egypt, with the Incas and Aztecs in the Americas, or in the classical East—with their mythic pantheons and great symbolic tales.

The same emotional and moral intelligence that orders creative "perspiration" tends to occupy center stage in adolescence with its deepening passions and pivotal struggles for identity. It can be felt with particular strength also in the beliefs and values of the European Middle Ages, times marked by feudal struggle and ardent moral conviction (and, today, in places where struggle and conflict seem to be forever recurring).

The same rational intelligence that comes forward for the "finishing and polishing" tasks of creativity takes new prominence in young adulthood, as we strive to create our unique place in the world of adult expectations. This more refined and refining aspect of intelligence stepped to the fore culturally with the Renaissance and the Age of Reason and, in the West, has held sway into modern times.

Of particular pertinence to the concept of Cultural Maturity, the same more consciously integrative intelligence that we see in the "seasoning" stage of a creative act orders the unique developmental capacities—the wisdom—of a lifetime's second half. And we can see this same more integrative relationship with intelligence just beneath the surface in our current cultural stage in the West in the advances that have most transformed understanding through the last century.

We associate the Age of Reason with Descartes' assertion that "I think, therefore I am." We could make a parallel assertion for each of these other cultural stages: "I am embodied, therefore I am"; "I imagine, therefore I am"; "I am a moral being, therefore I am"; and, if the concept of Cultural Maturity is accurate, "I understand maturely and systemically—with the whole of myself—therefore I am." Cultural

Maturity proposes that the discussion you have just read about intelligence's creative workings has been possible because such consciously integrative dynamics are reordering how we think and perceive.[24]

Creative Systems Theory Patterning Concepts

The creative frame I've begun to draw on in this chapter warrants some further general reflections before we apply it more directly in chapters to come. The use of a creative frame addresses a historically important truth-related quandary. I've proposed that culturally mature perspective takes us beyond the Modern Age's clockworks picture of reality's workings. But we are left with the essential question of just what is to replace it. If we are to effectively move forward, we clearly need a new defining notion. Creative Systems Theory proposes that reality—certainly the reality of human experience—is ultimately neither mechanistic nor mystical—but instead creative, and goes on to use a creative frame as the basis for a highly detailed pattern-language approach.

The use of a creative frame is not wholly original to Creative Systems Theory. For example, Alfred North Whitehead called creativity "the universal of universals" and made it central in his "process philosophy." Philosopher of science Karl Popper proposed something similar in claiming that "the greatest riddle of the cosmos may well be ... that the universe is, in a sense, creative." But Creative Systems Theory goes considerably further in using a creative frame as the foundation for detailed and rigorous conception.

The use of a creative frame is supported by reflections throughout this chapter. We've looked at how culturally mature truth is inherently "exploratory," how it is always as much about process as content. We've also observed how polarities relate in ways that are specifically

---

24   Note an important implication of this creative interpretation of intelligence: Recognizing and applying our multiple intelligences is not as easy as just deciding to do so. Many of intelligence's aspects knew their full expression only in times well past—for example, the intelligence of the body in tribal times, or the language of imagination and myth in civilization's "inspiration" stage. Engaging them necessarily requires a reach. Chapter Eight examines some of what makes that reach possible and what it involves.

"procreative." And we've just examined how the multiple aspects of human intelligence make our striking creative capacities possible.

Creative Systems Theory describes how Integrative Meta-perspective makes us newly conscious of—and newly responsible in—our natures as tookmaking, meaning-making beings. One result is a new, more explicitly generative picture of reality's workings. Creative Systems Theory goes on to apply the language of formative process to bring sophisticated, whole-box-of-crayons, "creative" systemic perspective to the workings of human complexity of all sorts—and specifically to the tasks of culturally mature decision-making.

Creative Systems Theory uses a creative frame to address multiple crux variables and also to provide sophisticated perspective for mapping multiplicity differences, both the differences of developmental processes over time and here-and-now contextual differences. In later chapters, we will examine Creative Systems patterning concepts in some depth and apply them to important challenges before us. For now, a quick glimpse will suffice:

Creative Systems Theory calls concepts that focus on "crux" distinctions *Whole-System Patterning Concepts*. Whole-System Patterning Concepts describe the degree to which an act or idea is "life-enhancing"—in the language of formative process, the degree to which a choice supports our creative growth and well-being. In the previous chapter, we made acquaintance with the most basic Whole-System Patterning Concept when I spoke of "crux" discernments being where culturally mature decision-making necessarily starts. Creative Systems Theory calls this most basic distinction the *Question of Referent*,[25] or, less formally, the question of aliveness. With Integrative Meta-perspective, this most basic of creative discernments replaces

---

25   Creative Systems Theory uses the word "referent" rather than a term like "truth" to emphasize all we may need to draw on—refer to—in making such bottom-line discernments. The specifically systemic discernments required beyond Cultural Maturity's threshold demand that we engage the whole of ourselves, all that we are capable of "referring to," all the diverse "feedbacks"—emotional feedback, intellectual feedback, spiritual feedback, bodily feedback, interpersonal feedback, cultural feedback—that we humans rely on to make our way in the world, applied in a newly conscious and complete way.

cultural dictates as our needed starting point in decision-making. It also takes us beyond postmodern arbitrariness, making life's inquiries not just experimental, but explicitly creative.

The notion of Capacitance briefly introduced in our examination of limits is similarly a Whole-System Patterning Concept. Capacitance measures generic capacity—the amount of creation/life a system can handle before being overwhelmed. It describes one of the most important kinds of limits we need to become aware of if we are to make intelligent choices and live healthy and effective lives. At any moment of choice, we want to know not just where the most vital options lie, but also whether we are up to what they might ask of us. In Chapter Nine, we will look more closely at the concept of Capacitance and its implications.[26]

In Creative Systems Theory, whole-box-of-crayons "multiplicity" distinctions are made with what the theory calls *Concepts of Creative Differentiation*. The theory delineates two basic kinds of creative differentiation concepts, what it calls *Patterning in Time* and *Patterning in Space*. Patterning in Time concepts address temporal multiplicity. In this chapter, our look at how polarity has its origins in the workings of formative process drew on Patterning in Time notions, as did reflections on how human intelligence functions to support and drive generative change. Patterning in Time distinctions delineate underlying processes in individual human development, make change in relationships of all sorts more understandable, and describe how various realms of human inquiry—science, government, education, religion—have evolved through history. Of particular importance for today, Patterning in Time observations provide perspective for making sense of the changes that define our time.

Patterning in Space distinctions give us Creative Systems Theory's complementary, here-and-now multiplicity notions. They describe how parts in human systems—at any particular time—also relate creatively.

---

26   With this later look at Capacitance, we will examine an important related phenomenon with direct pertinence to culturally mature leadership. Systems tend to respond protectively when they are pushed beyond their available Capacitance. The concept of *Creative Symptoms* in Creative Systems Theory describes this result. (See "Capacitance" in Chapter Nine.)

We saw Patterning in Space notions implied in my depiction of how our individual psyches "contain multitudes," a kind of internal multiplicity given foundational expression by our multiple intelligences. We can use creative Patterning in Space notions as effectively to help us more deeply understand how academic disciplines, departments in an organization, or cultural domains relate. Chapter Nine looks at how a creative frame makes possible a particularly deep and detailed perspective for understanding personality style differences.[27]

Besides providing guidance for addressing specific choices, a creative framing of truth also offers perspective for addressing the most big-picture of truth questions. It makes it possible for us to successfully answer all sorts of questions whose answers have before eluded us. As examples, in Chapter Eight we will look at how it offers a way to address the seeming incompatibility of free will and determinism, and also how it captures the worlds of science and religion in a way that makes clear that they are not so at odds as we have historically imagined. The whole of this book's companion volume, *Quick and Dirty Answers to the Biggest of Questions: Creative Systems Theory Explains What It Is All About (Really)* is organized around this further outcome of a creative frame.

A creative frame is not the only way to talk about the more dynamic and complete sorts of truth that Cultural Maturity describes and predicts. And in times ahead, we should arrive at other approaches to understanding that will prove important and useful. But any framing of truth capable of helping us as we go forward must successfully engage each of the demands presented in this chapter and that previous by our third threshold task. It must help us to recognize the necessity of being newly responsibility for the truths we apply; address both the crux and multiplicity aspects of how truth becomes systemic with Cultural Maturity's cognitive changes; think in ways that honor our living human natures; systemically bridge the polar assumptions of times past: and consciously incorporate intelligence's multiple aspects into how we make decisions. In addition, if we wish to develop detailed conceptual tools, we also need some "fulcrum concept"—such as the one that a creative frame provides—that can give order to our formulations.

What I can confidently claim with regard to the use of a creative frame is that it represents a particularly interesting and valuable contribution.

---

27 See "One 'Crayon' and Another."

With regard to ourselves, given that its foundation lies with what makes us not just alive, but alive in the incessantly and audaciously inventive sense that makes us human, a creative frame may, in fact, provide something quite precise. And the overarching comprehensiveness of its reach combined with the nuance and detail it often brings to understanding highlights its significant.

Can we extend this kind of claim further? Would it be appropriate for us to think of biological life, and existence as a whole, as ultimately creative? In a sense, perhaps so (this is a future topic[28]). But such conclusions leave us very close to common conceptual traps. Certainly we must take care that we don't simply project our time's new cognitive mechanism and make the results what it is all about, as Enlightenment perspective did with rationality and the presumed mechanical universe that followed from it. Better to say simply that whatever strategy we apply, it has to accomplish something similar to what a creative frame achieves.

The best argument for the power of a creative frame lies with its practical usefulness. The remainder of the book will put it to the test.

Leadership Reflections:
Precision, Simplicity, Possibility, and Purpose

A series of new-truth related questions that are particularly pertinent to leadership help to tie up loose ends before we move on to putting these basic truth reflections to work. The first concerns precision. We might reasonably ask whether the kind of truth that culturally mature perspective provides is as precise as the kinds of truth we have been accustomed to.

It is certainly the case that such truth doesn't offer the kind of last-word answers that we find with cultural absolutes and our various simple-answer ideologies. And thinking of truth as creative might seem even more to make choice less exact, less rigorous. But, in fact, Cultural Maturity's new truths are ultimately more precise, not less, than what they replace. The simple fact that more familiar kinds of precision today inevitably fail us offers a basic kind of confirmation. If the truths that come with culturally mature perspective provide useful guidance in our time,

---

28   See "Who We Are and What It All Means" in Chapter Eight.

as I've proposed that they do, then the precision question is largely answered. Culturally mature truth doesn't present final answers, but it does provide the feedback needed for wise consideration.

There is also how culturally mature truths are more precise in the nuance they bring to our distinctions. Truths we have before had at our disposal were blunt instruments at best compared to the highly context-specific discernment tools we have begun to look at here. In the end, culturally mature truths are more precise not just in being more specific, but also in the depth they bring to understanding. They offer new precision in the sense of bringing greater completeness to our appreciation of how things actually work.

The truths on which we necessarily base culturally mature social policy highlight this different, more creative sort of precision. I've drawn frequently on public policy concerns in these pages to provide illustration and will continue to do so. But the same policy that in one instance might be culturally mature can, in another instance, directly undermine the possibility of a positive outcome. It would be much easier if we could just say, "*This* is culturally mature policy, and *this* is not." Frequently we can. However, at other times when we ask if this or that policy choice would be culturally mature, the correct answer is, "it depends." That at first might seem a vague response, but in fact it holds in it just the kind of precision we are looking for. The needed follow-up question asks, "Depends on what?" Culturally mature truth is about what effective choice ultimately depends on.

> A Threshold Lesson: Culturally mature truths are not as cut and dried, nor are they as easily articulated, as the more absolutist truths of times past. They are also always contingent, often on multiple time and place considerations. But because they are more complete in what they consider than what they replace, they are also ultimately more precise.

A second question brings us back to our pursuit of Oliver Wendell Holmes's hoped-for "simplicity on the other side of complexity." I've claimed that culturally mature perspective makes possible understanding that, at least in practical application, can be simpler than what it replaces.

You don't need the specific truth notions we've looked at with the third threshold task to make a good start toward recognizing how culturally mature truth produces this result. We caught a glimpse with each of our previous threshold tasks. For example, with the first threshold task we saw how Whole-Person/Whole-System relationships become more straightforward than what they replace. The truths we draw on with Whole-Person/Whole-System relationships require that we take more into account, but at the same time, because they are not based on projection, they become less vulnerable to the drama that comes with mythologized perceptions. With our second threshold task we examined how Cultural Maturity requires that we surrender myths of limitlessness—our various dreams of specialness and magical possibilities—and, in doing so, to acknowledge and embrace a more accurate picture of reality. This degree of clarity would before now have been beyond us to tolerate, but again it presents a more straightforward, and thus in important ways simpler, reality than what we have known.

Ideas introduced with this chapter and that previous make a critical further contribution to this "simplicity on the other side of complexity" picture, one that should find growing importance in times ahead. The kind of pattern language discernments these reflections point toward are not only more accurate than what we have known, they are also more compact. Culturally Mature perspective offers that our ideas might represent more information, and more fully the right kind of information, with a few simple conceptual gestures. Such pattern notions require new ways of understanding. But their elegance also provides an important further antidote to overwhelm.

> A Threshold Lesson: Culturally mature truth, because it is not simplified, is necessarily more complex than what it replaces. But when we begin to grasp what it is about, we at least experience it as more straightforward. Eventually, if understood deeply, it can produce understanding that is functionally simpler than truth as we have known it.

A third question brings us back to whether we are up to what these new kinds of truth ask of us. It can seem initially that we may not be. Not only would such truths not have made much sense in times past, we would not have even recognized that anything like them is needed. At least it is clearly the case that we reside in an awkward in-between stage with regard to culturally mature truth's realization.

But it is also the case, as I have suggested, that such concepts can seem rather self-evident with reflection. Appreciating this easily startling juxtaposition of experiences further highlights the newness of these notions. It also further emphasizes the developmental nature of the processes that make them understandable. I've proposed that the reason that notions such as these, which stretch us so fundamentally, do not stop us cold is that they represent aspects of the new common sense that comes with Cultural Maturity's cognitive changes.

The kind of temporal relativity that gives us Creative Systems Theory's developmental/evolutionary frame provides a particularly good example of these contrasting experiences. I've suggested that the basic idea that culture might have developmental stages remains controversial in certain circles. But while a person can take issue with the specifics of the particular developmental/evolutionary frame I put forward in this book, with reflection, the general idea that cultures grow and develop in identifiable ways is hard to disagree with. When we look at all closely at either history or current cultural differences—as we will do in the next chapter—the fact of identifiable cultural stages with parallel underlying assumptions begins to seem self-evident.

Once we spot such pattern, it can seem remarkable that we have not recognized it all along—indeed, it can seem a bit scary that we have made important policy decisions without such understanding. In the next chapter, we will look at some of the dangerous mistakes we make when we do not take differences in cultural stage into account when making decisions. The simple explanation for why we have not seen such "obvious" understanding before now: Cultural Maturity's cognitive changes are needed for this obviousness to become apparent.

We encounter this same striking juxtaposition of experiences with more here-and-now pattern language distinctions—for example, with personality style differences. As with cultural stage differences, when we reflect on temperament differences at all deeply, we recognize that they are pretty obvious—differences are much greater than we have commonly imagined. Later we will examine how these distinctions can also be of immense consequence.[29] Yet we are now only beginning to deeply acknowledge the fact of temperament differences. Somehow

---

29   See "One 'Crayon' and Another" in Chapter Nine and Appendix D.

we've missed differences that on fresh examination become glaring. The explanation for how they have before been invisible to us appears to be the same. As with the stage distinctions of developmental/evolutionary perspective, applying such here-and-now pattern recognitions requires at least the beginnings of culturally mature sensibility.

Today, the distinctions that culturally mature truths require us to make can come much more readily than we might suppose. When such discernments become timely, we don't need to understand specific frameworks. We don't even need to consciously know anything about "crux" and "multiplicity" aspects of truth, culturally mature or otherwise, to begin making such distinctions. The changes that produce these new ways of thinking about truth come part and parcel with Cultural Maturity's new common sense.

> A Threshold Lesson: While culturally mature truths demand more of us both personally and conceptually, when we are ready for them, they are not that difficult to grasp. This is the case not just for basic principles, but also for more specific and detailed truths, at least when it comes to the particularly fundamental kinds of discernments that Creative Systems Theory patterning concepts address.

Given that culturally mature truth's task is not an easy one, I'll conclude these additional observations with some further reflections on what makes it all worthwhile. The most obvious reason the effort is worth it is just that Cultural Maturity's new kinds of truth have today become inescapably necessary—without them we will make unfortunate decisions. But as important, there is also how directly they address the experience of aimlessness that so commonly pervades our time. In part this result follows simply from the fact that these are truths that are now timely. But just as much, this outcome reflects the depths in ourselves that we necessarily engage in making such truth discernments.

Culturally mature truth includes the sort of arms-length truth ushered in with Enlightenment thought. Indeed, Cultural Maturity puts new emphasis on such truth's importance. But because culturally mature discernments are both more conscious and more deep and encompassing in their considerations, in a newly direct sense they engage questions at the level of value and purpose. With the Reformation, our Modern Age announced the end of secondhand gods—sacred experience no longer required a priestly intermediary. Culturally mature truth announces the end of secondhand meaning, meaning that requires a cultural intermediary. It engages what matters to us—ultimately what makes us human—with a completeness that before now has not been an option. In the process, culturally mature truth becomes, in itself, irrespective of the answers it might propose, an antidote to today's crisis of purpose.

Culturally Mature Truth—A Threshold Summary

We can frame either of our first two threshold tasks in terms of the third. Doing so helps summarize where we have come to this point with our inquiry as a whole before we move on to further kinds of evidence.

The first threshold task—confronting the need to better address complexity—translates directly into truth language. In addressing it, we gave special attention to the importance of leaving behind the ideological easy answers of times past, and thinking in more encompassing ways. We saw how the new relationship to complexity that results leaves culturally specific truths behind us, challenges any conclusion that grants a monopoly on truth to one part of life's systemic fullness (for example, one half of any polarity, one intelligence, or the conclusions of a particular cultural domain—science, religion, government, education, or art), and clarifies how more dynamic, rich, and complete kinds of truth are now becoming possible.

Truth language similarly helps summarize the second threshold task—learning to better factor real limits into our decision-making. Today's new truths provide the maturity of discernment we need if we are to effectively make sense of limits. They help us see how heroic and romantic myths of limitlessness today in fact constrain understanding. Part of the reward for successfully confronting the harsh realities of inviolable limits is the possibility of appreciating more dynamic and complete sorts of truth.

The chapters five and six have added important nuance and detail to truth's new picture. We've seen how needed new truths make severe demands—how they require a whole new order of responsibility, that our ideas better draw on the entirety of who we are, and that we think in fundamentally new ways about what makes something true. Ultimately they require that we craft wholly new kinds of conceptual frameworks. We've also seen how these are demands that we really can't escape. Without new ways of thinking about truth, we risk our future being determined by an increasingly dangerous, fragmented, and crazy mix of dogmatic ideologies and empty relativisms.

We've also examined more closely how culturally mature truth's new picture benefits us in essential, and often surprising, ways. In short, it means once again having guideposts. This new kind of guidepost doesn't provide final answers in the old sense, but we gain much more than we lose. I've pointed toward how culturally mature truth offers more precise, detailed, and encompassing understandings of both ourselves and the world around us. It also provides more meaning-filled understandings and, in the process, a newly provocative and compelling picture of the possible.

We can turn again to my friend's question: Do we face the end of civilization? We do, if we mean civilization in the sense of the past's one-size-fits-all answers and once-and-for-all solutions. But we also face something quite the opposite: the possibility of new, more mature and creative ways of understanding—truths that give fuller and more complete expression to who we are. Such truths require a great deal from us, but they also offer real hope that our immense human potential might be realized.

As with our previous two threshold tasks, we find in these observations not just useful guidance, but also important evidence for the concept of Cultural Maturity. The greater conceptual sophistication that our new-truth task describes could seem beyond us to effectively make sense of, much less to realize. That the concept of Cultural Maturity helps make this new-truth task understandable strongly supports Cultural Maturity's conclusions. And our beginning successes with making culturally mature truths manifest provides more in-the-trenches evidence.

In a similar way, too, our third threshold task offers encouragement. Certainly we find encouragement in the fact that needed truths are not only possible, their use is becoming increasingly common. We find encouragement, too, in how these new ways of thinking about truth relate to Cultural Maturity's broader challenge. While Cultural

Maturity's changes are needed for us to succeed with this additional threshold task, our successes immediately return the favor. Each time we effectively draw on culturally mature truths—even if we don't consciously know that this is what we are doing—in some small way we push beyond Cultural Maturity's threshold, and not just with regard to the question at hand, but also more generally.

We now turn to additional kinds of evidence and a more filled-out picture of where Cultural Maturity's changes take us.

Further Evidence

CHAPTER SEVEN

The Species Grows Up— Understanding Cultural Maturity as a Predictable Imperative

Something new is about to begin, something we glimpse only as a thin line of light low on the horizon...[that] may well open the way to future thought.
MICHEL FOUCAULT

YOU NOW HAVE MUCH OF Cultural Maturity's evidence under your belt. We've looked at how almost all of today's essential challenges require us to surrender the protective easy answers of times past and engage our three threshold tasks—more directly addressing complexity, acknowledging inviolable limits, and rethinking the bottom-line truths on which we base our choices. The fact that we see such parallels in what the new challenges require of us helps make clear that we are dealing with system-wide change. And the further fact that each of our threshold tasks stretches us so fundamentally affirms that what we see is change of a particularly essential sort.

The developmental analogy that gives the concept of Cultural Maturity its name has provided further evidence. We've looked at how each of the threshold tasks has a parallel in the developmental challenges of personal maturity. This observation supports the use of maturity as an integrating concept and also helps fill out our understanding of what effectively confronting today's cultural challenges requires of us. It also affirms the particular significance of the changes we see. I've described how personal second-half-of-life maturity involves not just a leap in how we understand, but a leap of unique consequence. In a related way, Cultural Maturity represents not just a critical next chapter in culture's story, but a chapter of particular significance.

But when it comes to Cultural Maturity and its significance, we can use all the evidence we can get. If the notion that our times require—and make possible—the kind of collective "growing up" I have described is only wishful thinking, then this inquiry is a waste of our time and a diversion from the tasks at hand. And if what I have described is but another form of ideology, it will lead us astray just as surely as any other.

We encounter some of the most solid further evidence in the recognition that we can understand the idea of a needed new human maturity not just as an observation about the particular challenges of our time, but as a set of changes we would expect to find at a particular stage in an extended, readily delineated, evolutionary progression. That is this chapter's approach. This more detailed temporal examination will help you better understand why we see Cultural Maturity's changes. It will also help you make deeper sense of just where these changes take us. And, as a bonus, it will present a vantage from which to understand our human story more generally.

The particular evolutionary perspective we will make use of draws on Creative Systems Theory's encompassing "pattern language" framework. I've described how getting beyond postmodern aimlessness requires that we better appreciate pattern—and pattern that is systemic in a whole-box-of-crayons sense. Besides further supporting the concept of Cultural Maturity, this chapter's reflections also highlight the importance of evolutionary perspective, and in particular, the developmental/evolutionary kind of perspective that becomes possible with Creative Systems Theory's application of a creative frame. By the end of the chapter, it should be inescapably clear that having perspective able to address culture in evolutionary terms will be more and more necessary as we go forward. Without understanding that is at least similar to that provided by the developmental/evolutionary frame that this chapter examines, it becomes very hard to effectively engage future challenges and make intelligent choices.

Terrorism—Getting It Right

I've promised to bring a more finely focused culturally mature lens to the challenge of terrorism. The topic of terrorism provides a particularly good entry point for this chapter's examination of developmental/evolutionary perspective. Effective decision-making in the face of terrorism becomes very difficult without a solid sense of how cultures evolve and where particular cultural groups reside in an extended picture of change.

Two weeks following the 9/11 attack on the World Trade Center in New York City, I sent out a white paper "alert" to 300 opinion leaders from around the world.[1] I warned of dangers that could result if we reacted without the needed maturity of perspective, and I outlined a "three-legged–stool" strategy.

Consistent with what we would expect with culturally mature perspective, the strategy I outlined is ultimately pragmatic—it is not "heroic" in the old definition. It is also a strategy that can be applied largely behind the scenes. In the end, it is common sense—simple and straightforward. But at the same time, making full sense of this simple strategy—and certainly its effective execution—demands an unusual degree of sophistication.

Below, I've briefly described this three-part strategy. To highlight the needed sophistication, with each part I will note how it requires that we get beyond common assumptions of both the political left and the political right. Later, I will reflect on how each also requires successfully engaging our three threshold tasks. I will also address how each part requires developmental/evolutionary perspective to be fully understood.

Policy to this point has sometimes paralleled this simple, pragmatic strategy, and it is coming to do so with greater frequency. But policy has also often stopped decidedly short.

A "Three-Legged–Stool" Strategy

Leg #1: Establish new boundary safeguards—such as at airports, borders, and ports—with a keen eye to the likelihood of unconventional approaches (surprise is key to what makes terrorism work). This is the "homeland security" piece. Here, though too often poli-

---

1   Later published in the February 2002 issue of the *Journal of Futures Studies*.

cies have been reactive in response to particular events rather than proactive (and often almost silly in going overboard in one arena while largely ignoring others[2]), the United States and other industrialized nations have made generally acceptable beginning steps. With this first leg, the Left has often not been happy with how these safeguards require at least limited curtailment of individual freedoms. The Right has had to face the fact that such safeguards will always be imperfect and how trying to make them perfect can in the end make us less safe rather than more. Effective boundary safeguards require a mature acceptance of limits to what is possible all the way around.

Leg #2: Pursue terrorists worldwide. This piece of the strategy can stretch the Left because of how much of it must be intelligence-based, and often military-based. It does so more specifically with how pre-emption (taking action not in response to harm, but in anticipation of harm) must necessarily be on the table with terrorism. The Right has to accept that effectiveness hinges on global cooperation. It also has to recognize that any strategy that confuses defeating "evil" leaders and nations with the more precise and nuanced actions required to effectively confront terrorism will produce the opposite of the desired outcome.

Leg #3: Address the root causes of terrorism. This third leg most explicitly requires developmental/evolutionary perspective, and just how it does again challenges the assumptions of both Left and Right.

Because liberals tend to like humanitarian approaches, at first blush addressing the causes of terrorism would not seem to present much concern to those with left-leaning political sentiments. But the most significant cause of global terrorism is not deprivation or oppression. It is the way in which globalization puts people who are different not just in belief and economic advantage, but also in the stage

---

2   We take off our shoes and carry liquids in little bottles at airports, while on trains, on subways, and on entering large buildings, people's actions currently receive minimal scrutiny.

in cultural development that they occupy, in inescapable proximity. At the least, the third leg requires the Left to accept limits to how effective humanitarian strategies can be. Cultural stage differences produce dynamics that even the most enlightened and generous of policies cannot alter. We also face simple economic constraints to what we can do.

The challenge that the third leg presents to the political right is more obvious, but the reason for much of it may be less so. In the end, the challenge to conservative assumptions has the same roots. The Right needs to accept that "softer" tactics such as making diplomatic efforts in world hot spots; addressing hunger, poverty, and powerlessness; and supporting education of the world's people (particularly women) may ultimately have the greatest effect on terrorism. The Right also must recognize that attempting to impose governmental forms that they may associate with freedom (and thus terrorism's opposite) will often only incite more terrorism. Certainly this will be the result when those forms are not appropriate to that particular culture's stage of development.

The Threshold Tasks

I've suggested that this three-step strategy is, in the end, common-sense. There is nothing dramatic or particularly original in it. But at the same time, it reflects a maturity of common sense that is still rare. The way each of our threshold tasks necessarily plays a role if we are to fully understand and effectively execute any of the legs in this strategy helps illustrate.

Addressing Complexity: I've described how each of the three legs of our stool requires us to get beyond the polarized solutions of traditional political ideology. Each leg also confronts a more fundamental, post-ideological systemic challenge: It requires us to avoid projection in how we think about terrorism and terrorists. Earlier, I noted the remarkable degree to which people have avoided responding to terrorism by making it the new communism. But this has not always been the case—and certainly not always with leaders.

It is very unlikely, for example, that the U.S. would have instigated the second Iraq war if leadership had applied the needed maturity of perspective. The belief with the second Iraq War that attacking Iraq and ousting Saddam Hussein might be an appropriate response to terrorism represents a prime illustration of confusing the defeating of "evil" leaders and nations with needed more nuanced and precise strategies. If the weapons-of-mass-destruction rationale was not outright deceit in support of an ideological agenda, certainly acting from it as the U.S. did reflected the kind of gross inability to evaluate risk that comes with mythologized perception. And no reasonable assessment could have reached the further conclusion used to justify involvement: that victory could be easily and quickly achieved.[3]

It is essential that we approach terrorism in ways that acknowledge the very real complexities presented by terrorism in today's world. If we do, our policies will be at least adequately effective, and "do no harm." Without such maturity of perspective, our actions, even if well intended, will very often make circumstances considerably worse.

Confronting Limits: Along with limits to past ideological assumptions—both of the sort that create political polarization and those that produce chosen-people/evil-other realities on the world stage—we also confront more specific terrorism-related limits. For example, each leg requires that we accept the fact that terrorism can only be limited and contained, not eradicated. I've described how, while terrorism can be horrendous, it is predicted by the realities of our time. We can establish boundary safeguards, but we can have real effect on the realities of terrorism only to the degree that we acknowledge the very real limits presented by world circumstances. Attempts at "perfect" solutions can only have unfortunate outcomes.

Effectively combating terrorism also requires that we accept limits to common ways of thinking about conflict. Certainly this is the case when it comes to thinking about how we prosecute those who commit

---

3   I suspect that history will judge the second Iraq War harshly. We could not have handed radical Islam a greater gift. And the larger ultimate damage done by the second Iraq War may lie not with the conflict at all, but with how it diverted attention and economic resources away from other pressing concerns.

terrorist acts. Usual assumptions restrict us to two options: Terrorism is an act of war and should be addressed militarily; or terrorism is best thought of as a criminal act and dealt with within the codes and structures of existing criminal justice systems. Neither frame is adequate. Terrorism is global and decentralized—not primarily a product either of national aggression (where a war model is appropriate) or internal transgression (where a criminal justice model effectively applies). We get into trouble if we choose either traditional frame as the "right" approach (and even more so if we hop back and forth between frames as it suits us). Effectively dealing with those who commit terrorist acts will require the crafting of new legal concepts.

And there is a more basic limit intrinsic to our common use of language that at least points toward the need for care in how we use our terms. The word "war" is powerful for how it can mobilize needed action. But it also quickly takes us back to the evil-other projective mechanisms that always before have accompanied warfare. We face the challenge of using language in a way that makes clear the seriousness of terrorism's threat and what is often a need for decisive action without in the process provoking outdated and ultimately dangerous psychological responses.

Rethinking the Truths on Which We Base Our Choices: Effectively addressing terrorism necessarily starts with keeping our eyes on what must ultimately be the prize. If our job is not just "fighting bad guys" (in either the war or the police-action sense) we must ask—with an uncommon directness and completeness—what, in the end, we want the confronting of terrorism to accomplish. The answer: Our actions must maximize global safety and human possibility. Miss this essential beginning step and we will fail with each leg of our three-legged-stool approach.[4]

Applying Developmental/Evolutionary Perspective

For this chapter's reflections, we need particularly to recognize how developmental/evolutionary perspective is required if we are to apply this three-legged–stool strategy with any effectiveness. I've described

---

4   My description of General Petraeus's leadership in Chapter One reflected asking this essential "Question of Referent."

how terrorism of the sort that these observations address is a natural consequence of the collision of cultures that reside at different developmental stages. Miss how this is so, and we easily act in ways that ultimately cause harm.

Without evolutionary perspective of some sort, the fact that we see terrorism at all—certainly the fact that it can take the forms that it often does—can be difficult to comprehend. The actions of a suicide bomber make no sense to someone who grows up with the individualist assumptions of Modern Age understanding—except as evidence of insanity or evil. Some historical reference—say, remembering back to the Christian religious fanaticism of the Crusades—at least makes the actions of terrorists more legitimately human actions. Evolutionary perspective helps us "hold life large" in ways that make projecting the less savory parts of ourselves less likely.

If we are to make good policy decisions, in the end we need not just a general appreciation that cultures evolve, but also more specific temporal frameworks that map change over time. A closer look at the wars in Iraq and Afghanistan—and similarities and differences of the challenges they presented—help illustrate.

The belief that the people of Iraq would celebrate the presence of U.S. soldiers—certainly for any length of time—would have been naïve enough were Iraq a modern nation. But the larger portion of the Iraqi people reside at a cultural stage analogous to the late Middle Ages in the West.[5] As will become clear with later reflections, this developmental reality made polar intolerance for occupying forces totally predictable. It also made the kind of antagonism between ethnic factions that we saw following the end of Saddam Hussein's rule what we should expect.[6] The implied nation-building goal of an eventual modern Western-style democracy similarly ignored cultural realities. The eventual, more

---

5   There is, of course, diversity within the Iraqi population. There are people who manifest modern culture sensibilities, and we also see earlier developmental sensibilities in some of the more tribal areas. But this general observation holds.

6   Struggle is a particularly defining characteristic of this stage in cultural evolution.

humble goal—a relatively stable government that provides some balance of influence between factions and an eventual basis for more representational authority—was more realistic.[7]

U.S. military action in Afghanistan was more justified, but from a developmental/evolutionary perspective, achieving success in the effort was predictably even more problematic. Most of Afghanistan's population resides in an even earlier cultural stage than what we see with Iraq.[8] The nation-building task in Iraq was primarily one of rebuilding (though often, as conceived by the West, with new kinds of institutions). The task in Afghanistan involved building governmental structures from the ground up.

Besides resulting in unhelpful—and often destructive—actions, a lack of developmental/evolutionary perspective can also leave us blind to what actually might be of benefit. Certainly it can leave us unable to appreciate cultural sensitivities that might make interventions more effective. But it can also lead us to miss ways in which change can work in our favor. It is quite possible that the kind of evolutionary change that we often see happening in other parts of the world would have eventually brought the fall of Saddam Hussein's regime. We have witnessed despots successfully swept aside who were less egregious in their atrocities. And while the situation in Afghanistan is more complex, we benefit greatly from being similarly attentive to the kind of change that is most ripe to happen there.[9]

---

7 Though we don't really know whether even this goal can be achieved. It is entirely possible that we have yet to see the carnage for which the second Iraq War will be most remembered.

8 In his book *The Wrong War*, Bing West, who spent ten years fighting in Afghanistan, describes how he reluctantly came to the conclusion that modern Afghanistan resides in the equivalent of about ninth-century Europe. Significant portions of Afghanistan's population reside in an even earlier equivalent time.

9 The situation we confronted earlier in the former Yugoslavia adds a further developmental reference point for applying an evolutionary lens to understanding conflict and its implications. The various parts of the former Yugoslavia resided at later times developmentally than I've described for Iraq and Afghanistan (spanning the equivalent of from about 14th to 18th century Europe). Consistent with the underlying develop-

Evidence, Evolutionary Perspective, and the Creative Function

Developmental/evolutionary perspective provides some of the best evidence for the concept of Cultural Maturity. Argument by analogy is understandably controversial. Indeed, even just thinking of culture as having developmental stages is controversial. Earlier I described how this kind of notion can—for very good reasons—arouse suspicion in certain circles. Some academic thinkers dismiss such pattern claims as "historicism" and reject any conclusions reached from them out of hand. But I think the evidence for such pattern, in fact, is close to irrefutable.

Personal maturity and Cultural Maturity are not the same. Indeed, as we shall examine later in the chapter, confusing the two can lead to traps in our thinking that directly undermine the needed greater maturity of perspective. But appreciating commonalities—and not just metaphoric here-and-now commonalities, but extended developmental patterns—provides a depth of insight into what Cultural Maturity requires of us that is hard to achieve in other ways. When we add related parallels with other human change processes, the argument by analogy becomes considerably more informative—and robust.

If Cultural Maturity's thesis holds up, whether we see such pattern becomes of much more than academic interest. Understanding such pattern provides one of the best ways to make sense of how otherwise baffling and overwhelming future challenges we've examined in these pages might be addressable. The possibility of a healthy and even survivable future may depend on whether the kind of developmental/evolutionary perspective we will examine proves accurate—and, in particular, whether it applies to our time. I've argued that Cultural Maturity presents the only option for the future that can provide real hope. I've also proposed that the developmental/evolutionary picture

---

mental dynamics of this time period, for many years Tito's "benevolent dictatorship" approach to governance effectively worked to provide coherence and order. The way in which the loss of Tito's defining influence brought conflict of a brutal sort was similarly consistent with what we would predict with this time period developmentally, as was how order was eventually effectively achieved through the establishment of multiple, independent nation states.

we will look at affirms that at least the potential for Cultural Maturity's changes is inherent in our natures.

In Chapter Six, I introduced a couple of approaches for getting at this more extended picture, each of which in different ways drew on a creative frame. The first focused on polarity. I described how formative processes of all sorts follow a predicable progression of polar relationships. The second approach focused on the recognition that intelligence is multiple. We discussed how human intelligence is structured to support our unique creative natures. The observations that follow expand on these reflections and look with greater detail and depth at how the ways we think and act follow predictable patterns through the course of any human change process.

Here I will give particular attention in these descriptions to change that manifests at a cultural scale. We will look at how we can make sense of cultural truth through history as a creatively predicted sequence of generative realities. And we will examine how Cultural Maturity's more integrative, whole-box-of-crayons kind of systemic perspective follows predictably—and predictably in our time—from this sequence.

The previous chapter's reflections on the role of polarity in how our cognitive processes organize experience have set the stage conceptually for this examination. I proposed that answering the question of why we think in polar terms in the first place provides pivotal insight for developing new ways of understanding and put forward an answer: The generation of polarity is necessary to formative process. The fact that historically we have thought in the language of polarity follows from our creative, tool-making, meaning-making natures. .

I also provided a beginning description of how this works. The first half of any formative process brings the newly created object or idea into being and, in the process, generates polarity. Over the first half of formative process, we see an evolving sequence of polarities, with each juxtaposition reflecting greater identification with the newly created form and diminishing identification with the context from which it originates. The second half reintegrates that which has now been made manifest with the context from which it originated, and in so doing establishes a new, now expanded whole. Extend this basic two-part picture like the bellows of an accordion and we get what I've called the Creative Function.

We readily recognize the two-part extended picture that the Creative Function describes with personal psychological development. The developmental tasks that define the first half of an individual's life are similar in that the underlying impetus with each is toward distinction and the establishing of identity. With childhood we begin discovering who we are, with adolescence we make our first forays into the social world, and during adulthood we establish our unique place in that world. Second-half-of-life maturing involves more specifically integrative tasks. It is about learning how to live in the world with the greatest perspective, integrity, and proportion.

Creative Systems Theory has more formal language for what I've described as the incubation, inspiration, perspiration, and finishing and polishing stages (see Figure 7-1). It calls them Pre-Axis, Early-Axis, Middle-Axis, and Late-Axis, respectively.[10] Later I will describe how this more formal language helps avoid confusion. It also helps us recognize important relationships when we make complex pattern language discernments.[11]

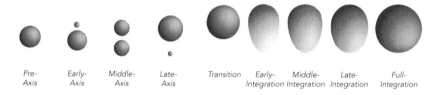

| Pre-Axis | Early-Axis | Middle-Axis | Late-Axis | Transition | Early-Integration | Middle-Integration | Late-Integration | Full-Integration |

Fig. 7-1. The Creative Function with Creative Stages[12]

The Creative Function presents a simplified picture. Stages can vary in length and emphasis depending on the kind of system and surrounding circumstances, and formative processes can be aborted

---

10   The use of the term "Axis" had it origins in early observations about how each stage as bodily experience organizes in a different way in relationship to the body's axis (see "The Evolution of the Body" in Chapter Ten).

11   See Chapter Nine.

12   Later, we will look at how the "map" the Creative Function provides is pertinent both to creative change and to here-and-now creative interrelationship (see "One 'Crayon' and Another" in Chapter Nine).

at any stage. But the general sequence holds with remarkable consistency. For our purposes, the important recognition is that it holds as predictably at a cultural scale as it does for more circumscribed formative processes such as the creation of a work of art or individual human development. It also strongly supports Cultural Maturity's conclusions.[13]

---

13   With the Creative Function again we confront representational limits and the need for "three-plus" representation. I think of the Creative Function as a culminating contribution in a sequence of increasingly sophisticated pictures of creative organization. The doorway diagram depicts polarity, the box of crayons describes our specifically human sort of complexity, and the Creative Function presents a more fully differentiated and explicitly creative picture.

We can adequately depict creation's first half, creative differentiation, as discrete circles (at least as adequately as with any paired-circle representation). In fact, opposing poles creatively interlink and each stage links to the next. But within any stage-specific slice, none of this is visible; colluding polar pairs can seem like the most extreme of opposites, and each polar juxtaposition will be experienced as complete and final truth. The representation thus comes close if our interest is reality as perceived through the eyes of each stage.

Beyond formative process's first half, representation works much less well. The Creative Function's midpoint describes the at once disorienting and fundamentally transforming reorientation that orders the beginnings of maturity in an individual life, and that the concept of Cultural Maturity proposes orders much that we see in present cultural times. Visual representation here provides some information, but as much through the lower pole's absence as what can be more concretely depicted.

As we proceed into formative process's second half, visual depiction fails us fundamentally. The complexities of maturity appear as an inadequate, and really misleading, dissolving of one pole into the next. (We've seen how mature systemic conception expands not just our appreciation for connections, but for the intricacies and dynamic interplays of real difference.) The function's representation fails completely at depicting Cultural Maturity—and, ultimately, because like previous depictions of polarity it is crafted from our juxtaposed circles, it fails to reflect the fact that formative process's workings are creative at all. Again, this failure is not a product of inexactness or because what the Creative Function depicts is ultimately mysterious. Rather, it is because the Creative Function reflects systemic conception of the needed new, more complete sort.

History—and Life—as a Creative Narrative

The descriptions that follow bring together observations about the workings of polarity, earlier reflections on the role of multiple intelligences in formative process, and previous conclusions about the systemic nature of contemporary challenges. To help fill out the creative picture, I've included as an additional example (along with the basic creative act, personal development, and cultural development) the generative process through which a new love relationship comes into being. (I could as easily have chosen the generative story of a friendship, an organization, a community, or a social movement.) I've chosen working on a piece of sculpture to make the simple creative act more vivid. (I was a sculptor before entering medical school.) [14]

Creation's Differentiation Phase

Creative "Incubation" (Pre-Axis)

 Formative processes begin with an unbroken whole, in a reality before the appearance of creation as form. The impulse to new form lies within, waiting for the right moment to break through into the world of the known. Here the primary intelligence is body intelligence.

In a simple creative act, like my working on a piece of sculpture, this is the incubation stage. I may have a vague sense that something is preparing to happen, but nothing is yet visible. If I'm sensitive, I can feel some of the primordial beginnings in my tissues—perhaps in an attraction to a certain kind of movement, a feeling of contained shape, a gentle expanding.

In a lifetime, this is the prenatal period and the first few months of life. The unbroken whole here speaks in the infant's relationship both to the mother and to itself. Even following birth, the bond to the mother is primary. The light of conscious volition, that evidence of first distinction of both self from self and self from other, is only preparing to awaken. The reality of the infant

---

14   This multi-layered developmental analysis was first presented in my book, *The Creative Imperative*.

is an unselfconscious creature world. To feel is to act; there is no separation.

In a new relationship, this is the time before there is anything really visible as relationship. I may have a sense of being open to the possibility of a new connecting. I may have even met the person and felt a certain "chemistry" in her presence. But the spark of conscious recognition has yet to ignite.

In the story of civilization, this incubation stage corresponds to Stone Age times. For the most part, this is a reality of our distant past, though there are still a few places on our planet—in the New Guinea highlands, the upper Amazon basin, some places in the Australian outback—where this primordial reality prevails.

The unbroken whole at a cultural scale has multiple layers—manifesting at once as the tribe, nature, and time. In early tribal realities, the "body" of the tribe is more accurately the primary organism, rather than the individuals who compose it.[15] At the same time, truth and nature exist as, in essence, a single thing. Tribal deities are simply the faces of nature set animate: the wind, the mountain, bear, eagle, coyote. Health is one's degree of harmony with this living nature. Knowing is one's bodily connection in and as this whole. And time similarly affirms this unbroken entirety. Existence takes place in an eternally cycling present. Each generation and each turning of the seasons reenacts a timeless story.

Creative "Inspiration" (Early-Axis)

 The next big slice in formative process makes the magic and numinosity of the creative most explicit. Newly created possibility now steps forth from mystery into the light. This dramatic movement fundamentally alters how we perceive the order of things. Truth becomes explicitly polar.

---

15   If a person breaks a taboo important enough to cause him to be expelled from the tribe, it is not uncommon for that person to simply go off and die. He doesn't need to kill himself. To be excluded from the womb of the tribal whole is tantamount to nonexistence.

And its primary mode of expression shifts from the kinesthetic to the symbolic, to the language of myth and metaphor.

In working with chisel and stone, this is the stage of first inspiration. What was before only a faint quickening is now visibly born. My task is to play with images and possibilities, to feel where in them the deepest power lies, and to risk giving that power first form.

In a lifetime, this is the magical world of childhood. In this stage, we see the first critical distinction in initial separation from mother and, in the first manifestations of individual consciousness, separation from the infant's more creature-like reality. Truth moves a bit more "into the light," organized now according to the laws of imagination. The critical work of the child is its play, trying out images of possibility on the stage of make-believe and let's pretend.

With intimacy, this part of the story has its beginning with the first blush of real attraction. Though we are still largely strangers, this is a magical time, filled with tentative first touchings and fantasies of the possible. Our connecting at this point is often more as numinous symbols than as mortals . . . a fair princess, a handsome prince.

With the story of civilization, this stage takes us to the time of early civilizations. It first manifests in the coming together of tribes into broader alliances, and reaches its full splendor with the classical high cultures. We see it historically in the mystical monumentality of ancient Egypt, the vibrant artistry of pre-Columbian Mesoamerica, and the great mythic tales of Olympian Greece and the rich philosophies that followed. We can also find current examples of this inspiration stage in culture—in places like Tibet (though Chinese occupation has tempered the inspiration) or Bali (though more so prior to the tourist invasion). This is the time of culture's initial flowerings.

Something more than just nature (spirit, essence, magic, beauty—no single word quite describes it) emerges as the new cultural referent in these times. Meaning speaks with particular directness through the language of myth, manifesting as epic tales and complex pantheons of major and minor gods. This is also a time of rich artistic potency. Art during this stage becomes not just expression, but in and of itself a form of truth. We see also philosophy's inspired beginnings.

Creative "Perspiration"(Middle-Axis)

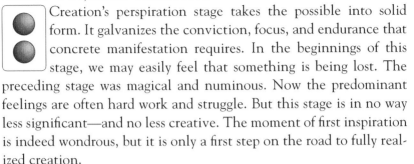

Creation's perspiration stage takes the possible into solid form. It galvanizes the conviction, focus, and endurance that concrete manifestation requires. In the beginnings of this stage, we may easily feel that something is being lost. The preceding stage was magical and numinous. Now the predominant feelings are often hard work and struggle. But this stage is in no way less significant—and no less creative. The moment of first inspiration is indeed wondrous, but it is only a first step on the road to fully realized creation.

With creative perspiration, the language of truth shifts from the mythic to the moral and the emotional. The work progresses by virtue of heart and guts. We can understand why the experience of struggle might be common by looking at the underlying polar dynamics. By the middle of this stage, the power of the newly created and the power of the context of creation have become equivalent. Reality exists as a polar isometric between at once opposite and conspiring forces.

As a sculptor, it is here that I most directly grapple with the hard demands of my calling. I must confront both the brute fact of the stone and my own limitations. Sometimes work proceeds with the patient rhythms and quiet satisfactions of the craftsman. Other times I rage. Over the course of this stage my relationship to the work changes, becoming both more vigorous and more expressive of the work as a human act.

In a lifetime, this stage marks entry into adolescence. Adolescence is a dramatic time, but also often an awkward and troubled time. The innocence of childhood must be left behind. It's a time for us to heroically challenge external limits and to establish inner ones. Emotions can be strong and contradictory. The reward for perseverance is an increasingly established identity and successful preparation for entry into the adult world.

In love, this stage takes on the tasks of relationship building. This process can be immensely satisfying—coming to better know the other person's gifts and peculiarities, beginning to build a life together. And again we commonly find contradictory feelings. The glow of the honeymoon period—when we view the other as a dream image—necessarily fades. This is the stage at which we most directly deal with questions of control and territory. It's here we decide who takes out the garbage.

This stage in cultural dynamics ruled in the West from the time of the Roman Empire through the Middle Ages and predominates today in much of the Middle East, as well as in parts of Eastern Europe, Asia, and Central and South America. We find great wonders that date from this stage, from the Roman aqueducts to Europe's great Gothic cathedrals. And equally we find struggle (and not infrequently pain and inhumanity)—the Crusades and the Spanish Inquisition, the European Dark Ages, and, in more modern times, often the tyranny of brutal dictatorships. The emotional and the moral assume new prominence. With the Middle Ages, Europe saw values like honor and chivalry newly revered, along with the first intimations of romantic love (though at this point it was unrequited love that was idealized—love held at a safe moral distance).

Cultural beliefs at this stage commonly have a fundamentalist ardency. A newly equal, and frequently ambivalent, balance between polar forces orders cultural experience. In the European Middle Ages, we see this polar tension in social structures that grew increasingly feudal: landed lords above, serfs and the otherwise impoverished below. Likewise, church and state (here in the form of kingly rule) became newly separate, newly equal in power, and ever more frequently at odds. And the ancients' many gods, with their differing proclivities, began to surrender their power to the notion of a single deity—or, more accurately, a dual deity: a monotheistic godhead on one side in eternal battle with the forces of evil on the other. In the modern world, one of the easiest ways to find perspiration stage cultural sensibilities is to note where conflict is common and particularly intractable.[16]

Again, we might regret that a certain magic has been lost. But this is not regression. The reward for this loss is increasingly established social structure. The Middle Ages gave us, with kingly rule, a new solidification of social organization, establishment of an institutional church, radical validation of rights with the Magna Carta, and increasingly formal structures of communication and commerce. We find related advances—and related contradictions—wherever perspiration stage developmental realities dominate in contemporary times.

---

16   As with terrorism and conflict in the Middle East.

Creative "Finishing and Polishing"(Late-Axis)

This progression has thus far taken us from the mystery of the formless, into magical possibility and first form, and then into a time of solidification of form. Now we give new form its finishing touches. Attention shifts increasingly to refinement and detail. Poles become even more separate, giving reality two nearly distinct faces. Truth becomes increasingly rational and material, defined in terms of logic and in terms of phenomena that can be seen and measured. And, at the same time, it becomes newly personal and subjective—the truth of aesthetics and even whim.

At this stage, as I face that piece of stone, I become newly able to objectively step back. The work now sits before me as a "piece," ready for completion. My focus shifts increasingly to issues of detail, to making sure all the elements are there and fit correctly together, to questions of aesthetic refinement and final nuance. Audience also becomes increasingly important. I need to give the newly created piece the delineation of voice required to communicate clearly.

In personal development, it is here that we face the tasks of adulthood. Adulthood challenges us to refine identity, to make essential decisions regarding career and family, and to give clarity and detail—and our personal stamp—to the way we live our lives. More than at any other time, it is at this stage that we can describe who we are in terms of things we can objectively see and measure—the structures we have given our lives and the forms of our actions. Adulthood is the most explicitly "in-the-world" stage of life.

Love at this stage becomes established and defined. We've sorted out the major issues of being together and reached general agreement on the roles and boundaries of the relationship—who does what, how, and when. We've largely stopped asking what our relationship will be, because it now is. Our attention shifts to details and fine-tuning. If we've chosen to continue together, love's connection at this point frequently has a feeling of acceptance and accomplishment not present in earlier stages.

In the story of civilization, this is the Modern Age, the last 400 years in Western Europe and at least an ingredient in the sensibilities of most cultural systems today. If classical times marked Europe's childhood, and the medieval period its adolescence, modernity

marked its coming of age. As culture engages finishing and polishing dynamics, oral and kingly truths give way to more materially
ordered realities—a personal reality of individuality, achievement,
and intellect; a social reality of law, industry, and economics; and a
physical reality of actions and their concomitant reactions. Institutions come to reflect a new appreciation for individual freedom and
personal initiative. Governmental forms become representative; religion entertains newly personal and direct relationships with the
divine; and economic competition becomes its own ethic, freeing
business from moral constraint. With the Modern Age in Europe,
we witnessed the Age of Reason and the growing prominence of
science with its new emphasis on the empirical. We also witnessed
reason's counterbalance in the Romantic Age, with its emphasis
on nature and the artistic (and on romantic love increasingly re-
quited). At this Modern Age stage, a sense of impending completion permeates culture. People speak of it being only a matter of
time until all of life's great mysteries find elucidation and individual
freedom is fully realized.

   To fully grasp the conceptual implications of this developmental
progression, we need to appreciate how the architecture of polarity
has evolved with it. The first half of the Creative Function maps
this evolution (see Figure 7-2). In tribal times, perception included
polarity, but polarity resided primarily in thought's background—
the major themes in human understanding were the unbroken
whole of nature and tribe. With the move into classical times in
both the East and the West, polarity assumed a more central role
in understanding, but poles remained conceptually close and were
not yet at odds. (The yin and yang of Chinese Taoist philosophy
or the entwined snakes of the Greek caduceus provide particularly
graphic illustration of this complementary sort of relationship, but
we could turn as readily to underlying assumptions in the dialec-
tics of Plato or Aristotle.) In the European Middle Ages, and in
present-day cultures where development resides in a parallel stage,
polarity becomes more explicitly about opposites. (Truth becomes
an isometric—though still ultimately co-generative—play between
clearly contrasting forces: feudal lords and peasants, church and

crown, good and evil.) With our Modern Age, poles become even more separate, and also, by virtue of that separateness, less obviously in opposition. (In a Cartesian reality, subjective and objective or mind and body are not so much in conflict as simply inhabitants of separate worlds.) While each kind of polar relationship can appear in a wide array of culturally specific manifestations, each brings with it predictable assumptions about how the world works.

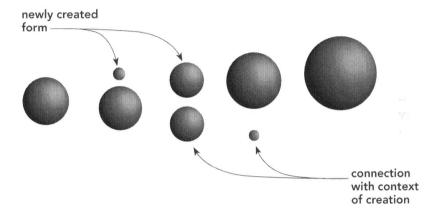

Fig. 7-2. Polarity's Evolution Through the First Half
          of the Formative Process

Creation's Integration Phase

Part of the "finishing and polishing" stage story is the belief that we have reached completion. The piece of sculpture is done. Identity is established. The hard work of relationship is over. We have brought understanding into the full light of reason. But, in a similar way to what we saw with intelligence's creative progression in Chapter Six, polarity has told but half of its story. Much that is most important in the "respiration" of creative life has yet to take place. It is these additional creative stages, and the additional kinds of polar relationships they involve, that give us Cultural Maturity and the kind of perspective this book draws upon.

I've described how formative processes have two halves. Polarity has very different significance depending on which half we inhabit. To fully appreciate how this is so, and before that, what just getting to such second-half realities requires, we need first to include an additional stage. More accurately, it is a time between stages. Appreciating this time of Creative Transition has particular importance for understanding our current time in culture and much that we now see around us.

Creative "Transition"

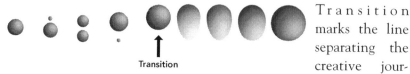

Transition

Transition marks the line separating the creative journey's two halves. Transitional changes are different from earlier developmental leaps in that they involve more than letting go of one stage and moving to another. They bring into question the entire developmental orientation (toward ever greater ascendancy, separation, and solidification of form) that has defined growth and truth. Transition is creation's Continental Divide. With Transition we reside at maturity's threshold, at a doorway joining two related but also fundamentally different worlds.

Transition can be a profound time—in its confrontations lie the seeds of wisdom. But it is also a time of disorientation and inescapable uncertainty. We stand at a precipice. Do we leap and trust that we will find solid ground? Do we go back? Proceeding depends on the gradual discovery of a new completeness in how we relate to both ourselves and our world.

As I enter this time of Transition as a sculptor, the piece stands before me essentially done—a crowning achievement. But what now? During the process of its creation I have come to be almost more the sculpture than myself. And now, suddenly, I must let it go. I could be tempted out of fear to cling to the piece, refuse its surrender. But if I do that, the piece becomes increasingly tired and purposeless, and I myself become increasingly absurd. I could just blindly walk away. But where do I go—indeed, is there any place to go?[17]

---

17   Transition may coincide with a creative manifestation's release into the world, or instead the needed severance may be more internal, a necessary letting go if the work is to proceed. Especially with greater maturity in

With individual development, we confront the unique and unexpected challenges of midlife. Just as we thought we were done growing up, the most fundamental of questions reappear and block our way. In time, this necessary questioning touches every part of our lives—our work, our love, ultimately our most basic ideas about who we are and how the world works. The sense of purpose we once took for granted can feel suddenly elusive. We ask, so who am I, really? And what really matters to me? At this point we have no way of knowing whether anything that lies ahead can again excite us as before. We can fear that being "over the hill" is what inevitably lies ahead. Some people respond to this uncertainty by abandoning what they have been—by getting a divorce, leaving their jobs. Others cling to old beliefs or try to return to their youth. But we have no real choice but to live with the uncertainty. When we attempt to hide from it, perversely, we only feel more empty and confused.

We see something similar with the midpoint in love as a creative process. Suddenly, just as we thought love's work was complete, the passions that have driven love can seem to elude us. The same sense of completion that before gave us pride can start to feel like habit, and the comfort of familiarity can begin to feel like taking each other for granted. We have become for each other all-too-familiar objects. Where to go from here? Stepping forward requires that we surrender that familiarity, and with it our dreams of perfection and completion. But is there anything beyond these things? We have no way to be sure. In fear, we often cling to what we know from before. But when we do, relationship becomes empty and stale.

In keeping with this developmental progression, much of what we see in the world today is consistent with Transitional dynamics. As a species, we stand at a precipice. Old answers are ceasing to work and, by all evidence, they will not be replaced by new ones, at least not of the same sort. What lies ahead? Anything? From the position of the

---

the artist's personal development (either in his life as a whole, or more specifically, his development as an artist), the piece's completion may wait until further seasoning has taken place. Whichever is the case, the underlying experience is similar.

apex of Transition we cannot know. We can try to cling to familiar truths—from the onward-and-upward story of material progress to religious predictions of final salvation or damnation. But when we do, we only become more absurd.[18]

Earlier reflections on postmodern thought—with its emphasis on the diminishing usefulness of final truths of every sort—highlight this Transitional predicament. I've proposed that while postmodern formulations shed light on our times, they assist us much less than we might hope. As far as helping us understand the future and its likely demands, in the end, they offer very little. Our developmental picture provides explanation. Such views eloquently address the Transitional quandary, but by themselves give us no way to understand what may lie beyond it—indeed, whether anything of real substance lies beyond it.

Creative "Integration"

 As we step over matutiy's threshold—whatever the creative scale—we leave Transition's precarious reality behind us. We are necessarily surprised by what we encounter—surprised that so much of creation's journey remains ahead, surprised at the magnitude of what it will ask of us, and surprised by the depth and richness of potential rewards. While Transition in one sense marks a completion, in another it marks a beginning—the start of a systemically mature creative life. We may have thought creation finished, or nearly so, but in fact we have barely approached its midpoint. Yes, the new object of creation (the piece of sculpture, personal identity, relationship as an entity, or culture as structure) stands shining before us. But it has yet to be significantly tested. Integration is about that testing and the creative changes that result—and not just in that object, but also in the systems that have done the creating.

---

18   And we really don't need to cling to encounter the absurd. Much that is absurd comes with the territory. See the concept of Transitional Absurdity in Chaper Eight.

The second half of the creative cycle reconnects the new creation with the personal and social contexts from which it was born. It is about bringing maturity to the creative process. We become newly able to step back from what we have created. We also become more able to step back from the whole of creative process' progression. And in stepping back, we also come to see with new depth and clarity. We come to appreciate where the process of creation has taken us, and what ultimately it has been about, in a way that before was not an option.

The word "integration" begins to describes what takes place, but this is not integration in any simple additive or averaging sense. The changes that we encounter in these Integrative stages are as fully creative as any seen before. They change everything—indeed, in a particularly fundamental sense.

You've seen how these changes manifest at a cultural level with the concept of Integrative Meta-perspective. I've described how Cultural Maturity's cognitive reordering involves not only a stepping back, but also a new depth and completeness of engagement. With these changes, our interest comes to lie increasingly not just with the newly created object, but that object in living relationship with all that surrounds it. Integrative Meta-perspective dramatically changes how we see the world. Indeed, as you've seen, it changes truth itself. At the least, we better appreciate the degree to which *how* we perceive affects what we perceive. And we better recognize how truths that before seemed separate or even adversarial—many of which are essential to our sense of identity and meaning—may in fact work as colluding partners.

Within the limits of any formative process' particular creative scale, Integration stage mechanisms propel us into a more conscious and explicitly complex and systemic—whole-box-of-crayons—world of experience. Previous to this point in development, this result would have been disorienting and overwhelming. As Integration stage dynamics become timely, we experience these changes as positive. They make possible a sophistication of understanding—and of life—that we could not have known before.

As I step back from that piece of stone and examine the finished sculpture that it has now become, I confront how the journey of its creation is in fact far from over. The piece may need further seasoning and, even if it does not, it has yet to be placed in the world. What will happen to it? Will it make the world a better place, be ignored, be destroyed? And in an important sense, it also has yet to be placed in me. Much remains to happen. On "completing" a piece of real significance, it is often years before I can say with any clarity what it is really about, what it has to teach. The conscious object of creation before was the stone. Creative maturity reveals that my engagement with it has always been as much about creating myself and, if it truly functions as art, about new possibilities in the creation of culture.

In our individual lives, the primary achievements of the first half of development—self-definition, the acquisition of skills and knowledge, perhaps creating a family—all in some way involve establishing ourselves as form. The developmental challenges of life's second half make real in ever-more-subtle ways the fact that creative Transition first made inescapable—that the role of such forms in the tasks of truth and identity is but a beginning. Truth as answer increasingly gives way to truth as relationship and pattern. We step back and become increasingly capable of a bringing a new big-picture depth, detail, and responsibility to our considerations. Questions that can't be answered in the old ways present themselves, questions of a newly contextual sort. We reexamine our professions, looking to see if they still provide challenge and fulfillment in our lives—and, as important, if they contribute in satisfying ways. We do the same with our relationships and our beliefs. In the process, who we are in each of these spheres deepens. Frequently our choices remain largely as before—it is primarily our relationship to our choices that changes. But sometimes, too, we make new choices, venture off in wholly new directions. Questions of perspective and meaning increasingly move to the forefront. When we say someone is mature, seasoned, or wise, we appreciate that that person has engaged and weathered at least the most important of life's Integration stage challenges.

With an intimate relationship, again we become newly capable of stepping back and newly capable, too, of appreciating what love of a deep sort is ultimately about. Love's second-half tasks give emphasis increasingly to the uniqueness of each person and to the unique needs of the relationship. Bonds become at once richer and more humble. As we become more fully ourselves, our connection can also become more full. But this can happen only with the acceptance of limits to what one person can be for another. Being together with integrity, caring, and honesty—however that might look—increasingly defines affection and commitment. We more deeply appreciate self and other as particular and complex beings.

The whole of this book has been about related changes that are predicted—and, I have argued, happening—at a cultural scale. The ability to engage each of Cultural Maturity's three threshold tasks follows from what we would expect second-half dynamics at a cultural scale to produce. Succeeding with the first threshold task—abandoning polarized assumptions and thinking in more encompassing, whole-box-of-crayons ways—can be thought of as a direct product of these more integrative creative mechanisms. Effectively addressing the second threshold task—acknowledging limits both to past ways of acting and to the heroic and romantic stories that have defined then—again reflects what this progression predicts. And successfully confronting our third threshold task—becoming consciously responsible, mature choice-makers and thinking about truth itself in new, more nuanced and context-specific ways—is similarly consistent with formative process' second-half challenges and the accomplishments that define successful engagement with them.

Do our times mark the end of civilization? In the sense of confronting Transition's threshold, they do. Our times mark the end of a progression that in its general trajectory has defined us since our beginnings as a species. From the near side of that threshold it can easily seem an end. There is no way of knowing whether anything lies beyond what we see, and every reason to assume we will find only problems ahead. But if we are able to step over Cultural Maturity's threshold, we see that a great deal potentially lies ahead. We can't know all the specifics or whether we can pull off what the future will require. But this developmental picture makes strong argument for the conclusion that the rewards for venturing forth could very well be not just exciting, but profound.

Figure 7-3 on the following page summarizes these observations.

THE CREATIVE CYCLE

CREATIVE STAGES	Pre-Axis	Early-Axis	Middle-Axis	Late-Axis	Transition	Integrative Stages
MAJOR PERIODICITIES						
A CREATIVE EVENT	Incubation	Inspiration	Perspiration	Finishing & Polishing	Presentation	Becoming "Second Nature" (Integration of the newly created form into self and culture)
A LIFETIME	Prenatal Period & Infancy	Childhood	Adolescence	Early Adulthood	Midlife Transition	Mature Adulthood (From knowledge to wisdom—integration of self as formed identity with the ground of being)
A RELATIONSHIP	Pre-relationship	Falling in Love	Time of Struggle	Established Relationship	Time of Questioning	Mature Intimacy (Relationship as two whole people—marriage of the "loved" and the "lover" within each person)
THE HISTORY OF CULTURE	Pre-History	Golden Ages	Middle Ages	Age of Reason	Transitional Culture	Cultural Maturity (Larger meeting of the form and context of culture)

Fig. 7-3. Patterning in Time

Implications

This creatively based developmental/evolutionary picture fills out our understanding of Cultural Maturity in multiple important ways. Certainly these reflections provide further evidence. The fact that we recognize parallels in both the creative workings of polarity over time and in the evolution of intelligence's mechanisms—two of the most fundamental of human processes—provides particularly solid support for the conclusions in these pages. And the fact that we can recognize larger patterns that capture our human narrative as a whole is certainly provocative.

These descriptions also help refine our understanding of Cultural Maturity's changes. If the assertion of parallel dynamics is accurate, we can use our experience from more circumscribed formative dynamics to guide us as we confront today's critical cultural choices. While we humans have not yet experienced culture's engagement with more mature creative mechanisms to any great degree, we have all had this experience with shorter periodicities. I've applied this approach in a limited way by drawing on the analogy with personal development with each of the three threshold tasks.

Another thing this developmental picture does is provide support for how I have described the cognitive changes that produce Cultural Maturity's new view of the world. We recognize something related with creative maturity whatever the creative scale. We see a new capacity to step back, and with that stepping back, the possibility of a less mythologized, no longer "parental" picture of how things work (whether the mythic "parent" in question is culture, a person who gave birth to us, or ourselves in any more individual process of creation[19]). In each case we see also a new and deeper engagement with our human complexity—with pertinent polarities, with our multiple intelligences, and in the specific context of that particular formative process, with our larger whole-box-of-crayons natures.

---

19 With any "creative act" of the more conventional sort, we must surrender equally beliefs we might have that make ourselves as individuals the sole parent/source of the creation and opposite sorts of beliefs that place that source of creation solely in some mythologized, and thus equally parental, notion of "mystery." In the process, creativity becomes both more "ordinary" and more ultimately worthy of our wonder.

This developmental picture also helps clarify a claim I've used to support the unique significance of Cultural Maturity's changes. I've proposed that culturally mature perspective should help us better understand our human story as a whole—past, present, and future. The changes that mark any formative process' second half offer us the opportunity to better appreciate how we got to where we have come—and through this, who we have been in getting there. Ideas presented in the next chapter will be needed to fully make sense of how this result comes about. But if Integrative Meta-perspective lets us step back from our natures as formative beings as I've described, it is reasonable to expect that culture's mature stages should help us appreciate, with new depth and completeness, both history to this point and what it means to be human.

This developmental/evolutionary picture is significant too for how it affirms Creative Systems Theory's specific explanation for why we see what I describe in this book—whether our interest lies with current circumstances or culture's larger story. We come back to Creative Systems Theory's assertion that what makes us unique is our audacious toolmaking, meaning-making—creative—natures. The whole of the developmental/evolutionary picture we have looked at follows predictably from the way change works in conscious creative systems.

One more thing this developmental picture does is help us address the long-term implications of the concept of Cultural Maturity. I've put primary emphasis in these pages on the concept's implications for today, on what it tells us about the challenges we now face and the capacities required to meet them effectively. But these developmental observations support the conclusion that we can also think of Cultural Maturity's changes as having more extended significance. If the picture I have outlined is correct, Cultural Maturity's threshold marks not just the beginning of a next chapter in the human story, but the turning of first pages in a new, second kind of story that in the end should define our ultimate human task.

Personal Maturity, Cultural Maturity, and the Mechanisms of Wisdom

Using personal maturity as analogy has served us well, but I've noted the importance of distinguishing clearly between personal maturity and Cultural Maturity. While we do see essential parallels—and not just metaphorical parallels, but also organizational parallels—there are also ways in which these two scales of maturity have decidedly different implications. The way I've used the word "wisdom"—a term that I've suggested effectively captures what the future demands of us—highlights one of the most important differences.

Earlier I observed that the word "wisdom" can be used in ways that are simply misleading. We will return to that kind of misinterpretation in the next chapter. But the specific differences between wisdom as it manifests in personal development and with Cultural Maturity are also pertinent to this book's reflections. Even when applied in ways that adequately grasp its meaning, the word "wisdom" has different significance depending on whether our interest lies with maturity of the personal or cultural sort. Personal wisdom, while of great significance, can be found at any cultural time. Culturally mature wisdom—and I cannot emphasize this too strongly—is something specific to our time. If we miss this distinction, we become immediately vulnerable to traps in our thinking.

Plato, Hippocrates, Christ, Lao-Tzu, and the Buddha were all wise people. But theirs was personal wisdom, the wisdom of individual maturity. Such wisdom has influenced us through history for very good reasons. Personal wisdom is a profound thing and is important to emulate. But the utterances of each of these wise people were made within the protective constraints of their cultural time. Established cultural guideposts—rarely questioned moral codes, clear gender roles, mythologized ethnic and national allegiances—circumscribed their assertions. And statements about the importance of humility (and thus the acceptance of limits to what we can know) were made within the surrounding context of ultimately deterministic (and thus ultimately limitless and certain) conceptions of order—whether voiced in the assurances of philosophical argument, divine omniscience, or being as an ultimate answer. In contrast, wisdom that has its origins in the mature stages of culture's evolutionary story produces results that before now we could not have known, much less made manifest. None of our three threshold tasks make complete sense—certainly any practical sort of sense for our time—restricted to wisdom as we have know it in times past.

An essential implication (as well as an important affirmation) of this conclusion concerns the age of people in whom we are most likely to encounter culturally mature insights. While frequently such insights are voiced by older people—personal maturity doesn't hurt—as often, and in many contexts more often, they are voiced by younger people. If the relationship between personal maturity and Cultural Maturity is as I suggest, this is what we would expect. I am reminded of Charles Dickens's observation that "each child is born into the world finer than the last." [20]

Values, Cultural Domains, and the Future

We can use our developmental/evolutionary picture not just to look to our human future as a whole, but also to provide perspective for re-thinking the assumptions of specific cultural domains. We've glimpsed more general domain-specific insights with earlier introductory thoughts about changes happening in spheres such as government and health care. But a developmental/evolutionary vantage lets us bring valuable further detail and refinement to our thinking.

Once we step over Cultural Maturity's threshold, how we think about cultural domains changes in a couple of explicitly systemic ways. First, domains stop being distinct categories of activities and become instead contrasting, but ultimately interrelated, crayons in culture's systemic box—aspects of here-and-now systemic "multiplicity." In addition, each domain/crayon itself becomes newly systemic, a particular expression of our particularly vibrant kind of living complexity.

In Chapter Eleven, I will offer a big-picture summary of changes in each of the major spheres of culture this book touches on—economics/business, science/technology, government, health care, education, the media, love and the family, art, and religion. At this point, we gain useful further insight into developmental/evolutionary change—and in particular, the kinds of developmental/evolutionary changes that

---

20   It is not unusual today to see leadership and surprisingly wise perspective coming from the millennial generation, the group just now stepping into adulthood. Millennials are known for being idealistic and often having activist tendencies. At the same time, in the same population we often see particular absurdities—for example, studies show that the millennial generation is particularly materialistic and surprisingly blind to the dangers of mass consumerism. But this is a predicted kind of juxtaposition (one we will later look at more closely—see "Transitional Absurdities" in Chapter Eight).

define the times in which we live—by looking briefly at a couple of spheres that have a particular kind of significance in our time: We've been especially likely to identify them with final truth.

I've described how, over the course of history, we've witnessed a progression from worldviews that most emphasize the more connectedness-focused, "left-hand," archetypally feminine aspects of our complexity, toward ways of thinking that give more difference-focused, "right-hand," archetypally masculine aspects of our complexity greater significance. Because more right-hand sensibilities predominate during Late-Axis times (becoming with Transition often in effect all that remains), we would expect spheres that most directly express archetypally masculine values to have had particularly dominant roles in recent times. Consistent with this, over the last century we have most often given a couple of spheres—first the world of science (along with its application in technology), and second, that of economics (and its application in business)—final truth status.

A conclusion I put forward in examining our third threshold task helps us appreciate just what, with each of these spheres, is beginning to become different. I proposed that once we step beyond Cultural Maturity's threshold, in an important sense every question becomes a moral/ethical question.[21] More commonly, we've divided concerns into those that are moral and those that are not. With our Modern Age, we've done so in a particularly explicit way. We've come to view the products of whole cultural domains as "value-free"—as good in and of themselves.

Science/technology and economics/business represent the two realms that in modern times we have most often seen as value-free. In fact, neither of these spheres has ever really been value-free. But while we have operated within the context of Modern Age values and beliefs, the fact

---

21   If for no other reason, this becomes the case because the concerns of any domain reflect only certain parts of our larger systemic natures. When we say questions from a specific domain have particular importance, we are claiming that one crayon has more significance than others. Right or wrong, we are making a statement of value. From the more encompassing perspective of Cultural Maturity, the belief that certain activities might be value-free thus stops being tenable. No thought or act escapes scrutiny.

that we've often acted as though they have been has rarely gotten us into great trouble. "The more scientific and technological advancement the better" and "the more economic benefit the better" have worked as acceptable rules of thumb. But today things aren't quite so simple—and in the future they will be even less so.

Let's take our two broad spheres one at a time. "More is better" still applies to science and technology at their best, but today such assertions need to be tempered by an acknowledgment of at least the more obvious kinds of limits. We are better appreciating that there are situations where technological solutions may present unacceptable risks, or where constraints may exist to how much science and technology we can afford. Many important future science- and technology-related creative insights will have as much to do with what is *right* to do as what we *can* do.

But as important for our reflections are limits that relate to how Cultural Maturity's changes alter how we think about the roles of science and technology, and, ultimately, how we think about scientific truth itself. Culturally mature perspective's whole-box-of-crayons vantage makes it clear that the kind of thought that underlies scientific and technological assumptions doesn't represent the whole of understanding. This does not make either science or technology any less significant. But it does bring attention to the importance of placing their contributions within a larger systemic context.

At the very least, we need to better tease apart where the kind of understanding that science and technology draws on can help us and where what it is good for may be limited. Nobel laureate Gerald Edelman put the larger, systemic picture this way: "Whatever we establish scientifically to be true, there is much in our experience that is of our own making and much of it the most precious part of our lives." There are a lot of things science can help us with quite wonderfully—and a lot of other things for which it really doesn't have much of great value to say.

Previous reflections on the ultimately "procreative" relationship of polar opposites help provide the needed perspective. Science does very well with concerns where "harder," more archetypally masculine sensibilities prove sufficient; that is, with most anything we can describe rationally or in terms of physical interactions, behaviors, or logical/mathematical constructs. But it does much less well whenever "softer," more archetypally feminine sensibilities play a significant role—as with self-understanding, human interactions, art, or spirituality. Einstein reminded us of the needed distinction in warning that "we should take care not to make the intellect our God; it has of course powerful muscles, but no personality." We are better seeing where problems may require more than scientific or technological solutions.[22]

Bringing this kind of larger perspective to how we think about science's role is essential. Often, today, we find thinking that becomes a narrow scientism—thinking that gives validity only to the explicitly material. At the least, this kind of thinking too easily abdicates science's larger moral responsibility. Later I will describe how it often leads to flagrantly erroneous conclusions.[23]

Ultimately, culturally mature perspective does more than just alert us to where science and technology may have limited application; it puts scientific truth itself in a new light. There is nothing particularly new in the observation that science can't explain everything. Thinkers of a more romantic or spiritual bent have emphasized this conclusion from early on in understanding's history. Whole-box-of-crayons systemic perspective goes further to present a fundamental challenge to past assumptions that made science's methodology objective and thus safe from fundamental questioning.

Science *is* objective in the sense that its conclusions are based on rational questioning and repeatable physical observation. But increasingly we recognize that even when what we study would seem quite appropriately the province of science, these approaches don't address or reflect all we need to consider. Timothy Ferris put this more basic limitation provocatively in his book *Coming of Age in the Milky Way*: "It is the faith of [classical] science that nature is rationally intelligible." An objectivity that leaves out essential pieces of the evidence represents a limited objectivity at best.

---

22   In recalling my visit to the 1962 world's fair in Seattle as a child, I remember how unquestioningly its exhibits assumed that problems of any sort could be solved by science and technology.

23   The best of scientists today do not fall for this ultimately ideological interpretation of science, but such thinking has found a new kind of popular audience of late (see "Postindustrial/Information Age Scenarios" in Chapter Nine and "Science and Technology" in Chapter Eleven).

The assertion that scientific thought confronts this more basic kind of limit might seem contradictory given how I've often used scientific advances as examples. But science's most basic notions can leave its best practitioners flailing for explanation. I've noted the challenge of thinking in ways that reflect that we are alive. The "what is life" question baffles even the best of scientists. (Commonly they just hand it off to philosophers, who in the end can do no better.)[24] And "explaining" quantum mechanics defies even those who are most brilliant and eloquent. Richard Feynman once commented: "I can safely say that nobody understands quantum mechanics." (And he should be able to understand it if anyone could.)

Key to this inquiry is the recognition that any truth that succeeds as culturally mature truth will, in the end, present a dilemma for science—at least for science of the classical sort. I've described how culturally mature truths of every sort ultimately "bridge" polarities, even truths of the most hard-nosed sort. If this conclusion holds, understanding leaves science in a pickle not just when it comes to more ephemeral concerns, but with concerns of every sort once we step over Cultural Maturity's threshold. Notice that science—at least when interpreted narrowly—runs into difficulties when it tries to address any of the notions I've drawn on to describe culturally mature truth: for example, responsibility (of the needed double sort), intelligence (in the multiple-intelligence sense), systemic thinking (of the newly dynamic and complete kind), creativity (in the fully encompassing definition), purpose (in the sense that addresses today's crisis of purpose), and maturity itself. Ultimately, it lacks the completeness of perspective needed to fully address any of our three threshold tasks. Traditional scientific truth remains single-crayon truth.

None of this is to diminish science. The fact that science can comfortably describe realities that "bridge" polarities (well, not always that

---

24   Biologist Gregory Bateson would often begin introductory biology classes by placing a live crab on a table at the front of the room and asking students how they knew it was a alive. He would then exit the room and leave them to ponder. On his return, he would respond to each student's answer by describing something that is not alive that also exhibits that characteristic. "It moves?" Certainly cars move. "It reproduces?" Crystals also reproduce. And so on.

comfortably), and often maneuver powerfully in such realities (as with the equations of quantum mechanics) is profound. But science's difficulty with explanation does leaves us with essential questions about how best to think about scientific truth beyond Cultural Maturity's threshold. Culturally mature science recognizes that exactly what makes science significant also restricts what it can accomplish. Culturally mature science is humble regarding its limits. And simultaneously, from that place of mature respect, it endeavors to reach as far as it is able into existence's deepest creative mysteries.

The other realm that we've commonly given value-free status to is the world of money—whether it manifests more abstractly in the ideas of economics or takes applied expression in the interactions of business. We use the familiar phrase "it's just business" to affirm this value-free status. In fact, the economic sphere, just by what it is, could not be more value-laden. But because money represents an ultimate material abstraction, it is not surprising that we might in modern times confuse it with truth. Like science, this is a crayon we have in recent times mythologized and given special importance. Indeed, today it has come to trump science in its assumed last-word significance—at least functionally (money increasingly defines what science gets done), if not always in our conscious beliefs. If there is one aspect of our human complexity that in our time we have made our God, this is it.

As with science, we like to think of the economic sphere as rational and a world apart from moral concerns—except perhaps where dishonesty comes into play. But the fact that we tend to think of the monetary realm as value-free is again a product of the times in which we live rather than truth in any final sense. Because we are unconscious of the power that it holds, we need to be particularly attentive to potential blindnesses and the importance of mature systemic perspective when it comes to economic concerns.[25]

It helps to put this need to think in larger ways with regard to the world of money in historical perspective. If we lived in the Middle Ages or in a tribal culture, we would find modern material values not just confusing, but unacceptable. In the Middle Ages, while material wealth had significant influence, simple greed was also considered one of the seven deadly sins. Within tribal cultures, the difference is even

---

25   See "Transitional Absurdities" in Chapter Eight.

more pronounced. In tribal societies, it is not acceptable for individual advantage to threaten the well-being of the group. These differences are of more than casual consequence. Much of the antipathy non-Western peoples often have for Western values lies in these differing views of competition and wealth, differences commonly perceived as having deeply moral significance.

A culturally mature reframing of the monetary realm starts with the importance, described earlier, of defining wealth—and human benefit more generally—in ways that are more systemically complete. A sign outside my local plumbing store provides the needed reminder: "Money will buy a pretty good dog, but it won't buy the wag of its tail." Cultural Maturity very specifically does not call for replacing materialism with some romanticized opposite. But it does very much call for more encompassing ways of thinking about and measuring human success. Progress in a culturally mature world continues to be about wealth creation, about the generation of new capital, but capital now comes to include all that goes into making human life ultimately rich and fulfilling.

Such reframing is pertinent not just to determining whether money-related practices will be just in the future, but also to whether the structures of business and economics, in the long term, will work at all. Earlier I suggested that our blindness to potential economic instabilities in the recent severe recession was a product of ideology as much as simple ignorance. Economics' reigning experts acted on the belief that free markets could largely regulate themselves, a belief that reflects an extreme right-hand—rationalist/materialist/individualist—worldview.

At the very least, such one-crayon perspective made financiers and the rest of us—very smart people included—vulnerable to dismissing, or not even seeing, potential risks. In 2004, then-chairman of the U.S. Federal Reserve Alan Greenspan proclaimed, "Not only have individuals become less vulnerable to shocks from underlying risk factors, but also the financial system as a whole has become more resilient"—this specifically in reference to the impossibly complex and highly interlinked financial instruments that played a central role in the 2007 meltdown.[26]

---

26   Some people did anticipate the problem. Warren Buffett warned that derivatives were "financial weapons of mass destruction carrying dangers, that while now latent, are potentially lethal."

It is forgivable that economic experts did not accurately forecast just when an economic downturn might occur. But that the greater portion of economic minds did not recognize fundamental instabilities—which in hindsight are glaring—suggests a more essential kind of blindness.

Modern economic thinking has made a start toward addressing economic questions in more systemic terms. For example, it increasingly recognizes the fact that economics is more than just a science of monetary exchange, that it is very much a social science, as much about human psychology as about rational behavior. And bit by bit, society as a whole is starting to confront the more basic recognition that economic wealth represents only part of what makes for a rich life. We are better seeing how our friendships, our families, and our communities contribute as much or more to a true sense of wealth. We are also at least beginning to grasp how the health of our physical and biological environments is also critical to our lives being worth living.

Particular economic and business questions are becoming more clearly moral/ethical concerns. And the "economic" question of how best to think abut wealth has become arguably our time's most pivotal and ultimately defining moral/ethical concern. Money is our common medium of exchange. If we are to act in ways that ultimately serve us, how we exchange it needs to directly reflect what to us most deeply matters. If extreme materiality exacerbates our time's crisis of purpose and has the potential to create instabilities that put us all at risk as I've proposed, then developing more encompassing—I could say moral—ways of thinking about the economic sphere becomes of ultimate importance.

For this chapter's developmental/evolutionary reflections, there is a common lesson to be learned from these two domains that we have viewed as "value-free." The future requires that we recognize how all questions are in the end moral questions—questions of value—and that we need to address them, whatever their source, with a new, more complete kind of systemic sophistication. Culturally mature perspective helps us appreciate how questions of every sort today represent aspects of our larger moral responsibility.

Leadership and Developmental/Evolutionary Perspective

The culturally mature leader's new-truth toolbox is not complete without temporal pattern language concepts at least related to the developmental/evolutionary notions we've touched on with this chapter. Culturally mature leadership requires that we always ask not just, "What is true?" but also, "What time is it?" Culturally mature perspective continually reminds us that "everything has its season."

Many of the most provocative leadership-related implications of developmental/evolutionary perspective concern leadership at a planetary scale. While globalization makes effective planetary scale leadership increasingly essential, the fact that the world's people reside at different cultural stages can make it very difficult to achieve the needed mutual respect, sophistication of communication, and depth of collaboration. Recognizing how belief evolves over time in predictable ways, and also how each stage-specific reality has its particular kind of validity, can help us better tolerate differences and even learn from them. It can also help us make good policy in the context of cultural stage differences.

I remember asserting during the Cold War that the old Soviet Union presented much less of a threat, at least in the long term, than most people assumed (while also emphasizing that the short-term threat of nuclear Armageddon was very real). The reason? Totalitarian communism is a governmental form specific to a particular period in cultural development (an early Modern Age substage), and the Soviet Union was beginning to progress beyond that period. I predicted that its political and economic forms would, with time, collapse under their own weight. It is impossible to know how much American policy contributed to hastening the collapse of the old Soviet Union. It is also impossible to know how much the Russian state will in the future attempt to again flex old totalitarian muscles—two steps forward and one step back tends to be how cultural change happens. But developmental/evolutionary perspective helps us appreciate the significant potential dangers that our previous exaggerated picture of communism's potential long-term influence created. It also supports the possibility of engaging conflict that may occur in the future more wisely.

A similar developmental/evolutionary analysis provides perspective for addressing future relations with China. China currently has an increasingly market-oriented economic system while at the same time retaining political structures of a largely totalitarian sort. While change in cultural functions such as economics and politics doesn't necessarily proceed at the same pace, in keeping with a culture's stage, they do tend ultimately to go hand in hand. With patience, we should see individual rights and more democratic principles increasingly becoming legitimate parts of China's cultural conversation.

I've described the importance of culturally mature developmental/evolutionary perspective if we wish to effectively address terrorism. Certainly such perspective helps us better understand countries and cultures where terrorism tends to have its roots. But just as important, developmental/evolutionary perspective helps us better understand ourselves in the face of terrorism and avoid unhelpful responses. Avoiding dangerously simplistic reactions toward the Soviet Union during the Cold War—where systems were not that far apart developmentally—was difficult enough. The fact that terrorism juxtaposes systems that reside at widely different developmental stages can dramatically compound the challenge. I've described how the actions of terrorists can appear simply crazy from the perspective of Modern Age belief.

What terrorism requires of us can seem decidedly unfair—and in an important sense is unfair. A person could claim that because extremists in the Islamic East see the U.S. as the Great Satan, it is naïve for us not to simply see them as enemies and act accordingly. Certainly it is true that even if we do an exceptional job at not polarizing and projecting in response to terrorism, only rarely, at least for now, will we get the same courtesy—maturity—in return. And it is certainly true also that much in terrorist acts—such as rapes and beheadings—is legitimately considered "evil" (in the sense of doing harm to life). But just as much it is true that immature, eye-for-an-eye thinking can only result in unfortunate outcomes.

I included the fact that the modern West has for the most part not responded to the terrorists' polar demonizations by returning the favor in Chapter One's list of Cultural Maturity "success stories." Developmental/evolutionary perspective is not essential to the needed wisdom and patience. But such perspective certainly helps. We tend not to have difficulty recognizing that "unfairness" is just how things work in relationships between individuals of different ages. We don't expect our children to think and act like adults. Today, we have to accept that even with the most wise and effective policy, it will take considerable time before suicide bombings and the like are no longer commonly seen as appropriate, even heroic, in their cultural contexts. Evolutionary perspective supports such acceptance.

Earlier I made reference to a further particularly important application of developmental/evolutionary perspective on the world stage. It helps us avoid imposing cultural forms—governmental, economic, religious—that are not timely and thus not appropriate. In the West, we are extremely vulnerable to viewing modern institutional democracy and free-market capitalism as ideals and making their dissemination an unquestioned goal of policy. It should now be clear that while institutional democracy and free-market capitalism each represent proud, indeed profound accomplishments, they are best understood as forms specifically appropriate to a particular stage in culture—and far from finished products. If we fail to appreciate this larger picture, actions taken with the best of intentions can result in decidedly harmful consequences.

Along with helping us make such big-picture distinctions, developmental/evolutionary cultural perspective also has important application with more specific and everyday leadership tasks. Whatever the issue, when we include the dimension of time in our reflections, our thinking comes to better capture what is important.

Barack Obama's speech during his first run for the U.S. presidency in response to criticisms of the arguably anti-American sermons of his pastor Rev. Jeremiah Wright provides a good example of how this simple addition can alter leadership's effectiveness. People found the speech deeply affecting. That they did was in large part a product of the fact that it included an acknowledgment of change. From Obama's March 2008 speech on race:

> The profound mistake of Reverend Wright's sermons is not that he spoke about racism in our society. It is that he spoke as if our society was static; as if no progress has been made; as if this country—a country that has made it possible for one of its own members to run for the highest office in the land and build a coalition of white and black, Latino and Asian, rich and poor, young and old—is still irrevocably bound to a tragic past.

Obama emphasized strongly the essential task of moving on. He also noted the importance of a certain understanding and forgiveness toward those who may cling to views from times past. That included

Reverend Wright, but he also included in this reference whites who may cling to past bigotries and fears. (Both Reverend Wright and his critics missed this necessary consideration of time.)

A full application of temporal perspective requires not just an evolutionary frame, but also the inclusion of a notion such as Cultural Maturity. In his bestselling book, *The Evolution of God,* journalist and scholar Robert Wright applies an evolutionary frame to historical changes in our ideas about divinity—a radical approach and an effort to be commended. His analysis works well until he gets to modern times and the challenges ahead. He accurately describes how we may see diminishing conflict not just between differing religions, but also between the beliefs of religion and science. But he implies that globalization, combined with a vaguely suggested "expansion of moral truth" provides adequate explanation for this more integrative result.

Wright's general conclusion is on target and important, but his explanation for how we get there doesn't work. Each expansion of the circumference of social organization through time—from tribe, to kingdom, to nation-state—has indeed resulted in reconciliation of differences with peoples we previously have made targets of our projections. But always before we've replaced more local evil empires with other more distant versions. Today the challenge is of a fundamentally different, deeper, and more encompassing sort—to leave behind the psychological need for enemies altogether.

I've described how globalization by itself is as likely to produce new conflict as mutual understanding. Not just globalization, but something akin to Cultural Maturity is required if we are to bridge conflicting religious beliefs. And globalization does nothing that would result in the bridging of more fundamental conceptual differences such as those that divide science and religion. Leadership that can help us bridge such fundamental divides requires not just an appreciation of similarities, but systemic perspective that can help us understand how differences and similarities have evolved—and the particular new ways in which they are evolving today.

CHAPTER EIGHT

Cultural Maturity from a Conceptual Perspective— Further Reflections

*All truths are easy to understand once you know them;
the point is to discover them.*

GALILEO

OVER THE COURSE OF THE BOOK, I've promised to return for a closer look at a handful of Cultural Maturity–related concerns that require us to draw further on Creative Systems Theory if we are to understand them fully. There also remain conceptual topics we need to touch on if Cultural Maturity and its changes are to make full sense. This chapter's further conceptual observations both help to solidify the concept of Cultural Maturity and provide important additional evidence of the concept's accuracy.

We'll begin by revisiting a conceptual quandary that accompanies the pivotal task of rethinking progress—and, in the end, thinking about the future at all: what I've called the Dilemma of Trajectory. I've described how familiar notions of what going forward entails would leave us at a dead end. We will look more closely at the Dilemma of Trajectory and more deeply examine how Cultural Maturity's cognitive changes reconcile it.

We will then turn to a couple of topics that each in its own way provides important additional support for Cultural Maturity's thesis. We will more closely examine how Cultural Maturity's cognitive reorganization alters the role and functioning of conscious awareness. Then, by examining the question of whether Cultural Maturity is best thought of as "revolution or evolution," we will take a more focused look at Cultural Maturity's changes at the level of process.

Next I will touch briefly on a result that has particular implications for our human experience of purpose, and purpose in our time—how some of the most absurd and dangerous of modern phenomena are developmentally predicted. Recognizing this fact doesn't make these phenomena any less absurd or dangerous, but by making unsettling circumstances more understandable, it at least offers a certain reassurance. By putting confusing realities in useful perspective, it also serves as further evidence for the concept of Cultural Maturity and the changes it describes.

Finally, providing a concluding counterbalance to the previous section's easily disturbing observations, I will describe how culturally mature perspective invites the possibility of addressing human quandaries that have always before left us baffled. We will see how it does so in ways that not only satisfy, but also inspire—offering additional important evidence for the concept of Cultural Maturity in the process.

Progress and the Dilemma of Trajectory

No question is more critical as we go forward than how best to think about and measure progress. I've emphasized the fact that progress' old "onward and upward" definition today serves us less and less well. This observation has pivotal importance. When the definition of progress that comes with a particular time in culture ceases to work, it becomes progress' opposite. It undermines advancement, makes us less.

The issue is more ultimately significant than just that our specifically Modern Age definition is no longer sufficient—though that certainly is true. The basic developmental orientation that has gotten us to where we are has stopped being sufficient. Creative Systems Theory calls this the Dilemma of Trajectory (see Figure 8-1). The Dilemma of Trajectory in part involves limits to what we can continue to do, but more specifically it describes how continuing with the human story as we have known it is really not an option.

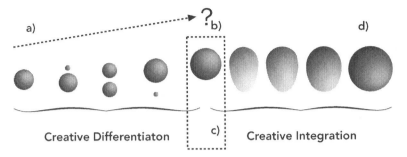

a) Cultural evolution's trajectory to this point

b) Transition (with right-hand sensibility at its peak and left-hand sensibilities largely eclipsed)

c) The Dilemma of Trajectory (with Cultural Maturity, or some similarly integrative process, needed to go on)

d) How Cultural Maturity reconciles the Dilemma of Trajectory

Fig. 8-1. The Dilemma of Trajectory

We can now take comfort in the fact that further options must exist. Our earlier examinations of Cultural Maturity's various threshold tasks each suggested the possibility of thinking about progress in more integrative ways. And the previous chapter's developmental/evolutionary picture provided a detailed description of changes consistent with this result. But while what we have seen is certainly suggestive of the conclusion that Cultural Maturity's changes might reconcile the Dilemma of Trajectory, it is only suggestive. In this chapter's next section we will look closely at just what more is needed.

But before we go there, we need first to more fully understand what creates the quandary that the Dilemma of Trajectory presents and what makes that quandary so consequential. The Dilemma of Trajectory confronts us with the essential question of whether the direction that has gotten us to where we are can, simply in some new form, get us where we need to go—whether we can make sense of what the future demands of us as an understandable extension of what we have known. The answer is yes ... and no. Progress in the general sense of increasing capacity and possibility will only become more important. But, at the same time, we face constraints to continuing forward as we have—and not just practical constraints, but also constraints of a more basic and inescapable sort.

Earlier, I proposed that the question of progress presents our time's ultimately defining limit. Our customary picture of history describes a steady, if sometimes bumpy, upward progression. History is about the rise of civilizations. We really can't continue on in this way. Beyond the damage that unthinking progress could wreak upon us, we confront limits of a more fundamental sort. We face limits to how far culture's story as we have conceived it (and not just recently, but at any time in the past) can take us. It is this more basic kind of limit that creates our Dilemma of Trajectory.

Polarity—and its changing significance over the course of history—provides a simple way to recognize this more fundamental kind of limit. The Creative Function describes how the evolution of culture to this point has produced ever-increasing separation between polar tendencies. For example, we've witnessed growing distinction over time between how we have thought of humankind and nature, mind and body, or the individual and the collective. Up until now, this evolutionary mechanism has served us—indeed, it has been key to culture's great advances. But it really can't continue. Going forward as we have would distance us from much that is most essential to us in ways that would be ultimately intolerable. A further separating of ourselves from nature, our bodies, or our shared humanity would sever us from much that most makes us who we are.

The recognition that polarity has an inherent symmetry—with more archetypally masculine, "right-hand' qualities set opposite to more archetypally feminine, "left-hand" tendencies—helps us refine our understanding of what threatens to be lost. Over the course of history, as part of the same process, we've seen archetypally masculine sensibilities (tied to separation and the new forms created) come to predominate while archetypally feminine sensibilities (tied to connectedness and original creative contexts) have faded in significance. If we continue going forward in this way, the archetypally feminine would cease to exist. With Transition in the Creative Function, this, in effect, is what we find. Much of what defines experience as we approach Cultural Maturity's threshold is a product of this near absence of archetypally feminine sensibilities.

People of extreme positivist or materialist philosophical persuasions might claim this outcome to be a good thing, being that it could seem to describe a final victory for the archetypally masculine. But most of the rest of us would not think it so (and the positivists and extreme materialists would not either, if they actually experienced what this result implies). We would not do well without the softer and more primal aspects of existence: the receptivity of our senses, the world of children, the artistic, our felt connectedness in community, the spiritual (however we interpret it). We recognize that life would lack meaning without these things. Indeed, at some level we recognize that life—certainly human life—would not exist without them.

Even if we can tolerate this reality as a short-term—Transitional—situation, we are left with the question of how we are then to proceed. Familiar ways of thinking restrict us to three options: going forward in a way that severs us from ourselves, collapse, or a romantic going back that in the end negates human accomplishment. While the noncommittal stance common with postmodern thought presents a "sort of" further option, in the end it only ignores progress' question. If today's new freedoms are to serve us, they can't be of the "anything goes" sort. Any new definition of progress must articulate a practical and purpose-affirming way to move forward.

We have good evidence that such a new definition is at least possible. If nothing else, there is the fact that progress' definition has evolved before. Our modern image of progress is in fact something quite new. With the previous chapter's developmental/evolutionary picture, we saw how each succeeding period in culture's story has articulated the human story, and at least by implication, the nature of advancement, in very different ways.[1]

Descriptions in earlier chapters of ways current changes involve a wholly new kind of relationship with experience support the further

---

1   History has altered not just what we think of as constituting progress, but also our relationship to the concept. Tribal peoples do not have notions like progress in the sense that we think of it. For them, truth is an eternal turning, each season following as always the one before it. In the Middle Ages, there was more of a sense of history, but nothing like the modern concept of progress' onward-and-upward arrow of achievement. Progress as we think of it is a Modern Age invention.

conclusion that rethinking progress in ways that are fundamentally new is at least an option. I've observed how Cultural Maturity involves stepping not just beyond our more recent truths, but dynamics intrinsic to how we conceived of truth at every previous cultural stage. Most immediately, this includes leaving behind our historical parent/child relationship with culture. But it also includes the cognitive changes that make this possible, how we are becoming able both to better step back from the whole of our complexity and to more deeply engage it. Integrative Meta-perspective replaces history's familiar picture in which each stage has produced greater identification with difference and the physical stuff of creation with a more integrative—whole-box-of-crayons—picture of going forward. This more embracing picture gets us very close to reconciling the Dilemma of Trajectory.

Creative Reengagement

But still only close. For this more integrative outcome to fully make sense, we need the additional ingredient I referred to earlier. Actually we have already begun to make its acquaintance. In Chapter Two, I observed that while this integrative outcome is most readily recognized in the bridging of here-and-now polarities, creative integration also has a more temporal component.

With Cultural Maturity, we leave the past behind—absolutely. But, at the same time, we gain fresh access to sensibilities more familiar in previous cultural periods. Creative Systems Theory calls this further aspect of Cultural Maturity's cognitive reordering *Reengagement*. Culturally mature perspective provides fresh access to aspects of experience that we knew intimately in earlier cultural times, but that for developmentally necessary reasons we have put behind us.

I've implied the importance of Reengagement and its contribution in previous observations. In Chapter Five, I described how culturally mature "crux" discernments address not just what matters in a particular moment, but in an important sense what matters ultimately. We can only address what matters ultimately if we have at least limited access to what may have most mattered in times past. Reengagement's role in needed understanding was also implied in my description of how history has evolved from times where archetypally feminine sensibilities played the larger role to times of archetypally masculine dominance.

This observation can make sense only to the degree the archetypally feminine itself makes deep sense. And certainly Reengagement was required for the previous chapter's temporal multiplicity reflections—for appreciating the way our developmental/evolutionary picture helps us understand not just the historical facts of past cultural stages, but also the sensibilities that underlay those facts.

Indeed, no major aspect of Cultural Maturity and its changes is fully understandable without Reengagement's contribution. The notion of "bridging," for example, makes only limited sense without at least the beginnings of Reengagement. Drawing only on earlier reflections, a person might conclude that we could effectively rethink progress simply by bridging pertinent polarities. But while in a limited sense this is true, bridging presents a glaring problem if each succeeding historical stage has involved increasing archetypally masculine prominence. At the point of Transition, with the archetypally feminine functionally eclipsed, just what are we to bridge with? We are left to bridge something with nothing, which is not bridging at all. Cultural Maturity's world of new possibilities would seem to remain wholly beyond our reach.

The notion of multiple intelligences confronts us with a similar dilemma. I've observed that culturally mature understanding requires at least a beginning connection with the multiple dimensions of cognition. But certain of our intelligences—indeed, all of our intelligences except the rational—witnessed their most prominent manifestations only in times well past: the body with our animistic beginnings, the imaginal in the time of the great myths, the emotional with the unquestioned moral ardencies of the Middle Ages. Just saying we should connect with our multiple ways of knowing puts us in the same predicament as proposing bridging as a solution: The dynamics of Transition leave us with nothing to connect with. Again, Cultural Maturity's changes remain beyond us even to contemplate.

For what we see to make sense—and for the Dilemma of Trajectory not to stop Cultural Maturity's argument cold (and perhaps stop progress cold)—we need the additional mechanism I've called Reengagement. Cultural Maturity's cognitive changes do more than just help us better understand the past, though they do that. They invite, and in fact require, a deeper connection with the past—or, more accurately, a deeper connection with aspects of ourselves to which we have had more ready access in times past.

Our developmental analogy again provides insight. Certainly, it helps us appreciate why Reengagement might be needed. Let's start there. I've described how growing up takes us through a sequence of maturational stages, and also how new developmental stages are about more than just becoming more adept; they offer entry into new worlds of experience. New stages make organizational "leaps." To understand why Reengagement is necessary, we need to add the further recognition that such leaps, along with offering new possibilities, also involve necessary forgettings—amnesias for realities we've moved beyond. With each organizational leap, doors close to past experience.

We see this kind of developmental amnesia in how adolescents have a difficult time making sense of the reality of young children, even though they have only just recently left this child world behind them. In a similar way, while we might expect young adults to be our great experts on the attitudes and needs of adolescence, it is often they who find adolescent assumptions most baffling.

With the amnesias that necessarily accompany individual development, we forget more than just memories. We disconnect from the organizing intelligences of the realities we have left behind—the primacy of body intelligence during infancy, of imagination during childhood, of special emotional and affiliative sensibilities during adolescence. We also disconnect from the values and ways of seeing the world that accompany each intelligence. With each developmental stage we distance ourselves from fundamental dimensions of our being. Such forgetting serves a critical developmental purpose: It keeps us from falling back into familiar but no longer timely worlds of experience. Growing up requires not just separation from family as home, but also separation from the ways of organizing experience that at different, earlier times have served as our cognitive/experiential homes.[2]

---

2   There is an important sense in which these amnesias are not absolute. We lose direct contact with earlier ordering principles, but at some level we still recognize their existence and significance. For example, while children universally believe in Santa Claus and the Easter Bunny (or

With personal development, our success with these necessary for-gettings sets the stage for Reengagement. In life's second half, we witness an almost opposite mechanism. Once the basic structures of identity and belief have been established, the protective doors provided by these developmental amnesias can begin to reopen. We no longer need to fear the past. Memories from earlier times in life often become newly available. And of more fundamental significance, maturity bit by bit reconnects us with those earlier ordering principles—the intelligences, values, aesthetics, and creative juxtapositions that have given each developmental stage its unique character and power. We reengage forgotten dimensions of who we are.

Many of the most rewarding delights of aging are direct products of such personal Reengagement. People's later years frequently bring a rediscovered child-like sense of playfulness and wonder. Aristophanes observed that "old men are twice boys." There is also the way grandparents often more readily connect with the worlds of their grandchildren than do the children's parents—a product at least in part of this Reengagement dynamic.

The perspective, compassion, humility—and wisdom—we associate with mature adulthood requires this gradual reconnecting. This is not wisdom's only source. There are also all the learnings that have come from a lifetime of experience. And there are the more specific learnings we've looked at that challenge us as we approach personal maturity's threshold—about the dangers of simplistic conclusions, the importance of appreciating limits, and the need to address truth and purpose more directly. But first-half learnings only provide cleverness if they don't include Reengagement. And the more specific learnings of mature perspective require Reengagement to make any deep sense. Pascal observed that "wisdom takes us back to our childhood" (a useful recognition as long as we appreciate that this is not all it does).

---

their culture's equivalents), and most adults think of such figures as fantasy at best, few parents try to convince their children of the irrationality of such belief. In some way, parents know that such "illusion" is essential to being children. They also recognize at some level that something very special lives in this illusion that they can only faintly recollect. Its elusive presence is much of what makes such childhood delight special to adults.

The dual mechanism I've described—first necessary amnesias, then later Reengagement—is in fact something we see with all human generative processes. Amnesias serve like cogs so the wheels of life do not turn backward during creativity's fragile early stages. Once form is sufficiently established, the past stops being something we need to keep at arm's length. It becomes instead a necessary part of mature understanding's larger, more complete picture. For this inquiry, the important recognition is that we should expect to see related dynamics in the evolution of culture. And we do.

We can readily recognize the first, "forgetting" aspect of this two-part process at a cultural scale. We see it in how difficult it can be for people who have not yet begun to engage Cultural Maturity's threshold to make useful sense of cultures at stages earlier than their own. It was not long ago, for example, that we in the modern West commonly denigrated people from tribal cultures—such as Native Americans in the United States—dismissed them as "pagan" or "savage." In doing so we were not just misperceiving these people, we were not really seeing them at all. More accurately we were projecting onto them unconscious parts of ourselves.[3] When we've romantically idealized earlier-stage peoples, in a similar way we've not been seeing what is actually there. Again we've been projecting aspects of ourselves in the present onto the blank slate of our ignorance.

More recently, most people, at least in the developed world, have begun to set such projections aside. Increasingly we are becoming able to see individuals from earlier cultural stages simply as human. And just as important, we are finding the experience of *real* difference newly fascinating. Temporal patterning observations like those I touched on earlier are becoming newly intriguing and obviously of value.

We find an everyday sort of support for Reengagement at a cultural scale in how almost anyone who spends any time in settings we would call not yet modern recognizes that much—and much of real significance—has been lost as well as gained in the phenomenon we call

---

3   In Chapter Ten we will examine a further mechanism that also plays a
     role in such denigration. (See "On the Nature of Nature" in the "More
     Patterning in Time—Particularly Intriguing Expressions" section of
     Chapter Ten.)

progress. There are clearly qualities and affinities present in these earlier realities that are not only important, but somehow essential to recapture if our future world is to be a healthy place. Few people remain happy for long if plunked down in a cultural reality earlier than their own. But going backwards is specifically not what we are talking about. The point is that sensibilities before forgotten—and forgotten for good reasons—are somehow now becoming newly pertinent.

The concept of Reengagement fills out what is wholly new with Cultural Maturity's cognitive changes in a way that is essential to complete understanding. Along with how Integrative Meta-perspective involves stepping beyond culture as parent and results in newly integrative relationships between here-and-now systemic aspects, it also involves something we have not seen before when it comes to the stage-specific truths we have left behind. This additional result applies to the truths of all previous cultural stage, but it is perhaps easiest to see with the rationalist, objectivist, materialist assumptions of Modern Age thought. Rather than discarding these truths the way we have traditionally discarded the assumptions of our previous age as we move into a new one, Cultural Maturity's cognitive changes make Modern Age perspective part of complexity's now expanded picture. In the end, Cultural Maturity does something similar with regard to past underlying truths of every sort.

It is essential that we not confuse Reengagement with things it is not. Certainly Reengagement is not about some romantic going back. Indeed, in the end it is not really even about reconnecting with the past. What we "reengage" with Integrative Meta-perspective is forgotten sensibilities as they are coming to newly exist in the present. Intelligence's multiple aspects, when consciously and fully engaged, provide fresh access to the sensibilities that defined our understanding of the world in previous cultural stages. In this way, Integrative Meta-perspective helps us both understand the truths of times past with a clarity that before we have necessarily lacked and, in a whole new way, draw on what has been most rich in previous truths.

We can think of Reengagement as producing a kind of temporal bridging. Combine here-and-now bridging with Reengagement, and we get a deeper understanding of—and ultimately, connection with—not just current complexities, but also human complexity as we have experienced it through time. The picture that results helps us understand how the Dilemma of Trajectory need not describe an end point. It becomes not just reasonable, but predicted, that we might be able to "progress" in ways specifically right for our time.

Rewriting History

One of the great rewards that comes with developmental/evolutionary perspective is a more systemic picture of history—as you saw illustrated in the previous chapter. Such perspective challenges us to revisit not just certain of history's facts, but also modern notions of what constitutes history. Oscar Wilde wrote, "The one duty we owe to history is to rewrite it." Cultural Maturity invites—indeed, demands—that we rewrite history. Culturally mature perspective rewrites both what we mean by history and our understanding of ourselves as participants in history.

Reengagement, and the broader perspective that comes with Integrative Meta-perspective more generally, alters our conventional modern picture of history in at least three ways. First, it helps us to see the past more accurately, to better recognize the particular gifts and blindnesses that have accompanied each chapter in culture's story. We could say that Integrative Meta-perspective makes us kinder toward the past—and often it does. But developmental/evolutionary perspective can also make for much harsher judgment. Certainly romantic idealizations don't easily survive the vantage it provides.[4] But even when romantic projection has not played a role in how we have described

---

4   Romantic idealization can make association with any cultural stage. New
     Age ideologies, along with the beliefs of environmentalists and feminists,
     often draw on idealized references to cultural times and places where
     archetypally feminine sensibilities held clear influence—for example,
     to tribal cultures, earlier agrarian societies, and classical Eastern belief.
     Adamant conservative and fundamentalist religious views can by infer-
     ence idealize almost medieval sensibilities (drawing on belief from a time
     previous to modern secular humanism and after the rise of monotheism).
     Academics tend to idealize the Age of Reason (or sometimes the an-
     cient Greeks). Later, with our examination of ways that personality style
     differences affect how we see the future, we will look at how different
     temperaments are prone to particular kinds of romantic idealizations (see
     "One 'Crayon' and Another" in Chapter Nine and Appendix D).

history, the sensibilities that have defined modern thought have caused us to miss much that is most important.

The lens provided by a rational/material worldview is able to describe only the most surface layers of history's full richness and complexity. History, in today's classroom, too often becomes little more than a chronicling of leaders, wars, and inventions. And what we have missed is often exactly that which is most essential *not* to miss if we wish to make sense of the values, motivations, and worldviews of premodern peoples (including ourselves prior to the Industrial Age). Our modern conception of history is, in the end, limited when it tries to describe the past, to the same degree—and for the same reasons—that Modern Age definitions of intelligence are limited if we wish to capture cognition's full complexity. The dissolving of cultural amnesias that comes with Integrative Meta-perspective provides a clearer and more complex, if not always so handy and self-affirming, picture of what has brought us to where we are.

Integrative Meta-perspective also reveals a more dynamic picture of history. This comes naturally from what we newly bring to the process of seeing. At the least, culturally mature developmental/evolutionary perspective helps us better put past events in context and sheds new light on how one moment of history ties to another—insights that can radically alter how we interpret events. Along with this, we better recognize how aspects of history to which we may have ascribed secondary importance at best—such as art, music, religion, moral belief, or the life of the body—in fact have considerable pertinence if we wish to understand history deeply. Good teachers of history have always used contributions from these various spheres to help make history come alive, and the best of historians have gone further, noting patterns and relationships. But with Cultural Maturity's cognitive reordering, these added ingredients stop being condiments and become explicit parts of the main meal.[5]

Finally, Integrative Meta-perspective gives history a new narrative depth. It helps transform history from a chronicling of events and beliefs to a multifaceted study of human purpose and our relationship to it.

---

5   Examples in Chapter Ten and Chapter Eleven draw on these added ingredients in ways that fill out our understanding of history in essential ways.

This kind of reflection has also always been a part of well-told history. But consciously bringing more of ourselves into the story changes the equation. History becomes more directly an inquiry into who we are as storytellers and makers of meaning. It also, by implication, becomes as much about the possible nature of meaning in the future as it is about the stories that have brought us to where we are today.

Integrative Meta-perspective also suggests a "historical" reward beyond history itself. It makes the study of history an important "hands-on" tool for acquiring culturally mature capacities. Just as bridging polarities, more deeply engaging the complexities of intelligence, or taking on any of Cultural Maturity's more specific threshold tasks can bring us closer to culturally mature sensibility, so too can a sufficiently deep engagement with where we have come from. Doing so provides a way to make contact with the fullness of our creative complexity.

A way in which I've personally applied history in my teaching reaps the rewards that come with each of these three ways culturally mature perspective rewrites history. It is notable for how directly it draws on developmental/evolutionary perspective. It is also notable because the primary language it makes use of—that of music—is not one an academic treatment of history would be likely to emphasize.

The inspiration for this approach came from an exceptional series of classes on world music that I took while in college. Today it is not uncommon to hear music from far-flung parts of the planet, but back then this was a rare and special experience. Each morning, with other students, I would listen to sounds that I'd never heard before but that were nonetheless deeply rooted in time and culture.[6] What I heard greatly moved me and provided many insights important to the later development of Creative Systems Theory.[7]

---

6   Robert Garfias, founder of one of the country's first ethnomusicology departments (at the University of Washington), taught these classes.

7   Recognizing commonalities tied to cultural stage helped refine my thinking about how culture has evolved. It also provided initial insights for Creative Systems Theory's framework for understanding temperament. I noticed that people with different personality styles tended to be attracted to music from different times in culture. The recognition—central to Creative Systems Theory—that related patterning principles underlie

Once each year during the Institute for Creative Development's brick-and-mortar years, I did a presentation that drew on those insights. I called it "An Evolutionary History of Music." Over the course of a day, I played music from each of culture's creative stages and engaged people—through story, dance, and conversation—in the underlying sensibilities of each stage. It became an anticipated event.[8]

My intent in doing this elaborate and lengthy presentation was to involve people in history in a way that would help dissolve the amnesias that have protected us from our full creative natures and, in this way, to support culturally mature understanding. Participants described the experience as bringing history alive in ways they had rarely felt. They also found that it gave them some of the most powerful and immediate appreciation for the larger—whole-box-of-crayons—complexities on which future human understanding and choice must be based.

A Ready Confusion

Most people who concern themselves with the future don't recognize the Dilemma of Trajectory and its considerable implications. And those who somehow do recognize that going forward as we have presents fundamental problems are most likely to respond by feeling a lack of hope. There can seem to be no meaningful way to proceed.

But there is also a kind of confusion that can come when people begin to recognize the creatively integrative changes that come with Cultural Maturity's cognitive reordering that can leave one just as short of where we need to go. I call it the "feminine mistake" (with apologies to Betty Friedan).

Because Cultural Maturity's picture of the tasks ahead gives new credence to the more connectedness-acknowledging, creatively germinal, left-hand, "archetypally feminine" aspects of our natures, people who ascribe to more left-leaning ways of thinking may at first confuse it with their own conclusions. This kind of misunderstanding is common enough that it is worth flagging. It should now be clear that views that identify

---

temporal and here-and-now human systemic differences had its origins in these observations.

8   You can view an edited video of the presentation at www.Evolmusic.org

with left-hand truths in the end come no closer to what Cultural Maturity requires of us than the most extreme right-hand kinds of ideologies.

We see this kind of misunderstanding most often with people whose belief systems are of the more spiritual, romantic, liberal/humanist, or philosophically idealist sort. With our examination of the "cognitive rewiring" that comes with Integrative Meta-perspective in Chapter Nine, we will look more closely at what is going on with each of these different, but related kinds of misunderstanding.[9] But tools we already have at our disposal provide an adequate shorthand. The diagrams in Figure 8-1 depict what we find with each of the kinds of belief just noted and contrast the results with culturally mature perspective.

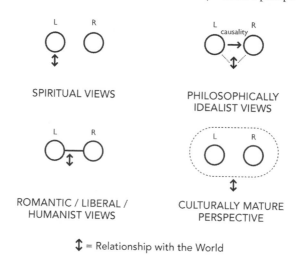

SPIRITUAL VIEWS

PHILOSOPHICALLY
IDEALIST VIEWS

ROMANTIC / LIBERAL /
HUMANIST VIEWS

CULTURALLY MATURE
PERSPECTIVE

↕ = Relationship with the World

Fig. 8-2. Left-Leaning Views Contrasted with Culturally Mature Perspectives[10]

With spiritual interpretations, left-hand truth becomes final truth. With romantic interpretations, along with related liberal

---

9   See " 'Cognitive Rewiring' " in Chapter Nine.

10   Polarity has both vertical and horizontal manifestations (a topic we will return to). For various purposes it works best to emphasize one or the other. With the Creative Function, vertical representation provides the least confusing approach. Horizontal representation is most appropriate when polar relationships expressly reflect contrasting left-hand and right-hand sensibilities.

and humanistic interpretations, right-hand sensibilities may have a strong presence, but the person most identifies with left-hand sensibilities.[11] With philosophically idealist interpretations, again both hands may have a significance presence, but left-hand sensibility is assumed to drive more right-hand experience and thus ultimately defines truth.[12] In contrast, with culturally mature understanding left-hand and right-hand sensibilities, rather than themselves defining truth, function as systemic aspects (of ultimately equal significance). Left-hand and right-hand sensibilities become "crayons" in the larger systemic "box."[13]

We can see additional examples of this kind of misinterpretation with common beliefs within specific realms of understanding. With our look at the Dilemma of Differentiation, I described how we often encounter something similar with popular versions of systems thinking. Along with mechanistic formulations, we also find more popular systems interpretations that reduce to an identification with

---

11   Indeed, the greatest weight can sometimes lie with right-hand sensibilities. Creative Systems Theory calls this kind of dynamic in which the half of a polarity that we identify with and the half we most embody are different "cross-polar." (See "Polar Traps" in Chapter Nine for a closer look at cross-polar dynamics.)

12   See "Transformational/New Paradigm Scenarios" and "'Cognitive Rewiring'" in Chapter Nine for a closer look at the mechanisms and implications of philosophical idealism.

13   I've given primary emphasis to the left-hand bias in describing these more limited viewpoints. But the further distinction implied in this use of the box-of-crayons metaphor is at least as important. With each of them there is as yet no defining "box," or at best such perspective is but vaguely present. (The encompassing circle in the "culturally mature perspective" depiction provides the box's representational equivalent.) The fact that these more limited views are ultimately ideological is what makes them ultimately different from culturally mature perspective—different not just in balance or degree, but fundamentally. The capacity with Integrative Meta-perspective to step back from all the "crayons" and engage a larger picture is what, in the end, distinguishes culturally mature understanding from any way of thinking that stops short of the needed sophistication, whatever the accompanying polar bias.

interconnectedness.[14] The popular equating of quantum physics with the ideas of Eastern philosophy or Western mysticism provides another example. Several of the early thinkers of modern physics recognized a relationship, but they didn't confuse them. In another way, we encounter a misguided equating of left-hand sensibilities with truth itself.

A further example relates directly to the recognition of intelligence's multiplicity. Popular interpretations of historically important, intelligence-related contributions can fall for a similar kind of trap. Following the emphasis that Sigmund Freud brought to unconscious processes, important thinkers gave special attention to intelligences other than the rational.[15] These early thinkers generally recognized that they were only highlighting the importance of a particular intelligence, not making that intelligence some last word. But their ideas have often been translated in ways that make more creatively germinal intelligences, or at least the conclusions that come from a more creatively germinal intelligence's particular perspective, in effect, truth itself—the body, the imagination, or the emotional becomes what it is all about. In the name of new understanding, we get only new versions of timeworn, ideological beliefs.[16]

---

14   Compounding the language problem, references to "living systems" thinking often reflect this kind of conceptual trap. At least by implication, we see different levels of organization—inanimate, animate, and more consciously creative—collapsed into a spiritually satisfying, but ultimately inconsequential "organic" unity To avoid this kind of trap, I am careful to emphasize that the kind of systems thinking we have interest in reflects the particular kind of life that makes us human.

15   I think in particular of Wilhelm Reich with body intelligence, Carl Jung with imaginal intelligence, and Carl Rogers and the early thinkers of humanistic psychology with emotional intelligence.

16   People who emphasize body intelligence can imply that the body doesn't lie. But while the body provides important information, and very much a kind of information that in our time we need to better connect with, certainly, too, the body does "lie" (in the sense that offering information can be partial and ultimately unhelpful—as with addiction). It is rumored that Carl Jung once quipped, in response to simplistic interpretations of his ideas (with their strong emphasis on imaginal intelligence)

We can often recognize when the "feminine mistake" intrudes in people's use of language. One example has particular pertinence to these reflections. It concerns how a person might use the word "wisdom." In the previous chapter, I touched on confusions that can result if we fail to distinguish between the kind of wisdom that comes with second-half-of-life tasks in personal development and that which comes with Cultural Maturity's changes. Another reason we need to take care with the word "wisdom" is that it so often crops up with interpretations that make left-hand sensibilities final truth.

In everyday usage, wisdom is often not really a "bridging" notion—or, if it does bridge, it does so in a way that is far from balanced, and thus ultimately trivial. We recognize this limited picture of wisdom in the way that people are more likely to associate statements of a spiritual sort with wisdom than observations that have more scientific origins. If truth's left hand doesn't get the last word, it certainly gets the greatest attention. I've emphasized that culturally mature wisdom is "wisdom of a more gritty sort." This more gritty sort of wisdom is at the least a more aware sort of wisdom—and thus aware of harsh realities. But it is also a more explicitly whole-box-of-crayons sort of wisdom, with all crayons—from the most poetic to the most hard-nosed—having influence.

Developmental/evolutionary perspective ties this additional way that the word "wisdom" can be misconstrued to how Reengagement can be similarly misconstrued. Wisdom statements—words people quote because they think them wise—don't find equal distribution through the course of history. Certainly such statements have not become more common with the passage of time as we might expect to be the case with utterances that have to do with understanding's big picture. Rather, they tend to come from early stages in culture—from Native American leaders like Chief Sealth; ancient Greeks like Plato and Aristotle; from the classical East, as with Lao Tzu or the Buddha; or

---

that he was certainly glad he was Jung and not a Jungian. Simplistic humanistic interpretations in psychology can, in effect, equate emotional intelligence with final knowing.

with the beginnings of the great monotheistic traditions and the words of Moses, Jesus, or Mohammad.

Individuals who are drawn to wisdom language—and particularly individuals who are vulnerable to equating wisdom with left-hand conclusions—commonly idealize these early stages in culture. Given that early cultural stages are when we most often find wisdom statements, in one sense this is reasonable, but it also in another way alerts us to this particular kind of trap. I've described how creative differentiation takes us from archetypally feminine beginnings in that unbroken whole to Transition's almost total archetypally masculine dominance. Thus, what we commonly think of as statements of wisdom tend to have their origins in times when the archetypally feminine is a stronger force than the archetypally masculine. Again, we see left-hand bias.[17]

An additional way to recognize this trap in how we might use the word "wisdom"—and a way to have fun delving even deeper into developmental/evolutionary perspective in the process—draws on the different ways left- and right-hand sensibilities relate to time. Chapter Ten describes how we experience time in predictably different ways depending on the context.[18] For now, it is enough that we notice how time relates to various ways we might use the word "wisdom." We commonly describe wisdom as something timeless, eternal. For example, we may talk of a "perennial philosophy." While part

---

17   This left-hand bias can be missed for a simple reason that we can recognize by drawing on developmental/evolutionary perspective at a further level of detail. At the time that such wisdom statements are made (here I am referring to personal wisdom statements), they in fact have the needed balance. But put in the larger context of cultural development, bridgings that come with personal maturity in these early times—along with the utterances that follow from them—are going to lean decidedly to the left. The concepts of yin and yang in traditional Chinese philosophy, for example, provide a balanced left-right image when set in their cultural context. But put in the context of cultural evolution as a whole, few would question that their emphasis is more spiritual than material. This is so even when "wise" utterances are not explicitly spiritual in nature.

18   See "The Relativity of Time in Time" in the "More Patterning in Time—Particularly Intriguing Expressions" section of Chapter Ten.

of the reason we do so is likely this fact that our observations often reference early-culture sensibilities, something in the left-hand bias of what we observe also leads us to speak this way.

Left-hand concerns—spirit, nature, the artistic, the world of children—by their nature lie more outside of time. This is particularly so with their most extreme expression in culture's early stages. Thus, when we identify with concerns of a left-hand sort, we are also more likely to see "real" truth as timeless. Right-hand concerns—science, invention, progress, the world of adults—lie specifically in time. In a related way, this is particularly so when these concerns manifest in modern times. I've emphasized that culturally mature truth is not at all timeless—except in the sense that it provides fresh access to sensibilities better known in times past. Culturally mature perspective—and wisdom—in cherishing and respecting each hand of truth equally, also takes into account both relationships to time. This is a further characteristic of the kind of truth we have interest in wherever we find it.

For this section's observations, these various reflections on wisdom simply remind us that our interest lies with wisdom of the whole-box-of-crayons sort. Such wisdom doesn't elevate one hand of truth. And certainly we can't get there by going back. Such wisdom is very explicitly about moving forward—and, in this, into a wholly new territory of understanding. In another way, we confront how the kind of understanding that we have interest in is of a fundamentally new sort.[19]

---

19   Now is not the only period when people have often harkened back to earlier times. Developmental/evolutionary perspective helps clarify how the systemic acknowledgment of more germinal sensibilities that comes with Cultural Maturity is different not just from what we find with current thinking that misses the mark, but also from other historical phenomena a person might confuse it with. This includes both the new attention to classical sensibilities that came with the Renaissance and also the Modern Age's later identification with romantic beliefs.

Creative Systems Theory proposes that the reaching back to classical times that accompanied Renaissance belief was a product of the creatively germinal time the Renaissance occupied in the then-emerging Modern Age. At the beginning of any creative stage, we find a natural affinity for germinal sensibilities wherever they might be found. When we are starting anything creative, we need to be "child-like." (See the description of creative sub-

A Threshold Lesson: Reengagement's role in Integrative Meta-perspective helps us recognize traps in our thinking. We must examine ideas to see if Reengagement makes a contribution. (It always plays a role in culturally mature systemic thought.) We also have to be sure that our thinking does not confuse the world as seen through the eyes of sensibilities we gain fresh access to with culturally mature perspective's fundamentally different and more challenging result.

Integrative Meta-Perspective and the Workings of Awareness

I've described the cognitive reordering that produces Cultural Maturity's changes as a stepping back that produces more encompassing awareness, combined with a new and deeper engagement with all that makes us who we are. To this point, I've given the greatest attention to making sense of what that deeper engagement involves and the more full and complete kind of understanding that results. Here we turn more specifically to changes in how we understand awareness.

We could well describe the defining task of culturally mature responsibility as that of being more consciously aware than in times past. And depending on what we mean by the word "consciously," that would be accurate. But this observation is of limited use—

---

stages in the "Creative Systems Analysis" section of Chapter Ten.)

Creative Systems Theory views the kind of thinking introduced with the Romantic Era differently. Romantic sensibilities emerged as a counterforce to the prevailing positivist worldview. Consistent with this, romantic descriptions were idealized and tended to involve projection. Images of the noble savage, for example, had less to do with tribal reality than the projection of unconscious aspects of modern reality onto tribal times. (In contrast to today, romantic interpretation in the Romantic Era was a major movement, not just one of many kinds of limited viewpoints.)

We can recognize both of these dynamics—resonance between parallel creative stages and romantic projection—in present realities. Along with engaging integrative processes, we are also, as with the Renaissance, taking first steps into new territory. And depending on our way of holding experience, we may be vulnerable not just to idealizing germinal sensibilities, but to treating the presence of germinal sensibility as a victory cry for our favorite slice of the creative pie.

indeed, it can easily lead us astray—if we don't appreciate how conscious awareness, too, is changing.

Changes in awareness' workings affect both how we understand and what we are capable of in ways that could not be more fascinating or more consequential. Appreciating these changes, besides helping us more fully understand Integrative Meta-perspective and all that it involves, has direct pertinence to a wide array of questions central to this inquiry.

For example, I've proposed that Cultural Maturity is ultimately about leadership. Awareness provides the leadership function in our psyches—at least as we have traditionally thought about things. Awareness is also quite obviously tied to how we think about individual identity. Shortly, we will examine how awareness' new significance plays a central role in the ways we are reconceiving both leadership and identity. We will also look at how awareness' new picture is directly pertinent to understanding the remarkable creative capacities that make us unusual, if not unique as a species.

But before we turn specifically to awareness and its changes, we should first briefly reflect on where we have come to thus far with the "what awareness more deeply connects with" half of the equation. With the concept of Reengagement, we have just added an essential piece to how we understand human complexity that is essential to understanding Integrative Meta-perspective and its implications—including awareness' new significance. And fully understanding awareness' new role requires a solid appreciation for how the various pieces we have looked at fit together.

The book's examination of the "what awareness more deeply connects with" side of things started in Chapter One with our look at the role of projection in the worldviews of times past and, with Cultural Maturity's threshold, the importance of re-owning the aspects of ourselves that with projection we've "given away." With Chapter Two, we looked at the more general "bridging" of past polar assumptions that happens as we move beyond ideological assumptions. With our examination in Chapter Six of how Cultural Maturity alters truth, we addressed the role of multiple intelligences in the new picture, and, with this, the power that comes with applying our various ways of knowing in a more conscious and integrative fashion. This chapter has added how we find further aspects of the needed larger picture in the earlier developmental realities to which Reengagement gives us fresh access.

It is important to reemphasize that these various ingredients— reincorporating projections, "bridging" polarities, the fact of multiple intelligences, and Reengagement—are not ultimately distinct. I have presented them separately only to help make Cultural Maturity's changes more readily understood. In the end, they represent different ways of describing the inclusion of the whole of our human complexity in what we consider—and ultimately in how we go about considering. They come together as the whole-box-of-crayons workings of our systemic natures. Framed in Creative Systems Theory terms, together they describe what we draw on in being toolmaking, meaning-making beings.

This section adds the essential recognition that Cultural Maturity's cognitive reorganization doesn't just alter the complexity that we can bring to bear when applying awareness, it also alters how we understand the nature and functioning of awareness. Integrative Meta-perspective's new, more complete picture of who we are and how we understand can make full sense only with an appreciation for awareness' new role.

The recognition that awareness is important to consider is nothing new. Pulitzer-prize–winning author John Noble Wilford beautifully summed it up: "Alone among all creatures, the species that styles itself wise, *Homo sapiens*, has an abiding interest in its distant origins, knows that its allotted time is short, worries about the future and wonders about the past." And awareness' significance has also always provoked debate—appropriately. Making sense of conscious awareness presents what might seem an unresolvable predicament. We have no way to step back from our subject. Using our conscious awarenesses to make sense of conscious awareness is a bit like trying to touch one's nose with one's nose. I like Ambrose Bierce's definition in his *Devil's Dictionary*. "Mind: A mysterious form of matter secreted by the brain. Its chief activity consists in the endeavor to ascertain its own nature, the futility of the attempt being due to the fact that it has nothing but itself to know itself with." Arguably, awareness and what it makes possible, is what philosophy is most ultimately about.

But awareness' significance has today become specifically different, and in ways that have major implications—in every part of our lives. To appreciate how this might be so, it helps to recognize that awareness' role has changed before. We tend not to think of awareness as something that changes, at least in any sense other than how learning can help us to be "more aware." But awareness' mechanisms do change, and they are just as specific to particular times in development (within formative processes of all sorts) as everything else we have looked at.

Some of the most celebrated of historical change-points are awareness-related. We cannot be in the presence of ancient cave paintings without pondering the emergence of reflective awareness, and wondering just how and when that emergence took place. And if a single change most defined the Renaissance and the ensuing Enlightenment, it was awareness' new, more "objective," from-a-balcony role. In a whole new sense, we came to regard awareness as triumphant. Everything we most identify with history's Modern Age—individualism, scientific objectivity, democratic governance, a more personal conception of the divine—can be seen to follow from this new role and its perceived ultimate significance.

The changes that come with Cultural Maturity's new picture of awareness are just as significant as any of those previous, and arguably more so. This is the case at least in the sense that Cultural Maturity provides perspective that helps us not just think in new ways, but also map the larger picture of how we have understood at previous times in culture's story. Awareness' new significance is also central to the new kind of conceptual orientation that comes with Integrative Meta-perspective. We've seen how this new orientation differs from what we have seen with all previous cultural stages, and also how it is essential to reconciling the Dilemma of Trajectory.

The pictorial representation of Integrative Meta-perspective I presented in Chapter Two (see Figure 2-1) included awareness's new role, but so much is going on in the diagram that awareness's implications could be missed. Figure 8-2 adds emphasis that highlights just how awareness' significance becomes different with Cultural Maturity's cognitive changes.

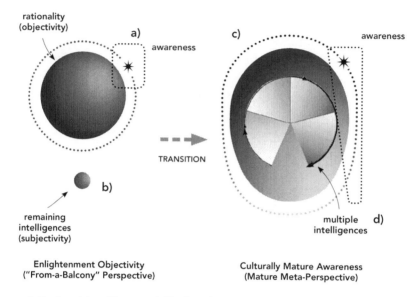

Enlightenment Objectivity
("From-a-Balcony" Perspective)

Culturally Mature Awareness
(Mature Meta-Perspective)

a) **Rational intelligence (allied with awareness to produce from-a-balcony objectivity)**

b) **The subjective (all remaining intelligences as experienced in Modern Age reality)**

c) **< -------- * -------- > Culturally mature awareness in its various more and less conscious permutations**

d) **Multiple intelligences (made newly explicit with culturally mature perspective)**

Fig. 8-3. Culturally Mature Awareness[20]

With Enlightenment objectivity, conscious awareness is appropriately depicted as coming from above—we perceive from "on high." But

---

20   We can now add a couple of observations that help clarify what this diagram describes. The size of the circles on the "Enlightenment, from-a-balcony-perspective" side of the diagram could cause confusion. I've depicted them as they are experienced in the final, Late-Axis stage of the first half of the Creative Function. Note in particular the diminutive size of the subjective pole. Part of what we discover with formative process' mature stages is the ultimately great expanse and significance of what we have thought of as the more subjective side of experience. In Late-Axis reality, the larger part of that expanse is experienced only unconsciously.

this is not so, at least in the same sense, with culturally mature awareness's new picture. Indeed, "location" comes to have a whole different kind of significance. Culturally mature awareness requires that we step back, but as I've described, it is just as much about deep and complex engagement. The dotted line in the "Culturally Mature Awareness" side of the diagram is intended to communicate some of this at once more ultimately "objective" and more deeply involved relationship. Awareness manifests itself in more and less conscious forms depending on the creative contexts in which it takes expression. (As we would expect, again we encounter limits to explicit representation.)

Expanding on earlier reflections helps further claify this new cognitive picture. With Enlightenment objectivity, awareness became not just elevated, but mythologized. I've described how the Enlightenment's grand task was to bring all of understanding into the light of awareness. Enlightenment thought made a new polarity ultimate truth: awareness, seen as linked with the rational, set in opposition to the subjective, a catch-all category to which all other intelligences along with simple errors in understanding were relegated. This identification of truth with awareness and rationality was seen as a culminating achievement.

Culturally mature perspective celebrates this achievement as, in its time, liberating us from the stultifying constraints of medieval belief, but it challenges its finality. With Cultural Maturity, the way awareness functions changes even more fundamentally. First, awareness comes to stand separate from intelligence as a whole—including rationality. In this sense it becomes even more "objective." And, at the same time, awareness becomes newly able to engage intelligence's full complexity. Subjective and objective are bridged, and intelligence presents a newly complete—differentiated and integrated—picture.

Our experience of awareness changes in fundamental ways with this new kind of cognitive organization. It is a kind of shift that we are more and more coming to recognize. Certainly, this is the case in my field, psychology. Few truths become more obvious when practicing the craft of the psychotherapist than how different the reality of conscious awareness is from the exalted way that the conscious mind has tended to view itself. Actually, the fact that conscious awareness is limited in what it can grasp is exactly as it should be. The larger part of our functioning works best without volition's interference. (Recall the story of the centipede who walks gracefully with her hundred legs until praised for her exquisite memory.)

A central achievement of modern psychology and psychiatry has been the elucidation of more complex and multihued pictures of our inner workings. Linking awareness and will back in the middle of the last century, psychiatrist Carl Jung put it this way in his book *Man and His Symbols:* "Where there's a will there's a way is the superstition of modern man." He went on to observe that "what we commonly call 'self-knowledge' is a very limited knowledge." The oft-used psychological metaphor that compares the psyche to an iceberg, part visible, part submerged, gets us started in the right direction (though unless applied carefully, it remains polar and polarizing[21]). Awareness' new task is first to help us recognize as much of life's multihued complexity as we are able, and then to assist us in making the most life-affirming choices from the options revealed.

How do we best talk about awareness' new kind of function? Again we confront limits to usual representation, but a creative frame quite effectively captures what is new. In the end, awareness' function has always been creative, to support our toolmaking, meaning-making natures. But Integrative Meta-perspective makes that role explicit. It also increases creative possibility. Awareness' new, more explicitly creative role is more humble in the sense that it must give up its claim to final clarity. But at the same time it gains in its power both to support creative potency and to support that potency being applied in the most ultimately life-affirming ways.

We can usefully draw on acts that are "creative" in the more everyday use of the word to help appreciate this at once more humble and more powerful role for awareness. A question: What becomes awareness' purpose with a great work of art or music? Is it to create the

---

21   Thinking of the unconscious this way, as therapists often do, in the end gets in the way of the mature systemic perspective that effective, cutting-edge therapeutic work requires. Notice how the whole-box-of-crayons image, or simply recognizing the role that multiple intelligences necessarily play in cognition, results in a more multilayered and multihued picture.

work? Given that awareness can produce only what it knows, that would not be creative at all. Is it simply to get out of the way? Such passivity has never produced anything of value. Awareness must itself function creatively.

Awareness' new definition is different from awareness' more familiar Enlightenment interpretation in the same way that the function of conscious awareness in sculpting or musical composition is different from what it might be in constructing a bridge. The artist's responsibility is not to craft a predefined product (no matter how elegantly)—that would not be composition. Rather, it is to help bring forth the commitment, sensitivity, and perspective needed for the artistic effort.

This new, more explicitly creative role for awareness becomes essential once reliable handholds stop being available—whether we are creating relationships, communities, organizations, or societies. Mature responsibility becomes a measure of the imagination, courage, and integrity we bring to all of our personal and collective choices. We may not get to know what the ultimate outcome of our efforts will be. But we can know that anything that helps us bring these qualities to bear increases the likelihood that what results will enhance life.

I promised to return for a closer look at the central role awareness's new picture plays in new ways we are conceiving of both leadership and identity. We now have the needed preparation.

Awareness' new picture helps fill out previous reflections about how the demands and possibilities of leadership are changing. The Modern Age picture made conscious awareness leadership's source. With leadership in ourselves, awareness became captain of the cellular ship. With leadership in the world it became truth's determiner. In the new picture, awareness still provides "leadership," but it is now leadership of the more specifically creative sort this book is about. I've described this sort of leadership, as I have awareness' new role, as at once more humble and more powerful. With awareness' new picture, we see more clearly why this juxtaposition of terms is appropriate. With awareness's new definition, truth in our old triumphant, arms-length sense necessarily abandons us. And, at the same time, as we gain the ability to more deeply engage the whole of our complexity and think more systemically, our creative options increase dramatically. In the end, this shift fundamentally alters the demands—and possibilities—that come with leadership of every sort.

In a related way, awareness' new picture helps fill out previous reflections on the changing nature of identity. Our look at the Myth of the Individual in Chapter Two confronted us with how relationships of times past have been of the two-halves-make-a-whole sort and challenged us to think about identity in more systemically complete ways. Later, I described the traps we get into when we confuse some notion of an inner or "true" self with the larger complexity that ultimately makes us who we are—and how we just as much miss the boat when we make behavior what it is all about. We can think about how identity is becoming different in another way by recognizing how identifying with awareness, certainly in the sense that makes it half of a polarity and the end of the story, results not just in an unsatisfying definition, but in a definition that ultimately leaves us estranged from much that ultimately makes identity matter.[22]

There is another significant implication that is important to at least touch on. Culturally mature awareness's both more ultimately objective and less arms-length vantage means that we can never fully leave ourselves out of truth's picture. In an important sense noted earlier, truth becomes "participatory." A "fact" becomes as much a product of who is doing the understanding as whatever we wish to make sense of. This is not at all to make truth just subjective.[23] But it does mean that responsible decision-making becomes more personal and requires greater perspective. Earlier I spoke of how culturally mature truth al-

---

22   Integrative Meta-perspective in a related way alters how we think about human will. Traditionally we have thought of will and awareness as one and the same. With Integrative Meta-perspective, we recognize how they never really have been. We better appreciate, for example, how we often discover what is important to us only after we are well on our way to acting on it. Later we will examine how our emerging picture of the body further supports this more creative picture of will and intent. (See "The Evolution of the Body" in the "More Patterning in Time—Particularly Intriguing Expressions" section of Chapter Ten)

23   In popular writings, the observation that new truth is more "participatory" often reduces to little more than this.

ways "depends"—how our conclusions must always be tied to the contexts in which we make them. Part of that context is ourselves and the lenses through which we see.

Some version of this recognition is almost always present in the best of contemporary thought. Twentieth-century perspective in the social sciences emphasized that we could understand other cultures, other individuals, or even ourselves, only through the filters of our own biases and through the necessarily limited mechanisms of our own understanding. Nothing more defined twentieth-century art than the idea that its purpose had as much or more to do with the viewer's unique response as with any notion of artistic statement. And while our involvement in the truths we apply is most obvious when the topic is ourselves, we find this recognition also in the hard sciences. The classical physicist studied his or her quarry as if from beyond a sheet of plate glass and the classical biologist as if it lay on a dissection table. In contrast, the best of twentieth-century science argues that the observer can never be wholly cleaved from truth's equation. I think of Werner Heisenberg's famous assertion that "what we observe is not nature itself, but nature exposed to our method of questioning."

This less arm's-length relationship with truth immediately inserts uncertainty into truth's equation. It also adds an important further level of nuance to culturally mature truth's responsibility-twice-over demands. We become responsible not just for the truths on which we base our choices (and the act of choosing itself), but also for understanding the particular perspective from which we are making our determinations. This additional level of responsibility is essential to recognize if we are to effectively grasp the implications of awareness' more explicitly creative role and not confuse what I have described with interpretations that fall short of what is needed.

I've described how today we see important beginning steps towards this more filled-out kind of "creative" picture. We are becoming capable of thinking in culturally mature "pattern language" terms—of making effective Whole-System discriminations and also of better appreciating both temporal and here-and-now contextual variables. I've proposed that not only does Integrative Meta-perspective make culturally mature crux and multiplicity observations possible, this more sophisticated and nuanced kind of discernment comes with the territory. In the end, it comes part and parcel with awareness' new, more explicitly creative significance.[24]

> A Threshold Lesson: Awareness' new significance is key to what makes culturally mature perspective possible. It is also central to the appreciation and application of a creative frame and to the new more sophisticated and nuanced ways of thinking we need to effectively address the challenges before us.

Revolution or Evolution

These thoughts on the workings of awareness and on our cognitive functioning more generally help answer two questions implied in earlier reflections on culturally mature leadership. Both involve how to best think about the change processes that produce culturally mature capacities.

The first question asks whether it is best to think of culturally mature change as something "we make happen" or something that "happens naturally." If the answer is of the "make it happen" sort, we've got a lot of work to do, likely much more than is possible to do. If the answer is that it "happens naturally," we need only get out of the way so we don't interfere and mess things up.

Obviously the answer, as with any creative process, is "both." But our "both" answer has some particular implications with specific importance to culturally mature leadership. As far as the "happens naturally" side of things, I've emphasized that the potential for Cultural Maturity's changes is built into us—and how, if it is not, it is hard to be

---

24   Awareness' new picture can be misinterpreted in ways that lead to an array of unhelpful conclusions. More left-hand interpretations can make it all about process. More postmodern interpretations can make it all about uncertainty. And more right-hand interpretations can use awareness' limts to argue for an ultimately deterministic world. (See "The Evolution of the Body" in the "More Patterning in Time—Particularly Intriguing Expressions" section of Chapter Ten for a decription of how awareness' limits can be used by people whose thinking collapses into a narrow scientism to argue for the conclusion that in the end we are "biochemical puppets"—and also further clarification of why this argument ultimately fails.)

optimistic about the future. But this chapter's reflections add an essential further recognition. Cultural Maturity's changes make awareness and intent critical in a sense we have not seen before.

Awareness and intent always play some role in creative change. But we've just seen how Integrative Meta-perspective gives awareness a new, more ultimately consequential kind of significance. The newly encompassing responsibility that accompanies culturally mature truth in a similar way implies a more significant role for intent. I wouldn't be writing this book if I didn't believe that a new level of awareness and intent were critical today. And if you did not agree, likely you would not still be reading it.

Contrasting today with earlier times in culture supports this greater role for both awareness and intent. While the fact that Renaissance changes were important was not lost on people in their time, anything close to the full nature of that importance was not appreciated until a long time later. Much in the implications of Cultural Maturity's changes is well beyond what we can now grasp. And much in those changes may happen in spite of us. But to a much larger degree than with new culture stages in times past, foresight must play a role. In the end, a greater capacity for foresight—along with a greater willingness to act from it—comes close to defining what Cultural Maturity is about.

Our second leadership-pertinent question is related and concerns how we should expect to experience Cultural Maturity's changes: Put simply, is this revolution or evolution? Again, the answer is of a "both" sort. And again, necessarily, it stretches conventional understanding. Neither revolution nor evolution as we customarily think of them, even applied in combination, quite captures what Cultural Maturity's very particular developmental/evolutionary changes ask of us.

There are certainly ways in which Cultural Maturity is revolutionary. I've argued that the changes that mark Cultural Maturity's threshold are more fundamental than anything we have seen before. I've described how the Dilemma of Trajectory presents a unique circumstance, and how Integrative Meta-perspective reorders our internal complexities in a wholly new, specifically integrative way. These are changes of a unique—and radical—sort.

But at the same time, just how the changes that mark Cultural Maturity's threshold are unique also makes them less explicitly disruptive than changes we encounter with other major developmental/evolutionary change-points. Rather than breaking from the past in a traditionally heroic sense, they break new ground through being more complete. The appropriate imagery is different from early America's revolutionary armies, the overthrow of kingly rule in Europe, or more recently, bloody street clashes in the Middle East.

The developmental metaphor again provides a simple reference. "Growing up" in the first-half-of-life sense of becoming an adult requires revolutionary change in the traditional heroic sense. It is about emancipation—about stepping beyond the constraints of parental authority. Depending on how authoritarian our parents have been, this may not require overt rebellion. But if adolescents aren't at least a bit rebellious, we should be concerned that they are not doing their (developmental) job.

Maturity in the second-half-of-life sense that provides Cultural Maturity's analogy is ultimately more radical in that it represents a more fundamental kind of change. But it doesn't require battle—we are already free. While midlife can be highly disorienting, and we may make wholly transformative changes in our lives, if then we must fight, it is only with our inner demons, fears that can keep us from maturely engaging our full potency. Second-half maturity in our personal lives requires greater awareness and new courage, but ultimately it is simply about seeing in more complete ways what, before now, we have not yet been ready to see.

In the end, Cultural Maturity could not be more revolutionary. But as with personal maturity, it is ultimately as much about inner revolution as outer revolution. This is not to make it about inner change as opposed to outer change—if we miss how it is about both, we fall for predictable conceptual traps. However, Cultural Maturity is very much about fundamental changes at the level of who we are. With Cultural Maturity's changes, there is no "other" to defeat. Cultural Maturity is about becoming more complete in all our inner and outer understandings.

This is also revolution that takes place not over just weeks or months, or even decades. While we must engage Cultural Maturity's initial requirements in short order if we are not to suffer most unfortunate consequences, Cultural Maturity's demands will extend well into the future. Indeed, if the analogy with second-half-of-life tasks in individual development holds, they should define the whole of our human future.[25]

Transitional Absurdities

An additional piece of theoretical evidence draws on a dynamic that for quite a while I questioned. Only recently have I written about it. I now think that in fact it is quite important. It offers an explanation for much of what we can find most disturbing in current human behavior. It also helps us understand how what we see may have more benign—or at least more addressable—implications than we might fear.

It is hard to ignore that much that goes on in our times seems not at all sane. And we must not ignore this fact—we pay a high price when we do. At the same time, acknowledging how often our actions seem nonsensical easily leads only to cynicism—and often of an imperviously self-righteous sort. A recognition that follows directly from the concept of Cultural Maturity assists us in getting beyond both unhelpful responses: Many phenomena particular to our time that may appear ludicrous, if not disastrous, in their implications are predicted by Cultural Maturity's mechanisms. Some of these phenomena are simple reactions to complexities that stretch us beyond what we are yet able to tolerate, or to limits we would prefer to deny.

---

25   These differences provide further insight with regard to the kind of distinction I made earlier in the chapter in describing how views that identify with left-hand truth can sometimes, at least initially, be confused with culturally mature perspective. It is not uncommon for such left-leaning views to interpret changes ahead for the species in cataclysmic terms. Indeed, people of more liberal/humanist inclination, and also individuals who hold spiritual beliefs of the more philosophically idealist or New Age sort can be, in their own ways, as prone to dystopian predictions as religious fundamentalists with their visions of an impending Armageddon. Not infrequently, in a similar way, they also at least imply images of collapse and regeneration. Such mythic, death-and-resurrection imagery should be a red flag that the changes being described are wholly different from Cultural Maturity—and really not anything new at all. We've had predictions of great cataclysms and rebirths regularly through history. (See "Scenarios for the Future" in Chapter Nine.)

But many relate more directly to the Dilemma of Trajectory. They express where our evolving two-handed relationship to truth predictably takes us. I call them Transitional Absurdities.[26]

You've seen how creative Transition's threshold presents a strange circumstance. The archetypally masculine has almost wholly eclipsed the archetypally feminine. We stand in a world of all content and no context, of all right hand and no left, of life as ultimate abstraction stretched ever more distant from the foundations of experience. Transitional Absurdities are products of this circumstance. The most striking of them reflect it directly. Transitional Absurdities of a more postmodern sort may expressly question these circumstances, but because postmodern thinking so often fails to see that it remains unable to take us beyond the circumstances it challenges, postmodern Transitional Absurdities can present particularly problematical examples.

Applying the concept of Transitional Absurdity requires care. As with other tools of critique, it can become a repository for any phenomenon that our particular worldview might find aversive. We must understand it as a very specific concept requiring very particular discernments. When we do, it provides important perspective. I've implied examples previously. As a start, I would include the following on my list:

- *The unending triviality of mass consumer culture.*
  (Human value becomes increasingly tied more to things and surface titillation than to anything substantive.)

- *Our truly amazing ability to ignore damage done to the earth's environment and to deny potential ecological catastrophes.*
  (Our ability to hide from the obvious when it comes to environmental destruction is remarkable.)

- *The superficial pettiness that defines much of modern politics and our bewildering willingness to accept it as leadership.*

---

26   This is another formal Creative Systems term.

(So often the important questions are not even voiced, much less usefully addressed—this in the face of leadership challenges that could not be more immense or pressing.)[27]

■ *The common belief in certain circles that new technologies alone can solve the world's problems.*
(This belief requires that we ignore the obvious fact that the ability to invent and the capacity to use invention wisely are not at all the same.)

■ *How readily we confuse artificial stimulation with information—and meaning.*
(Related is how easily we accept the most superficial of electronic human contact as relationship.)

■ *The curious assumption that unfettered greed can produce stable economic systems that serve the larger good—along with how we make money our God more generally.*
(Not only do unregulated systems commonly result in perverse incentives, because they are based on "one-handed" notions of order, they are also ultimately unstable.)

---

27   Earlier I posed the question of whether the extreme polarization that marks contemporary politics is best thought of as a transitory phenomenon that will correct itself as voters see its harmful effects, or whether, instead, it has more fundamental significance. The concept of Transition predicts that at a certain point, compromise, even if we can achieve it, ceases to produce useful answers. At that point, partisan pettiness would be appropriately thought of as Transitional Absurdity. If Transitional dynamics do play a major role in what we encounter today, the extreme polarization we now see may eventually contribute to government, as we have known it, simply ceasing to work. In time, we may come to think of it as anticipating the eventual realization of government's needed next stage. We encounter a further government-related Transitional Absurdity in how the power of global corporations is coming to trump the influence of participatory governance of any sort.

▧ *Religious doctrines that in their focus on "prosper-
ity" and individual success have more to do with material benefit and self-aggrandizement than anything
spiritual.*
(Just as remarkable is how easily people can miss the
contradictions.)

▧ *How alienated we can be from our bodies—as we
see with today's obsession with the most surface aspects of physical appearance (witness our current in-
fatuation with plastic surgery), rampant obesity and
drug abuse, and the use of sex to sell almost every
kind of product.*
(We have become alienated not just from our bodies as experience, but of ultimately greater significance, also from
our bodies as intelligence.)

▧ *The replacement of traditional moral codes with an
"anything goes" brand of moral relativism.*
(Too often we replace rules designed to protect the greater
good with beliefs that reduce to the narrowest sort of self-
interest.)

▧ *How advertising has become our time's dominant art
form.*
(In terms of dollars spent, hands-down, the primary use
of imaginal intelligence today has become the selling of
products.)[28]

▧ *The huge gap that exists between our claims to highly
value children and the choices we make in relation to
them.*
(We see this gap in how we let media and advertising
exploit children, and also in the low priority we give

---

28   Chapter Eleven's look at the future of art examines how this situation
     turns art's traditional cultural function on its head.

education in modern society—realities that can legitimately be considered child abuse.[29])

We can understand each of these "absurdities" as what we would expect when a challenging of traditional assumptions intersects with developmental dynamics in which only the faintest vestiges of more archetypally feminine and primordial sensibilities remain to ground our choices.[30] The attraction of the trivialities of mass consumer culture reflects consumer culture's role as a last meager remnant of connection in community (and an ultimately material, right-hand expression of it). Consumerism also represents a last faint residue of the archetypally feminine power of receptivity (material consumption being the most surface form of "taking in"). Our denial of environmental vulnerability follows predictably from our degree of dissociation from nature (and a complementary extreme hubris). And the dumbed-down pettiness of modern politics reflects a reality in which only the most superficial of concerns is likely to get real attention (and in which "democratic" decisions go ever more exclusively to the highest bidder).

That we can ignore how invention has always been Janus-faced in its implications is similarly an expected consequence of an isolated right-hand worldview (in which the object of creation becomes truth itself). A culture in which artificial stimulation trumps substance is what we would expect when life is lived at only the most surface layers of experience. And the fact that we make a virtue of greed and consider it a reliable foundation for social institutions reflects an individualism divorced from human connectedness, and money made ideology.

---

29 Chapter Eleven looks at these realities more closely as they pertain to the future of both education and parenting.

30 Placing the concepts "archetypally feminine" and "primordial" together in this way can initially cause confusion. The Creative Function helps clarify. With original unity—formative process' starting point—the two concepts, at least from a big-picture perspective, are essentially the same. With further creative stages, this stops being the case—the archetypally feminine becomes an aspect of each more manifest reality. The point here is that Transition eclipses left-hand sensibilities wherever we find them.

And we can go on. When we confuse the fruits of faith with economic success, we see reflected what has become most sacred in our isolatedly material world. And our obsession with plastic surgery and the like (and a pill for every ill), our epidemic of obesity and drug abuse, and our increasing use of sex to sell everything—literally everything—reflects an extreme form of dislocation from any semblance of bodily awareness. (Were we really obsessed with sex, we would spend our time doing it and getting good at it, not buying products that serve as artificial substitutes.) An anything-goes brand of moral relativism is in the end but a particularly narrow form of isolated individualism. Advertising's status as our time's ultimate art form makes creatively germinal sensibilities the servant of extreme materialism. And the gap between what we say and what we do when it comes to children reflects a dismissing of the developmental times that most embody more primordial sensibilities.

With some Transitional Absurdities, what most stands out is how right-hand sensibilities have themselves become truth (for example, with the way money has become ultimate ideology, and how readily we assume that new technologies, by themselves, can be our salvation.) With other such absurdities, it is the near absence of truth's left-hand that is most obvious (for example, when we are oblivious to the harm we do to nature or to how disconnected we have become from our bodies). Or it may be the degree to which we live life at the surface of things that is most apparent.[31] (We see this in our rush-rush, multitasking lives; in our equating of artificial stimulation with significance; and in how readily we confuse the most superficial of electronic human contact with relationship.)

We can usefully apply the concept of Transitional Absurdity to today's broader crisis of purpose. In part what we see is a function simply

---

31   With Chapter Five's extended example, I proposed that today's common confusing of artificial stimulation with meaning has deeper origins than just the power of new information technologies. In Chapter Ten, I will map how we carry excitation closer to the body's surface with each succeeding stage in the first half of any formative process. Transition gives us this dynamic's extreme. When we live on life's surface, we become particularly vulnerable to mistaking surface excitation for significance and to such confusion's addictive exploitation.

of the loss of familiar truths. But I suspect Transitional disconnectedness plays the ultimately more consequential role. Actions come to have no meaning when estranged from their contexts. And freedom severed from deep human relationship and the flesh from which our toolmaking capacities arose becomes empty at best. Transitional realities are not just absurd; if we extend them any great distance into the future, they potentially become our undoing.

While the negative implications of the concept of Transitional Absurdity are most obvious, there are important ways, too, in which the concept is consistent with hope. We derive at least limited reassurance from recognizing that such blindnesses and insanities are predicted. The creative necessity of Transition means that we need not think of them as evidence that we have gone irreparably astray. Moreover, the concept of Cultural Maturity suggests that solutions exist. Indeed, it suggests that Transitional Absurdities can be thought of as marking not just the necessity, but also the possibility, of further stages in our understanding. It also proposes that, in the end, a single solution works for all of these absurdities: the "growing up" that Cultural Maturity describes.[32]

So how do we put these contrasting implications of the fact of Transitional Absurdity together? Like it or not, we get a demanding picture. The way Transitional Absurdities carried very far into the future put us so directly at risk raises some obvious questions about what we should anticipate in the decades immediately ahead. While Cultural Maturity promises important new possibility, at the same time, Transitional dynamics suggest most unpleasant outcomes if these absurdities continue on to any great degree. And Transitional dynamics will surely influence what we see for some time to come. At any major cultural change-point we tend to hold onto old realities well beyond

---

32 I've observed how we've seen important culturally mature contributions throughout the last century. Because of the growing effect of Transitional Absurdities in our time, Cultural Maturity's current influence can sometimes seem less than what it has been before. In fact, Cultural Maturity's influence is greater than at any time in the past. But it is certainly true that Cultural Maturity's more nuanced realizations are today often eclipsed by the shrillness and postmodern arrogance of Transitional Absurdities.

their timeliness. Overshooting the mark is pretty much how things work—partly out of fear and denial, partly because systems are not homogeneous. And there will always be great diversity in how far along individual people are toward realizing new possibility. [33]

The next chapter examines further mechanisms that are similarly predicted that can lead to results we might not prefer. If they don't result directly in poor choices, certainly they could blind us to the perspective necessary to ask the needed questions. In the decades immediately before us, we should see inspiring examples of culturally mature leadership and much in the way of good and wise decision-making—at all levels—that will move us deeply. But certainly we will also encounter absurdities, instabilities, and sometimes tragedies. Some of what we may face could try us mightily.

The recognition that much in our time that is absurd follows from the predicted workings of change can be misinterpreted in a couple of ways that have implications for leadership. Certainly it doesn't mean that we should dismiss dangerous absurdity, assuming that it is just "part of the process." It also doesn't mean that we should ignore absurdity, even when it clearly is Transitional in origin. The recognition of Transitional Absurdity does mean that we need to be careful not to imply reasons for what we see that might make matters worse (most ideologies have such reasons at the ready) and that we must be even more vigilant in engaging Cultural Maturity's threshold—and getting beyond it.

Notice that the fact of Transitional Absurdities in further ways serves as evidence for the concept of Cultural Maturity. That the concept of Cultural Maturity predicts such absurdity and also puts it in historical perspective is no small accomplishment. There is also the way in which the notion of Transitional Absurdity alerts us to how, in multiple parts of our lives, we are headed in directions that are ultimately unworkable, with no options that can save us other than the kinds of changes that the concept of Cultural Maturity describes. The latter is a harsh

---

33   These dual tendencies also play out within ourselves. Earlier I made reference to the millennial generation's contradictory tendencies. We see such contradictions in differences between individuals and also within individuals.

sort of evidence, but in another way it makes Cultural Maturity the only game in town.

Unexpected Rewards

A final kind of theoretical evidence expands on earlier, more philosophical reflections and provides a certain counterbalance to the previous section's easily unsettling observations. While a lot of the benefits we see with the needed new maturity of perspective are straightforward—for example, the simple fact that it helps us make sense of our time—many of the rewards of culturally mature understanding, including some of those that are most significant and serve as the most provocative evidence for Cultural Maturity's changes, are less obvious. One of those rewards has particularly intriguing implications. It concerns questions whose answers in times past have proved especially elusive. Culturally mature perspective frequently provides answers—indeed, often quite simple answers.

How might this be so? It is a result that follows naturally from where Cultural Maturity's cognitive changes take us. Because questions whose answers elude us in this way are almost always in some way about what makes us who we are, they require systemic perspective. More specifically, they require systemic perspective of the whole-box-of-crayons sort—and this just if we are to ask them in ultimately useful ways. When we step over Cultural Maturity's threshold we become able, at the very least, to better frame our concerns.

It is beyond this book's scope to examine pertinent philosophical issues in great detail, but a few of particular pertinence to our inquiry provide a good conclusion for this chapter's theoretical musings.[34]

Free Will and Determinism:

Let's start with an eternal philosophical question that the kind of creative interpretation of awareness' function that we examined earlier in this chapter directly reconciles: the apparent contradiction of free will and determinism. It is a quandary that leaves traditional thought tied in knots. In *The Open Universe: An Argument for Indeterminism,*

---

34 My book *Quick and Dirty Answers to the Biggest of Questions* elaborates on each of these and more.

Karl Popper posed the dilemma this way: "Common sense inclines, on the one hand, that every event is caused by some preceding event, so that every event can be explained or predicted. On the other hand, common sense attributes to mature and sane human persons ... the ability to choose freely between alternative possibilities of acting." If we live in an ultimately mechanistic universe—and ultimately, too, if we live in a wholly unitary one—every result should be predetermined (either by simple cause and effect, or by some version of divine intent or fate). Yet in our everyday world, we experience choice to be free. Clearly both results can't be true.

To address this quandary in useful ways, we must first step back and recognize that free will versus determinism has all along been a falsely framed dichotomy. To think of free will as ultimately free in the end translates into but another kind of determinism—just determinism where we get to do the determining. When we appreciate that awareness works creatively, how we think about human will changes accordingly. With the more humble, but ultimately more powerful, sort of leadership that comes with culturally mature awareness, free will stops being free in the same sense. We may be free to choose, but contingency and unpredictability cannot be escaped. We have no guarantee that the outcome of our choosing will look anything like what we intend.[35]

Similarly, in a creatively ordered reality, determinism as we have more traditionally thought of it abandons us. Causality continues to link events, but it loses its cut-and-dried predictability. Every choice happens in a context, and not just a simple cause-and-effect context, but a multilayered, dynamic, uncertainty-permeated systemic context. When our concern is human choice, that inherent indeterminism necessarily involves not just the particular dynamism of living systems, but also the audaciously creative ordering processes that make us human.

From a culturally mature perspective, free will and determinism, as conventionally conceived, are revealed to be ideologies, isolated crayons

---

35   That doesn't necessarily mean it will be worse than what we intend. Earlier I described how Integrative Meta-perspective separates intent from awareness. Sometimes our system as a whole is smarter than "we" are ("we" in the sense of who we think we are when we identify with conscious awareness).

in the systemic box. Once we are over Cultural Maturity's threshold, each become part of a larger picture. Free will and determinism each loses its past surety, but in exchange for our "loss" we get a more dynamic, more life-affirming picture of human determination.[36]

Science and Religion:

Arguably the most fundamental of eternal questions—certainly the most debated of them—concerns how best to think about the often-warring views of science and religion. Most crudely the question asks, which of these polar interpretations is right? Better we ask how, if at all, they might relate to one another. Culturally mature Creative Systems Theory proposes that they very much relate, and that they do so at the deepest levels of understanding. Indeed, it proposes that these alternative worldviews have all along been engaged in an unwitting conspiracy.

We made a start toward this kind of conclusion with earlier reflections on the workings of polarity. I've claimed that while we tend to think of polarity in terms of two beliefs in opposition, polarity at its most basic juxtaposes unity on one hand with difference on the other (Robert Pirsig's "handful of sand before the sorting began" and "the piles and the basis for sorting and relations then"). I've proposed that it is this most basic polarity that in the end defines the relationship between the spiritual on one hand and the material on the other.

If we add creative language, the result is a more nuanced articulation of this relationship. Framed creatively, our diverse interpretations of the spiritual dimension become time- and place-specific expressions of formative process' more archetypally feminine "left-hand" (expressed at a cultural scale in the practices and beliefs of religion).[37] The various

---

36 Creative Systems Theory calls change in creative systems "meta-determinant." Creative outcomes are never predetermined, but at the same time, creative processes follow predictable patterns and are always in some way linked to what has come before.

37 Chapter Eleven examines the future of religion in terms of two defining questions: Is there a God? And how do we best understand the creative role played by spiritual/religious experience? Here our concern is the latter kind of question.

ways we talk about the material—in our categories and taxonomies, and in simple observations about life's concrete facts—reflect reality as seen through a complementary archetypally masculine, "right-hand" lens (expressed at a cultural scale with science, and at a far right-hand vantage, with the more extreme forms of scientism).

Chapter Eleven looks at how science and religion have each evolved over time, and how they have done so in ways consistent with a creative interpretation. Science—from Aristotle to today's world of quarks and quasars—and religion—from its animistic beginnings to modern monotheism and beyond—have each progressed in ways that reflect what the Creative Function would predict. As important is the recognition that scientific belief and religious belief have been juxtaposed in creatively predictable ways over the course of history. In our cultural beginnings, they tended to speak nearly as one (certainly in tribal realities, but also with most Early-Axis societies); later they were more often stridently at odds (in Middle-Axis times such as the European Middle Ages); later still, they often tended more to ignore each other's existence (as with Modern Age Cartesian dualism). Developmental/ evolutionary perspective supports the conclusion that however irreconcilable the beliefs of science and religion have often seemed, behind the scenes, they have been in collusion, working together to drive the evolution of human values and understanding.

The language of narrative helps bring this creative relationship alive. We can think of religion and science as history's two great "creation story" storytelling traditions. We've told creation stories since our beginnings around the tribal campfire. Today we find our most dramatic, big-picture "how it all came to be" imagery in our modern picture of cosmological creation. This contemporary creation story doesn't end with our (perhaps) Big-Bang beginnings. It includes the amazing and mysterious emergence of life, as well as the immense new creative capacities that arrived with conscious awareness. In keeping with the material's greater reign in our time, we tend to assume that this progression describes a wholly scientific story. But we can think of all of history's great encompassing stories as versions of this story—told in ways appropriate to their time, place, and perspective.

Our past stories have taken the forms they have in part because of each time's practical constraints (for example, the invention of the telescope dramatically altered what we could see). But even more, they have taken the forms that they have because of the developmentally specific sensibilities that at different times have ordered our worldviews (that is, our early animistic and much later Enlightenment interpretations were different not just because of what we knew, but because of *how* we knew).

When we add a creative interpretation of the science/religion polarity, we see that these two stories have also taken the forms they have because of the internal vantages from which they have been told. Science and religion become alternative big-picture storytelling perspectives. Religious/spiritual traditions have observed creation's story from a more left-hand creative vantage, and with the more symbolic and specifically experiential—"faith-based"—languages of the more germinal aspects of intelligence. Scientific and more materialist philosophical traditions have simultaneously observed creation's story from a complementary more right-hand vantage, and with the more concrete and rational languages of our more manifest modes of knowing. From a more integrative evolutionary perspective—particularly when change is framed creatively—we can appreciate how, all along, science and religion have been parts of a single larger story.

Culturally mature perspective doesn't let either science or religion off easily. It challenges both the mechanistic/objectivist underpinnings of classical science and the parental assumptions of traditional faith. It similarly challenges simple Cartesian separate-worlds dualistic interpretations—objective made cleanly distinct from subjective. But for the future, it suggests intriguing possibilities for both science and religion.[38] Certainly the concept of Cultural Maturity supports more encompassing interpretation. It also supports the conclusion that in the future we will conceive of both science and religion in ways that are more dynamic and complete, and thus more fully reflective of existence's wonder.

Who We Are and What It All Means:
A creative frame also invites conjecture with regard to the ultimate science- and religion-related eternal question: our place in the larger scheme of things. From a scientific viewpoint, we can appropriately

---

38   See "Science and Technology" and "Religion and Spirituality" in Chapter Eleven.

ask—as many great thinkers have asked—"Are we but a speck in an essentially purposeless universe, an odd, momentary impulse of no real ultimate significance?" Or do we better think of ourselves as God's special children, as most religions through time have somehow seen us? A creative perspective offers a third option—neither quite so random nor quite so grand, but arguably more intriguing.

While Creative Systems Theory's primary interest is human systems, it applies in a less direct way to thinking about existence more generally. Certainly it helps us understand why we have seen our physical and biological worlds in the particular ways we have at different times in history.[39] It helps clarify, for example, how with Late-Axis culture we came increasingly to view all of existence as a great machine—Descartes's clockworks universe.

Cultural Maturity's more dynamic, systemic picture, in the end, similarly reorders how we think about everything. The third option just noted follows from where that reordering takes us. In an important sense, we can think of existence as a whole as creative (here in the most encompassing sense of being dynamic and self-organizing). Reframed, our question becomes, What is our place and significance in creation?—as creation becomes what the "scheme of things" is ultimately about.

We can crudely but usefully think of existence in terms of three "emergent" phenomena: there is inanimate creation[40]; there is life; and there is this odd addition, conscious life (including ourselves and to lesser degrees other higher life forms). A creative interpretation proposes that we might best think of it all like Neapolitan ice cream. Each layer is the same stuff (here creation instead of ice cream), while at the same time, each layer is fundamentally different.[41] Each layer beyond inanimate creation is distinguished by a "creative multiplier"

---

39   See "On the Nature of Nature" in Chapter Ten.

40   This includes ongoing physical generativity such as that reflected in the quote by Ilya Prigogine in Chapter Four and described in his Nobel Prize–winning work in thermodynamic chemistry.

41   In another way, culturally mature perspective simultaneously increases our appreciation for both interconnectedness and for difference.

(or several creative multipliers working together) that radically increases the rate at which creative reorganization can take place. In the case of life, this is natural selection and the learning/adapting capacities that come with life's workings. In the case of ourselves, it is the option of fresh creation happening with every new "aha" that arises with conscious awareness and our unique toolmaking, idea-making, meaning-making prowess.[42]

Our place in the larger scheme of things? At the least we are a fascinating bit of creative innovation (with the jury still very much out on just how ultimately successful). If we want to be more grand, we could claim ours to be a rather special sort of creative innovation. We are the only creature, at least on our particular earth, that is not just consciously aware, but aware of itself as part of something that has evolved and continues to evolve. In an interesting sense, through us, creation, not just as fact but as process, has become conscious of itself.

This does not guarantee that our behavior will not bring our demise—and a literal end of civilization. Our time on the planet has been extremely short. And the dramatic creative capacities that are our great gift may very well also be the end of us. But in our time, this generative story continues—in new ways, and with new implications for what may transpire. Cultural Maturity has its basis in the possibility—and necessity—of a more aware and more deeply engaged relationship with our creative, toolmaking, meaning-making natures. Homo sapiens— "man the wise"—is perhaps coming to better deserve his audaciously proclaimed status. If this book's assertions have touched at all close to the truth, our future well-being depends on it.

---

42 Creative Systems Theory uses the term *Creative Causality* to describe the underlying generativity shared by these various levels of organization. Creative Systems Theory was originally called "The Theory of Creative Causality."

CHAPTER NINE

How Our Thinking Can Go Astray— Separating Wheat from Chaff as We Look to the Future

The first principle is that you must not fool yourself,
and you are the easiest person to fool.

RICHARD FEYNMAN

ONE OF CULTURALLY MATURE PERSPECTIVE'S MAJOR CONTRIBUTIONS lies in how it helps us separate ideas that can serve us in times ahead from those that miss the mark and can only ultimately get in the way. Having good compare-and-contrast tools at our disposal is essential to culturally mature leadership. Most obviously, such tools help us evaluate information. But they also help us identify common traps in our own attitudes and beliefs, and thus ensure that our understandings are up to Cultural Maturity's challenge. In addition, they help us determine the best places to put our energies, and assist us in choosing wisely when picking with whom to collaborate in our efforts.

With regard to evaluating information, besides helping us judge specific claims, having good comparison tools also helps us anticipate what information might and might not be of value depending on the information's source. Everyday information can have different kinds and degrees of reliability depending on the medium through which it reaches us—whether it comes from Fox News, a "progressive" (left-liberal) radio station, a church sermon, or a scientific journal. And within particular fields, we encounter predictable differences in the underlying assumptions both of specific individuals and of broader schools of thought.

Good comparison tools help us predict where culturally mature contributions might be present and also to recognize important contributions when they show up in unexpected places. And even when no culturally mature contribution is present, identifying which "crayon" in complexity's box that a piece of information comes from helps us to appreciate what usefulness there still might be to glean.

This chapter starts by briefly reviewing observations from previous chapters pertinent to the compare-and-contrast task. It then contrasts the concept of Cultural Maturity with other ways of thinking about the future. For comparison, we will look at the five most common futures "scenarios" (to use a favorite term of futurists), the most frequently encountered pictures of what may lie ahead for the species. With each we will give particular attention to the kinds of assumptions that produce each scenario's conclusions.

Next we examine a handful of more specific compare-and-contrast tools. We will look at how the language of polarity can be used to distinguish common traps. We will reflect on how an understanding of temperament helps us map different ways in which people's thinking can stop short of Cultural Maturity's needed systemic completeness. And we will examine what we can learn from observing overall systemic capacity and what happens when we exceed it.

I will then present a particularly powerful "hands-on" approach that directly supports culturally mature understanding. Along with examining its practical usefulness, we will look at what this approach can teach us about how culturally mature understanding is different from ways of thinking we might confuse it with. Then I will make comparison with one specific conceptual viewpoint—the perspective of philosophical pragmatism—to illustrate making some particularly fine-grained distinctions. I will conclude the chapter by applying these wheat-from-chaff tools to the tasks of culturally mature leadership.

These various comparative observations must necessarily be of a brief, snapshot sort. But even this bare outline should help you more safely and effectively make your way in the territory ahead. At the least, these various comparison tools will help you better appreciate what culturally mature perspective is not. But each of them also provides perspective for refining your understanding of Cultural Maturity and making it more directly a part of your experience. In addition, these observations offer a further layer of evidence. Culturally mature perspective's ability to place more limited viewpoints within a larger frame provides important further support for the concept of Cultural Maturity and the sophistication of its viewpoint.

Ideology, Systems, and Big-Picture Perspective

I've put forward observations directly pertinent to our compare-and-contrast task throughout these pages. In getting started, I emphasized that culturally mature truths differ fundamentally from beliefs of an ideological sort. I described how this includes ideological beliefs that reflect here-and-now conclusions of a systemically partial sort, beliefs that take one crayon in a time's systemic box and make it the whole of truth. And it also includes ideological beliefs where the roots are more temporal, beliefs that reflect the assumptions of a particular stage in culture's story. Over the course of the book, I've further broken down these different ways ideology can manifest. And I've described cues we can use to help us recognize ideology's presence.

With regard to ideology of the here-and-now, one-crayon-versus-another sort, you've seen how the "crayons" involved may be ones that express commonly found advocacies and animosities—such as with conflicts between nations or ethnic groups, or with political party affiliations. We've also looked at how ideology of the one-crayon-versus-another sort may be more conceptual, but still be as much a reflection of taking one aspect of human complexity and giving it last-word status—such as what we find when we identify with thoughts or feelings, masculine or feminine, or either science or religion as some last word.

As far as belief that identifies with the assumptions of a particular stage in culture's story, the reference can be to any stage, but I've given particular emphasis to the importance of recognizing how such ideological limitations apply as much to Modern Age (Late-Axis) realities as they do to the assumptions of any previous period. We can think of this challenge to Modern Age ideology in terms of stage-specific new capacities such as those around which I've organized the first half of this book. We can also think of it in terms of cultural narrative—for example, with the essential distinction between culturally mature narrative and heroic/romantic or postmodern stories of how things work. And we can think of it, too, in terms of modern institutions and the ways of thinking that underlie their workings. I've emphasized the importance of leaving behind the common assumption that familiar institutional forms—whether governmental, economic, scientific, or religious—represent endpoints and ideals.

I've also implied wheat-from-chaff distinctions that have more specifically to do with conceptual challenges we encounter at Cultural Maturity's threshold. In particular, I've discussed how we must clearly distinguish the kind of systemic perspective needed to address the critical tasks before us from both engineering models, no matter how complex, and ideas that confuse the needed systemic inclusiveness with simple connectedness. Concepts that alert us to quandaries that challenge familiar ways of thinking at the most fundamental of levels— such as the Dilemma of Trajectory, the Myth of the Individual, and the Dilemma of Representation—similarly provide important compare-and-contrast insights.

A last kind of distinction concerns where we should look if we wish to find contributions that succeed at being culturally mature. It should now be clear that we can look almost anywhere. Because culturally mature thought reflects perspective "whose time has come," we should expect to see Cultural Maturity's beginnings in every cultural sphere, and at every level of activity from the most conceptually rarefied to the most applied and everyday. And we do. While culturally mature innovation requires unusual Capacitance, we've seen how it has arisen from a great variety of sources.

But I've hinted at a surprise when it comes to seeking out culturally mature contributions that is important to note if we are to make best use of this chapter's reflections. Given the serious nature of the questions to which we have given attention, we might reasonably assume that we would find the best of culturally mature thought in the hallowed halls of academia. In fact, while many of the Cultural Maturity "success stories" I have noted have had academic origins, the academic world has commonly not been the rich source of such thinking that we might imagine, nor has it always been accepting of culturally mature contributions even when they have been put forward by academic figures. The reason is historically understandable. Academia as we know it came to prominence with our Modern Age. Not just its structures and approaches, but also its defining assumptions tend to reflect this history.

Two Modern Age advances are particularly significant in this regard. First is the separation of the medieval world's at best faintly differentiated realms of knowledge into clear and distinct disciplines. The second is the elevation of rationality and its identification with objective understanding. Each of these historically pivotal advances easily becomes a stumbling block when the task is culturally mature perspective. As more and more often today the critical challenges are systemic, interdisciplinary inquiry becomes increasingly essential. Academia is beginning to recognize the importance of breaking down traditional boundaries between spheres of understanding, but it still has a long way to go. And with regard to the more basic challenge of better bringing the whole of our cognitive complexity to bear when taking on complex questions, we rarely see more than a start.

For our task, academia's limitations do not need to be an obstacle. They simply alert us to the importance of expanding where we look. This recognition that there is no one locale where culturally mature contribution is most likely to be found provides another important reason to have good compare-and-contrast tools. Given that we can find culturally mature contributions in the most unlikely of places, it becomes especially important to have reliable ways of knowing when we have encountered the real thing.

Scenarios for the Future

Our first more specific comparative lens—contrasting Cultural Maturity's predictions with other ways of looking at the future—provides a particularly good big-picture vantage for refining our understanding of Cultural Maturity and its implications. I will juxtapose five of the most common ways of thinking about what may lie ahead. The first two— We've Arrived and We've Gone Astray scenarios—in opposite ways stop fully short of Cultural Maturity's threshold. I will touch on them just briefly. We will look more closely at the remaining three—what I will call Post-industrial/Information Age, Postmodern/Constructivist, and Transformational/New Paradigm scenarios. Each of these at its best approaches Cultural Maturity's threshold. But, as we shall examine, each is also vulnerable to conceptual traps that can lead our thinking far astray and none, in the end, fully addresses our three threshold tasks.

An observation I made in the book's introductory chapter provides a glimpse of these alternative ways of thinking about the future and how what they describe is fundamentally different from what we find with the concept of Cultural Maturity. I've described how conventional ideas about the future tend to be of two basic sorts: notions that view the trajectory that has gotten us to where we are as essentially sound, and notions that claim that there are fundamental problems. We've Arrived and Post-industrial/Information Age scenarios fall into the first camp. Each in different ways interprets history's journey to this point as advancement and views the future as its logical consequence—either because we've reached that journey's triumphant culmination or because the future extends out along the same general path. We've Gone Astray and Transformational/New Paradigm scenarios most often fall into the second camp. They consider something to be fundamentally wrong or broken in our current human narrative—though the best of New Paradigm views may regard modern-day truths as simply outdated, rather than misguided. Depending on whose views we are talking about, Postmodern/Constructivist scenarios can produce a grab-bag of results—hiding mildly optimistic predictions, suggesting ultimately "gone astray" sorts of conclusions, or being simply noncommittal.

The concept of Cultural Maturity directly challenges each of these basic orientations toward the future. With regard to the first, more history-affirming kind of interpretation, it makes clear that continuing on as we have cannot work for times ahead. With regard to the second, more condemning conclusion, the concept of Cultural Maturity emphasizes that each past cultural stage—including our most recent—while it has had its particular partialities and blindnesses, in its time has also taken us generally forward. The concept of Cultural Maturity also argues that further productive stages, at least as potential, lie ahead. It contrasts with Postmodern/Constructivist formulations in providing an overarching explanation for why this might be so, and also by helping us formulate needed new ways of thinking.

A more detailed look at our five scenarios:

We've Arrived Scenarios

Advocates of We've Arrived conclusions regard the present as a cultural end point, as most people through history have done with regard to their particular present. They assume that current institutions and ways of thinking—political, religious, scientific, or economic—at most need a bit of further polishing.

Modern Western We've Arrived scenarios elevate (alone or in combination) the structures and assumptions of established democratic forms, free-market capitalism, contemporary monotheistic religion, material progress, scientific objectivity, individualism, and modern aesthetics. Such belief defines much of modern consensus reality. It may be ardently held or just assumed. A We've Arrived scenario's prescription for the future? We should keep doing what we are doing—and see if we can get others to follow our example.

While the concept of Cultural Maturity strongly affirms the achievements of the Modern Age, it makes clear that there is no more reason to assume that we've arrived at some culminating truth in our time than in any age previous—and every reason to hope that we have not. Culturally mature perspective regards neither modern institutional structures nor modern social values and aesthetics as last chapters. It argues that carrying modern Western culture's great successes unmodified into the future—in particular its onward-and-upward conception of progress and its extreme materialist, individualist values, but also its specific institutional structures—would, in fact, have most unfortunate consequences. It also counsels against assuming that modern Western cultural forms represent ideals to which people everywhere, irrespective of their cultural context, should ascribe.

We've Gone Astray Scenarios

Advocates of We've Gone Astray conclusions believe almost the opposite—that in some significant way humanity has failed. Often the implication is not just that we have made mistakes in judgment or policy, but that we have erred fundamentally.

We've Gone Astray scenarios take their most radical form in the predictions of impending Armageddon put forward by certain extreme religious groups and in popular culture portrayals of dystopian cataclysm. But other more restrained We've Gone Astray interpretations—such as those we see with the more pessimistic of environmentalist positions, with romantic and idealist[1] philosophical beliefs, and

---

1   Philosophically idealist views are most characterized by their claims for a yet-to-be-realized, ideal cultural end point, but as I noted in the previous chapter, they often include the assumption that getting there will be preceded by a time of destruction.

commonly with the more entrenched views of both the political left
and the political right[2]—can translate into an "it's all going to hell in
a handbasket" cynicism that, while not as terminal in its predictions,
can be as severe in its criticism (and often just as limiting when it
comes to useful action).

We've Gone Astray scenarios produce different advice depending
on who is offering it. For some, the task is simply to fix what we've
broken. For many, the answer lies in going back to the values and
assumptions of some earlier time. For others, as with We've Arrived
adherents, it means there is really nothing to do—in this case, because
the damage has already been done. We have gone so far astray that we
are beyond redemption.

Culturally mature perspective views We've Gone Astray scenarios as
inappropriately condemning and, in the end, diversions from the true
magnitude of what the future asks of us. It affirms that modern times
often find us in denial about much that desperately needs attention.
And it agrees that we have made plenty of mistakes. But it also argues
that most of the dilemmas we confront are the result not of our failings,
but of our successes.

Culturally mature perspective also makes clear that going back is not
an answer, even if we wish to retrieve things we appropriately perceive
to be lost. It supports the claim that important truths—for example,
about nature, about the sacred, about community, and more—have
been "forgotten." But at the same time, it emphasizes that the natural
trajectory of cultural systems, like that of individuals, is growth—and
that that is what we have seen.

Culturally mature perspective also warns of a particular danger that
accompanies We've Gone Astray conclusions—how they can work as
self-fulfilling prophecies. We see this danger most explicitly with views
that make endgame scenarios inevitable expressions of God's will. But
we can encounter something just as incapacitating and self-fulfilling

---

2   We tend to think of politically conservative views as most likely to iden-
    tify with the past and be critical of the present, but people of liberal/
    progressive bent can be vulnerable to a particularly debilitating sort of
    self-righteous cynicism (often accompanied by it own kind of romantic
    idealization of the past).

with reactive cynicism. The cynic gets to feel right and superior while taking no real action that might make things different.

Post-industrial/Information Age Scenarios

Post-industrial/Information Age interpretations treat invention as the fundamental driver of cultural change and emphasize the transforming effects that inventions of the future will have on every aspect of our lives. In the end, they make technology the solution. Such views are common in popular culture and academic thought, and find special favor in futurist circles. The digital revolution has given such beliefs a new generation of adherents.

The concept of Cultural Maturity affirms technology's essential role in future possibilities and applauds many Postindustrial/Information Age ideas. But at the same time it directly challenges much in Post-industrial/Information Age interpretation. Most obviously, it does so in cautioning against the assumption that the consequences of invention will necessarily be positive.[3] It reminds us that inventing is not the same thing as using invention wisely. It also emphasizes that technological solutions will rarely in themselves be sufficient for addressing the tasks ahead.

The most limited of Post-industrial/Information Age thinking contributes little to this inquiry. It simply extends the Industrial Age's onward-and-upward story. But Postindustrial/Information Age thinking can also alert us to many of the questions culturally mature perspective addresses. Indeed, the best of Post-industrial/Information Age thought can put forward ideas that are nearly as far-reaching in their implications as those we have looked at here.

We see this result for two very different reasons. First, there is the fact that emerging technologies often serve to support and catalyze Cultural Maturity–related changes. Global access to technologies that make possible greater resource efficiency, for example, will be critical to long-term environmental sustainability. And emerging technologies can support not just needed changes in what we do, but also in how we think. For example, decentralized information technologies thrust

---

3   The best of Post-industrial/Information Age formulations do not make this assumption.

us into a systemically networked reality that just by its structure transcends conventional expertise and authority.

The second reason we may see related predictions has to do with unwarranted conclusions. Post-industrial/Information Age thinkers can predict outcomes that, while accurate and helpful, are not really supported by Post-industrial/Information Age interpretation. One example: Theorists who observe some of the more positive effects of decentralized information technologies just noted sometimes then talk as if the kinds of psychological and social changes needed for the future will follow naturally from them. This conclusion is not supported, certainly not if we are talking about the depth of psychological and social changes required if we are to bring needed wisdom to future decision-making. Indeed, these changes, by themselves, can work to fuel the addiction to artificial stimulation and pseudo-significance that presents Transition's greatest danger. Certainly, by themselves, they do nothing to counter it.

Culturally mature perspective applauds the contributions made by the more sophisticated of Post-industrial/Information Age thinkers. And, at the same time, it warns even those who make an effort to think in more encompassing ways that they may need to reexamine their explanations if their ideas are to hold up—and, more important, if their ideas are to ultimately serve us as we go forward.[4]

Post-industrial/Information Age interpretation and the concept of Cultural Maturity more explicitly part company regarding the common Post-industrial/Information Age assumption that technological innovation is what ultimately drives cultural change. Culturally mature perspective affirms the importance of technology as a driver of change, but it also emphasizes that this explanation in isolation leaves out much of what is most significant—for understanding change, and more importantly, for usefully addressing the future. It argues that, more accurately,

---

4   Alvin Toffler and John Naisbitt, who provided some of the best early futures-oriented thinking for a popular audience, addressed broad social concerns. And some of the more insightful commentators on the information revolution—Nicholas Negroponte and Bill Joy come immediately to mind—reflect on specific social issues. But more than the common assumptions of Post-industrial/Information Age perspective is needed to get very far with such analysis.

the causality goes both ways. Invention catalyzes change, but what we are capable of inventing is also always a function of who we are and how we are able to understand and perceive. In particular, innovation reflects our time in culture's story.[5] With regard to today's needed changes, invention helps drive and support Cultural Maturity, but it is just as true that invention sufficiently innovative to push us toward needed changes could not happen—and certainly would not be supported—without the new sensibilities and perspectives that Cultural Maturity begins to make possible.

Another way in which culturally mature perspective takes issue with Post-industrial/Information Age assumptions concerns just what needed changes in how we understand, if recognized, entail. I've described how the best of Post-industrial/Information Age thinking affirms the importance not just of technical advancement, but also of new ways of thinking, and how there can be similarities in the kinds of conceptual changes proposed. We often see emphasis, for example, on the importance of systemic understanding. But here, again, limiting assumptions about how things work—in this case, a strong mechanistic bias—tend to get in the way of the needed sophistication of conceptual perspective. What we encounter is rarely more than systemic understanding of the engineering sort.

We can miss the strong ideological component that commonly permeates Post-industrial/Information Age conclusions—this for a now familiar reason: Technology includes much that we most mythologize in our time. Post-industrial/Information Age assertions can simply appear smart and logical. The hidden ideological thread becomes most apparent when such interpretation takes a utopian turn—think of science fiction–like prognostications from the middle of the previous century that claimed that we should all by now be living in glass-enclosed cities and flying around in personal transporters. We also encounter this ideological component in knee-jerk conclusions that with any close examination become questionable at best. Consider the common assumption in artificial intelligence circles that computers will soon become

---

5   An illustration: China had all the technical prerequisites for an industrial revolution 2,000 years ago. However, it lacked the materialist, individualist values needed to make such change acceptable and successful. Today, we see no such lack.

more intelligent than we are. In a purely computational sense, they are already more intelligent—indeed much more so. But belief that they might become more intelligent than we are in the ways that are most important to us—and certainly when it comes to the wisdom-related cognitive capacities that will be increasingly important to us in the future—reflects decidedly limited, and ultimately ideological ideas about the nature of intelligence.[6]

Today, the pivotal influence of digital technologies often combines with Transitional dynamics (and the narrow scientism that we often see with such dynamics) to produce particularly extreme forms of techno-utopianism. We see this most dramatically with anything-is-possible special effects imagery in the media. But we also encounter it in views expressed by acknowledged serious thinkers. I think, for example, of recent claims that artificial intelligence will make eternal life finally possible—by offering the option of wholly

---

6   I've emphasized how Integrative Meta-perspective celebrates the richly multifaceted nature of human intelligence. Successful forays into the world of chess by IBM's computer "Deep Blue" were dramatic, but they reflected a much more limited sort of processing than that used by human chess players (and chess reflects an activity that, while sophisticated, doesn't require the kind of sophistication that human activities of a less purely technical sort require). Advances since have added further complexity, and through greater application of divergent processing they have introduced additional "creativity." But even the most sophisticated "intelligent" computers reflect a basic misconception about how human cognition works.

None of this is to say that computers becoming more intelligent than we are in the sense that they already are might not have immense consequences. And some might not at all be positive. Physicist Stephen Hawking believes artificial intelligence will eventually out-compete human intelligence and be the end of us. This is not an unreasonable prediction. We can readily create self-organizing and self-propagating computer programs that can grow and mutate endlessly. And unlike human intelligence, there is nothing inherent in such programs that would have them wish to make wise or moral choices. (In Chapter Twelve, I will elaborate on how the moral ingredient intrinsic to human intelligence's creative workings is critical to any hope for a healthy future.) If we want wise or moral consequences, we will have to specifically design such inclinations into them. And because of inherent limitations to doing so, we will also have to always maintain ultimate oversight.

disembodied existence. Besides being a conclusion that again depends on a naïvely simplistic picture of intelligence, we see a kind of ultimate limits-denying ambition that is a giveaway for ideology. Extreme expressions of a technological gospel can titillate, but they are best thought of as Transitional Absurdity.

Post-industrial/Information Age interpretations, while often helpful, most often stop well short of providing the completeness of perspective our times demand. Indeed, because such interpretations tend to leave out so much that needs to be considered as we go forward—in particular, just how fundamental and personal that change must be—they often work to hide from us the depths of what our times require. In the end, too, they stop short at the level of "story"—they fail to provide ultimately compelling images for the future. Technological advancement is wonderful, but it is only part of what we need for a future that is worth living.

Postmodern/Constructivist Scenarios

I introduced postmodern perspective in Chapter Five. There I observed how the best of formal postmodern thought successfully approaches Cultural Maturity's threshold. But I also emphasized that postmodern ideas vary greatly in their success at stepping over it, or even usefully recognizing its implications. Postmodern/Constructivist perspective today gives us at once some of the best and some of the weakest of future-related thought.

I've described how postmodern belief had its start in the philosophical ponderings of existentialism. With the growing influence of social constructivism in the later part of the twentieth century, it came to be a central influence in academic circles. Today, postmodern sensibility has come to define much of popular culture, helping take us beyond the heroic/romantic narrative that until recently defined the larger portion of shared cultural expression. But while on both fronts—more formal thought and popular expression—postmodern perspective makes important contribution, in each case, it stops ultimately short of where we need to go.

Formal Postmodern/Constructivist ideas share with the concept of Cultural Maturity the questioning of the absoluteness of past ways of understanding. They emphasize our time's loss of familiar cultural guideposts, and challenge final, "essentialist" truths in general. And they point out accurately that beliefs vary widely between cultures, evolve over time, and are subject to human manipulation. But Postmodern/Constructivist ideas fail to help us understand at all deeply why today we see such fundamental questioning of past belief. And of particular importance, rarely do they offer much of real substance to replace what they insightfully recognize has been taken away.

The best of formal Postmodern/Constructivist thought does make a start at looking forward. The claim that we "construct" the realities we live in at least implies the possibility of crafting our world in more effective ways. Postmodern/Constructivist thinkers also often make predictions that are at least generally consistent with more systemically conceived options—for example, how institutions and assumptions of the Modern Age will give way to more fluid and pluralistic cultural structures, and how understanding in the future will be more and more often characterized by multiple perspectives and often by contradiction.

But fears of falling back into old absolutes severely limit Postmodern/Constructivist thinking. Even the most fully developed ideas stop short of the critical next step. They fail to help us think with the needed complexity and new sophistication—to "construct" our personal and collective realities in the needed "post-essentialist" ways. Indeed, Postmodern/Constructivist beliefs often directly interfere with efforts to go further. Postmodern/Constructivist thinkers tend to assume that there are no universal truths, only truths specific to particular times and places. I've described how formal Postmodern/Constructivist thinking can get stuck in an immediate skepticism toward anything that might look like an overarching concept.

This skepticism has admirable roots. Overarching ideas in times past have had their origins in narrow and often self-serving belief. But postmodern thought's common distaste for big-picture conception—indeed conception of any substantive sort—undercuts its ability to contribute creatively to the larger conversation. Postmodern theorists tend to be better at critique than they are at providing useful perspective. And often theirs is a most limited—indeed, limiting and deadening—kind of critique. Identification with our ultimate inability to know for sure and with different-strokes-for-different-folks notions of diversity ultimately undermine efforts to effectively move forward.[7]

Over the last couple of decades, Postmodern/Constructivist sensibility has come simultaneously to have less of a hold in academic circles and a growing influence in spheres of popular expression. With contemporary art, music, humor, and popular cultural more generally, we see increased use of irony and a mixing of influences often from far-flung sources. As with the earlier, more formal postmodern contribution, this popular influence has at once invited the beginnings of more complex and multifaceted sensibility and resulted in efforts that often contribute much less than they claim. Too often, today, we find popular expression that confuses the glib, ironic, and often simply random with substance.[8] At worst we get expression that is little more than artificial stimulation in the name of significance.[9]

Put in developmental language, the Postmodern/Constructivist contribtuion, whether of a more formal or more popular sort, reflects well the unsettling realities of cultural development's Transition stage. When timely, it helps us get beyond the past's heroic/romantic

---

7 There are thinkers of Postmodern/Constructivist bent whose contributions I draw on and whom I very much respect—for example, Richard Rorty in the philosophical sphere and the many important contributors to constructivist perspective in education. But Postmodern/Constructivist views, even at their best, can provide but a start toward understanding either the present or the future.

8 Postmodern sensibility increasingly permeates not just entertainment, but also more serious forms of popular expression. For example, it has had growing influence in the offerings of public media. I think of Ira Glass's "This American Life" on National Public Radio as first introducing postmodern irony and contradiction to the public media world. Today, such sensibilities permeate more and more of public media programming, particularly that which attempts to reach a "younger demographic." While initially this aesthetic was new and made a contribution, all too often today it translates into a glib, difference-for-its-own-sake cleverness that says very little while pretending to be profound. I see this as a trap that threatens to undermine public media's ability to function as a resource we can rely on to point us toward what is important.

9 See "The Media" in Chapter Eleven.

assumptions, challenge ideology, and confront worlds that may seem only contradictory from the perspective of what we have known. But in the end, Postmodern/Constructivist beliefs fail to grasp at all clearly what, if anything, may lie beyond Transition's threshold. When this failure is extreme, we find sensibility that becomes, in effect, Transitional Absurdity.

Transformational/New Paradigm Scenarios

The last grouping is made up of thinkers who frame our future task in terms of "changes in consciousnes" or new scientific and spiritual "paradigms." It includes both efforts that make a serious and concerted attempt to understand cultural change and a wide array of highly simplistic and ultimately unhelpful popular interpretations. Transformational/New Paradigm ideas at their best encourage us to think radically about what the future will require of us. At their worst, they present intractably ideological conclusions that are not in the end new at all.

Transformational/New Paradigm thinking can share important characteristics with culturally mature perspective. This fact both alerts us to where contributions may lie and, because we find such similarities with both the best and worst of such thinking, emphasizes the importance of taking particular care in teasing apart specifics. Transformational/New Paradigm thinking highlights the need for change that makes a fundamental leap. It also most often argues that needed changes are as much about ourselves and how we think as they are about what we might do or invent. And, almost always, too, it acknowledges the importance of seeing interconnections that before we have ignored, and better including more archetypally feminine, left-hand values and sensibilities, along with those of a more right-hand sort.

Transformational/New Paradigm thinkers have sometimes brought these recognitions together in ways that at least knock on Cultural Maturity's door. Transformational/New Paradigm perspective at its best is represented by historically significant contributors to big-picture understanding. I think immediately of Jean Gebser, Carl Jung, Erich Neumann, and Joseph Campbell.[10] More recently,

---

10   Joseph Campbell was an important early teacher/mentor of mine. (See

leadership theorists with Transformational/New Paradigm inclinations have also made important contributions.[11]

At the same time, Transformational/New Paradigm ideas—certainly those commonly found with popular, New Age sorts of views—frequently have nothing at all to do with Cultural Maturity. Commonly, they really have nothing to do with the future. More accurately they represent modern explications of timeless romantic, philosophically idealist,[12] or mystical beliefs. In Chapter Eight, I made reference to how the beginnings of Reengagement can have people confuse various timeworn views that make left-hand sensibility primary with needed new understanding. With unfortunate frequency, Transformational/ New Paradigm ideas reflect polarized identification with the archetypally feminine and miss that the truth claims that result get us no closer to culturally mature perspective than do ideological beliefs of a solely mechanistic sort. Even Transformational/New Paradigm views that succeed at being helpful are commonly limited by their strong left-hand biases. They may ask important questions, and in so doing take us up to Cultural Maturity's threshold. But their picture of the future most often then collapses into what is ultimately left-hand belief.

We can miss the left-hand bias with certain Transformational/New Paradigm writers because they make science their primary focus. The essential difference from science-related references in this book is that with the more simplistic of Transformational/New Paradigm scientific

---

"The Evolution of Intelligence" in Chapter Ten.)

11   For example, Margaret Wheatley and Peter Senge.

12   I've described how philosophical idealism views history as progressing toward some social or spiritual ideal. Hegel's views illustrate philosophical idealism that posits a social ideal. With simplistic Transformational/New Paradigm thought the ideal is more spiritual. We find a good example of philosophical idealism of the more spiritual sort in the early twentieth century thinking of **French philosopher and Jesuit priest Teilhard** de Chardin who postulated that history would end at a spiritual enlightenment–like "Omega Point." Both left-hand and right-hand sensibilities are acknowledged with philosophical idealism, but the left-hand (essence or spirit) is seen as the ultimately determining force, driving and shaping the right-hand world of manifest forms.

writing, science ends up reduced to interpretation that makes interconnectedness if not what it is all about, certainly primary.[13] Transformational/New Paradigm interpretations of science can be as limited and ultimately unhelpful as the narrowest kinds of scientism—just limited and unhelpful in an opposite way. Earlier I described how we find a similar kind of simplistic interpretation with popular systems writing that reduces to little more than an elaborate way of arguing for ultimate unity.

Transformational/New Paradigm ideas often find significant overlap with We've Gone Astray interpretations, more so than Transformational/New Paradigm supporters, with their commonly upbeat identification with things inspirational, wish to admit. People of more romantic or philosophically idealist inclination can fall into either camp or vacillate back and forth. In a Chapter Eight footnote, I observed how, when people who make left-hand sensibilities primary look to the future, they are often drawn to images of collapse and resurrection. People who ascribe to Transformational/New Paradigm views can be some of the quickest to see the future in cataclysmic terms—whether physical cataclysm such as environmental catastrophe or fundamental failure of past worldviews.[14]

Sometimes Transformational/New Paradigm views interpret history in ways that are at least superficially similar to what I've described with developmental/evolutionary perspective. Indeed, some of the best of such thinking depicts early cultural stages in ways that can be quite helpful.[15] But, at least with more simplistic interpretations, when we

---

13   I've observed how notions like entanglement and the participatory role of the observer in physics can be simplistically interpreted in this way. Transformational/New Paradigm scientific interpretations also often gives particular attention to "paranormal" kinds of phenomena. Sometimes we find good and interesting science. But as often, a left-hand agenda means that data must be taken with a considerable grain of salt.

14   I remember being surprised at a conference I attended in the late 1990s on the Y2K millennium computer bug to find that the people who seemed most sure that the Y2K bug would have devastating consequences were not the Information Age computer types, but rather those of a more Transformational bent.

15   I've described how an appreciation for archetypally feminine sensibilities is necessary for a deep understanding of history's early stages. Even where we find helpful observations, however, we must stay alert, given the left-

turn to making sense of our times and the challenges ahead, we tend to find descriptions that have more to do with utopian wishful thinking than anything really possible. What gets put forward as radical in its implications is instead all-too-familiar idealized projection, some hoped-for new Golden Age. The result tends to be a picture of the future that, even if it were realizable, we would not want.[16]

---

hand bias of such views, to where romantic projection may masquerade as accurate description.

16   The conclusion that we would not want this kind of outcome even if it were a possibility should be obvious from earlier big-picture reflections on the kind of thinking that the future will require. But we find a particularly concrete kind of support in a characteristic we commonly find even with the most well meant of Transformational/New Paradigm belief. Like ideology more generally, it tends to attract people with specific personality styles.

Drawing distinction between culturally mature perspective and a version of Transformational/New Paradigm perspective that has found particular popularity of late, what is commonly referred to as "integral" thought, highlights this result. The language might seem to suggest conclusions similar to what we see with Cultural Maturity, but while we find people who identify with such perspective often sincerely attempting to address the future, such thinking most often has its roots in a spiritual form of philosophical idealism. At best the result is ideas with a strong left-hand bias. At worst we find all too familiar New Age ideology, just dressed in fancier clothing. We also find that such views predictably attract specific kinds of people (in this case, people who have personality styles in which particular, more left-leaning sensibilities prevail).

Later in this chapter, we will examine the general notion that ideological views tend to attract people with specific personality styles (and Appendix D examines this recognition in depth). At this point, the important recognition is that the greater portion of Transformational/New Paradigm thinking—including that of the "integral" sort—miss the mark not just because it may not be wholly "balanced," but also because, in making the native sensibilities of certain temperaments more enlightened, it is ultimately self-serving in the "chosen people," ideological sense. With regard to the future, we do not benefit from further "chosen people" worldviews, even if they are advocated with the best of intentions.

(In my earliest writings, I sometimes used the word "integral" to refer to systemic understanding that bridges polarities. I've since stopped using the term—replacing it with terms like "integrative" and "systemic" to

A Threshold Lesson: The concept of Cultural Maturity directly challenges more familiar ways of thinking about the future. Understanding just how it does takes us a long way toward the needed sophistication of perspective.

Polar Traps

The recognition that culturally mature perspective "bridges" the polar assumptions of times past points us toward a more basic—simple, yet powerful—comparison tool. Ideas that don't successfully bridge—and there are lots of ways this can happen—necessarily stop short of the needed maturity of perspective. Recognizing ways in which this can happen helps us identify traps in our thinking. It also helps us more fully appreciate where bridging takes us and develop approaches that support getting there.

We can apply this kind of recognition to the scenarios I've just described. Each in its more simplistic manifestations reduces to polar argument. We've Arrived and We've Gone Astray views form the polarity that gives us the Dilemma of Trajectory—all is well juxtaposed with destruction and collapse. The more extreme of Postindustrial/Information Age and Transformational/New Paradigm interpretations reduce to opposing right-hand and left-hand ideologies.

Postmodern/Constructivist conclusions, in their common inability to get beyond critique, can be, in their own odd way, the most intractably polar. They often reflect what I referred to in an earlier footnote as cross-polar dynamics—the pole they consciously ally with and the pole they most embody may not be the same. A good place to see this easily confusing circumstance is in the way Postmodern/Constructivist thinkers can simultaneously identify with the impossibility of knowing for sure and assume a stance that produces a particularly intractable sort of dogmatism.

Creative Systems Theory provides a framework for making highly detailed polar trap distinctions. We can think of the Creative Function's picture of interplaying polar juxtapositions as not just a map of complexity, but also as a map of the various ways we protect ourselves from complexity's demands—a recognition we will return to shortly.

---

avoid confusion with this fundamentally different kind of worldview.)

For now, we can apply a simpler polar trap approach. It is based on the observation that there are three basic ways in which polarized belief, whatever the pertinent either/ors, can get in the way of culturally mature understanding. It gives us a compact and highly useful compare-and-contrast language.

Creative Systems Theory calls these three ways in which our thinking can stop short *Separation Fallacies*, *Unity Fallacies*, and *Compromise Fallacies*.[17] The earlier doorway image helps clarify how each of these three basic ways of thinking misses the mark and also how they relate one to the other (see Figure 9-1).

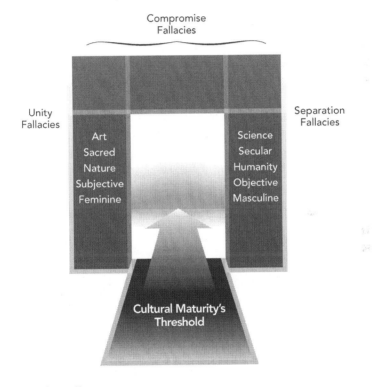

Fig. 9-1. Polar Fallacies

---

17   My 1991 book, *Necessary Wisdom*, uses this most basic sort of fallacy framework to help tease apart common traps in how we think about broad spheres of human activity such as love, leadership, morality, medicine, science, religion, and global relations.

Separation Fallacies fall off the right side of Cultural Maturity's threshold. They identify with the archetypally masculine. In doing so they equate truth with difference—with perceived fundamental distinctions such as between men and women, the material and the spiritual, the intellect and the emotions. They also give greatest value to the more creatively manifest side of the pertinent polarity (here men, the material, and the intellect). Some common Separation Fallacies: We are each wholly unique, individual. Experts have the answers. Final truth is what can be rationally articulated and objectively demonstrated. Man is wholly separate from nature and has rightful dominion over it. Change is a simple product of cause and effect.

Here we've seen Separations Fallacies suggested with positivist and behaviorist views, and also with ideas that reduce to a narrow science. We've also encounter Separation Fallacies with technological gospel beliefs that make invention the assumed answer to future problems and with extreme materialist economic models that idealize unfettered free markets.

Unity Fallacies fall off the left side of Cultural Maturity's threshold. They identify with the archetypally feminine. Related Unity Fallacies might include: In the end, we are all one (differences are ultimately irrelevant). The ordinary person knows best (better than leaders and institutions). Final truth is what we know from within. The task is to always to live in accord with nature. Everything happens for a reason, even if that reason remains mysterious (it is all connected). Unity Fallacies argue against distinction and emphasize oneness. They may claim a transcendence of polarity, but in fact they very specifically take sides. They give their allegiance to the softer, more creatively germinal hand of creation—to the spiritual over the material, feelings over facts, the timeless over the specific.

Here we've seen Unity Fallacies suggested with romantic, liberal/humanist, philosophically idealist, extreme environmentalist, and New Age views. Any of the results that come with what I have called the "feminine mistake" reflect Unity Fallacy conclusions.

Compromise Fallacies split the difference. A few related Compromise Fallacies are: We are all different in our own ways ("different strokes for different folks"). Good decisions come from everybody having an equal say. There are lots of kinds of truth, and each has its merits. Nature can be different things to different people. In the end, life is what we make of it. Some Compromise Fallacies advocate a safe, additive middle ground. Others argue correctly for multiple options, but give us nothing to help us beyond this accurate but meager observation—they claim to address diversity but fail to address what makes differences different. Compromise Fallacies take us beyond black and white, but in the end only replace it with shades of gray.

Here we've seen Compromise Fallacies manifest most explicitly with Postmodern/Constructivist interpretations. But we also see them any time a person takes a polarity—content and process, masculine and feminine, or mind and body—and observes simply that both sides are true without also articulating just how they might both be true, and at least a bit about where that result takes us.

Polar fallacies of any of these three types represent shorthand concepts. For starters, no one type of fallacy is as distinct from the others as the labels might suggest. Look closely and you'll see, for example, that Unity Fallacies commonly carry a hidden Separation Fallacy, and that Separation Fallacies similarly often carry a hidden Unity Fallacy. A person who sees his own group as chosen and a conflicting group as evil succumbs to a Unity Fallacy with regard to his compatriots and a Separation Fallacy in relation to his adversaries.

In addition, there are in fact many versions of each type of fallacy. Some are common with certain personality styles and specific views of the future, some with others. We can talk, for example, of multiple, very different kinds of Unity Fallacies. We find an intellectual sort of Unity Fallacy in academic and liberal thought that sides with the underprivileged and polarizes against conservatives and corporations. We find a more ardent sort of Unity Fallacy with fundamentalist religious beliefs that ally with "family values" and polarize against moral relativism and intellectual elites. And we often see a more specifically spiritual sort of Unity Fallacy with advocates of New Age or back-to-the-land philosophies. In this chapter's next section, I will describe how we can draw on more detailed "multiplicity" pattern language concepts to tease apart just what is different about particular versions of the three basic types of polar fallacy and why different versions manifest in the specific ways that they do.

We encounter another kind of added complexity in the way certain kinds of thinking, depending on who is doing the thinking, can be used to argue for any one of these basic kinds of fallacies. I've described how systems thinking can be used equally well to justify right-hand and left-hand conclusions. If we make systems thinking only about recognizing the fact that numerous apples-and-oranges variables commonly come into play, it just as readily becomes an argument for Compromise Fallacy. Chaos theory, and with it the sciences of complexity more generally, because it introduces uncertainty into an essentially mechanistic picture of reality, can similarly be used to support each of these ultimately unhelpful results. Chaos theory can be used to argue for a narrow scientism (to support the conclusion that even the most indeterminate of processes can be understood in ultimately right-hand terms), for spiritual conclusions (to argue for a universe in which what can't be known is part of everything), and for a postmodern kind of Compromise Fallacy (to support the claim that nothing can be known for sure). For the same reason—that introduction of ultimate uncertainty into understanding's equation—the postmodern thesis itself can be used to argue for each kind of conclusion depending on its advocate. Various postmodern theorists lean decidedly to the right in their conclusions (libertarian thought has strong postmodern aspects), others to the left (academic postmodernists can be almost Marxist in their sentiments), and others can just as dogmatically assume that the task with everything is to split the difference.

The box-of-crayons image helps clarify what is going on with polar fallacies and just why even the most innocent-seeming versions leave us fundamentally short. The situation with Unity Fallacies and Separation Fallacies is straightforward. Either a more left-hand or a more right-hand "crayon" is calling the shots. Compromise Fallacies can at first be a bit trickier to make sense of, but the mechanism is again ultimately straightforward. With Compromise Fallacies, opposite parts communicate directly with one another and collude. As with Unity and Separation Fallacies, the box—Integrative Meta-perspective—is absent. Rather than the new vibrancy of hues that comes with Cultural Maturity, we find only shades of gray.[18]

Polar fallacies of any sort tend to reflect general tendencies. While sometimes what we encounter with a polar fallacy is a consequence

---

18   See " 'Cognitive Rewiring' " later in this chapter for more filled-out descriptions of underlying cognitive mechanisms.

only of momentary misunderstanding, more often what we see is a product of underlying psychological/cognitive pattern. If we are vulnerable to polar traps, we will tend to fall for the same general sort of trap whatever the question we consider. Recognizing polar traps most obviously helps us better discern when culturally mature perspective is lacking. But by alerting us to what more is required if our thinking is to have the needed systemic sophistication, it also helps us better appreciate where Cultural Maturity's threshold is to be found, and to perhaps get a toe over it.[19]

A Threshold Lesson: We can learn a lot about ourselves by identifying polar traps—and even just polar leanings—to which we might be vulnerable. We can also learn a lot by looking not just at ourselves, but also at related tendencies in groups we may identify with.[20]

---

19   In the Introduction, I noted how writing this book required that I deal with the conundrum that culturally mature capacities are required to fully understand culturally mature capacities. People of multiple persuasions could read (at least superficially) what I have written with regard to each of the three threshold tasks and believe that they agree with all that I have said. In various footnotes, I've observed how this could be so, often giving special emphasis to misunderstandings we might find with someone of liberal/humanist inclination. (I've described, how liberal/humanist thought is a place where we are especially likely to find confusion with culturally mature perspective). This section's look at polar fallacies helps bring these observations together. In each case, I was describing a particular sort of Unity Fallacy.

With the first threshold task, I warned of confusing getting beyond us-versus-them assumptions on the world stage with "siding with peace." With the second threshold task, I noted the kind of traps environmentalists can get into if they think of sustainability only in simplistic "small is beautiful" terms. With the third threshold task, I emphasized the critical difference between thinking of purpose and identity in terms of getting at some essence or core of truth and drawing on culturally mature truth's more dynamic and complete kind of referent.

20   Language can be a giveaway. For example, postmodern academic terminology like "essentialist" and "construct" should at least alert us to the possibility that a group may identify with Compromise Fallacies. When

One "Crayon" and Another

When it comes to the compare-and-contrast task, the recognition that culturally mature perspective is systemic in the whole-box-of-crayons sense does more than just help us tease apart the underlying mechanism of our various kinds of polar traps. The box-of-crayons image points toward more differentiated wheat-from-chaff distinctions. We appropriately ask about whether a particular "crayon" in complexity's larger multiplicity, either overtly or covertly, ends up with the last word.

This kind of systemic multiplicity distinction applies in a general way when considering any kind of diversity. We know that a group made up only of men or only of women, or only of people of one age or one ethnic/cultural background, is going to be vulnerable to certain partialities, if not outright fallacies. Similarly, any inquiry that extends beyond the most specialized focus is going to lack needed depth and complexity if it does not include voices from diverse disciplines.

I've found personality style diversity particularly useful for making one-crayon-from-another wheat-from-chaff distinctions. In Chapter Six, I introduced the recognition of how strikingly different we can be from one another other by virtue of temperament and remarked on how boggling it might seem that until very recently we rarely paid much attention to such difference. I also offered an explanation for this past lack of awareness. Deep appreciation for temperament differences requires Integrative Meta-perspective.[21] The converse is also true. A

---

words like "consciousness" or "transformation" are used with any great frequency, Unity Fallacies most likely lurk. And too great an emphasis on a notion being "scientific" should raise flags that the conclusion being proposed may more accurately reflect a Separation Fallacy—the more ideological sort of belief I've called scientism (though in some cases such emphasis may reflect the opposite—Unity Fallacy conclusions using pseudoscience as justification).

21   Any subtlety of differentiation has come only in the last fifty years. Previously we tended either not to recognize difference—to think only in terms of normality (us) and subtle variations from normality—or to polarize in the face of difference—to make difference about health versus pathology. Recognizing such differences with any sophistication can happen only with at least a beginning capacity for whole-box-of-crayons "pattern" discrimination.

deep appreciation for temperament difference provides a valuable tool for appreciating when culturally mature perspective is present and, if it is lacking, just why.

If we combine a general understanding of temperament differences with an appreciation for the trouble we can get ourselves into when we give one temperament in the systemic box final-truth status, the result is a subtle and powerful basis for making wheat-from-chaff distinctions. And attention to temperament difference can support not just a better appreciation of where ideas stop short, but also a deeper understanding of Cultural Maturity itself—indeed, the direct experience of it. It can serve as a "hands-on" approach for realizing culturally mature perspective.

A brief story illustrates these two layers of significance and how they relate. During the Institute for Creative Development's bricks-and-mortar years, I offered an annual yearlong training program designed to teach leaders (in the broadest sense) the skills and capacities needed for culturally mature leadership. I carefully selected participants according to two criteria. The first criterion was whether a person was up to the task. For many people, the magnitude of the questions we might address in combination with the challenge presented by culturally mature perspective to familiar ideologies would be too much to handle. Beyond that, I selected for maximum diversity.

In part, I was interested in diversity as we commonly think of it: diversity of gender, ethnicity, class, and area of expertise. But more deeply, I was interested in the diversity of temperament—personality style. I knew that if we were going to engage questions that required whole-box-of-crayons perspective, we would greatly benefit from having all of the "crayons" directly represented in the room. Having this completeness of temperament diversity present meant that just our being together supported the systemic stretch that culturally mature perspective requires.

On first walking into the room, participants would often be startled at how many of those present were people with whom they would normally not have had contact—at least close contact. At the same time, because each person in the room was someone capable of the level of engagement and inquiry our task together called for, it was not really possible for anyone to dismiss anyone else, even a person toward whom one might feel knee-jerk antipathy in another context.

Having that diversity—and that particular sort of diversity—present provided a ready mirror for identifying traps and fallacies. The limitations inherent in any single-temperament perspective became quickly apparent. And participants gradually began to appreciate how certain kinds of ideological beliefs tended to accompany particular temperament. People learned to identify common temperament-related traps. They also came to appreciate what each person needed to do to get beyond the traps to which he or she was natively most vulnerable.

Having that completeness of temperament diversity in the room also directly supported the broader development of culturally mature perspective. Working together produced appreciation and respect for the aspects of creative complexity—the particular crayons in the box—that each person represented. It also supported everyone present beginning to better recognize and more consciously hold the whole box. This translated into greater effectiveness when dealing with particular issues. It also translated into greater ability to understand and apply Cultural Maturity's changes more generally.

Almost any temperament framework can help with appreciating systemic multiplicity in this sense. For example, many people find the Myers-Briggs personality typology, commonly used in business and educational settings, insightful. But it helps greatly if the framework we apply expressly reflects Integrative Meta-perspective.[22] And it helps even more if we have a framework whose "pattern language" structure is specifically designed for the task. The Creative Systems Personality Typology (CSPT), because it has its foundation in the creative underpinnings of human complexity, succeeds on both counts.

The CSPT is a highly detailed framework. Appendix D presents an extended examination of both its particulars and its implications.[23] But a quick look here helps illustrate the power of

---

22   I think, for example, of the value of having an appreciation for the fact of multiple intelligences as an integral part of the temperament framework. Different intelligences come into play differently with various temperaments. A colleague refers to the more general need to address "deep diversity."

23   And those interested in learning more about the Creative Systems Personality Typology can visit the CSPT website (CSPTHome.org). My

temperament as a compare-and-contrast approach. It also further supports the particular usefulness of a creative lens. The CSPT addresses the different ways each of us holds the "crayons" of creative complexity. (I could say that the typology indicates which crayon each of us represents, but as you will see, things aren't that simple). It provides a concise language for making critique that might otherwise take pages of commentary.

I've described how culturally mature multiplicity patterning distinctions are of two sorts—those that pertain to temporal relativity and those that describe systemic differences of a more here-and-now sort. The CSPT makes discernments of the latter type—what Creative Systems Theory calls Patterning in Space (see Figure 9-2). It proposes that temperament differences reflect the way each individual preferentially embodies different parts of formative process' mechanism. Just as we can speak of "inspiration," "perspiration," and "finishing and polishing" creative stages, we can talk of people who derive their gifts (and their blindnesses) from their specific connection with these very different creative realities.[24]

---

short book, *The Power of Diversity: An Introduction to the Creative Systems Personality Typology*, also provides more detailed description.

24   In an earlier footnote, I described how Creative Systems Theory is unique in observing a creative relationship between temporal and here-and-now contextual variables. Appreciating this relationship makes it possible to recognize all manner of interconnections and causal patterns that otherwise would be impossible to see. Appendix D's more detailed look at the Creative Systems Personality Typology provides examples that highlight the power of this recognition.

If we are to avoid confusion in applying these observations, we need to be clear that while the distinctions that define the CSPT apply the same creative language as Patterning in Time discernments, Patterning in Time and Patterning in Space represent different kinds of concepts. A common beginner's mistake is to assume that "later" personality styles are somehow more evolved than "earlier" ones. If we appreciate how development and temperament reflect different concerns, we don't fall for this kind of trap. Each of us in the course of personal development (and within any endeavor we undertake) goes through the same sequence of organizing realities. At once, each of us, whatever our developmental stage, has special affinity for certain creative realities.

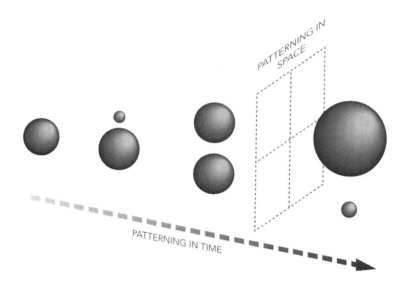

Fig. 9-2. Patterning in Time and Space

We can use temperament differences understood in this way both to better understand each temperament's particular contributions and to predict, and more accurately interpret, conceptual traps. No temperament has a leg up when it come to Cultural Maturity. Each major temperament group is equally capable of culturally mature perspective. But each temperament group also has specific kinds of naïve thinking—and outright fallacies—to which it is especially vulnerable. Here is the briefest of glimpses at how the CSPT slices the temperament pie with the addition of formal Creative Systems Theory language:

The first big slice includes the various Early-Axis temperament types, people who live preferentially in more "inspiration stage" realities. "Earlies" tend to be most drawn to experience that involves imagination and possibility. They often contribute as artists, as innovators in the sciences, in work with young children, or as leaders in the "information revolution." Think Albert Einstein, Georgia O'Keeffe, or Steve Jobs.

The second big slice (Middle-Axis temperaments) is made up of people who derive their worldview from more "perspiration stage" preferences. "Middles" are most in their element with activities that involve commitment and heart. They often contribute as teachers, as managers in business, as ministers, in athletics, in the military, or in government. Think George Washington, Mother Teresa, or Colin Powell.

The third big slice (Late-Axis temperaments) is made up of people who most engage life with "finishing and polishing" sensibilities. "Lates," more than other temperaments, tend to value worldliness, intellect, style, and material success. They often contribute as entrepreneurs and business executives, in academia, as political leaders, as artists of more classical sensibility, and in entertainment and the media. Think John Kennedy, Elizabeth Taylor, or Walter Cronkite.

The CSPT also differentiates polar "aspects" within each broad temperament group. It describes how some people manifest more "upper-pole" and others more "lower-pole" sensibilities. Upper-pole types tend to live more "in their heads," and when it comes to imagination, to manifest its more visionary and spiritual aspects. Lower-pole types live more in their feelings and in their bodies. The CSPT also makes more horizontal polar distinctions. It speaks of some people being more "inner" (more receptive and reflective), and others being more "outer" (more expressive and action-oriented).[25] These aspects differentiate each broad temperament group into four basic subgroups (see the diagram in Figure 9-3).[26]

---

25 "Inner" and "outer" refer roughly to the kinds of distinctions suggested by the common terms "introvert" and "extrovert," but the CSPT provides a more nuanced picture. It addresses what creates these differing tendencies and also describes how they manifest in different ways with different temperaments. (See the "More Patterning in Time—Particularly Intriguing Expressions" section of Chapter Ten, and Appendix D.)

26 Chapter Ten's examination of the creative evolution of the bodily experience clarifies how this upper/lower, inner/outer language is more than just metaphorical. It reflects different ways of living in our bodies. (See "The Evolution of the Body" in the "More Patterning in Time—Particularly Intriguing Expressions" section of Chapter Ten.)

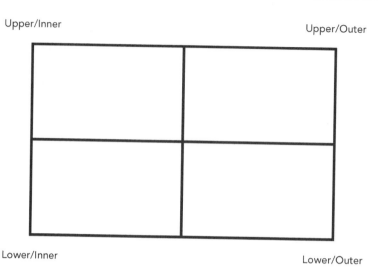

Upper/Inner   Upper/Outer

Lower/Inner   Lower/Outer

Fig. 9-3. Polar Aspects

Besides providing a detailed framework for appreciating differences, the CSPT also gives us a nuanced language for teasing apart conceptual traps. Earlier, I promised to draw on creative patterning notions to add further detail to our understanding of polar fallacies. I then identified a variety of different kinds of Unity Fallacies—those we are more likely to find with the ideas of liberal intellectuals, those common with fundamentalist religious thought, and those we more frequently see with back-to-the-land or New Age advocates. These various types of Unity Fallacies have their origins respectively in more "finishing and polishing stage" (Late-Axis), "perspiration stage" (Middle-Axis), and "inspiration stage" (Early-Axis) sensibilities and are predictably most found with temperaments that live largely in the analogous slices of experience.

We could tease apart a parallel sequence of temperament-related Separation Fallacies and Compromise Fallacies. And we could go further and identify more "upper," "lower," "inner," and "outer" manifestations of each kind of fallacy. For example, the highly materialist Late/Upper/Outer Separation Fallacies that we might find with a corporate CEO are very different from the more fanciful, Early/Upper/Outer Separation Fallacies we might encounter with a person who delights in technological-gospel imagery of the more sci-fi sort.

We can also use personality style to help tease apart traps that link to more temporal multiplicity variables. In an earlier footnote, I observed that romantic idealization can make reference to any cultural stage. People who romantically idealize earlier cultural stages do so in predictable ways. The recognition that temperament is tied to the aspects of formative process we most live in and identify with points toward why this might be so and provides us with a further compare-and-contrast tool. People with more "inspiration stage" (Early-Axis) temperaments are most likely to idealize "inspiration stage" times in culture, people with more "perspiration stage" (Middle-Axis) temperaments tend to be drawn to "perspiration stage" times in culture, and people with more "finishing and polishing stage" (Late-Axis) temperaments more commonly feel affinity with "finishing and polishing stage" times.

In first introducing Creative Systems Theory Patterning in Space notions in Chapter Six, I described how they can help us not just better understand temperament, but also here-and-now diversity of belief and activity of almost any sort. We can use them, for example, to map out differences in political or philosophical ideology, the various parts of a business organization—administration, manufacturing, marketing, etc.—and how they function together, or the systemic relationships of various cultural domains such as education, government, science, and religion.

We can bring the CSPT together with such more general here-and-now diversity observations in ways that provide insight into just why such diversity manifests as it does. We find that certain temperaments are most drawn to different kinds of beliefs and spheres of activity. This recognition can help us better understand the particular contributions—and particular blindnesses—that can come with different kinds of ideas and the activities of parts of larger systems.

This kind of recognition points toward some fascinating compare-and-contrast tools. For example, a close look reveals that the contrasting beliefs of differing schools of thought in any field tend to mirror the personality style biases of its originator. As illustration, in my field of psychology/psychiatry, B.F. Skinner was a Late/Upper/Inner, Sigmund Freud a Middle/Upper/Inner, and Carl Jung an Early/Upper/Inner. These men's contributions to modern psychology each directly reflect what we would expect from their temperaments' systemic proclivities.

And the people most attracted to each contributor's work tend to reflect these same general proclivities.

An appreciation of temperament differences gains special significance with the growing need for culturally mature leadership. To lead effectively, we need to understand not just our own specific "crayon" and the blindnesses it can produce, but also our particular temperament's significance in diversity as a whole. Especially when collaboration is required, sensitivity to other people's specific gifts and vulnerabilities becomes similarly essential. We need a solid sense of how we can use crayons together and how we can best draw on such interrelationship when confronting different sorts of creative challenges.

My brief story about convening groups for workshops illustrates how understanding temperament diversity can also directly support the realization of culturally mature perspective. If personality style differences reflect the parts of creative complexity that different people preferentially inhabit as the CSPT proposes, then a deep appreciation for temperament diversity and the ability to be newly conscious and responsible in the whole of our creative natures—the ability that Creative Systems Theory proposes ultimately defines Cultural Maturity—become closely related capacities. Having temperament diversity in a room substantially increases the likelihood that decision-making will be of a culturally mature sort. It also works directly to catalyze broader culturally mature understanding.

Some of the most intriguing implications of the link between temperament and systemic complexity concern new ways in which diversity is adding to our lives. In my therapeutic work with couples, I've been increasingly fascinated, for example, with how often today people choose partners with temperaments very different from their own. Fifty years ago this was rarely the case. Back then, when we said "opposites attract," this almost always meant opposite in the sense of different polar tendencies within the same basic temperament group. In our time, it is increasingly common for people to feel attracted to potential partners from different temperament groups than their own. Such cross-type attraction is most common when individuals are beginning to live their lives as a whole in culturally mature ways.

The concept of Cultural Maturity predicts this change. If love's attraction comes ultimately from our ability to make each other's lives more, and "more" today increasingly means the ability to hold the whole of systemic complexity, then we would expect differences that before might have produced only confusion and conflict to become, today, newly attractive. Adding temperament diversity to love's equation doesn't at all make love easier. Whole-Person love by itself is demanding enough, and the Whole-Person task becomes particularly daunting when the other person lives not just in his or her own particular uniqueness, but in a territory of experience that even with the best of efforts we can never understand as directly as our own. But in a whole new, particularly timely and significant sense, we become constant "teachers" to each other.

In today's world, a sophisticated understanding of temperament— both the gifts and limits that come with particular ways of being in the world—becomes increasingly essential. And it does so with almost every kind of creative challenge we face, from the newly systemic demands of the contemporary workplace, to what is needed for healthy and fulfilling love, to the broader tasks of collective decision-making.[27]

---

27 In Chapter Six, I made reference to how we can make a first crude cut through political difference by characterizing the ideological beliefs of the Right as, on average, more archetypally masculine and those of the Left as, on average, more archetypally feminine. I noted then that temperament provides a more nuanced lens for recognizing such pattern and promised to return for a closer look. A quickest of overviews: People of Early-Axis temperament (where the archetypally feminine is strongest) will almost always lean to the political left in their allegiances (though they may also choose to not be political). Late/Outers and Middle/Upper/Outers (the temperaments where the archetypally masculine manifests most strongly) are most likely to identify with the political right. Late/Inners (those with the most archetypally feminine in that axis) will tend more to the political left. The other Middle-Axis temperaments present a particularly interesting situation—one that helps illumine some of the nuance in how creative relationships work. The greater number of Middles are conservatives, in spite of the fact that we might expect Middles, from this analysis, to split about evenly. The reason sheds light on the curious fact that we often see the less economically advantaged of conservatives making political choices that might not seem in their self-interest: Middle/Lowers tend to ally with the stability and felt sense of control that comes with the Middle/Uppers' worldview (like a football player might with the words of his coach, a congregant might with the

Appendix D presents a more detailed look at the Creative Systems Personality typology that provides a more visceral feel for these significant differences in how we embody our humanness. It also focuses a finer lens on the particular gifts that people of different temperament bring to the tasks of Cultural Maturity, and also the specific traps to which they are most vulnerable.

Capacitance

For these reflections on temperament to be ultimately useful, we need a Creative Systems Theory patterning concept that I briefly introduced earlier, what the theory calls *Capacitance*. The temperament story I just used to highlight how personality style diversity can be applied as a hands-on tool for developing culturally mature perspective suggested the importance of considering Capacitance. I mentioned that I selected participants for training programs according to two criteria. Temperament diversity was one. But before that was whether a person was "up to the task"—that is, whether the activities we were engaged in together might be too much for a particular would-be participant. Capacitance is a "crux," Whole-System patterning concept.

"Up to the task" might seem like a terribly general criterion, but framed in the language of Capacitance, it becomes highly specific and a measure that we can't ignore. Capacitance implies a level of awareness. But more than that, it refers to a person's overall capacity to take in, tolerate, and engage life. Earlier I used the metaphor of a balloon. Capacitance describes the size of the balloon, the "volume" of life a system can handle before things become too much. The concept could not be more important—for its practical usefulness, for its theoretical implications, and also for what it contributes to needed compare-and-contrast distinctions.

It helps to understand Capacitance in relationship to the first Whole-System Patterning Concept I introduced, what Creative Systems Theory calls the Question of Referent (or simply "aliveness," if

---

beliefs of her minister, or a soldier might with the assertions of his commander), even though more left-leaning views that more expressly advocate support for those who are less "on top" in life might seem more appropriate. Appendix D's observations help fill out these brief references.

our interest lies less with the question than with where we look to find its answer). Capacitance is more specifically quantitative. It concerns how *much* truth—how much "aliveness"—we can handle.[28]

The concept of Capacitance is not about particular capacities—even general ones such as intelligence. Rather it is about what we are systemically capable of.[29] In first introducing Cultural Maturity's cognitive reorganization, I observed that it requires not just stage-specific changes but also, as with any new cultural chapter, a more general increase in capacity. "Capacity" as I then used the word referred to Capacitance, to overall systemic capacity.[30]

It is rare in my work as a therapist that I don't at some point talk with clients about Capacitance and the importance of effectively managing it. As traditional cultural guideposts less and less define the structures of our daily lives, attention to Capacitance—both how much we have available and the Capacitance demands our lives make of us—becomes key to crafting our lives in ultimately healthy ways. The importance of a concept like Capacitance comes into particularly high relief with the recognition of how, with today's ever more rush-rush existence, living over one's Capacitance has for many people become not just the norm, but a dangerous addiction. We can add the fact that today we often accept doing so as normal to my list of Transitional Absurdities. Attention to Capacitance gives us the feedback we need to live our personal lives in healthy and sustainable ways.[31]

---

28   In the 1992 film *A Few Good Men*, Tom Cruise's character is asked, "You want answers?" In response to his reply, "I want the truth," he gets the now famous line, "You can't handle the truth." Capacitance describes truth in this "how much you can handle" sense.

29   Like other "crux" truth concepts, Capacitance is specifically a bridging, whole-box-of-crayons, maturely systemic notion.

30   See the Creative Systems Theory website (www.CSTHome.org) for a more thorough examination of the concept of Capacitance.

31   For some people I work with in therapy, learning to live consciously within their Capacitance becomes the work's most defining theme. I advocate for what I call the "80 percent rule"—approaching one's day with a 20 percent buffer. Eighty percent might seem like a conservative starting point. But there are always surprises. And going over 100 percent of

Just as much, the concept of Capacitance today provides essential insight when we are making societal-level decisions. As ideological beliefs and traditional institutional structures begin to break down, effective social policy hinges on our ability to understand what is possible and what is not. Capacitance is often what most determines possibility. Crafting approaches that are most likely to be helpful requires a keen sensitivity to Capacitance limits and to differences that may exist in the Capacitance available to different systems.

The concept of Capacitance helps us more conceptually in multiple ways. In Chapter Six we examined the bare-boned truth task of addressing moral questions without traditional guideposts. Drawing then on our first kind of "crux" discernment, I proposed that moral choices are those that are most "life-affirming." If we combine the concepts of aliveness and Capacitance we get a more precise way to think about moral decision-making: Acts that support and promote systemic aliveness and the Capacitance needed to make it manifest are moral; acts that diminish systemic aliveness and the Capacitance needed to make it manifest become immoral. Of course, in real life, things aren't quite as simple as this statement implies—systems are always multiple and overlapping—but the general principle holds.[32]

Capacitance is never healthy. In the end, we need available Capacitance not just to avoid undue stress, but also so that we can live our daily lives in the most deep and fulfilling ways. A life lived over one's Capacitance quickly becomes reflexive and superficial. When we honor the 80 percent rule, we soon realize that most of life's great joys happen within that 20 percent buffer. We can only have fresh experience if we have Capacitance to spare. Henry David Thoreau observed that we should leave "wider margins for life."

32   Creative Systems Theory uses the term "violence" in a related way. Violent acts are those that result in actual damage to a system's Capacitance (more than just momentary disruption). Violence in this most basic sense can take both archetypally masculine and archetypally feminine forms. Archetypally masculine violence damages Capacitance through direct insult. It may take the form of physical assault, damaging words, or the explicit thwarting of possibility. Archetypally feminine violence does its damage more covertly. It may take the form of undermining, passive aggression, emotional entanglement, or seductiveness. Either kind of violence can prove the more damaging depending on the context.

The concept of Capacitance also assists us conceptually by providing a further way to understand how the Dilemma of Trajectory need not represent the end of the road. Capacitance is the one thing that increases in a consistent way over the entire course of formative process. (In the Creative Function, Capacitance is represented by the volume within the circles.) This steady increase occurs irrespective of the leaps that mark transitions between creative stages.[33] Critical to looking forward culturally, it also continues with Cultural Maturity's more integrative kind of trajectory. Another way of thinking about the Dilemma of Trajectory is that our old "onward-and-upward" definition of progress has lost its connection with Capacitance. Cultural Maturity's new trajectory, by making possible a continued increase in Capacitance, quite specifically carries on progress's tradition. The task we face in rethinking progress involves finding ways of thinking about growth that successfully reflect what, in our time, makes us personally and collectively "more"—what, in fact, produces actual and necessary growth in Capacitance. If we frame progress in terms of Capacitance, we are no longer limited when looking to the future to images of heroic achievement or collapse.

My assertion at the beginning of this section that we need the concept of Capacitance if personality style distinctions are to prove ultimately helpful highlights Capacitance's importance as a compare-and-contrast tool. Capacitance has compare-and-contrast implications in the sense that it is what ultimately defines what anyone is capable of. And it has more specific compare-and-contrast implications when it comes to understanding temperament. Temperament distinctions can be highly misleading unless they are accompanied by Capacitance-related observations. A person who has the requisite sensibility for a certain kind of contribution may nonetheless lack the Capacitance needed to effectively carry out that contribution's tasks or to function effectively in the relationships it requires.[34]

---

33   We can think of development as proceeding in a similar way to how the growth of a snake involves it periodically shedding its skin. The snake's skin represents stage-specific beliefs and developmental tasks. The snake's expanding girth represents growing Capacitance.

34   Appendix D examines Capacitance-related personality style differences.

We find Capacitance's most ultimately significant compare-and-contrast contribution in the recognition that Cultural Maturity is directly tied to Capacitance. This is no more the case with Cultural Maturity than with any other developmentally related cultural change-point. But being conscious of Capacitance's role—something we become capable of only with Cultural Maturity—provides important perspective if we are to successfully support culturally mature change.

The implications include both "bad news" and a very important kind of "good news." On the bad news side, we have to accept that without sufficient Capacitance, culturally mature perspective is simply not possible. Cultural Maturity's changes require that we be able to engage a certain magnitude, or "volume," of experience. If there is not adequate Capacitance, Cultural Maturity's challenge can only overwhelm. But the reverse is also the case when it comes to Capacitance and Cultural Maturity: At a certain Capacitance, Cultural Maturity's conclusions become almost self-evident, a recognition with critical implications for culturally mature advocacy. We find that we often don't have to advocate for culturally mature changes separately. Specific interventions can help, but it can often be enough to simply support the needed growth in a system's Capacitance.

I should briefly include a Capacitance-related notion that is important to understanding the behavior of systems. Creative Systems Theory describes how systems pushed beyond their available Capacitance respond protectively, and do so in characteristic ways. For example, the system may become reactive, anxious and withdrawn, undermining, or combative. Creative Systems Theory calls these responses *Creative Symptoms*.

The general concept of Creative Symptoms is pertinent to systems of every sort, but it is most developed for the psychological sphere. Creative Systems Theory describes how we can understand the greater portion of patterns that psychologists have historically described using the language of psychopathology as protective mechanisms utilized by people of different personality styles when they confront circumstances that require more Capacitance than they have available.[35]

---

35   See Appendix C and the Creative Systems Theory website (www. CSTHome.org).

A critical example of how the concept of Creative Symptoms comes into play at a cultural scale brings attention to a unique danger we face as we look to the future. One way that systems that are challenged to more than their available Capacitance protect themselves is by polarizing. Polarizing helps keep the challenge to Capacitance at a safe arm's length. In times past, when this happened at a major social-system level, while it diminished effectiveness, it really didn't change things that much. It only increased polarization that was already part of consensus reality. The result might be a war. But it was likely a familiar kind of war.

Today, as polarization directly undermines the needed maturity of perspective, this sort of response becomes newly problematic. One of the great dangers we face in our time is that today's array of newly God-like challenges—along with the more encompassing task of Cultural Maturity—will stretch Capacitance beyond what we can tolerate. The resulting polarization and projection could distance us from the needed maturity of perspective just as such maturity has become imperative.

A Threshold Lesson: Being attentive to and carefully managing personal Capacitance is essential to wise leadership in our individual lives. It is also essential to contributing in culturally mature ways. Effective in-the-world leadership requires sensitivity to the Capacitances of both the systems in which we lead, and systems with which we may interact.

"Parts Work"

A kind of hands-on approach that I draw on extensively in my work offers a way to get beyond only thinking conceptually about what culturally mature outcomes might look like and step directly into Cultural Maturity's world of experience. In doing so, it provides a further valuable compare-and-contrast tool. I call the general methodology simply "Parts Work." Related methods are used in several schools of psychological practice,[36] but Creative Systems Theory adds specific

---

36 Most notably the Gestalt Therapy of Fritz Perls and Roberto Assagioli's
    Psychosynthesis.

"rules" that make this kind of approach not just a handy psychological technique, but a sophisticated, culturally mature perspective–producing methodology.[37]

Parts Work places the different crayons in the relevant systemic box physically in the room and challenges the individual or group one is working with to establish a culturally mature relationship with them. I apply various forms of this approach in working with individuals in therapy, when training leaders, and in think tank environments when engaging groups wishing to take on cultural issues in culturally mature ways.

The example that follows comes from individual therapy done with a respected biologist and environmentalist. It starts with work at a personal level, but then transitions to address perspective needed more broadly for effective culturally mature leadership:

> Bill's father had died. The immediate reason Bill had come to me was the depression that the loss had evoked. But with time, along with addressing grief, he recognized a further concern—what he described as a war within himself.

> Bill's father had left him a beautiful piece of land that had been in the family for generations. Bill loved the place and planned to construct a cabin and move there when he retired. But new zoning regulations had made the land unbuildable. Suddenly, his plans were on hold. He felt deeply sad—and angry. The particular situation disturbed him, but even more disturbing to him ultimately was the way his response to it had left him torn from the comfortable moorings of a once-unquestioned set of beliefs. He was known for banging heads with property rights proponents and more often than not emerging victorious. Now disparate internal voices were advocating not just different social policies, but two very different—and contradictory—views of the world. Bill found distress and confusion in this conflict and asked if we could somehow explore it.

---

37   The chapter's next section examines these rules and how they have this result.

I agreed. But I recognized that such work would present some difficulties. Bill was an exceptionally intelligent man with well-thought-out beliefs that were not easily questioned. We would have to do more than just talk if I was to be of help.

I began by having Bill imagine that the warring parts were like two characters on a stage. I asked him to describe everything he could about each character—what it wore, its age, the expression on its face. Then I had him invite them into the room. The environmentalist sat stage left, sensitive features, longish hair. The property rights advocate stood more distant, stage right, stockier in build, baseball cap tucked between his crossed arms. After a bit, he too sat down.

I instructed Bill to turn to the two figures and describe the issue he wanted to address. After a bit of initial self-consciousness, Bill proceeded to talk with them about the land, the new regulations, the deep conflict he felt. Then I suggested that he go over to each chair and speak as that character—become it and give voice to what it felt about the questions at hand. I had him return to his own chair when each character had said its piece and from there to respond to the chair that had spoken and follow up with any further questions he might have. I instructed him to let himself be surprised by what each character might say.

This back and forth went through several iterations, first Bill speaking, then in turn, each of the parts. The character in the left chair spoke of the importance of protecting the environment in its natural state. The character on the right argued that government had no right to dictate what a person did with private property. Both expressed a longing to live in such a beautiful place. As the dialogue progressed, Bill's relationships with each of them deepened. He became increasingly able to find a place in himself where he could both respect what each character had to say and see limits to its helpfulness.

After some time, Bill again turned to me. He said he felt a bit disoriented, but that the conversation had helped. He commented that much of what the two characters said had indeed surprised him—and moved him. He found it particularly enlightening that each character seemed essentially well-intentioned. Before he had framed the environmental/property rights conflict as a battle between good and ignorance (if not worse). The work showed him that it was more accurately a battle between competing goods. Initially, it had been hard for him not to identify with the environmentalist, but, with time, he recognized that in fact each figure had important things to say.

The brief piece of work hadn't given Bill a final answer for how to approach the property issue. But it had given him a more solid place to stand for making needed decisions. He had begun to see a more full and creative picture.

Later I asked Bill what broader implications the exercise might have for his professional efforts. We decided to continue with the hands-on approach. I tossed him particularly thorny questions that pitted environmental concerns against property rights concerns. His task was to hold his Whole-Person chair, and from there to use his two "consultants" to help him determine the most effective and fair approach. The result in each case was a deeper understanding of the dilemmas involved and, in several instances, novel solutions.

This example is highly simplified. Such work most often involves more parts than just two,[38] and it may take several months of work before a person can sit solidly in the Whole-Person—whole-box-of-crayons, Integrative Meta-perspective—chair. But the example illustrates a general type of method that is both straightforward and highly effective.

---

38   Sometimes more parts are appropriate simply because the questions at hand involve more than two aspects. But it is also the case that people with different personality styles tend to work best with different degrees of differentiation. With some temperaments, having just a couple of characters in the room will prove most effective; with others, as many as seven, eight, or more.

As a therapist, I draw frequently on this kind of approach. I don't know of other techniques that apply all of intelligence's multiple aspects so simply and unobtrusively. I also don't know of other ways of working that so directly support culturally mature perspective. It does so not just through what is said, but through every aspect of the approach, even the layout of the room. Of particular importance, the fact that I as a therapist speak only to the Whole-Person chair (one of those rules) means that my relationship with the client directly models and affirms Whole-Person relationship. Through the work, culturally mature perspective and responsibility become directly acted out and embodied.

Ongoing work with this kind of approach alters not just how a person engages specific issues, but also how he or she engages reality more broadly. The work becomes like lifting weights to build the "muscles" of culturally mature capacity. One of the litmus tests for success with this kind of approach is the appearance of culturally mature shifts with regard to questions that have not been directly discussed.

This same general kind of approach can also be applied to working with more than one person. I often use related methods when assisting groups where contentious issues have become polarized, or with groups where people wish to address many-sided questions that require careful, in-depth inquiry. When working in this way, I place individuals or small subgroups around the room to represent the various systemic aspects of the question at hand (the various characters/crayons). Another subgroup, seated in a circle around the smaller groups, is assigned two tasks—first to engage these subgroups in conversation to clarify their positions, and then to articulate a larger systemic perspective and explain how that perspective could be translated into right and timely action.

These various Parts Work techniques might seem to represent a specifically psychological kind of methodology. But in potential, they have much broader application. Because of the particular ways they are structured and the Whole-Person relationship the facilitator maintains with the individual or group doing the work, such approaches could ultimately be used anywhere engendering culturally mature capacities is an appropriate objective. I think most immediately of educational settings. While today we are not at the place where people would be

comfortable utilizing these kinds of approaches in schools,[39] it could
be powerful to do so. Such methods would be most obviously a good
fit where the task was interdisciplinary learning. But in the end they
could be just as useful with education that focuses on particular kinds
of knowing, such as religious education or the education of scientists.

"Cognitive Rewiring"

An essential recognition about the kinds of conceptual traps I've described in this chapter helps clarify why techniques like Parts Work can
be as powerful as they are. The concern with such traps is more than just
misplaced thinking. First, they reflect not just ideas, but how we hold
reality. But as important, from the perspective of the person succumbing
to the trap, not only does the thinking involved not feel misplaced, as
experience it isn't misplaced. It reflects "authentic" truth as perceived
from the perspective of the part/inner character/crayon involved.

This fact presents a major dilemma both for therapeutic work with
individuals and with broader cultural change efforts. One of the cardinal
rules of Parts Work is that I, as the therapist, do not talk to parts, only
to the Whole-Person chair. If a person's ideological identification means
that he or she is engaging me from a crayon or part, there becomes, in
effect, no way to make contact, much less connect in a way that could
produce change. One reason that Parts Work has the dramatic results that
it does is that it offers a way to get beyond this quandary. It is structured
in a way that makes Integrative Meta-perspective its natural outcome.

A good way to understand how the Parts Work approach produces
this outcome is to think of it in terms of a specific kind of "cognitive
rewiring." Briefly examining this rewiring process highlights a couple
of key contributions that Parts Work makes that are directly pertinent
to our compare-and-contrast task. First is how Parts Work offers not
just methodology, but a practical "definition" for culturally mature
understanding (a significant accomplishment given the Dilemma of
Representation). Second is how Parts Work provides a powerful tool
for understanding how culturally mature perspective differs from other

---

39   In a parallel sense to how Modern Age institutions take care to separate
     church and state, traditional education does its best to keep the aca-
     demic and psychological separate.

ways of thinking. The distinctions it implies get at what is necessarily different with culturally mature perspective in particularly direct ways.

Three additional cardinal rules beyond my rule that I don't talk to a person's parts set the stage for these further recognitions. Each is a rule that the person doing Parts Work necessarily follows. When the goal is culturally mature perspective, these rules apply to understanding as a whole. With work that engages primarily at the level of personal maturity, they also apply, but in a more circumscribed way, with concerns limited to individual experience.

Rule #1: Parts don't talk to parts, only to the Whole-Person chair.

Rule #2: Only the Whole-Person chair relates to the world. The parts don't get to interact with the world. All communication with the world (including with me) happens through the Whole-Person chair.

Rule #3: The Whole-Person chair is (creatively) in charge. It is from here that final decisions about what matters and what is to be done are made. In conversing with a part, the person listens to what the part says and makes use of the information—or not—depending on whether the message is helpful or not helpful. The person then makes needed determinations and is ultimately responsible for them.

These rules define a new set of systemic relationships—both internal systemic relationships and just how the person relates to the world. Prior to crossing Cultural Maturity's threshold, parts often talk with each other, and the Whole-Person chair is capable only of sporadic leadership. One consequence is now familiar: Experience organizes as polarity—whether that of polar ideology, or, at the level of overarching narrative, that of heroic/romantic explanation. Prior to crossing Cultural Maturity's threshold, parts also relate to the world with, again, the Whole-Person chair providing at best infrequent leadership. The result is a view of the world defined by two-halves-make-a-whole relationships and by projective idealizations and demonizations.

With Cultural Maturity, the Whole-Person chair assumes both final responsibility and ultimate leadership. At the same time, it establishes a new depth and creative richness of connection with each of the parts. The new kind of cognitive "wiring" that results takes place in a related but more limited way with maturity in individual development. With Cultural Maturity, it manifests in a way that redefines our relationship to experience as a whole.

It is important to appreciate just how fundamentally different this result is from what came before. (See the diagram in Figure 9-4.) The rules I just described help clarify what is different. Rule #1 cuts the "wires" through which the internal dramas of times past took place. Rule #2 cuts the "wires" that produce related external dramas and, by making the only "wire" that connects with the world that which takes expression from the Whole-Person chair, establishes mature responsibility and authority. Rule #3 makes it so that parts now link in a direct and explicitly creative manner to the Whole-Person chair and produces the possibility of newly complex and rich understanding. Taken together, these rules and the rewiring that results produce a new kind of leadership.

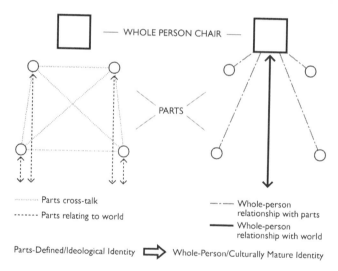

Fig. 9-4. **Cognitive Rewiring**

This outcome doesn't require a technique like Parts Work. Such "rewiring" underlies culturally mature capacities however we might acquire them. And it is there with new leadership wherever we find it—whether it is that which gives us culturally mature personal identity, that which produces Whole-Person relationships, or that needed for effective culturally mature leadership in the world.

Notice that the kind of leadership that results from this rewiring process is very specifically the new, more "creative" sort that this book has been about. It is neither leadership in the old, more right-hand, command-and-control sense, nor leadership only in the sense of allowing, getting out of the way, or facilitating process. Rather, it is the more demanding, both more dynamic and systemically aware, kind of leadership on which our future depends.

The fact that this rewiring process provides a concrete definition for culturally mature understanding has particular significance for our compare-and-contrast task. I've described how ideological views take aspects of systemic complexity and make those aspects the whole of truth. Culturally mature understanding becomes what we get when we sit solidly in that Whole-Person, Integrative Meta-perspective chair. This posture doesn't give us final answers. But it does result in us better asking the right questions—questions that have the potential to lead to useful answers.

This rewiring picture also helps make previous more specific compare-and-contrast distinctions more concrete. Dynamics that underlie the most explicit of Separation Fallacies and Unity Fallacies are easiest to recognize. With the most basic of Separation Fallacies, a right-hand—more rational, scientific, or economically materialist—part directs the show. We see the most basic of Unity Fallacies when a left-hand—more spiritual or emotional—part prevails and interacts directly with the world.

Compromise Fallacies are a bit more complicated, but viewed through the lens of this rewiring picture, how they work provides insight into an array of less obvious kinds of conceptual traps. With Compromise Fallacies two parts talk with each other (rather than with the Whole-person chair) and in various ways split the difference in their conclusions. Just how they split the difference will determine the kind of belief system that results. For example, with liberal/humanist belief, the conversation emphasizes more left-hand values (we often see a blurring of compromise and left-leaning conclusions with liberal/humanist positions). With postmodern belief of the different-strokes-for-different-folks sort, the conversation is going to be more balanced. And we commonly see a more right-hand bias along this same continuum with more libertarian conservative beliefs.

With philosophically idealist belief, left-hand parts again talk with right-hand parts, but the left-hand part has a special status—it is assumed to be the ultimately causal force. Depending on the particular kind of philosophically idealist belief, the "voice" that speaks to the world may talk from a variety of points on the left/right continuum. I've described how various philosophically idealist views may frame the future in more spiritual or more political terms (and political conclusions can themselves span the left/right spectrum[40]).

For our compare-and-contrast task, the important recognition is that each these various patterns produces a fundamentally different result than what we find with Integrative Meta-perspective. In no case does the Whole-Person chair hold the needed defining authority. And in no case are multiplicity's aspects drawn on in ways that can give their diverse creative contributions full expression.

Several important apparent contradictions touched on earlier become more understandable with this rewiring picture. The first brings us back to the question of whether culturally mature perspective is more complex or simpler than what it replaces. Cultural Maturity's cognitive rewiring produces a result that is more complex in the sense that it requires greater Capacitance and also in the way that it more explicitly draws on a diverse array of creative elements. But in the sense that internal and external conflicting tendencies give way to a single, encompassing locus of determination, it is also simpler.

A further apparent contradiction concerns the question of whether what we then see describes greater or less control. The answer to this question provides key support for a creative frame. Again we find that both result. That single point of determination in one sense very much means greater control—certainly it makes us more explicitly responsible and in charge. But "in charge" comes to have new meaning. Rather than greater control in the conventional sense, what we see is something ultimately much more significant: greater creative effectiveness and power.

A key result suggested earlier is important both to understanding this more creative kind of control and to perceiving it as something we might want. Having the Whole-Person chair in charge does not diminish the power of parts as would be the outcome with control in

---

40   The ideas of both Marx and Hitler were ultimately of this sort.

the more traditional sense. The Whole-Person chair's new solidity and authority allow each part to be most fully potent. Previously, the potential danger of doing damage to the person's systemic completeness kept parts from fully manifesting their significance. With Integrative Meta-perspective, this danger disappears. Integrative Meta-perspective creates the ability to at once better manage the whole of our complexity and to draw most powerfully on that complexity. Using the box-of-crayons image, we become able not just to hold the whole box, but also to draw on the contributions of each of the crayons in ways that deeply tap each hue's particular vibrancy.

Addressing a potential confusion that could come with these reflections confronts us in another way with an essential systemic observation that I touched on with our initial look at culturally mature truth. We reasonably ask whether it is best to picture culturally mature truth as something that we find "at the center," like the arrangement of chairs in Parts Work might suggest, or whether we more accurately think of truth as something that surrounds experience's complexity, like with the crayon's encompassing box. The question brings us back to a way I've described the conflicting positions of more humanistic and more behavioral interpretations. We also again encounter the Dilemma of Representation. In fact, as we would predict, each representation reflects an equally important part of what ultimately defines truth. The same holds for leadership and ultimately for identity. If we miss this larger systemic picture, we fall for predictable traps in our thinking.

Pragmatism

Making comparison with notions that have close parallels with the concept of Cultural Maturity can provide particularly fine-grained compare-and-contrast insights. Pragmatism makes a good such point of comparison. Pragmatism has formal philosophical roots,[41] but its basic meaning has become part of common usage. It proposes that the truths that are most helpful are so not because they are true in some absolute sense but because they get us where we need to go.

---

41   In fact, pragmatism has uniquely American roots—in the late nineteenth- and early twentieth-century ideas of Charles Sanders Pierce, William James, Oliver Wendell Holmes, and John Dewey.

We can describe culturally mature truth as pragmatic truth, but to do so accurately, we need to use the word "pragmatic" with appropriate sophistication. Cultural Maturity calls into question many of pragmatism's common associations and stretches and challenges much in pragmatism's more philosophical formulations.

Culturally mature truth and pragmatic truth are similar in that the interest of each is truth stripped of ideology. Mythologized truth is dramatic—heroic, romantic, claiming of the absolute. Mature systemic truth is "just what works." With both culturally mature perspective and pragmatism, beliefs become tools, ways of thinking that if used well move us toward what matters. Beliefs help us find what works, and we craft new beliefs to support changes in what may work best, but beliefs are not in themselves truth.

Culturally mature truth is different from pragmatic truth as commonly conceived in that it is about "just what works" in a specific temporal context—within a culturally mature reality. This recognition alerts us to what can be a dangerous flaw when pragmatism is simplistically conceived. By ignoring the Questions of Referent, pragmatism can fail at mature truth's "responsibility twice over" task. It is a solid step forward to say that truth is "what works." But we gain little—indeed, make ourselves open to harmful consequences—if we leave unanswered the question, "toward what end?" If we ignore this further critical piece, pragmatism can be used to support almost any conclusion.

If we make our referent undiluted power, pragmatism becomes justification for a narrowly Machiavellian ethos. If we make our referent wealth alone, then both generosity and truthfulness become threats to success. If we make our referent always being agreeable so that we will not offend, then we have a kind of pragmatism that may make us momentarily safe, but which also makes us pushovers. Any ideology can serve as pragmatic truth's yardstick. A person can be a liberal pragmatist, a conservative pragmatist, a scientific pragmatist, or a fundamentalist pragmatist. It all depends on where we believe last-word truth to lie.

More formal explications of pragmatism tend to avoid the worst excesses of this trap. But they share with postmodern philosophical views more generally that while they help us with surrendering past cultural absolutes, what they offer to replace them tends to be severely limited. [42] Richard Rorty put it this way in *The Consequences of Pragmatism*: "[Pragmatists] see certain acts as good ones to perform under the circumstances, but doubt that there is anything general and useful to say about what makes them all good."

Culturally mature pragmatism requires us to consciously examine the feedback we use to determine if something does, in fact, work. It also requires that we make whether our choices serve culturally mature ends our measure of "what works." It is right that we should strive to succeed and to avoid failure. Culturally mature pragmatism simply adds, "but what is success, and what does it mean to fail?" And most important for the challenges of today, it asks whether we are measuring the kind of success and failure pertinent to a healthy and sustainable future. Only truths that in the end support culturally mature possibilities remain pragmatic.

We can usefully think of what culturally mature pragmatism involves in terms of truth's complementary "crux" and "multiplicity" tasks. Culturally mature pragmatism necessarily starts by consciously asking the pertinent bare-boned, crux truth questions. We need to inquire about both the direction "what works" takes us—answer the appropriate Questions of Referent. We also need to ask about the Capacitance available for understanding what works and for getting the needed work done. Given that our interest lies with culturally mature crux distinctions, such discernments become necessarily of the bridging, whole-box-of-crayons sort.

And culturally mature pragmatism is also necessarily a highly differentiated and context-specific, multiplicity-sensitive pragmatism. It is deeply attentive to how what is most life affirming—and thus ultimately pragmatic—will be different at different times and places. That includes at different times both in our personal development and in culture's evolving story. It also includes more here-and-now, one-crayon-as-opposed-to-another distinctions such as we see with temperament differences. Culturally mature pragmatism is alert to all the various kinds of multiplicity distinctions that might be pertinent.

The observation that culturally mature leadership is pragmatic reminds us of the importance of being attentive to a confusion that can get in the way of appreciating culturally mature leadership that

---

42 Pragmatism can be appropriately thought of as a postmodern philosophical view.

I noted earlier. I've emphasized that culturally mature leadership can seem less sexy than leadership based on ideology. It can seem rather "ordinary." We must know how to distinguish the "ordinariness" of mature pragmatic leadership—which demands exceptional Capacitance—from the ordinariness of leadership that is in fact just—well—ordinary. If we fail to understand the difference, we may not recognize culturally mature leadership when it is right in front of us, or we may badly misconstrue its significance.

A Threshold Lesson: The observation that culturally mature thought finds parallels in the thinking of philosophical pragmatism helps us recognize ideological traps and provides a valuable further compare-and-contrast tool—though only if the clear reference is to pragmatism of a systemically complete sort.

Comparison and Advocacy

Let's conclude with some last reflections on the implications of our compare-and-contrast observations for culturally mature leadership. We appropriately start with ourselves—with stepping back and reflecting on possible blind spots in our own leadership assumptions. As Richard Feynman put it in the quotation that introduced this chapter, "the first principle is that you must not fool yourself."

Some questions you might ask to support your effectiveness as a culturally mature leader: Of the five scenarios for the future I described, does one come closest to how you have most often seen things? (And if so, does Cultural Maturity's picture require that you question past beliefs?) Do you see your own thinking in any of the polar traps I've described? (And if your answer is yes, how would a more systemic view change how you think, how you relate, and the values you hold?) What are some of the specific gifts and potential blindnesses that come with your particular personality style? (And does your picture of the world change when you attempt to step outside your most native viewpoint and apply a more whole-box-of-crayons perspective?) How about Capacitance—are you generally up to what Cultural Maturity's challenge requires? (And how are you most likely to respond when you are not?) Reflecting on "Parts Work" and its implied "cognitive rewiring," how far along do you feel you are when it comes to living your life from a culturally mature Whole-Person/Whole-System vantage? And if your thinking succeeds at being pragmatic, how close does it come to meeting the requirements of a culturally mature pragmatism?

This chapter's compare-and-contrast observations are pertinent to every aspect of culturally mature leadership. Certainly they are pertinent to effectively making culturally mature decisions. Good comparative tools help us evaluate both our own choices and the choices of others. The importance of having effective comparative tools available multiplies when the leadership task requires not just good decision-making, but also the effective communication of culturally mature concepts and conclusions. The ability to tease apart beliefs and their implications can be critical to successful making what one has to say understandable. It can also be essential to the well-being of the change agent.

In Chapter Four's brief look at the role appreciating limits necessarily plays in effective culturally mature advocacy, I observed that attention to limits can be particularly important when working with groups. It is a place where having good comparative tools available becomes especially critical. While the best of thinking in most fields today takes on questions that require culturally mature perspective and often makes good progress in engaging them, it remains rare to find groups of any size in which a commitment to understanding of a culturally mature sort is the norm. The thinking of almost any group that attracts great numbers of adherents will reflect belief that takes one part of understanding's systemic entirety—one crayon or several in collusion—and gives the result dominion over the whole.[43]

I am particularly aware of this kind of limitation when I am invited to speak at conferences. Most conferences attract people who share the same

---

43 We confront the same limits-related reality with any form of mass communication, whether written—with magazines, newspapers, or books—or with radio and television. Such communication requires a "critical mass" of readers/listeners/viewers. That scale of audience is going to be generated either through a lowest-common-denominator, mass-consumer approach that threatens no one (with its appeal being that it requires little in the way of Capacitance), or through the attraction of groups of the ideologically like-minded. The Internet makes possible greater diversity of opinion. It also offers the potential for more substantive content. But, as we will later examine, that potential is as yet rarely realized. (See "The Media" in Chapter Eleven.)

basic worldview. This may or may not be in an obvious ideological sense, but people tend to be drawn together by shared assumptions and values.

Communicating culturally mature conclusions usefully becomes particularly challenging if an audience, whether consciously or unconsciously, tends to identify with one side of a key polarity. Even if a presentation is in fact quite balanced, the audiences can readily assume that the presenter advocates the ideology opposite to their own. (This is why leaders in the political sphere capable of culturally mature perspective commonly suffer the double insult of getting attacked from both sides, the political right and the political left, simultaneously.) The change agent must be prepared for this and be ready to respond in ways that are most likely to produce creative results. Good compare-and-contrast tools can help us avoid the worst of ambushes, even if they can't always guarantee fulfilling outcomes.

An observation I made in this chapter with our look at Parts Work and the cognitive rewiring that comes with culturally mature perspective provides important insight for understanding this kind of limit and its implications. When we attempt to communicate with a person or group that holds an ideological position, in the end we are "talking to a part." Remember the cardinal rule in Parts Work that one doesn't talk to parts, only to the Whole-Person chair. When engaging advocates of an ideological position, we can easily assume that if we simply communicate clearly our more complete view will be recognized and appreciated. But given that from the perspective of the "chair" the person or groups occupies, what the ideological position describes is precisely how the world looks—complete and authentic experience—the person or group's most "honest" response is likely to be that the problem is yours. If the person or group is of more right-hand persuasion, the conversation is likely to end with at least the conclusion that your thinking is rather mushy—not sufficiently rigorous. In a similar way, if the a person or group is of extreme left-hand persuasion, the conversation can end with the conclusion that you are too much in your head—or perhaps not aware enough spiritually—to really understand.

A further observation filled out in this chapter highlights how sacred cows can be put in jeopardy even without any obvious difference of opinion being expressed. The challenge to belief can communicate simply through the greater Capacitance that culturally mature perspective reflects. I've described how systems pushed beyond their Capacitance react protectively. The culturally mature advocate faces the additional "unfair" fate that ideas expressed with the greatest care and eloquence, sometimes precisely because they are important and expressed eloquently, may push an audience beyond its Capacitance and interfere with the possibility of being heard.

A person who wishes to advocate for culturally mature understanding needs to be continually making comparative discernments. Doing so requires being sensitive to when sacred cows are being challenged, to the likely responses when they are, to the Capacitance limits, and to options that might exist for getting beyond potential impasses. All the compare-and-contrast tools we have looked at are directly pertinent.

The culturally mature advocate's task, ultimately, is to find some way to get at least the beginnings of a shared experience of Integrative Meta-perspective into the conversation. Put in Parts Work terms, some kind of connection must be made with the other person or group's Whole-Person chair. If there is sufficient Capacitance, lots of ways exist to do this. Simply finding a shared objective that can result in actions that win for everyone can often get most of the way there. Sometimes using simple metaphors like the box-of-crayons image can provide the needed shared perspective.

Comparative observations can also help us devise more sophisticated approaches that directly support shared understanding. Such approaches may apply specific techniques like those I described in the Parts Work example. But they may also draw more generally on the kind of appreciation for systemic difference that underlies this chapter's compare-and-contrast reflections.

For example, I've described how we can use temperament diversity not just as a compare-and-contrast tool, but also to directly catalyze systemic perspective. When I convene think tank groups to deal with major emerging cultural issues, I try, as I do with training programs, to select participants not just for diversity of expertise, but also for diversity of temperament. The needed maturity of perspective is much easier to attain if the required systemic complexity is embodied in the participants.

When consulting with organizations, I often do something related by convening groups that draw on people from throughout the organizational system. The R & D and information technology parts of the organization tend to contribute more "inspiration stage" (Early-Axis) types, the more hands-on workforce and management more "perspiration stage" (Middle-Axis) types, and the marketing department and executive ranks the more "finishing and polishing" (Late-Axis) types. Bringing together different parts of the organization by itself promotes good communication and systemic perspective. But the temperament diversity component also helps tap a breadth of sensibility and a vitality of creative energy difficult to access in other ways.

Diversity of a more developmental, cultural-stage sort can also assist us when our goal is culturally mature understanding. Certainly having people in the room who represent pertinent cultural stages is important if the issue at hand directly affects them. But if the concept of Reengagement holds, such presence can be helpful for deeper reasons. It can help support the needed complexity of perspective. High Capacitance here is key if conversations are to be most productive. But even where Capacitance is not universally high, if enough people are present who can hold culturally mature perspective, the involvement of different cultural-stage representatives can directly support the needed fullness of systemic understanding.[44]

An observation I made previously in relationship to an earlier compare-and-contrast distinction—that between maturity of the personal and cultural sorts—provides a fun conclusion for these reflections. I noted as evidence for the fundamental difference between personal maturity and Cultural Maturity the fact that young people often grasp new realities—including Cultural Maturity—more quickly than their parents. This observation has a fascinating—and provocative—implication, one that is most obviously pertinent to education, but which also helps further fill out our general understanding of Cultural Maturity.

A person might reasonably ask, given that our concern is mature understanding, whether culturally mature curriculum would not best be left for graduate-level classes (or even restricted to continuing education).

---

44   Notice an interesting consequence if the Creative Systems claim that developmental differences and temperament differences have related origins is accurate. Having different temperaments in the room can help us with the creatively more demanding stretch of "bridging" different-stage cultural realities.

In fact, culturally mature curriculum should begin on day one. The kind of "growing up" we have interest in involves the whole of culture as a system, and the earlier we start, the better. Some of the people who have worked closest with me in developing these ideas—particularly those related to temperament—are teachers of young children.

Learning to make culturally mature "crux" and "multiplicity" truth discernments, for example, appropriately serves as the core of education at any age. To teach crux distinction skills, a preschool teacher might ask: "Sarah, which of those stories did you like best? And can you tell us anything about why you liked it?" And contrary to what we might think, we can begin just as early to teach about systemic multiplicity, about context and human difference. That same teacher might ask Evan and Jane and Walter "and which story did each of you like best?" She might then comment on how interesting it is that different people like different stories and wonder aloud just why that might be. Later, when looking together at the tadpoles in the tank in the room she might turn to Evan, a somewhat quirky kid who is often made fun of and tends to get left out of classroom conversations, and say: "Evan, you liked the story with the funny creatures in it. I bet you know a lot about tadpoles. Can you tell us about them?" Complement that with chances for others to similarly highlight their gifts—and with conversation that reflects on just how these diverse gifts are different, and also how different gifts can work together—and we are well on our way toward a curriculum that not only teaches about Cultural Maturity's needed larger holding of systemic complexity, but embodies it.

CHAPTER TEN

Timeliness and Possibility

There is an instinct for rhythmic relations which
embraces our … entire world of forms.
FRIEDRICH NIETZSCHE

THIS CHAPTER ADDRESSES A HANDFUL OF TOPICS that add substance to Creative Systems Theory's underlying conceptual picture, in particular that picture's developmental/evolutionary, Patterning in Time aspects.

The most obvious importance of Patterning in Time notions lies with how they help us better understand the way change in human systems works, and with this, how fundamentally different experience can be at different points in any human developmental process. Each of this chapter's various topics, from a slightly different direction, helps fill out Creative Systems Theory's picture of developmental change and it mechanisms.

But for this book's inquiry, there are also important further kinds of pertinence. In addition, these topics will each in its own way help solidify the argument for Cultural Maturity. I've proposed that if the progression from more left-hand to more right-hand determination that occurs over the first half of any human formative process accurately applies to the story of culture, then some kind of specifically integrative mechanism like that described by the concept of Cultural Maturity becomes the only option for going forward. Each topic will help put the Dilemma of Trajectory in relief and bring further attention to the fundamental reordering needed for us to proceed.

These various topics will also each help deepen understanding of the more general power and importance of a creative frame. By expanding on previous creative-frame-related observations, they will help confirm the importance of a creative frame not just for today, but also for its significance in the larger story of understanding.

These additional reflections begin with a deeper look at the multiple aspects of intelligence, including a more detailed examination of how our various ways of knowing manifest at different points in formative process. Then, to come at Creative Systems Theory's evolutionary picture of cultural change in a more academic/intellectual way than I have previously, I will use Patterning in Time notions to map the history of philosophical understanding. Next, providing a counterbalance to the rational intelligence bias of the previous section, I will touch on four Patterning in Time topics, each intriguing in its own right, that highlight the role of more creatively germinal contributors to formative process. We will examine how the meaning of time creatively evolves (time's relativity in time); how, through history, we have conceived of and related to nature; patterns we see in how architecture has evolved through time (and how the shapes we create reflect how we hold experience more generally); and just what it means to live in—and be—a body (and how the answer changes depending on when in developmental time we look).

Next, I will touch briefly on several topics that support the application of Creative Systems Theory Patterning in Time concepts—and Creative Systems patterning concepts more generally. I will address how we can make even more fine-grained Patterning in Time distinctions than those I have presented thus far. I will also outline how we can use various Creative Systems patterning concepts together to produce highly detailed systemic analyses of human systems of all sorts. And I will describe how everyday language can capture at least the main contours of the kinds of observations that Creative Systems Theory's patterning concepts reflect. I will conclude with a couple of examples that apply Creative Systems patterning concepts to the task of promoting culturally mature capacities in organizations.

Some of this chapter's chronicling of stage-specific realities may at times feel repetitive. But this repetition is for a good cause. Beyond the various kinds of pertinence just mentioned, there is one more noted earlier. A deep engagement with creative patterning's larger picture helps us not just more fully grasp, but more directly embody, what Cultural Maturity is about.

In this chapter, I will often draw on material from earlier writings, in particular from my first book, *The Creative Imperative*. *The Creative Imperative* took a deep-dive look at creative organization and includes important material I have not written about since that time. I encourage readers who have a serious interest in the thinking of Creative Systems Theory to read it. Besides documenting the theory's beginnings, *The Creative Imperative* also provides the most detailed written descriptions to date of many important Creative Systems Theory notions. This chapter also at times draws on my second more applied work, *Necessary Wisdom*.

The Evolution of Intelligence

I've emphasized the central significance of the fact that intelligence has multiple aspects and the importance of understanding how those aspects come into play in different ways in different circumstances. Integrative Meta-perspective's ability to take us beyond the limitations of Enlightenment understanding's from-a-balcony worldview has its roots in how it produces the ability to more consciously engage the whole of intelligence.

This newly aware, encompassing, and engaged relationship with intelligence's multiplicity is key to understanding any of the new kinds of truth concepts that come with culturally mature perspective. Patterning in Time concepts require that we more consciously draw on the different intelligences—and different juxtapositions of intelligences—that order understanding in different creative stages. Patterning in Space concepts similarly require sensitivity to the different ways in which intelligence organizes with different kinds of here-and-now creative relationships. And while Whole-System Patterning concepts don't involve the same one-crayon-from-another kinds of distinctions, they too require that we draw on the whole of our cognitive complexity and do so in an integrated way that is only now becoming possible.

Attempting to make sense of intelligence's multiple aspects played a key role in my early thinking. The fact that intelligence has multiple aspects was then only beginning to be appreciated. I recognized that creative processes drew on a variety of different kinds of knowing, and did so in different ways at different creative stages. I also recognized that I would need to give some special attention to intelligence's more creatively germinal aspects, as they tend to be especially foreign to people. At our time in culture, people are rarely very conscious of intelligence's more kinesthetic/body and imagination/symbol-making aspects, and if they are at all conscious of these aspects, they tend not to think of them as intelligence.

I saw that if I was to deeply understand intelligence's multiplicity, particularly these more germinal aspects, I would need to seek out some unusual and highly innovative people to learn from. During my residency, I studied in depth with Joseph Campbell, one of modern time's greatest contributors to our understanding of symbol, myth, dream, and imagination. I also studied with important practitioners who were attempting to bring the body more directly into the psychotherapeutic process.[1] I wanted to understand as deeply as possible just what each intelligence brings to understanding and how our various intelligences worked together to made us who we are.

Important insights came to me during this time of initial reflections on intelligence and its relationship to formative process. Early on, my primary interest lay with creative process as we customarily think of it—what we see with art or invention. But as I was introduced in my training to developmental psychology—and, in particular, more systemic developmental thinkers such as Jean Piaget and Lawrence Kohlberg—it became clear to me that a similar intelligence-related progression worked beneath the surface with our personal formative stories. The surprising recognition that we see a similar cognitive progression with culture's story came soon thereafter—and with it, Creative Systems Theory was born.

Thus far in this book, my descriptions of the various intelligences as described by Creative Systems Theory have been brief. I've given greater attention to the Creative Systems Theory thesis that our multiple intelligences work together to support and drive human formative process. Because of the central importance of the concept of multiple intelligences if we are to make deep sense of a creative frame, I introduced my first book, *The Creative Imperative*, by attempting to articulate what made each aspect of intelligence particular and the nature of each

---

1   Most notably Stanley Keleman, an earlier innovator in the "bioenergetic" approach to body psychology.

aspect's contribution. I don't think I've since done a better job of introducing intelligence's creative multiplicity—particularly its nonrational aspects. Here I include edited excerpts from these early writings.

The Intelligence of the Body:

> *God guard me from those thoughts men think*
> *In the mind alone:*
> *He that sings a lasting song*
> *Thinks in a marrow-bone.*
>
> WILLIAM BUTLER YEATS

The earliest knowing in any life process is bodily knowing. Developmental psychologist Jean Piaget speaks of the early intelligence of the child as "sensorimotor" knowing. The infant's reality is organized kinesthetically, as interplaying patterns of movement and sensation. Similarly, bodily understanding organizes reality in the earliest stages of culture. To a tribal person, truth lies in one's bond with, and as, the creature world of nature. We live from this same place in the beginning moments of any process of creative manifestation. The first moments of new creative possibility are felt as "inklings," kinesthetic sensings of life. In this first stage of creative reality, intelligence is "cellular."

Body in this most germinal stage in creation is very different from the body as we conceive of it through the isolated and isolating eye of Modern Age understanding. It is much more than simply sensation; also much more than simply anatomy and physiology; and more than one side of an either/or: body versus mind, body versus spirit. In this first stage of formativeness the body is not something we have, but who we are. It is our intelligence. It is how we organize our experience of both ourselves and our world.

While we don't usually give the knowing of bodily reality much status in formal thinking, it has a central place in the concrete experience of our lives. For example, if you say you love someone and you are asked how you know, eventually you will begin to talk in the language of the body. You know you feel love because when you are with that person your "heart" opens, there is a warm expanding in the area of the chest.

This experienced "heart" cannot be found by dissection, but it is undeniably very real, very close to what is most essential in us.

While we are often unconscious of this organically kinesthetic aspect of experience, it never escapes us totally. We give it colorful expression in our "figures" of speech. We speak of feeling "moved" or "touched," of being "beside ourselves" or feeling that something is "over our heads." If we take the time, a lot of this sort of experience is available consciously. As a simple example, if I attune to it, I am aware that I feel my bodily connection to different people at different times in quite different ways. With one person I may be most aware of a sense of fullness and solidity in my belly or shoulders. With another, the vitality may be most prominent as a sense of animation in my eyes and face, or erotic arousal in my genitals. With some people our meeting touches very close to the core of my body; with others the bodily experience of meeting may feel much more peripheral, more "superficial."[2]

The Intelligence of Imagination, Symbol, and Myth:

> *Dreams are the true interpreter of our inclinations.*
>
> MICHEL DE MONTAIGNE

Symbol—the vehicle of myth, dream, metaphor, and much in artistic expression—also speaks from close to the beginnings of things, though not quite so close. When a storyteller utters the words "Once upon a time…," it is more than simple convention. The words are a bidding to remember an ancient fecundity and magic.

The symbolic, as I think of it, is both the organizing truth and the chief mode of expression in the second major stage of formative process. As myth, it serves as truth's most direct expression in the times of early high cultures: in ancient Egypt, early Greece, for the Incas and the Aztecs of pre-Columbian Mesoamerica. As imagination, it defines the reality of

---

2   We might commonly think of the word "superficial" as disparaging. Here I use it only to refer to the more surface layers of body experience. See "The Evolution of the Body" later in this chapter for an examination of how, with each creative stage, experience organizes closer to the surface of the body.

childhood: the essential work of the child is its play, the trying out of
wings of possibility on the stage of make believe and let's pretend. The
symbolic is present in a similar way with the beginnings of any creative
task. It organizes reality in the stage of inspiration, that critical time when
bubblings from the dream work of the unconscious give us our first visible
sense of what is asking to become.

Joseph Campbell described the mythic aspect of the imaginal this
way in Myths to Live By: "It would not be too much to say that myth
is the secret opening through which the inexhaustible energies of the
cosmos pour into human cultural manifestation. Religion, philosophies,
social forms of primitive and historic man, prime discoveries in science
and technology, the very dreams that blister sleep boil up from the basic
magic ring of myth."

The Intelligence of Emotion:

> *The perception of beauty is a moral test.*
>   HENRY DAVID THOREAU

The next intelligence in this development sequence is more familiar
to us than the first two. It is one step closer to the rational sensibilities
that today we are most likely to identify with truth. This is the language
of emotions.

While we tend to be more conscious of emotional intelligence, beginning to think of the affective realm as intelligence stretches usual
understanding in a couple of key ways. First, emotional intelligence
becomes an integral part not just of our feeling lives, but also of our
conceptual understanding of how cognition works. In the past, we
have specifically cleansed the emotions from our theoretical formulations so that our ideas would have the rigor needed for objective truth.
Second, we necessarily engage the emotional in a deeper sense than
we are accustomed to. The emotional as we have known it in our current stage in culture is only a faint vestige of the feeling dimension at
its full grandeur as a primary organizing reality.

The emotional is what orders truth in the third major stage of formative process. When emotional intelligence is preeminent, life is imbued
with a visceral immediacy, and strong ethical and moral responses. We

can feel its presence in the fervencies and allegiances of adolescence. It is there in a similar way in the crusading ardency and codes of honor and chivalry of the Middle Ages. And we see it in the courage to struggle and the devoted commitment necessary to take any personal experience of creative inspiration into manifest form.

With more formal thinking in modern times, at best we acknowledge the most surface layers of this part of us. We treat the emotional as decoration, or regard it only as a pleasant diversion from the real stuff of understanding. That somehow we must reengage this aspect of ourselves as an integral part of how we know truth becomes obvious if we examine the issues that now confront us as a species. Solving the dilemma of our future will require a keen sensitivity to the fact of human relationship and deep levels of personal integrity and ethical responsibility. It is our emotional selves that most appreciate and understand these sorts of concerns.

The early chapters of *The Creative Imperative* gave special attention to these more creatively germinal aspects of intelligence that in common usage we might not think of as intelligence at all. But over the course of the book, I also filled out the rational, and in particular what the rational looks like when we think of it not as intelligence itself, but as one essential aspect of intelligence's larger picture. The following further reflections are drawn from these later observations.

The Intelligence of the Intellect:

> *Cogito ergo sum——I think, therefore I am.*
>
> RENÉ DESCARTES

The rational (rational/material intelligence) is what we measure with IQ tests and most engage and reward in traditional education. It is the intelligence of syllogistic logic——if A, then B, then C. In creative work, it comes most strongly to the fore with formative process's time of finishing and polishing. With individual psychological development, it orders adult understanding. In modern times, it represents the kind of cognitive processing that we equate almost exclusively with intelligence.

That we specifically elevate the rational in Late-Axis culture doesn't mean that rational processing doesn't have an important place in the cognitive processes of earlier cultural times. But depending on the cultural stage, the underlying premises of our "logic" will have their roots in the pertinent (often decidedly nonrational) organizing sensibilities. In earliest times, for example, our "logic" will reflect underlying animistic (body intelligence) assumptions. Imagine two cave dwellers discussing the various creatures depicted on a cave wall.

What becomes different with Late-Axis culture and its Age of Reason is that the underlying premises of our logical assertions come to have their roots as well in rational/material assumptions. Rationality becomes allied with awareness and perceived together with it as, in effect, truth itself. With Late-Axis from-a-balcony perspective, the rational sits in polar juxtapositon to the irrational, a catchall category for all the previously reigning intelligences. This supremacy for rational intelligence is regarded as culminating and alters how we understand everything about our worlds. We come to think of causality increasingly in terms of actions and their concomitant reactions, identity in terms of logical thought ("I think, therefore I am"), and wealth and progress almost exclusively in terms of material acquisition and technological innovation.

Beyond One Intelligence, One Stage:

In order to keep things simple, throughout most of this book, I've spoken as if we can identify each intelligence with a particular creative stage. But if we wish to bring nuance and sophistication to our thinking, we need to recognize how each intelligence has a role to play at each creative stage. It is true that particular intelligences most define understanding at particular creative stages. But in a way similar to what I just suggested for rational intelligence, with each stage within any particular scale of formative process each intelligence manifests in a particular way as part of the larger sensibility that orders that stage's generative task.

As a further example, let's take imaginal/symbolic intelligence as it takes expression at different stages in culture. In tribal times, while imaginal/symbolic intelligence takes a back seat to bodily knowing, it nonetheless has an important role, manifesting as animistic imagery with its clear message of inseparability from nature (remember our cave dwellers). With Early-Axis culture, imaginal/symbolic intelligence steps forward to become intelligence's most determining voice. It is here that we find pantheons of gods, great mythic tales, and, more so than at any other time, artistic expression treated as a direct expression of truth. With Middle-Axis culture, while imaginal/symbolic intelligence again takes a more secondary role—in this case to emotional/moral intelligence's now defining presence—it continues to contribute. Myth's numinosity gives way to the more explicitly moral sensibilities of legend—think of the medieval tales of the Knights of the Round Table. And while art ceases to be itself a definer of truth, it continues to serve powerfully as a language for religious sensibility. With the Late-Axis times, imaginal/symbolic intelligence is still valued, but it comes to have clearly diminished significance. We now relegate it to the separate-world reality of the subjective. We may still appreciate it—indeed, the arts can have an elevated presence. But increasingly the imaginal's role is decorative.[3]

The chart in Figure 10-1, from *The Creative Imperative*, summarizes the ways each of the primary intelligences identified by Creative Systems Theory takes expression at different stages in formative process.

A Creative History of Truth

One of Creative Systems Theory's particularly provacative truth-related contributions is the way it helps us put specific truths in historical perspective. We can apply the Creative Function to help delineate how various kinds of truth—scientific truth, religious truth, artistic truth, our ideas about government, education, or the truth conclusions of the human body—have evolved through time. The way the Creative Function provides a big-picture vantage for thinking about philosophy's more encompassing sort of truth highlights how Patterning in Time notions can also help us tease apart truth's workings more generally.

Creative Systems Theory immediately alerts us to limits inherent in such an endeavor. Philosophy, even when interpreted very broadly, as here, means ideas that can be verbally articulated and put into some rational form (even if their focus is the nonrational[4]). Thus, while philosophy claims to

---

3   With current, more Transitional times, the imaginal assumes an even more surface kind of significance. Think of Walt Disney–style fantasy and video games.

4   In modern times, the rational bias then often manifests in a way that ironically can put even greater emphasis on the rational. We can see

INTELLIGENCE AND THE FIRST HALF OF THE CREATIVE CYCLE

CREATIVE STAGES

CREATIVE LANGUAGES (* = Primary Organizing Language)

	Pre-Axis	Early-Axis	Middle-Axis	Late-Axis
The Body	*The Creature Body, the Body as Nature	The Body as Essence, the Body of Ritual, the Spirit or Dream Body	The Visceral/Muscular Body, the Body of "Heart and Guts"	The Physical Body, the Body as Appearance
The Symbolic	Animism – the Symbolic as a Language of Nature	*Myth – the Symbolic as a Language of Ritual and Spiritual Relationship	Legend – the Symbolic as a Language of Moral Order	Fantasy – the Symbolic as a Language of Romanticism and Idealism
The Emotional	Feeling as Harmony with Nature	Feeling as Inspiration, Essence, and Primal Passion	*Feeling as Visceral Emotion	Feeling as Sentiment and Pleasure
The Intellect	Participatory Conciousness	Magical and Aesthetic Thought	The Logic of Right and Wrong	*Rational, Mechanistic Thought

Fig. 10-1. Multiple Intelligences and Creative Stages

be about truth itself, the perspective from which it views truth often limits what it is capable of seeing. John Keats voiced the limitation as a rhetorical question, "Do not all charms fly at the mere touch of cold philosophy?"[5]

But once we recognize its limitations, philosophical truth provides a valuable window. It is at least representative of broader understanding. And because it tends toward verbal descriptions and logical analysis, philosophy is more amenable to brief synopsis (ignoring for the moment the fact that philosophers are rarely brief) than, say, the historical "beliefs" of art, government, or religion.

The Creative Function provides a crude but provocative way to "map" the history of philosophy. Such mapping has its basis in the recognition that we can think of philosophical tradition as having left and right hands (or a least traditions that lean variously to the right or left). Philosophy refers to these two fundamental currents in different ways—the transcendental as opposed to the empirical, the approach of the idealist or the romantic as opposed to the positivist or the materialist. Each at times flows into the other, but the simplification supports understanding. Jean Gebser described the situation this way: "Idealists and materialists are like two children on a seesaw who have been teetering back and forth for two thousand years."

The more left-hand current includes thinkers such as Plato and philosophers of more religious bent who believe that what we can ultimately most rely on is inner experience, whether mental or spiritual. The more right-hand current includes thinkers who in one way or another

---

detailed, lengthy treatises on the limits of rationality. The length of such treatises and the fact that we would refer to them as treatises makes the rational's continued preeminence clear.

5   Because rationality represents the most creatively manifest of intelligences, we might be drawn to conclude that philosophy is a solely right-hand activity. But our picture needs to be more nuanced. Creative Systems Theory affirms that philosophy is largely an upper-pole activity (in the Creative Function and in ourselves, an activity of the head more than the body or emotions). But it also delineates how each pole has more reflective (inner) and expressive (outer) aspects. Philosophy most draws on the inner aspect of upper-pole sensibilities. This additional recognition is essential to appreciating what philosophy observes in general, and, in particular, to what happens to philosophy at Transition's threshold.

believe we rely ultimately (or at least most usefully) on our senses, such as the early natural philosophers, Aristotle, and most of modern science.

Creative Systems Theory expands on this recognition by applying the observation that polarities organize creatively. The history of ideas becomes a chronicling of the diverse ways in which this two-handed interplay has been perceived through time, and from different perspectives at any particular point in time. If nothing else, this approach offers the possibility of synopsis and an antidote to that common lack of brevity in philosophical writings. Two basic changes shape this philosophical trek through time, both now familiar.

The first is that gradual shift from left-hand to right-hand emphasis over the course of creative differentiation. Left-handed cosmologies predominate in earliest cultural periods, while more right-handed worldviews come to the fore as we move toward the present. The second is the role of cultural stages. Incubation, inspiration, perspiration, and polishing tasks give each hand identifiable characteristics depending on which hand predominates. These creative tasks translate into the animistic thought of tribal times, the more magical thought of the earlier civilizations, the morally focused philosophies of the Middle Ages, and the opposed material and romantic perspectives of the Modern Age.

The descriptions that follow are highly (even absurdly) abridged. But more detailed analysis is best left for other writings. Because of space limitations, I will mention thinkers without great elaboration. Readers may find some familiarity with philosophical thought's key figures and traditions to be helpful, but the most important recognitions concern the suggested underlying patterns.

Many people would consider where we must start not to be philosophy. Tribal (Pre-Axis) times precede written language. But the animistic assumptions of Pre-Axis realities produce a consistent conceptual world. Here we find a reality in which left-hand sensibilities almost wholly define experience. It is not that right-hand elements are denied; rather, simply, it is that they are not yet strongly present. All is seen as connected—tribe, nature, spirit, time—and these connections define truth. People may assume more right-hand and left-hand roles—a tribal chief's duties are more "secular" than those of a shaman. But differences manifest within an almost entirely unitary holding of experience.

The cosmologies of civilization's early rise (Early-Axis) more overtly acknowledge both hands of truth, but the left hand retains dominance. The magical and mythic beliefs of ancient Egypt, the Incas and Aztecs, classical India,[6] or Olympian Greece each, to varying degrees, gave final word to the archetypally feminine. Plato's philosophy belongs in this left-hand tradition, though he conceived of truth's left hand more in terms of mind than spirit. In Plato's cave, external reality is a play of shadows cast by internal essences—the "forms" or "ideas." Aristotle, along with the earlier Greek natural philosophers, focused more outwardly, on phenomena that could be understood with the senses: the natural world, speech, behavior. Their thinking laid the foundation for modern scientific thought. But even Aristotle's ideas made but a start to the right. Aristotle saw divine action as what began it all—the "unmoved mover"—and invisible causal forces behind motion of every sort.

With culture's perspiration stage (Middle-Axis), the strength of truth's two hands became more balanced. Because philosophy tends to take expression from the more inner, reflective side of our rationality (in contrast to politics or economics), medieval philosophical writings tend still to lean toward the archetypally feminine. This continued left-handed emphasis is particularly evident in expressly theistic formulations such as the fourth-century ideas of St. Augustine of Hippo or those of medieval mystics such as Meister Eckhart or Hildegard of Bingen. But the Middle Ages saw also a manifesting of expressly secular philosophy. While St. Thomas Aquinas's ideas were deeply grounded in religious principle, they followed on and extended the tradition of Aristotle. William of Ockham went even further in pressing against the constraints of orthodox religious cosmology.

With the Modern Age (Late-Axis), archetypally masculine philosophical sensibilities moved forefront. In the empiricism of Bacon, Locke, and Hume, right-hand æsthetics were assumed to shape the left. Positivist formulations, such those of Saint-Simon and Comte, relied almost exclusively on truth's right hand, as did the more extreme of materialist and early scientific views (Hobbes and Laplace).[7]

---

6   Creative Systems Theory views classical Eastern philosophy as emanating from this stage.

7   I say extreme because most early scientists, and most we associate with the birth of the Scientific Age, were religious people.

Dualism became explicit in the seventeenth-century thinking of Descartes[8] (and in a less absolutely cleaved form in the ideas of Leibniz). We see the greatest right-hand preeminence in current times with the claims of extreme behaviorism and scientism that material explanation is all we need.

Modern Age left-hand cosmologies arose either as a counterbalance to or reaction against this new right-hand supremacy. The most important include modern forms of idealism (Berkeley, Kant, and Hegel) along with eighteenth- and nineteenth-century romanticism (Rousseau, Schelling, and Goethe). Idealist cosmologies acknowledge the validity of both of truth's hands and assume that they interact—but, as I've described, truth's left hand in the end drives the right and determines truth. Spinoza's equating of God with nature set the stage for romanticism's polar response to the growing dominance of right-hand sensibilities.

Note that this progression brings us eventually to the critical impasse that has been central to this book's argument for Cultural Maturity. As left-hand sensibilities surrender their dominance to right-hand beliefs, eventually we confront the Dilemma of Trajectory. Thought's history describes a step-by-step replacing of mysticism by "hard truth." Modern thought represents a final victory for from-the-balcony objectivity (and assumes that future thought will simply reap the rewards of that victory). We are left with the question of whether there is anywhere left to go.

At the least, we are left with the question of whether philosophy has anywhere left to go. If extreme advocates of right-hand truth are correct and right-hand truth is all there ever really was (the left hand was just a pleasant illusion), then in effect we've arrived. Philosophy has appropriately reached the end of its usefulness—it is now a historical artifact, its functions now replaced by economics, science, and technology.

Certainly philosophy confronts difficulties. (It is understandable that today we might find so few job openings for philosophers.) At

---

8   We might assume dualism to give equal weight to each hand. However, which hand ultimately predominates is a function of dualism's larger context. The separate-worlds ideas of Descartes, while expressly affirming of religion's place, represented an important victory for distinction over connectedness.

Cultural Maturity's threshold, the empirical and the transcendental threads each reflect their respective Transitional Absurdities. An extreme objectivity that leaves out half of the data can hardly be considered objective. And an extreme subjectivity that leaves out the subject—at least in any embodied sense—is ultimately empty.[9] And as you've seen, Transition's picture presents more than just philosophical problems. A world defined only by right-hand values is likely not consistent with survival.

The way in which the concept of Cultural Maturity resolves philosophy's Transitional predicament is now familiar. Integrative Meta-perspective does three things with regard to philosophy's right- and left-hand traditions. First, it challenges either hand's claim to be the last word. Second, it steps back and affirms a more dynamic and encompassing picture. (It proposes that even just making right- and left-hand truths separate but equal—as with Cartesian dualism—is not enough.) And finally, it emphasizes the importance of not just systemically reframing here-and-now differences, but also finding fresh ways to understand how differences have taken expression through time (that task of Reengagement that is necessary if bridging is to make any real sense given the Dilemma of Trajectory).

Cultural Maturity describes how these changes provide a way to go on. It also opens the door to a greater sophistication of understanding all the way around. We've seen how Integrative Meta-perspective makes possible pattern language concepts that, in a way that before now would not have been possible, give expression to human experience's full whole-box-of-crayons complexity.

In this newly integrative picture, neither hand gets away unscathed. But the truth of each hand becomes more robust, more multihued in conception, and more extensive in its appropriate concerns. In some small way, we see this with any "bridging." It is true in especially striking and consequential ways for the particularly defining systemic relationships that through history have been the concern of philosophy.

---

9   None of this fully negates philosophy. In an earlier footnote, I observed how philosophy is never just a right-hand pursuit, how it always also includes reflective elements. But it does leave philosophy hanging by a thread.

Figure 10-2 briefly summarizes this creative progression.

Cultural Stage[10]	Left-hand Preeminence		Right-hand Preeminence
Pre-Axis	Animism		
Early-Axis	Plato, the more spiritual classical Eastern philosophies [the more secular of Eastern philosophies – Taoism, for example – can be thought of as dualistic]		Aristotle, Democritus, Confucious
Middle-Axis	St. Augustine, Meister Eckhard, Hildegard of Bingen		William of Ockham, Thomas Aquinas
Late-Axis	Kant, Schelling, Rousseau, Hegel, Bergson, Teilhard de Chardin		Descartes [or dualism], Newton, Locke, Hume, Compte, Mars, and the modern analytic philosophers
Transition	The more extreme of New Age and environmental beliefs	The more extreme of postmodern beliefs	Scientism,[11] extreme behaviorism, the technological gospel
Early Integration[12]	The more mature of religious, Transformational/ New Paradigm, and environmental perspectives	The more mature of postmodern perspectives	The cutting edge of modern science, and the more mature of Post-Industrial/ Information Age perspectives

Fig. 10-2. Philosophy and Patterning in Time

---

10   When the more "horizontal," left-hand versus right-hand aspect of polarity is most pertinent, it helps to turn the Creative Function on its side. Philosophy, because of its conscious rational formulation, is uniformly an upper-pole activity. Philosophical differences thus reflect more inner versus outer dynamics.

11   While scientism is not limited to Transitional times, it gains wider acceptance with Transitional dynamics (the archetypally feminine pole so diminished as to exert little influence).

12   See "Scenarios for the Future" in Chapter Nine.

Reflecting on this big-picture interpretation and how it helps us, a person might appropriately ask whether culturally mature perspective is itself accurately thought of as philosophy. The postmodern argument for the end of philosophy—at least as a pursuit of final abstracted truths—is legitimate. And culturally mature truth is never just philosophical. It is always as much about politics, science, sociology, religion, or art. But with regard to the question of what makes truth true, its concerns certainly parallel those of philosophical inquiry.

Wherever we end up with our answer, culturally mature perspective succeeds in bringing fresh life to the philosophical enterprise. We find a result similar to what we encountered for the broad study of history. Culturally mature systemic perspective offers that philosophical inquiry might be newly vital and substantive. At the least, Cultural Maturity makes the "big picture" newly relevant—indeed, essential.

What culturally mature truth gives us is necessarily more humble than the ultimate answers to which classical philosophy aspired. But it succeeds in providing new appreciation for the wonders (along with the wondrous absurdities) of being human. And it offers a kind of practical applicability that philosophy has rarely been able to achieve. Perhaps a time will come when parents no longer cringe—appropriately—when they hear that their children have chosen philosophy as a college major.

More Patterning in Time—Particularly Intriguing Expressions

Let's now turn to a small handful of additional Patterning in Time–related topics. Each is intriguing in its own right. And each also, because it focuses on a concern for which more creatively germinal aspects of intelligence are key to understanding, offers valuable additional insight for our inquiry.

Certainly, each topic helps us more deeply appreciate the creative realities these particular intelligences give us access to. I've described how, in our time, the sensibilities that order formative process's earliest stages are particularly difficult for us to understand and consciously access. These additional Patterning in Time topics, by bringing particular attention to ways these more primordial sensibilities have helped us, work to further fill out our understanding of developmental/evolutionary process. (At the least, each offers a certain counterbalance to philosophy's more rational bias.)

There is also a further contribution that comes from how each topic highlights more germinal realities. There is a way it contributes to understanding where Integrative Meta-perspective's more systemically complete picture takes us. I've noted the importance sense in which culturally mature understanding bridges not just here-and-now polarities, but also more temporally, how in the end it is about getting our minds around formative process as a whole. We need to take some care with this further kind of insight if we are not to fall for traps. I've emphasized that Reengagement is not at all about going back. In the end, it is not about the past at all. But if the concept of Reengagement holds, these topics should at least provide further useful glimpses into what the future's needed more dynamic and complete ways of holding experience will require of us.

The Relativity of Time in Time

In clarifying the particular kind of wisdom that comes with Cultural Maturity in Chapter Eight, I promised to return to the observation that how we relate to and experience time is different at different times and places. Time presents an additional example where culturally mature perspective helps us address a concern that always before has left us a bit baffled. It also offers valuable additional insight into how truth, more generally, patterns in time.

Just what is time? We can't ask the question without being confronted with contradiction. A watched pot never boils, yet time flies when you are having fun. Time is the "best medicine" (Ovid) and also "all devouring, all destroying" (Jonathan Swift). Time in the ecstasy of sexual passion can feel eternal, while waiting in line it can feel like an eternity. Saint Augustine's words in his *Confessions* most famously express the conceptual frustration: "What then is time? If no one asks me, I know; if I want to explain it to someone who does ask me, I do not know." Luis Borges put time's endless paradoxes more poetically: "Time is a river that carries me along, but I am the river; it is a tiger which devours me, but I am the tiger; it is a fire that consumes me, but I am the fire."

And today time is entering the human conversation in a way that might seem only to confuse the situation further. Modern physics presents a newly fluid picture of time—with relativity, time expands and contracts and gets equal billing with the three dimensions of space.

Certainly time has becomes a "timely" topic as our rush-rush world leaves us with never enough of it.

Cultural Maturity's cognitive reordering offers that we might engage time in deeper and more complete ways than was possible in the past. These changes can at first seem to make time even more difficult to grasp, but in the end they make it newly possible to understand fully. The important recognition when it comes to our day-to-day perception of time is that time is not always the same thing.

Culturally mature perspective brings together our often very different relationships to time and makes them part of a larger, at once more detailed and more integrated picture.

In the here and now, culturally mature perspective "bridges" common polar relationships with time. It links the time of "being" with the time of "doing," the sacred time of the priest with the time of Galileo's desire "to measure everything measurable and to make everything measurable that is not yet measurable." We discover that time, like truth as a whole, has left and right hands. Integrative Meta-perspective helps us better use those hands in concert.

Culturally mature perspective also stretches our understanding of time out over time, helps us appreciate time's developmental dimension. Time as experience is itself "relative in time"—a contextual relativity that we all at some level recognize. The time of the young child fascinated with the odd amblings of a caterpillar goes on forever. The time of the adult who needs to be on time and not waste time is much more linear and lockstep. And the time of life's last years is different still, more tempered and better able to respond to circumstances. Creative Systems Theory's creative frame offers a way to map this relativity of time in time.

Appreciating time's relativity over the course of culture's developmental story has direct pertinence to the critical task of rethinking progress. While I've used progress as a general notion, I've also stressed how, in the way we think about it, progress is a specifically modern concept. Our onward-and-upward image of progress requires the more goal-oriented sensibilities that arrived on culture's stage with time's Modern Age definition.

Time in Pre-Axis cultures is circular (or even more immediately, timeless—as in the almost psychedelic "dream time" of the Australian Aborigines). Time is measured by the repetitive turning of seasons and the enactment of ritual. In an important sense, past, present, and future exist simultaneously (ancestors are commonly seen to reside in a parallel here and now). The durational is clearly secondary to the eternal—to time as timelessness, to what we might call deep time.

Time in Early-Axis cultures begins to acquire a more overt sense of progression, though time as the timeless retains its strong influence. We witness the advent of more formal "timepieces"— ritual observatories like Stonehenge, the stone calendar wheels of the Aztecs. Such structures marked duration, but with them, it was time's cycles that most commanded our attention. And the mystical awe with which these structures were regarded makes clear the continued power of left-hand sensibility. Still, time as experience has distinctly evolved, becoming a spiral more than a circle. The perceived relationship of the living and the dead again provides a good lens for understanding (our perceptions of death and of time are intimately linked). Death in Early-Axis times is thought to be followed not by life in a parallel world, but by reincarnation (or something similar). We return to where we started, but now in altered form.

In Middle-Axis cultural times, time as progression and time as timelessness juxtapose more as equals. With the advent of monotheism, death no longer means returning to where we start, but going to some distinct afterlife. The world of forms—personal identity, invention, and time as something we can delineate— stands increasingly delineated, with the timeless now inhabiting a separate heavenly world. Timepieces become more precise (and less overtly sacred)—from the sundial and the hourglass to, in the thirteenth century, the first mechanical clocks. Time has not become totally divorced from the sacred—the impetus for the creation of mechanical clocks was the need for medieval monks to know the time for prayer (an ironic beginning for the device that would become the lord of secular time). But time has become something we can separately consider.

Time in Late-Axis culture becomes our familiar linear time, the time of being on time, of not wasting time, the time purely of duration. It is time as division, the time of parts, each second equal and adding to the next. It is the time of classical science—measuring an object's speed from here to there—and the time of commerce—as Francis Bacon said, "time is the measure of business as money is of wares." (With their needs for reliable minute-to-minute, and even second-to-second accuracy, science and commerce were the primary drivers for the development of modern timepieces.) While primordial time connects, links all in the timeless, linear time separates, cleanly cleaves one moment from the next. It is secular time, but in our own ways we deify it. We organize our days around it, make it "of the essence." Ironically, while we tend to assume that linear time represents the real meaning of time—time finally stripped of its mysticism—a person could argue equally well that its inception marks a final extraction of time from life's equation. (In a Newtonian world, the three dimensions of space define truth, and time, like art or spirit, becomes something separate, and secondary).

We could map out a similar creatively contextual picture of time's significance for Patterning in Space differences. For example, people with different temperaments do not experience time in exactly the same way. The time of the artist differs from that of the businessman as fundamentally as that of the child and the adult (and, as Creative Systems Theory predicts, in a related way).

What is the future of time? Certainly in times ahead we should become better able to recognize time's elasticity of meaning. The temporal wars between the eternal and the durational should increasingly find resolution in more encompassing ways of thinking about time. We should become better able to appreciate the particular values and states of experience that accompany different relationships to time. With regard to progress, we should more and more recognize the price we pay, and will increasingly pay, for making time (with money) our secular deity.

Our various definitions of time come together in the importance of addressing questions of timeliness. Note that all Creative Systems patterning concepts are in one way or another about what makes something "right and timely." Prior to now, culture as parent gave us one-size-fits-all rules that made the great majority of time-related determinations for us. We encounter such predetermination with common assumptions related to age. More recently we encounter it with the expectations of the nine-to-five workweek. With Cultural Maturity, our temporal options expand and come to lie increasingly in our own hands. They also come to exist in the context of a deepening appreciation for how diverse aspects of experience live in time in very different ways.

On the Nature of Nature

Another question that highlights the power of Patterning in Time perspective asks how we best understand and relate to nature. We could think of it too as an eternal quandary—it is a question that has always fascinated us, and also has often presented answers that contradict. Certainly, how we answer it today has critical implications as we move into the future. Our times challenge us to an essential growing up in our relationship to nature.

Previous reflections on limits introduced the challenge. We've seen how we must relate to nature differently for the sake of human survival and the health of the planet. We also need a shift in our relationship with nature for a further equally important reason. We need it for the sake of our souls. John Muir once said, "I only went out for a walk and finally concluded to stay till sundown. For going out, I found I was really going in." We too are nature. In forgetting nature, we, in a very important sense, forget ourselves as well. The task is not only to better protect nature, but to develop a new and deeper kind of relationship with and understanding of nature.

Developmental/evolutionary perspective helps us in multiple ways with this essential task. At the least, it makes clear that our understandings of our biological and physical and worlds have never been as objective and final as we have thought them to be. Our beliefs have always been as much about polar projection as actuality, or at least as much about the lenses through which we have been able to see as what we have endeavored to see. Is the creature world a "peaceable kingdom" (and thus to be emulated), or "red in tooth and claw" (something to fear and, if possible, to tame)? Is the physical world animate and spiritful (and thus best treated as an expression of the divine), or is it dead and inert (and thus regarded at best as a resource for fulfilling human needs)?

Developmental/evolutionary perspective also helps us more clearly grasp what we need to leave behind—and, just a bit, where we need to go. The common conclusion in modern times that nature is in effect a machine would have seemed ludicrous within any other cultural period. But it makes perfect sense in the context of the kind of cognitive perspective that has given us Modern Age reality. With the recognition that the way we see nature is time-specific, it also makes perfect sense that further ways of understanding and relating to nature, in potential, lie ahead. Integrative Meta-perspective's larger picture at least helps us begin to understand what we need to get in touch with in ourselves if we are to think about nature and our relationship to it in the needed new ways.

What is nature—at least to us? And how does our answer to that question now need to change? Creative Systems Theory maps how our perceptions of nature differ as a function of any Patterning in Time (or Patterning in Space) variable. The way it does provides valuable insight for going forward.

In sketching this progression, I will give particular emphasis to an aspect of change's creative mechanism that before I've only implied. In addition to amnesia between creative stages, we also encounter a more vigorous kind of dynamic—the newly created content (the archetypally masculine pole) actively pushes away its creative context (the archetypally feminine pole). We encounter this active pushing away with any formative process, but it is particularly easy to recognize in our historical relationship with nature.

The reason for this pushing away is related to what I described for developmental amnesias. The attraction of creation's origin can be so powerful that it threatens to undermine needed separation. This pushing away manifests most strongly with later parts of Middle-Axis dynamics and the early parts of Late-Axis dynamics. Then it can translate into active denigration. With Early-Axis, the creative context's role is primarily nurturing. With Late-Axis, increasingly separation is sufficiently established that there is little need to fear falling back.[13]

---

13   This mechanism helps make some previous observations more understandable—for example, how later stage cultures have often not just dismissed tribal people, but actively oppressed them. It also helps us understand

The basic contours of the evolving sequence of relationships with nature that Creative System Theory describes should now feel familiar:

The view of nature in early tribal (Pre-Axis) times was far from that of today. Rather than an inert resource to be utilized, nature—as mountain, river, forest, and soil—was cherished as the divine source of all life. Mortals stood small in relationship to her mysterious immensity.

With the rise of early civilizations (Early-Axis times in culture), we saw the first real separation from nature. Animism gave way to ascendant pantheons of gods, and man came to inhabit a realm that seemed fully distinct from the creaturely. Nature and humanity were no longer seen as one. And at the same time their perceived relationship remained strong. The early Greek gods were viewed as ascendant above nature, but it was never forgotten that they were born from Gaia, the earth. The Eleusinian Mysteries, while beyond animism, embodied a deep awe of nature and expressed a message of shared consciousness between matter and humanity.

Humanity's relationship with nature first grew overtly contentious in the period we identify with the rise of monotheism. That rise took expression in at once a more forceful ascendancy of the divine and a new ascendancy of man. The divine now stood as a singular lord on high. And mortals, while still respectful of nature's power, saw themselves now as sovereign over her. From the book of Genesis come these words: "Be fruitful and multiply, and replenish the earth and subdue it; and have dominion over the

---

dynamics that play out in specific spheres—such as what we see in relationships between genders at various cultural times. Witness veils and burkas today in the Islamic Middle East. Historically their presence protected both men and women from the possible consequences of that original primal power. From the perspective of our time, they look only like evidence of oppression. Certainly historically they reflected differing status and differing levels of freedom. How best to think about them now presents a fascinating Patterning in Time exercise.

fish of the sea and over the fowl of the air and over every living thing that moveth upon the earth."

This voice of dominion would continue to rise in volume, calling out with ever-greater force for the taming of nature. Nature's wildness became increasingly something to control and conquer. By the early Renaissance, we heard statements such as this from French poet Bossuet: "May the earth be cursed, may the earth be cursed, a thousand times be cursed because from it that heavy fog and those black vapors continually rise that ascend from the dark passions and hide heaven and its light from us and draw down the lightning of God's justice against the corruption of the human race."

Later centuries brought a significant further distancing from nature. Much of the moral condemnation subsided, but this occurred less because humanity had come to terms with nature's power than because we had put nature's power sufficiently at arm's length that it no longer threatened. We had risen far enough above our creaturely origins that nature could be seen, for all intents and purposes, as inert. With the scientific revolution and the Industrial Age, our bodies increasingly became things we had rather than were; animal behavior became the product of instinct and reflex; and the earth became an assortment of material resources to be exploited for the practical tasks of human achievement. This mechanistic picture of nature was tempered by the Romantic Age's idealization of nature, and in important ways still is. But what we saw with the Romantic Age was more reactive and compensatory than anything that really helped us understand nature more deeply.

The task ahead? Certainly, we need a next step in how we think about our relationship with nature. The question today becomes less whether we will achieve a more culturally mature relationship with nature than how much we will make ourselves and the other inhabitants of our planet suffer on the road to achieving it. As the Roman poet Horace wrote, "You may chase Nature out with a pitchfork, but she will ever hurry back to triumph in stealth over your foolish contempt."

With barely our toes over Cultural Maturity's threshold, we can only begin to grasp what a needed "growing up" in our relationship with nature asks of us. We can know that in some way we must remember our connection with nature. We can also know that we must do so in a way that fills out rather than diminishes our appreciation of the uniqueness of our human natures.

The recognition that the reality of each previous cultural stage at least points toward something we need to keep in mind helps us take our thinking a bit further. As was clear in Pre-Axis and Early-Axis times, in the future we must more deeply grasp how, in the end, we are part of nature, indeed how there is an important sense in which we are ultimately responsible for nature's well-being. To effectively assume that responsibility and make good choices, we also need to step back from nature as with Middle-Axis sensibility, though now not in a moral posture fueled by fears of chaos and regression, but in a way than can help us better see with perspective and make hard choices.[14] We also need the more Late-Axis kind of stepping back that can address nature "objectively" as a resource, though now not simply in the sense of something to exploit. A sustainable use of resources requires sophisticated scientific understanding of resource relationships along with a keen appreciation of the ways in which economic factors influence how resource sustainability can best be

---

14   When I was in my early twenties, I had an experience that has ever since helped me appreciate this piece's importance. I come from pioneering stock, my ancestors some of the first to make it over the Oregon Trail into what is now Washington State. I was reading some of the family journals written along the trail. Suddenly I realized that these brave people had had a very different—indeed, almost opposite—idea of nature than the reverential view that I, as a young environmentalist, had taken for granted. They respected nature, but they treated her as anything but precious. Nature to them was clearly less friend than worthy adversary. I also realized that their posture toward nature, while harsh, had a rightness that mine lacked given the context. For tasks such as crossing snow-covered mountain passes and rafting the Columbia River with wagons and livestock, my more reverent attitude would have been more hindrance than help.

achieved. All of these ingredients are essential to the maturity of systemic perspective we will need if we are to be effective planetary stewards going forward.

Architecture and the Developmental "Anatomy" of History

I've noted that I was a sculptor before I turned to the kind of endeavor this book represents. I've always been struck by the way in which architecture's more monumental physical expressions are similar to sculpture in reflecting not just functionality, or even some abstract sense of beauty, but how, at the time and place of their creation, we are coming to hold reality. Appreciating deeply how this is so requires that we engage experience from the kind of body intelligence a sculptor necessarily draws on. The following observations are excerpted from *The Creative Imperative:*

> The evolution of architecture, particularly architecture that is regarded by the people of its time as in some way sacred or special, makes a fascinating lens through which to observe the creative metamorphosis that gives us the "rise of civilization." In modern times, people often assume that architecture's changes through time are products largely of invention, of what we had become capable of building. More accurately, particular shapes move us when they speak from how we are coming to experience and shape reality as a whole. Similarities noted below not only cut across cultural traditions, they reflect patterns found everywhere at parallel stages in culture.

> In earliest prehistory (early Pre-Axis), the most common ritual dwelling was the earth itself. The "medicine" of early Stone Age people—drawings and ritual objects—has been found most often in the deep recesses of caves. It was apparently these caves, and such sites as sacred wells and burial mounds, that were the most common places for the shaman's "discourses" with the primordial powers of nature. Sculpturally, the sacred forms in this most archetypally feminine of periods were spherical containers and gentle mounds.

With the beginnings of Early-Axis sensibility, attention began to shift upward. Ritual spaces increasingly became ritual structures, and these structures specifically places for conferring with the heavens. The neolithic stone circles of Europe provide some of the earliest examples, while the pyramids of Egypt and Mesoamerica are somewhat later, and the temples of early Greece and the ritual dwellings of the classical East—Buddhist stupas, Hindu temples—somewhat later still. The architectural mass remains in secure juxtaposition to the earth's belly, but now there is a clear verticality. Worshippers stand below and gaze upward.

Approaching Middle-Axis times, places of worship increasingly reflect an equal structural affinity with Above and Below. The domes of the Byzantine period very nearly balance in their upward might the weight of the foundation and sanctuary beneath. In the uplifted towers and high rounded arches of Romanesque architecture, we see the first gestures toward real ascendant preeminence, a statement made fully manifest by the last centuries of Middle-Axis culture in Europe in the Gothic cathedral's surging buttresses and poetic spires.

With the beginnings of Late-Axis culture, we find two important architectural themes. The first is the continuation of upward movement. The second is the secularization of the ascendant. The most powerful gods of industrial high culture reside in the material realm, not the church. The culminating form of this period is the skyscraper. With its glass and steel purity, it is a perfect monument to objectivity and rational abstraction.

With Transitional times, we have taken one further step. The skyscraper continues to have an important place, but it is joined by an even more ascendant image: the spaceship. The spaceship is a ritual dwelling in which humans not only contemplate the heavens, they inhabit them.

Looking ahead? We see beginnings of further steps. The postmodern sensibility in architecture directly questions Late-Axis orthodoxies. And in keeping with the idea that earlier stages might have lessons to teach, it makes at least a start at entertaining aesthetics from earlier times. The worst of postmodern architecture presents little more than a hodgepodge of influences. But the best can bring together diverse aesthetics in truly striking and inspiring ways. In an earlier footnote, I mentioned Jørn Utzon's Sydney Opera House and Frank Gehry's Guggenheim Museum in Bilbao. I look forward to what more the future may bring.

The Evolution of the Body

With questions like "What is time?" and "What is nature?" this sequence of developmental/evolutionary reflections has brought us close to some of life's most eternal quandaries—and up against some of today's most important concerns. The question "What is architecture?" might seem less basic and consequential. But as seen through the sculptor's body intelligence sensibilities that I made reference to in introducing the question, our interest is in important ways the same as that which confronts us with the next question—arguably the most basic and primal question we could ask: What is a body? (In each case, we want to better understand how we shape, and are shaped by, experience.)

On the surface, the question "What is a body?" might seem simple to answer. We need only look down; there it is. In fact, the question is not at all simple. Certainly it is perplexing philosophically. The body is at once something we have and something we are—not an easy fact to reconcile. And the question increasingly confronts us in eminently practical ways—when we consider the body scientifically and medically. We are used to inquiring about how neurons work, about the biochemistry of digestion, or about the role of genes in disease. But increasingly we recognize we have only begun to understand the body's rich systemic complexity.

Part of the reason we have more to learn is simply that there is research yet to be done. But the reason, at least that we could miss all that we do, has as much to do with how we think. I've observed our Modern Age tendency to view a machine model of understanding as sufficient and culminating. And Transitional culture, with its near absence of lower-pole sensibility, would be expected to distance us even further from anything more than the most rudimentary action-reaction notions of bodily functioning. I've described how disconnected we can be from bodily experience as a particularly consequential Transitional Absurdity.[15]

The importance of understanding living systems in ways that better reflect the fact that they are alive applies in a way that has particular significance to the question of what it means to support good bodily functioning. If health and healing are about anything, they are about enhancing life. We've always known at some level that healing was more complex than fixing broken anatomy. I am reminded of Benjamin Franklin's quip, "God heals and the doctor takes the fees." But before now, the implications have most often been more than we could handle.

The notion that we can speak of the body as "intelligence" has similarly become newly important. And similarly it stretches us in fundamental ways. I've commented on the trickiness of talking about the body as a way of knowing, given how in our times we have so little connection with the body as experience. But I've also emphasized the essential role that body intelligence comes to play with culturally mature understanding. In particular I've emphasized its pivotal significance in a creative picture of cognitive functioning.

When we "bridge" mind and body—as culturally mature perspective always does—the question of just what it means to have a body becomes a new sort of question. It also, in a whole new way, becomes a question of deep significance. The what-is-a-body question presents anther eternal quandary for which developmental/evolutionary perspective offers new insight. Creative Systems Theory not only invites

---

15   See "Transitional Absurdities" in Chapter Eight.

us to consider a larger picture, it provides us with a way to map body realities and body dynamics.

Here, very briefly, I will draw on Creative Systems Theory's framing of bodily experience in a couple of ways. First, I will address the different ways we experience bodily intelligence at different stages in any formative process. I will then turn to how, with each stage in formative process—including culture as a formative process—we not only experience what it means to have a body in particular ways, we inhabit our bodies in particular ways.

I've spoken of each creative stage being ordered by a different intelligence. Earlier in this chapter I added a further level of detail by outlining how each intelligence—bodily intelligence included—manifests in each stage, but in different ways. The following descriptions, drawn from *The Creative Imperative*, fill out this progression. It also links the progression to how health and healing have been perceived at different times in culture's story:

> Creative Systems Theory calls the body of earliest times the "creature body." This is the body that knows the tribal dances and that moves in harmony with the beings of the forest, the skies, and the oceans. Disease in tribal cultures is most often thought to follow from breaking taboos. Beneath the surface of taboos we find actions that violate and put at risk the fundamental inseparableness from tribe and nature. Treatment is primarily through ritual and the application of healing herbs, its purpose to restore that inseparableness.

> Creative Systems Theory calls the next body the "energetic body." Here the body becomes less creaturely and more a vessel of energies and essences. We find this layer of bodily perception and conception today in the acupuncture meridians of traditional Chinese medicine and the chakras of India's yogic traditions. Disease in early classical times, in both East and West, is thought to result from imbalances between energetic tendencies. Healing can be through manipulation, meditation, or herbal remedies, its purpose being to reestablish inner balance.

> Creative Systems Theory calls the third body in this developmental sequence the "visceral/muscular body." From late classical

Greece until well into the Modern Age, the body in the West was conceived of in terms of emotion-laden fluids—blood, phlegm, yellow bile, black bile. (Here lie the roots of words like "bilious" and "phlegmatic.") Disease, then, was thought to have its origins in sinful acts or conflicted relationships and to manifest as blockages in the movement of these fluids. Healing practices— the administration of medicines, crude surgery or manipulation, religious absolution—were designed to remove these blockages.

The final body in this sequence—or at least the one we know from most recent times—is our familiar body of anatomy and physiology, the Modern Age's body as great machine. Modern medicine views disease as damage to that machine—the cause being variously trauma, microbes, genetic defect, or wear and tear. The purpose of healing, whether through surgery or the prescribing of drugs, has been to repair broken tissues and restore its functioning.

Which is the real body? Were early conceptions simply naïve? In major ways, certainly they were—especially when it comes to implications for health and healing. The greater portion of the knowledge we draw on today, including discoveries as basic as the role of bacteria and viruses in disease, is remarkably recent. But Creative Systems Theory suggests that differences in how we've understood the body may also reflect our complexity as much as our past ignorance. If the concept of Reengagement holds, we would expect each of our earlier ways of understanding the body to have at least something to teach. Indeed, given that modern cultural realities have inherently the weakest connection with bodily experience, we might expect earlier ways of thinking about the body to provide some particularly useful insights.

When it comes to health care, earlier views of the body at the least point toward the importance of including more than just physical factors in our considerations. The perspective of the "visceral/muscular body" adds that we must also consider a person's general emotional/moral well-being and the health of relationships. The perspective of the "energetic body" adds that we must include too a person's sense of balance and life direction. And the perspective of the "creature body," adds that we also need to take into account the health of one's felt connection with nature, spirit, or group—with things larger than oneself. A person might object that these factors have more to do with psychology than medicine—and at least from an isolatedly "physical body" perspective, that would be accurate. But when we begin to bridge mind and body, these observations begin to have larger consequences. If the future of medicine is about anything, it is about learning to address the body as *somebody*.

Medicine can also learn from how these various "bodies" suggest a more animated, indeed intelligent, picture of bodily functioning. Increasingly today we recognize that other aspects of the body than just the nervous system are "intelligent"—in the sense that they learn and also direct complex evolving processes. I think in particular of the immune system (that among other things constantly creates new antibodies to fight disease), the digestive system (that manages an intricate ecosystem of supportive microorganisms), and the endocrine system (that organizes complex hormonal responses). We are just beginning to grasp what this more dynamic—indeed, "creative"—picture of bodily response may mean for the future of medicine. But we can be sure that engaging the body as *somebody* must also better include the whole of how we, as bodies, choose, learn and communicate.

And specific interventions from earlier times can be at least provocative—perhaps invite is to entertain options we might not have thought of. For example, I find it fascinating that while Western medicine has begun to make limited use of acupuncture, it has yet to explain acupuncture's effectiveness in any satisfying way. We can't help but wonder what even greater mysteries we have yet to explain—or even recognize.

It is important to appreciate that we've never really just studied the body—objectively stood back from it—even the modern scientific body. We've always studied mind/bodies, albeit of different sorts (and being mind/bodies ourselves, never from a purely objective perspective). Creative Systems Theory proposes that how we experience our bodies today reflects a particular time-relative and space-relative relationship between mind and body. It also proposes that this felt relationship is changing. I suspect that in the twenty-first century, the body will provide many of humanity's most dramatic and important new learnings.

The second way of approaching who we are as bodies turns to an important way that we can use how bodily experience organizes creatively to help us more deeply understand Creative Systems patterning concepts. I've emphasized that every Creative Systems concept requires each of our multiple intelligences if we are to fully understand its implications. Bodily intelligence contributes to understanding in some particularly graphic ways. We can think of Creative Systems patterning concepts not just as useful abstractions, but as ways of describing different ways of being in our bodies. Creative Systems Theory maps this dynamically systemic picture. It describes how what it means to be embodied evolves in a characteristic manner over the course of any formative process, and how it also similarly manifests in characteristic ways with here-and-now creative differences.

I've observed how polarity has both more horizontal and vertical aspects. The words are more than just metaphorical. They reflect different ways experience is embodied.[16] The diagram in Figure 10-3—from *The Creative Imperative*—depicts how horizontal polarity manifests differently depending on when and where we find it. It can be applied equally well to Patterning in Time and Patterning in Space observations.

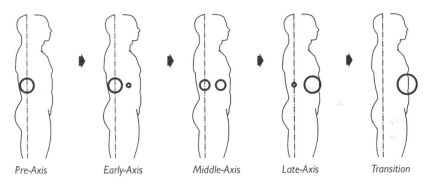

Pre-Axis   Early-Axis   Middle-Axis   Late-Axis   Transition

Fig. 10-3. The Evolution of Horizontal Polarity[17]

---

16   We encounter horizontal polar dynamics expressed in a particularly concrete way bodily with my description of how some people's temperaments are more "inner" while others are more "outer." In a related way, we encounter more vertical polar dynamics bodily with how one person's temperament may seem more "upper," more in his head, while another person acts in ways that are more "lower," more from the gut.

17   Creative Systems Theory uses the terms "inner" and "outer," rather than the more familiar terms "introvert" and "extrovert" to avoid lumping together

The diagram in Figure 10-4 adds vertical polarity to the representation and depicts how horizontal and vertical polarity together generate our felt experience of ourselves and how we perceive our worlds. Also from *The Creative Imperative*, it similarly can be applied to both Patterning in Time and Patterning in Space observations.[18]

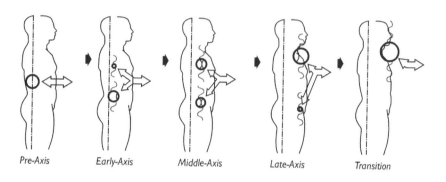

| Pre-Axis | Early-Axis | Middle-Axis | Late-Axis | Transition |

Fig. 10-4. The Evolution of Horizontal and Vertical Polarity

How does our actual experience of being embodied change with Integrative Meta-perspective? We become more in touch with bodily experience, certainly, better able to read our body's cues and derive fulfillment from the life of the body. There are also deeper rewards. A client described the changes this way. He observed that early in his life he had felt rooted in his beliefs. Then those beliefs were challenged and he went through a period where he felt that he had no roots. As he developed more culturally mature sensibilities, increasingly he felt "rooted in the fact of rootedness." The way Reengagement gives us a

temperaments that are in fact fundamentally different. The diagram in Figure 10-3 points toward why this more differentiated picture is important. It follows from the creative organization of temperament that even the most "outer" of Earlies will often be more "inner" than most Lates, and conversely that even the more "inner" of Lates will be more outer than most Earlies. (See Appendix D and the CSPT website for more detailed reflections on "inner" versus "outer" differences.)

18   *The Creative Imperative* and the Creative Systems Theory website each describe this evolution of body sensibility in greater detail.

new, more complete relationship to bodily experience is key to how Cultural Maturity provides an answer to today's "crisis of purpose."[19]

Finer Distinctions

I've presented only the basic contours of the various kinds of Creative Systems patterning concepts in this book. In fact, each can be understood in much greater detail, and often these more fine-grained distinctions prove especially valuable when it comes to the practical tasks of application. In keeping with this chapter's emphasis on Patterning in Time observations, let's take a quick look at how such detailed discernments can support our understanding of developmental processes—and, here in particular, of history as a developmental process.

These more fine-grained Patterning in Time distinctions have their basis in the recognition that creative stages are themselves creative processes and organize creatively. Thus we can identify creatively ordered substages within larger change processes. The following excerpt from

---

19   We find a more cultural-level affirmation of this relationship to questions of purpose in how Integrative Meta-perspective's more vital and dynamic picture of the body in a further way helps us address ultimate philosophical quandaries—for example, the seemingly contradictory relationship of free will and determinism touched on in Chapter Eight. Numerous studies over the last thirty years have demonstrated how choice often precedes conscious awareness. (We find, for example, that we can measure neural impulses consistent with action before we are consciously aware that we have chosen to take action.) Scientism types have used this observation to argue that free will is an illusion, that, in effect, we are "biochemical puppets."

But if we combine this chapter's more complete picture of the workings of the body with a creative understanding of conscious awareness and intelligence, the results of these studies become exactly what we would expect to find. I've described how Integrative Meta-perspective detethers awareness from will or intent. Much that we see in daily life in fact makes no real sense without the recognition that conscious awareness and will are not the same (in the same way that awareness and identity are not the same). Conscious awareness serves a powerful purpose, but it functions too slowly for many essential tasks. It is also not sufficiently nuanced in its perceptions. Think of the shifting movements of a skilled running back in football. His steps are "intentional," but they also happen more quickly, and are more subtly crafted, than movements he could "choose" to make in a wholly conscious manner.

The Creative Imperative describes creative substages within our most recent cultural stage (see the diagram in Figure 10-5).

If you look closely within modern Late-Axis culture, you can see quite distinct Early-, Middle-, and Late-Axis substages. First came a period of initial inspiration and discovery. This was the time of Galileo, Newton, and Descartes, and the emergence of the scientific paradigm; of Michelangelo, da Vinci, and Raphael, and the beginnings of Europe's artistic renaissance; of Columbus, Cortez, and Magellan, and the birth of a new age of exploration; and of Martin Luther, and the first suggestions of a new, more personal kind of relationship with the divine. After this came a period with a decidedly more Middle-Axis flavor, the Age of Empire. We saw then struggles between the great European powers for dominance in the new world, open conflict between social classes, and the first establishment of the structures of industrialization. The last two hundred years, what we might call the Age of Technology and Individualism, has been most definitively Late-Axis, with the final establishment of democratic institutions, a new elevation of the individual in the writings of people like Thomas Paine and Jean-Jacques Rousseau, the realization of universal education, and the full flowering of scientific preeminence.

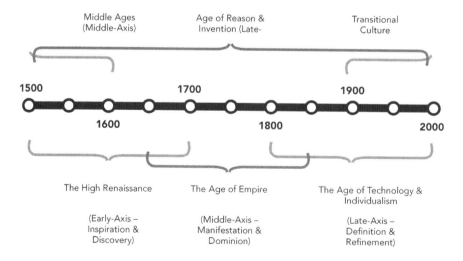

Fig. 10-5.   Major Subrhythms in Late-Axis Culture

Within any substage, we can also identify even smaller creative fluctuations. As a rough rule of thumb, if we look back thirty to forty years, what we witness will often seem surprisingly familiar. Shortly, I will describe how these further distinctions today don't provide the additional precision we might wish them to. But for our purposes, they are at least conceptually interesting. The following description of fluctuations in the later part of the twentieth century in the United States comes from *The Creative Imperative* (see the diagram in Figure 10-6):

> Within Transition's changes, we can observe much smaller cycles that imbued this aesthetic with qualities from various earlier creative stages. In the '60s and early '70s, Early-Axis sensibilities flavored the emerging Transitional picture: the magic youth of the "flower child," strong advocacy of matriarchal values such as peace and reverence for nature, neo-pagan sexual norms, and fascination spiritually with both Eastern and Western mystical thought. The mid-'70s and early '80s were marked by values of an increasingly Middle-Axis sort: renewed fundamentalism and moralism in religion, mounting conservatism in politics, and in music the sudden popularity of Middle-Axis forms such as country music that had been previously largely ignored. With the mid-'80s and '90s we witnessed a growing emphasis on more Late-Axis, individualistic and materialistic values. Increasingly the "best and the brightest" went to Wall Street.

What we encounter with the beginnings of the twenty-first century is suggestive of a further turning of this thirty- to forty-year cycle. Radical innovation again prevails—in this case, that of the digital revolution. In the '60s and early '70s, when people wanted answers they looked to gurus, antiwar leaders, and hip psychologists. With the beginnings of the twentieth century, they looked instead to the wizards of high tech.[20]

---

20 We can find this kind of pattern within the thinking of particular domains as well as with broad cultural tendencies. For example, Arthur Schlesinger, Jr., in his book *The Cycles of American History,* describes how, in the political sphere, liberal and conservative dominance has

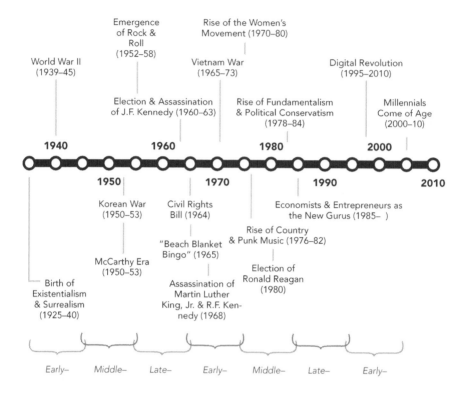

Fig. 10-6. Rhythmic Fluctuations Over the Last Seventy-Five Years

I just noted that for the practical tasks of decision-making this level of detail today tends not to provide the additional precision we might wish. Partly this is because such rhythmic fluctuations take place in the context of a growing complexity of other factors that affect what we see (for example, globalization). But as much it is because of how Transitional dynamics "flatten out" such fluctuations. Such rhythmic dynamics require the involvement of both left-hand and right-hand sensibilities to manifest in any deep way. With left-hand sensibilities largely eclipsed, creative substages are going to manifest less visibly and more often be overshadowed by other factors.

alternated predictably over the course of American politics. He proposes that they move in roughly thirty-year cycles.

Engaging Systems

I'll conclude this chapter's reflections by touching briefly on three topics that each in different ways involves applying Creative Systems Theory to the practical tasks of creatively engaging systems that we are parts of—of being a change agent in them, or more generally supporting the system's health and well-being.

First, I will outline how various Creative Systems patterning concepts are as pertinent to understanding the functioning of systems as the Patterning in Time distinctions that I have here given greatest attention. Next, to bring the task of application more down to earth, I will describe how we don't need formal Creative Systems language to make many of the most import kinds of creative discernments. I will conclude with a couple of examples that illustrate how the most powerful kinds of intervention most always involve approaches that engage both the process and the content sides of the creative equation.

Creative Systems Analysis

Any system, or set of related systems, can be described by using a multilayered application of Creative Systems patterning concepts. Such Creative Systems analysis provides perspective that is often hard to get in other ways. Because Creative Systems notions are based on underlying organizing principles, such analysis can help us get at what, beneath the surface, is most fundamentally important in any situation. Also, because all Creative Systems concepts are based on the recognition that human systems are creatively ordered and share a common language, such analysis often makes it possible to address highly complex phenomena in surprisingly simple ways. For the same reason, the use of a creative frame means that such analysis is inherently dynamic in a way that honors our living, human natures.

It is beyond the scope of this book to examine such analysis in any detail, but a quick look at the kinds of distinctions that tend to prove most helpful with different kinds of systems helps fill out this chapter's reflections. For this inquiry, the important recognition is that whatever kind of system we wish to examine, and whatever level of detail is pertinent, in some way each of Creative Systems Theory's basic kinds of patterning distinctions provides important information.

Below I've outlined the kinds of discernments that might be most important when applying Creative Systems patterning concepts to systems of different scales.

Individuals: When the system in question is an individual, temperament and Capacitance discernments tend to provide the most immediately useful information. But we can't leave out stage in personal development. And all manner of patterning observations related to larger systems may have importance—for example, the Patterning in Space function of a person's profession (being a teacher, a salesperson, or a lawyer require drawing on different sensibilities). More contextual developmental observations may also be pertinent—for example, those that relate to a person's personal and workplace relationships. And the creative stage and emerging critical questions that define a person's larger cultural context will of course have significance. With psychotherapeutic work, a person's internal Patterning in Space complexity (his psychological aspects and how they relate), symptom patterns seen when the person is stressed, and the growing edge of a person's development (where potential new aliveness resides) all gain special importance.

Relationships: With relationships, to the above more individual identity considerations we add how the temperaments of those in relationship may be similar and different, the relative Capacitances of the people involved, the developmental stage of the relationship (inspiration stage, perspiration stage, and finishing and polishing tasks make very different demands that affect people of different temperaments in different ways), and the creative edge of the relationship as process—where potential for new aliveness in the relationship most resides. Cultural Patterning in Time context is a major variable when it comes to relationship options (this is so at any cultural time—for example, whether intimate bonds are determined by matchmakers or romantic choice—but in our time, with the new potential for Whole-Person relationship, it takes on particular importance).

Organizations: A full analysis of the health and functioning of an organization draws on all of Creative Systems Theory's patterning tools. With regard to Patterning in Time, particular attention needs to be given to the developmental stage of the organization and the creative stage at which key projects reside (with the personal life stages of key personnel and of the organization's target population, if it has one, also often being important factors). Cultural-scale Patterning in Time variables may become centrally important if an organization functions internationally, or if culturally mature leadership and organizational functioning are considerations (as they more and more must be for any organization that wants to be vital in our time and attract the best people).

Patterning in Space organizational concerns include the organization's creative role (Early-Axis, Middle-Axis, and Late-Axis organizations require different kinds of organizational cultures and different approaches to leadership and management). They also include the temperaments of key people, how those temperaments match or don't match the expectations and demands of particular organizational functions, and the potential synergies and conflicts that temperament differences in particular relationships might be expected to produce.

Whole-Systems organizational concerns include the Capacitance of the organization as a whole and the Capacitance demands of the particular challenges the organization faces. They also include the Capacitances and creative edges of key people. And they include sensitivity to ways in which the system as a whole, as well as specific individuals within it, can respond when stressed beyond available Capacitance. Key to the organization's vitality is attention to where the growing edge of the organizational culture's contribution lies—where new organizational aliveness/creative substance is most likely to be found.

Nations and the Planet: Cultural-scale Patterning in Time observations here provide the most important distinctions. They alert us both to our own social group's defining tasks and also to what relationships with other people who may reside at different developmental stages may require of us. Patterning in Space observations that have to do with the functions of different aspects of culture—government, business, science, religions—can help support culturally mature changes within specific spheres. Capacitance discernments also have an essential place—from understanding the Capacitance demands of particular cultural challenges to the ultimate question of whether we as a species can make manifest sufficient Capacitance to effectively confront (bring sufficient wisdom to) the challenges before us.

Everyday Language

While this kind of formal analysis serves a valuable function, we can make the same kinds of distinctions in less formal ways. I've described how the task of Creative Systems patterning notions is to help us discern the choices that are "right and timely." We can get a long way toward doing so without fancy conceptual notions.

Discernments of the Whole-System patterning sort involve asking the pertinent Questions of Referent and inquiring about available Capacitance. Once we begin becoming comfortable with thinking more systemically, we don't need formal notions to make these kinds of discernments. They require simply that we ask what most matters to us, and that we check to see if we can stretch sufficiently to handle pursuing it.

The kinds of discernments made with Creative Systems Theory's Patterning in Time and Patterning in Space concepts alert us to the importance of giving attention to the contexts in which we make our choices—how, while truth as we usually think of it is about what, how much, or how many, truth is always ultimately as much about when and where. While formal notions help us be precise, again more informal ways of thinking about temporal and spatial context often prove quite sufficient. Three informal kinds of observations, what I call the "rhythm," "boundary," and "container" aspects of culturally mature truth, address the more specifically contextual concerns that Patterning in Time and Patterning in Space concepts alert us to.

The word "rhythm" brings attention to context in the temporal sense. At a personal scale, many daily concerns in the end ask rhythm questions—for example, sensing when to go to sleep and to awaken, or the best times to eat throughout the day. Other rhythm variables extend over time, but generally repeat—for example, the right rhythmic relationship between time alone and time spent with others, or the best balance between more structured and less structured activities. All Patterning in Time determinations in the end have to do with being attentive to rhythms. We are happiest and healthiest when we honor what is timely in the various formative processes that make up our lives.

Boundary choices have to do with how we engage other systems—our relational yeses and nos. They involve equally the ability to make our boundaries "hard and fast" when necessary and to surrender and dissolve boundaries when appropriate. A key characteristic of Cultural Maturity is that it makes us more personally responsible for our boundaries. It also makes us more conscious of boundary relationships and more able to craft our boundaries in increasingly subtle and dynamic ways. One result is that we become able to be both closer and more fully separate in relationships of all sorts. While having formal Patterning in Time and Patterning in Space notions at our disposal certainly helps us make boundary discernments with the needed new sophistication, the concept of boundary serves us well as a more general notion.[21]

---

21   Our boundary responsibilities include not just outer boundaries, but also inner boundaries, boundaries in our internal relationships with aspects of ourselves. I introduced the importance of internal boundaries with Chapter Nine's examination of Parts Work and the "cognitive rewiring" that comes with Integrative Meta-perspective.

I often use the concept of stress to illustrate how skills with making outer and inner boundaries relate. We can think of stress being of two kinds: the positive stress of creative challenge and the negative stress that produces stress hormones. If we can make both good outer boundaries and good inner boundaries, we can be sure that the greater portion of stress will be of the positive sort.

When we encounter something that might produce stress in the negative sense—for example, a person saying something we could interpret as insulting—we have two kinds of options. We can establish an outer boundary. This could be either by confronting the person or by just getting out of the line of fire. We might also decide from our Whole-Person chair that there is really no great concern, that the "problem" is a part within ourselves unnecessarily feeling threatened. (If the person making an insulting comment is a schizophrenic standing at a street corner, taking his comments personally misperceives the situation.) Then the needed boundary is an internal one, with the part that is reacting in an ultimately unhelpful way.

The formula with regard to negative stress is simple (though not always easy to execute). We need to be ready to make internal boundaries when parts react to situations where there is no real threat. And our parts need to know that we will make external boundaries when such boundaries are needed. Do these two things, and the stress that remains in our lives will be of the creative sort.

The notion of containers refers to the structures that define a system's relationships and activities. Containers include physical structures such as where we choose to live (our house, our neighborhood, even our country). They also include relationship structures (a marriage, what for us constitutes community, the relationships of our workplaces). In addition, they include beliefs, our ideational containers—how we think about experience to a very large degree determines the experience it is possible for us to have.

Most rhythm, boundary, and container questions were not personal concerns in times past. Cultural dictates took care of such choices for us—through assumed moral dictates, gender and class roles, and broadly shared assumptions about the workings of daily life. The more experimental world of culturally mature choice makes being attentive to such context concerns increasingly essential. Very often, these are the things we can control. When we get them right, what we can't control has the highest likelihood of working to our creative benefit.

As a therapist, I find rhythm, boundary, and container questions to be always forefront in my mind. For example, when I work with couples, very early on I always in some way inquire about the rhythms that define their relationship—in particular, how much time they spend together and how much apart, but also how much time they spend doing different kinds of things when they are together. People tend to want to first focus on the content of their relationship—who said this, who said that, who did what to whom. But very often the result of such focus is further entanglement rather than communication. (Put in Parts Work terms, the result tends to be parts talking with parts.) When couples get rhythms right (and right rhythm can be very different for different couples), conflict often "magically" disappears.

Much of conflict in relationship has its roots in fears of the simple rhythms that good relationships require. Conflict protects us not just from the vulnerability of getting too close, but also from the risk of real separateness (it is hard to stop thinking about someone you are in conflict with). Getting the rhythms right makes us face our vulnerabilities—which may not be easy. It stretches Capacitance. But it also gives relationship a new simplicity—the ease of being together in ways that simply honor who we are.

Along with asking about rhythms, I'm also keenly interested in whether boundaries are honest and honored. People often assume that being a loving person and being "open" means not having boundaries. In fact, the most loving thing we can do is be knowledgeable about and respectful of boundary needs (in ourselves and others). We always make boundaries. The only question is whether we do so consciously and caringly or covertly—and often unpleasantly. Relationships are much more likely to be healthy when boundaries are made in straightforward ways, and when boundaries are respected.

And, just as much, I'm concerned about the integrity and appropriateness of the relationship containers. I want to know whether the structures in which relationship takes place acknowledge each person's unique makeup. I also want to know whether these structures honor who these two unique people are together. Too often the containers we end up with are more a reflection of parental or societal expectations than what would produce the most loving and creative life. In a culturally mature reality, container questions must be asked consciously. No two culturally mature relationships end up looking exactly the same.

Greater sophistication in our understanding of rhythms, boundaries, and containers supports—indeed is essential to—Whole-Person relationships between individuals. And, in the end, it is just as important when it comes to relationships between systems at a larger scale—communities, organizations, or nations.

Certainly this is so when dealing with social conflict. Too easily, we get caught up in the content of differences and beliefs—and with less-than-helpful consequences. Focusing our attention instead on context variables often produces much better outcomes. This is particularly the case if our interest lies with long-term benefit.

I think of how dramatically globalization and the collision of cultures at different stages of social evolution make demands on Capacitance. Polarization—and a high risk of catastrophe—can become almost inevitable. If we wish to preserve peace, good intelligence, well-trained armies, and a commitment to honest diplomacy are all important. But perspective that focuses as much on the contexts of interactions as the content, and does so from a systemic vantage, is essential to effective policy.

This includes attentiveness to rhythms—certainly those of cultural stage differences, but also how quickly allegiances can shift and the changing realities that accompany even the most limited of change processes. It also includes sensitivity to boundary relationships—which as globalization and the changes of Cultural Maturity make traditional ethnic and national bounds less and less useful, must be understood with ever-greater sophistication. In addition, it requires that we be always aware of the containers available to us and which ones may provide the highest likelihood of effective communication. As globalization and the possibility of more culturally mature relationships come increasingly to define the world situation, we are more and more often called on to craft new kinds of cultural containers, ones better able to hold the complexity and magnitude of the challenges this new world presents. Such new cultural containers can, in potential, take a variety of forms—such as new governmental mechanisms, non-governmental organizations that can bring multinational cooperation to addressing social issues, globally integrated information systems to help head off disasters, or conferences and think tank processes that bring together the best hearts and minds to address difficult issues.

The best of diplomacy pays attention to all these variables. But having language that explicitly combines context and content concerns helps us do so more consciously and creatively, whether that language is informal or that of more detailed culturally mature conception.

Process Techniques

I've given particular emphasis with this chapter to new kinds of discernments that come with Creative Systems Theory's contribution. You could say I've given greatest emphasis to the "content" rather than the "process" side of that contribution, though such language really only helps us if we recognize that every Creative Systems concept is simultaneously about content and process. I'll conclude with a couple of examples that illustrate interventions that more specifically engage the process side of the creative equation.

I've previously touched in limited ways on the particular way the process dimension manifests with culturally mature change. For example, Chapter Six examined the ultimately "exploratory" nature of culturally mature truth. And Chapter Nine's look at "Parts Work" approaches examined how not only do particular kinds of processes provide the most powerful and reliable ways to get to culturally mature understanding, these processes may in the end give us the most concrete "definitions" for such understanding.

It is important to recognize that with both of these previous illustrations, we see process in a sense that is more significant than just something we do alongside content—process becomes about more than just how we get things done, with truths remaining essentially constant. In each case, process also has deeper significance than just how we get from one truth to another—it refers to more than just the methods by which we facilitate change, even change that involves leaps in paradigm. Whenever an approach we use draws on process in a culturally mature sense, process and content work together as left and right hands within a larger systemic picture.

The two additional examples I include here come from the world of organizational systems. They address the important leadership question of how we might best work for culturally mature change in organizations—of all sorts.

Thinking in the organizational development world has given increasing emphasis to process in recent decades. Previously, organizational thinking was almost entirely analytic—about teasing apart how an organization functions and suggesting changes that might make it function better. But while process-related approaches have had growing influence, most often they too have fallen short of what is needed for culturally mature change. At best, they get up to Cultural Maturity's threshold in the postmodern/contructivist sense of facilitating greater dialogue and transparency. At worst, they represent only a contrasting advocacy for polarity's left hand. They can end up siding with process in opposition to content, or they can be more about getting rid of hierarchies and boundaries than anything that could produce truly new kinds of outcomes.

My purpose with these two additional examples is not to argue for specific new techniques. These examples simply illustrate methods that have worked for me. Each demonstrates an approach that engages an organizational system in a way that both increases Capacitance and, in potential, results in culturally mature capacities. With each, attention to process and content have ultimately equal significance. The process dimension is most obvious in each case, but the application of culturally mature patterning concepts is also required if the process technique is to be effective.

The first comes from work I did some years back with a public television station. The station wanted my help with determining directions it might want to go with its cultural contribution, and also with regard to how it was functioning as an organization. I suggested putting together an ongoing "internal think tank." I selected people for the think tank from throughout the organization, interviewing people so as to get representation from each major part of the company. I also selected for high Capacitance and attempted to get significant temperament diversity. We met once a month for over three years. The group's assigned task started with identifying the questions that were most important both with regard to the role and functioning of the station and to the broader future of public television The group then rolled up its creative sleeves and took those questions on. The approach proved powerful.

Notice that while someone from the outside might be most be struck by the actively questioning, process aspects of what we were doing, success with the effort depended directly on the application of culturally mature patterning notions. At the heart of what we did was keeping the ultimate Question of Referent always at the forefront—our task was to address the concerns that could most enhance the station's contribution. Selecting for high Capacitance was important to the effective engagement with those concerns, as was consciously bringing creative diversity into the room, both the diversity of representation from each department and temperament diversity. Behind the scenes, that fact that I was being attentive to Patterning in Time variables as they related both to the station's growth and the growth of the group further supported effectiveness.

Our work together did not alter the organizational structure or basic organizational functions in any obvious way. (Sometimes culturally mature organizational change significantly alters the structure of an organization, but often it doesn't need to.) We simply added—with the ongoing "think tank" group—a new organizational element. Two things were key to that element's creative influence. First, the organization's positional decision-makers, the CEO and the COO, were active participants. The decision-making hierarchy was not changed, but those making final decisions had ongoing creative input from the larger group, and formal leadership was held accountable just by the fact of continued involvement in the group. Also, participants were

instructed to find ways to engage people in their departments in a related inquiry process—at the very least to ask people to assist in identifying questions that could be brought to the larger think tank group.
The result supported the station as a whole becoming an increasingly
conscious, continually evolving, creative system.

The second example describes an experiential approach designed
to be used with leaders of organizations. Because everyone is this in a
sense—we each play roles that affect the well-being of larger systems
(at least our communities and our families)—anyone who is interested
in developing culturally mature capacities can find the technique helpful. I'm particularly likely to make use of this approach when working
with a group with whom I have the luxury of working over time. I
include it because it is rare to find organizational methods that actively
and strategically apply multiple intelligences. The approach makes use
of all the major intelligences while also drawing necessarily on patterning concepts.

The technique begins by having participants close their eyes and
imagine their organization as some kind of "vehicle" (in the largest
sense—real or imaginary, mechanical or living) moving within its environment. This could be anything from a spaceship coursing through a
galaxy to a turtle making its way across a grassy field. I ask participants
all kinds of questions about their vehicle images—such as how they
would describe its movement, what challenges or threats might exist in
the surrounding environment, and if there are other similar "vehicles"
nearby. I then ask them to physically embody the image and to move as
it, learning all that might be gleaned in the process. Finally, I give each
participant a large sheet of paper with instructions to draw the image
and to write down any observations that might have significance from
these reflections.

And that is just a first step. Next I ask participants to include in their
drawing key individuals and groups within the organization (including
themselves), placing them in or about the vehicle image. I also have
participants draw lines between these various aspects of the system to
represent interrelationships. If participants have some familiarity with
Creative Systems Theory patterning concepts, I may then ask them to
evaluate the systemic aspects they have depicted in terms of Capacitance, developmental variables such as people's ages, and Patterning

in Space notions such as temperament and the creative "crayons" that various parts of the organization represent.

And we've not yet gotten to the most important parts. I then have participants describe what defines the "vehicle's" purpose (the appropriate defining referent) and where important "creative edges" (possible growth points) may lie. I request that they answer these questions not just with words, but by drawing on the intelligence that might be most helpful—using the body to express possible changes in the movement quality of the vehicle, using image or metaphor to describe changes in the vehicle's structure or appearance, or using emotional intelligence to give voice to changes in the quality of various relationships on or around it.

At this point, I will often take one person aside and work with that person and his or her organization more individually using the group as a whole to assist me. Group members role-play the various elements in the individual's drawing. I then have the person I am working with experiment with making changes in what these elements do, how they relate, or where they are located on the vehicle. I may also invite the people representing different elements to engage the person about how they experience suggested changes and to give any feedback that might help the person rethink his or her leadership role. This part of the approach will vary greatly depending on the situation and can be very dynamic.

Finally, I return to the larger group. I have participants summarize what they have learned about the life of their particular organization and its current creative needs and challenges. In particular, I have people describe what they have learned about what is being creatively asked of them personally. I may also ask about parallels they see in what various participants in the group encountered with their particular organization/system and how those parallels may relate to the larger challenge of culturally mature leadership.

This second kind of approach is more experiential and hands-on than many leaders will find comfortable. But when facilitated well, and with sufficient preparation both conceptually and in terms of understanding the power of drawing on multiple intelligences, it can be startlingly effective. Notice that once again we have an approach that emphasizes process, but that requires creative patterning observations to be successful in any deep way.

Pattern, Complexity, and Meaning

All of this chapter's patterning concept–related topics have been in various ways about better holding the whole of our uniquely human complexity—as evolutionary beings, in our individual choices, and in relationships, organizations, and institutions of all sorts. Besides adding detail to previous reflections, each has also further highlighted how Cultural Maturity's results, while demanding and dramatic in their significance, are also ultimately straightforward, even ordinary. In the end, these various observations have simply been about better taking into account all that needs to be considered.

An experience that people often have when doing Parts Work reflects this easily paradoxical-seeming outcome. At a certain point—as people just begin to recognize the whole-box-of-crayons task—it is not uncommon for them to in some way ask me, "Is that all there is?" I confirm that indeed it is, that living effectively from that Whole-Person chair is "as good as it gets." Integrative Meta-perspective requires that we accept that life does not have magic answers. But as the person continues working, the process more and more reveals a further truth. It makes clear that life itself is a magical answer. And it does so in ever-deeper ways. Both realities—the major significance and the ordinariness—become increasingly obvious.

CHAPTER ELEVEN

The Future of Cultural Domains

*I hold that man is most in the right, when he is most closely
in league with the future.*

HENRIK IBSEN

I'VE USED THE CHANGES that are happening and predicted in various specific realms of understanding and action as examples throughout this inquiry. I've proposed that the fact that we tend to view current ways of thinking and current institutional structures as ideals and endpoints extends to every aspect of our personal and collective lives. I've also emphasized how current forms, wherever we find them, can't be end points, how further changes necessarily lie ahead. And I've described common threads that run through needed changes.

In this chapter, I use changes within specific realms to help bring together where the book's reflections have taken us and to add an important additional layer to the argument for the concept of Cultural Maturity's accuracy and significance. I'll start by briefly visiting a broad realm that has provided many of our most clear-cut Cultural Maturity examples, what the academic world calls the social sciences—including history, anthropology, archeology, political science, philosophy, psychology, and sociology. That the social sciences have provided important examples is not surprising given that they are each in different ways about understanding just what it means to be human. These observations provide useful summary and set the stage for further reflections.

The larger portion of the chapter draws on what I have previously referred to here as cultural domains—basic spheres of human activity.

We can think of "domains" in this sense as primary Patterning in Space worlds within culture as a system. I will address changes that are reordering nine such domains—business and economics, science and technology, government, medicine, education, the media, love and the family, art, and religion.

Rewriting the Social Sciences

I've described how Integrative Meta-perspective makes it possible to understand our humanness in more complete ways. In doing so, it challenges us to revisit—indeed to fundamentally rewrite—the social sciences. I've given particular attention to how culturally mature perspective alters how we think about history, philosophy, and the more specifically human nature–focused disciplines of psychology and sociology.

With regard to history, I've described how, in modern times, we've tended to make history a chronicle of leaders, wars, inventions, and the occasional grand idea. I've also described how culturally mature perspective argues for a more dynamic and systemic view of history, one that better draws on the whole of intelligence. One result is a more specifically "developmental" picture that highlights the very different ways we have thought and acted at different points in the human story. History—along with history-related disciplines such as anthropology, archeology, and political science—becomes a wholly difference pursuit when we view it through a developmental lens, and certainly when we view it through Creative Systems Theory's specifically creative lens.

With our look at philosophy, I observed how, since its beginnings, philosophy has been about making rational sense of the biggest of human questions. I also described how Cultural Maturity's challenge to rationality's past last word status presents a direct challenge to philosophy. We looked at how a creative frame makes understandable why at various times we have held particular kinds of philosophical beliefs and lets us map the history—and to a limited degree the future—of philosophy. Integrative Meta-perspective can be thought of as providing a whole new kind of "philosophical" vantage.

I've given particular attention in this book to how Cultural Maturity's changes alter the worlds of understanding traditionally claimed by psychology and sociology. We've looked at how culturally mature perspective requires us to fundamentally rethink both the workings of human relationship and what it means to be an individual. I've emphasized the power of Whole-Person patterning concepts, how they help us more directly address human purpose, and in particular, the practical importance of the concept of Capacitance. I've described how Cultural Maturity's changes make possible a new, fundamentally deeper and more accurate understanding of human differences. And I've made the claim that if we wish our psychotherapeutic methodologies to support culturally mature outcomes, we need to apply fundamentally different kinds of approaches than psychologists and psychiatrists have drawn on in times past.

Besides requiring that we alter psychological understanding and how we apply psychological concepts, culturally mature perspective also presents a direct challenge to much in psychological research. What happens when we add new insights with regard to human diversity makes a particularly good illustration. Because the largest portion of research to this point has been normative—based on the assumption that "normal" is a single thing—the simple recognition of how dramatically temperaments can be different from one another brings a major portion of traditional psychological research into question.

Of all spheres of understanding, the social sciences have been most influenced by the postmodern contribution. Most of the references to postmodern thought in this book have come from the social sciences. With each of these references, we've seen the same juxtaposition of significant benefit and major limitation that we encounter with postmodern understanding more generally. The postmodern contribution has radically challenged Modern Age assumptions. And at the same time, with each social science sphere we have touched on, it has proven to be severely limited in its ability to provide a useful alternative.

Cultural Domains

Let's now examine the nine domains—basic spheres of human activity—I just noted: business and economics, science and technology, government, medicine, education, the media, love and the family, art, and religion. Given that the best of thinking and innovation within any of these realms only takes baby steps beyond Cultural Maturity's threshold, these reflections will necessarily raise more questions than they answer. But even just good questions can serve us powerfully as we venture forth.

These observations will often draw specifically on Creative Systems Theory patterning concepts. With each domain, I will address its Questions of Referent—reflecting on how we can best think of that domain's systemic significance. I will also briefly put each domain's contribution in developmental—Patterning in Time—perspective. In addition, I will expand on several Patterning in Space–related observations noted earlier that concern how the ways in which we think about cultural domains change with culturally mature systemic perspective. First is how we stop thinking of domains as separate and distinct and view them instead as systemically interrelated aspects of culture as a system—"crayons" in culture's systemic box. Second is how culturally mature perspective helps us think about each domain itself more systemically, better appreciating the whole of its complexity and dynamism.

This chapter's reflections also draw on a further Patterning in Space observation that adds important perspective for understanding how specific domains serve us, the ways in which various domains interrelate, and what we should expect to see in times ahead. We find that domains—as we always find with contrasting systemic "crayons"—differ in the balance between right-hand and left-hand sensibilities that they reflect (this balance set in the context of the right-hand/left-hand balance of the cultural stage in which we encounter any particular domain). Earlier I drew on this recognition to provide insight into the ultimate relationship between scientific and spiritual/religious understanding.

Here this recognition will give us the remainder of the chapter's structure. I will begin these domain-specific observations with spheres where the archetypally masculine wields greatest influence (economics and business, science and technology), move to spheres where the defining sensibilities are more balanced (government, health care, education, the media, love and the family), and conclude with spheres where the archetypally feminine has the more defining presence (art and religion). This is not a linear progression—again, our box-of-crayons image provides the best representation. But recognizing underlying left/right influences offers a shorthand approach to seeing relationships.

Until now in this book, I've given greatest attention to domains in which right-hand sensibilities have a strong influence—for the simple reason that within them changes are most easily grasped. Here I will often go into particular depth with domains where left-hand sensibilities play a more significant role. Underlying dynamics there can be trickier to delineate, and, in our times, with the archetypally feminine having diminished significance, understanding presents particular challenges. Developmental/evolutionary observations made over the previous few chapters in the book should make changes in these spheres more readily understood.

Some of the more provocative observations in this chapter have to do with what we experience in particular domains at this specific time. I've described how we exist today at an awkward in-between point in Cultural Maturity's changes. This fact can make what we encounter confusing. On one hand, with growing frequency we find new, often inspiring culturally mature capacities and insights. But at once we confront Transitional dynamics that can seem contradictory, and that when extended beyond their timeliness easily become Transitional Absurdities. Often it is the latter, more disconcerting kind of influence that makes the most noise and thus seems to have the greater significance. With each domain, I will reflect on both more inspiring and more disconcerting influences.

Besides briefly examining each domain's systemic function, its "creative" history, and what we can usefully say about its future, here I will also address that domain's particular role in supporting Cultural Maturity. Just as culturally mature understanding and leadership extends to every profession and domain of understanding, so does every domain have its contribution to make to Cultural Maturity's broader changes. I'll introduce each section with a brief statement about that domain's larger leadership task.

All of these reflections must be understood with an awareness of inherent limits. We must always keep in mind, for example, that the contributions that Creative Systems Theory and the concept of Cultural Maturity make are of a big-picture, long-term sort. I will sometimes draw on front-page news issues, and often the book's ideas can help put such concerns in perspective. But I will give such issues only brief mention for the purpose of supporting and filling out the more overarching perspective that our tools best provide. I will also make all the chapter's observations humble to limits inherent in even the best of big-picture thinking. What we can say at this point about the long-term, while more than we might imagine, is necessarily less than at times we might wish.[1]

Economics and Business

Essential leadership tasks: Economists, bankers, and business leaders must work to establish sustainable economic systems that succeed for all the world's people—and for the planet as a whole. The most forward-thinking among them will provide leadership with that most pivotal task of reformulating profit and progress.

The answer to the economic sphere's Question of Referent? In the end, economies are simply about the exchange of value. In Chapter Seven, I described how material wealth represents the most abstract, right-hand measure of value, and how today it has come to define what economies are about—and, in effect, what human value is most about. I also began to put the economic sphere in broader evolutionary perspective, and with this, to describe how our relationship to material wealth necessarily becomes different with Cultural Maturity's changes.

A brief evolutionary summary: Material wealth has always had importance, but consistent with its ultimate right-hand contribution, in very early historical periods its significance remained secondary to more basic determiners of value such as connection with nature and tribe, religious edict, and the bonds of blood and family. Native American potlatches involved the exchange of wealth, but their primary purpose was the solidifying of tribal bonds. Over time, we saw growing separation of the monetary from the social, but the process has been gradual. Earlier I noted how medieval belief made greed one of the seven deadly sins. With the more commerce-based world of the Modern Age, material wealth came increasingly to define the primary bottom line for our actions. Today, money represents much more than just a medium of exchange. It has become the aspect of experience that

---

1   You can find further domain-specific reflections on the Cultural Maturity blog (www.CulturalMaturityblog,net) and on other Creative Systems Theory websites (see www.CreativeSystems.org).

we most mythologized—in effect, our determining ideology. As we approach Transition, this equating of material wealth with value often reaches a startling extreme.

I've proposed that this particularly defining Transitional dynamic—like any dynamic carried beyond its timeliness—increasingly puts us in danger. I've described how it has become a major contributor to today's crisis of purpose. I've also argued that it can't continue even to serve us economically, how it plays a major role in modern economic instabilities, producing inevitable house-of-cards dynamics.

The structural question of just what kind of economic system might most benefit us in the future is beyond both the scope of this inquiry and what we can now grasp at all adequately. It is quite possible that major changes of a structural sort will really not be that important.[2] We can reasonably assume that future economic models must be more systemic in the sense of being more fully global in their scope.[3] Future economic models will also clearly need to better support long-term benefit along with short-term profit. But it is too early to know whether basic economic mechanisms will need to be that much different from what we see today.

But there is a lot of a less structural sort we can say. The most important recognition brings us back to that Question of Referent. With Cultural Maturity's changes, we should find ourselves increasingly appreciating and applying more fully systemic referents. At a macroeconomic level, that means replacing wholly monetary measures such as GDP with referents that better take into account all that contributes to well-being—not just material growth, but also the health of our families and communities, the continued vitality of natural environments,

---

2   This is not to say that structural innovations such as new kinds of currencies or new more cooperative economic approaches might not play significant roles, only that new structures are not necessary for the most important kinds of change.

3   As nation-states less and less define our primary collective boundaries, we should see changes that reflect both greater uniformity and greater decentralization. We will need more generally accepted economic rules and expectations for global commerce, and also new ways of establishing more local and regional economic relationships.

and our larger sense of human purpose. Personally, it means the kind of maturity in relating to money that I described in Chapter Four—the ability to be smart about money, and at the same time to appreciate money as simply a resource we use to support a meaningful life. Today we see at least beginning progress on both of these fronts.

We can also assume that future models must be more attentive to limits—for example, to the danger of having economic institutions that are too big to fail. When we begin to think of profit not just in terms of short-term gain, but in terms of long-term benefit, this greater maturity in the face of limits becomes obviously important—and not just socially, but also economically. For example, while addressing climate change may involve significant short-term costs, if we think at all long-term it becomes clear that climate change denial would prove ultimately much more costly.

Many of the most important needed changes in the economic sphere have to do with how we think about the economic sphere's relationship to other cultural domains—in particular, government. In this chapter's section on governance, I will address the most critical challenge in this regard: the need to confront money's current hold on the workings of government. But we also need to learn to think more systemically about how the economic sphere and government relate when it comes to crafting effective economic policy. Here we encounter one of the most important needed "bridgings" when it comes to social policy. Culturally mature perspective makes it clear that free market purism ultimately can't work, that it leads to benefit primarily for the rich and a lack of attention to shared assets such as infrastructure, health care, and the environment. But culturally mature perspective makes it equally obvious that ill-conceived regulation can undermine economic vitality in ways that are damaging all the way around. Cultural Maturity's changes should help us better appreciate the complementary roles that freedom and limitation each necessarily play in fair and sustainable economic policies, and through this, to help us develop more pragmatic, and ultimately creative, policy approaches.

Changes we see today more specifically in the world of business add important further elements to this evolving picture. Some of the most valuable new thinking about leadership in recent years, for example, has come from the business world. That we find such innovation springing from the world of business—where values tend not to be the initial concern—might seem a surprise. But it very much makes sense. Globalization and technological advancement have had particularly immediate effects on business, requiring it to deal with ever more rapid change and an increasingly networked world. More than any other sphere, business quickly pays the price if leadership is not up to the task.

We should expect to continue to see leadership innovation coming from the world of business in times ahead. If for no other reason, this will be the case because businesses want to attract the best of workers, and increasingly the best of workers will be those with culturally mature capacities. To appeal to such workers, business leadership and business structures must better reflect and more directly draw on culturally mature beliefs and values.

While in our time we see the beginnings of both more systemic ways of thinking about wealth and more creative leadership in the economic sphere, we also see some of the most unsustainable of Transitional dynamics. In particular, the growing discrepancy between rich and poor presents one of today's most glaring—and ultimately dangerous—Transitional Absurdities. Inequality itself is not the problem—within limits, it spurs individual initiative and wealth creation. But extreme inequality threatens democratic institutions and results in ultimately unstable economies. It is quite possible that the harshest lessons about economic limits in times ahead will come from ignoring the instabilities that such discrepancies inevitably create.

Science and Technology

Essential leadership tasks: Scientists must provide leadership in addressing the growing number of planetary challenges that require sophisticated scientific insight, while never hiding from the deep questions of ethics and values—and understanding itself—that will inescapably accompany advances that serve us.

The domain of science is concerned with understanding what is "out there." It is not quite as abstractly right-hand as the world of money has today become. But it comes close in modern times with its almost exclusive concern with what can be materially measured.

Because of this right-hand orientation, we can miss the deep ways in which scientific belief has evolved. But it very much has evolved over the course of culture's story, and in ways consistent with this book's broader developmental picture. While Aristotle's early contributions gave new attention to the materially concrete, a left-hand "unmoved mover" remained primary. Medieval science, which understood the body in terms of visceral humors and at least entertained the practices of alchemy, was about mysticism as much as it was about science as we think of it today. Science in the sense of repeatable, physical measurement appeared with the Age of Reason and the solidification of Late-Axis sensibilities. I've described how this new focus had profound influence, and not just within science. Science's new, arm's-length—"objective"—kind of understanding became our generally acknowledged model not just for scientific truth, but for truth of all kinds.

Over the last hundred years, science has evolved further, and in ways that have continued to provide conceptual leadership. I've frequently here drawn on contributions from the sciences, and often from as far back as the beginnings of the last century—for example, the initial discoveries of relativity and quantum mechanics in physics, and early systems thinking in biology. With each of these advances we witnessed not just wholly new insights in that field, but important steps toward addressing the more formal task of culturally mature conception.

This cutting-edge role could seem surprising, given that we might expect the hardest of pursuits to be the last affected by more integrative changes. One explanation is similar to that which I just put forward to explain why it is not surprising that business has contributed important innovations when it comes to leadership. Scientific inquiry, as apposed to inquiry in "softer" realms of understanding, allows immediate demonstration of an explanation's usefulness.

But there is also a fascinating further explanation consistent with a creative frame. In the section on art, I will address how advances in the arts, because they draw on the most germinal aspects of intelligence, often presage advances in other spheres. While we tend to think of the hard sciences as almost art's opposite, the most abstract of scientific thinking can often similarly draw on the most germinal aspects of ourselves. We see this with scientific thinking that attempts to deal with the rarefied worlds of the very large or the very small—the most primordial aspects of the physical (as with relativity and quantum mechanics). We see something similar with thinking in biology that requires getting close to making sense of life itself (as with early systems ideas).

This major contribution to Cultural Maturity's task acknowledged, it is also true that scientific perspective, at least of a classical sort, can—and often does—stop decidedly short when it comes to the needed new maturity of understanding. Early on, I brought attention to the limits that traditional scientific understanding, with its mechanistic assumptions, inherently confronts. In particular I've emphasized how these limits come into play where the focus of inquiry is not just life, but the particularly dynamic kind of life we are by virtue of being human. I've made the assertion that no culturally mature concept—whatever its concern—can be effectively grasped if our thinking stays limited to the mechanistic assumptions of a traditional scientific worldview.

Integrative Meta-perspective directly challenges the basic assumptions of Modern Age science. Indeed, the concept of Cultural Maturity itself remains beyond us to effectively grasp if understanding remains limited to classical assumptions. In Chapter Seven, I described how traditional from-the-balcony perspective runs into difficulties when it tries to make sense of any of the notions I've drawn on to develop the concept of Cultural Maturity. In each case, deep understanding requires a systemic completeness of perspective that classical science cannot achieve.

With Chapter Nine's look at Post-industrial/Information Age scenarios I went further to describe how ideas based on a classical science worldview can explicitly get in the way when it comes to the kind of thinking the future requires. I observed how, with Transition, science's approach can be taken to an ideological extreme—becoming a narrow scientism and producing only naïve and simplistic conclusions. Again, the limitations of such thinking are most obvious when it comes to ourselves—for example, what we see with the unhelpful, even silly conclusions that arise from thinking in the cognitive sciences that fails to understand intelligence as anything beyond complex computation.[4]

---

4   Two areas of scientific inquiry—cognitive science and evolutionary biology—are today often used to reach conclusions about phenomena that

But we also find thinking today at the cutting edge of the hardest of hard science that smells suspiciously like Transitional Absurdity.[5]

The technological sphere similarly presents a good-news/bad-news picture when it comes to the tasks of Cultural Maturity. Digital technologies provide a good example. I've described how the dynamically networked reality of digital technology is very much in keeping with needed new ways of understanding—how we can think of it as both a reflection of new understanding and a force that supports further understanding. At the same time, digital technologies can be applied in ways that produce the worst of artificial stimulation in the name of meaning. With Transition, they can also lead us to subscribe to some of the most naïve of limits-denying techno-utopianism.

Going forward, scientific inquiry and technological advancement will be critical to addressing all manner of concerns with major implications for our future well-being. To the degree to which new insights have their roots in culturally mature perspective, with its appreciation for both multiple ways of knowing and the fact of real limits, science can also be expected to contribute in important ways to the

---

before have been considered outside science's reach. While sometimes these conclusions add to understanding in helpful ways, just as often they reflect particularly superficial, ultimately quite naïve and nonsensical thinking. For example, it was a common belief among neuroscientists not long ago that dreams were nothing but random neural stimulation (a conclusion that has since gone out of favor). More recently, a respected evolutionary biologist made the well-publicized claim that music is empty "ear candy," with no evolutionary significance. I find it impossible to grasp how anybody who has either had a dream or made music could reach such conclusions.

5   I will be fascinated to see the ultimate fate, for example, of the currently popular notion in theoretical physics of a "multiverse" (the idea that there exist, in potential, an infinite number of universes). The concept had it origins in attempts to stretch classical models to make pieces fit that before did not seem reconcilable. The way it presents a picture that makes any option a possibility (if you need a different truth, you need only locate the requisite universe) makes what it proposes suspiciously similar to what we find with the "anything goes" conclusions of postmodern relativism. Time will tell whether we are seeing good science or simply a related kind of Transitional nonsense.

development of fresh ways of understanding. We can think of the patterning concepts introduced in this book as "scientific" in this new, more complete sense.

Government and Governance

Essential leadership tasks: It is the job of political leadership to place before us culturally mature images of possibility, to take tough stands in the face of very real limits, and to provide initiative in the crafting of institutional structures that are more creative, consciously systemic, and accountable.

Governance has to do with how collectively we make choices, and in particular how we make choices that have to do with more right-hand social functions such as economies, armies, and infrastructure.[6] Government's Question of Referent asks what kinds of values, discernments, and institutional structures do we draw on, at particular times and places, if we are to best make such choices.

The fact that governance's story is evolutionary, that the answer to its Question of Referent has gone through stages, is not hard to grasp. We recognize a progression from tribal rule, to the times of god-kings, to the authority of emperors and kings (who were not quite divine, but not just mortal, either), to the emergence of more democratic principles and governmental structures. A more fine-grained lens can help us also appreciate more intermediary structures—for example, the way more authoritarian governmental forms, from right-wing dictatorships to modern communist authoritarian regimes, reflect dynamics at the intersection of Middle-Axis and Late-Axis sensibility.

Key to Cultural Maturity's argument is the recognition that while Late-Axis governmental forms reflect profound achievement, they don't represent the final accomplishments we tend to assume them to be. We've examined how familiar assumptions of democratic governance as we have known it leave us short of the sophistication that future governmental leadership will require. We've also begun

---

6   Education, art, and religion each also involve collective choice, but collective choice that more often includes ingredients of a more left-hand sort.

to look at new capacities that will be critical to effective government going forward.

One necessary to the ability to more directly address government's Question of Referent has particular importance: the capacity to step back and think of government less in terms of defining structures and more in terms of governance, the functions that government serves. Such perspective lets us address government in terms of its broader systemic significance and also more effectively discern where changes may be needed.

Some of the needed changes we've examined involve bringing more systemic sophistication to the internal functioning of government. I've emphasized the importance of getting beyond the extreme left-versus-right bickering that has more and more come to characterize political discourse. While success in this regard has thus far been limited, people increasingly recognize that the degree of petty partisanship we see today cannot continue. I've also highlighted the importance of realizing more Whole-Person/Whole-System leadership—and "followership"—in the political sphere. I've observed how we can have mixed feelings with regard to these changes—we can want leaders to get off their pedestals, and then not be happy when they do. But we are making good beginning headway toward appreciating political leaders as simply people who have hard jobs—and with Transitional times, often nearly impossible jobs.

Government's new picture also necessarily includes learning to address how governments relate to one another more systemically. I've given particular emphasis to the importance of stepping beyond our past need for "evil others," and the concomitant need to view our own kind as "chosen people." Government's picture should also increasingly involve changes in the boundaries that determine governmental influence, both where those boundaries reside, and how we experience their significance.

As an example, in times ahead we should find the nation-state less and less serving the same role as ultimate definer of collective identity. Culturally mature perspective's multifaceted systemic picture predicts what might seem contradictory trends—both of which we are witnessing. First we should see increased identification at larger, more regional or even global scales. Even if we don't specifically identify as global citizens, the growing number of issues that we will need to address at a global scale means new, more broadly based approaches to decision-making will be essential. And at the same time we should witness renewed appreciation for local traditions and bonds. Combine these two trends with how more and more entities—from non-governmental organizations and multinational corporations to terrorist groups—define themselves in ways that cut across traditional boundaries, and the need to think about governance in more dynamic and multi-dimensional ways becomes inescapable.[7]

One observation has served in a particularly striking way to highlight the fact that we are dealing not just with refinements to old ways of thinking, but a wholly new chapter in government's evolutionary story: the recognition that what we have witnessed thus far in the governmental sphere is not really "government by the people"—at least in any Whole-Person sense. I've described how the Myth of the Individual applies directly to government and has profound implications for governance's future. I've argued that realizing something more akin to authentic "government by the people" represents one of Cultural Maturity's most defining tasks.

Earlier in this chapter, I made reference to the importance of rethinking money's hold on the workings of government. This task links directly to the challenge of realizing more authentic "government by the people." What we see today with modern democracies is much closer to one-dollar-one-vote than one-person-one-vote. A recent study from Princeton and Northwestern Universities made news by reaching the conclusion that the U.S. is really less a democracy than an oligarchy.[8]

---

7   In Europe we've witnessed of late at once both the European Union and an array of regional separatist movements. The effort toward independence in Scotland is particularly noteworthy in that if it had succeeded, we would have seen separation happening through popular vote—as apposed to civil war.

The growing number of transnational entities suggests the likelihood of a kind of change going forward that would radically alter how we think about law. In times ahead, we may find such entities, rather than applying the laws of particular nation-states, establishing their own unique legal relationships between one another.

8   *Testing Theories of American Politics: Elites, Interst Groups, and Average Citizens* by Martin Gilens (Princeton University) and Benjamin I. Page (Northwestern University).

The observation that large corporations and wealthy individuals wield political influence far beyond that of people with lesser means should not be a surprise. But the extent of the demonstrated discrepancy helps tie what we see to observations here about needed next steps in how we conceive of government and governance (as well as previous reflections about the dangers presented by economic inequalities and their implications for the related sphere of economics).

As with economic structures, a needed next stage in the evolution of governance does not necessarily mean radical new forms. But certainly it means deeply rethinking how our forms work and entertaining more systemic ways of understanding them. It also means recognizing that we must get beyond government-related Transitional Absurdities— such as the partisan shrillness that can make arriving at effective policy nearly impossible and the extreme hold that money has on governmental functioning—if government is to benefit us going forward.

Medicine (and Health Care More Generally)

Essential leadership tasks: Health care professionals need to ask deeply what it means to offer quality, universally available care in the face of inescapable economic limits. They also need to provide leadership in helping us think much more expansively and creatively about what the enhancing of health ultimately entails.

My own professional background has meant that health care questions have already received considerable attention—in particular with Chapter Four's look at implications of the health care delivery crisis and Chapter Ten's look at how our understanding of the body has changed through history. I will keep further reflections brief and primarily of a summary nature.

The basic answer to health care's Question of Referent is straightforward: Health care is about keeping people healthy. But it is also true, as I've observed, that how we have thought about health and healing has not always been the same. I've described how, with each cultural stage, we have come to view not just the human body, but health care's task in significantly different ways. I also described how the assumptions of modern "scientific medicine" [9] are consistent with what we see in other spheres with the most recent, Late-Axis stage in this sequence.

Two changes have been especially critical to what we witness today. In keeping with Modern Age machine model thinking, we have come increasingly to view health care as the fixing of broken anatomy and physiology. And, particularly over the last century, we have seen significant changes in the status afforded the practice of medicine and, with this, in how we think about medicine's role in culture. It was not long ago that surgery was commonly done by barbers. We have come increasingly not just to better respect medicine, but also to mythologize it.

In part, this elevated status has been a product of major successes. Particularly important were successes that followed from the germ theory of medicine—first, the transforming application of sterile technique, and later, the discovery of antibiotics. And certainly more recent successes such as the growing prevalence of organ transplantation and new insights coming from the biotechnology revolution have also contributed. But this newly elevated status has also reflected how, with the Modern Age, we've come to mythologize any activity we associate with science. As medicine has more and more been thought of as a scientific pursuit, we've gradually come to describe its cultural role in grand heroic terms. Health care has come to be about defeating death and disease—and, as I've observed, this essentially at any cost.

With many of the Cultural Maturity–related health care challenges I've made reference to, we have made at least solid first steps. We haven't progressed as far with confronting death directly as the effective addressing of spiraling health care costs will require. But health care professionals today are gradually becoming more comfortable speaking about death with their patients, and hospice care has become an increasingly respected aspect of health care's contribution. And the doctor/patient relationship is one of the places where the value of more Whole-Person leadership is being most recognized. We increasingly appreciate the importance of physicians being able to listen to their patients as well as

---

9   I put these words in quotes because much less of standard medical practice is supported by well-done science than we tend to think.

write orders, and patients are coming both to take greater responsibility for their care and to be better informed so that they can do so effectively.

We are also seeing at least the beginnings of the kind of rethinking of health care's big picture that I made reference to with the rationing care exercise in Chapter Four. Certainly we are coming to better recognize the value of prevention. This includes preventive screening, but also, and at least as important, making good lifestyle choices—eating healthy foods, getting adequate sleep and exercise. We are also better appreciating the roles that psychological factors such as stress play in personal well-being. And we are beginning to better recognize that a healthy environment is key to health—both a healthy physical environment (we are getting better, for example, at seeing the health dangers presented by environmental pollutants) and a healthy social environment (for example, we are beginning to better appreciate poverty's major role as a risk factor for diseases of almost every sort).

The kind of deeper thinking about the mechanisms of health and healing I made reference to in Chapter Ten is more rare, and often when intriguing questions are raised, polar traps distort conclusions. But here, too, we see at least beginning headway. In particular, discoveries derived from attempts to tease out the complex workings of the immune system (often spurred by the AIDS epidemic), along with new insights from efforts to understand the genetic underpinning of disease, have forced medicine to think about bodily processes in more dynamic ways.

The world of health care, too, has its Transitional Absurdities. More often than not, modern medicine has continued to apply a "great machine" model to bodily functioning, even while the best of thinking in other spheres has learned to leave such antiquated thinking in the past. (My medical training, while the best available, was in effect the training of a highly educated plumber or electrician.) Particularly striking is our ability to celebrate each new, more expensive medical advance while rarely raising the question of whether the advance is something that we can ultimately afford. Such denial is understandable given the new relationship to death that effectively confronting health care limits will entail. But it has stopped being helpful, or even really sane.

Education

Essential leadership tasks: Educators have front-line responsibility in Cultural Maturity's changes. They must teach the capacities necessary to life in a culturally mature world. They must also inspire the courage and commitment required for taking on the tasks of this needed greater maturity. In effect, they must work to make us all futurists.

With Chapter Five's examination of the crux aspect of truth, I described how there is a sense in which education's purpose has always been the same: to teach the skills and sensibilities needed to live aware and productive lives. But I also emphasized that what an aware and productive life requires has evolved, how with each stage in culture what such a life entails—and thus what effective education entails—becomes different.

Today, this has become the case in particularly consequential ways. Because education has essential implications for every other domain, bringing culturally mature perspective to understanding education's place in culture's story—and in particular, its future place—has special significance. Education's necessary new bottom-line purpose follows directly from this book's thesis. Education's referent going forward must be to foster the capacities needed to live in—and create—a culturally mature world.

As with other domains, developmental/evolutionary perspective helps put education's new defining task in context. Education's cultural beginnings emphasized the body-centered learnings of nature and tribal ritual. Imagine a father, spear raised in his hand, hunting a lizard, his son behind him mimicking his movements (with no words spoken). From civilization's early rise to medieval times, education became increasingly moral and philosophical; for example, with monastic education.[10] Education of a more specifically academic sort, with its emphasis on verbal/rational understanding and logical problem solving, is more recent. I've described how modern Western education derived its power through providing the literacy needed for democratic governance and the skills required for an industrial age.

---

10   This was for the limited number of elites who had access. For most people, education was more everyday and practical.

Culturally mature education—education that educates for the capacities a culturally mature future will require—represents a further essential step. It is beyond our scope to go into great detail about the specifics of what such education might involve, but we can readily identify important pieces. Some of these pieces most concern the content of education. With others, changes in how we approach education—education as process—have greatest significance.

As far as education's content, we should first note that such education appropriately includes some very traditional educational curriculun. Learning that focuses on established knowledge in diverse fields—history, science, literature, mathematics, and more—should have no less a place in times ahead. Future curriculum must also address essential abilities such as the skills needed to maneuver in a digital age that, while new, may often be largely technical in nature.

But there are also needed new learnings more particular to Cultural Maturity's changes. Many follow directly from reflections in this book. If nothing else, the concept of Cultural Maturity argues for bringing the future more fully into education. Until now, education has emphasized what is and what has been. The present and the past continue to be just as important in a culturally mature reality, but arguably what most defines culturally mature education is the greater awareness and responsibility it brings to future concerns. Some of the best education I've observed uses grappling with particularly thorny future challenges as the starting point for more specific kinds of learning.

One of the most defining necessary changes in education follows from the pivotal recognition that the larger portion of challenges before us require systemic solutions. Education that can support a culturally mature future must be multidisciplinary. Not long ago, education that spanned disciplines was thought of as lacking rigor. Today we are better appreciating how education that does not span disciplines tends to be irrelevant.

If Cultural Maturity's argument holds, we should also find each of our three threshold tasks increasingly informing the content of education. Better recognizing when ideological beliefs leave us short will be necessary to education's ability to provide the needed completeness of perspective. Emphasizing the deep importance of limits will be essential to education that reflects not just knowledge, but mature—

wise—understanding. And appreciating the need to bring both new responsibility and greater attention to nuance and contingency when it comes to the truths we apply will provide a necessary foundation for more specific learning.

And certainly something like the concept of Cultural Maturity—whatever language and characteristics we use to describe needed changes—must in some way infuse curriculum. Culturally mature education must be able not just to bring perspective to the larger human story, but also to help us understand the particular significance of our current time in that story. It must help us appreciate what is involved with being newly conscious in writing culture's story and making culturally mature choices in all parts of our lives. The best of education will inspire because it effectively shines light on the profound importance of the times in which we live and the immense promise that successfully addressing today's challenges holds for the future.

Much that will be most important for culturally mature education will have to do with educational process as much as the content of education. For example, we should find education focusing increasingly not just on the accumulation of information, but more and more on what we are able to do with it—on critiquing information and discerning where meaning lies, on applying information in ways that support collaboration, and on learning to use information wisely. In part, this shift will come from the simple fact that the digital revolution makes information of all sorts more widely available—information has stopped being a scarcity. But it will also be driven by a growing need (and growing capacity) to engage information creatively—essential to a world in which change is ever-present and in which solutions must be not just multidisciplinary and systemic, but also dynamic in their conception.

Some of the most import process-related changes in education follow from observations in these pages about the more here-and-now "multiplicity" aspects of truth. I've emphasized the importance of better bringing the whole of intelligence, not just our rationality, into both what we learn and how we learn. Multidisciplinary learning of the depth we have interest in is impossible without it, as is ultimately addressing any question that requires systemic perspective. Appreciating that intelligence has multiple aspects challenges many of the

most basic assumptions of modern academic education. Certainly it
challenges how we think about what makes the answer to any question right. It also encourages the application of more dynamic and
exploratory educational methods.

We also once again confront the critical importance of better appreciating individual differences—of all sorts. Education needs to be
cognizant of how different people's worlds of experience can be depending on their ethnicity, gender, or socioeconomic background. And
education represents the sphere where the particular significance of appreciating personality style diversity comes into highest relief. Education has made a start with regard to this specific sort of diversity by
acknowledging that we don't all learn in the same ways. But education
has a very long way to go in recognizing how deeply we can be different at the level of temperament. Greater sensitivity to differences of all
these sorts will be important both to better supporting each student's
unique contribution and to more deeply appreciating how differences
can add to who we are together. (I've noted how learning that brings
attention to the power of difference can start on day one.)

Cultural Maturity's new picture inherently brings into question beliefs that with Transitional times have become commonplace in educational circles. One is the assumption that uniformity of instruction
and "setting a high bar" will result in educational excellence. The use
of uniform standards, with universal testing to demonstrate proficien-
cy, has a place as a safety net for students and for identifying failing
schools. But too great a use of such methods too easily translates into
one-size-fits-all education that can undermine the depth and creativity
in learning that the future will require. Education that successfully supports learning to take responsibility for the truths we apply and thinking in more complete ways must be able to tap into each learner's passion for life and also be responsive to the very different ways a passion
for life may manifest in different situations and with different students.
Too often, in "setting a high bar," we fail to apply the foresight and
complexity of perspective needed to understand excellence in ways
that can ultimately serve us.

Beyond these changes in educational content and teaching approach, I predict we will also witness dramatic changes in the basic
structures in which education takes place in years ahead. We should

see such changes both with higher education and with education for younger students, but for different reasons.

With higher education, the need for structural changes will come in part from developmental/evolutionary changes I've described. The lecture halls of times past tend not to be a good fit with highly interdisciplinary learning and with education that emphasizes process as much as content—education that is more hands-on and two-way. But structural changes in higher education will come as much from broader social and technological changes, in particular from spiraling costs and from the digital revolution. These factors should combine to drive us toward a very different kind of higher education picture, certainly a more multifaceted picture with multiple options available to different people depending on their needs.

It is likely that online education will, with time, make higher education as we have known it for most purposes seem simply antiquated. I am not at all suggesting that online education is somehow "the answer." But even with fairly traditional content, 400 students and a professor in a university classroom is rarely a good use of resources. (The most common critique of online education is that it lacks personal contact. In fact, personal contact of any significant sort was lost years ago.) In my experience, approaches that in some way combine digital content with opportunities for face-to-face exchange will for most purposes provide the best results—for example, combining the best instructors in the world, teaching electronically, with the use of small groups that meet together for more personal and in-depth inquiry.

In the far-off future, large universities will likely stop being the primary places where higher education takes place. Universities will also likely stop being the primary place where we certify learning. This additional shift has the potential to be even more transformative. It will benefit learning, certainly. When education and credentialing becomes separate processes, learning can be acquired in varied ways without penalty. It will also support society deriving the greatest benefit from learning. When employers draw on more diverse measures than simply degrees, the result ultimately is a more multifaceted and dynamic—and in potential more educated—workforce.

Changes ahead with education for life's earlier years should be just as dramatic. Here the needed new picture is more specifically dependant on

Cultural Maturity's changes. It starts with the recognition that education that prepares young people for the future will often be costly. I've proposed that just " raising the bar" does not produce higher-quality education. Countries with the best educational systems give teachers high status and spend generously on education. Additional ingredients important to the culturally mature education of young people do not come cheap—for example, making education more dynamic and exploratory; engaging learning at the level of purpose; and being more deeply responsive to human differences. Culturally mature education for young people will requires making education a very high societal priority—a significantly higher priority than we do currently, at least in the United States.

We legitimately ask how we can afford this new picture. The answer necessarily lies in the larger question of how we view children and their importance. I find it striking how blind we can be to the gap that exists between the idealized way we often speak about children and our behavior when it comes to creating environments that really serve them. I think of this gap as an important further example of Transitional Absurdity. Transitional dynamics inherently distance us from childhood experience and what makes it particular.

If this is an accurate way of understanding what we see, then there is also good news. We should expect the cognitive changes that come with Cultural Maturity to help us better appreciate both the sensibilities that make childhood unique, and the unique contributions that young people bring to our lives. The needed priorities should follow.

The Media

Essential leadership tasks: The news media—both traditional and in all its new, increasingly decentralized forms—will be critical to effectively confronting Cultural Maturity's challenge. They must clearly articulate the new questions, provide the informational resources a culturally mature populace requires, and go beyond just balanced reporting to engage essential issues with an unswerving focus and creativity that at this point is rare. Popular media also have an essential role. They must stand opposed to the artificial-stimulation-as-substance diversions that today too often pass as communication, and put forward images that can model and inspire culturally mature lives.

The news media's obvious systemic function is to help us be informed. But it also has a deeper role that is key to addressing its future. In the Middle Ages, we looked to the church and to the crown for the guidance we needed to make our choices. They functioned as our "trusted agents." In modern times, the news media, when at its best, has taken over this trusted agent role, functioned as the source we can look to for information we can rely on.

The news media's story through history by itself adds in only limited ways to previous observations. We could examine how different intelligences have predominated in what we have found important to communicate at different times in culture, but that is now a familiar topic. And while I could describe how means of communication have evolved—from drumbeats, to wandering minstrels making their rounds among medieval villages, to the advent of movable type, to the digital revolution—this is largely a technical history. For this look at the future of media, historical perspective's most important contribution is to affirm the importance of the news media's trusted-agent role—how it has functioned in modern times to provide us with key information we have needed to live safe and productive lives. Culturally mature media must necessarily continue this trusted-agent tradition, but now at a new level of sophistication. Going forward, the media must provide reporting and interpretation able to support people making culturally mature choices in both their personal and collective lives.

In identifying this essential task, we need to acknowledge how very far the news media today often are from succeeding at it. Of cultural functions we have looked at, the news media are probably most blind to how badly their current practices fall short of what real leadership in a culturally mature world requires. The news media's approval ratings are rarely much above ratings we give politicians—and for good reason. Too much of what we call news is sensationalized "if it bleeds, it leads" journalism—the latest murders, rapes, and disasters.[11] Arguably, this is

---

11 Notice the direct relationship to the task of finding a new maturity in relationship to death that we examined with the health care delivery challenge. "If it bleeds, it leads" journalism works because we reflexively associate images of death and destruction with significance—this in spite of the fact that death, being something that eventually happens to each

barely news at all, if by news we mean something new, information that tells us anything we did not previously know.[12]

In Chapter One, I observed how even when the news media do take on serious issues, what we find tends to fall well short of culturally mature journalism. Most often reporting takes the form either of ideological advocacy or, in the name of fairness, voicing one predictable ideological position followed by its opposite. I've described how even the best of journalism too often confuses "balanced reporting" with the kind of systemic perspective needed if we are to arrive at the needed new, more creative and complete kind of understanding.

Today's increasingly diverse and decentralized digital media options invite new possibilities, but they also present new dangers. The most obvious danger lies with the creation of "gated communities" of the like-minded. But there is also how the sheer amount of information can make us vulnerable to confusing quantity with significance—a Transitional trap. Information overload can also have us simply stop listening. And nothing in a more diversified media environment, by itself, protects us from the sensationalizing of content and the confusion of empty stimulation with news—indeed, this danger increases.

The most significant new possibility lies with the way new types of media can help us develop resources to filter and triage information. Our trusted agents no longer need to be established figures—such as Walter Cronkite in his time—with the resources of major networks behind them. New media modalities invite the development of media resources that specifically highlight information able to help us create a culturally mature world. This is a possibility that we have yet to significantly realize. It is essential that we successfully do so.

Changes in popular media similarly involve both new dangers and

---

of us, could not be more commonplace.

12   I can tell you the likely number of murders and rapes that will happen in the upcoming year. If rates are increasing, that could be news. And if an event happens in one's own neighborhood or city, that too might be news. But if an event takes place in some far-off locale, as is most often the case with content on the evening news, describing it tells us nothing—indeed, less than nothing.

new options. The business of popular media is the telling of stories. Old stories necessarily leave us short. But we also have the option of telling new kinds of stories.

I've observed how modern (Late-Axis) storytelling has most often applied either heroic (putting a man on the moon) or romantic (Romeo and Juliet) narratives and how each of these most familiar kinds of narrative has derived much of its attractiveness from idealization, projection, and dreams of limitlessness. I've also described how the growing influence of postmodern narrative in contemporary popular media has begun to take us beyond these two options. Such more Transitional storytelling has often challenged past idealizations in important and creative ways.

But I've emphasized, too, how we can't stop there. Transitional storytelling can translate into a difference-for-its-own-sake, ironic-glibness-in-the-name-of-profundity sensibility that produces at best cleverness, at worst a self-satisfied superficiality that reflects, and serves to perpetuate, Transitional Absurdity. While such ultimately unhelpful Transitional dynamics are often not of great concern—being more silly in their consequences than significant—they can also present real dangers. I've described how entertainment media with growing frequency draw on psychological mechanisms that differ little from those of addicting drugs. In doing so, they contribute to what is arguably our time's most destructive form of Transitional Absurdity.[13]

Fortunately, there is nothing to keep us from telling new kinds of stories. I often challenge friends and colleagues in the entertainment world to expand their thinking to include culturally mature narrative and to reflect on how such new storytelling can be translated into effective expression. We see bits of culturally mature narrative in the best of contemporary popular media—stories of people, often in very different ways, seeking personal meaning in a world where traditional guideposts are not as helpful as in times past; of relationships in which people not only step outside the bounds of expectations, but attempt to engage one another in more complete (Whole-Person) ways; of people look-

---

13   The entirely predictable "artificial stimulation" can reflect an ultimate extension of either more right-hand or more left-hand themes—explosions, shootings, and car crashes on one hand; reality TV's wholly consumptive emotional titillation on the other.

ing toward the future in a manner that steps beyond outdated heroic imagery (and equally its polar twin, dystopian imagery) and provides authentic hope and creative inspiration for going forward. It is true that culturally mature narrative can initially seem less sexy than what it replaces. But, for the simple reason that culturally mature possibility describes what is becoming creatively right and true in our times, more and more we should find storytelling that draws on culturally mature themes compelling—and ultimately, most "sexy."

I'm a strong advocate for media literacy classes in the schools. Good media literacy classes continue to be rare, and I think it is essential that media literacy insights inform education at all levels. I have particular interest in how media literacy becomes essential in our digitally interconnected world. The topic highlights the important relationship between the content of this section and that of the section previous.

The emphasis with media literacy curriculum has changed in recent years in ways that have sometimes caused conflict between media literacy advocates. Not long ago the primary focus was learning to "deconstruct" media so that students could better recognize biases and not be exploited by the media—particularly by television with its too often numbing, even addictive effects and, within media of all sorts, by advertising's distorting influence. The emphasis was largely protective. Newer media literacy advocates tend to be more positive and proactive, giving greatest attention to how digital media offer the possibility of endless media options and of students' creating their own media.

Today, a next step has become essential. We reside in an easily confusing, in-between place when it comes to the promise of the digital revolution. We see dramatic new freedoms, and at once realities that are often decidedly less helpful than we like to imagine. What we encounter with new media—both with news media and popular media—is too often empty stimulation more than substance, and content that is at best an inch deep and many, many miles wide.

I sometimes suggest a simple exercise for teachers to do with students that captures what is needed, in a way that draws on the best of the two media literacy traditions. The teacher challenges each students to put together a website[14] that can function as a trusted agent—that provides

---

14   It doesn't need to be a website. For certain students a drawing with arrows

links to information (and entertainment) that the student finds personally most useful and important (most life-affirming). Students then engage in discussion about why they chose to include what they did, and also about what they found to be missing that should somehow be included. This simple exercise not only captures what needs to be at the heart of good media education, it begins to get at the timely task for all of us if digital technologies—and the media more generally—are to serve us in a culturally mature world.

Love and the Family

Essential leadership tasks: In relationships of all sorts, including the most personal, we all need to be leaders. That means learning to love as whole people. It also means creating child-rearing environments that support the development of Whole-Person identities and rich and full cognitive capacities in our children.

Some of the most important culturally mature leadership happens closest to home. In Chapter Two, I put current changes in our experience of love in developmental/evolutionary perspective. I observed that while romantic love represents a major step beyond love in which the choice was made by one's family or by a matchmaker, it remains two-halves-make-a-whole love. I also described how, as a psychotherapist, I today find people increasingly seeking out more Whole-Person bonds. Such bonds stretch us by requiring that we surrender the idealized imagery of times past and know both ourselves and the person we are with more complexly. But they also offer the possibility of a depth and creativity of connecting that we have not known before.

I've observed, too, how the same changes that produce this result also fundamentally alter our experience of personal identity. They challenge us to think about who we are in ways that don't confuse projected aspects of ourselves with the personalities of people around

---

or some other form of expression might provide the best medium. And it is quite possible that someone reading this book twenty years from now will have a hard time remembering just what a website is.

us. They help each of us better appreciate—and more deeply engage with—our own, unique whole-box-of-crayons complexities.

We most readily recognize how this deeper engagement with our personal complexities pertains to love and the family with today's growing acceptance of diversity in gender roles. In fact, we are rethinking not just roles, but gender itself. Through most of human history we have assumed that men and women have clear and wholly separate natures. With the contemporary acceptance of gay marriage, and with it, alternative ways of defining gender identity, this polarized picture is rapidly breaking down. We are becoming increasingly comfortable with thinking about gender identity and sexual orientation in terms of a diverse array of options, and options that can change over time.[15]

The way Integrative Meta-perspective alters our experience both of love and of identity has immediate implications for the kind of leadership family life today requires. Certainly it makes us more conscious in making family life–related decisions and increases options. Whether to be married at all has become a legitimate question. And there is that critical choice of whether or not to have children—something that has never before really been a matter of choice. We are becoming increasingly capable of the depth of self-knowledge needed to ascertain whether having children is the most creative use of our particular lives.

We also face the possibility—and considerable challenge—of parenting in more Whole-Person ways. Whole-Person parenting will become increasingly important if our children are to develop the capacities necessary to lead effectively in their lives. This does not at all mean "permissive" parenting. It does mean child-rearing that respects the uniqueness of each child and supports each child in honoring and developing his or her particular identity.

The Reengagement with child sensibilities I noted in the section on education should play an increasingly significant role in making such more Whole-Person child-rearing possible and its value more obvious. Too often, today, people either give children little importance, or they give their children undue importance in ways that make

---

15   One popular social media website recently decided to offer more than thirty descriptive phrases that people could choose between to describe their gender and/or sexual orientation.

those children only extensions of themselves.[16] In the end, these two equally dismissive ways of relating to children are but opposite sides of the same Transitional coin. Integrative Meta-perspective provides an antidote. When we better appreciate the sensibilities that make children children, the importance of more deeply valuing children—as children—becomes common sense.

Cultural Maturity not only alters the choices we make as lovers and family members, in the end it fundamentally redefines both love and the family. These particular changes in turn provide some of the most powerful teachers of culturally mature possibility. In learning to relate to one another in more Whole-Person ways, we come to experience reality as a whole with the needed greater nuance and sophistication.

The Arts

Essential leadership tasks: Given that part of the function of art has always been to give voice to the newly possible, those in the arts have some particularly fascinating roles to play going forward. And the fact that thinking more creatively is so central to Cultural Maturity means that there is a new way in which we all, in the broadest sense, need to become artists.

Earlier I promised to give some extended attention to domains where left-hand sensibilities play the stronger role. Such realms have always been more elusive to fully grasp—such is the way of the archetypally feminine—and Transitional dynamics make them decidedly more so. Culturally mature perspective invites us to understand the contributions such domains make with new depth and detail. The artistic—painting and sculpture, music, dance, literature—represents one of these more left-hand domains.

Art's Question of Referent asks just what makes something art, and more, what makes a piece good or even great art. Framed more systemically, it asks about how art serves us and what is going on when it serves us most powerfully. Art's significance has been a question of eternal

---

16   And often, in effect, material objects to polish and perfect (for example, starting to prepare children for Harvard in preschool).

debate, and final definition inevitably escapes us. But culturally mature perspective makes art's function newly amenable to scrutiny.

Art would still be of value if its purpose were simply to create things of beauty. But mature perspective suggests that its significance is deeper—and in ways with particular pertinence to culture's emerging tasks. Art's deeper contribution follows from the fact that art takes expression from the most germinal of intelligences—the body, the imaginal, and the more internal aspects of the emotional. That deeper contribution has a couple of parts. First, art functions as an "advocate" for, and reminder of, the more germinal realms and values tapped by the artistic endeavor. It provides us with a collective ongoing link with left-hand sensibilities. The second kind of contribution is less obvious, but it has particular importance for this inquiry. I've noted how art fulfills a visionary function. It connects us with new possibilities. Rainer Maria Rilke counseled the artist: "Fear not the strangeness you feel. The future must enter you before it happens."

We find the most familiar example of this visionary function in how the art of the Renaissance anticipated advances in science and government that we did not see until centuries later. This visionary function is a product not of exceptional capacity on the part of artists (though exceptional art requires exceptional capacities), but rather of the creatively germinal intelligences that predominate in the artistic personality. When we call something art, we claim that in some way it gives voice to truths just peeking over the horizon. Good or great art is art that serves this anticipatory function in especially powerful ways—in the psyche of the individual, but also, and particularly, for the "psyche of culture."

Art's developmental/evolutionary story confronts us immediately with an apparent contradiction that we find with all more left-hand contributions. A person could argue equally well that early forms or modern forms are most significant—early forms on the basis of the preeminence of the underlying sensibilities, and modern forms on the basis of the stage in cultural development. It is hard to disagree with the assertion that the artistic had its most dominant significance in times well past. The central role that dance has played in tribal societies and that mythic imagery played in the daily lives of ancient Egypt or ancient Greece reveals a decidedly more defining presence for the artistic than we find in today's world. But, at the same time, it is also clear that Modern Age forms reflected an aesthetic "sophistication" we had not seen previously.

This apparent contradiction follows quite "logically" from how the relationship between left-hand and right-hand sensibilities evolves over cultural time. I've described how history to this point follows a progression from more left-hand dominance toward increasing right-hand dominance. Domains where left-hand sensibilities are strongest have greatest influence early on. But, as with all spheres, such left-hand domains manifest with particular refinement in culture's "finishing and polishing" stages.

A more detailed examination of why we see this apparent contradiction adds further nuance to our now-familiar developmental/evolutionary progression. And art's origins in sensibilities of a more left-hand sort means that a closer look at the story of art through history will provide important further insights for understanding Integrative Metaperspective's specifically integrative changes.

I've described how, early in culture's evolution, the sensibilities that underlie artistic expression are primary. In tribal realities, it is difficult to separate art and cultural identity—particularly art that takes expression in movement and sound. To not know the dances and songs—the most direct voices of bodily reality—is unthinkable. Artist Barnett Newman proposed that "man's origin was that of the artist." Arguably, the birth of art—in cave paintings and the like—is synonymous with the birth of reflective consciousness.

Somewhat later, with the rise of early civilizations—and imaginal intelligence now primary—we see art at once becoming a bit more distinct and reaching its greatest visual preeminence. We can't picture classical Greece, the ancient cultures of Mesoamerican, or the artistry of classical China or Japan without also imagining sculpture that many would say has not been equaled, and deeply compelling written and painted images—of gods and goddesses, harvests and rituals, heroic deeds. Art in these early times is not quite truth, but it is venerated as a direct route to truth.

With each succeeding stage, while art has arguably gained in its refinement, it has also stepped further from center stage. In medieval times, art still commands great appreciation—what could be more inspiring

than the aesthetic intricacy and monumental power of a Romanesque
or Gothic cathedral? But at the same time, art's influence in the Middle
Ages becomes secondary. The institutional church and the crown now
hold sway. Art exists to proclaim their wonder and dominion.

With the Modern Age—and archetypally masculine preeminence—
we see a dramatic further refinement of aesthetic and some of history's
most significant artistic accomplishments. The Renaissance (Late-Axis
Europe's Early-Axis substage) witnessed an artistic exuberance not seen
since classical times. But art also moved to a still more secondary role. It
became something separate, something to give pleasure, to decorate—a
treasured but ultimately subordinate function to those of commerce, science, government, and culture's other harder endeavors.

With the Modern Age, we also see right-hand sensibilities influenc-
ing artistic expression in a variety of more specific ways—to art's benefit or diminishment, depending on one's view. Art became increasingly
an activity of experts. (All children make art—in childhood, the more
germinal aspects of intelligences are primary, irrespective of cultural
stage. But in modern times, growing up means setting such activities
aside, unless a person makes the dubious choice of becoming an artistic
professional.) Also art became much more the expression of the individual as opposed to an expression of collective (animistic or divine)
forces. (For the first time, we find the larger portion of visual art signed
and musical composition, at least of an upper pole as opposed to music
of the more folk/traditional sort, attributed to specific composers.) We
also saw more specific changes that directly impacted the art itself. For
example, we witnessed the advent of three-point perspective, and with
it visual art reflecting a more material and objective vantage (more
similar to that of a photograph).

As we venture into Transitional times and face the challenges of
Cultural Maturity, expression in the arts can seem schizophrenic. At
times, art's more recent contribution has very much reflected its past
visionary function. But just as often, art has come to seem irrelevant,
even absurd. As with other spheres at Transitional times, we commonly
encounter overlapping realities.

A lot in the art of the last century gave articulate expression to
essential aspects of Cultural Maturity's new challenge. I think of how
the cubist works of Pablo Picasso and Georges Braque emphasized

multiple perspectives. The writings of Samuel Beckett, James Joyce, D.H. Lawrence, and others introduced a newly participatory aesthetic (where what we see is explicitly as much about ourselves as what we might be looking at). We see truth's new dynamism reflected in Salvador Dali's melting watches and the impermanence of much performance art. And we recognize what I've called Reengagement in the inspiration that Wassily Kandinsky, Aaron Copland, Stephen Reich, and others found in the artistic expression of earlier cultural times.

But at the same time, for most people, art has had diminishing significance through the last century. Few people can name major figures in the visual arts of the last fifty years. And much of twentieth century visual art that people recognize may seem baffling, if not ludicrous. (Campbell's soup cans and toilets as art?) The arts that do have effect on people's lives today tend to be either classical forms that appeal to a limited audience or expression (mostly musical) that is highly commercialized, often more a product of mass culture (who will be the next blond teenage pop diva?) than anything that serves art's underlying cultural function.

Even with its diminished significance, however, art's cutting edge has often continued to reflect art's primordial task. Part of that task in our time has been to chronicle its own demise—or, more accurately from the perspective of Cultural Maturity, the predicted effect that Transitional dynamics will have on artistic sensibility (and left-hand understanding as a whole). Twentieth century artists challenged art itself—both what makes something art and art's role in culture—certainly art with a capital A. We hear Dadaism's proclamation: "Art is dead—long live art." Pop art's claim to status as high art left us to ponder whether everything is art, or perhaps nothing.

Creative Systems Theory proposes that the reason such art has left most people baffled is only in part that good art always does. Some of what more is involved relates to what we find at Transition with any domain. Art becomes increasingly existential—its strength that it effectively challenges what before has been mythologized, its weakness that it is yet unable to really replace what has been taken away. But as much or more of the reason reflects Transition's odd requirement of art that it take expression from a reality in which the more archetypally feminine sensibilities that have been art's primary source have become nearly absent. We can understand the triviality of much of art today as an expression of Transitional Absurdity.

What lies ahead for art? A person might appropriately ask whether art as experience will ever again claim the potency of times past. Cultural Maturity proposes its now familiar answer to such questions—it will and it won't. If the creative dissolving of past amnesias (Reengagement) predicted for other more left-hand cultural functions—community, spirituality, our human connection with our bodies and nature, or the experiential world of children—similarly re-enlivens artistic sensibility, art should derive new attention and respect. Reengagement should reconnect us with the germinal dimensions that give rise to art. But the integrative dynamics that produce culturally mature perspective, as you've seen, always also exact a (major) price. They challenge notions that make any one part of the whole distinct or supreme. For art, we would expect that to translate into a surrendering of special status, the death of art with a capital A.

If Cultural Maturity's predictions are accurate, we will likely connect with art more deeply in the future—art in all its guises, from the most formal to the most personal or alternative. But at once such connecting will be of a more humble, less mythologized sort. Art in a culturally mature reality becomes an increasingly human enterprise, newly cherished, but at the same time no longer elevated and separate. As part of these changes, we should see the boundaries that separate the artist and the non-artist becoming more permeable. The professional artist should still be highly valued. But, too, we should come to view the artistic—or more precisely, the germinally creative—as something each person appropriately claims (and, as with a muscle group, learns to exercise). We see at once "bridgings" of the art and the everyday, and the artist and the non-artist.

We should also see other more aesthetic bridgings. Art will likely continue its forays across the boundaries of traditional disciplines—linking visual art with theater with music with the written word—as we have seen with performance art over the last half century. We should also encounter further creative links between the artistic work of different cultures—of both the same and different cultural stages. (Digital media should dramatically accelerate both of these integrative processes.) And certainly, we will see deeper links between the artistic and the technological as we are already beginning to witness with current explorations in new media.

Temperament-related Patterning in Space observations highlight a further kind of bridging. With increasing frequency, we should find people of artistic temperament contributing outside the formal bounds of art. In times ahead, every profession should have a growing need for people who are good at the new—both comfortable with change and facile with the imaginative capacities needed to envision the possible. If business needs to be more entrepreneurial, it needs more people natively skilled at imagining the yet unimagined. And a few more imaginative types might greatly help the CIA stay ahead of the ingenuity of terrorists.

One arts-related Transitional Absurdity has particular relevance to this inquiry. We reasonably ask what art's dominant form is today. The answer: If we define "art" in terms of the sensibilities expression draws on, and define "dominant" in terms of dollars spent, then, hands down, today's dominant art form is advertising.[17]

This answer—at once obvious and unsettling—presents an essential quandary. If art's purpose is to presage, to aesthetically lead, then advertising's ultimate effect is precisely the opposite of art, at least as defined by art's historical mandate. Advertising promotes extreme material values that can no longer serve us. And its purpose, rather than to provide insight and guidance, is to mislead, making it hardly a solution to today's crisis of purpose.[18] Advertising's hold on the modern

---

17 Advertising's power derives from its use of the trusted and largely invisible grammar of art—metaphor, image, movement, sound, and feeling. This power can be amplified today by how distanced the average person has become from these languages (and thus both unconscious of their workings and often hungry for their sustenance).

18 Put bluntly, advertising is a form of lying. Classes on advertising teach that one should never say anything logical in an advertisement—for the simple reason that doing so would encourage people to think and question (and then likely not buy the product). Instead, advertising juxtaposes images of what a person is supposed to buy with images of fulfillment: "Salems are springtime fresh" (this from when tobacco companies were well aware of smoking's health effects); "Coke is it" (as obesity becomes

psyche represents a particularly consequential Transitional Absurdity. We know we are being misled, but this does not seem to diminish advertising's effect.

This contradictory picture confronts us with an important follow-up leadership question: What, if we value art—and our well-being more generally—do we best do with advertising's lock on the artistic? The question is particularly relevant to this inquiry, as addressing it at all deeply requires that we venture into the territory of each of our domains—besides art, business and economics, certainly (advertising is a business pursuit); science (we need to ask about the cognitive effects of advertising); government (are there public policy implications?); obviously both education and the media (there could not be a more important media education topic); and religion (is this not one of the pivotal moral issues of our time?).

A person might appropriately argue that the correct answer to the follow-up "what do we do" question should be to do nothing. If the purpose of art is to mirror what most defines culture, then advertising, given these highly material times, is just art doing its job. But if art's purpose is not just to mirror, but to presage, then advertising fundamentally fails at art's task. And it ultimately fails us in a deeper way. I've proposed that what ultimately makes an act moral is the degree it supports and furthers life. Art in its dominant guise today not only fails as art, it fails the test of morality.

I've mentioned that I am a strong advocate for media literacy curriculum in schools. The importance of having a more conscious relationship to advertising's influence is a major reason why. Advertising's capacity to inform remains an essential element in the workings of a free market and will continue to be in the future. But becoming more conscious of advertising's effects—and, when necessary, reigning in its excesses—will be essential to a psychologically and spiritually healthy future. If, with Cultural Maturity's changes, we can become more conscious of and facile with the languages of aesthetic expression, we should become more capable of such creative management (both with regard to advertising and to the media more generally).

---

more and more an epidemic). Ultimately, advertising promotes our time's most dangerous lie: that consumption in and of itself brings fulfillment.

Religion and Spirituality

Essential leadership tasks: Religious leaders need to firmly denounce doctrinal polarizations, help us step beyond outdated moral absolutism, and challenge us to engage the larger questions of purpose and well-being that will determine whether we ultimately honor what in ourselves and the world around us is most sacred.

What lies ahead for the world of spirituality and religion if Cultural Maturity's predictions hold? Spiritual/religious[19] experience has had an important place in the human endeavor throughout history. And religion's future presents most intriguing questions.

As with art, a somewhat more extended look is warranted—for ultimately related reasons. To an even greater degree, we confront left-hand sensibility's inherent elusiveness. Again we encounter the need to think in terms of a developmental trajectory that might seem contradictory. And religion's developmental/evolutionary story, like that of art, provides important further insights for understanding culture's larger story.

People who give special importance to spiritual/religious experience will find this examination at once affirming and disconcerting. The concept of Cultural Maturity strongly acknowledges the importance that at least the roots of religious experience have for the future. It also identifies multiple important future roles. And at the same time, the concept of Cultural Maturity challenges religion in fundamental ways. It doesn't confront religion any more severely than we've seen with other spheres, but the central place religion holds in many people's lives can give this challenge particular significance. For many people, the church (the synagogue, the mosque) has served as a primary refuge from Cultural Maturity's easily overwhelming demands. And while

---

19   Creative Systems Theory describes how people of different temperaments tend to use different words—"spirituality," "religion," or even something more general. Earlies (people with Early-Axis temperaments) will commonly prefer the term "spirituality." Middles are more likely to use the term "religion." And Lates can be drawn to either term or prefer instead to use words such as faith, philosophy, or ethics.

newer, alternative forms of spirituality may claim to take us forward, rarely do they effectively get us over Cultural Maturity's threshold.

Addressing the future of spirituality/religion presents us with two kinds of questions that are important to distinguish. The first is most familiar: Does God—or however we think of ultimate spiritual/religious authority—exist? Culturally mature perspective is humble to the fact that this is a question that even culturally mature understanding cannot ultimately answer. It does invite us to ponder how the Cultural Maturity's challenge to understand authority in ways that leave behind the parental imagery of times past might alter how we conceive of such authority. But it is limited in what more it can say.

The second question asks what the role of spiritual/religious experience has been through history and how that role may now be changing. Here culturally mature perspective has a great deal to tell us. Answering this second questions also at least puts the first question in larger perspective.

Engaging it necessarily starts with religion's Question of Referent—we need to ask how, ultimately, spiritual experience serves us. The simple notion that there is a Question of Referent to ask about by itself challenges traditional assumptions. Conventionally, religious truth is God's word (or the word of Allah, the utterance of a polytheistic pantheon, the inclinations of a collection of animistic forces, or whatever) and that is that. No larger perspective is needed—or desired.

In Chapter Eight, I framed religious experience's referent creatively. I proposed that we can think of our diverse interpretations of the spiritual dimension as time- and space-specific expressions of the far extreme of archetypally feminine, "left-hand" sensibility as it manifests at a cultural scale. This might at first seem a terribly abstract way to speak about religion's function. But if we examine spiritual/religious thought and practice over the course of the human story, we find strong support for this interpretation.

Four shared motifs stand out through history: Spiritual/religious experience finds particular significance in how things come to be ("in the beginning"), in community (with congregation and communion), in how things are connected (indeed, all things), and in right thought and behavior (with ethics and morality). Each of these motifs in different ways reflects the relatedness-affirming values that characterize the archetypally feminine, left-hand side of fundamental polarity. In Latin, *re-ligare*, the root of the word "religion," means "to connect." William James put it this way: "In mystic states we both become one with the Absolute and we become aware of our oneness."

We must be careful with such reframing not to just psychologize the sacred, a negation of the spiritual of which the social sciences have often rightfully been accused. The spiritual in Creative Systems Theory's interpretation represents more than just projection from within ourselves (though the images we attach to our beliefs may be just that). Rather, it marks our felt connection with every aspect of creative context—the personal, interpersonal, and cultural, certainly; and, at least metaphorically, also the biological, and the cosmos as a whole.

But if we take needed care, we can effectively use a creative framing of spiritual/religious experience to at least make sense of religion's past—its progression over time from animism in our Pre-Axis beginning, to polytheism with Early-Axis culture, to a more fundamentalist monotheism with the emergence of Middle-Axis developmental sensibilities, to monotheism of a more personal sort with Late-Axis culture. Creative Systems Theory describes how this progression follows predictably from how, in the Creative Function, formative process's left hand manifests through the stages of creative differentiation. Religion's history becomes an evolving story of how, collectively, we have connected with connectedness.

And we can go further—a creative interpretation provides important perspective for both understanding current circumstances and looking toward religion's future. To make sense of how it does, it is important to appreciate how the historical picture I have just described confronts us with the same potentially confusing dynamic that we just encountered in reflecting on the history of art. We reasonably ask whether religion has become more or less significant over time. Certainly, each chapter in religion's story to this point has brought more conceptually sophisticated understanding (or at least more philosophical and differentiated understanding). But at the same time, with each stage, the sacred, along with other left-hand functions, has diminished in the attention accorded it and in its relative potency as a cultural force.

We can recognize this dynamic with the changes that accompanied the arrival of the Modern Age. With the Reformation, spiritual truth shifted from the realm of decree to that of individual experience and belief—a radical and important step forward. Before then, intermediaries had always stood between individuals and the sacred (a shaman, a god-king, a priest). But at the same time, religion lost the cultural centrality it had held in the Middle Ages. Its influence was replaced increasingly by science, philosophy, government, and the marketplace.

If we extend this creatively predicted dynamic, where takes us at least makes how deeply religion has been questioned over the last century more understandable. We've seen how the influence of left-hand sensibilities not only decreases over the course of history, with Transition it becomes largely eclipsed—a situation that would seem not to bode well for things spiritual. If this direction were to continue unmodified, we would appropriately pronounce God dead. Respected thinkers through the last century and earlier have argued just that. Friedrich Nietzsche proposed that, "A casual stroll through the lunatic asylum shows that faith does not prove anything." Noting religion's role in world conflict, Bertrand Russell argued good riddance to any notion of divine causation: "[If life has] deliberate purpose, the purpose must have been that of a fiend. For my part, I find accident a less painful and more plausible hypothesis."

This would be the end of the story if it weren't for important further notions that also come with a creative frame—in particular, the Dilemma of Trajectory and how Cultural Maturity's cognitive changes reconcile it. Integrative Meta-perspective supports the conclusion that the underlying sensibilities of religious/spiritual experience are inherent in who we are—they can't really be lost. (Truth's left hand is necessary for anything creative.) More, if the concept of Reengagement holds, the contribution of spirituality's root experience should in fact grow in times ahead. I've described how the more left-hand sensibilities that the spiritual has traditionally helped link us with will be very much needed in the future.

For people who identify strongly with religious belief, this picture presents reason for celebration. If the concept of Cultural Maturity accurately defines today's fundamental challenge, in the future the sacred should manifest with even greater significance than in times past. But as I have suggested, the concept of Cultural Maturity does not at all let religion off unscathed. The price for this renewal is high—extremely so.

The doorway to this deepened spirituality can open only to the degree we are willing to reexamine much in the very foundations of belief.

Certainly the concept of Cultural Maturity brings into question culturally specific notions of the sacred. It argues that life in the future will be most unhappy if we cannot transcend differences of belief. This is especially the case where such differences make one religion true and all others false.

In addition, religion confronts Cultural Maturity's challenge to truth's past parental/mythologized status. Inherently that challenge includes spiritual truth. Whether manifest in the more maternal imagery of animism and mysticism or in the sterner and more philosophical images of patriarchal religious structures, the incarnate forms of sacred authority have served as mythic protectors, shielding us like children from the all-too-easily overwhelming complexities and ambiguities of mortal life. Cultural Maturity's changes call into question the value of this kind of protection. Integrative Meta-perspective repeats the Reformation's call for responsibility in a further, quite ultimate way.

There is also an arguably even more fundamental kind of dislocation that comes with Cultural Maturity's changes. It follows from Integrative Meta-perspective's whole-box-of-crayons picture. Culturally mature systemic perspective challenges the notion that spiritual truth lies at the center of truth's equation (as it does for scientific truth and the truths of any other approaches to knowing—but again, for many people that it might for religion can feel particularly consequential). With Cultural Maturity, it no longer works to think of the spiritual as some ultimately defining core of experience, as life's essence. The kind of experience that through history we've described in spiritual/religious language becomes one crayon in the systemic box—very much an essential crayon, but only one of many we must draw on. Integrative Meta-Perspective views spiritual experience as an important aspect of truth, but only that, an aspect. If we make the spiritual some last word today, it not only fails as truth we can rely on, ultimately it fails as spiritual truth—which, to be the real thing, must honor the particular truth challenges of its time.[20]

---

20 Recognizing this larger picture is a common experience with Parts Work—one that can have considerable impact. People discover that spiritual sensibility doesn't reside in the Whole-Person chair—rather, it

For our time, the concept of Cultural Maturity predicts something very similar to what we witness today—an often conflicting mixture of doubt, dogmatism, and fresh curiosity. Many people find themselves deeply questioning religion, at least as conventionally conceived. Some of their concerns are fairly immediate—for example, the sexual and financial transgressions of church leadership that grace the pages of our morning newspapers. But their doubts can also be more far-reaching.

We also witness more fundamentalist beliefs becoming newly attractive for many people (while at the same time people are turning away from mainstream religious institutions). The way I've framed religion's systemic contribution suggests a dual explanation—one cause regressive, the other a reflection of emerging needs. The more absolutist doctrines of fundamentalist belief (whether Christian, Jewish, Islamic, or other) work as a defense mechanism, providing a bulwark against today's new uncertainties and the loss of clear moral guidelines. And at the same time, such persuasions also often offer a deepened sense of devotion, ritual, and community—things missing and missed in people's lives (and missing in most more liberal forms of religion).

We also see a third trend. A growing number of people recognize the deep importance of the spiritual/religious in their lives, but at the same time are uncertain as to what to do with that recognition. Ultimately, they may or may not find their answers within established traditions. A 2009 Pew Forum report describes a slight drop in overall church attendance over the last fifty years accompanied by a dramatic increase (from 22 percent to 48 percent) in people who describe themselves as having had a personal "religious or mystical" experience.

---

sits to the left, respected, but very specifically a part. Here, I've used the language of polarity to highlight this same result. I described how creative polarity at its most fundamental juxtaposes oneness on one hand with the making of distinctions on the other. Previous reflections on systemic understanding got us to the same recognition in another way. I emphasized how a defining characteristic of culturally mature systemic understanding is that it simultaneously increases our appreciation for interconnectedness and our appreciation for difference. (Earlier, I pointed out a related shift at a personal level with the recognition that culturally mature perspective challenges psychological notions that make "the self" some internal—and sometimes eternal—essence.)

As far as the future, the concept of Cultural Maturity, at the very least, tells us a lot about what will not be helpful going forward. It makes clear that none of our usual more comfortable postures in relation to spiritual/religious experience will be able, ultimately, to get us where we need to go—not religious absolutism, not atheism (its own kind of "religious" absolutism[21]), not agnosticism (in the end but a Compromise Fallacy), and not even conventional dualism that keeps sacred and secular in safely separate worlds. And as I've described, more contemporary spiritual formulations rarely get us any closer. Each of these options equally protects us from the necessary magnitude of a maturely conceived world.

The concept of Cultural Maturity can also take us a bit further. The conclusion that we should see fresh acknowledgement of the more receptive/connectedness side of the creative is consistent with a deeper valuing of experiences we might more generally describe as spiritual: loving relationships, peaceful surroundings, life lived at a sustainable pace, and the "spirit" of creative and intellectual pursuits. For some people this might translate into a renewed appreciation of specifically religious belief, for others not.

The concept of Cultural Maturity also supports that we should see new and deeper acknowledgement of faiths beyond one's own heritage. Ecumenical acceptance is a start. But we should also see a growing interest in how spiritual persuasions relate one to the other and, as here, the very different ways that spiritual/religious experience has taken expression through history.[22]

---

21   Adamant atheism sells books, but its absolutist claims ultimately fail us as fundamentally as do any other claims that deny limits to what we can know.

22   This kind of historical reflection provided one of my most valued early experiences of culturally mature perspective. During a trip to Ireland (the country where my pioneering ancestors started their journey), I visited sacred sites from over five thousand years of history: Stone Age passage graves, Celtic stone circles, medieval Christian monasteries, modern churches. Near the end of the trip, as I walked along a beach, I felt myself struggling to simultaneously hold the profoundly different realities of these experiences. The feelings were often not comfortable, but the moments of "aha" that occasionally permeated the struggle and frustra-

In addition, the concept supports the conclusion that we should find ourselves able to draw in new ways on spiritual/religious sensibilities when addressing important challenges. Three examples most stand out. Each requires that we fundamentally rethink assumptions that have historically been inseparable from spiritual/religious belief. But with each, if we can make the needed stretch, the root sensibilities of spiritual/religious experience can provide valuable assistance.

The first example returns us to that critical task of getting beyond our historical need for enemies. Religious values traditionally emphasize peace ("God is love"), humility ("blessed are the meek"), and tolerance. The difficulty (and needed stretching), of course, lies with the fact that our gods historically have reserved their love for our own kind. Religion has played as big a role as politics in defining the world in "chosen people/evil other" terms—and some would argue that it has played a bigger role.[23] To realize its potential as a force toward peace, religion must embrace a more inclusive "us." At the level of ecumenical perspective—and sometimes in ways that are more overtly integrative—it is doing just that. I'm reminded of Reverend Desmond Tutu's role with South Africa's Truth and Reconciliation Commission.

The second topic looks again to the task of culturally mature moral decision-making. I've described how today's loss of clear cultural guideposts means that

---

tion—moments that somehow creatively linked these very different realities—helped me begin to grasp the potential richness of a culturally mature engagement with spiritual experience.

23 Creative Systems Theory disagrees with the common assertion that religion is the cause of such animosity. It is accurate that most wars have been in some sense "holy wars." But what polarizes is the system as a whole—religious belief is simply the aspect to which we often give special attention. This recognition has important practical as well as theoretical implications. A logical conclusion of the argument that makes religion the problem is the claim that transcending our need for religion would produce a more peaceful world. It wouldn't. Creative Systems Theory proposes that the critical variables are instead cultural stage and Capacitance. The key to getting beyond demonic projection lies in the end neither with religion nor with political ideology, but with the more encompassing task of embracing a larger, more complete and systemic social identity.

even the most familiar moral concerns make new demands. I've also empha-sized how questions of every sort have today become questions of value—in the largest sense moral/ethical concerns. Because moral understanding has traditionally been the province of religion, spiritual belief, at least if maturely conceived, should be able to help us navigate what should be an ever-more-demanding moral/ethical landscape.

But of course, "at least if maturely conceived" is no small addendum. Different religious traditions may view what is good and what is evil quite differently. And even if traditional belief is not held dogmati-cally, it generally stops well short of the subtlety and nuance that to-day's increasingly complex and often highly situation-specific moral/ ethical concerns require.[24] Cultural Maturity affirms that religion has a critically important potential role to play in bringing a moral voice to today's conversations. And at the same time, it emphasizes that that voice can make useful contribution only to the degree that it speaks from a maturity and subtlety of systemic perspective that people of reli-gious conviction often still find difficult to welcome.[25]

The third topic is death. I've emphasized how a new maturity in our relationship to death will be necessary to effectively address the health care delivery crisis. I've also hinted at how this aspect of Cultural Ma-turity has broader implications—for example how greater maturity in our relationship with death might greatly diminish our vulnerability to artificial-stimulation-masquerading-as-meaning dynamics in the me-dia. Helping us deal with death has been a primary function of religion

---

24   I've described how culturally mature morality requires us to be newly sensitive to timeliness and context—to better recognize how what is life-giving for one person or in one situation may not at all be life-giving in another. It also requires us to acknowledge that even on the best of days, and with the best of guidance, spiritual or otherwise, we can never know for sure that our choices are right.

25   This more sophisticated moral perspective applies to religious sensibility itself. Clashing faiths are not the only place spiritual/religious Unity Fal-lacies can lead to naïve and dangerously self-serving conclusions. I've de-scribed how violence takes both left-hand and right-hand forms. People who fall for spiritual/religious Unity Fallacies often have a hard time rec-ognizing and respecting boundaries, and thus can be prone to inflicting archetypally feminine violence on those around them.

though history. The difficulty in this case is that one of the main ways in which religion has helped us cope with death is by protecting us from it—certainly from how fundamentally death challenges us to confront limits to what we can know and control.[26]

But with Cultural Maturity, new access to the more creatively germinal sensibilities that spiritual/religious experience draws on should at least invite a more reflective relationship to death. The way Cultural Maturity makes uncertainty part of common sense should also make the ultimate uncertainty presented by death more tolerable. The potential for important leadership with regard to this critical developmental/evolutionary challenge becomes an expected result. I've described how hospice care represents one of the areas where medicine is making important steps in becoming more accepting of death. Hospitals with religious affiliation are often doing some of the best work in this regard.

Beyond these basic observations, our ability to predict the future when it comes to religion, as with other domains, is limited. We will almost certainly still have traditional churches, mosques, and synagogues well into the future—though their significance in culture may change. (If spiritual experience remains important, we will continue to need places that engender it. Traditional structures should at the least be historically revered.) And spiritual practice such as prayer and meditation should similarly still have a role—perhaps an expanded one. (If the spiritual is a kind of knowing, then we should increasingly value approaches that help us access such knowing.)

We will likely also see a deepening appreciation of relationships between spiritual/religious sensibilities and the contributions of other cultural realms. At least conceptually, this extends all the way to the ultimate spirituality-related polarity—that which has traditionally cleaved sacred and secular: science and religion. The best of thinkers

---

26 Each stage in the evolution of spiritual/religious understanding has provided us with a ready picture of what happens after we die—with Pre-Axis cultures, that we rejoin nature and the ancestors in a kind of parallel world; with Early-Axis times, that we undergo reincarnation, whether as creatures or again as people; with the Middle-Axis early rise of monotheism, that we enter heaven or hell depending on our life choices; and with the more liberal monotheism of Late-Axis times, at least that we go to a better and happier place.

in our time have appreciated the important role of each—and in many cases also at least some level of complementarity.[27] I've argued that most views that claim to bridge the science/religion polarity fail—in the end, collapsing one pole into the other in the name of integration. But I've also described how more encompassing perspective is consistent with Cultural Maturity (and pointed toward how a creative frame provides a conceptually solid starting point for developing such perspective).

Creative Systems Theory's more detailed formulations highlight one last new accomplishment that will be essential if future spiritual/religious understanding is to be up to the task—part of the "multiplicity" aspect of culturally mature perspective. We need more differentiated understandings of belief and practice. I've proposed that a full maturity of perspective requires an appreciation of the larger story of religious sensibility through time, and also the ability to make sense of the very different ways in which sacred experience manifests within that story's various chapters. Each accomplishment involves a considerable stretch with regard both to our general ability to tolerate complexity and our capacity to think in maturely systemic ways.

This more differentiated result presents a particular challenge we encounter with other more left-hand aspects of our lives (for example, with art or love). It requires us to "think" a whole lot more than we are accustomed to when it comes to questions of faith. Addressing religion's Question of Referent, teasing apart how faiths from different times and places are different and how they may relate to one another, theorizing about how spirituality might relate to science and other concerns—these things involve making subtle distinctions.

People of more spiritual/religious inclination might not at first find this call for more nuanced discernment very appealing—even they may feel that what it asks is antithetical to what the spiritual is about. There are two keys to such discernment becoming attractive. First is the recognition

---

27   I think of Einstein's famous assertion that "Science without religion is lame; religion without science is blind." Pope John Paul, went similarly beyond simple dualism when he said, "Science can purify religion from error and superstition. Religion can purify science from idolatry and false absolutes."

that bringing detail to culturally mature understanding is about "thinking" in a fundamentally different sense than that which deadens faith. This is not just rational analysis, but inquiry that draws on the whole of who we are.[28] Second is how, once we are into culturally mature territory, a more conscious and differentiated picture becomes increasingly essential to our spiritual discernments being helpful.[29] Ultimately, it supports a fundamentally more rich, abundant, and powerful spirituality.[30]

Religion's success with making its important contribution to the future depends on the courage and fullness we bring to our spiritual inquiries. I am reminded of Alfred North Whitehead's observation that "Religion will not regain its old power until it can face change in the same spirit as does science." There is hope for this task in who we are. While we tend to think of religion as a conservative force in culture, it is important to remember that religion at its best has always too been about the possible. As Langston Hughes put it, "We build our temples for tomorrow."

---

28 Cultural Maturity wholly agrees that religion must be in the end about experience, not analysis. But it also argues that the sort of analysis described here—specifically integrative discernment of pattern—presents no threat. Indeed such analysis cannot be left out if religion in the future is to continue to carry out its historically critical, specifically sacred task.

29 This further step gains particular significance when we interact with people whose religious practices derive from cultural stages different from our own. I've described how our historical need for evil others can be dangerously compounded by a propensity to make our particular time in culture's story right and true and to denigrate the realities of other stages (earlier stages, certainly, but it can go both ways).

30 Such distinctions are not just theoretically interesting; addressing them is necessary to any full realization of culturally mature spiritual/religious experience and understanding. It is an observation that applies ultimately to every realm of understanding. (In the end, the "crux" and "multiplicity" distinctions that Integrative Meta-perspective makes possible are as much a "threat" to more right-hand spheres as to more ephemeral concerns.)

Going Forward

CHAPTER TWELVE

The Legitimacy of Hope

It is all a question of story....

THOMAS BERRY

AT THE BOOK'S BEGINNING, I asserted that the concept of Cultural Maturity helps us in three essential ways—each of major significance. It provides a new guiding story; it helps us understand essential tasks that lie before us and the skills and capacities we will need if we are to effectively address them; and it points toward the wholly new kind of thinking that future challenges will require of us. Over the course of the book, I've attempted both to clarify the implications and to substantiate the importance of each of these contributions.

The book's reflections have all been in some way about seeking out a new guiding story, if not determining that new story's precise words, then at least making sense of what writing it effectively and wisely will require of us. Continuing with cultural historian Thomas Berry's words that introduce the chapter: "The Old Story—the account of how the world came to be and how we fit into it—sustained us for a long time. It shaped our emotional attitude, provided us with life purpose, energized action, consecrated suffering, integrated knowledge, and guided education. We awoke in the morning and knew where we were. We could answer the questions of our children. But now it is no longer functioning properly, and we have not yet learned the New Story."

We've examined how the concept of Cultural Maturity makes understandable just why the particular story we are now leaving behind is limited. We've also looked at how the concept of Cultural Maturity articulates a new guiding narrative that provides essential help as we look to the future. We've seen how it takes us beyond both the denial of essential challenges and the cynicism and hopelessness that is a common response to getting past denial. We've also observed how the concept of Cultural Maturity helps us avoid naïve wishful thinking, whether of the sort that makes a favorite political ideology the solution, or of the spiritual or technological magical-answer sort. Cultural Maturity's new guiding narrative describes a rich and compelling way forward.

We've seen too how understanding the new tasks that come with Cultural Maturity and making sense of the skills and capacities needed to effectively engage them provides practical "guidebook for the future" direction. It offers identifiable actions and ways of thinking we can practice. And we've observed how, when understood deeply, needed new skills and capacities become not just tools required if we are to function effectively in a culturally mature world; they become hands-on methods for realizing Cultural Maturity. They come together as Cultural Maturity's new, more complete and nuanced way of leading and being in the world.

Making a solid start at examining both the necessity and possibility of fundamental new ways of thinking has helped clarify Cultural Maturity's significance in the larger story of understanding. It has also helped make the depth of the challenges presented by Cultural Maturity's changes more inescapable. And getting a beginning sense of how Creative Systems Theory succeeds at the needed new kind of conception has at the least raised intriguing possibilities.

Three further questions bring together these various observations and invite concluding reflection: First, what evidence do we have that the concept of Cultural Maturity is right? Next, how do we best place the concept of Cultural Maturity in time, both appreciate the time frame in which it has pertinence and understand when we should see needed future changes? And, finally, if the concept of Cultural Maturity holds up, should we be hopeful as we look to the future?

Summarizing the Evidence

At one level, the concept of Cultural Maturity doesn't require much evidence or explanation. The need for the species to "grow up" in some basic way has become impossible to ignore. We human beings do a lot of childish things, many of them simply not consistent with our ultimate survival, much less with a sane and vibrant future. The planet as a whole will do well in the long term whether or not we humans make wise choices. And the species will also most likely endure without Cultural Maturity's changes, or at least through the necessary trials if the needed changes are a long time in coming. But if we don't bring greater maturity to a great many issues, and quite quickly, the centuries immediately ahead for us will not be good.

We find more specific supporting evidence in the observation that has provided much of the structure for the book's inquiry—the way an identifiable set of common "threshold" tasks runs through the critical questions of our time. We've seen how even when the challenges ahead could not seem more different, the skills and capacities needed to confront them share striking similarities. This observation supports the conclusion that what our times ask of us can be summarized with a single notion. And clear parallels between those tasks and the tasks of maturity in an individual lifetime support at least the metaphorical use of the word "maturity" to describe the needed changes.

We've also examined parallels between stages in individual development and culture's narrative to this point. And we've looked at related parallels found with human formative processes of all sorts. The recognition of developmental parallels shifts the status of a needed collective "growing up" from simple metaphor to extended analogy. We've seen how this shift solidifies the argument for the concept of Cultural Maturity and helps fill out the notion's implications. It also provides hints for developing culturally mature frameworks for understanding.

We've examined, too, how we can understand Cultural Maturity's changes not just in terms of changes in belief and behavior, but also in terms of a specific sort of cognitive reordering. Appreciating Cultural Maturity's cognitive changes helps make understandable the unique significance of the changes that our times are about. It also helps us better make sense of the new capacities and new ways of thinking that Cultural Maturity makes possible and why their realization might be predicted.

In addition, we've seen how the more mature perspective that follows from this cognitive reordering reconciles fundamental quandaries not addressable in other ways. Particularly pertinent as far as evidence is how the concept of Cultural Maturity offers a way past the Dilemma of Trajectory, the recognition that neither going forward as we have, nor going back, can get us where we need to go. The ability to address this—plus other quandaries, many of a more eternal sort—makes the concept's conclusions particularly convincing.

And we've looked, too, at how culturally mature perspective provides an overarching vantage for understanding competing views of the future and, more generally, for separating the wheat from the chaff in our thought processes. This last achievement doesn't by itself constitute proof. But it does support the encompassing significance of culturally mature understanding and further adds to the concept of Cultural Maturity's persuasiveness.

Early on, I observed that for me the most compelling evidence for Cultural Maturity's thesis is more basic. I don't see another way of framing the human task that can effectively take us forward. None of the contrasting scenarios I have described can produce a future that is ultimately healthy or, if extended far into the future, likely survivable. If I have not missed something important, Cultural Maturity becomes the only real option.

Time Frames

Three time-related concerns have importance if we are to fully make sense of the concept of Cultural Maturity and its implications. First is the time span question—over what period of time the concept has pertinence. Next, we need to know the particular significance of our times in Cultural Maturity's changes. And finally, we need a sense of just how rapidly we should expect to see additional changes of a culturally mature sort.

The time span question concerns both beginnings and duration. It is critical to answer if we are to effectively engage the challenges ahead. As far as the "beginnings" part of the question, I've observed that we saw first glimpses as early as the initial decades of the twentieth century and also emphasized the importance of this kind of recognition if we are to avoid cynicism. While people today can feel frustration that change is not happening more quickly, we have in fact made a solid start. Acknowledging changes that have already taken place also helps us avoid confusing the concept of Cultural Maturity with wholly different ways of thinking, such as beliefs that see the future only in terms of culture being broken and needing repair, or in terms of radical, all-changing transformation.

At the other end of the time span question, I've described how the concept of Cultural Maturity should have pertinence well into our human future. Indeed, if it is appropriate to associate culturally mature perspective with the whole of the second half of the Creative Function, as I have suggested, then at least Cultural Maturity's general orientation pertains to the entirety of our human future. This recognition of extended significance helps us appreciate how Cultural Maturity's changes have an ultimate kind of importance. It also helps us value the limited "baby steps" toward Cultural Maturity's realization that we have so far achieved.

This brings us to the question of the particular significance of the times in which we live. For a number of reasons, the next twenty to fifty years should prove especially important. For readers of this volume, this will be true if for no other reason than that this is the time period in which our efforts can have direct effect. It is also the case that our times present us with a striking array of critical challenges for which action sooner rather than later will be essential if we are to avoid tipping-point consequences. In addition, a growing number of people are today becoming capable of, and in their own ways committed to, culturally mature perspective.

The decades immediately ahead will confront us with the essential task of going from current circumstances, in which well-developed culturally mature capacities are limited to exceptional people, to a reality in which the need for a new Cultural Maturity—or however we popularly come to speak of this necessary "growing up"—comes to broadly reshape how we humans think and act. Arguably, we could not live in more fascinating or consequential times.

As far as the pace at which further changes might take place, we face major unknowns that could significantly alter how such change plays out. The combination of inescapable challenges and the growing number of people capable of mature perspective could conceivably result in much faster change than we might imagine. We could see a "critical mass" phenomenon. Other factors could also slow progress, some considerably.

I noted an important example in introducing the concept of Capacitance. The fact that so many critical concerns—new economic
complexities and potential instabilities, climate change, globalization's
challenges, terrorism and the proliferation of dangerous weaponry, and
more—confront us simultaneously makes immense demands. And
Cultural Maturity's changes themselves make Capacitance demands.
I've described how systems challenged beyond what they can handle
often protect themselves by polarizing.

If we can effectively manifest the needed perspective and Capacitance, change could happen quickly. But it is not inconceivable that
advancement could stall or even, at least temporarily, reverse.

The Question of Hope

Should we be optimistic as we look to the future? The concept of
Cultural Maturity, if accurate, just by its existence confers a certain
kind of hope. It affirms that effectively addressing the potentially
overwhelming tasks before us is a legitimate option. And having a
new kind of story that can guide us in practical ways going forward
is clearly consistent with hope. If in addition it is true, as I have proposed, that the potential for needed changes is built into who we are,
then hope is even more warranted. Certainly what we see is consistent
with possibility.

But possibility, of course, answers only half of hope's question. We
are left with whether we can pull off the needed further changes—or,
at least whether we can do so soon enough to avoid calamity. I can
think of numerous more specific scenarios—beyond the more general
reactive response to Capacitance's challenge just noted—in which new
possibilities could be thwarted, or at least made very long in coming.[1]

---

1   For example, economic instabilities could spiral so far out of control
    that attempts to address climate change would be essentially abandoned.
    Global food shortages, pandemic, and the destabilization of fragile gov-
    ernments could result in planetary chaos. If the industrialized world fails
    to maintain culturally mature perspective in the face of international
    terrorism, it is not impossible that globalization's promise will be eclipsed
    by a prolonged "clash of civilizations." Today's broad availability of cat-
    aclysmic weaponry further amplifies the risks. Potential domino-effect
    scenarios in the Middle East, for example, with multiple nations (and

If we deny the importance of the tasks that the concept of Cultural Maturity highlights, or to any major degree stop short of engaging them responsibly, human life in times ahead could be unpleasant and brutish—and in ways we cannot now even imagine.

Without question, our future will not be easy. The juxtaposition of so many critical challenges and the continued prominence of Transitional sensibilities (and often absurdities) means that times ahead will be not just particularly significant and particularly fascinating, but quite often particularly crazy. Certainly we will now and then stumble along the way, causing ourselves and the planet's other species anguish in the process.

We can take limited, if not wholly comforting, encouragement from the inevitability of so many of the challenges that our times present. Foresight is much the best approach, but even if we fail to choose wisely now, eventually the need for something like what the concept of Cultural Maturity describes should become inescapable. The question, in the end, becomes less whether we should be hopeful about Cultural Maturity being realized than how long it will take for us to bring forth the courage and commitment its manifestation requires.

I think that in fact the evidence is very good that, sooner rather than later, culturally mature capacities will become common and, with growing frequency, be a basis for policy. If nothing else there is the simple fact of the human species' profound innovative capacities. While we've often hidden from difficult questions, history shows, too, that when given no option but to invent, we have an amazing ability to rise to the challenge.

We also have evidence more specific to this book's reflections. I've proposed that the nature of human intelligence makes us not just inherently creative beings, but also inherently moral beings, concerned ultimately with choices that are life-affirming.[2] There is also how at

---

possibly more soon) possessing nuclear weapons, make an Armageddon-like picture much more possible than we like to admit.

2   Earlier, I contrasted this circumstance with artificial intelligence. The encouragement this circumstance provides needs to be tempered by the fact that the dynamics of Transition can leave us estranged from aspects of intelligence that are necessary for this result. But if what I have described

least the potential for Cultural Maturity's changes is built into us, and with this, the way needed new capacities are not that hard to grasp when we are ready for them. If we are natively primed for the tasks ahead in the way this book's observations suggest, then that needed courage and commitment should be more in the cards than we might imagine.

In addition, we confront that essential sense in which Cultural Maturity becomes the only game in town. The fact that there is really no fork in the road should at the very least sharpen our attention. At a certain point, we should find the need for broadly encompassing culturally mature change increasingly obvious, and where such change potentially takes us more and more compelling.

I've noted an important further factor that supports successfully bringing forth what is required—and doing so sooner than we might think. It has to do with Cultural Maturity's particular significance in the larger human endeavor. If the needed "growing up" were only about survival, the tasks ahead would justify appropriate diligence. And if it were about survival plus the possibility of a generally healthy and sustainable future, this even more would justify deep courage and committed effort. But I've argued that Cultural Maturity is about something more fundamental, and fundamentally compelling—about a next chapter in our human story of potentially great, indeed profound, importance. Cultural Maturity's new common sense gives our personal lives a whole new depth of meaning, and the human enterprise as a whole a new order of significance. With that recognition, Cultural Maturity stops being one possibility to ponder and becomes, instead, the only option that makes any sense at all.

---

is accurate, Cultural Maturity's changes should make this moral consequence increasingly central both to how we think about human identity and to the concrete descisions we make as a species.

Appendices

An Introductory "Stretching Exercise"

WHEN I LEAD WORKSHOPS ON THE FUTURE, I often begin with a brief exercise. It makes a good introduction for instructors who might wish to use this book as text for classes.

Identify two or three challenges, concerns, or problems that you feel our species must at least begin to successfully address over the next ten to twenty-five years.

Your choices could span from the most personal of concerns to the most global. All that matters is that each issue be something you care deeply about. You would feel personally troubled and pained if we failed to confront it successfully.

Ask yourself what will likely be needed to effectively engage each of these concerns. What skills, perspectives, policies, values, technologies, acts, or abilities will be required? Take time to reflect in depth.

Be aware of your own thinking process as you explore options. Notice if you tend to be drawn most immediately to particular kinds of solutions. For example, some people jump to more "external" answers: new laws, appropriations for social programs, or new technologies. Others are most drawn to answers of a more "internal" sort: deeper psychological awareness, a return to traditional values, or a "shift in consciousness." If one kind of solution alone isn't enough, be as specific as you can about what part of the task remains to be addressed.

Let yourself be surprised by what you come up with. Often the awarenesses that turn out to be most important don't fit into ready categories or require that language be used in unusual ways. If the pieces don't immediately come together, try framing the question or problem in a different way. New challenges often require not just new answers, but new ways of articulating the questions.

Ask yourself if any of the needed skills, perspectives, policies, values, technologies, acts, or abilities you listed are new. Which have always been part of being good citizens and leading healthy lives? Which require new sensibilities and capacities?

Examine the claims you make here very closely. Some people are overly quick to see the need for radical change. If you claim that some capacity is new, be very clear what makes it so. At the other extreme, many people share with Marcus Aurelius the assumption that there is "nothing new under the sun." If this is more your tendency, closely examine the terms and concepts you have used—for example, love, community, freedom, individuality, or morality. Look to see if these terms have the same meanings in the contexts you are using them as they did twenty, fifty, or a hundred years ago.

Finally, notice any similarities between what your two or three challenges will require of us. Do common threads exist? If so, do these threads have any relationship to each other—do they in any way suggest a coherent fabric? And taken together, do they offer any useful information about the larger task of our time?

Frequently Asked Questions

THIS FAQ SUMMARY BRIEFLY ADDRESSES QUESTIONS often asked by people new to the concept of Cultural Maturity. Some are questions that may be asked by people who have never heard of the concept. Others are questions that commonly come up once people have started working with the notion.

What is Cultural Maturity?

The concept of Cultural Maturity describes changes that are reordering today's world, and also further changes that will be necessary if we are to have a healthy and rewarding human future. The concept helps us make sense of why these changes are important, what they ask of us, and how further changes are more likely than we might imagine. Cultural Maturity is a specific concept within Creative Systems Theory's more overarching picture of how human systems grow and change.

Can you briefly summarize the concept's thesis?

The concept of Cultural Maturity proposes that our times challenge us to confront a critical next stage in our collective human development—put most simply, to engage an essential, and now newly possible, "growing up" as a species. This growing up takes us beyond what has always before been a parent/child relationship between culture and the individual. Cultural Maturity's changes involve leaving behind the protective cultural absolutes of times past and assuming a new level of responsibility in all parts of our lives. They also involve engaging the more demanding and complex—but ultimately more rich and full—kinds of understanding and relating that doing so begins to make possible.

Why do we need such a notion?

Most immediately, the concept of Cultural Maturity provides perspective for making sense of our easily confusing times. It offers a compelling picture for going forward. It also provides practical guidance for making good decisions in all parts of our personal and collective lives. It helps us delineate the new characteristics that effective thinking, relating, and acting in times ahead must have. In addition, it helps us separate the wheat from the chaff in our ideas about the future and what times ahead will require of us.

What is the evidence that the concept of Cultural Maturity is correct?

Several different kinds of evidence support the concept. Some evidence is empirical. If we list the most critical challenges ahead for the human species, we find that effectively addressing them—or even just adequately understanding them—requires the greater maturity of perspective that the concept of Cultural Maturity describes. We find further evidence in the way in which many of the most defining advances of the last century have reflected at least first steps toward the new kinds of thinking and relating that the concept of Cultural Maturity predicts.

Additional kinds of evidence are more "developmental." We find that the challenges described by the concept of Cultural Maturity have direct parallels in the tasks that define second-half-of-life developmental changes in our individual lives (and ultimately in the mature stages of any human change process). We can understand Cultural Maturity as a developmentally predicted set of new capacities and realizations.

Some of the most important evidence concerns inescapable realities. Something at least similar to what the concept describes is essential to moving forward for reasons deeper than just the need to effectively address new challenges. It turns out that continuing forward on history's past trajectory is really not an option. Doing so would distance us irretrievably from essential aspects of who we are. Cultural Maturity—or something that can provide a related kind of result—becomes, in effect, the only viable way to proceed.

The concept seems more psychological than most thinking about the future. I guess that makes sense, since you are a psychiatrist. But isn't that unusual?

Ultimately the concept of Cultural Maturity concerns the "psyche of culture"—who we are collectively and the particular challenges that today confront us. But there is also a more specifically psychological aspect. Cultural Maturity is not just about various ways of looking at the future, but also about how the particular ways we understand and hold experience affect how we see the future (and also the present and the past). Cultural Maturity involves changes not just in what we think, but *how* we think—developmentally predicted cognitive changes.

The notion that our times bring into question past culturally specific beliefs sounds a lot like what we hear with postmodern arguments. Is Cultural Maturity just different language for the same kind of conclusion?

The concept of Cultural Maturity begins with some related observations. But in the end it fundamentally challenges—or at least fundamentally extends—the postmodern thesis. Cultural Maturity and postmodern thought similarly bring attention to how our times require us to step beyond culturally defined beliefs. But postmodern perspective does not adequately answer why we should see this challenging of past cultural truths. It also fails to provide much if anything to replace what it quite accurately observes has been taken away. The concept of Cultural Maturity specifically addresses why we see the changes we do, and it proposes that the challenge ultimately is not just to surrender past sureties, but to think, relate, and act in some fundamentally new—at once more demanding and more possibility-filled—ways.

You argue that culturally mature perspective requires us to think about social questions more systemically. But you also emphasize that we need to be wary of conceptual traps when using systems language. Could you clarify a bit?

The kind of systems thinking we are most used to is the kind that good engineers draw on. But human questions are not just engineering questions—we are not machines. Culturally mature perspective invites us to think in ways that directly reflect that we are alive—and more than just this, that we are alive in the particular sense that makes us human. If we ignore these needed new steps in our thinking—or misinterpret their implications—we end up with misleading and unhelpful conclusions.

Is Cultural Maturity just another way of talking about the transformations of the Information Age?

There are links. But Cultural Maturity's picture is more encompassing and warns us that thinking in Information Age terms alone can't get us where we need to go. Culturally mature perspective makes clear that very few of the important concerns before us can be resolved solely by technological means. It also challenges the common assumption that invention is the ultimate driver of cultural change. It argues that culture, just as much, shapes what we are able to invent and how we use what we invent. And while much in the information revolution supports Cultural Maturity's changes, much also has the potential to fundamentally undermine culturally mature possibility. If we miss these differences, we can end up pursuing ends that we ultimately would not at all want.

Is Cultural Maturity what people are referring to when they speak of "new paradigm" understanding?

That depends on how a person uses the phrase "new paradigm." The phrase can describe the best of new understanding. But it is also often used to refer to simplistic liberal/romantic, spiritual, or philosophically idealist beliefs masquerading as culturally mature systemic perspective. Such beliefs are not really new, and they tend to advocate for outcomes that would not be possible to achieve and, more to the point, that we would not ultimately want to achieve.

You propose that we can think of Cultural Maturity in terms of changes in how human cognition functions. Could you say more about this?

Historical perspective helps clarify. The Renaissance insights that ushered in our Modern Age in a similar way involved not just new ideas, but whole new ways of thinking—indeed, a reordering of how our cognitive processes work. The from-the-balcony kind of objective perspective that defines Modern Age thought was the result. Cultural Maturity's cognitive changes are related. But they produce a more encompassing—objective in a more fully systemic sense—kind of perspective.

A good way to understand this result turns to what culturally mature understanding requires that we draw on in ourselves. Today's new, more systemic questions demand that we bring more aspects of intelligence—more of our own systemic complexity—to bear if we are to successfully address them. Rarely can the intellect alone get us there.

We can see this need to draw on more aspects of who we are in the way in which most all of today's new questions are questions of value. For example, we need to better appreciate how having amazing new technologies and knowing how to use them wisely are not at all the same things. The intellect alone is great for addressing questions that just require knowledge. Wisely addressing questions of value requires a more complex kind of engagement.

This appreciation for the importance of bringing more of ourselves to bear helps get at the difference between the kind of systemic thinking that culturally mature perspective makes possible and the more mechanical, gears-and-pulleys systems thinking of good engineering. Rationality alone is quite adequate for describing systems understanding of the mechanical sort. But if we wish to apply the new more dynamic, life-acknowledging (and human-life acknowledging) kind of systemic understanding that future questions will increasingly require, we need the whole of intelligence, applied in newly conscious and integrated ways.

You propose that the kind of systemic thinking that culturally mature perspective makes possible produces not just more complete ways of understanding, but also new kinds of truth concepts. Can you explain this?

Culturally mature systemic perspective not only makes possible new kinds of concepts, it makes it clear that these new ways of understanding will be critical to making good choices in times ahead. As one-size-fits-all cultural guideposts lose their usefulness, we need concepts that help us understand what matters in more encompassing ways. We also need concepts that help us better address the multifaceted complexity of today's challenges.

The evolutionary kind of thinking that underlies the concept of Cultural Maturity is one example of the latter. Evolutionary perspective will have growing importance as our global world more and more requires good communication between cultures at different stages in their development. Equally important are concepts that help us make more here-and-now systemic distinctions. Such concepts will be key to helping us understand the very different ways in which different people—whether by virtue of ideology, temperament, or the sphere in which their contribution manifests—see their worlds.

I think I get your argument for a more dynamic and complete kind of systemic understanding. But trying to think about it makes my head swim. A simple definition would be helpful.

It is appropriate that it might initially make one's head swim. We are talking not just about new ideas and new policies, but new, more mature ways of holding reality. We aren't used to all that this involves—including that fact that definition in the traditional sense can't adequately capture our quarry. But with familiarity, people find culturally mature understanding more precise and more complete than what we have seen before. When fully grasped it is often also experienced as simpler than what it replaces.

Could we say that Cultural Maturity is about being more interdisciplinary in our perspective and more relativistic in how we think?

Certainly Cultural Maturity affirms the importance of multidisciplinary inquiry. It argues that most of the important questions of our time require it. One of the reasons the academic world often provides less leadership than we might prefer when it comes to the future is how impenetrable the walls between academic disciplines often remain. (Another reason is the common assumption in academia that rational understanding is sufficient.)

Culturally mature truth is relativistic in the sense that it is contextual. It recognizes that a great multiplicity of factors commonly come into play with any question that matters. But it is explicitly not relativistic in the "different strokes for different folks," anything-goes sense. It is about bringing greater discernment to critical concerns, not less.

Can you say more about how such perspective translates into everyday decision-making?

A couple of simple but ultimately quite sophisticated conceptual tools help capture the new kind of systemic thinking that comes with culturally mature perspective. They also help us avoid confusing culturally mature understanding with things it is not.

First is how such thinking inherently "bridges" familiar assumptions. It draws a circle around conclusions that we have tended to think of as polar—such as us versus them in relationships between countries, mind versus body, masculine versus feminine, or matter versus energy. Thinking in polar terms worked very well for the tasks of times past—indeed, it was critical to addressing them. The concept of Cultural Maturity describes how continuing to think in polar terms in the future will more and more often leave us not just unable to answer critical questions, but unable to ask them in useful ways.

"Bridging" is a different kind of notion than we might assume. It results in neither compromise nor simple agreement. And it is certainly different from simple oneness. In the end, it increases our appreciation for both difference and commonality. The polarity of political left versus political right makes a helpful example. Our current disgust with partisan pettiness reflects the need for more mature perspective. In the end, not only do the limited views of each polar extreme leave us short, simple compromise—splitting the difference—gets us no closer to the kind of mature systemic view we have interest in. We need to be able to address and make sense of a larger, more dynamic and creative picture.

The second simple yet sophisticated conceptual tool helps us think with greater detail and also provides a particularly good image for the cognitive reorganization that produces Cultural Maturity's changes. Think of a box of crayons. The box represents culturally mature perspective. The crayons represent the multiple systemic aspects that make us who we are—such as our multiple intelligences. In application, we can think of the crayons' various colors as the multiple systemic aspects intrinsic to any complex human system—such as the parts of an organization or the various domains that make up culture as a system (government, science, religion, education, art, etc.). Culturally mature decision-making involves being conscious of a question's multihued complexity and drawing on the whole of our own complexity when making choices.

You emphasize the importance of better appreciating limits.
Yet at the same time you say Cultural Maturity is about
thinking more expansively. Could you explain this apparent
contradiction?

Cultural Maturity is very much about a new relationship to limits—
of all sorts. It is about better appreciating planetary limits. It is about
a new respect for limits inherent in the dynamics of relationship—
whether between lovers or between nations. It is also about appreciating ultimate limits to what we as humans can know and control.

At the same time, culturally mature perspective makes clear that a
maturely conceived relationship to limits expands possibility. For example, with regard to environmental limits, while culturally mature
perspective affirms that a new ethic of sustainability will be essential,
it also makes clear that a mature understanding of sustainability is not
(and cannot be) about doing with less. It must be about an ultimately
fuller, and more fulfilling, understanding of more.

You speak of Cultural Maturity as a simple notion,
but it doesn't sound simple to me. Is it or isn't it?

There are ways in which it is simple. It is a single-brushstroke notion
that we can apply to very different questions. Also, many of Cultural
Maturity's underlying characteristics are, in fact, familiar to our experience. We can know a lot about them from the mature stages of other
human developmental processes. When such changes at a cultural
scale are developmentally timely, we can experience them as surprisingly straightforward. But simple does not mean easy. Cultural Maturity requires us to hold experience with a mature fullness not possible
in times past. At the very least, culturally mature perspective requires
us to surrender assumptions (often favorite ones) and step into new
territories of experience.

Cultural Maturity is a specific concept within Creative Systems
Theory's more overarching picture of how human systems
grow and change. Do I need to understand Creative Systems
Theory to make use of the concept of Cultural Maturity?

No. As a simple metaphor or analogy, the concept of Cultural Maturity works fine as a stand-alone concept. While the concept of Cultural

Maturity is a formal Creative Systems Theory notion, there is no need to either understand or agree with the theory's ideas to make effective use of it.

Creative Systems Theory does, however, add to the more basic concept. It helps us understand why Cultural Maturity's challenges are to be expected and exactly what they ask of us. And while all the more nuanced aspects of Cultural Maturity's demands follow directly from Cultural Maturity as a concept, very often the devil is in the details. Creative Systems Theory provides simple language for making many of the important distinctions. Creative Systems Theory can also help us think about systems at a level of detail that the concept of Cultural Maturity by itself does not provide.

Creative Systems Theory also has particular significance because it models one successful effort at culturally mature conception. In addition it represents an approach that can be applied in highly sophisticated ways to a wide variety of questions. But the concept of Cultural Maturity, when understood deeply, requires no support from Creative Systems Theory.

Could you say more about how the concept of Cultural Maturity provides hope for the future?

Most immediately, the concept of Cultural Maturity supports hope by articulating a practical and compelling story for the future. It makes clear that there is very much reason to go on. It also provides specific guidance for going forward—it helps us understand the challenges before us and the capacities needed to effectively engage them. In addition, the concept of Cultural Maturity supports the conclusion that success with the tasks before us is not just some idealized fantasy, or something only in our far-off future. It describes how the potential for the kind of thinking, relating, and acting that the future requires is inherent in who we are. And the fact that many of the most defining advances of the past hundred years reflect the beginnings of culturally mature sensibility supports the conclusion that we are already a good distance on our way—even if we have not had overarching perspective for understanding just what we have been up to.

APPENDIX C

A Glossary of Selected Creative Systems Terms

CREATIVE SYSTEMS THEORY PRESENTS an overarching framework for understanding purpose, change, and interrelationship in human systems. It offers a newly dynamic kind of understanding able to provide important guidance in addressing the increasingly nuanced systemic questions that more and more define the human experience. With regard to this inquiry, it provides key conceptual perspective— Cultural Maturity is itself a specific concept within Creative Systems Theory. Creative Systems Theory also provides us with an example of broadly encompassing culturally mature conception. This appendix offer brief definitions of Creative Systems Theory terms that are applied in this book.

A Creative Frame:

Creative Systems Theory proposes that what most defines us as humans is our toolmaking, meaning-making—"creative"—natures. It goes on to describe how human intelligence is structured to support creative change and how human systems of all sorts are organized in ultimately creative ways. (The term "creative" here refers to the scientific as much as the artistic, to completions as much as beginnings—in short, to formative process wherever we find it.)

The use of a creative frame applies most directly to human systems. Creative Systems Theory uses a creative frame to develop a detailed "pattern language" for making highly detailed human systems–related distinctions. In a more basic way, a creative frame is also pertinent to biological and physical systems. Creative Systems Theory describes how, in a way similar to how the cognitive changes that gave us Modern Age belief altered our understanding of existence as a whole, made it all a "great machine," the cognitive changes we see today result in a more dynamic—in the broadest sense "creative"—picture of reality's workings.

Cultural Maturity:

Creative Systems Theory delineates how Modern Age institutions and ways of thinking are not the ideals and end points we commonly assume them to be—indeed, how they can't be if our future is to be bright. The theory describes how human developmental processes of all sorts—from individual growth, to change processes in relationships, to the evolution of culture—progress in related, creatively ordered ways. It goes on to propose that we can understand the times in which we live in terms of a series of creatively predicted, "developmental" tasks and changes. It calls today's new creative challenge Cultural Maturity.

The concept of Cultural Maturity makes analogy with the particular kind of maturity both needed for and a product of passage into a lifetime's second half. Cultural Maturity challenges us to step beyond the absolutist, one-size-fits-all beliefs that come with relating to culture as a symbolic parent. And it makes it possible to think in more dynamic and complete ways. Creative Systems Theory describes how parallel "developmental" changes mark the first substages of the second half of any human formative process.

Integrative Meta-perspective:

The cognitive reordering that accompanies Cultural Maturity's changes produces what Creative Systems Theory calls Integrative Meta-perspective. Integrative Meta-perspective involves a dual process—more fully stepping back from, while at the same time more deeply engaging, the whole of our human complexity. Of particular importance, that dual process involves more fully stepping back from and more deeply engaging the multiple aspects of intelligence. With Modern Age understanding, we stepped back and looked out—as if from a balcony—over a new, rationally understandable world. With Integrative Meta-perspective, we more fully step back—from the rational as well as other aspects of intelligence. We also more deeply engage our complex cognitive natures. Integrative Meta-perspective makes it possible to see ourselves, and everything around us, in more fully systemic ways.

Intelligence (as described by Creative Systems Theory):

Creative Systems Theory describes how the diverse aspects of intelligence are creatively related and work together to support and drive the mechanism of human formative process. The theory delineates four primary kinds of intelligence. Each kind of intelligence is present in some form throughout any formative process, but each finds strongest expression in a particular creative stage.

The first, *Somatic/kinesthetic Intelligence*, is body intelligence. It finds strongest expression in creation's "incubation" stage. *Symbolic/Imaginal Intelligence* is the intelligence of myth, dream, and imagination. It finds strongest expression in creation's "inspiration" stage. *Emotional/Moral Intelligence* is affective intelligence. It finds strongest expression in creation's "perspiration" stage. *Rational/Material Intelligence* is intellectual intelligence. It finds strongest expression in creation's "finishing and polishing" stage.

Creative Systems Theory describes how intelligence manifests in different ways at different times and places. It also delineates how the ways in which we make sense of our worlds follow from how this is so. Creative Systems Theory proposes that making sense of today's essential questions requires at least a beginning ability to more consciously apply the whole of intelligence.

Whole-Systems Perspective:

Creative Systems Theory describes how we can understand human experience at every scale—from the personal, to relationships, to the familial, to the cultural, to the global—as systemic. It also describes how we can understand the various ingredients that make up any of these spheres—for example, business, education, religion, or art within culture as a system—as contrasting generative aspects within that particular systemic whole.

Beyond emphasizing the importance of thinking in systemic terms, Creative Systems Theory also clarifies how the kind of systems thinking required by the challenges we face is necessarily of a new sort. Today's questions require more than the kind of systems thinking used by good engineers. While such thinking is often adequate for day-to-day usage, it necessarily stops short if we wish to effectively describe living systems, and certainly if we wish to describe human systems. (And ultimately it stops just as short for addressing physical systems.) A creative frame offers a way to understand systems that directly reflects our living, human natures.

Creative Systems Theory describes how ideas that fall short of the needed systemic sophistication leave us trapped in ideology—if not the us-versus-them ideologies of now-outmoded advocacies, at least the more overarching ideological simplifications that come with Modern Age heroic/romantic belief. It describes how we can understand modern-day, limiting assumptions of all sorts—from those that accompany how we think about government and economics to those that produce common traps in how we conceive of love—in terms of the importance of learning to think and act in more systemically complete ways.

Creative Differentiation:

Creative Differentiation refers to the dynamics that characterize the first half of any human formative process. The new content buds off from its creative context, grows, and evolves. With each succeeding stage, it becomes more defined and more separated from the context from which it arose.

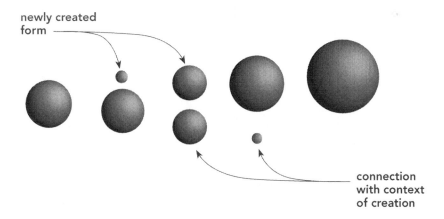

newly created
form

connection
with context
of creation

Fig. C-1. Creative Differentiation

Creative Integration:

Creative Integration refers to the dynamics that characterize the second half of any human formative process (or that second half as a concept). The newly created content reconnects with its original context, in the process seasoning, maturing, and contributing to a now expanded context.

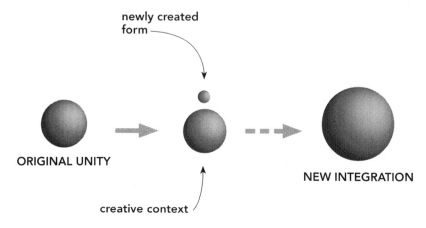

Fig. C-2. Creative Differentiation and Integration

The Creative Function:

The Creative Function is a visual depiction of formative process in human systems as conceived by Creative Systems Theory. The Creative Function represents formative process as an evolving progression of creatively related polar relationships.

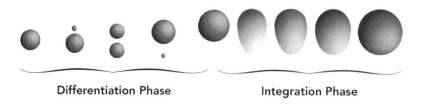

Fig. C-3. The Creative Function

Creative "Bridging"

Culturally mature understanding systemically draws a circle around concepts that we've traditionally described in polar terms—such as political left versus political right, freedom versus constraint, art versus science, humankind versus nature, or matter versus energy. The concept of "bridging" comes together with the idea of a creative frame in the recognition that polarities have a predictable symmetry. Polarities characteristically juxtapose a "harder," more right-hand, more archetypically masculine element with a "softer," more left-hand, more archetypally feminine ingredient. The result of bridging becomes not just systemic, but systemic in a specifically "procreative" sense. Bridging is a product of how today's time in cultural change reflects creative integration at an ultimately defining scale, at the level of culture and understanding as a whole.

The Dilemma of Differentiation:

The Dilemma of Differentiation refers to the quandary of how to make distinctions without reducing how we understand to the mechanistic—putting everything into "this versus that" categories. The Dilemma of Differentiation also alerts us to how avoiding distinction altogether—making everything about connectedness (in the hope of escaping mechanism's trap)—gets us no closer to where we need to go. Creative Systems concepts get beyond the Dilemma of Differentiation by defining difference (and connectedness) in creative terms.

Creative Causality:

Creative Systems Theory describes how the history of understanding reflects evolving juxtapositions of more "right-hand," archetypally masculine, and more "left-hand," archetypally feminine, ways of understanding how things work. Integrative Meta-perspective's more dynamic and systemic picture of how things change and relate represents a third, encompassing option beyond mechanistic "action and reaction" causality and the "all is connected" causality of spiritual belief. The term "Creative Causality" refers to this more fully systemic picture as causality as viewed through a creative frame. The term applies most directly to human systems, but it is ultimately pertinent also to new, more dynamic understandings of the biological and the physical. Creative Systems Theory was originally called the Theory of Creative Causality.

"Whole-Box-of-Crayons" Perspective:

A simple box of crayons provides an ultimately quite precise way to represent culturally mature systemic understanding. Integrative Meta-perspective involves stepping back so we can hold the whole systemic "box"—getting our minds around all the pertinent systemic elements. At the same time, it involves deeply engaging those various systemic elements—all the various "crayons"—so that we can apply them in the most ultimately creative ways.

Culturally Mature Truth:

Culturally mature perspective challenges us to step beyond the absolutist truths of times past and makes it possible to understand truths of all sorts in more dynamic and systemic ways. It also reveals new kinds of truth concepts and emphasizes their importance for effectively addressing the questions before us.

Creative Systems Theory identifies two basic kinds of new-truth notions. *Whole-System Patterning Concepts* are Whole-System measures. They are of three types: the *Question of Referent* (what the theory calls "aliveness," for short), Capacitance (generic capacity), and *Creative Symptoms* (protective responses that occur when situations threaten to overwhelm Capacitance). *Concepts of Creative Differentiation* help us better understand generative processes and relationships within and between systems. Of these, *Patterning in Time* concepts address temporal relationships. *Patterning in Space* concepts address here-and-now creative relationships.

All Creative Systems truth notions are in some way concerned with what is creatively "right and timely." They help discern what, at any point in time, best supports generativity and larger well-being. Truth in this sense (you can think of it as a system's growth-producing and life-sustaining "creative edge") represents a fine balance. When systems retreat from their creative edges they become stagnant. But if they push too far beyond them, they risk being overwhelmed, immobilized, or even destroyed.

The Question of Referent ("aliveness"):

The Questions of Referent is the basic feedback we use for making decisions. The concept can be applied to truth whenever or wherever we find it but is particularly pertinent to truth in a culturally mature reality—when culturally defined measures stop being enough. Decision-making then requires both a more conscious relationship to the referents we use and the application of more fully integrative/ systemic referents.

We need to draw directly on truth in this most basic creative sense if we wish to address wealth beyond material accumulation, learning beyond the mere acquisition of facts and skills, or health beyond the simple absence of disease. Truth in the sense of "aliveness" is only in part tied to particular actions or beliefs. Every thought, feeling, image, and sensation that exists can, in some context, express what is most alive (most ultimately creative).

Capacitance:

Capacitance measures a system's overall capacity—think of a balloon that if stretched too far, could break. Capacitance replaces more specific notions of potential such as skill, IQ, or health. We can talk about a system's average Capacitance. We can also talk of the Capacitance available to a system at a particular moment.

Creative Capacitance is the one thing that increases consistently over the course of any human formative process. Cultural Maturity, like all developmental dynamics, is a Capacitance-dependent notion. Without sufficient Capacitance, culturally mature perspective is largely impossible. And at a certain Capacitance, culturally mature conclusions become increasingly self-evident.

Creative Symptoms:

Creative Symptoms refer to how human systems respond when challenged to a quantity of "aliveness" greater than their Capacitance (if they are not able to grow in response or to consciously protect themselves in some way—by making a boundary or choosing to leave the situation). Creative symptoms are unconscious protective mechanisms. They function by getting the system out of the line of fire—by moving it above the creative challenge (by intellectualizing, for example), below it (perhaps by the system becoming depressed), inside of it (the system might unconsciously withdraw), or outside of it (by the system becoming preoccupied with something safer, for example). The concept applies to human systems at all scales.

Patterning in Time:

Patterning in Time concepts describe how change in human systems is creatively ordered and conforms to predictable patterns. Creative Systems Theory delineates how a parallel sequence of creative ordering principles and sensibilities manifests over the course of human formative process of all sorts—from invention, to individual development, to the growth of a relationship, to organizational change, to the evolution of culture. Patterning in Time concepts can be used to tease apart highly complex processes and make highly nuanced discriminations. Being creatively framed, they allow detailed delineation while increasing our appreciation for the dynamic, life-imbued (and human life-imbued) nature of what we observe.

Patterning in Space:

Patterning in Space concepts describe creative differentiation within and between human systems at any one point in time. They can be used to help us better understand contrasting aspects of the individual psyche, personality differences between individuals, the functions of different parts of an organization, or how various domains in culture—such as government, business, art, science, education, or health care—function and interrelate. As with Patterning in Time notions, Patterning in Space concepts help us delineate highly complex processes while deepening our appreciation for their creative dynamism.

Whole-Person/Whole-System Relationship:

In contrast with "two-halves-make-a whole" relationships, in which bonding happens through the mutual projection of systemic parts (an evil other, a projected gender ideal), in culturally mature relationship each participant maintains its systemic completeness. The term "Whole-Person/Whole-System Relationship" pertains to human relationship wherever we find it—between intimates, between parents and children, between leaders and follows, between organizations, or between one country and another.

Culturally Mature Leadership:

Culturally Mature Leadership is Whole-Person/Whole-System leadership. With culturally mature leadership, leaders (and in ideal situations, also those being led) maintain their systemic wholeness. The leader succeeds in stepping beyond both polarized identification within the pertinent system (for example, management versus labor) and between systems (for example, ally versus enemy). The culturally mature leader may be a strong advocate—indeed, the ability to advocate strongly increases with culturally mature capacity—but that advocacy is held within a mature systemic perspective.

Whole-Person Identity (and the Myth of the Individual):

With Cultural Maturity, identity comes to reflect who we are as systemic wholes. Whole-Person identity is a necessary corollary of Whole-Person relationship. Note that this recognition directly challenges how we have thought of individuality in modern times. The kind of individuality we have until now identified with—what we see idealized with romantic love and traditional heroic leadership— in fact reflected but half of what identity becomes when understood systemically.

Meta-determinacy:

The recognition that determination in creative systems bridges usual notions of predictability and unpredictability. Creative outcomes are not predetermined—nothing more marks creative processes than the fact that one cannot know ahead of time exactly what they will produce. But they are also not simply uncertain. Creative processes are highly patterned, and the products they produce are always in some way linked to what has come before. (Creative processes are predictable/unpredictable in the same sense as the last word in a conversation or the last note in a piece of improvised jazz.)

Systemic Scale:

The Systemic Scale of a particular system is the defining circumference of the system (for example, individual, relationship, family, organization, region, or planet).

Systemic Level:

The Systemic Level of a particular system is the organizational level as defined by major emergent properties (inanimate, versus animate, versus conscious).

Creative "Reengagement":

Reengagement describes a dynamic intrinsic to Creative Integration. Creative Differentiation involves necessary amnesias for developmental realities that we have progressed beyond (so that we will not fall back into the familiar). With Creative Integration we see a reconnecting with these forgotten underlying sensibilities (a mechanism critical to Integrative Meta-perspective's more complete and dynamic picture). Reengagement is not at all about going back. What we "reengage" is forgotten sensibilities as we experience them in the present.

The Dilemma of Trajectory:

Over the course of Creative Differentiation, archetypally feminine values and sensibilities diminish in influence, while archetypally masculine values and sensibilities become increasingly dominant. At Transition, the archetypally feminine in essence ceases to exist. With this circumstance, it is not possible to continue "progressing" in the same way we have known. Creative Integration resolves the dilemma.

The Dilemma of Representation:

The Dilemma of Representation describes how usual approaches to both language and pictorial depiction inherently stop short when it comes to representing Creative Systems (and culturally mature conclusions more generally). This result is specifically not a reflection of the outcome being somehow mysterious. Rather, it is a product of the necessary systemic complexity and completeness.

Polar Traps:

The concept of polar traps uses the language of polarity to describe the basic ways that we can fall short of culturally mature understanding. Creative Systems Theory identifies three basic kinds of polar fallacies, distinguished by the polar leaning with which they tend most to identify. Unity Fallacies identify with the archetypally feminine. Separation Fallacies identify with the archetypally masculine. And Compromise Fallacies split the difference.

Pre-Axis:

The Pre-Axis stage is creation's "incubation" stage. Somatic/ Kinesthetic Intelligence predominates. (With Patterning in Space, Pre-Axis refers to the systemic elements that most embody Pre-Axis sensibilities as they manifest at a particular point in time.)

Early-Axis:

The Early-Axis stage is creation's "inspiration" stage. Symbolic/Imaginal Intelligence predominates. (With Patterning in Space, Early-Axis refers to the systemic elements that most embody Early-Axis sensibilities as they manifest at a particular point in time.)

Middle-Axis:

The Middle-Axis stage is creation's "perspiration" stage. Emotional/Moral Intelligence predominates. (With Patterning in Space, Middle-Axis refers to the systemic elements that most embody Middle-Axis sensibilities as they manifest at a particular point in time.)

Late-Axis:

The Late-Axis stage is creation's "finishing and polishing" stage. Rational/Material Intelligence predominates. (With Patterning in Space, Late-Axis refers to the systemic elements that most embody Late-Axis sensibilities as they manifest at a particular point in time.)

Transition:

Transition is the midpoint of formative process—where processes of Creative Differentiation and Creative Integration meet. With culture as a creative process, this is where we find Cultural Maturity's "threshold."

Integrative Stages:

Integrative Stages are the stages in the second half of any formative process. Because integrative stages manifest in different ways depending on Patterning in Space variables, one term is used to refer to integrative dynamics as a whole.

Transitional Absurdities:

Transitional Absurdities are the nonsensical ways in which reality can appear with Transition's near absence of more creatively germinal (archetypally feminine) values and sensibilities. Some examples: How readily we ignore damage done to the environment, the extreme material values of modern times, and how disconnected we can be from our bodies.

Cross-polar Dynamics:

The term "cross-polar" refers to dynamics in which a system identifies with the pole opposite to that which it most inhabits. Cross-polar dynamics are often present in liberal/humanist and postmodern belief. (With liberal/humanism, we can find a strongly intellectual and idealized identification with the underprivileged. With postmodern writings. we can see lengthy, hyper-rational arguments for the inadequacy of the rational and for the impossibility of ultimately knowing anything.)

Archetypally Masculine and Archetypally Feminine Violence:

Creative Systems Theory defines violence as any action that results in damage to Capacitance. Archetypally masculine violence damages Capacitance through direct insult. It may take the form of physical assault, harshly condemning words, or the simple impeding of possibility. Archetypally feminine violence works more covertly. It may take the form of undermining, passive aggression, emotional entanglement, or seductiveness. Depending on the context, either kind of violence can prove the more damaging.

Creative Systems Analysis:

Any system, or set of related systems, can be examined using a multilayered application of Creative Systems Patterning Concepts. Because Creative Systems notions are based on underlying organizing principles, such analysis can help us get at what is most fundamentally important in any situation. Also, because all Creative Systems concepts are based on a single notion—that human systems are creatively ordered—such analysis often makes it possible to address highly complex phenomena in surprising simple ways. And the use of a creative frame means that such analysis is inherently dynamic in a way that honors our living, human natures.

Temperament, Creative Contribution, and Conceptual Traps

We must select the illusion which appeals to our temperament....
CYRIL CONNOLLY

IN CHAPTER NINE, I INTRODUCED the Creative Systems Personality Typology. Here I will describe the distinctions it makes in a bit more detail. I do so in part to provide a further feel for how nuanced the patterning concepts that become available to us with culturally mature understanding can be. More specifically with regard to the leadership tasks of Cultural Maturity, I do so to provide further insight into the particular creative contributions each temperament most brings to the challenges ahead, and also into where each is most vulnerable to conceptual traps.

Creative Systems Theory proposes that, in a way similar to how organisms have ecological niches, we as individuals live our lives in a predictable array of creatively ordered psychological/social niches. The Creative Systems Personality Typology delineates these different niches and how experience of being human differs in fundamental ways depending on which niche we inhabit. The Typology provides a particularly deep and sophisticated approach to understanding temperament differences.

Understanding Temperament

It is remarkable how different reality looks through the eyes of people with different temperaments. As Lucretius said many centuries ago, "What is food for one man is to the other poison." Because we are so used to our own perspective, we can miss how fundamentally this is so. Either the fact of difference doesn't register, or we attribute differences we see to other people's ignorance or misunderstanding (or sometimes their superiority). With Chapter Nine's reflections, I made a start at describing how this situation is changing, how these changes relate to Cultural Maturity, and the importance of theses changes for the leadership tasks before us.

The ability to deeply delineate temperament differences assists us in multiple ways. Certainly, it helps us understand both ourselves and others, and, in the process, to better get along. But there are also broader cultural benefits. The Creative Systems idea that human differences mirror the systemic elements—the multiple crayons in the box—needed for systems to function as creative wholes has huge implications if we wish our collaborative efforts to have culturally mature outcomes. More personally, recognizing such creative complexity around us can help catalyze the internal systemic integration needed for culturally mature thought. I may never be a jazz musician, a professional football player, or an advertising executive, but if I can begin to understand what makes these people who they are, and better, if I can even slightly embody their felt realities, their presence can help me more deeply engage creation's full systemic complexity in myself.

With each of the descriptions that follow, I will address that temperament's ordering creative dynamic, mention some familiar people as examples, list professions that people with that basic temperament often assume, and discuss general characteristics, strengths, and weaknesses. These descriptions are simplified. For example, while I will talk in terms of discrete categories—Early-, Middle-, and Late-Axis personalities, and within these people whose personality style emphasizes Upper or Lower, Inner or Outer aspects—only rarely do we find pure types. It is similar to what we see with color. We may say a color is green. But at the same time, we know that there exist many different greens—indeed, that there is no absolute line that makes one color blue-green and another greenish-blue. And while we can talk about commonly seen professions or beliefs, major exceptions exist to every such behavioral generalizations. Indeed, the exceptions are often where the most interesting and useful discoveries lie. I walk into a room of CEOs and expect those present to be Lates, but many are not. I assume that a firefighter who comes to see me as a client is a Middle, but instead he is an Early. In each case the equation changes dramatically.

Following each basic description, I will more specifically address the strengths and blindnesses that that particular temperament brings to the tasks of culturally mature leadership. Some of the most powerful compare-and-contrast tools shift our attention from ideas we have to who we are in having them. I've described how differing conclusions represent more than just alternative intellectual interpretations. Our conclusions have as much to do with "where we come from" as the logic we use to arrive at our beliefs.

A deep appreciation for personality style dynamics can help us evaluate not just the conclusions of individuals, but also the degree to which the beliefs of particular groups succeed at being culturally mature.

I've described how the thinking of most schools of thought and most formal organizations—at least to this point in our history—is ideological, how it reflects taking one part of systemic truth and making it the whole truth. Consistent with this, particular temperaments are characteristically drawn to particular schools of thought and particular organizations. Conceptual traps of a fundamental sort almost certainly lurk when strong advocacy is limited to people of one or two basic personality styles. The temperament diversity attracted by a way of thinking or a social movement provides one of the most accurate tests for Cultural Maturity.

Each major temperament group is equally capable of culturally mature perspective. And depending on the system's Capacitance, each major temperament group is equally vulnerable to naïve thinking or outright fallacies. Combine an appreciation for how various temperaments organize experience with a recognition of how what we are likely to see changes depending on Capacitance, and we get a particularly powerful lens for making needed wheat-from-chaff distinctions.[1]

Pre-Axis Patterns:

 Pre-Axis patterns differ from other temperament dynamics in that they rarely manifest in modern times in healthy individuals (the one exception being people with a strongly Pre-Axis cultural background). We encounter Pre-Axis dynamics most frequently in people who have significant psychological

---

1   Those interested in a more detailed look at the Creative Systems Personality Typology and its implications for culturally mature leadership can visit the CSPT website at www.CSPTHome.org.

or neurological limitations. (Because they are principally of interest to those in the therapeutic professions, they are beyond the scope of this brief discussion of normal variation.)

Early-Axis Patterns:

 Early-Axis temperaments reflect a special affinity with the inspiration stage in formative process—that period when the buds of new creation first find their way into the world of the manifest. The reality of Early-Axis individuals is born from the organizing sensibilities of possibility and imagination.

A few quotes capture Early-Axis sensibilities and values. From Albert Einstein: "He who can no longer wonder, no longer feel amazement, is as good as dead." From Miles Davis: "I'll play it first and tell you what it is later." From Henry David Thoreau: "It is life near the bone where it is sweetest." From Orson Welles: "I don't say we all ought to misbehave, but we ought to look as if we could." From Tom Robbins: "In the haunted house of life, art is the only stair that doesn't creak." And from Pablo Picasso: "Everything is miraculous. It is miraculous that one does not melt in one's bath."

Where do we find Earlies? Often they work with young children (grade-school teachers, day-care workers). Frequently they become artists—visual artists (particularly those of more abstract inclination), dancers (particularly those whose aesthetic tends toward the improvisational), musicians (most jazz musicians, some classical and rock-and-roll musicians), or writers (particularly poets and most writers of science fiction). Earlies make important contributions in the sciences. (Many of science's major innovators have been Earlies—though the larger number of scientists are Lates.) Recently they have starred in the high-tech revolution.[2] Most people who teach reflective techniques such as meditation and yoga are Earlies. (It is they who are most attracted to things spiritual, particularly practices with roots in Early-Axis cultures.)

---

2   Their role in Information Age innovation has provided this temperament, which is historically least often associated with mainstream success, with new stature and influence, and often great wealth. You can think of it as a kind of "revenge of the Earlies."

A few famous Earlies: Leonardo da Vinci, Georgia O'Keeffe, Rainer Maria Rilke, Stephen Hawking, Bill Gates, Carl Jung, Isadora Duncan, Albert Einstein, Mary Cassatt, Jonathan Winters, Antoine de Saint-Exupery, May Sarton, Groucho Marx, Pablo Neruda, Anäis Nin, Howard Hughes, Alan Watts, Robin Williams, John Coltrane, Boris Karloff, Emmett Kelly, Gary Larson, Pablo Picasso, Buckminster Fuller, Frank Zappa, Nikola Tesla, Jack Nicholson, and Mrs. Saunders (my Kindergarten teacher). More notorious Earlies include Charles Manson and Rasputin.

This listing necessarily skews toward the more manifest Early-Axis types—which in no way implies that they have greatest importance. As is the case with every axis, Uppers and Outers are most in the world and thus tend to be most visible. It is only with the more universally manifest world of Late-Axis personality structures that we see Lower/Inner personalities acknowledged historically, and even then they are underrepresented. Mrs. Saunders is the only Early/Lower/Inner in this list.

Imaginal Intelligence, the intelligence of symbol, myth, and metaphor, predominates in the cognitive processing of Earlies (for the modern Early, imaginal intelligence as experienced within the Rational/Material Intelligence context of today's Late-Axis culture). Edgar Allan Poe captured the inner world of the Early when he wrote: "All that we see or seem is but a dream within a dream." The magical and imaginative dimensions of this intelligence predominate in the more manifest Early-Axis temperaments (Early/Uppers and Early/Outers). The mythical and mystery-centered dimensions hold sway in the psyches of Early/Lowers and Early/Inners.

As we might expect, Earlies tend to feel a special attraction to the beginnings of things. Of all axes, they are most comfortable with situations where the unknown outweighs the known. Often their contributions are quite visionary. (Jonathan Swift reminds us that "vision is the art of seeing things invisible.") As we would expect with archetypally feminine sensibilities dominant, Earlies tend to be drawn more to interconnections than differences, and to things that are fluid more than things that are fixed. Their greatest contributions often derive from their fascination with underlying principle and pattern. (I am reminded of Albert Einstein's famous assertion, "I am interested in God's thoughts; the rest are details.") Earlies can take great joy in the nonsensical and contradictory.

(From Lewis Carroll in *Through the Looking Glass:* "'Contrariwise,' continued Tweedledee, 'if it was so, it might be; and if it were so, it would be: but as it isn't, it ain't. That's logic.'"). Earlies, particularly Early/Lowers, tend to be more comfortable in their bodies than other temperaments and derive particular fulfillment through bodily experience. (Indeed, for many Earlies, body and spirit can be hard to distinguish.) Earlies generally feel a more immediate connection with nature than other temperaments, and greater comfort with solitude (whether alone in nature or just with themselves). I am reminded of the familiar words of Yeats:

> I will arise and go now, to Innisfree,
> And a small cabin build there, of clay and wattles made,
> Nine bean-rows will I have there, a hive for the honeybee.
> And live alone in the bee-loud glade.
>
> THE LAKE ISLE OF INNISFREE

Of all temperaments, Earlies have the most permeable boundary structures (which we would expect, given that Early sensibilities are the least manifest). This can make an Early-Axis person seem fragile or frail and can present difficulties in situations where strong boundary structure is needed. At the same time, this energetic porousness is the source of many of the Early's great gifts and strengths—such as intuitiveness, sensitivity to interconnections, and an ability to "go with the flow."

On meeting an Early, one is often first stuck by a childlike quality. Early-Axis people have a special appreciation for childhood sensibilities both in themselves and in the world around them. While a certain non-conformism is a common Early-Axis trait, its origin is less rebellion than a certain mistrust of—and even ignorance of—adult convention.

With Early/Uppers, qualities such as imaginativeness, intuitiveness, charisma, and spiritual and artistic sensitivity predominate. Early/Uppers make manifest the sensibilities of the "magical child." Where Inner aspects predominate, the Early/Upper's "artistry" is most internal. We often see Early/Upper/Inner sensibilities in poets, painters, and in people drawn to the more ascendant and ascetic of Eastern spiritual practices. I think of the words of Pablo Neruda—"My only obligation is this: to be transparent."

Where Early/Upper/Outer aspects are stronger, the Early/Upper's imaginativeness manifests with greatest visibility—through more dramatic forms of artistic expression or through scientific or technical invention. It is here we find the notorious "mad professor." Note this description of Nobel physicist Theodore B. Taylor from *The Curve of Binding Energy* by Johns Mcphee: "She found him attractive—tall, gangling with a broad forehead, a somewhat parted chin, and great thoughtful brown eyes, which often seemed to be focusing on something no one else could see."[3]

With Early/Lowers, attributes like connection to nature and mystery, a deep capacity to nurture, and spontaneity are most prominent. We see simultaneously embodied the playful aspects of the child (as opposed to the numinous and magical) and the child's connection with the primordial. Early/Lowers find a comfort with darkness not seen with other temperaments. I think of Antoine de Saint-Exupery's description of night as "when words fade and things come alive."

With Early/Lower/Outers, what often first strikes us is their capacity for abandon. Spontaneity and the ability to improvise come easily. Here, mythically, we find the wild man and wild woman. Early/Lower/Outers often manifest as the more improvisationally-inclined of musicians and dancers. Salvador Dali once exclaimed, "I do not take drugs—I am drugs."[4]

Qualities like the ability to nurture and a delight in the mysterious predominate with Early/Lower/Inners. Such people often manifest creatively through artistic expression, frequently of a deeply personal sort. Many contribute through work with children—attracted either

---

3   Dr. Taylor was a participant in the nuclear waste think tank that I described in Chapter Six.

4   Early/Lowers in particular tend to identify with the social margins—in the past, as bohemians or hippies, and more recently as "goths" or as inhabitants of the "grunge scene." (Early/Lowers are the most likely to wear their hair long—men certainly, but also women, particularly in their later years—and to wear unconventional attire.) Many homeless people are Early/Lowers (in part because Early/Lowers tend not to be as adept as others at material success, in part because the street can feel more inviting than the rigidity of the workplace).

to selflessly serving the children's "magic" or to the possibility of living immersed in the unformed. They also often find fulfillment in work with animals. Early/Lower/Inners in particular would appreciate these words of poet Izumi Shikibu: "As I dig for wild orchids in the autumn fields, it is the deeply bedded root that I desire, not the flower."

Common weaknesses of Earlies parallel their strengths. Earlies often have a difficult time finding satisfaction in the traditional work world. They tend to like more freedom than most jobs provide and are often a bit too eccentric or original in their thinking to fit in well. They also often lack the facility with detail and the comfort with repetitive tasks that the workplace so often demands.

Earlies also run into problems because of difficulties they can experience in distinguishing between dreams and dreams made manifest. (They may either not appreciate the difference, or simply not be good at carrying tasks to completion. A recent newspaper column jokingly referred to an obviously Early-Axis person as "planning impaired.") Earlies also often do poorly in situations that involve significant conflict or struggle. They can lack the boundary solidity, the "thick skin," needed for drawn-out combat, or for just the often "hardball" realities of modern life.[5]

Earlies are much more likely than Middles or Lates to feel awkward in social situations. Even more expressive Earlies can seem quite introverted and a bit "nerdy." Earlies also frequently find societally expected forms of commitment either challenging or not of real interest. Relationship can be very important, but it must somehow complement the Early's creative, primordial, and spiritual sensitivities to be long-lasting.

When I do personality style workshops, I often ask people to write down words and phrases that capture the experience of their particular temperament. Some statements from the mouths of Earlies: "It can help if I have others around who can take my wild brainstormings and put them into reality"— "I've often named the cars I've owned. The

---

5   The Early's creative intensity can also be a two-edged sword. George
     Bernard Shaw observed only half tongue-in-cheek that "The true artist
     will let his wife starve, his children go hungry, and his mother drudge for
     his living at seventy, sooner than work at anything but his art."

ones I remember most fondly are not the ones that ran best, but those with special or quirky personalities."—"I am most happy when things have a sense of almost sacred balance."—"I can feel least alone when I am by myself."—"My hair has a mind of its own."—"People sometimes think I am sad or depressed when actually I am just deep inside myself, and in fact most happy."—"In having children, I particularly love the almost vegetative state of pregnancy and very early mothering."—"I love things primordial: the roar of the ocean, the musky smell that lingers after sex."

Some descriptive words for the four Early-Axis quadrants:

Upper/Inner   Upper/Outer

intuitive, spiritual, philosophical	artistically creative, scientifically innovative, charismatic
love of nature and mystery, nurturing, reflective	spontaneous, improvisational, love of the "wild"

Lower/Inner   Lower/Outer

When it comes specifically to the tasks of culturally mature leadership, as with all temperaments, Earlies natively both make particular contributions and have particular blindnesses. On the positive side, high-Capacitance Earlies can be especially adept at looking toward the future. They have the personality style that is by nature most visionary and most interested in the "big picture." This is also the temperament most natively comfortable with uncertainty and most open to the kind of fundamental change Cultural Maturity represents. Earlies also tend to be particularly adept at recognizing pattern and interrelationship.

At the same time, Earlies can be especially vulnerable to Unity Fallacies, most commonly of the more spiritual/mystical or environmental variety, but sometimes, too, those of a more liberal/progressive sort.

Because Early-Axis temperaments are those most natively influenced by the archetypally feminine, interpretations often bias significantly to the left. When Earlies romanticize a culture from previous times, most often it is an Early-Axis stage culture (where spiritual values and mythic sensibilities tend to predominate). Where Capacitance is low, left-hand traps can become pretty much the norm.

Depending on the individual, Earlies can be attracted to almost any of the scenarios for the future I have described, but they tend to espouse versions that are specific to and predictable from Early-Axis sensibility. Of all temperament groups, Earlies are the least likely to ascribe to We've Arrived scenarios.[6] In contrast, attraction to We've Gone Astray scenarios is fairly common—of all groups Earlies are the most likely to experience Transition in terms of a crisis of purpose and can respond to its demands with depression or even suicide.

Early/Uppers can be attracted to Post-industrial/Information Age scenarios, particularly versions that focus on digital technologies (at the extreme, succumbing to beliefs of the techno-utopian sort).[7] Early/ Uppers can also be drawn to Postmodern/Constructivist conclusions. They tend to be both more comfortable than most temperaments with the positive contributions of postmodern interpretation (finding appeal in its challenging of cultural convention and its openness to multiple viewpoints) and particularly vulnerable to the seduction of existential non-commitalness. Of the various temperament groups, Earlies are the most likely to be attracted to Transformational/New Paradigm scenarios, both versions that provide useful insight and interpretations that are at best diversions.

---

6   Because Earlies tend to find such delight in possibility and the unorthodox, neither the status quo nor the institutional hold native appeal. And what attraction We've Arrived interpretations might hold comes up against the strong archetypally masculine bias of modern values and institutions. The identification that some Early/Upper/Outer scientists feel with a traditional scientific worldview is the one common exception.

7   Early/Upper/Outers can also be particularly attracted to evolutionary science and the sciences of complexity. Such attraction can result in views that make important headway into culturally mature territory. But we also see interpretations that use indeterminacy and self-organization to argue for a narrow scientism.

Middle-Axis Patterns:

Middle-Axis temperaments reflect a special affinity with the "perspiration" stage in formative process—that period where new creation struggles into crude, but now solid, manifestation. While Earlies identify most with the first improvisational sparks of creation, Middles find greatest meaning turning sparks into usable fire. This includes the ability to provoke and nurture the flames—blow air on them so they will heighten—and, simultaneously, to contain the flames, so that the fire burns usefully and safely. The Middle-Axis fire both performs work and warms the hearth of community.

Following are a few words from familiar Middles. From Albert Schweitzer: "A man can only do what he can do. But if he does that each day, he can sleep at night and do it again the next day." From Margaret Mead: "One of the oldest human needs is having someone wonder where you are when you don't come home at night." From Douglas MacArthur: "In war there is no substitute for victory." From Abraham Lincoln: "The better part of a one's life consists of his friendships." From Winston Churchill: "This is a lesson: never give in—never, never, never, never." From Samuel Johnson: "Great works are performed not by strength, but by perseverance." And from Jesse James: "Everybody loves an outlaw. At least they never forget 'em."[8]

Where are we most likely to find people with Middle-Axis temperaments? Middles often become teachers, managers in business, military officers, social workers, athletes and coaches, union bosses, ministers or priests, physicians (about an equal balance of Middle/Upper and Late/Upper), politicians (a similar balance), policemen and firefighters, bankers, loggers, owners of family businesses, machinists, miners, and carpenters. In addition, Middles make up the greater portion of stay-at-home parents. (It is with Middle-Axis that we find the strongest identification with home, family, and community.) Women who think of themselves first as wives and mothers are commonly Middles,

---

8   Note how we find very similar sentiments with the Middle-Axis stage in cultural development (from the Koran: "God helps those who persevere"—from Proverbs 24:16: "For a just man falleth seven times and riseth up again.") and with Middle-Axis functions within a cultural stage (from Aesop and the moral voice of fable—"Slow and steady wins the race.")

as are the most devoted husbands and fathers. Middle-Axis individuals of both sexes frequently play strong roles in their neighborhoods and churches, and in social service organizations. Most of the "real work" in society is done by Middles.

Some better-known Middles include Teddy Roosevelt, Mother Teresa, Margaret Thatcher, Joe Louis, Billy Graham, George Washington, Babe Ruth, Eleanor Roosevelt, Chris Evert, Thurgood Marshall, Florence Nightingale, Colin Powell, Roy Rogers and Dale Evans, Aretha Franklin, Clint Eastwood, Bella Abzug, Julia Child, Queen Victoria, Tugboat Annie, Johnny Cash, Jimmy Carter, J. Edgar Hoover, Frederick Douglass, Hulk Hogan, Cesar Chavez, Golda Meir, Mary Lou Retton, Rush Limbaugh, Boris Yeltzin, Betty Friedan, Norman Schwarzkopf, Willie Nelson, Bear Bryant, Jimmy Hoffa, Barbara Bush, and Fred and Ethel Mertz. More notorious Middles include Joseph Stalin, Adolf Hitler, Ma Barker, and, as above, Jesse James.

Again, lower-pole figures—particularly Lower/Inners—are not well represented in this list. But Middle/Lower is where we find many of the most important, if unheralded, figures in our lives: the neighborhood police officer or firefighter, the friend who is there no matter what, the parent who puts a special note in a child's lunch box.

Emotional/Moral Intelligence, the intelligence of heart and guts, orders the Middle's world (as Emotional/Moral Intelligence manifests within Late-Axis culture). The stuff of heart holds sway in Middle/Inner and Middle/Lower temperaments—where the archetypally feminine is strongest. Harder sensibilities—the stuff of guts and fortitude—dominate with Middle/Upper and Middle/Outer temperaments.

Middle-Axis dynamics move us firmly into the human dimension. Early-Axis and Late-Axis realities are each in their own ways abstracted from the personal. Early-Axis sensibilities are more concerned with the pre-personal reality of creative buddings; Late-Axis sensibilities are more concerned with the post-personal worlds of the intellectual, the social, and the material. Middle-Axis sensibilities operate right in the middle, engaged directly in the tasks of mortal existence.

With Middle-Axis dynamics, we see a strong capacity for hard work, deep emotional and moral convictions, and the ability to persevere and to sacrifice when necessary. (Napoleon Bonaparte once said, "The first virtue in a soldier is endurance of fatigue; courage is only the second virtue.") Middles are attracted to the basic ("home is where the heart is"). Loyalty is an especially valued trait. The phrase "salt of the earth" would rarely be used except to refer to a Middle-Axis person. Middle-Axis creativity tends to be less that of glaring originality than of the application of new possibility to what exists. The most skilled craftspeople are Middles. With some notable exceptions, Middle-Axis people tend to be incrementalists rather than leapers. "A bird in the hand is worth two in the bush" is a Middle-Axis sentiment. Here lie the best day-to-day, hands-on problem solvers, whether in the halls of Congress, in the office, in the home, or on the factory floor.

Middles tend to respect strong moral fiber and often speak with a bluntness not found with other temperaments. (Charles de Gaulle admonished that "people get the history they deserve.") Middle-Axis personalities tend toward the traditional in their values—though this does not necessarily translate to conservative (for example, environmentalists are often Middles). Humility and unpretentiousness are often strong values (though bravado can prevail with outer aspects). It is not uncommon for Middle-Axis parents to warn of the dangers of getting "too big for your britches." Teddy Roosevelt said it well for the political sphere: "Speak softly and carry a big stick." (Note the tendency toward sayings and homilies in these descriptions. Homilies are a peculiarly Middle-Axis art form—"A stitch in time saves nine," "People who live in glass houses shouldn't throw stones," "Haste makes waste," etc.) Middles tend to love a good story and are often particularly adept at telling them.

Middle-Axis dynamics juxtapose opposites in near equal balance. Like two ends of a teeter-totter, opposites simultaneously battle and collude. In the Middle-Axis psyche, strength struggles against weakness, thoughts against feelings, good against evil, domination against submission, control against abandon, honor against dishonor. Meaning for a Middle is a reflection of timely balance (though often of a struggled sort) between such isometrically interplaying forces. The reward for this creative push-pull is the realization of substance and the satisfaction of a job well done.

Words we might associate with Middle/Upper personalities include fortitude, courage, uprightness, fairness, and moral conviction. Middle/Uppers are often strong leaders. With Middle/Upper/Outers this tends to be organizational leadership—the leadership of politicians, captains of industry, coaches, military officers. We hear both the fortitude and the generosity of spirit often found with Middle/Upper/Outer sentiments in these words of George S. Patton: "Wars may be fought with weapons, but they are won by men. It is the spirit of the men who follow and the man who leads that gains the victory."

Middle/Upper/Inner leadership tends to manifest at a more personal level. Upper/Inner sensibilities are common in teachers, managers, and religious leaders. Middle/Upper/Inner leadership has a strong moral component. It is compassionate, but also resolute. Benjamin Franklin observed that "sin is not hurtful because it is forbidden, but it is forbidden because it is hurtful."

People of Middle/Lower temperaments are often most known for their perseverance, loyalty, capacity to support or nurture, and their often-irreverent sense of humor.[9] Middle/Lowers place great importance on relationship.[10] For Middle/Lower/Inners, the most defining relationships tend to be with friends, family, and immediate community. Besides being good parents, Middle/Lower/Inners often contribute through working as teachers (particularly with children and adolescents), as social workers, as behind-the-counter salespeople, in nursing, or in the food industry. These words of Johann Wolfgang von Goethe capture the dedication common to Middle/Lower/Inner temperaments: "It is not doing the thing we like to do, but liking the thing we have to do, that makes life blessed."

For Middle/Lower/Outers, the key relationships tend to be with community in a broader sense, with team members, or even more broadly, with one's ethnic group or nation. Middle/Lower/Outers are

---

9   Middle/Lower/Outers in particular enjoy the jostling camaraderie of a good joke, story, or put-down. Boxer Jack Dempsey once offered the following piece of practical wisdom: "Some night you'll catch a punch between the eyes and all of a sudden you'll see three guys in the ring against you. Pick out the one in the middle and hit him, because he's the one who hit you."

10   But they are not known for being romantics. A Czech proverb (here Middle both in Time and Space) counsels, "Do not pick your wife at a dance, but in the field among the harvesters."

capable of strong bonds of allegiance. They are the loyal fans scream-
ing at a football game. Middle/Lower/Outers become farmers, soldiers,
police officers, carpenters, and professional athletes. It is they who do
the hands-on protecting and heavy lifting of society. They like to get
things done. Henry Wadsworth Longfellow's familiar poem, "The Vil-
lage Blacksmith" reflects Middle/Lower values:

> Under a spreading chestnut tree
> The village smithy stands;
> The smith a mighty man is he,
> With large and sinewy hands;
> And the muscles of his brawny arms
> Are strong as iron bands.
>
> His brow is wet with honest sweat,
> He earns what'er he can,
> And looks the whole world in the face,
> For he owes not any man.

Shortcomings again tend to express the flip side of common
strengths. For example, because Middles have less of both the intuitive sensitivity common in Early-Axis patterns and the refinement and
differentiation found with more Late-Axis sensibilities, the attitudes
and beliefs of some Middles can seem to others coarse or simplistic, a
conclusion reinforced by the common Middle-Axis tendency toward
concreteness. (Middles are notorious for retelling all the details of an
event rather than summarizing and abstracting.)

The Middle's great capacity for control can also be an impediment—
indeed, sometimes his or her undoing. The Middle/Upper's need to
be on top (both of others and of his or her own impulses) can make it
hard for the Middle either to surrender authority or to let go of control
sufficiently to find fulfillment. When we say someone is too "high and
mighty," it is most likely a Middle/Upper we are talking about. The
Middle/Lower's tendency to feel most safe (and in control) if someone
else is in charge can also be limiting. If Middle/Lowers are not careful,
they can become passive or undermining of authority (as Michel de
Montaigne said, "Obstinacy is the sister of constancy.") The need for

occasional release of control can make alcohol attractive for both Uppers and Lowers, with the potential for abuse.

Identifying words and phrases given to me by Middles include "A good education is the key to a productive life. Teachers are our real heroes."—"Politics has to do with power, who has it and who doesn't."—"Never say die."—"The caterpillar does all the work, and the butterfly gets all the publicity."—"Children, family, and God. In these lie life's true riches."—"I like people who are plainspoken, people who are unpretentious and forthright."—"Shit or get off the pot."—"There is nothing more precious than a good friend."—"A good leader has to be willing to make tough, often uncomfortable decisions. You will not always be loved, but in the end you will be respected."—"A penny saved is a penny earned."—"I know how to be there for others."—"You play the cards you're dealt."—"Few things give me more pleasure than working in my garden."

Some descriptive words and common qualities for the Middle-Axis quadrants:

Upper/Inner   Upper/Outer

moral stature, aptitude for mentoring and teaching	natural leadership ability, organizational adeptness, action orientation
unpretentiousness, commitment to home and community	toughness, loyalty, capacity for hard work

Lower/Inner   Lower/Outer

When it comes specifically to the tasks of culturally mature leadership, on the positive side, high-Capacitance Middles are some of the people most adept at social leadership. Even when culturally mature perspective is yet limited, the Middle's ability to keep things together, along with their valuing of people and their respect for fairness, can provide great benefit. When these attributes combine with the Capacitance needed for culturally mature understanding, relationship, and action, such benefit increases dramatically.

At the same time, low-Capacitance Middles can feel particularly threatened by culturally mature ideas and be especially reactive in their responses to them. Because Middles have a high native need for control and order, the surrendering of familiar realities that Cultural Maturity requires does not tend to come easily for Middles. And the isometric organization of polarity within Middle-Axis dynamics (with right- and left-hand poles at near-equal potency) means that projective responses to being pushed beyond Capacitance can be particularly intense in expression.[11] The fact that Middles tend to feel strong moral conviction and to manifest their beliefs in action amplifies both the richness of potential contributions and the risks when blindness and denial prevail. Romantic idealization most commonly makes reference to either more Middle-Axis times within Late-Axis culture or, at least by implication, the medieval sensibilities that gave us kingly rule and the establishment of monotheism.

People with Middle-Axis temperaments are the most likely to ascribe to We've Arrived beliefs. When such beliefs are held by high-Capacitance Middles, rather than being overly ideological, they tend to reflect the Middle's basic tendencies to leave things that don't need to be changed unchanged, and to focus attention on doing the work that needs to be done. Low-Capacitance Middles, on the other hand, are often ardently polemic in their We've Arrived beliefs. Particularly in times of major social perturbation such as today, the Middle's native tendency toward conservatism can quickly translate into unquestioning identification with current social forms.

Middle/Upper/Outer We've Arrived beliefs tend to focus on strongly archetypally masculine institutional structures—

---

11 We can see adamant Fallacies of both the Unity and Separation sort, and often simultaneously (for example, a person expressing strongly felt Unity Fallacies with regard to their own kind, and equally strongly felt Separation Fallacies with regard to groups that they see as different).

government, business, the military. With Middle/Upper/Inner We've Arrived interpretations, religious and/or educational institutions tend to get the greater emphasis. Where We've Arrived conclusions appeal to Middle/Lowers, they tend to center more around traditional notions of family, community, and morality. There can be identification with traditional institutions,[12] but the resonance is less with institution as structure than with the bonds of association and moral belief that such institutions represent.

It is with low-Capacitance Middles, and in particular Inner/Lower examples, that we tend to see the most extreme of We've Gone Astray interpretations. This can take the form of intractable cynicism. It can also manifest in the form of end-time religious proclamations. Post-industrial/Information Age scenarios can also have strong attraction for Middles, in particular Middle/Upper/Outers. (Engineers tend to share this temperament.) Postmodern/Constructivist ideas tend to have much less appeal (given their emphasis on uncertainty), but this is not always the case. Some of the best of applied constructivist thinking is found in school settings.[13] Transformational/New Paradigm scenarios tend to have the least appeal for Middles. The strong archetypally feminine contribution in such views can make even the most developed scenarios look suspicious from a Middle-Axis vantage.[14]

While Middles can have the hardest time being comfortable with the depth of change that Cultural Maturity entails, they also have a unique advantage when it comes to culturally mature perspective. The fact that they sit in the middle (between Early and Late) can make a balanced, if not necessarily integrative, view seem reasonable. If Middles have sufficient Capacitance, it is they who most

---

12   Religious institutions in particular appeal to Middle/Lower/Inners. Middle/Lower/Outers are more likely to profess strong nationalistic sentiments.

13   Middle-Axis personalities and values predominate in K-12–level educational environments.

14   The establishment of Middle reality requires that the less formed world of Early sensibility be kept at arm's length.

quickly realize that the result is common sense. Some of the people I know who are best at articulating Creative Systems ideas in simple, obvious-seeming ways are Middles.

Late-Axis Patterns:

 Late-Axis patterns reflect a special affinity with the finishing and polishing stage in formative process—the developmental period that turns our attention to questions of detail. Rational/material intelligence orders experience, bringing emphasis to the intellect and to the more refined (manifest) aspects of the emotional and the aesthetic. Because Late-Axis is the most natively outer of the personality style axes, of all temperaments, Lates tend to function most easily and efficiently in the external world.[15]

Here are a few words from well-known Lates. From Francis Bacon: "Reading maketh a full man, conference a ready man, and writing an exact man." From Alfred, Lord Tennyson: "'Tis better to have loved and lost than never to have loved at all." From Elizabeth Cady Stanton: "In a word, I am always busy, which is perhaps the chief reason I am always well." From John F. Kennedy: "In times of turbulence and change, it is more true than ever that knowledge is power." From Bill Blass: "When in doubt wear red." From Ted Koppel: "Look ... ours is a business of appearances, and it's terribly important to appear to be self-confident ... the minute you give evidence of doubt, people are going to eat you alive." From Alexandre Dumas: "Nothing succeeds like success." From T.H. Huxley: "Science is nothing but trained and organized common sense." From Sophie Tucker: "I have been rich and I have been poor. Rich is better:" And from Bertrand Russell, "To be able to fill leisure intelligently is the last product of civilization."

Lates often become professors, writers, lawyers, CEOs, scientists, fashion models, ballet or modern dancers, Wall Street financiers, marketers, or actors. More than with any other axis, various individuals can differ widely in their inclinations. Within Late-Axis we find the people who are most rational in their perspective, and also those who

---

15   See the diagram in Chapter Ten.

tend most toward the romantic. We find the people who are most materialistically driven, and at the same time many of those most committed to artistic and intellectual pursuits where monetary remuneration is often slight. We find the people most aggressively in the world, and also many of those most internal and reflective in their proclivities.[16]

Some familiar Lates include Walter Cronkite, Marie Curie, Carl Sagan, Julia Roberts, Sammy Davis, Jr., Elizabeth Taylor, Jonas Salk, Donald Trump, Alistair Cooke, Frank Sinatra, Bertrand Russell, Mikhail Gorbachev (who is really more Middle than Late, but notable because he embodied significantly more Late than any previous Soviet leader), Ted Turner, Harry Belafonte, Gloria Steinem, Woodrow Wilson, Johnny Carson, Steve Martin, Peter Lynch, Clark Gable, Kenneth Clark, Mikhail Baryshnikov, Peggy Fleming, William F. Buckley, Norman Rockwell, and Robert Redford.[17] Less savory Lates tend to engage in white collar crime, so are less visible and less often prosecuted than Early and Middle lawbreakers—I think immediately of those who engaged in investment bank excesses during the "great recession."

Of all temperaments, Lates tend to move most effectively in the world of form and structure—whether the sphere is ideas or professional accomplishment. When we say that someone is scholarly or intellectual, most often we are referring to a Late. Lates tend to be socially comfortable and speak persuasively. And, more than other temperaments, they tend to be materially successful. They are the most natively competitive[18] and the most likely to value external reward.

Lates can be quite creative, but their creativity tends to be of a different sort than the whole-cloth originality of Earlies. Late-Axis scientists are more likely to be recognized for the skill of their experimental work or their ability to bring together existing work to reach new conclusions. Late-Axis visual artists, dancers, and musicians tend

---

16   A look to the Creative Function helps explain. It is with Late-Axis that we see the greatest natural separation between poles.

17   The word "celebrity" almost always refers to a Late.

18   Note the subtle but often quite consequential distinction between the Late's competitive tendencies and the Middle's need for control.

to work from established traditions or written scores and make their primary creative contributions through refinement and subtlety of aesthetic expression.

Lates tend to value and manifest the skills of social discourse more than other temperaments. This can take highly formal expression—etiquette and the fine art of diplomacy come naturally to many Lates. (From Lord Chesterfield: "Politeness and good breeding is absolutely necessary to adorn any, or all, other good qualities or talents.") As often, it manifests in a simple ease and comfort in the social sphere. Lates commonly have an unusual degree of interpersonal adeptness and flair. When we say that someone has "personality" or "style," when we say that someone is sophisticated or looks "sharp," we are usually referring to a Late. More than other temperaments, Lates attend to physical appearance. (Ralph Waldo Emerson reflected on having "heard with admiring submission the experience of the lady who declared that the sense of being perfectly well-dressed gives a feeling of inward tranquility which religion is powerless to bestow." Estee Lauder offered this advice: "Never just 'run out for a few minutes' without looking your best. This is not vanity—it is self-liking.")

The qualities that most stand out with Upper-pole Late-Axis personalities are clarity of thought, verbal facility, and the ability to deal easily and effectively with the material world. With Late/Upper/Inners, the more intellectual of these qualities stand out. University professors, scientific researchers, and nonfiction writers commonly have Late/Upper/Inner personalities. The Late/Upper/Inner quadrant is also where we find the greatest appreciation for the formal. Refinement and etiquette are Late/Upper/Inner notions. (In the words of Lady Montagu, "Civility costs nothing and buys everything.")

With Late/Upper/Outers, more external and material concerns take center stage. It is here we find the individuals who are most facile with money and the complexities of the business world—corporate executives, economists, media moguls, and stockbrokers. While for Late/Upper/Inners the intellect resides most comfortably in the ivory tower, Late/Upper/Outers apply it to the most worldly concerns. (In the words of Donald Trump, "As long as you are going to be thinking anyway, think big.")

With Late/Lower temperaments, qualities such as gregariousness, talent, sensuality, and emotional presence often most stand out. Of all personality groups, Late/Lowers are most likely to enjoy being "on stage." People in the performing arts almost always have at least some Late/Lower in their makeup, as do the great majority of fashion models and television entertainers. Late/Lowers often have a rich sense of the dramatic, as well as the smoothness and presence needed to pull it off. Sophia Loren once observed that "sex appeal is fifty percent what you've got, and fifty percent what people think you've got."

Where the balance is toward Inner, the dramatic focus highlights emotional and aesthetic nuance. Late/Lower/Inner is the most common personality style of people involved in the performing arts—dancers, actors. Novelists and visual artists of a more realist bent also often find their creative source in Late/Lower/Inner sensibilities, as do interior and fashion designers.[19]

With Late/Lower/Outers we find the people with the greatest capacity to project and be visible. Late/Lower/Outers are those most successful at marketing and promotion (both of things and themselves). Where there is balance between Upper and Lower tendencies, we can find "serious" media personalities, such as television newscasters. More expressly lower-pole personalities define the entertainment industry—"glamour" and "celebrity" are Late/Lower/Outer words. The more glittery and flamboyant of actors and actresses have Late/Lower/Outer personalities, as often do the more packaged and promoted of popular musicians. In more day-to-day manifestations, Late/Lower/Outers may work for advertising agencies or sell high-end clothing or real estate.

Partialities again express the flip side of common strengths. Lates who are either highly intellectual or materialistic can have a difficult time with emotional closeness, or anything that requires creative depth. It is not so much that they fear these things (as can be the case with Early/Uppers and Middle/Uppers) than that they often live a long way from where these things reside. Also, Late/Uppers can lose perspective in their obsession with detail and the ideal. The other side

---

19   Even the most Inner of Late-Axis personalities may pursue what might seem Outer pursuits. Because Late dynamics are the most manifest, even sensibilities that are particularly internal may manifest in the world of form.

of the Late/Uppers' valuing of objectivity and excellence is a common tendency to be perfectionistic and often overly critical. Achievement is the Late/Upper's great two-edged sword. While the Late/Upper tends to do very well at climbing the ladder of success, often he or she has a difficult time stepping away from it.

Late/Lower failings are related, but more personal. Excessive outgoingness can translate into feeling distant from oneself—and paradoxically also from others. Breezy can become only superficial; smooth only slick; romantic seductively manipulative. (Oscar Wilde, a Late/Lower who often played humorously with the gifts and blindnesses of Late-Axis life, quipped, "In matters of grave importance, style, not sincerity, is the vital thing.") Competitive spirit can become cattiness and backbiting. (A Hollywood actress once remarked of a fellow actress, "There goes the good time that was had by all.") Isolation can be compounded by the Late/Lower's reluctance to "look bad" by admitting aloneness or confusion. Late/Lowers are often tormented by self-doubt—particularly in relation to physical appearance (which is ironic in that it is they who most easily succeed at accepted standards of beauty). Late/Lower/Inners especially can become frightened and withdrawn. Not surprisingly, eating disorders are especially common in Late/Lower young people. For related reasons, Late/Lowers often have a difficult time with the changes of life's later years.

Some words from the diverse world of Late-Axis sensibility: "I like to relax by listening to classical music or reading a good book."—"I was usually quite popular in school. I am still the person who can take a dull party and bring it to life."—"I don't like to admit it, but I can be pretty competitive. I like to win."—"I feel very at home in the world of ideas."—"I make lists. Sometimes I even make lists of lists."—"I like to feel classy and put-together. Presentation can make all the difference."—"I would make a good television news person."——"In the end, most of the world's problems are economic."—"I like performing. I love the feeling that comes from connecting deeply with an audience."—"Diamonds are a girl's best friend."—"I can be a bit excitable. People say they like this in me. They think I'm a fun person. But sometimes it gets in the way. I get scattered and people think I am less intelligent than I really am."——"I love the feel of silk pajamas."

Some descriptive words and common qualities for the Late-Axis quadrants:

Upper/Inner   Upper/Outer

intellectual, articulate, good at synthesis	worldly, financially adept, publicly expressive
romantic, emotionally sensitive, æsthetically nuanced	able to strongly project, emotionally articulate, persuasive

Lower/Inner   Lower/Outer

When it comes specifically to the tasks of culturally mature leadership, on the positive side, high-Capacitance Lates tend to be the people who are most adept at putting ideas about the future into words and into action. Most books about the future are written by Lates, and the larger portion of academic futurists, particularly those who focus primary attention on the future of business, government, or technology are Lates. Where Lates are capable of culturally mature perspective, we find some of the most articulate expression of ideas and some of the most facile translation of ideas into policy.

Low-Capacitance Lates, on the other hand, can be some of the people least able to recognize the limitations of modern belief. Part of this blindness derives from how little felt dissonance can exist between the convictions of people with Late-Axis temperaments and the normative assumptions of contemporary (Late-Axis) reality. But as much of this circumstance derives also from the way Late-Axis understanding tends to organize from the more surface layers of experience. Low-Capacitance intellectual views can lack the depth needed to grasp emerging complexities. And low-Capacitance social interactions can be strongly influenced by popular-culture values.

Lates can identify with any of the five scenarios, but given the Late's primary engagement in the more creatively manifest aspects of formative process, We've Arrived and Post-industrial/Information Age scenarios predictably find the greatest number of adherents. Where Lates romantically idealize, they most often elevate Modern Age achievements and institutions.[20] Late-Axis We've Arrived views tend to focus on political and economic structures more than religious belief (the more archetypally mascline aspects of culture as structure). Post-industrial/Information Age scenarios that focus on science and technology are often accepted almost without question. It is common for Lates to simply assume that technology is culture's driver and that the future will be defined by the influence of new technological advances.

With Late/Upper/Outers, the temperament constellation most natively linked with financial, media, and global institutional leadership, we find We've Arrived and Post-industrial/Information Age interpretations almost exclusively. With Late/Upper/Inner sensibility we find greater variety. This is the temperament most common in professorial ranks. We can see an ultimate sort of intellectual We've Arrived interpretation with logical positivist and extreme behaviorist worldviews (Enlightenment belief finds culminating expression). We also see We've Arrived interpretations with a more liberal-humanist flavor (with modern forms of the arts and humanities getting closer to equal billing with harder realms of activity and inquiry).

Postmodern/Constructivist interpretation can also find strong advocacy among those of Late/Upper/Inner sensibility (both its most clear and useful expressions and its common reduction to an empty intellectualism). And Late/Upper/Inner tendencies can sometimes produce a kind of We've Gone Astray attitude based more on a hyper-rational alienation from meaning rather than the romantic underpinnings more common with such scenarios. Late/Upper/Inners can also be attracted to a secular humanism with either liberal We've Gone Astray or more Transformation/New Paradigm leanings.

We've Arrived adherents can also be found among Late/Lowers. Those of Late/Lower/Outer tendency will focus more on the accomplishments of

---

20   The one exception is the way Late/Upper/Inner academics often idealize the democratic achievements of the early Greeks.

the arts and humanities, modern media, and entertainment, and on the sensibilities and values of material culture. People with more Late/Lower/ Inner tendencies can also be attracted to We've Arrived interpretations, but generally with less emphasis on the more extroverted expressions of media and materiality. In addition, We've Gone Astray interpretations of the more philosophically romantic sort can be found. On occasion, Transformational/New Paradigm beliefs can appear with Late/Lower/Inner dynamics—indeed, it is here that we find some of the most extreme of New Age transformational interpretations (actress Shirley MacLaine is a Late/Lower/Inner[21]).[22]

---

21   There is a natural link between Early/Upper and Late/Lower dynamics. Early/Uppers represent the most achetypally masculine pattern within the most archtypally feminine axis, while Late/Lower represent the most archetypally feminine pattern within the most archetypally masculine axis. This interesting relationship produces, simultaneously, intriguing similarities and what can be startlingly extreme differences.

22   An additional pattern beyond the simple association with polar tendencies that I noted earlier is common with Lates and can be confusing. In "cross-polar" dynamics, the polar sensibilities a person identifies with and the pole a person most speaks from are not the same. Cross-polar patterns are found with each temperament axis. (You can see a common Middle-Axis cross-polar dynamic, for example, in the posture of the self-righteous victim, who identifies with being oppressed while at the same time criticizing from a position of "on-high" moral superiority.)

      But the dual fact that Late-Axis mechanisms natively emphasize the archetypally masculine and that verbal expression is a predominantly upper-pole function means that, in Late-Axis, strong identification with the archetypally feminine frequently results in cross-polar dynamics. Late-Axis academic positions that derive from left-hand sensibilities often manifest as a highly intellectual anti-intellectualism. (The worst of Postmodern/Constructivist thought gets tangled in this sort of contradiction.) Something similar is commonly seen with Late-Axis political expression. One can find views that, because they are ultimately anti-authoritarian, undermine their own authority (thus the often amazing ability of Democrats in the United States to shoot themselves in the foot in their attempts to win elections and to get anything substantive accomplished). Late-Axis cross-polar Unity Fallacies are common in liberal-humanist advocacy.

In Summary

This has been but a crude outline of the Creative Systems Personality Typology and its implications for culturally mature leadership. As far as the specific temperament descriptions, it is important to keep in mind that we find grand exceptions in every case, and that while it can be useful to talk of pure types, they are rare. Most often we find Earlies with some Middle or Middles with some Late.[23] And even when temperaments are quite extreme, they are never just Upper or just Inner. However polarized the dynamic, Upper and Lower, Inner and Outer tendencies are each always present. To appreciate our difference with any subtlety, we need to think not in terms of boxes, but balances and interplays.

As far as the implications for culturally mature leadership, the important recognition is that, given necessary Capacitance, all temperaments have equally significant roles to play. High-Capacitance Earlies are the most likely to provide us with needed fresh ideas. Middles are most likely to question innovation and are often the last to get on board. But when a new idea passes the scrutiny of a high-Capacitance Middle, it is likely a good one—and Middles are some of the best at putting good new ideas into practice. High-Capacitance Lates contribute a keen analytical eye. In addition, they are especially adept at popularizing, which is essential when the time arrives for important new ideas to reach a broad audience. If you want potent culturally mature decision-making, put a team together that includes solid representatives from each axis.

Cross-polar dynamics do not preclude culturally mature perspective. They simply reflect one way in which the creative balance between poles can manifest. But because cross-polar assertions are often contradictory, cross-polar fallacies can be particularly tricky to tease apart and get beyond.

23 An example: Middle/Upper/Outer tends to predominate in the personalities of politicians, but to be successful, politicians also need at least a touch of the Late's greater aptitude for detail, abstraction, and marketing. We could imagine a continuum with John F. Kennedy, Franklin Roosevelt, and Woodrow Wilson on the Late-Axis end; Abraham Lincoln and Harry Truman more toward the Middle; and more narrowly conservative figures such as Richard Nixon and George W. Bush almost pure Middle.

References

(I have limited references to instances where understanding context might help with clarity.)

Introduction

p. 4. Johnston, Charles. *The Creative Imperative: Human Growth and Planetary Evolution*. Celestial Arts, 1984.

p. 6. Johnston, Charles. *Hope and the Future: An Introduction to the Concept of Cultural Maturity*. ICD Press, 2014.

p. 6. Johnston, Charles. *Quick and Dirty Answers to the Biggest of Questions: Creative Systems Theory Explains What It Is All About (Really)*. ICD Press, 2013.

p. 13. Havel, Václav. "The Need for Transcendence in the Postmodern World." Speech presented at his acceptance of the Liberty Medal, Independence Hall, Philadelphia, July 4, 1994.

p. 13. Einstein, Albert. "Why Socialism?" *Monthly Review*, May 1949.

p. 43. Hugo, Victor. *Historie d'un Crime*. 1877.

Chapter 1

p. 52. Friedman, Thomas. "Are We Home Alone?" *New York Times*, March 21, 2009.

p. 62. Emerson, Ralph Waldo. *Ralph Waldo Emerson: Selected Journals*. Library of America, 2010.

p. 70. Lawrence, D.H. *Pansies: Poems by D.H. Lawrence.* Penguin, 2002. (First published in 1929.)

p. 71. Muir, John. *My First Summer in the Sierra and Selected Essays.* Library of America, 2011. (First published in 1911.)

p. 74. Holmes, Oliver Wendell. *The Essential Holmes.* University of Chicago Press, 1987.

p. 81. Anderson, Walter Truett. *The Truth About the Truth.* Tarcher/Putnam, 1995.

p. 86. Heisenberg, Werner. *Physics and Philosophy: The Revolution in Modern Science.* Prometheus Books, 1999. (First published in 1958.)

p. 88. Brooks, David. "An Economy of Faith and Trust." *New York Times,* January 15, 2009.

Chapter 2

p. 91. Frost, Robert. "Mending Wall." In *The Poetry of Robert Frost.* Henry Holt and Co., 1969. (First published in 1914.)

p. 96. Whitman, Walt. *Song of Myself.* Counterpoint, 2010. (First published in 1855.)

p. 107. Fitzgerald, F. Scott. *The Love of the Last Tycoon.* Simon and Schuster, 1995. (First published in 1941.)

p. 107. Johnston, Charles. *Necessary Wisdom: Meeting the Challenge of a New Cultural Maturity.* Celestial Arts, 1992.

p. 117. Pirsig, Robert. *Zen and the Art of Motorcycle Maintenance: An Inquiry Into Values.* Bantam, 1974.

Chapter 3

p. 144. Wilson, Edward. *The Future of Life*. Alfred A. Knopf, 2002.

p. 145. Brand, Stewart. *Whole Earth Discipline*. Viking, 2009.

p. 150. Planck, Max. *The Universe in the Light of Modern Physics*. Nubu Press, 2011. (First published in 1931.)

p. 151. Friedman, Thomas. "The Inflection Is Near?" *New York Times*, March 7, 2009.

p. 156. Wordsworth, William. "The Excursion." In *William Wordsworth: The Major Works*. Oxford University Press, 2008. (First published in 1814.)

p. 156. Niebuhr, Reinhold. "Serenity Prayer" (originally untitled). In *The Essential Reinhold Niebuhr*. Yale University Press, 1987.

p. 164. Korzybski, Alfred. *Science and Sanity*. The Institute of General Semantics, 2010. (First published in 1933.)

Chapter 4

p. 182. Santayana, George. "The Life of Reason." In *The Essential George Santayana*. Halcyon Press, 2010. (First published in 1905-1906.)

p. 186. Descartes, René. *Discourse on the Method*. 1637.

p. 186. Korzybski, Alfred. *Science and Sanity*. The Institute of General Semantics, 2010.

p. 187. Broad, C.D. *The Mind and Its Place in Nature*. The Humanities Press, 1951.

p. 189. Prigogine, Ilya. *Order Out of Chaos: Man's New Dialogue with Nature*. Bantam Books, 1984.

Chapter 5

p. 211. Csikszentmihalyi, Mihaly. *The Evolving Self*. HarperCollins, 1993.

p. 213. Saint-Exupéry, Antoine de. *The Little Prince*. Houghton Mifflin Harcourt. 2013. (First published in 1943.)

p. 217. Sartre, Jean-Paul. *Being and Nothingness*. Gallimard, 1943.

p. 217. Lyotard, Jean-François. *The Postmodern Condition*. Manchester University Press, 1984. (First published in 1979.)

p. 221. Schrödinger, Erwin. *What is Life?* Cambridge University Press, 1992. (First published in 1944.)

p. 224. Bertalanffy, Ludwig von. *General Systems Theory*, George Braziller,1968.

p. 224. Bateson, Gregory. *Steps to an Ecology of Mind*. University of Chicago Press, 2000. (First published in 1972.)

p. 230. White, T.H. *The Once and Future King*. Ace Trade, 2011. (First published in 1958.)

Chapter 6

p. 253. Dyson, Freeman. *Disturbing the Universe*. Sloan Foundation Science Series, 1981.

p. 263. Bohr, Niels. In his first meeting with Werner Heisenberg in 1920, in response to questions on the nature of language, as reported in *Discussions about Language* (1933).

p. 263. Goleman, Daniel. *Emotional Intelligence*. Bantam Books, 1995.

p. 264. Gardner, Howard. *Multiple Intelligences: New Horizons in Theory and Practice*. Basic Books, 2006. (First published in 1993.)

p. 273. Whitehead, Alfred North. *Process and Reality*. Edited by D.R. Griffin and D.W. Sherburne. The Free Press, 1978.

p. 273. Popper, Karl. *The Open Universe: An Argument for Indeterminism*. Routledge, 2012. (First published in 1982.)

Chapter 7

p. 295. West, Bing. *The Wrong War*. Random House, 2011.

p. 321. Ferris, Timothy. *Coming of Age in the Milky Way*. Perennial, 2003. (First published in 1988.)

p. 322. Feynman, Richard. *The Character of Physical Law*. The MIT Press, 2001. (First published in 1964.)

p. 324. Greenspan, Alan. "Banking." Speech presented to the American Bankers Association Annual Convention, New York, October 5, 2004.

p. 324. Buffett, Warren. Annual Letter to Shareholders of Berkshire Hathaway, Inc., 2002.

p. 328. Obama, Barack. "A More Perfect Union." Speech presented at the National Constitution Center, Philadelphia, March 18, 2008.

p. 328. Wright, Robert. *The Evolution of God*. Little, Brown and Company, 2009.

Chapter 8

p. 339. Aristophanes. "The Clouds." In *The Complete Plays of Aristophanes*. Bantam Classics, 1984.

p. 339. Pascal, Blaise. *Pascal's Pensees.* CreateSpace, 2012. (First published in 1669.)

p. 342. Wilde, Oscar. *The Critic as Artist.* Mondial, 2007. (First published in 1891.)

p. 347. Reich, Wilhelm. *Character Analysis*, Farrar, Straus and Giroux, 1980.

p. 348. Rogers, Carl. *On Becoming a Person*, Constable and Robinson, 2004. (First published in 1961.)

p. 354. Wilford, John Noble. *The Riddle of the Dinosaur.* Knopf, 1985.

p. 354. Bierce, Ambrose. *The Devil's Dictionary.* Public Domain Books, 2011. (First published in 1906.)

p. 358. Jung, Carl. *Man and His Symbols.* Dell, 1968. (First published in 1964.)

p. 374. Popper, Karl. *The Open Universe: An Argument for Indeterminism.*

Chapter 9

p. 390. Naisbitt, John. *Megatrends 2000.* William Morrow, 1990.

p. 390. Toffler, Alvin. *The Third Wave.* Bantam, 1991. (First published in 1980.)

p. 390. Negroponte, Nicholas. *Being Digital.* Random House, 1995.

p. 395. Rorty, Richard. *Contingency, Irony, and Solidarity.* Cambridge University Press, 1989.

p. 396. Gebser, Jean. *The Ever-Present Origin.* Ohio University Press, 1986.

p. 396. Jung, Carl. *The Undiscovered Self*. Little, Brown and Company, 1957.

p. 396. Neumann, Erich. *The Origins and History of Consciousness*. Bollingen, 1949.

p. 396. Campbell, Joseph. *The Hero with a Thousand Faces*. Second edition with revisions. Princeton University Press, 1968. (First published in 1949.)

p. 397. Wheatley, Margaret. *Leadership and the New Science*. Berrett-Koehler, 1992.

p. 397. Senge, Peter, *The Fifth Discipline*. Doubleday, 1990.

p. 421. Perls, Fritz. *Gestalt Therapy Verbatim*. The Gestalt Journal Press, 1992. (First Published in 1969.)

p. 421. Assagioli, Roberto. *Psychosynthesis*. Viking,1969.

p. 431. Pierce, Charles Sanders. *Philosophical Writings of Peirce*. Dover, 2011.

p. 431. James, William. *Pragmatism*. BiblioBazaar, 1995. (First published in 1907.)

p. 431. Holmes, Oliver Wendell. *The Path of the Law*. Public Domain Books, 2012. (First published in 1897.)

p. 431. Dewey, John. *Experience and Education*. Touchstone, 1997. (First published in 1938.)

p. 433. Rorty, Richard. *Consequences of Pragmatism*. University of Minnesota Press, 1982.

Chapter 10

p. 444. Campbell, Joseph. *The Power of Myth*, Anchor, 1991.

p. 444. Keleman, Stanley. *Your Body Speaks Its Mind*, Center Press, 1981.

p. 445. Yeats, William Butler. "A Prayer for Old Age." In *Yeats's Poetry, Drama, and Prose*. Scribner, 1983.

p. 446. Montaigne, Michel de. *Michel de Montaigne: The Complete Essays*. Penguin, 1987.

p. 447. Thoreau, Henry David. *Henry David Thoreau: Collected Essays and Poems*. Library of America, 2001.

p. 448. Descartes, René. *Meditations and Other Metaphysical Writings*. Penguin, 1999.

p. 452. Gebser, Jean. *The Ever-Present Origin*.

p. 463. Muir, John. *My First Summer in the Sierra and Selected Essays*.

p. 466. Bossuet, Jacques Bénigne. *Politics Drawn from the Very Words of the Holy Scripture*. Cambridge University Press, 1991. (First published in 1709.)

p. 479. Schlesinger, Arthur. *The Cycles of American History*. Houghton Mifflin, 1999.

Chapter 11

p. 526. Rilke, Rainer Maria. *Letters to a Young Poet*. Norton, 1993. (First published in 1929.)

p. 536. Nietzsche, Friedrich. *The Antichrist*. Tribeca Press, 2009. (First published in 1895.)

p. 536. Russell, Bertrand. "Do We Survive Death?" In *Why I Am Not a Christian and Other Essays on Religion and Related Subjects*. Allen and Unwin, 1957.

p. 544. Whitehead, Alfred North. *Process and Reality.* Edited by D.R. Griffin and D.W. Sherburne. The Free Press, 1978.

p. 544. Hughes, Langston. "The Negro Artist and the Racial Mountains." In *The Collected Poems of Langston Hughes*. Vintage Classics, 1995.

Chapter 12

p. 547. Berry, Thomas. *The Dream of the Earth.* Sierra Club Books, 1988.

Words of Thanks

I would like to thank people who, over the years, have played particularly key roles in the development of Creative Systems Theory or who have provided important support in my efforts. In no particular order, my deep appreciation goes out to Larry Hobbs, Rick Jackson, Lyn Dillman, Brenda Kramer, Joseph Campbell, Robert Garfias, Ilya Prigogine, Stanley Keleman, Chogyam Trungpa, Sandra Wood, Pam Schick, Peggy Hackney, Janice Meaden, Sue Lerner, Dean Elias, Ron Hobbs, Marcy Jackson, Steve Boyd, Dona McDonald, Tom Engle, John Palka, Colleen Campbell, David Moore, and Dan Senour.

I also wish to give special thanks to my editors Kathy Krause, Rebecca Gleason, and Jan Bultmann for their skilled and committed help in making inherently challenging material as clear and accessible as possible, and to Teresa Piddington for help in the proofreading stages. I also want to thank Les Campbell for his beautiful work designing the book's cover, internal layout, and diagrams.

INDEX

ICD Press is the publishing arm of the Institute for Creative Development. Information about the Institute and other Institute publications can be found on the Institute website www.CreativeSystems.org.

The Institute for Creative Development (ICD) Press
4324 Meridian Ave. N.
Seattle WA 98103
206-526-8562
ICDPressinfo@gmail.com

34091388R00355

Made in the USA
San Bernardino, CA
18 May 2016